The Tales of Canterbury

The Tales of Canterbury

COMPLETE

GEOFFREY CHAUCER

Edited by
Robert A. Pratt
University of Pennsylvania

HOUGHTON MIFFLIN COMPANY · BOSTON
Atlanta   Dallas   Geneva, Ill.   Hopewell, N. J.   Palo Alto   London

Printed in the U.S.A.

Library of Congress Catalog Card Number: 72–9380

ISBN: 0-395-14052-8

To Venca of Canterbury

Contents

Introduction ix

Acknowledgments xxxv

The Order of the Tales xxxv

The Language of Chaucer xxxvii

Suggestions for Reading Chaucer xxxvii

Illustrations xxxix

For Further Reading xli

The Tales of Canterbury

General Prologue 1

The Knight's Tale 26

The Miller's Prologue and Tale 78

The Reeve's Prologue and Tale 98

The Cook's Prologue and Tale 108

The Man of Law's Introduction, Prologue, and Tale 111

The Shipman's Tale 141

The Prioress's Prologue and Tale 152

The Prologue and Tale of Sir Thopas 160

The Prologue and Tale of Melibee 166

The Monk's Prologue and Tale 208

The Nuns' Priest's Prologue and Tale 232

The Wife of Bath's Prologue and Tale 252

The Friar's Prologue and Tale 284

The Summoner's Prologue and Tale 294

The Clerk's Prologue and Tale 311

The Merchant's Prologue and Tale 342

The Squire's Introduction and Tale 372

The Franklin's Prologue and Tale 390

The Physician's Tale 412

The Pardoner's Introduction, Prologue, and Tale   420

The Second Nun's Prologue and Tale   438

The Canon's Yeoman's Prologue and Tale   454

The Manciple's Prologue and Tale   481

The Parson's Prologue and Tale   487

Chaucer Takes His Leave   557

Comment on the Text   561

Basic Glossary   581

Introduction

Geoffrey Chaucer began the book which he called *The Tales of Canterbury* at a time when he had already achieved success and confidence as a poet and had matured as a man of business and court affairs. At the start, writing had been the occupation of his leisure; but by the mid-1380's his career had so shaped up that the duties of his official posts were less taxing and literature could have more of his attention. At the same time, the tone of his writing became less conventional and more original and lively, less bookish and more closely related to the world about him and his experiences in that world for half a century.

Chaucer had been born into an England that was in a state of excitement and ferment, and the span of his life (c. 1343–1400) coincided with a time of war, plague, rebellion, and social change. A few years before Chaucer's birth, King Edward III (reigned 1327–77) asserted his claim to the crown of France and launched the series of bloody and exhausting campaigns which were to be known as the Hundred Years' War. Edward III's great victories in the harbor of Sluys in Flanders (1340), and on the fields of Crécy (1346) and Poitiers (1356) in northern France, strengthened the status of England as a European power and helped arouse a new national pride. Such glorious achievements, however, were not to be repeated until the victory of King Henry V at Agincourt in the next century (1415). After Poitiers, England's activities in the Hundred Years' War brought truce, compromise, and disaster. Edward's fruitless ambition ruined the Florentine banking house of the Bardi and drained the financial resources of England. In 1348 most of Europe, including England, was struck by the terrible Black Death (bubonic plague), and recurrent epidemics took the lives of about half the population of England. War, pestilence, and famine exhausted the land; the conditions of peasants and other workers went from bad to worse. Attempts to fix prices and wages speeded up the economic and social disintegration that led to the Peasants' Revolt in 1381, when a mob marched on London with fire and bloodshed in the hope of somehow improving their lives, only to fail ignominiously in their negotiations with the skilled soldiers and diplomats of the Crown. Thus in Chaucer's day the stability and order which marked the feudal system at its height was showing strong signs of disintegration. At the same time professional men, such as lawyers and physicians, were achieving new social and financial recognition. The bourgeoisie was rising in status and wealth: artisans were organizing into occupational guilds and social fraternities, and merchants were able to conduct business dealings on a vast scale.

The Church, with its hierarchal government from the distant Papacy at Rome through archbishop, bishop, archdeacon, and down to the parish priest and vicar, tended to lose control over many of its clerics. The "regular" clergy—monks, nuns, and friars—too often allowed devotion and service to be overshadowed by personal desires. Thus Chaucer's century saw the ideals of Christianity somewhat clouded by corruption and avarice, bringing about conditions which eventually led to the Protestant Reformation and to the Counter Reformation.

Along with political, social, and moral change, language also was a source of some confusion in Chaucer's day, for England was a land of not just one language, but three. The native tongue, the speech of countryside and street, was English, but even that varied greatly from one part of the country to another, so much so that the speakers of northern and southern dialects sometimes could scarcely understand each other. The second language, French, had been brought across the Channel by the Norman conquerors three centuries before. For two of these centuries French had been the language of the nobility, of fashionable society, and (together with Latin) of government documents and official business. In Chaucer's century, however, the speakers of French were generally bilingual and were quite at home with English, which by now had absorbed many French words. The third language was Latin, the language of learning, of the universities, the Church, and the law. Medieval Latin had less complex sentence structure than classical Latin and for learned men had become a comfortable, fluent mode of expression that knew no national barriers and helped to keep the Western world and the Church together. These three languages—English, French, and Latin—thus belonged to different levels of society and ways of life, and a man's background and career would naturally determine which language or languages were his.

John Chaucer, the poet's father, was a wealthy vintner, a wholesale merchant and importer of wine; he might have chosen for his son a career in business, or law, or the Church. Instead he early arranged a career at court; the first glimpse provided by official records (our chief source for the poet's life) reveals Chaucer as a page, in parti-colored hose, member of the household of Elizabeth Countess of Ulster, wife of Prince Lionel, second son of King Edward III. In that year young Geoffrey received elegant clothing in May in London, and money for "necessaries at Christmas" at Hatfield in Yorkshire. Also in Elizabeth's train was "Philippa, daughter of Pan'," evidently the Philippa—daughter of Sir Paneto de Roet—whom Chaucer was later to marry. Chaucer's important acquaintance with the powerful John of Gaunt, fourth son of Edward, must have commenced at least this early, for John was guest in the Hatfield household that Christmas.

In 1359–60 when the King and his sons invaded northern France, Chaucer took part in the fruitless campaign, was captured by the French but soon ransomed, and later in 1360 carried letters for Prince Lionel from Calais to England.

Then we lose sight of Chaucer for six years. He may have been in Ireland with Lionel, who was there as King's Lieutenant; but more likely he was a student in London at the Inner Temple, the law school which not only prepared young men for the legal profession as such, but also afforded training for a business, diplomatic, and official career such as Chaucer was to pursue for the rest of his life. There are traces of an Inner Temple record (now lost) that he was fined "for beatinge a Franciscane Fryer in fletestreate," a punishment which could have been meted only to an actual student at the Temple. At all events, he was in Navarre in 1366, and is mentioned as yeoman in the King's household in 1367 and as squire the next year; that he was now married is shown by the mention of Philippa Chaucer as "damoiselle" of Queen Philippa in 1366.

Chaucer's greatest patron was to be not Lionel nor Edward III but John of Gaunt, Duke of Lancaster, who in 1369 led another futile French campaign, in which Chaucer took part. While the army was abroad, John's first duchess, Blanche, died of the plague. It must have been soon afterward that Chaucer wrote an elegy, *The Book of the Duchess,* for presentation to Blanche's bereaved husband. In 1372 and 1374 Philippa Chaucer received pensions indicating that she was in attendance on John of Gaunt's second duchess, Constance of Castille; in 1374 Chaucer received a pension from John, and from the King a daily pitcher of wine which was commuted in 1378 to a handsome annual pension. In the 1380's Philippa received a number of New Year's gifts from the Duke; she may have died shortly after receiving her annuity of 1387—the last known record of her.

Between 1368 and 1378 Chaucer made several trips to the Continent in order to take part in diplomatic missions for the King. In both 1368 and 1370 he was abroad, destination and business unknown. In 1372–73 he went first to Genoa to arrange a commercial agreement between that city and England, and then to Florence on secret business for the King. During 1376 and 1377 he made three or four trips to France, evidently to negotiate for peace, and to arrange a marriage between the newly crowned King Richard II and a daughter of King Charles V of France. In 1378 he went again to Italy, this time to Bernabò Visconti, Lord of Milan, and to the English condottiere Sir John Hawkwood, then in Bernabò's service, concerning the King's war in France; thus for a second time the poet must have felt the impact of the new literature of Italy, the writings of Dante, Petrarch, and Boccaccio, which gave him new material and refreshing inspiration. Meanwhile in 1374 he had accepted an important position which he held until 1386: Controllership of Customs and Subsidy of Wools, Skins, and Hides in the Port of London. Likewise in 1374 he was given rent-free a house over Aldgate; it was probably here during this period that he wrote such poems as *The House of Fame, The Parliament of Fowls,* and *The Book of Troilus.*

The years 1385 and 1386 brought significant changes in Chaucer's worldly affairs and in his literary activities. Leaving the Custom House, he moved to the country south across the River Thames, where he became Justice of the Peace for the county of Kent and one of the two members of Parliament, "Knights of the Shire," for Kent. About this time he planned and started to write *The Tales of Canterbury,* his most extensive and famous work. For about two years, beginning in 1389, he was Clerk of the King's Works, in charge of royal buildings and repairs thereto, and in 1391 he was made deputy forester of the royal forest of North Petherton in Somersetshire. He may have lived here in the Park House for the greater part of eight years, writing most of *The Tales of Canterbury,* though he was in London on several occasions and was at least once in Kent. At Christmas 1395 he was in attendance on John of Gaunt's son, Henry Earl of Derby. When this patron later became Henry IV, the poet addressed to him "The Complaint of Chaucer to His Purse," a witty *tour de force,* complaining that his dear lady, his purse, has become light, and at the same time complimenting the new king on his accession to the throne. On the day of his coronation, 13 October 1399, Henry granted Chaucer 40 marks yearly for life in addition to the annuity of £20 granted by Richard and confirmed by Henry. On December 24 the poet took a long lease on a tenement in the garden of the Lady Chapel of Westminster Abbey, where he apparently lived until his death in October 1400. He was buried in the East Aisle of the South Transept of the Abbey; around his tomb other men of letters were later buried, thus forming Poets' Corner.

For a full understanding and appreciation of Chaucer's achievement, we must realize that when he was a young man, noble households of England were probably less familiar with poetry written in English than with that written in French—on either side of the Channel. Thus when Chaucer, in his early teens, was in the midst of a noble family, in the company of fashionable lords and ladies, he was in a courtly atmosphere conducive to the study and writing of the types of courtly poetry so popular in France and so often imitated in England: songs, lays, roundels and complaints, envoys and ballades—all written in complex stanza forms. These little poems were sometimes witty and amusing expressions of love, sometimes sad protestations of the hopelessness of ever winning the lady's favor. Likewise popular were the love visions—the most famous of which, *Le Roman de la Rose,* Chaucer later translated. These delicately wrought love visions told of a poet who fell asleep in lovely surroundings, to waken in a conventionalized perfect landscape, ornate with singing birds and delicate flowers, inhabited by ideal figures who often personified such allegorical abstractions pertaining to love as Beauty, Youth, Jealousy, Reason, and Cupid. The influence of these courtly French conventions can be seen especially in such of Chaucer's early poems as *The Book of the Duchess, The House of Fame,* and *The Parliament of Fowls,* and later in the Prologue to *The Legend of Good Women.* It is to Chaucer's credit that, while under the influence of this genre, he allowed fresh air to flow into the idealized gardens, forests, and meadows, that he infused his characters with some vitality, and that he injected humor and some keen first-hand observations of his own. Indeed, by the time that, in his full maturity, he penned the love poem "To Rosemounde," he was able to view the artificialities of the French tradition with an eye satirically jaundiced and a pen brilliantly sharp.

French was a language which Chaucer could read and write, and presumably speak, with ease; he was also familiar with Latin in both its classical and its medieval forms. Hence another early literary influence on him, and one that continued with increasing intensity for many years, was the classical world as he experienced it, for example, in the poetry of Ovid, Virgil, and Statius, and as he found it reinterpreted by medieval writers. Of these poets his favorite from the beginning was the irrepressible Ovid, with his quick fancy, his narrative skill, his vast fund of mythological lore, and his sometimes serious, sometimes cynical preoccupation with love. Chaucer knew Virgil too, with his stateliness, his humanity, and his vigorous yet delicate poetic power. Even the early dream visions, written in the medieval French tradition, came under the spell of these two poets; for their stories form subordinate sections of *The Book of the Duchess* and *The House of Fame,* and form the actual "legends" of *The Legend of Good Women*—those "Saints' Legends of Cupid" which begin with the martyrdom of Cleopatra. Chaucer's use of classical story continued right into *The Tales of Canterbury.* There the series of tragic falls of great men, authentic tales of horror and the supernatural assigned by Chaucer to the Monk, includes several victims of Fortune from classical myth and history: Hercules, Zenobia, Nero, Alexander, Julius Caesar, and Croesus, though some of the stories are derived from medieval retellings. Roman history forms the basis of the Physician's Tale—Livy's account of Virginia, retold in *Le Roman de la Rose.* One of the last poems written for *The Tales of Canterbury* was the Manciple's parodic recasting of Ovid's story of Phoebus, his adulterous wife Coronis, and the tell-tale raven.

Another important influence of learning on Chaucer's poetry was his intimate knowledge of the *De Consolatione Philosophiae* of Boethius (d. 524). Sometimes called the last of the Roman and first of the Christian philosophers, Boethius offered a work at once familiar, elevated, and rewarding, which fascinated and impressed literate men throughout the Middle Ages, and which was translated, in turn, by King Alfred, Chaucer, and Queen Elizabeth I. Chaucer's labor of translation, accomplished in the midst of his poetic career, made him intimate with the treatise; its thoughts and phrases are echoed again and again in his later poetry. Particularly notable are the passage in Book IV of *Troilus and Criseyde* where Troilus discusses predestination and free will (a problem glanced at by the Nuns' Priest in discussing the perils of Chauntecleer); certain profound thoughts in the Knight's Tale, especially Arcite's query concerning the vanity of human wishes, Palamon's questioning the fairness of divine providence, and Theseus' pronouncement on the relationship of the human condition to time and eternity; certain passages which set the tone of the Monk's Tale; and such short poems as "The Former Age" and the "Balade de Bon Conseyl" or "Truth." "The Former Age" belongs to a long primitivistic tradition as old as Hesiod and still with us in Henry Miller's pipe dream of a Golden Age on the island of Corfu in *The Colossus of Maroussi.* In "The Former Age" Chaucer reworks and modernizes (or should we say "medievalizes") ideas of Boethius so that they bear on his own time. In a different manner he does this also in "Truth," a poem brilliant in imagery, sonorous in tone, and lofty in spirit. Another short poem, "Chaucers Wordes unto Adam, His Owne Scriveyn," is a humorous chastisement of the copyist who let errors slip into the texts of *The Troilus* and *Boece* which he transcribed for Chaucer.

Chaucer's knowledge of Latin and especially of French enabled him to translate extensively from those languages, thus bringing many significant works to a wider English audience than they would otherwise have had. His most famous translation, the *Boece,* was based on Jean de Meun's translation into French and also on the *De Consolatione Philosophiae* itself. Similarly, the story of Griselda, forming the Clerk's Tale, he based on a French translation of Petrarch's *Griseldis* and also on the Latin original. The *Melibee,* with its plea for arbitration rather than fighting, was translated from Renaud de Louhan's free, abridged French version of Albertano of Brescia's *Liber Consolationis et Consilii.* The Parson's Tale is evidently a translation of a French confessional manual on penitence and the seven sins, but with the addition by the poet of enlivening illustrative details. That Chaucer translated *Le Roman de la Rose*—presumably in its entirety—is indicated by his reference to it in the Prologue to *The Legend of Good Women* (the god of Love says, "in pleyn text, withouten nede of glose, Thou hast translated the Romaunce of the Rose") and by Eustache Deschamps' *Ballade* addressed to Chaucer ("de la Rose . . . en bon Anglès le livre translatas"); but we have no more than 1705 lines that can, even with reservations of doubt, be attributed to him. In the Prologue to *The Legend* Chaucer writes also of his translations—now lost—of the pseudo-Origen *Homilia de Maria Magdalena,* and the *De Miseria Humane Conditionis* of Innocent III. In his so-called Retraction which follows the Parson's Tale, Chaucer makes mentions of his "translacions" in a manner which suggests that others have been lost too. Whether *A Treatise on the Astrolabe* was a fresh, original adaptation of materials from Messahala and Sacrobosco, or was simply a paraphrase or translation of a Latin treatise known to Chaucer but not to us—in either case he was once again making basic materials available in English. The very bulk of all these works of translation makes us realize that Chaucer must have spent hundreds and hundreds of hours turning treatises and poems into his native tongue for the benefit of his less gifted countrymen. Just how important to Chaucer was this basic task—the dissemination of learning and moral wisdom—is suggested by the fact that the pieces specifically mentioned above must have totaled nearly a half (close to 45 per cent) of his literary output. It is no wonder that Eustache Deschamps in his *Ballade* addressed to Chaucer called him a Pandarus—a go-between—to "those ignorant of the language" (Aux ignorans de la langue, Pandras), and as the refrain to his *Ballade* wrote:

Grant translateur, noble Geffroy Chaucier!

In addition to Latin and French, Chaucer also came to know Italian, perhaps in the course of his official journeys to Italy, and three Italian writers helped shape the course of his literary career—Dante, Boccaccio, and Petrarch. Boccaccio, as we shall see, provided Chaucer with the plots of two of his finest poems; and together these three Italian poets revealed to him psychological insight, vividness, sensuousness, and lyricism that were richly influential on his poetry. By comparison, literature in English had apparently little influence on Chaucer; but there are a few echoes from such works as the *Travels* of Sir John Mandeville, *Sir Gawain and the Green Knight,* and the *Confessio Amantis* of Chaucer's friend, John Gower; and Chaucer had evidently heard read aloud portions of the famous Auchinleck Manuscript (a fourteenth-century collection of romances and other writings); for echoes from its versions of rimed romances are found in the tales of the Wife of Bath, the Franklin, and the Merchant, and above all in the rime of Sir Thopas, wherein the poet parodies the genre.

We can have no idea whether Chaucer ever used French as a literary language; certainly his natural propensity seems to have been for English, and in this he must have received encouragement from some of his patrons. Although the nobility of England used English, French had long been the fashionable language for literature, and only during the fourteenth century did the fashion change. In 1367 Parliament was first addressed from the throne in English rather than French, and after that date English replaced French in the courts of law. By using English rather than French in writing poetry for a noble and courtly audience, Chaucer gave an impetus to English as a medium for literature in England. Substantial writings in Middle English first appeared in any quantity in the thirteenth century and, except for the rimed romances, these were mainly didactic or religious. By the latter half of the fourteenth century a considerable body of material had appeared, including *Piers Plowman,* Langland's lengthy satire on political and social conditions, presented with religious overtones; the discussion of grace and salvation in the form of a symbolic elegy called *Pearl;* and, presumably by the same author, the sophisticated courtly romance of adventure, love and honor, and the supernatural, *Sir Gawain and the Green Knight.* Along with the writings of Chaucer, these poems represent a surgent use of English for the literature of England after two centuries dominated by Latin and French.

Consideration of three of Chaucer's earliest long poems—*The Book of the Duchess, The House of Fame,* and *The Parliament of Fowls*—reveals that their literary background is French (with some classical influence and with some Italian influence in the latter two), but that Chaucer has humanized the conventional elements in his own inimitable manner. His first poem that can be dated with any certainty is *The Book of the Duchess,* the elegy written for the bereaved John of Gaunt after the death of his first duchess, Blanche of Lancaster (September 1369). In this elegy the poet dreams that he encounters in a forest a mourning knight whom he tries to console; especially moving are the knight's sorrow, his story of his love and courtship of his lost lady, and the description of her person and character. Thus Chaucer used the conventional French setting and form as a vehicle for genuine emotion, with praise for Blanche and consolation for John. *The House of Fame* likewise has the dream framework, together with other poetic devices long familiar to Chaucer and his audience, and with brilliant imagery suggested by Dante. Accomplished with rich humor, the result is altogether delightful as a talkative eagle takes the dreaming poet in his clutches on a whimsical, half-philosophical, half-jocular space-trip past the constellations to the Palace of Lady Fame

in search of tidings of love. In *The Parliament of Fowls*—an allegorical royal court-
ship in which most of the people are depicted as birds—the ideal vision is vitalized
by a rich sensuousness learned from Boccaccio, by lively satire directed against
various classes of society, and by the colloquial chattering of birds who, in the con-
ventional dream poems of France, would have been merely decorative. Yet in these
writings, as in the Prologue to *The Legend of Good Women,* Chaucer shows that
he had well served his poetic apprenticeship in studying and imitating such poems
as *Le Roman de la Rose;* for this courtly tradition had stimulated in the poet a
sensitivity to ideal beauty and a mastery of colorful detail that were never to desert
him.

After these three examples of poetry presented in a dream framework came two
of Chaucer's most successful poems—*Troilus and Criseyde* and the Knight's Tale
—with stories both purporting to be of ancient origin, but actually based on *Il
Filostrato* and *Il Teseida,* writings by his somewhat older contemporary, Giovanni
Boccaccio (1313–75). Boccaccio's two historical romances were pseudo-classical
stories complete with Greek and Trojan personages and with decorative settings
supposedly representing ancient Troy and Greece. Chaucer enriched his two poems
with materials from Statius' epic, the *Thebaid;* and from the medieval *Roman de
Thèbes* and Benoit's *Roman de Troie,* both of the twelfth century. His reworking of
his source materials was so complete that the final results were virtually original ar-
tistic creations.

Medieval historians often asserted that Western Europe had been settled by the
survivors of demolished Troy; in fact London was sometimes called Troia Nova
(New Troy). Thus Chaucer's audience was bound to be fascinated by a love story
which took place during the last tragic years of Troy, especially when he claimed
to have in hand as his source a Latin account by an ancient writer, Lollius, whose
book no one else had seen—at least in recent times. Actually Chaucer used Boc-
caccio's *Filostrato,* and even more closely a translation of it into French prose—
Le Roman de Troilus et de Criseida—purportedly by Beauvau, Seneschal of Anjou.
Boccaccio had taken from Benoit the story of the faithless Criseyde's desertion of
Troilus, Prince of Troy, for the Grecian warrior Diomede; to this story he had
prefaced his own account of Troilus' falling in love with Criseyde, his wooing
of her with the aid of her cousin Pandarus, and his triumphant winning of her
love, all apparently based on Boccaccio's own love-affair with an unidentified
widow named Giovanna. Chaucer followed the outlines of Boccaccio's plot, but
made extensive changes, omissions, and additions; and into the work he infused
characterization and psychological insight, dramatic dialogue, rich humor, an
atmosphere of high romance, and a telling sense of the moral significance of the
problems and decisions of the characters. Whereas *Il Filostrato* is presented in a
style not at all lofty or ornate, Boccaccio had filled *Il Teseida* with elements of high
style and epic grandeur; and in the *Troilus* Chaucer to a large extent incorporated
a similar tone, again and again deliberately imitating Boccaccio's epic invocations,
similes, classical allusions, and heightened descriptions; yet the poem, far from
having epic pretensions, has a total effect of high romance. Again, Chaucer
deepened the implications and import of his poem by making his characters and
his audience perpetually aware of the planetary forces at work in the universe, and
by putting in the mind of Troilus philosophical questions raised in the *De Con-
solatione Philosophiae* of Boethius. In the introductory stanzas of the poem we are
told the outcome of the events—that Troilus will fall in love with and win Criseyde,
that later he will lose her, and that she will be faithless. Like the spectators of

Greek tragedy we are thus placed in the godlike position of knowing more of their fates than do the characters themselves.

Chaucer endowed his three main characters with depth and feeling, and their humanity far exceeds that of their counterparts in Boccaccio's *Il Filostrato*. Pandarus, now the lady's uncle, is a connoisseur of human nature, a humorist who can make himself the butt of his own jokes, a master of practical though not ultimate wisdom, and one of Chaucer's greatest comic creations. Perhaps Chaucer's crowning achievement in this poem is his complex characterization of Criseyde, whom many have felt to be among the most winning and lovable women in fiction, the more so because of her inner need which makes her, at the last—with sorrow in her deed and full awareness of its implications—accept the love of the headlong and slightly brutal Greek whom she has not the strength to resist. If Criseyde never gave herself fully to Troilus, his tragedy was to have given his complete unselfish love to a woman not worthy of such devotion; his was a blindness of heart which only after death yields to an awareness that this world of earthly love is vanity fair.

In technical skill, human feeling, and narrative force, Chaucer reached new heights in the *Troilus,* which was probably written in the early 1380's, when he was about forty. Yet even this poem, like his earlier ones, leaned heavily upon traditional materials, models, and principles of composition. Likewise his next substantial poem, *The Legend of Good Women,* shows the use of well-known literary materials and motifs, but with fresh outlook and treatment. For us the most significant feature of *The Legend* may be that it probably represents Chaucer's first experience in the formal framing of a collection of stories. Echoing certain details in *The Parliament of Fowls,* the poet declares that his love for old books is such that he can be drawn from them only by a May morning and in particular the daisy, which he praises enthusiastically. Falling asleep, he dreams that the God of Love, dressed in silk and crowned with a sun, approaches him in a meadow with the Queen Alceste, who is costumed like a daisy. The god accuses him of frightening men from love by such poems as *Troilus and Criseyde* and his translation of *The Romaunt of the Rose;* Alceste in turn defends him by citing such writings as *The House of Fame, The Parliament,* the story of Palamon and Arcite (shortly to appear as the Knight's Tale), and his translations of *Boece* and the Legend of St. Cecilia (later the Second Nun's Tale). The penance is imposed that Chaucer write, year by year, a legendary, a book of saints' lives,

a glorious legende
Of goode wymmen, maydenes and wyves,
That weren trewe in lovyng al hire lyves;
And telle of false men that hem bytraien.

Thus are introduced the stories of the martyrs of love: "Incipit legenda Cleopatrie, Martiris, Egipti regine" (Here begins the Legend of Cleopatra, Martyr, Queen of Egypt); then Thisbe, Dido, Medea, Ariadne, and five other good women, the last story unfinished. This book Chaucer is told to give to the Queen, at Eltham or Sheen—the sites of two of the royal palaces favored by Queen Anne. *The Legend of Good Women* represents the first appearance in English of the pentameter couplet which Chaucer was soon to use with such success and variety in *The Tales.*

Even if *The Legend of Good Women* was (as its Prologue implies) commanded by someone at court, it benefited Chaucer by encouraging him almost immediately to create a more elaborate frame for a greater number and variety of stories. Soon after he started work on *The Tales of Canterbury* (in the late 1380's) three further influences came into play and helped determine the nature and tone of much that he wrote. There was a tendency to free himself from conventional, bookish plots and to revert somewhat to his earlier practice of apparently formless but actually cogent and artfully designed organization, with a new richness based on maturity and wisdom—a matter which must come up for discussion a little later in connection with the tales themselves. Further there was a somewhat related tendency to draw materials more than ever before from the world about him. In addition there also developed a rather extensive interest in science. Traces of each of these dominating interests or tendencies are of course found earlier, but each of them came to a fruitful climax in the 1390's and affected Chaucer's work on *The Tales of Canterbury.*

It is possible to trace an ever-increasing ability of the poet to turn for material and inspiration to the everyday scenes and people he knew so well. More and more the imaginary world of his reading—dream vision, old story, rules of poetics, and artificial imagery—is supplemented and finally overbalanced by the real world that he had come to know over the years, the world of the court, of warfare, of countryside and city, of dikes and ditches, of the Custom House by Thames-side which led to the ends of the known earth. As his poetic power developed, Chaucer had allowed more and more of this real world to infuse his poetry; finally, when about 1386 he planned *The Tales of Canterbury,* there came a significant turning point: he freed himself from dependence on the literary past and looked to life itself for his subject matter and method of organization. It was as if he cried "farewell my bok" and "welcome, . . . every good felawe." He now sketched with his eye on the men and women about him, and described the gestures and actions that belong to life itself.

There had been premonitions of this realism quite early: certain passages in *The Book of the Duchess,* the humorous words of the rather human eagle in *The House of Fame,* and the lively talk of some of the birds in *The Parliament of Fowls.* Even more direct and natural were the interchanges of Criseyde and Pandarus, which owe their subtlety and vivacity entirely to Chaucer rather than to Boccaccio or other previous writers. The full and bursting bloom of Chaucer's realism, however, comes with *The Tales of Canterbury.* We may well ask what brought about the poet's realization that here was a medium and a method—new and untried, to be sure—in which he could achieve his greatest success as artist, poet, and creator. In part the answer is to be found in recent Italian literature: in the influence of the *Divina Commedia,* the regions of which Dante had peopled with unforgettable contemporary men and women, often echoing the bitter political strife of his native city of Florence; and probably in the influence of the *Decameron,* the stories of which reflect Boccaccio's realistic view of life. There were, too, such English writings as *Piers Plowman,* where many lines and phrases offer sharp glimpses of English life in Chaucer's time. But the ultimate answer is more probably to be found in the fact that the poet did not read his books and dream forever in a castle tower looking down on Maytime gardens and meadows, but instead devoted a tremendous amount of interest, energy, and time to a wide variety of worldly matters, and allowed his remarkable mind to range over an equally wide variety of intellectual interests. During his multifarious career, Chaucer had shared experiences with many of his pilgrims, and had been brought close to others. Thus he had seen military service on the Continent, like the Knight "in his lordes werre," and like the Squire in "Artoys and Pycardie." Like the Squire, "he koude songes make and wel endite"—in fact had made "many a song and many a lecherous lay," well exemplified in his humorous love poem "To Rosemounde." Like the Yeoman, he knew forestry at first hand. From the Custom House on the bank of the Thames he knew many a Merchant and Shipman; like the Merchant, he had traveled; and he had been rewarded for detecting a smuggler. Like the Clerk and the Wife of Bath, he had traveled to Italy; and like the Clerk, had many books. Like the Lawyer he had evidently studied at a Temple, where he must have been intimate with "lerned men . . . of lawe expert and curious," as well as with at least one manciple.

Thus Chaucer's activities and interests reveal a breadth of experience and knowledge unusual in a man of his time, or indeed of any time. He not only fulfilled what was to be the Renaissance ideal of courtier, soldier, and scholar; he was busy as an amateur scientist who carved for himself a modest niche in the history of science; and he was also diplomat, politician, businessman, translator, and poet. If the poetry of Chaucer presents the world and its people with an immediacy, truth, and vividness achieved by few poets, some of his success must be attributed to the intensity of his life, and to the wide range of his interests.

Of the scientific interests reflected in Chaucer's writings we must particularly note alchemy, medicine, and astronomy and astrology. Chaucer was widely read in these subjects and made use of them in his poetry with accuracy and ease. It has been demonstrated that he knew well a number of basic alchemical treatises and had detailed knowledge and understanding of the purposes, materials, and processes of alchemy. One must bear in mind that the poet is not to be identified with his ignorant and blundering creation, the Canon's Yeoman. The Yeoman's knowledge of alchemy is superficial and his list of alchemical terms is garbled, though he does his best to describe the process of "silver citrinacioun." (The Yeoman's story of the tricks of the "false chanoun" in its presentation of this avaricious charlatan ironically travesties the serious alchemist, but it reveals no knowledge of alchemy as such.) The Yeoman's last hundred lines—his moralistic conclusion—are a parody of the writings of alchemists, whose words are here so distorted as to denounce alchemy and to recommend leaving it alone, the very opposite of what the cited treatises actually do, for they urge the alchemist to continue his investigations and not to despair. The Yeoman is depicted as ignorant and as believing that all alchemists are cheats; but in his presentation of the Canon whom he served for seven years, again and again in spite of himself he permits glimpses that give the impression that this learned man is a serious worker, a sincere investigator. Thus the poet uses his knowledge to present characters in dramatic conflict and to conjure up in the reader's mind speculations concerning alchemy. His extensive interest in the subject is part and parcel of his tremendous curiosity concerning nature, whether in the physical body of man, or in the stars, or in the relationships of microcosm and macrocosm.

Chaucer's mastery of medical terminology and his understanding of medieval medicine are revealed in *The Tales of Canterbury:* for example, the description in the General Prologue of the well-read Doctour of Phisik, whose medical knowledge is firmly "grounded in astronomye"; the detailed description of the illness of Arcite in the Knight's Tale; Dame Pertelote's elaborate justification of her prescription of digestives, emetics, and laxatives for her husband in the Nuns' Priest's Tale; and the careful descriptions, in the General Prologue, of the Pardoner's strange condition and the Summoner's terrible disease. Likewise Chaucer's knowledge of astronomy and astrology permeates his writings: many poems, tales, and links contain allusions to the planets or their influence. Chaucer opens *The Tales of Canterbury* with the sun running its course through the zodiacal sign of Aries. Mars,

Venus, and Saturn play major roles in the Knight's Tale. The crucial trick in the Miller's Tale is brought about by a supposed display of judicial astrology by "hende Nicholas," clerk of Oxford (another Nicholas, astronomer of Oxford, is mentioned by Chaucer in his *Treatise on the Astrolabe:* Nicholas of Lynne). The Host delights in telling the time of day by estimating the position of the sun; the Nuns' Priest's Chantecleer is his eager rival. The wife of Bath's lecherous, bold character she attributes to the influential positions of Venus and Mars at her birth. Further, in 1391 Chaucer wrote a substantial scientific treatise, among the very first in English: his *Treatise on the Astrolabe* (an instrument to help determine the apparent positions of heavenly bodies) has been described as "the oldest work written in English upon an elaborate scientific instrument," and as "still one of the best and most lucid accounts of the astrolabe." It was to have contained tables and conclusions "after the kalenders of the reverent clerkes, Frere J. Somer and Frere N. Lenne," of Oxford. (About 1380 John Somer had composed an astronomical calendar for Joan, mother of Richard II; and in 1386 Nicholas of Lynne had prepared one for John of Gaunt.) Then about 1392 or 1393 there was composed *The Equatorie of the Planetis,* a treatise on a related instrument, which offers further evidence that Chaucer was somehow involved with a group having determined astrological interests. For *The Equatorie,* although in a prose style unlike that of Chaucer, is nevertheless somehow connected with him and with the contemporary scientific group at Oxford: it presents a table of planets, assigned to John Somer, dated 31 December 1393; and it also contains a reference to the root (*radix*) of Chaucer, suggesting some connection between him and the tables of *The Equatorie,* perhaps referring to some lost tables with that root, possibly prepared for him by John Somer or Nicholas of Lynne. Thus, *The Equatorie* comes from the same intellectual ferment or circle as the *Treatise on the Astrolabe.* At about this same time we first find in Chaucer's writing evidence of a thoroughgoing interest in judicial astrology as such, not only in integrating the discordant forces at work in the personality of the Wife of Bath, but also in setting up the background for the Man of Law's Tale. There the narrator declares:

> *Imprudent Emperour of Rome, allas!*
> *Was ther no philosophre in al thy toun?*
> *Is no tyme bet than oother in swich cas?*
> *Of viage is ther noon eleccioun,*
> *Namely to folk of heigh condicioun?*
> *Nat whan a roote is of a burthe yknowe?*

Just as a slide rule is an instrument used to speed mathematical calculations, so an "equatorie of the planetis" is a mechanism used to speed calculations of the position of the planets at a given time—the calculations necessary for preparing a horoscope. Judicial astrology interested such personages as Joan of Kent, her son Richard II, and his uncle John of Gaunt. Despite a pious disclaimer in the *Treatise on the Astrolabe,* one may ask whether in the Man of Law's Tale and elsewhere Chaucer may not have been promoting himself as a sort of possible court astrologer: he had the knowledge; he used judicial astrology dramatically in *The Tales of Canterbury;* he also commended it in the Man of Law's Tale; both here and elsewhere in his poetry, Chaucer's creatures move against the background of the planets in their courses through the twelve signs of the zodiac. Thus the planetary spheres and the zodiac form the celestial frame of *The Tales of Canterbury,* while the mundane frame, with perpetual celestial overtones, is that of a pilgrimage to the shrine of St. Thomas à Becket.

The literary device of gathering a group of stories within the frame of a large situation or story is found in such Eastern collections as the *Panchatantra,* the *Katha Sarit Sagara, Kalilah and Dimna,* the *Seven Sages,* and, most famous of all, the *Thousand and One Nights.* In the course of the *Odyssey* the hero recites tales. In the *Metamorphoses,* Ovid presents tales within tales; for example, his story of the daughters of Minyas frames three stories which these maidens tell, including the story of Pyramus and Thisbe. It has been suggested that this episode, with its framing device, may have helped both Boccaccio and Chaucer design their framed story collections. Of Boccaccio's various accomplishments in the framing of stories, the best known is the *Decameron,* with its company of ten young people who flee the Florentine plague and each of whom tells a story on each of ten days, making the total of a hundred. Chaucer must have heard about this famous collection during his two journeys to Italy, the first of which took him to Florence itself. Less well known was the *Novelle* of Giovanni Sercambi of Lucca; but this collection is of interest because the men and women of the frame travel about Italy instead of sitting in a garden like those of the *Decameron.* Finally, mention should be made of Chaucer's friend John Gower, in whose *Confessio Amantis* the priest of Venus instructs and advises the confessing lover with over a hundred tales purporting to illustrate different sins. Examination of these various story-collections serves chiefly to emphasize the originality and brilliance of Chaucer's frame and of the changes he rings upon its basic design. The individual storytellers are presented with a rich vitality that is without precedent; and the clashes and frictions that develop among them, as they amble toward their destination, give this collection an extra dimension not found in any other.

Chaucer's entire framework for the tales is apparently a simple and natural one; but it is actually complex and far-reaching in its results. It consists first in the assembling of the company of pilgrims at a real inn of Chaucer's day, the Tabard, at Southwark, on the south shore of the Thames opposite London, there to begin the final stage of their pilgrimage to the shrine of the martyred Thomas à Becket at Canterbury, a ride of three or four days to the east along the most heavily traveled portion of the Pilgrims' Way. In Chaucer's day the pilgrimage was already a venerable institution. While the greatest of all shrines to be visited was the holy city of Jerusalem, there were many lesser ones throughout Europe; and of these, the most famous and popular in England was the shrine of St. Thomas at Canterbury. Originally conceived as a means of doing penance, giving thanks, or securing religious indulgence, the pilgrimage became at least for some a pretext for everything from a harmless if worldly vacation to an opportunity for every kind of irresponsible and licentious gaiety. As J. S. P. Tatlock said, the medieval pilgrim was little more than a sanctified tramp with the ictus on "tramp"; in this Chaucer's pilgrims are typical—the motives of few of them are primarily religious. Rather they seem drawn by the urge to get out on the road after the cold confinement of winter, to join fellow human beings on a holiday excursion not necessarily holy in all respects—but nevertheless leading to the shrine of St. Thomas at Canterbury.

In the fiction of the frame, the pilgrims are gathered together by chance; actually they are most carefully selected in variety of origin, interest, and character, and for potential sympathies, quarrels, contrasts, and other interplay. Chaucer tells us that they go to Canterbury "from every shires ende of Engelond"; and this particular company gives the impression of coming from all England: the Shipman "wonynge [dwelling] fer by weste" from Dartmouth in Devonshire; the Wife of Bath from Somersetshire; the Clerk from Oxford; the Sergeant of the Law, if he is to be identified with Thomas Pinchbeck (as J. M. Manly suggested), from Lincolnshire; the Reeve from Norfolk; the Cook and (I suppose) the Guildsmen, from London; and the Manciple, the Pardoner, and the Prioress from its close vicinity. The Franklin, the Parson, and the Plowman are quite evidently from the country. Again the pilgrims represent widely ranging walks of life, from the Knight (whose eminence is suggested, in part, by lines 52–53) to the humble Plowman (who carts dung to the fields); from the eminent Sergeant of the Law (who need not bare his head before the King) to the London Cook of ill repute. Likewise they afford a moral range from the heights (the good Parson) to the depths (the Pardoner, whom Kittredge called "an assassin of souls"), and an equally wide intellectual range. Thus the company participating in this pilgrimage is a little world of men, a little England, as it were; a group brought together to travel for a brief time down the road of life together.

Chaucer had apparently intended to describe a gathering of twenty-nine men and women who, together with him, make a round total of thirty. Just as the Tabard Inn serves as the focal gathering point of these pilgrims, so does the actual host of the Tabard, Herry Bailey, serve as the organizer of the pilgrims into a company of competing storytellers, thus setting up the "plan" of the tales themselves; and he arranges to call on all the pilgrims in turn to tell their stories. The Parson's Prologue indicates that Chaucer, when he wrote it, planned to have each pilgrim tell one story on the journey to Canterbury and to close the "feeste" with the Parson's Tale as the company neared Canterbury. At another stage Chaucer evidently intended to have some pilgrims tell more stories than one, as shown by the words of the Host to the Franklin:

> "What, Frankeleyn! pardee, sire, wel thou woost
> That ech of yow moot tellen atte leste
> A tale or two, or broken his biheste."

In the General Prologue, however, Chaucer presented the ambitious scheme of having each pilgrim tell four tales apiece, two on the way to Canterbury and two on the return trip to Southwark, outdoing Boccaccio's total in the *Decameron*. On the one hand, some critics feel that the generous number of one hundred and twenty tales represents Chaucer's first plan, and that it was later replaced by the more feasible total of thirty. On the other hand, it is altogether possible that as he completed tale after tale, Chaucer's ambition correspondingly grew, and that he revised the General Prologue to match even before he had completed twenty-four tales. In either case, there seem to be no hints in the course of the actual links and tales that Chaucer ever introduced a single line deliberately intended for the homeward journey; and the Parson's Prologue and Tale are far better suited for the approach of the pilgrims to the shrine in the Cathedral than for their return to supper at Herry Bailey's Tabard Inn at Southwark.

But the Host not only plans the program of tale-telling as a whole: he also intends to call in turn upon each member of the company for the promised contribution. He comments on many of the tales, and often calls upon the next teller; but again and again these highly individualistic personalities are too much for him, and, in the long run thrusting themselves forward, they initiate the telling of as many tales as he does. Far from forming a static group, the pilgrims give free rein to their whims, desires, and other idiosyncrasies, so that, by his careful art, Chaucer has made his fiction of stories framed in the setting of a pilgrimage seem lively and real.

He sets up his description of the Canterbury pilgrims by telling us that at the Tabard Inn he had so spoken with every one of them that he right away became one of their company; he then decides to tell us

> al the condicioun
> Of ech of hem, so as it semed me,
> And whiche they weren, and of what degree,
> And eek in what array that they were inne.

And so Chaucer focuses our attention on pilgrim after pilgrim until we see them so vividly and get to know them so well that we too feel ourselves to be a part of this fascinating company. In the portraits or sketches, practically every detail is one that could have resulted from personal observation (appearance, dress, characteristic behavior, or mannerism), or from talking with the "sondry folk" and learning from each of his past life, beliefs and opinions, preferences, and the like; or from a combination of these and the pilgrim-poet's personal judgment ("so as it semed me"). The pilgrims are described as they were on the road, during the actual pilgrimage: for example, the facts that the Miller "broghte us out of towne" with his "baggepipe"; that the Reeve ever "rood the hyndreste of oure route"; their mounts and their individual styles of riding; and we may assume that various other details, too, were supposedly noted by Chaucer during the days these people passed in one another's company.

Again and again Chaucer particularly tells us, or clearly implies, that a bit of information comes from the lips of his subject: as when he writes of the Friar:

> For he hadde power of confessioun,
> As seyde hymself, moore than a curat;

or tells of the Pardoner's pillow-case "Which that he seyde was Oure Lady veyl"; or the poet will quote and immediately comment, as with the Summoner:

> "Purs is the ercedekenes helle," seyde he.
> But wel I woot he lyed right in dede. . . .

The description of the Parson allows us to overhear this good man offering Chaucer his *apologia pro vita sua:*

> This noble ensample to his sheep he yaf,
> That first he wroghte, and afterward he taughte.
> Out of the gospel he tho wordes caughte,
> And this figure he added eek therto,
> That if gold ruste, what sholde iren do?

In short, Chaucer's descriptions often echo or reflect self-revelatory monologues which the poet has elicited from his subjects; and which he passes along to us with sufficient comment to show that he is not taken in, that there is more than meets the ear.

Chaucer generally gives the impression that he is wholly objective, reporting what he has learned from the pilgrims, dryly listing cold facts; but again and again he slips his tongue into his cheek; somehow we catch a warning to be careful how we interpret. Thus we are not directly told whether the Squire curled his hair. Nor are we directly told that the Monk has a mistress; but there are puns and vivid details enough to make a direct statement unnecessary. The Merchant is insulted in line after line, all delivered in a genteel, almost complimentary manner. At times the poet implies his thoughts by careful juxtaposition of apparently irrelevant details: of the Friar (ll. 212–14); of the Cook (ll. 385–87), with the almost apologetic "as it thoughte me" possibly suggesting, in a tease, that the audience might have a different opinion.

On other occasions Chaucer hazards a guess: the age of the Squire; that the Yeoman was a forester; the weight of the Wife's coverchiefs; and he perpetually reminds us that his observation and his judgment are contributing factors in these portraits. Likewise his deliberate choice is to be found in the order in which he presents the portraits. Some of them, quite naturally it seems to us, after the fact, fall into groups, either because they are related (Knight and Squire; Parson and Plowman) or are friends (the Sergeant of Law and the Franklin, presumably; the Guildsmen; the Summoner and the Pardoner); or because their roles in life were similar (the regular clergy; the final group of rascals).

It soon becomes obvious that this grouping of pilgrims in the General Prologue often reveals contrasts and underlying conflict. Thus Chaucer begins with a dignified representative of feudalism and of chivalry—the gallant man on horseback—who for some is the epitome of the Middle Ages, when knighthood was in flower. Over the span of half a century he has served his King and his God; he has fought for Edward III against the French in the Hundred Years' War, he has fought against the Lithuanians in the Baltic region, he has crusaded against the Moslems from one end of the Mediterranean to the other—from Algeciras and Morocco to Asia Minor and Alexandria. More noteworthy even than the Knight's tremendous military career as vassal of the King and crusader for God is his character: he loves "chivalrie, trouthe and honour, fredom and curteisie," and, as Chaucer sums him up in one all-enveloping line, "He was a verray [true], parfit, gentil knyght."

If this knight of tournament, siege, and battlefield appears to neglect the court and boudoir, the lack is more than made up by his elegant and accomplished son, the fashionable Squire, who loved so hotly that at night "He slepte namoore than dooth a nyghtyngale." The Squire is mindful not only of fighting but also of love; his skill with his sword has been devoted to winning his lady's favors. His chief accomplishments belong to the castle and to times of peace; he jousts, to be sure, but is especially devoted to singing, dancing, drawing, dressing in style, and to making poetry and love.

Thus in father and son are opposed two complementary phases of chivalry; likewise the perpetual conflicts of age and youth, of older and younger generations; and again, two stages in the development of knighthood itself. Far from static, the two portraits offer a complex of conflicting purposes and ideals; for Chaucer was aware of many of the transitions that occur as individuals mature, and of the transitions which obtained during his time when the medieval world was giving way to tendencies that led toward the modern world.

A method of portraiture somewhat different in its texture, and perhaps more complex in its total effect, is that of the Prioress. Just as the Knight, his son the Squire, and his servant the Yeoman, form a group, so the next pilgrims described also form a set of three, not bound together by ties of blood or companionship, but nevertheless fittingly portrayed in sequence as a sort of triptych—three members of the "regular" clergy, the Prioress, the Monk, and the Friar. The daily lives of the regular clergy were guided and bound by a religious "rule" (Latin, *regula*), in contradistinction to the secular clergy, such as the parish priest, the "Persoun of a toun," who lived in the world (Latin, *saeculum*). The three portraits form a series of gradual contrasts, beginning with the quiet, devout Prioress, who daintily imitates the ladies of the court, whose charity and pity amount to mawkish sentimentality, who sings divine service quite properly, and whose rosary carries the motto cut in gold (forbidden metal) *Amor vincit omnia*. Second is the manly Monk, a gourmet with no interest in the monastic duties of study and manual labor, but a lover of venery (hunting; the work of Venus), with his swift greyhounds, and his gold pin in the form of a love-knot. The Friar, in turn, is presented in the longest and most complex portrait of the entire collection, with several motifs in counterpoint: his relations with and attitudes toward various types of women, toward rich and poor, toward the sick and the sinful, and above all toward his vows of chastity, poverty, and obedience, and toward his duty of serving man and God.

The portrait of the Prioress is marked by a rather subtle ambiguity which leaves the reader with facts which he (rather than Chaucer) must interpret and which defy a simple one-dimensional explanation. Her oath is such a small and delicate one (by St. Loy, patron of courtiers and of goldsmiths), yet still an oath. Her second language is French rather than Latin. Her table manners seem perfectly commendable; yet to the detail they match the famous directions, offered by the old Duenna in *Le Roman de la Rose,* telling what a woman should do to attract a man. She is full of charity and pity—for bleeding mice. Thus to the final ambiguity of the love that conquers all, we are left uncertain whether the mind and heart of the Prioress are devoted more to God or to a courtly life that can never be fully hers. She is as difficult to know through and through as are many real people; and the complexity of her relationship to the religious life is intensified by contrast and comparison with the Monk and the Friar. Her personality is further enriched for us by the tale she tells and also by the tale of the Nuns' Priest.

For Chaucer's art of characterization extends far beyond the portraits presented in the General Prologue. One way in which he extends and deepens our impression of the pilgrims is through their activities and conversations in the links between the tales, their repartee and quarrels with the Host and with one another. The Reeve gets into conflict with the drunken Miller; the Friar teases the Wife of Bath; the Host teases Chaucer and later the Monk; the Knight interrupts the Monk and acts as peacemaker between Pardoner and Host. The successive links offer gradual revelations concerning Herry Bailey: his treatment of the different pilgrims, his oaths, his pretensions as a literary critic, glimpses of his homelife, and much more. Yet another way in which the pilgrims reveal their personalities is through the stories they tell: some of these fit the professions of the tellers; some appear to derive mood, color, and motivation from traits of the tellers as they were presented in the General Prologue, and to develop these traits and related ones into well-rounded personalities. In addition, several figures such as the Reeve, the Wife, the Pardoner, and the Canon's Yeoman, tell about themselves in dramatic monologues of varying length which serve as prologues to their tales. Again, quarrels, rivalries, or other interplay stir several pilgrims to tell stories satirizing one another—as for example the Miller and the Reeve, or the Friar and the Summoner. But the variety of methods used by the poet in different combinations cannot be summed up in any cut-and-dried listing: we are perpetually challenged to be alert for new methods of character revelation, sometimes counterpointed against each other with overwhelming richness.

The first tale of all is told by the pilgrim whose portrait heads the series in the General Prologue, the "verray, parfit, gentil knyght." For the satisfaction of his audience—medieval and modern—longing for the good old days when knighthood flourished, he offers a medieval romance of chivalry and love, reconciling and uniting, as it were, the interests and ideals of both Knight and Squire. In his story the noble duke Theseus (a knight and a famous conquerer much like Chaucer's own knight) is arbiter and master of ceremonies and of destinies for two young heroes whose desires, propensities, and accomplishments are like those of his son, the Squire. The reader who so desires may discover in the Knight's Tale a sympathetic understanding of the personality and interests of the Squire, a broader humanity in the Knight than was at first glance apparent in the portrait of the General Prologue. Thus the portrait enhances the tale, and the tale in turn enriches the portrait. Knight, Squire, and Knight's Tale exist for one another, and by their interrelationships form a total which is greater than a simple summation.

It is clear that the Knight's Tale fits both the profession and the personality of its teller; but there are no remarkable ambiguities here: the tale could belong to any good knight, to any worthy representative of chivalry. And insofar as the Prioress's Tale is a miracle of the Virgin, told in her honor, it would be a suitable tale for any devout nun or prioress, for any worthy representative of the religious life. But there are also qualities of the tale which make it eminently suitable for this particular prioress, and so in turn it intensifies her personality for us. Critics have suggested that a thwarted mother-instinct is revealed both by the "smale houndes" to whom she fed "rosted flessh, or milk and wastel-breed" (fine white bread), and by the choice of hero for her tale, the little schoolboy; and have found her interest in his martyrdom to be matched by her attitude toward the bleeding mouse and the dead or beaten hound of the General Prologue. In the tale, even as in the prologue, it may be that her charity and pity have a limited range. The contrast between the Prioress and the Monk is brought back to mind by her comment to the effect that the abbot was a holy man, "As monkes been, or elles oghte be." Such details as these, taken together, heighten the impression given of the Prioress in the General Prologue, and reveal that her tale fits not only her profession, but also her personality—belongs not only to the Prioress, but also to the woman within the robes.

But this is not all: accompanying the Prioress on this pilgrimage are another Nun, who was her secretary and assistant (her "chapeleyne"), and the Nuns' Priest who was attached to their convent. These two are the only tale-tellers who are not introduced to us by means of formal portraits in the General Prologue (excepting of course, the Canon's Yeoman, who joins the company later at Boghtoun under Blee). Although the completely literate Second Nun is the only pilgrim who claims to have translated her story (to avoid idleness, the nurse of vices), hers is a somewhat colorless even if devout personality; yet she serves as a modest and useful foil to her superior. On the other hand, the tale that the Nuns' Priest offers the pilgrims vividly reveals a vibrant and brilliant personality, and something of his opinion of the Prioress, too. Here, as everywhere else, Chaucer's methods of presentation invite the reader to take an active part in understanding and interpreting the world of *The Tales of Canterbury*.

The Nuns' Priest's Tale, then, is outstanding in its revelation of the character of its teller. One of its notable features is satire: in the course of his rambling narrative of the cock and the hen and the fox, often interrupted by seemingly irrelevant digressions, Sir John satirizes a multitude of things, among which are the tales of several preceding storytellers, the Shipman, the Prioress, Chaucer, and the Monk; stock descriptions of heroes of romances; theories of dreams; the excessive contemporary interest in emetics and laxatives; the medieval tendency to cite "authorities," "sentences," and "ensamples" from old books—as proof in an argument; elaborate similes; scholastic disputes concerning God's foreknowledge and man's free will; the advice of women; the manuals of rhetoric and the rhetorical devices taught in medieval schools; and the custom of drawing a moral from every story—ending with "Haec fabula docet. . . ." Thus, by the time his tale is ended, we come to know a good deal of the mind and temperament of "this sweete preest, this goodly man sir John," who has framed his tale in the milieu of the other tales and their tellers, and at the same time in a universe rich with theories, concepts, and forces of which the protagonist cock is blithely unaware.

Another figure revealed to us chiefly by indirection is that of Chaucer, who presents the portraits and other information in the General Prologue with an apparently casual objectivity—and likewise the subsequent links and tales; and takes the limelight as storyteller, after a tease from the Host, with the protest that he knows only one rime, which he learned long ago. This Tale of Sir Thopas proves to be such doggerel that the Host can barely endure two hundred lines of it. First the hero's person is described in a series of similes that echo the similes of other rimed romances—though this is the only one where the hero's face is as white as fine white bread ("payndemayn"). What kind of knight is this, with "lippes rede as rose" and hair and beard "lyk saffroun," the orange-yellow spice used to color pies, meats, and confectionery? To his noble pastimes, Sir Thopas adds low-bred wrestling, and he hawks with a goshawk, appropriate for yeoman rather than knight. The topaz is the gem of chastity, and maidens long for our hero in vain. He rides through a forest full of wild beasts such as the lecherous hare, full of aphrodisiac spices, and full of singing birds—especially the "thrustel," whose song had long been known to incite pleasures of the flesh.

> Sire Thopas eek so wery was
> For prikyng on the softe gras,
>   So fiers was his corage,
> That doun he leyde him in the plas. . . .

It is now we learn he had dreamed all night that an elf-queen shall be his "lemman" (sweetheart, mistress, concubine); and soon his hunt for her is on. Sir Thopas meets a three-headed giant called Sir Olifaunt, and promises to return tomorrow in armor to fight him. With a deft twist of the David-Goliath motif, Sir Olifaunt casts stones at Thopas from a sling. Our hero rushes home to prepare. He listens to romances and eats spices while breeches, shirt, and armor are loaded onto him piece by piece, for four doggerel stanzas. Finally, a lily-flower stuck in his helmet, Sir Thopas rides forth to get a drink of well-water—and Herry Bailey calls a halt: he can stand no more. Chaucer has done his best; the plot, to be sure, has barely begun; we have not yet met the heroine; the jog-trot of the stanzas is not much worse than that of the rimed romances Chaucer must have listened to many an evening as a member of a captive audience in some courtly hall. But apparently Herry Bailey had a low opinion of such heroes as Horn, Guy, and Pleyndamour, and of the audiences that welcomed them; so of "the flour of roial chivalry" we know no more. Chaucer's second attempt, his "litel thyng in prose," the nine- or ten-thousand-word Tale of Melibee pleased Herry Bailey more.

Two of the pilgrims who reveal their natures in long prologues as well as in their respective tales are the Pardoner and the Wife of Bath. The Pardoner boasts of the methods whereby he extracts money from his victims, caring not at all what becomes of their souls which he has bargained to save; and he crowns all with the murder story, the exemplum, with which he enforces and enriches his sermon against avarice and other sins. The perversion of the Pardoner's soul may in part be due to maladjustment of his personality—he is a *eunuchus ex nativitate*—to the world of normal men and women, against whom he takes subtle revenge. His relationship with the vicious Summoner intensifies the sordidness of the Pardoner's life, and reminds the audience how far each fails to perform his ecclesiastical duty. The song they sing together—"Com hider, love, to me"—is particularly ironic for the Pardoner, whose high voice belies the virility of which he brags. This is the man who at another moment tells the Wife of Bath that he is about to marry and asks her advice!

In the General Prologue we became aware of the many husbands and pilgrimages of the Wife of Bath; of her gay clothing, her fair, bold, red face, her large hips, her laughter, and joking; and her knowledge of the "olde daunce" of the art of love. These, however, are only hints of what is to come when she reveals herself in the prologue to her tale. First comes her sermon in defense of marrying as often as she is widowed, her cry of "Welcome the sixte!" and her defense of marriage as opposed to virginity. If all this tends to make marriage seem attractive, her reaction to the Pardoner's interruption sounds the notes of woe and tribulation, and so does her description of her conduct toward her three rich old husbands, and her treatment of the unfaithful fourth. She must love, and she must wield the whip; she must dominate, and she must succumb. She was born under the influence of Venus, and also under Mars. Venus gave the Wife lecherousness, but Mars gave her sturdy hardiness. The complexity of her character, and its contradictions, give her an added dimension of reality. She tells of courting her fifth husband Jankyn, the clerk of Oxford; of the death and burial of her fourth husband; and of the "book of wikked wyves" that Jankyn had brought down from Oxford: how he read it aloud by the fireside until she could endure no more; of their final climactic brawl, and their treaty: how she won governance of house and land, and of his tongue, and of his hand; and how he, in turn, agreed to burn the book. Says she: "After that day we hadden never debaat."

Still more of Alice's character is revealed by the tale she tells, and even by the little sermon on gentilesse, poverty, beauty, and old age which she permits her fairy-tale heroine to preach before the denouement in order to teach the hero all he needs to know. Further touches are added to the portrait of the Wife of Bath by her contacts with other pilgrims during various links and tales. The Pardoner's interruption affords a bit of repartee; the Friar's teasing comment on her prologue prompts Alice to tease him back when she starts her tale; the Clerk, after telling of the patient wife Griselda, in part for Alice's benefit, sings a song in her praise—a masterpiece of mock-encomium. The Merchant refers to her in his tale. The Franklin, in turn, has Dorigen praise the conduct of maidens, wives, and widows in terms which put to shame the way in which Alice played each of these roles. On one special occasion—in the short poem "Lenvoy de Chaucer a Bukton"— her personality even bursts out of the Canterbury pilgrimage and *The Tales,* when Chaucer, writing to his friend Bukton, who was about to marry, cries out to him: "The Wyf of Bathe I pray yow that ye rede Of this matere that we have on honde." Thus she seems to have belonged to the vivid milieu of the poet and his audience as well as to *The Tales,* where her ideas stir up such a variety of comments on marriage, "sovereynetee," "gentillesse," and related problems. Here, in short, is a figure involved in dramatic clashes of speech and action and principle. Her extensive travels and experiences give the impression of a woman living in a wide world. The story of her life, with its glimpses of earlier years, and its hints and promises for her future, has the effect of giving her an extension in time as well as in space. Her essential mystery deepens as we are made aware of the cosmic background of the planets; and when she tells her tale, successive shadowy alter egos loom behind her in deepening perspective: old Alice on the Canterbury road, the young Alice in her memory and in the fields; the "olde wyf" of the tale, the heroine transformed to be young and fair, and the "elf-queene" who "daunced ful ofte in many a grene mede." Chaucer has gone beyond all precedent in endowing the Wife of Bath with humanity, and with life, and in his presentation of the golden splendor of her personality, wherein Venus, and Mars, and the "Queene of Fayerye" contend for "sovereynetee."

A somewhat different method of self-revelation is found in the Reeve's dramatic monologue which precedes his tale: he boasts of his impotence in language so figurative that Herry Bailey thinks that he has heard a sermon based on Holy Writ. But the Reeve, together with the Miller, is even more significant as an example of one of Chaucer's more complex methods of characterization. The reeve of a manor was apt to come into conflict with the local miller, especially if either was dishonest; but the two figures portrayed by Chaucer appear to have been personal enemies as well; the characteristics of each are revealed by the portraits in the General Prologue, by their quarrel in the links, by the story each tells, and by the story told on each by the other. Thus it has long been recognized that the background, physique, character, and personality of Osewold the Reeve are reflected in the portrait of old John the carpenter of the Miller's Tale, whose adventures both in anticipation and in retrospect so stir up this man, who in youth had been a carpenter, that one may with some justification suspect that he himself has been thus cuckolded and that Robin the Miller knows it. Likewise the portrait of "deynous Symkyn" in the Reeve's Tale clearly offers a personalized reprise of salient characteristics of Robin the Miller of the General Prologue, so similar are the two millers in their wrestling, weapons, thieving, gay apparel, piping, and drinking. What has not been so clearly understood, however, is the fact that the Reeve's Prologue is both a reflection of and a commentary on the Miller's Tale as well as an introduction to the tale that follows. In the Reeve's Prologue are to be found such echoes of the preceding tale as the figure of the colt. Alisoun had been thus described:

> *Wynsynge she was, as is a joly colt;*

and when Nicholas "heeld hire harde by the haunchebones," "she sproong as a colt dooth in the trave"—that is, in the travail, the wooden frame at the blacksmith's forge, when being shod for the first time. The Reeve in turn says:

> *But ik am oold, me list not pley for age;*
> *Gras tyme is doon, my fodder is now forage. . . .*
> *And yet ik have alwey a coltes tooth.*

Soon, in his tale, the Reeve allows the manciple's horse to run into the swamp to the "wilde mares." Again, Alisoun's mouth is described as "sweete as . . . hoord of apples leyd in hey," while Osewold the Reeve compares himself to the rotten fruit "open-ers" lying "in mullok or in stree." Alisoun and Nicholas make melody until the bell of lauds; in his prologue Osewold uses the ancient symbol of the bell to stress his impotence. The theme of fire and coals, used effectively several times in the Miller's Tale (as in the forge scene just mentioned), is likewise picked up by the Reeve in his prologue.

In the tales told by the Friar and the Summoner, Chaucer exploits to the full the personal and professional animosities that motivate these rascals; but the obvious interrelationships are not the only connections between the two tales. The Friar, in his tale, has the fiend virtually award the summoner a doctorate in demonology; how then can this Friar deny the Summoner's description of hell and Satan which immediately follows? But this is not the only use that the Summoner makes of the Friar's Tale. At the climax, when old bedridden Thomas awards his gift to the wheedling Friar John, the Summoner borrows for his figure of speech not the "trombetta" of Dante's Malacoda, but (from the first crisis in the Friar's Tale) a "capul drawing of a cart." At the second crisis of the Friar's Tale, the summoner is after the poor widow's cloth—her "panne" (Latin *pannus*), her "clooth"; and sure enough, in the final scene of the Summoner's Tale a new gown cloth is to be awarded to the lord's squire Jankyn if he can solve a difficult problem in aerodynamics and sensation. Solve it he does, and by means of a cart wheel, again stolen from the Friar. One such bit of filching might pass as coincidence; but a total of three seems too deliberate to ignore.

Thus *The Tales of Canterbury* cannot be considered merely a collection of stories, or of pilgrims designed to tell them. The bringing together of teller and tale gives each a significance not found in either by itself, and the whole is greater than their sum. The framing of the tales puts them in perspective and directs our view. They are framed as coming from each teller's experience, background, knowledge, his world of prejudices, desires, ideals, and love, or his animosities, his weaknesses, his hypocrisies. They are further to be viewed in relation to the pilgrim audience, some of whom are addressed or hit at in particular; and in relation to the Host, Herry Bailey, whose comments are sometimes irrelevant, sometimes banal, usually self-revealing. Set off against these personalities, these segments of society, each tale takes on a deeper significance in its own right.

Chaucer not only shows his skill by placing each tale in an external setting which gives it added richness; he likewise puts into each tale an internal setting—of background and atmosphere—in which the events take place. Although the setting of the Knight's Tale is presented at length by means of extensive descriptions inherited from classical epic and medieval romance, for most of his subsequent tales Chaucer presented settings in just a few lines, perhaps a few at the beginning, and then single lines or phrases as the tale progressed. After the opening description of the old widow's cottage and yard, the setting of the Nuns' Priest's Tale is handled in about a dozen lines. The overpowering milieu of the Pardoner's Tale is wrought by means of an absolute minimum of descriptive terms, whose sharp and memorable impact on the reader is heightened by the apparent casualness with which the tavern, the crooked way, the oak, and the next street in the town are brought to his attention. In the Miller's Tale the poet enriches our glimpses of Oxford, day and night, by using figures of speech which present simultaneously to the mind's eye both the scene of the immediate action and also another scene. Thus during Alisoun's first scene with Nicholas we are simultaneously made aware of a colt being shod at a forge; later the melody of these two lovers continues until lauds, when "freres in the chauncel gonne synge"; and Absolon's expectant stance in chips and shavings reminds us how the carpenter has labored all day to prepare the tubs. Again and again the Wife of Bath's Prologue and her Tale offer vivid settings, all accomplished, as it were, in passing, with an art that conceals itself. More subtle than the presentation of these formal bits of description is the creation of atmosphere in certain tales. Sometimes a realistically worldly setting is enhanced by a gradually discovered otherworldly background, offering a mysterious depth to the tale. The bourgeois figures, Sir Thopas, the Merchant, and the Wife of Bath, lead us to three highly individualized fairylands, while the Squire and the Franklin offer realistic settings in which magic flourishes before our very eyes. The sophisticated Nuns' Priest, in turn, permits bird and beast to converse in the old widow's farm yard. The world of death overshadows the Pardoner's Tale; while the ordinary, everyday environment of the Friar's Tale suddenly vanishes to reveal the horrors of hell. Each of these otherworldly backgrounds is crucial to its tale, and in each Chaucer's art deserves thoughtful attention. For example, in the Friar's Tale we walk along the Yorkshire road and watch a summoner, who pretends to be a bailiff, reveal that he is worse than the fiend, who has assumed the form of a yeoman; and the ground beneath our feet somehow feels less secure because of continuous intimations of another world, so far and yet so near. The yeoman-fiend says:

> *My dwellyng is in helle,*

and tells the curious bailiff-summoner somewhat of devils and hell, and how the devils sometimes "been Goddes instrumentz," so that standing precariously on earth we become aware of both heaven and hell. Finally, when the tale reaches its climax, the summoner is given an opportunity to repent—and refuses. Then it is that the fiend declares to the unrepentant summoner:

> *Thou shalt with me to helle yet to-nyght,*

a line that offers vivid echoes of and contrasts sharply with Christ's words to the repentant thief, "Verily I say unto thee, Today shalt thou be with me in Paradise" (Luke xxiii.43):

> *Amen dico tibi, hodie mecum eris in Paradiso.*

Thus simply and effectively the old exemplum is given new overtones, the Yorkshire countryside is given a cosmic background, and the utter depravity of the summoner is emphasized beyond belief.

Again, the poet opens some tales in ways which take us elsewhere from the present time and place, and thus prepare for the unusual quality, values, and tone that are to follow. The Clerk's Prologue leads us first to Padua and the late Petrarch; and then summarizes Petrarch's "prohemye," with its strange and sonorous geographical names—

> *To Emele-ward, to Ferrare, and Venyse—*

and their Miltonic effect of removal to a world strange to us in more ways than one. The Knight's Tale opens with a double summary of Theseus' conquest of the Amazons, a repetition with slight variations, taking us from Athens to Femenye and back, in such a manner that we are completely transported to the ancient, chivalric dukedom where the romance transpires in a mood of perpetual springtime. The Pardoner's Tale opens with a description of the sinful tavern in Flanders during the plague, and the wicked exemplum with its pious sermonizing is intensified by this macabre presence of the Black Death, which throughout Europe had incited some to riotous living in desperate attempts to seize whatever moments remained of life, and stirred others to remorse and guilt and new depths of religious feeling. Throughout the tale we are conscious of these two worlds, the moral and the licentious, and in the end they meet head-on when "the feend" has permission to destroy the revelers. The Squire's Tale and the Franklin's each has its special way of transporting us to the scene of the story. The Wife of Bath accomplishes this in a *tour de force* that is somewhat complex but altogether effective: her introduction of limitour and incubus at once compliments and teases Friar Huberd, takes us back to the days of "Kyng Arthour," sets the tone for the rape in the woods with which the tale opens, and prepares for the denouement in all its beauty and terror. (It is left for the Merchant to reveal just what sort of creature the "queene of Fayerye" really is.)

Some of the tales gain richness from the connotations of the names of characters. Chaucer accepted from predecessors the names "Custance" and "Chauntecleer," which fit the personages to whom they belong. On the model of "Chauntecleer" (which in Old French signifies "one who sings clearly, loudly") Chaucer concocted the name "Pertelote," which seems to signify "one who ruins, confuses, destroys ('perte') someone's lot or fate ('lote')": in other words she is "hominis confusio." The suitability of the name "Thopas"—that is, topaz, symbolizing chastity—has already been mentioned. Father Beichner has shown how the portrait of Absolon in the Miller's Tale is intensified by the reputation for beauty and effeminacy that his scriptural namesake enjoyed throughout the Middle Ages. His rival Nicholas has the name of the patron saint of students. Turning to the Merchant's Tale, we should note that in Chaucer's time May was the third month of the year, and January nearly the last—facts which enforce the correspondence of the names to the respective ages of the two characters. The appropriateness of the names of January's brothers, Justinus and Placebo, need not be stressed. January's squire Damian shared the name of St. Damianus who, along with his brother St. Cosimus, was favored by a cult (persisting as late as the eighteenth century at Isernia, in southern Italy) as a virtual patron saint of generative power, and on their feast day was offered phallic *ex-voti* made of wax. Such significant names as these not only bring to the characters connotations from the real world outside the tales, but also give the tales a satiric tone of cynicism and a forceful narrative quality of anticipation; some of Chaucer's audience, on hearing the names of Absolon and Damian in the stories, must have expected the worst. In the same tales another effective device, the descriptive epithet, intensifies the struggles of such figures as the "sely carpenter," "hende Nicholas," "joly Absolon," and "fresshe May."

Chaucer's conventional manner of tale-telling was to retell another man's story with the book open before him but with fresh purpose and new unity. The Knight's Tale, for example, is a complete reworking into medieval romance of Boccaccio's long pseudo-epic, *Il Teseida*. The Man of Law's Tale is a concentrated and heightened redaction of the rambling account of Constance found in *Les Cronicles of Nicholas Trevet*. The Physician's Tale is a redaction of Livy's historical account of the conflict of Appius and Virginius, but is based chiefly on Jean de Meun's version (in *Le Roman de la Rose*), which stresses the wickedness of the judge; but Chaucer adds a new emphasis on the beauty, personality, thoughts, and emotions of the heroine Virginia. In retelling the legend of St. Cecilia the poet selects from standard accounts those details which heighten her reverend faith, her chastity, her busyness in active good works (especially her persistent teaching and proselytizing), and her defiant audacity in the face of earthly authority. The Clerk's

Tale of Griseldis follows Petrarch's expansion of the last novella of Boccaccio's *Decameron,* but with new subtle emphases on values cherished and championed by the Clerk as he reacts to the views of Alice of Bath. Thus in this series of redactions of venerable stories about the classical and more recent historical past, Chaucer was no slavish translator. These standard plots, already treated successfully by previous writers, he improved by slight subtractions, additions, expansion or omission of passages, or modifications of the action; by a reworking of characterization; by more vivid settings and atmosphere, and by the enrichment of theme and significance. But the basic, well-tried stories laid in Troy, Athens, pagan or Christian Rome, or the Marquisate of Saluzzo, were clearly and pointedly recognized as modernizations (if you will), or at least fresh retellings, of narratives already presented in other tongues by great "auctours."

In turning from tales with recognizable sources, rewritten with one or more books—French, Italian, or Latin—open before him, to tales for which only analogues survive, we must note first that for some tales there is no recognizable source plot at all. Chaucer apparently worked various materials together on his own for the rime of Sir Thopas, the Wife of Bath's Prologue, the Canon's Yeoman's Prologue and Tale, and the unfinished tales of Cook and Squire. For others there are analogues scattered about the world; and the poet may have read one or more of these, but he may quite as likely have simply heard the stories he retold; he may have kept them in his head rather than in his library. There is nothing particularly bookish about the plots of the tales told by the Miller, Reeve, Wife of Bath, Friar, Summoner, Merchant, Franklin Squire, or Pardoner. These recall fabliau, fable, novella, tale, and exemplum, from all over Europe and from the Orient too. For the most part, Chaucer took from these analogues only the barest outlines of anecdotal plots, and most of these are presented with such originality, are so embellished with decorative and thematic digressions, and are so apposite to the personalities of one or more pilgrims, that the original sources seem almost to have been forgotten in the vibrant syntheses of apothegm, anecdote, and folklore, classical, scriptural, scholastic, and scientific learning, and vivid details of contemporary life.

Just as through the very existence of the tales told by the pilgrims Chaucer adds reality to the tellers themselves and to the pilgrimage, so the tales gain verisimilitude and vividness by his perpetual device of tales within a tale. Thus the Wife of Bath's lurid anecdotes from Valerius Maximus and from Jankyn's "book of wikked wyves" help make her account of her adventures with the five husbands seem authentic autobiography. Her metamorphosis of Ovid's tale of Midas' ears (perverted to show that women cannot keep secrets) makes her personality and homelife more vivid, while the curtain lecture of the "olde wyf" of Alice's fairy story has the effect of making fairyland good enough to be true. Chauntecleer is the more believable because of the biblical, classical, and medieval narratives that he foists upon his innocent wife. The vividness of the Pardoner's Tale is intensified by the presence of the time-worn exempla in its moral introduction. Dorigen's complaint not only reveals her puzzlement in the face of an extraordinary dilemma, but also builds a contrast between her noble aims and ideals and her goodness, and the callousness, lasciviousness, and promiscuity of the Wife of Bath. The two sermons of the wheedling friar John in the Summoner's Tale, the anecdote of the stumbling astronomer in the Miller's Tale, the examples in the Manciple's Tale, and other digressions in other tales, all enhance the total effect of the teller, his tale, and often other pilgrims.

In each minor episode, in the dramatic clashes in the links, and in the larger construction of each tale, Chaucer shows his mastery of plot. The Knight's Tale is far more unified and direct than Boccaccio's *Teseida*, its source. The climax of the Miller's Tale is so neat that the casual reader may be unaware of the deftness and skill by which the two separate plots crash together when a colter from the hot forge causes Nicholas' cry of "Water!" In the swiftness and economy of the Pardoner's Tale, from opening scene to denouement, we recognize one of the world's masters of plot. The manner in which Chaucer ends that story reminds us of Dante, both Francesca's words, "That day we read no more" ("quel giorno più non vi leggemmo avante"), and Ugolino's "then hunger was more powerful than grief" ("poscia, più che il dolor, potè il digiuno").

Yet there is more than this. The Knight's Tale, before it is ended, brings thoughts on the nature of life and death:

> *This world nys but a thurghfare ful of wo,*
> *And we been pilgrymes, passynge to and fro.*

Theseus discourses on the order of the universe, and on sorrow yielding place to joy. In the Miller's Tale the learned world of the irreverent Nicholas is set against the obscurantism of the pious carpenter John; and motifs of religion, both sincere and hypocritical, are counterpointed against lust and melody of flesh and the world. The Prioress's Tale, too, may have undercurrents. The topsy-turvy world of the Nuns' Priest's Tale questions all kinds of values, including some concerning literature, learning, and men and women; whereas the Wife of Bath raises questions which touch the very foundations of medieval religious life and those of the institution of marriage, including church doctrine as laid down by St. Paul: "Let women be subject to their husbands as to the Lord." All these themes are heightened through carefully presented ironies, as when in the Pardoner's Tale there lurks unsuspected in the gold a spiritual death far worse than the physical death the rioters vowed to find. Thus the pilgrims and their tales cover a wide range, from the black depths of the Pardoner's soul to the sublime ideals of the Knight and the Parson.

In the first canto of the *Commedia,* Dante leaves *il cammin di nostra vita* to be guided by Virgil and then Beatrice through Inferno, Purgatorio, and Paradiso; Chaucer and his fellow pilgrims hold to the road and journey of this life. Chaucer's scene of action is the real world of fourteenth-century England, but with a distinction: the tellers and tales are set in that very special condition of travelers and traveling where good fellowship and undue frankness are often born of the knowledge that the companionship is of the journey only and of a holiday time set apart from ordinary daily life. And so, their spirits liberated, men are brought out of themselves and stimulated to reveal themselves, first to the poet, and then to the entire company. Thus he is enabled more or less to sum up the existence of each pilgrim to this particular point in time, this fixed point of pilgrimage which thus becomes a point of reference, not in the eternity of the next world, but in the forever-now—the special fixed eternity—of the poem. This time is not the epic time in which destiny gradually unfolds, but is a momentary time, the time of a lightning flash in which the poet simultaneously transfixes and illumines the scene and presents it for perpetuity in a sudden revelation of setting, character, speech, and action. Like Dante, Chaucer presents the essence, the essential living qualities of people, caught in an eternal moment. Dante indicates the decisiveness of the moment by making it the result of divine judgment upon the individual; Chaucer indicates the decisiveness of the moment by brilliantly singling it out from the progress of the earthly pilgrimage itself, choosing the occasion of the particular Canterbury pilgrimage within the all-inclusive pilgrimage of life, so that the one both symbolizes and is the other. Thus the illumined moment has an intensity matched only by that of the pilgrims themselves. Dante makes this world credible through his description of the next; Chaucer makes the next world credible through his descriptions of men and women in this world, again and again revealing the future—both here, as in the Wife's Prologue, and in the hereafter, as in the comedy of the Friar's Tale and the tragedy of the Pardoner's. If Chaucer does not seem often to condemn the wicked, he does something far more powerful and effective as again and again he forces the omniscient reader to pass the final judgment.

One of the factors motivating Chaucer and contributing to his success was the brilliant and appreciative audience for which he wrote. Describing the golden age of gothic genius in England, John Harvey, when he had examined the rich throng of artists who moved in late fourteenth-century London, claimed that this was a galaxy of talent and genius seldom rivaled in Western Europe. This world challenged the best that was in Chaucer, and in *The Tales of Canterbury* he met this challenge with the greatest intellectual and artistic activity of his career. Here one of his mastering aims seems to have been to discover and seize and present men and women from every possible new angle, and to employ all the devices of his skill and ingenuity to bring them to life. He created tales, tellers, settings, and filled all with themes, counterthemes, digressions, allusions, and casual details in a rich abundance that offers all things to all readers—a variety of values, moral, poetic, and human. In this crowning achievement Chaucer has lifted each pilgrim out of his habitual environment and set him up, in a new perspective or relationship, on the road leading from this world to "Jerusalem celestial." Each representative of mankind in *The Tales of Canterbury* is found working out his destiny, each searching for his kind of satisfaction in life. Here each is seen, caught between the poles of opposite values, between earth and eternity, illumined for all time in the bright sunlight of the poet's vision, intellect, and art.

Acknowledgments

My particular indebtedness to F. N. Robinson and to J. M. Manly and Edith Rickert is described in the Comment on the Text (p. 561). In preparing text, glosses, and notes I am indebted to the scholarship of these and many other Chaucerians, including such previous editors as W. W. Skeat and A. C. Baugh; to the *Oxford English Dictionary;* and to the *Middle English Dictionary* and its Editor, Sherman M. Kuhn. My colleagues Harold S. Stine and James L. Rosier have aided me with information and advice. I have received suggestions and encouragement from Rev. Paul E. Beichner, C. S. C., Edgar Hill Duncan, and Bartlett J. Whiting, and likewise from Joseph A. Yokelson and my wife, each of whom also helped with proof.

The Order of the Tales

Although the order of the tales in the various manuscripts shows a variety of patterns, certain tales are firmly and consistently linked together by their epilogues and prologues so as to form internally integrated groups. Thus the links connecting the tales of the Shipman, the Prioress, Chaucer, the Monk, and the Nuns' Priest are indisputably genuine, and are used in the manuscripts so consistently to link these particular tales that there can be no doubt we have here a clearly established Group of tales, or, considered from the point of view of the manuscripts, a clearly established and integrated Fragment. There are nine or ten such Groups (or Fragments)[1], and the only question concerning the order of the tales is that of the sequence which Chaucer intended for these Groups.

In his Oxford edition Skeat followed the order used in the "Six-Text" edition of the Chaucer Society, lettering the "Groups" from A to I. F. N. Robinson followed the order of the Ellesmere manuscript, which was the basis of his text, and numbered the "Fragments" from I to X. Several kinds of evidence suggest that the order used for the present text represents Chaucer's intention at the time of his death. This "1400 Order," with Robinson's and Skeat's designations for the Fragments (or Groups) is as follows:

I	(A)	Prologue, Knight, Miller, Reeve, Cook.
II	(B¹)	Man of Law.
VII	(B²)	Shipman, Prioress, *Thopas, Melibee,* Monk, Nuns' Priest.[2]
III	(D)	Wife, Friar, Summoner.
IV	(E)	Clerk, Merchant.
V	(F)	Squire, Franklin.
VI	(C)	Physician, Pardoner.
VIII	(G)	Second Nun, Canon's Yeoman.
IX	(H)	Manciple.
X	(I)	Parson.

[1] Presumably IV (E) and V (F) should be considered as one Group.

[2] So many scholars have made use of Skeat's line numbers for the Shipman-Nuns' Priest sequence of Tales that I follow Robinson's method of appending them with asterisks.

This order, which was first proposed by Skeat, following suggestions made by Henry Bradshaw, is supported by evidence provided by the fact that in the course of *The Tales* Chaucer and the other pilgrims mention places along the road from Southwark to Canterbury. For example, about two miles from the Tabard Inn the company stops at a brook or spring called the Wateryng of Seint Thomas (I 826), cuts are drawn, and the Knight begins the storytelling. In the link between the Miller's Tale and the Reeve's, the Host cries,

> *Lo Depeford! and it is half-wey pryme.*
> *Lo Grenewych, ther many a shrewe is inne!* (I 3906–07)

Thus early in the collection of stories Chaucer reinforces the idea of a real journey along the actual road from London to Canterbury by stressing both the time of day (about 7:30 A.M.) and the towns through which the pilgrims are passing (about five miles along). In the link between Chaucer's Tale of Melibee and the Monk's Tale, the Host cries,

> *Lo, Rouchestre stant heer faste by!* (VII 1925)

indicating that the company has traveled about thirty miles and is about halfway to Canterbury. In the interlude between the Wife of Bath's Prologue and her Tale, the Summoner promises

> *tales two or thre*
> *Of freres, er I come to Sidyngborne* (III 846–47)

(about ten miles beyond Rochester); and later at the conclusion of his story he declares,

> *My tale is doon; we been almoost at towne.* (III 2294)

The Canon and his Yeoman overtake the pilgrims at Boughton in the Blean Forest (about seven miles from Canterbury; VIII 556–57, 587), and the Manciple begins his story at Harbledown (about two miles from Canterbury; IX 1–3). Here is an impressive series of clear allusions to places, the order and locations of which were perfectly familiar to Chaucer and his audience, who could be expected always to recognize easily just how far along the Pilgrims' Way the company had traveled. Yet in the complete manuscripts of *The Tales,* while the places near Southwark and those near Canterbury appear in correct order, the two crucial passages—those naming Rochester and Sittingbourne—appear in incorrect order. There is evidence that during the development of *The Tales of Canterbury* Chaucer at various times changed the arrangement and order of tales: for example it seems very likely that at one time the Man of Law was immediately followed by the Wife of Bath. It should be noted that the two crucial passages which name Rochester and Sittingbourne were prepared when Fragment VII and the III–IV sequence were reaching final form; for the *Melibee*-Monk link was written only after the cancellation of the Nuns' Priest's Endlink and the cancellation and presumable replacement of the original Clerk's Endlink; and the words between the Summoner and the Friar were written only when their tales were inserted between those of the Wife of Bath and the Clerk. Thus it was at a late stage in the development of *The Tales* that Chaucer shaped these sequences into their present form, apparently imagining the Monk, Nuns' Priest, Wife of Bath, Friar, and Summoner as telling their tales along the road between Rochester and Sittingbourne.

Other kinds of evidence supporting the "1400 Order" include analysis of the tradition of tale-order in the various manuscripts (all of the fifteenth century); compelling internal evidence for the Man of Law-Shipman sequence; and the fine artistic appropriateness of the Nuns' Priest-Wife of Bath sequence. Indeed, through this last juxtaposition, the related problems of celibacy, women, marriage, wives, and "sovereynetee" start with Chaucer's own Dame Prudence (in the *Melibee*), and Herry Bailey, and the antifeminist Monk, and then develop easily and naturally from the story of the vainglorious cock, whose multiplicity of wives is echoed by Alice of Bath's desire for many husbands, and whose flourishing of "auctoritees" is matched by her public airing of her own "experience." Thus whatever Chaucer might have planned and done had he lived longer, he seems by 1400 to have conceived and developed a definite arrangement for the groups of tales so far written.[2]

The Language of Chaucer

In Chaucer's time the form of speech varied in different parts of England, but with sufficient regularity to present five rather distinct dialectal regions: Northern, East Midland, West Midland, Southern, and Kentish. Particularly along the boundaries of these areas, dialectal admixture and variation usually occurred. An easily recognizable feature of the Northern dialect, for example, was the retention of Old English long *ā* in such words as *bān* (*bone*) and *hām* (*home*); another such feature was the Northern third person singular in *-s* (*makes*) as opposed to *-eth* (*maketh*), which still held on in London and the South; there were also typical Northern forms such as *slyk* (*such*) and *whilk* (*which*). By means of a deft use of these and other Northern characteristics in the speech of the two Northumbrian students Aleyn and John, Chaucer added humor and local color to the Reeve's Tale. The poet of *Pearl* and *Sir Gawain and the Green Knight* wrote in the North West Midland dialect; and the author of *Piers Plowman* in South Midland. John Gower and Geoffrey Chaucer wrote in the South East Midland of London, a dialect with a slight admixture of Kentish. It was their good fortune that this Middlesex dialect became the basis of the English we speak and write today, and these two poets did their part in giving their language literary prestige.

Suggestions for Reading Chaucer

"Poetry," said Robert Frost, "is what gets lost in translation"; and Kenneth Rexroth, concerning Chaucer: "Both wit and music are missed." In this book the text and the glossing are placed side by side so as to enable the modern reader to experience at first hand the direct and powerful thrust of Chaucer's poetry, the enchantment and the rough-and-tumble of his world, and the delicately presented nuances of his wit, his characters and their speech, and his music. This marginal glossing is supplementary to the Basic Glossary (pp. 581-587), with which the

[2] Some of the background for these remarks may be found in *PMLA*, 66 (1951), 1141-67; 68 (1953), 1142-59; and pp. 45-79 of *Studies in Medieval Literature in Honor of Albert Croll Baugh*, ed. MacEdward Leach (Philadelphia: Univ. of Pennsylvania Press, 1961).

reader should become familiar as soon as possible, noting especially the words marked with asterisks.

The reading of Chaucer can be greatly facilitated if the student will watch for and learn, again as soon as possible, the chief features of this language which at first make it seem a little unfamiliar. For example, we soon see that adverbs end not only in -ly (and -lich) but also in -e (study, for example, these lines in the General Prologue: 77, 94, 97, 124, 129, 148, 149, 230). Some nouns have no ending for the genitive singular (for example, *lady*, 88; *fader*, 781). There are some plurals without endings: *deer, sheep, freend, yeer* (but also *yeres*), *hors, caas,* and *paas,* for example; a few plurals end in -en (or -n): *asshen, been* (also *bees*), *eyen* or *yen, hosen* (also *hoses*), *toon* (also *toos*). The third personal singular possessive pronoun is the same for the neuter as for the masculine: *his* (rather than *its;* see line 8). In Chaucer the forms of the third person plural are *they* (nominative), *hir(e)* or *her(e)* (genitive; see line 32); and *hem* (dative and accusative; see line 11). In the third person singular of the present indicative occur some interesting contractions of which the following are typical: *bit* for *biddeth* ("bids"), *fint* for *findeth* ("finds"), *halt* for *haldeth* ("holds"), *rit* for *rideth* ("rides"), *stont* for *stondeth* ("stands"). Both the infinitive and the plural sometimes end in -en (or -n; line 12 shows an example of each). There is an imperative ending in -eth (see line 788). The past participle sometimes begins with the prefix *y-* (see lines 8, 25) and may end in -e(n), or -d or -t. One should note the position of the adverb (immediately after the verb instead of at the end of the clause) in such lines as 791, Miller's Prologue 3119, and Pardoner's Prologue 345. The negative adverb *ne* combines with certain verbs to form such contractions as *nas* (*ne was*), *nere* (*ne were*), *nolde* (*ne wolde*) and *nyste* (*ne wiste*); see the Basic Glossary under the letter *n* (p. 584). The intensive double negative may be observed in lines 131, 251, 321, and 428; yet the fact that "two negatives make a positive" sometimes affords the possibility of a *double entendre* (Nuns' Priest's Tale, 3266). Finally, the reader should watch for words which look familiar but whose meanings have changed since Chaucer's time: for example, *coy* (119), *letten* (889), *verray* (72).

Chaucer's language had this advantage over ours: that in general it was spelled as it was pronounced, and pronounced as it was spelled. Another difference is that the English vowels had not yet broken away from their standard European pronunciation (that of Latin, German, French, or Spanish, for example). Hence we can attain a rough approximation of Chaucer's speech by pronouncing all the letters in each word (including the final *e,* which may be pronounced like the *a* in *China;* within the verse final -*e* is elided before a vowel or a silent *h,* and at other times may be slurred); and by pronouncing the vowels in the "Continental" manner. Once these principles have been mastered, it is possible to give Chaucer's verse a rhythm close to that which he intended, and to listen to the music of his poetry. Thus the *a* in *name* and *fame* is to be pronounced like the *a* in *father* (and the final *e* lightly sounded as already described). In general a diphthong is to be pronounced by sounding the two vowels of which it is composed, gliding from the first to the second; for example, *au* (or *aw*) as in *cause,* is pronounced like *ow* in Modern English *now; ei, ey* (also *ai, ay*) like *ay* in *day; oi, oy,* like *oi* in *boil;* and *eu, ew,* like *u* in *mute.* The doubling of a vowel (*caas, baar*) indicates length in time, not a change in sound; and so the *oo* of *soote* and *roote* is to be pronounced like the *o* in *note;* likewise *goode, bookes;* the same sound should be used for *com, corage* (the *a* stressed), *wol, wold.* The *l* of *wold* we no longer pronounce in Modern English; in such words we have kept the old spelling but lost the old pronunciation. All the consonants are to be pronounced in Middle English words, not only in *wold,* but also in such other words as *half, palmer, knife, knotte,* and *knyght.* (The letters *y* and *i* are equivalent and interchangeable.) The *gh* in *knyght* was pronounced like German guttural *ch* (as in *Knecht*) or Scottish *ch* (as in *loch*). The letter *c* before *a, o,* or *u* is pronounced as in *cat;* before *e* or *i,* as in *city; g* before *a, o,* or *u,* as in *go;* before *e* or *i* as in *age.* The *r* was trilled. These are rough and ready suggestions, intended merely to enable the student to make an approximation of Middle English pronunciation; for a closer approximation, including the important distinctions between open and close $\bar{e}$ and between open and close $\bar{o}$, he should consult F. N. Robinson, *The Works of Geoffrey Chaucer* (2nd ed., 1957), pp. xxx–xxxii; or such fuller descriptions as those found in S. Moore and A. H. Marckwardt, *Historical Outlines of English Sounds and Inflections* (1951) or H. Kökeritz, *A Guide to Chaucer's Pronunciation* (1962).

Chaucer's poetry was read aloud and heard more often than read silently, and one of its features is a natural pause (or caesura) in the midst of each line. The predominant beat of the verse is iambic (˘ ´); and the basic number of feet, five. But Chaucer varied the rhythm of his verse from the norm in a variety of ways: by adding or omitting syllables, by replacing iambs with other feet, such as trochees (´ ˘) as in the opening line of *The Canterbury Tales;* by having an extra caesura; and by perpetually shifting the position of the caesural pause. As a result, the rhythms range from those of everyday conversation to those of dignity, pomp, or tragedy. The student should read much of the poetry aloud, in as natural a manner as possible, with a full consciousness of its meaning and its emotional impact.

Illustrations

The institutions and individuals listed below have kindly given permission for reproduction of the following:

The Ellesmere portrait of Chaucer (frontispiece): Huntington MS. 26.C.9.
   Huntington Library, San Marino, California.

The Martyrdom of St. Thomas à Becket (p. xlvi): the Carrow Psalter, MS. W.34, fol. 15^{v}.
   Walters Art Gallery, Baltimore.

The Helm of Sir Richard Pembridge (p. 2).
   Courtesy of the Royal Scottish Museum, Edinburgh.

Diagnosis-Prognosis by Astrology (p. 14): MS. Crawford 9.14.5, fol. 37^{r}.
   Crawford Collection of the Royal Observatory, Edinburgh.
   Courtesy of the Astronomer Royal for Scotland.

Emilia in the Garden (p. 30): Codex NR. 2617, fol. 53.
   Österreichische Nationalbibliothek, Vienna.

The Prioress' Tale (p. 156): MS. Eng. poet. a. 1, fol. 124^{v}.
   Copyright Bodleian Library, Oxford.

The Attack on Prudence and Sophie (p. 168): MS. fr. 1165, fol. 66^{r}.
   Bibliothèque Nationale, Paris.

The Wheel of Fortune (p. 209).
  Deborah M. Borst, photographer.
  Courtesy of the Dean and Chapter of Rochester Cathedral.
A Medicinal Herb (p. 239): MS. Lat. 337, fol. 125^r.
  Bayerische Staatsbibliothek, Munich.
The Fox Chase (p. 251): MS. Douce 360, fol. 21^r.
  Copyright Bodleian Library, Oxford.
The Children of Venus (p. 270): MS. Rawlinson D. 1220, fol. 31^v.
  Copyright Bodleian Library, Oxford.
Satan in Hell, by Francesco Traini (p. 296): Camposanto, Pisa.
  Anderson print from Alinari.
Cassone panel with scenes from *Decameron* X.x, by Pesellino (p. 319).
  Accademia Carrara di Belle Arti, Bergamo.
The *hortus conclusus* in the *Speculum Humanae Salvationis* (p. 365): MS. M 766, fol. 25^r.
  Pierpont Morgan Library, New York.
The magic horse in *Méliacin* (p. 381): MS. fr. 1589, fol. 7^r.
  Bibliothèque Nationale, Paris.
The decapitation of Virginia (p. 419) MS. Royal 20 D. I, fol. 235^r.
  Copyright British Museum, London.
Part of a chest-front depicting scenes from the Pardoner's Tale (p. 435): Private collector.
  The Raymond Fortt Studios, Kingston-upon-Thames, Surrey.
Eight scenes from the life of Saint Cecilia (p. 443): Uffizi Gallery, Florence.
  Alinari.
The laboratory of John Norton (p. 461): Additional MS. 10302, fol. 1^r.
  Copyright British Museum, London.
The Cook (p. 479): Huntington MS.26.C.9; Oxford MS.
  The Huntington Library, San Marino, California; The Philip H. & A. S. W. Rosenbach Foundation, Philadelphia.
Jerusalem Celestial (p. 489): The Cloisters Apocalypse, fol. 36^v.
  The Metropolitan Museum of Art, The Cloisters Collection, New York.

In selecting illustrations I have received suggestions from Francis L. Utley and Curt A. Zimansky, and also from *A Mirror of Chaucer's World* by Roger S. Loomis, whose lead I follow for the Prioress's Tale, the *Melibee*, and the choice of manuscript for the Canon's Yeoman's Tale. My former colleague Loren MacKinney long ago introduced me to medical illustrations, including those used for the Doctour of Phisik and the Nuns' Priest's Tale. Kenneth Sisam, in his edition of that Tale, introduced Chaucerians to the Douce fox chase; and Manly, in his *Canterbury Tales,* to Pesellino's cassone panel depicting Griselda. Robert Hughes' *Heaven and Hell in Western Art* is useful for Satan (Part 3; note that *The Last Judgment* by Giusto di Menabuoi is found on p. 205 instead of 180), and for the *hortus conclusus* (chapter 2); for the latter see also Alfred L. Kellogg in *Speculum,* 35 (1960), 275–79. Three scholars have generously sent me information: Brian Spencer, Assistant Keeper of The London Museum, on the carved scenes from the Pardoner's Tale; Edgar Hill Duncan, on the alchemical laboratory of John Norton; and Dorothy Miner, late Librarian and Keeper of Manuscripts of The Walters Art Gallery, on the Carrow Psalter.

For Further Reading

F. N. Robinson, ed., *The Works of Geoffrey Chaucer* (2nd ed., 1957). The standard edition.

J. M. Manly and E. Rickert, *The Text of the Canterbury Tales* (8 vols., 1940). Critical text, together with all variants, based on all known manuscripts.

J. M. Manly, ed., *Canterbury Tales by Geoffrey Chaucer* (1928). Helpful introduction on Chaucer and his times; vivid notes on medieval life.

R. K. Root, ed., *The Book of Troilus and Criseyde by Geoffrey Chaucer* (1926). The standard edition of Chaucer's tragic romance.

A. C. Baugh, ed., *Chaucer's Major Poetry* (1963). Valuable glossary, sections on Chaucer's language and versification, and notes.

E. T. Donaldson, *Chaucer's Poetry: An Anthology for the Modern Reader* (1958). Perceptive comments on selected tales.

BIBLIOGRAPHIES

E. P. Hammond, *Chaucer: A Bibliographical Manual* (1908).

D. D. Griffith, *Bibliography of Chaucer: 1908–1953* (1955).

W. R. Crawford, *Bibliography of Chaucer: 1954–63* (1967).

A. C. Baugh, *Chaucer,* Goldentree Bibliographies (1968).

BACKGROUNDS

M. Bowden, *A Commentary on the General Prologue to the Canterbury Tales* (2nd ed., 1967). The most efficient and inclusive guide to the portraits of the pilgrims.

W. F. Bryan and G. Dempster, eds., *Sources and Analogues of Chaucer's Canterbury Tales* (1941). Discussion and texts of the literary background of each tale.

M. Chute, *Geoffrey Chaucer of England* (1946). Readable biography together with historical and social background.

M. M. Crow and C. C. Olson, *Chaucer Life-Records* (1966). The documentary evidence concerning Chaucer's life.

W. C. Curry, *Chaucer and the Mediaeval Sciences* (2nd ed., 1960). Facts essential for an understanding of certain pilgrims and tales.

J. H. Fisher, *John Gower: Moral Philosopher and Friend of Chaucer* (1965). Important for an understanding of Chaucer as well as of his friend and fellow poet.

R. D. French, *A Chaucer Handbook* (2nd ed., 1947). Translations or summaries of many sources and analogues, as well as introductory information.

J. Harvey, *Gothic England: A Survey of National Culture, 1300–1550* (1948). Architecture and other arts of Chaucer's world; extensively illustrated.

Robert Hughes, *Heaven and Hell in Western Art* (1968).

M. Hussey, *Chaucer's World: A Pictorial Companion* (1967).

J. J. Jusserand, *English Wayfaring Life in the Middle Ages* (new ed., 1930). Vivid descriptions and discussions, illuminating the pilgrimage and the pilgrims; illustrated.

R. S. Loomis, *A Mirror of Chaucer's World* (1965). Nearly 200 pictures of objects and miniatures related to Chaucer and his poetry.

Loren MacKinney, *Medical Illustrations in Medieval Manuscripts* (1965).

F. P. Magoun, Jr., *A Chaucer Gazetteer* (1961). Identification of the places named by Chaucer.

J. M. Manly, *Some New Light on Chaucer* (1926). Investigations of records of real people closely similar to the pilgrims.

G. Mathew, *The Court of Richard II* (1968).

W. A. Pantin, *The English Church in the Fourteenth Century* (1955).

G. A. Plimpton, *The Education of Chaucer* (1935). Excellent reproductions of many pages of various types of manuscripts of Chaucer's time, including a complete primer.

A. L. Poole, ed., *Medieval England* (rev. ed., 2 vols., 1958). Valuable chapters by various experts on different phases of life in Medieval England; illustrated.

E. Power, *Medieval People* (1924). A gallery of realistic portraits including a sensitive study of the Prioress.

E. Rickert, *Chaucer's World,* ed. C. C. Olson and M. M. Crow (1948). Passages from contemporary official and private documents and from literature; excellent illustrations.

D. W. Robertson, Jr., *Chaucer's London* (1968).

A. Seton, *Katherine* (1954). An historical novel concerning Chaucer's sister-in-law who was mistress and finally third duchess of the powerful John of Gaunt. Although the sketch of Chaucer is disappointing, the background is very well handled—especially the Peasants' Revolt.

E. F. Shannon, *Chaucer and the Roman Poets* (1929). Chaucer's knowledge and use of such poets as Virgil and Ovid.

D. Taylor, *Chaucer's England* (1968).

G. M. Trevelyan, *England in the Age of Wycliffe* (4th ed., 1909). Detailed account of the influence of Wyclif on Chaucer's England and of the Peasants' Revolt.

INTERPRETATION AND CRITICISM

M. Bowden, *A Reader's Guide to Geoffrey Chaucer* (1964).

B. H. Bronson, *In Search of Chaucer* (1960).

G. K. Chesterton, *Chaucer* (new ed., 1948).

N. Coghill, *The Poet Chaucer* (1949).

G. Dempster, *Dramatic Irony in Chaucer* (1932).

G. L. Kittredge, *Chaucer and His Poetry* (1915).

W. W. Lawrence, *Chaucer and the Canterbury Tales* (1950).

G. L. Lowes, *Geoffrey Chaucer and the Development of his Genius* (1934).

R. M. Lumiansky, *Of Sondry Folk: The Dramatic Principle in The Canterbury Tales* (1955).

K. Malone, *Chapters on Chaucer* (1951).

C. Muscatine, *Chaucer and the French Tradition: A Study in Style and Meaning* (1957).

C. A. Owen, Jr., ed., *Discussions of the Canterbury Tales* (1961).

H. R. Patch, *On Rereading Chaucer* (1939).

D. W. Robertson, Jr., *A Preface to Chaucer* (1962).

R. K. Root, *The Poetry of Chaucer* (2nd ed., 1922).

B. Rowland, ed., *Companion to Chaucer Studies* (1968).

R. J. Schoeck and J. Taylor, eds., *Chaucer Criticism: The Canterbury Tales* (1960).

S. Sullivan, ed., *Critics on Chaucer* (1970).

J. S. P. Tatlock, *The Mind and Art of Chaucer* (1950).

E. Wagenknecht, ed., *Chaucer: Modern Essays in Criticism* (1959).

The Tales of Canterbury

Here bygynneth the
book of the
tales of Caunterbury.

Whan that Aprill with his shoures soote   soote: sweet.
The droghte of March hath perced to the roote,
And bathed every veyne in swich licour   veyne: vein; sap-vessel. **swich:** such.
Of which vertu engendred is the flour;   licour: sap.
Whan Zephirus eek with his sweete breeth   5 Zephirus: the west wind. **eek:** also.
Inspired hath in every holt and heeth   inspired: breathed on; quickened.
The tendre croppes, and the yonge sonne   holt: wood. **croppes:** shoots.
Hath in the Ram his half cours yronne,   yronne: run.
And smale foweles maken melodye,   foweles: birds.
That slepen al the nyght with open eye   10
(So priketh hem Nature in hir corages);   priketh: spurs. **hem:** them. **hir:** their.
Than longen folk to goon on pilgrimages,   corages: hearts. **goon:** go.
And palmeres for to seken straunge strondes,   straunge: foreign. **strondes:** shores.
To ferne halwes, kowthe in sondry londes;   ferne: distant. **halwes:** shrines.
And specially from every shires ende   15   kowthe: known.
Of Engelond to Caunterbury they wende,
The hooly blisful martir for to seke,
That hem hath holpen whan that they were   hem: them. **holpen:** helped.
      seeke.   seeke: sick.
   Bifil that in that seson on a day,   bifil: it befell.
In Southwerk at the Tabard as I lay   20 lay: lodged.
Redy to wenden on my pilgrymage
To Caunterbury with ful devout corage,   corage: heart.
At nyght was come into that hostelrye   hostelrye: inn.

---

4. Of which vertu: By power of which.

7. yonge: because its annual course had recently started with the vernal equinox in the zodiacal sign of Aries, the Ram, about March 12. Here, as elsewhere in his writings, Chaucer indicates time by reference to a natural timepiece, the motions of heavenly bodies. The zodiac (a circular zoo) is an imaginary celestial belt in which lie the courses of the sun, moon, and planets. The apparent annual path of the sun runs through its center (8° from either side). The zodiac is divided into 12 equal parts, each 30° in length, and each named for a constellation. At the vernal equinox, the sun is at the first point of Aries (the Ram); roughly a month later the sun enters the sign of Taurus (the Bull); and so on through the other ten signs in the course of the year.

8. halfe cours: i.e., the second half course, that occurring in April.

13. palmeres: professional pilgrims.

17. martir: Thomas à Becket, Archbishop of Canterbury, was murdered in 1170 and canonized three years later. The scene of his martyrdom was the object of many pilgrimages for centuries. **blisful:** full of the bliss of heaven; beatified.

20. Tabard: the Tabard Inn in Southwark, across the Thames from London.

The Martyrdom of St. Thomas à Becket: This representation of the martyrdom of St. Thomas (29 December 1170) is an illumination of East Anglian origin (c. 1250–60) in the Psalter from the Benedictine Priory of St. Mary and St. John of Carrow, Norwich. In front, his shield emblazoned with a bear rampant, Reginald Fitzurse, leader of the knights, strikes a blow which dashes off St. Thomas's mitre. Behind and to the right, William de Tracy's descending sword wounds the arm of the faithful Edward Grim, who carries the cross-staff of the archbishop. Behind Tracy, Richard Le Bret strikes a blow which severed the crown of the martyr's head; the sword broke in two (actually on hitting the pavement). To the left of these three stands Hugh de Moreville in black helm.

Wel nyne and twenty in a compaignye,
Of sondry folk, by aventure yfalle — 25   aventure: chance. yfalle: fallen.
In felaweshipe, and pilgrimes were they alle,
That toward Caunterbury wolden ryde.   wolden: would.
The chambres and the stables weren wyde,   wyde: spacious.
And wel we weren esed atte beste.   esed: entertained. atte beste: in the
And shortly, whan the sonne was to reste, — 30   best manner possible.
So hadde I spoken with hem everichon   hem: them. everichon: everyone.
That I was of hir felaweshipe anon,   anon: immediately.
And made forward erly for to ryse,   forward: agreement.
To take oure wey ther as I yow devyse.   ther as: where. devyse: tell.

    But nathelees, whil I have tyme and space, — 35   space: leisure, opportunity.
Er that I ferther in this tale pace,   pace: pass, go.
Me thynketh it acordaunt to resoun   me thynketh: it seems to me.
To telle yow al the condicioun   acordaunt to resoun: reasonable,
Of ech of hem, so as it semed me,   suitable. hem: them.
And whiche they weren, and of what degree, — 40   whiche: what. degree: rank.
And eek in what array that they were inne;   eek: also.
And at a knyght than wol I first bigynne.   than: then. wol: will.

    A Knyght ther was and that a worthy man,
That fro the tyme that he first bigan   fro: from.
To riden out, he loved chivalrie, — 45   riden out: go on expeditions.
Trouthe and honour, fredom and curteisie.
Ful worthy was he in his lordes werre,
And therto hadde he riden, no man ferre,   therto: moreover. ferre: farther.
As wel in cristendom as in hethenesse,

---

39. so as it semed me: as it seemed to me.

46. trouthe: loyalty. **honour:** glory, achievement. **fredom:** generosity. **curteisie:** courtesy, sportsmanship.

47. his lordes werre: the King's war against France, the Hundred Years' War.

52–53. The Knights of the Teutonic Order held annual banquets in Prussia before they raided in Lithuania and Russia (l. 54). **the bord bigonne:** sat at the head of the table. **alle nacions:** the representatives of all nationalities.

56–66. The Knight fought against heathen also at each end of the Mediterranean (**the Grete See**). Algeciras, near Gibraltar, in the Kingdom of Granada, was besieged by Christian Crusaders from 1342 until its capture from the Moors in 1344. There was further fighting against the Moors in Benmarin (a part of Morocco) and Tlemcen (in Western Algeria: see l. 62), in the forties, sixties, and eighties. Aided by many other Christians, King Peter of Cyprus captured Antalya (**Satalye:** l. 58) in Asia Minor in 1361; conquered Alexandria (l. 51) in 1365; and attacked Ayas (**Lyeys:** l. 58) in Asia Minor in 1367. The Lord of Balat (**Palatye,** in Asia Minor: l. 65) was a heathen bound in friendly treaty to King Peter.

The Helm of Sir Richard Pembridge: This stark helm, with its broad sights, the numerous holes pierced for breathing, and over the knight's left brow the slight remaining trace of a dent from a "jelous stroke," brings us close to the Knight and the knights in his Tale. In passage after passage Chaucer assumes that his audience is almost physically aware of arms and armor; but from his period little survives. The only headpiece comparable to this rare example is the "helmet of the leopard" of Edward the Black Prince at Canterbury.

The helm was made for a worthy knight, Sir Richard Pembridge (d. 1375), who served valiantly as captain "in his lordes werre" (l. 47 and note)—the campaigns in France of Edward III. He fought at Sluys (1340), Crécy (1346), and Poitiers (1356), and in the campaign of 1359–60 (in which Chaucer was captured; see Inroduction). He was in the group sent to Dover by Edward to receive Peter of Cyprus when he came to seek knights and funds for his crusading (see note for ll. 55–56, and *De Petro Rege de Cipro,* Monk's Tale, ll. 2391–98, and note). Sir Richard was later made Knight of the Garter and Warden of the Cinque Ports. His helm hung over his tomb in Hereford Cathedral for more than four centuries and is now in the Royal Scottish Museum, Edinburgh.

And evere honoured for his worthynesse.   50
At Alisaundre he was whan it was wonne.
Ful ofte tyme he hadde the bord bigonne
Aboven alle nacions in Pruce;
In Lettow hadde he reysed and in Ruce,   reysed: raided.
No Cristen man so ofte of his degree.   55
In Gernade at the seege eek hadde he be   eek: also. be: been.
Of Algezir, and riden in Belmarye.
At Lyeys was he and at Satalye,
Whan they were wonne; and in the Grete See
At many a noble armee hadde he be.   60   armee: armed expedition. be: been.
At mortal batailles hadde he been fiftene,
And foughten for oure feith at Tramyssene
In lystes thries, and ay slayn his foo.   thries: thrice. ay: always.
This ilke worthy knyght hadde been also   ilke: same.
Somtyme with the lord of Palatye   65   somtyme: once.
Agayn another hethen in Turkye.   agayn: against.
And everemoore he hadde a sovereyn prys;   prys: reputation.
And though that he were worthy, he was wys,
And of his port as meeke as is a mayde.   port: deportment.
He nevere yet no vileynye ne sayde   70   vileynye: rudeness; evil.
In al his lyf unto no maner wight.   maner wight: sort of person
He was a verray, parfit, gentil knyght.   verray: true. parfit: perfect.
But, for to tellen yow of his array,   array: equipment.
His hors were goode, but he was nat gay.   hors: horses. gay: richly attired.
Of fustian he wered a gypon   75   fustian: thick cotton cloth.
Al bismotered with his habergeon,   bismotered with: stained by.
For he was late ycome from his viage,   late: recently. viage: expedition.
And wente for to doon his pilgrymage.

   With hym ther was his sone, a yong Squier,
A lovere and a lusty bacheler,   80   lusty: gay.
With lokkes crulle as they were leyd in presse.   crulle: curly. as: as if. presse: device
Of twenty yeer of age he was, I gesse.   for curling.
Of his stature he was of evene lengthe,   evene: average. lengthe: height.
And wonderly delyvere, and of greet strengthe.   delyvere: agile.
And he hadde been somtyme in chyvachie   85   chyvachie: cavalry raid.
In Flaundres, in Artoys, and Pycardie,
And born hym weel, as of so litel space,   born hym: conducted himself. space:
In hope to stonden in his lady grace.   time. lady: lady's.
Embrouded was he, as it were a meede   embrouded: embroidered. meede:
Al ful of fresshe floures, whyte and reede.   90   meadow.
Syngynge he was, or floytynge, al the day;   floytynge: fluting.
He was as fressh as is the month of May.   fressh: fresh, lively.

---

68. though . . . wys: though he was brave, he was prudent.
70–71. nevere . . . no . . . ne . . . no: intensive quadruple negative.
75–76. The gypon was a tunic worn under the habergeon (armor for breast and back).
80. bacheler: bachelor; aspirant to knighthood; youth.
85–86. Probably the expedition conducted by the Bishop of Norwich in 1383.

Short was his gowne, with sleves longe and
    wyde.
Wel koude he sitte on hors and faire ryde.   faire: well.
He koude songes make and wel endite,   95
Juste and eek daunce, and weel purtreye and   juste: joust. eek: also.
    write.   purtreye: draw.
So hoote he lovede that by nyghtertale   hoote: hotly. by nyghtertale: at night.
He slepte namoore than dooth a nyghtyngale.   namoore: no more.
Curteis he was, lowely, and servysable,
And carf biforn his fader at the table.   100   carf: carved.
    A Yeman hadde he and servantz namo   he: the knight. namo: no more.
At that tyme, for hym liste ride so;   hym liste: it pleased him to.
And he was clad in cote and hood of grene.
A sheef of pecok arwes, bright and kene,   arwes: arrows.
Under his belt he bar ful thriftily,   105   bar: bore. thriftily: carefully.
(Wel koude he dresse his takel yemanly: dresse: set in order, prepare. takel:
His arwes drouped noght with fetheres lowe)   gear; weapons.
And in his hand he baar a myghty bowe.
A not heed hadde he, with a broun visage.   not heed: head with hair cut short.
Of wodecraft wel koude he al the usage.   110   visage: face. koude: knew.
Upon his arm he baar a gay bracer,   bracer: arm-guard.
And by his syde a swerd and a bokeler,   swerd: sword.
And on that oother syde a gay daggere
Harneised wel and sharp as point of spere;   harneised: adorned.
A Christofre on his brest of silver sheene.   115   sheene: bright.
An horn he bar, the bawdryk was of grene;   bawdryk: baldric, belt.
A forster was he, soothly, as I gesse.   forster: forester. soothly: truly.
    Ther was also a Nonne, a Prioresse,
That of hir smylyng was ful symple and coy;   symple: unaffected. coy: quiet.
Hir gretteste ooth was but by Seinte Loy;   120
And she was cleped madame Eglentyne.   cleped: called.
Ful wel she soong the service dyvyne,
Entuned in hir nose ful semely,   semely: in a becoming, pleasing man-
And Frenssh she spak ful faire and fetisly,   ner. fetisly: gracefully, elegantly.
After the scole of Stratford atte Bowe,   125
For Frenssh of Parys was to hire unknowe.
At mete wel ytaught was she with alle: at mete: at meals.
She leet no morsel from hir lippes falle,
Ne wette hir fyngres in hir sauce depe;   depe: deeply.
Wel koude she carie a morsel and wel kepe   130   kepe: take care.

---

95. **songes make:** compose the music.   **endite:** write, compose the words.
101. **Yeman:** yeoman, attendant.
106. **yemanly:** in a manner befitting a yeoman; handsomely.
115. **Christofre:** a small image of the patron saint of foresters.
120. **Seinte Loy:** St. Eligius, patron saint of courtiers and goldsmiths.
123. **Entuned in hir nose:** This mode of nasal intonation is traditional with the recitative portions of the church service.
125. **After . . . Bowe:** i.e., as it was spoken in the Stratford nunnery, just outside London.

That no drope ne fille upon hir brest.

In curteisie was set ful muchel hir lest.

Hir over-lippe wyped she so clene

That in hir coppe ther was no ferthyng sene

Of grece, whan she dronken hadde hir
draughte.   135

Ful semely after hir mete she raughte.

And sikerly she was of greet desport,

And ful plesaunt, and amyable of port,

And peyned hire to countrefete cheere

Of court, and to been estatlich of manere,   140

And to ben holden digne of reverence.

But, for to speken of hir conscience,

She was so charitable and so pitous

She wolde wepe, if that she sawe a mous

Caught in a trappe, if it were deed or bledde.   145

Of smale houndes hadde she that she fedde

With rosted flessh, or milk and wastel-breed.

But soore wepte she if oon of hem were deed,

Or if men smoot it with a yerde smerte;

And al was conscience and tendre herte.   150

Ful semely hir wympel pynched was,

Hir nose tretys, hir eyen greye as glas,

Hir mouth ful smal, and therto softe and reed;

But sikerly she hadde a fair forheed;

It was almoost a spanne brood, I trowe;   155

For, hardily, she was nat undergrowe.

Ful fetys was hir cloke, as I was war.

Of smal coral aboute hir arm she bar

A peire of bedes, gauded al with greene,

And theron heng a brooch of gold ful sheene,   160

On which ther was first writen a crowned A,

And after *Amor vincit omnia.*

   Another Nonne with hire hadde she,

That was hir chapeleyne.

   A Monk ther was, a fair for the maistrie,   165

An outridere, that lovede venerie,

A manly man, to been an abbot able.

---

fille: fell.

muchel: much. lest: delight.

over-lippe: upper lip.

ferthyng: farthing, a very small silver
   coin, one-fourth of a penny.

mete: food. raughte: reached.

sikerly: surely. desport: geniality.

port: port, behavior.

estatlich: dignified, stately.

holden: held, esteemed. digne: de-
   serving. conscience: tender feeling,
   sensibility. pitous: pitying, compas-
   sionate.

deed: dead.

wastel-breed: fine white bread.

soore: sorely. hem: them.

men: someone. yerde: stick.
   smerte: smartly.

wympel: headdress. pynched: pleated.

tretys: well formed, graceful.

therto: moreover.

spanne: span. trowe: think.

hardily: certainly.

fetys: neat, elegant. war: aware.

bar: carried.

peire of bedes: set of beads, rosary.

brooch: ornament. sheene: shining,
   bright.

chapeleyne: secretary and assistant.

a fair . . . maistrie: an extremely fine
   one. venerie: hunting; pursuit of sex-
   ual pleasure. able: suited.

---

131. no . . . ne: intensive double negative.

139–40. peyned . . . court: took pains to imitate the behavior of the court.

146. houndes hadde she: In general, nuns were forbidden to keep dogs.

152. eyen greye: blue-gray eyes.

159. gauded . . . greene: The "gauds," large beads for the Paternosters, were green.

162. *Amor vincit omnia:* "Love conquers all." Cf. Vergil, Eclogue X, 69: *Omnia vincit Amor.*

164. The text of O′ completes the line with the words **and preestes thre;** Chaucer must have left the line unfinished, for his portrait of the other nun is barely started, and there was clearly only one priest accompanying the prioress.

166. outridere: a monk who looked after the estates of the monastery.

Ful many a deyntee hors hadde he in stable,   deyntee: elegant
And whan he rood, men myghte his brydel
    heere
Gynglen in a whistlynge wynd als cleere   170 gynglen: jingle. als: as.
And eek as loude as dooth the chapel belle   eek: also.
Ther as this lord was kepere of the celle.   ther as: where.
The reule of Seint Maure or of Seint Beneit,   reule: monastic rule.
By cause that it was old and somdel streit   somdel: somewhat. streit: strict.
This ilke Monk leet olde thynges pace,   175 ilke: same. pace: pass away.
And heeld after the newe world the space.   space: course, custom.
He yaf nat of that text a pulled hen,   yaf: gave. of: for. pulled: plucked.
That seith that hunters ben nat holy men,   ben: are.
Ne that a monk, whan he is recchelees,   recchelees: neglectful of duty and dis-
Is likned til a fissh that is waterlees,—   180 cipline. til: to.
This is to seyn, a monk out of his cloystre.
But thilke text heeld he nat worth an oystre;   thilke: that. nat: not.
And I seyde his opinion was good.
What sholde he studie and make hymselven   what: why.
    wood,   wood: mad.
Upon a book in cloystre alwey to poure,   185 poure: pore over, examine closely.
Or swynken with his handes, and laboure,   swynken: work.
As Austyn bit? How shal the world be served?   Austyn: St. Augustine. bit: bids.
Lat Austyn have his swynk to hym reserved!   swynk: work.
Therfore he was a prikasour aright: prikasour: hunter on horseback.
Grehoundes he hadde as swift as fowel in   aright: indeed. fowel: bird.
    flight;   190
Of prikyng and of huntyng for the hare   prikyng: tracking by footprints.
Was al his lust, for no cost wolde he spare.   lust: pleasure.
I seigh his sleves purfiled at the hond   seigh: saw. purfiled: trimmed at the
With grys, and that the fyneste of a lond;   edges. grys: a costly gray fur.
And, for to festne his hood under his chyn,   195 festne: fasten.
He hadde of gold wroght a ful curious pyn;
A love-knotte in the gretter ende ther was.
His heed was balled, that shoon as any glas,   balled: bald.
And eek his face, as he hadde been enoynt.   as: as if. enoynt: anointed.
He was a lord ful fat and in good poynt;   200 in good poynt: in good condition;
His eyen stepe, and rollynge in his heed,   stout. stepe: protruding.
That stemed as a forneys of a leed;
His bootes souple, his hors in greet estaat.   estaat: condition.
Now certeinly he was a fair prelaat;
He was nat pale as a forpyned goost.   205 forpyned: wasted by suffering.
A fat swan loved he best of any roost.   goost: spirit.

---

172. **celle:** subordinate monastic establishment.
173. St. Benedict, the father of western monasticism, established Monte Cassino in 529; St. Maurus was his disciple.
196. He had a very elaborate brooch made of gold.
202. **That stemed . . . leed:** i.e., his eyes gleamed like a furnace under a caldron.

His palfrey was as broun as is a berye.

A Frere ther was, a wantowne and a merye,   wantowne: gay; wanton.
A lymytour, a ful solempne man.   solempne: pompous; distinguished;
In alle the ordres foure is noon that kan   210   merry. kan: knows.
So muche of daliaunce and fair langage.
He hadde maad ful many a mariage   maad: arranged.
Of yonge wommen at his owene cost.
Unto his ordre he was a noble post.
Ful wel biloved and famulier was he   215
With frankeleyns over al in his contree,   frankeleyns: wealthy landholders.
And with worthy wommen of the town;   contree: region.
For he hadde power of confessioun,
As seyde hymself, moore than a curat,
For of his ordre he was licenciat.   220
Ful swetely herde he confessioun,
And plesaunt was his absolucioun:
He was an esy man to yeve penaunce,   yeve: give.
Ther as he wiste to have a good pitaunce.   ther as: where. wiste: knew.
For unto a povre ordre for to yive   225   povre: poor. yive: give.
Is signe that a man is wel yshryve;   yshryve: shriven.
For if he yaf, he dorste make avaunt,   yaf: gave.
He wiste that a man was repentaunt;   wiste: knew.
For many a man so hard is of his herte,
He may nat wepe, althogh hym soore smerte.   230   hym soore smerte: it may pain him.
Therfore in stede of wepynge and preyeres
Men moote yeve silver to the povre freres.   men: one. moote: must, ought to.
His typet was ay farsed ful of knyves   typet: scarf; hood; cape. farsed:
And pynnes, for to yeven faire wyves.   stuffed. yeven: give.
And certeinly he hadde a murye note: 235
Wel koude he synge and pleyen on a rote;   rote: rote, a stringed instrument.
Of yeddynges he baar outrely the pris.   yeddynges: songs, ballads. outrely:
His nekke whit was as the flour-de-lys;   utterly, entirely. pris: prize.
Therto he strong was as a champioun.
He knew the tavernes wel in every town   240
And every hostiler and tappestere   hostiler: innkeeper. tappestere: bar-
Bet than a lazar or a beggestere;   maid.
For unto swich a worthy man as he
Acorded nat, as by his facultee,

---

208. Frere: friar.
209. lymytour: a friar licensed to hear confessions and preach in a certain area.
210. ordres foure: i.e., Dominicans, Franciscans, Carmelites, and Augustinians.
211. daliaunce: gossip; mirth; playfulness; amorous or wanton behavior.
212–13. He hadde . . . cost: i.e., he found husbands and dowries for women whom he had seduced.
220. licenciat: a man licensed by the pope to hear confessions and administer penance.
227. if he yaf . . . avaunt: if the man gave, the Friar dared to boast.
242. Better than he knew a leper or a beggar woman.
244. as by his facultee: in view of his official capacity or position.

To have with sike lazars aqueyntaunce.   245   sike: sick. lazars: lepers.
It is nat honest, it may nat avaunce,   avaunce: profit one.
For to deelen with no swich poraille,   poraille: poor people.
But al with riche and selleres of vitaille.   vitaille: victuals.
And over al, ther as profit sholde arise,   over al: everywhere. ther as: where.
Curteis he was and lowely of servyse.   250
Ther nas no man nowher so vertuous.   vertuous: capable.
He was the beste beggere in his hous;
[And yaf a certeyn ferme for the graunt;   252ᵃ   yaf: gave. ferme: fixed payment.
Noon of his bretheren cam ther in his
         haunt;]   252ᵇ   haunt: limit.
For thogh a wydwe hadde noght a sho,
So plesaunt was his *"In principio,"*
Yet wolde he have a ferthyng, er he wente.   255   ferthyng: farthing.
His purchas was wel bettre than his rente.
And rage he koude, as it were right a whelp.   rage: behave wantonly.
In love-dayes ther koude he muchel help,   love-dayes: arbitration days.
For ther he was nat lyk a cloysterer   muchel: much.
With a thredbare cope, as is a povre scoler,   260   cope: cape. povre: poor.
But he was lyk a maister or a pope.   maister: one in authority.
Of double worstede was his semycope,   semycope: short cloak.
That rounded as a belle out of the presse.   presse: mould.
Somwhat he lipsed, for his wantownesse,   lipsed: lisped.
To make his Englissh sweete upon his tonge;   265
And in his harpyng, whan that he hadde songe,
His eyen twynkled in his heed aryght,   aryght: right well.
As doon the sterres in the frosty nyght.   doon: do. sterres: stars.
This worthy lymytour was cleped Huberd.   cleped: called.

  A Marchant was ther with a forked berd,   270
In motlee, and hye on horse he sat;   motlee: motley; parti-colored cloth.
Upon his heed a Flaundryssh bevere hat,   hye: in a high saddle.
His bootes clasped faire and fetisly.   fetisly: elegantly.
His resons he spak ful solempnely,   solempnely: impressively, pompously.
Sownynge alwey th' encrees of his wynnyng.   275   sownynge: proclaiming.
He wolde the see were kept for any thyng   kept for: guarded against.

---

246. **honest:** honorable; respectable; appropriate to persons of standing.
246–47. **nat . . . no:** intensive double negative.
251. **nas:** was not. (nas no . . . nowher: intensive triple negative.)
252ᵃ. I.e., he gave a fixed payment to his convent for the privilege of begging within assigned limits. The bracketed lines, found in 5 MSS., may be genuine but canceled by Chaucer.
254. *In principio:* from John i,1; used as a blessing and as a formula for warding off evil spirits.
256. **His purchas . . . rente:** What he picked up amounted to more than his legal income.
257. **as . . . whelp:** exactly as if he were a puppy.
259. **cloysterer:** a religious remaining in his cloister.
262. **double worstede:** a stout worsted cloth 45 inches wide (see Baugh).
269. **lymytour:** see l. 209 and note.
270. **Marchant:** wholesale exporter and importer.
274. **resons:** opinions, remarks.

Bitwixe Middelburgh and Orewelle.
Wel koude he in eschaunge sheeldes selle.

sheeldes: "écus," French gold coins.

This worthy man ful wel his wit bisette:

wit: mind. bisette: employed.

Ther wiste no wight that he was in dette, 280

wiste: knew. wight: man.

So estatly was he of his governaunce

estatly: dignified. governaunce: management; demeanor.

With his bargaynes and with his chevyssaunce.
For sothe he was a worthy man with alle,

for sothe: in truth.

But, sooth to seyn, I noot how men hym calle.

noot: (ne woot) know not.

  A Clerk ther was of Oxenford also, 285
That unto logyk hadde longe ygo.
As leene was his hors as is a rake,
And he was nat right fat, I undertake,

nat right: not at all.

But looked holwe, and therto sobrely.

holwe: hollow. therto: moreover.

Full thredbare was his overeste courtepy; 290

overeste: outermost. courtepy: short coat.

For he hadde geten hym yet no benefice,
Ne was so worldly for to have office.

have office: accept secular employment. hym was levere: he had rather.

For hym was levere have at his beddes heed
Twenty bookes, clad in blak or reed,
Of Aristotle and his philosophie, 295
Than robes riche, or fithele, or gay sautrie.

fithele: fiddle. sautrie: psaltery.

But al be that he was a philosophre,

al be that: although.

Yet hadde he but litel gold in cofre;
But al that he myghte of his freendes hente,

hente: get.

On bookes and on lernynge he it spente, 300
And bisily gan for the soules preye

gan preye: prayed.

Of hem that yaf hym wherwith to scoleye.

yaf: gave. scoleye: study.

Of studie took he moost cure and moost heede.

cure: care.

Noght o word spak he moore than was neede,

o: one.

And that was seyd in forme and reverence, 305

in forme: formally.

And short and quyk and ful of hy sentence;

quyk: lively.

Sownynge in moral vertu was his speche,

sownynge in: tending toward.

And gladly wolde he lerne and gladly teche.
  A Sergeant of the Lawe, war and wys,

war: prudent.

That often hadde been at the Parvys, 310
Ther was also, ful riche of excellence.

---

277. Orwell, a port near Ipswich, was nearly opposite the port of Middelburg on the island of Walcheren, Netherlands.

278. Wel . . . selle: Only the royal money changers were permitted to make a profit on exchange. sheeldes: worth about half a noble (today between thirty and forty dollars).

282. chevyssaunce: dealings for profit (the word connotes dishonest proceedings).

285. Clerk: university student.

286. He had proceeded to logic, one of the fundamental parts of the medieval university curriculum.

297. philosophre: with a play on the cant sense of "alchemist."

306. sentence: significance; sentiment; instruction.

309. Sergeant of the Lawe: a member of the highest degree of lawyer, the King's legal servants.

310. at the Parvys: probably the porch of St. Paul's, where lawyers met their clients for consultation.

Discreet he was and of greet reverence—
He semed swich, his wordes weren so wise. swich: such.
Justice he was ful often in assise, justice in assise: circuit judge.
By patente and by pleyn commissioun. 315 pleyn: full.
For his science and for his heigh renoun, science: knowledge.
Of fees and robes hadde he many oon.
So greet a purchasour was nowher noon: purchasour: acquirer (of land).
Al was fee symple to hym in effect; in effect: in fact.
His purchasyng myghte nat been infect. 320 infect: invalidated.
Nowher so bisy a man as he ther nas,
And yet he semed bisier than he was.
In termes hadde he caas and doomes alle
That from the tyme of kyng William were falle.
Therto he koude endite, and make a thyng, 325 endite, make: write, compose. thyng:
Ther koude no wight pynche at his writyng; deed. pynche: find fault with.
And every statut koude he pleyn by rote. koude: knew. pleyn: fully.
He rood but hoomly in a medlee cote, hoomly: plainly.
Girt with a ceint of silk, with barres smale; ceint: cincture, sash.
Of his array telle I no lenger tale. 330

   A Frankeleyn was in his compaignye.
Whit was his berd as is the dayesye; dayesye: ("day's eye") daisy.
Of his complexioun he was sangwyn.
Wel loved he by the morwe a sop in wyn; by the morwe: in the morning. sop:
To lyven in delit was evere his wone, 335 i.e., of bread. wone: wont, custom.
For he was Epicurus owene sone,
That heeld opinioun that pleyn delit pleyn: full, perfect.
Was verray felicitee parfit. verray: true. parfit: perfect.
An housholdere, and that a greet, was he;
Seint Julian he was in his contree. 340 contree: region.
His breed, his ale, was alweys after oon;

---

315. patente: royal letter of appointment. A pleyn commissioun gave him jurisdiction over all kinds of cases.

317. The fees and robes were gifts of clients.

319. fee symple: unrestricted possession.

321. nowher . . . nas: nowhere . . . was not (intensive double negative).

323–24. He knew accurately all the cases and judgments since the Conquest.

326. If the portrait describes the Sergeant of Law named Thomas Pinchbeck, the word "pynche" is a pun.

328. medlee: cloth of mixed weave, sometimes parti-colored.

331. Frankeleyn: wealthy landowner, country gentleman.

333. complexioun: temperament; combination of humors, i.e., the four body fluids which were supposed to determine a person's health and temperament. sangwyn: a ruddy face was one of the signs of the sanguine "complexioun," in which the humor blood predominated (see also Knight's Tale, I. 2168; Squire's Tale, I. 352). The other "complexiouns" were the choleric (see I. 587, and Nuns' Priest's Tale, II. 2928, 2946, 2955), in which the humor choler predominated; melancholy (see Knight's Tale, I. 1375; Nuns' Priest's Tale, II. 2933–35), in which the humor black bile predominated; and the phlegmatic, in which phlegm predominated.

336. He was an epicure, devoted to luxurious living.

340. Seint Julian: patron saint of hospitality.

341. after oon: according to one standard, uniformly good.

A bettre envyned man was nevere noon.
Withoute bake mete was nevere his hous
Of fissh and flessh, and that so plentevous,
It snewed in his hous of mete and drynke,   345
Of alle deyntees that men koude thynke,
After the sondry sesons of the yeer,
So chaunged he his mete and his soper.
Ful many a fat partrich hadde he in muwe.
And many a breem and many a luce in
    stuwe.   350
Wo was his cook but if his sauce were
Poynaunt and sharp, and redy al his geere.
His table dormant in his halle alway
Stood redy covered al the longe day.
At sessiouns ther was he lord and sire;   355
Ful ofte tyme he was knyght of the shire.
An anlaas and a gipser al of silk
Heeng at his girdel, whit as morne milk.
A shirreve hadde he been, and a countour.
Was nowher swich a worthy vavasour.   360

An Haberdasshere and a Carpenter,
A Webbe, a Dyere, and a Tapycer,—
And they were clothed alle in o lyveree
Of a solempne and a greet fraternitee.
Ful fressh and newe hir geere apiked was;   365
Hir knyves were chaped noght with bras
But al with silver; wrought ful clene and wel
Hire girdles and hir pouches everydel.
Wel semed ech of hem a fair burgeys
To sitten in a yeldehalle on a deys.   370
Everich, for the wisdom that he kan,
Was shaply for to been an alderman.
For catel hadde they ynogh and rente,
And eek hir wyves wolde it wel assente;
And elles certeyn they were to blame.   375
It is ful fair to been ycleped "madame,"
And goon to vigilies al bifore,
And have a mantel roialliche ybore.

A Cook they hadde with hem for the nones
To boille the chiknes with the marybones,   380

Glosses (right column):

envyned: stocked with wine.
bake mete: tarts; meat pies.
mete: food.
deyntees: delicacies.
after: according to.
mete: dinner.
muwe: mew, cage (for fattening).
breem: bream. luce: pike. stuwe: fish-pond.
but if: unless.
dormant: fixed in its place, always ready for company.
sessiouns: i.e., of justices of the peace.
anlaas: short dagger. gipser: pouch, purse. morne: morning.
shirreve: sheriff. countour: overseer of taxes for a shire. swich: such.
Webbe: weaver. Tapycer: weaver of tapestry. o: one. lyveree: livery.
solempne: distinguished, impressive.
geere: equipment, apparel. apiked: adorned. chaped: mounted.
everydel: every bit, altogether.
kan: knows.
shaply: suitable, likely.
catel: property, goods. rente: income.
ycleped: called.
ybore: borne, carried.
for the nones: for the occasion.
chiknes: chickens. marybones: marrow-bones.

---

356. **knyght of the shire**: representative of his county in parliament.
360. **vavasour**: substantial landowner below the rank of baron.
364. **fraternitee**: The fraternity of which these five pilgrims all wore the livery was a social and religious guild. Its vigils (l. 377) were services on the eve of guild festivals.
369–70. Each of them seemed a good burgess to sit on the raised platform in a guildhall.
372. **alderman**: officer of a city; or officer of a guild.
379. For two portraits of the **Cook** see p. 000.

And poudre-marchant tart and galyngale.
Wel koude he knowe a draughte of Londoun ale.
He koude rooste, and sethe, and broille, and
     frye,

sethe: seethe, boil.

Maken mortreux, and wel bake a pye.

mortreux: stew. pye: pie, pastry.

But greet harm was it, as it thoughte me,   385
That on his shyne a mormal hadde he,
For blankmanger, that made he with the beste.

harm: pity. thoughte me: seemed to me. shyne: shin. mormal: an itching, suppurating sore.

   A Shipman was ther, wonynge fer by weste;
For aught I woot, he was of Dertemouthe.

Shipman: shipmaster. wonynge: dwelling. woot: know.

He rood upon a rouncy, as he kouthe,   390
In a gowne of faldyng to the knee.

rouncy: great strong horse.
faldyng: coarse woolen cloth.

A daggere hangynge on a laas hadde he

laas: cord.

Aboute his nekke, under his arm adoun.
The hoote somer hadde maad his hewe al broun;
And certeinly he was a good felawe.   395
Ful many a draughte of wyn had he drawe

drawe: drawn.

Fro Burdeux-ward, whil that the chapman sleep.

sleep: slept.

Of nyce conscience took he no keep.

nyce: foolish. conscience: scruples. keep: heed.

If that he faught, and hadde the hyer hond,
By water he sente hem hoom to every lond.   400
But of his craft to rekene wel his tydes,
His stremes, and his daungers hym bisides,

stremes: currents. hym bisides: near him.

His herberwe, and his moone, his lodemenage,
Ther nas noon swich from Hulle to Cartage.

nas: (ne was) was not.

Hardy he was and wys to undertake;   405
With many a tempest hadde his berd been shake.
He knew alle the havenes, as they were,
Fro Gootlond to the cape of Fynystere,
And every cryke in Britaigne and in Spayne.

Britaigne: Brittany.

His barge ycleped was the Maudelayne.   410

barge: vessel. Maudelayne: Magdalen.

   With us ther was a Doctour of Phisik;
In al this world ne was ther noon hym lik,
To speke of phisik and of surgerye,

to speke of: with regard to. phisik: medicine.

---

381. **poudre-marchant:** a tart flavoring powder. **galyngale:** a flavor prepared from sweet cyperus root.

387. **blankmanger:** creamed fowl with a rich sweet sauce.

389. **Dertemouthe:** Dartmouth, on the Devonshire coast.

390. **as he kouthe:** as (well as) he knew how.

396–97. **Ful many . . . sleep:** The Shipman stole wine which he was carrying from Bordeaux for a merchant (**chapman**).

400. I.e., by drowning.

402. **daungers:** dangers to navigation, such as submerged rocks.

403. **herberwe:** harbor, i.e., harbors in general. **lodemenage:** pilotage, and perhaps navigational skill in general.

404. **Hulle to Cartage:** Hull, on the Yorkshire coast; Cartagena, Spain, on the Mediterranean.

408. From Gotland (in the Baltic Sea) to Cape Finisterre (the northwest point of Spain).

411. **Doctour of Phisik:** physician. **phisik:** medical science.

Senach sagt es Etliche nützliche
vnderscheyde von dem firmament vnd
von den hymeln vnd das yt ze mercken
Nt heß abraham
daz er ansehe den
hymel vnd sein
derzierde die der
hymel hett vnd
solt got ermanen
vnd sein allmäch-
tigkeyt · Die 12.
zaichen sullent
vns andächtig

For he was grounded in astronomye.
He kepte his pacient a ful greet deel   415
In houres by his magik natureel.
Wel koude he fortunen the ascendent
Of his ymages for his pacient.
He knew the cause of every maladye,
Were it of hoot, or coold, or moyste, or drye,   420
And where engendred, and of what humour.   engendred: originated.
He was a verray, parfit praktisour: verray: true. praktisour: practitioner.
The cause yknowe, and of his harm the roote,
Anon he yaf the sike man his boote.   anon: immediately. boote: remedy.
Ful redy hadde he his apothecaries   425
To sende hym drogges and his letuaries.   letuaries: electuaries, remedies.
For ech of hem made oother for to wynne—
Hir frendshipe nas nat newe to bigynne.   nas: was not.
Wel knew he the olde Esculapius,
And Deyscorides, and eek Rufus,   430
Olde Ypocras, Haly, and Galyen,
Serapion, Razis, and Avycen,
Averrois, Damascien, and Constantyn,
Bernard, and Gatesden, and Gilbertyn.
Of his diete mesurable was he,   435   mesurable: moderate.
For it was of no superfluitee,
But of greet norissyng and digestible.   norissyng: nourishment.
His studie was but litel on the Bible.
In sangwyn and in pers he clad was al,   sangwyn: red cloth. pers: bluish cloth.
Lyned with taffata and with sendal;   440   sendal: thin silk.
And yet he was but esy of dispence;   esy of dispence: slow to spend money.

---

414. astronomye: what we call astrology.

415–16. He took care of his patient during the various stages (houres) of a disease by means of natural magic (i.e., by practices based on astrology).

417–18. The images were talismans representing the signs of the zodiac or symbolically associated with them. Their virtue depended on the positions of the planets at the time when they were made. He could well find or place them in a favorable position (fortunen).

420. These four elementary qualities or contraries combined in pairs to produce the four elements, and also combined in the four humors: hot-moist (Air; blood); hot-dry (Fire; choler); cold-dry (Earth-melancholy); cold-moist (Water; phlegm). See note for l. 333, above.

423. The cause and the source of his disease known.

429–34. The physician has studied the most reputable medical authorities. The legendary Aesculapius, Dioscorides, Rufus, Hippocrates, and Galen were Greek; Hali, Serapion, Rhazes, Avicenna, Averroes, and Damascenus were Arabic; the rest were fairly recent European authorities. John of Gaddesden, Merton College, Oxford, had died in 1361.

435–38. He nourished his body rather than his spirit (cf. Summoner's Tale, ll. 1844–45).

"For he was grounded in astronomye": Although later (1464) and from a distance (Germany) this picture well expresses a view universal in Chaucer's world. MacKinney (Medical Illustrations in Medieval Manuscripts, pp. 22–23) thus comments on it (his "Fig. 17. Diagnosis-Prognosis by Astrology"): "In both medical and astronomical manuscripts one finds illustrations of professors gazing at the stars. . . . Our miniature is a typical representation of medical astrology; a physician studies the sky, consulting his book for the diagnostic-prognostic interpretation. On the book one can make out only a few letters, apparently in roughly scribbled Latin." The anonymous German text below offers instructions concerning the medical uses of astrology and an explanation of its divine origin.

He kepte that he wan in pestilence.

that: that which.

For gold in phisik is a cordial,

for: because. cordial: medicinal

Therefore he loved gold in special.

stimulant.

    A good Wif was ther of biside Bathe,   445

But she was somdel deef, and that was scathe.

somdel: somewhat. that was scathe:

Of clooth-makyng she hadde swich an haunt,

that was a pity. haunt: skill.

She passed hem of Ypres and of Gaunt.

passed: surpassed. hem: them.

In al the parisshe wif ne was ther noon

That to the offrynge bifore hire sholde goon;   450

And if ther dide, certeyn so wrooth was she,

That she was out of alle charitee.

Hir coverchiefs ful fyne were of ground;

ground: texture.

I dorste swere they weyeden ten pound

weyeden: weighed.

That on a Sonday weren upon hir heed.   455

Hir hosen weren of fyn scarlet reed,

hosen: hose, covering for feet and

Ful streite yteyd, and shoes ful moyste and newe.

legs. streite: tightly. yteyd: tied.

Boold was hir face, and fair, and reed of hewe.

She was a worthy womman al hir lyve:

Housbondes at chirche dore she hadde fyve,   460

Withouten oother compaignye in youthe,—

withouten: without; in addition to.

But therof nedeth nat to speke as nowthe.

as nowthe: at present.

And thries hadde she been at Jerusalem;

thries: thrice.

She hadde passed many a straunge strem;

straunge: foreign, distant.

At Rome she hadde been, and at Boloigne,   465

In Galice at Seint-Jame, and at Coloigne.

She koude muche of wandrynge by the weye.

koude: knew.

Gat-tothed was she, soothly for to seye.

Upon an amblere esily she sat,

amblere: a saddle horse.

Ywympled wel, and on hir heed an hat   470

ywympled: covered with a wimple.

As brood as is a bokeler or a targe;

targe: shield.

A foot-mantel aboute hir hipes large,

foot-mantel: outer skirt.

And on hir feet a paire of spores sharpe.

In felaweshipe wel koude she laughe and carpe.

carpe: chatter, gossip, jest.

Of remedies of love she knew per chaunce,   475

per chaunce: perchance.

For she koude of that art the olde daunce.

    A good man was ther of religioun,

---

442. pestilence: the Black Plague, which nearly halved the population of England in the epidemics of 1348, 1361, 1369, and 1376.

443. "Aurum potabile" was supposed to be an excellent medicine; it was also very expensive.

445. biside Bathe: probably St. Michael's juxta Bathon, a suburb famous for weaving.

448. The cloth of Ypres and Ghent was highly thought of.

457. moyste: perhaps moist with oil (S. M. Kuhn).

460. The ceremony at the church door included any transfer of property and so was particularly important from the Wife's point of view.

465–66. The Wife's pilgrimages took her to the shrine of the Virgin in Boulogne; the shrine of St. James at Compostella in Galicia; and the shrine of the Three Kings, and perhaps that of the Eleven Thousand Virgins, at Cologne.

468. gat-tothed: with teeth set wide apart. To have the teeth set far apart was a sign that a person would travel, and would be bold and lascivious.

476. She was artful and knowing.

And was a povre Persoun of a toun,   povre: poor. Persoun: parson.
But riche he was of holy thoght and werk.
He was also a lerned man, a clerk,   480   clerk: scholar.
That Cristes gospel trewely wolde preche;
His parisshens devoutly wolde he teche.
Benygne he was, and wonder diligent,
And in adversitee ful pacient,
And swich he was preved ofte sithes.   485   preved: proved. sithes: times.
Ful looth were hym to cursen for his tithes,   looth were hym: he was loath.
But rather wolde he yeven, out of doute,   yeven: give. out of doute: doubtless.
Unto his povre parisshens aboute
Of his offryng and eek of his substaunce.
He koude in litel thyng have suffisaunce.   490
Wyd was his parisshe, and houses fer asonder,
But he ne lefte nat, for reyn ne thonder,   lefte: ceased, omitted.
In siknesse nor in meschief to visite   meschief: misfortune.
The ferreste in his parisshe, muche and lite,   ferreste: farthest. muche and lite: high
Upon his feet, and in his hand a staf.   495   and low.
This noble ensample to his sheep he yaf,   yaf: gave.
That first he wroghte, and afterward he taughte.
Out of the gospel he tho wordes caughte,   tho: those.
And this figure he added eek therto,   therto: moreover, besides.
That if gold ruste, what sholde iren do?   500
For if a preest be foul, on whom we truste,
No wonder is a lewed man to ruste;   lewed: unlearned, ignorant.
And shame it is, if a prest take keep,   keep: heed.
A shiten shepherde and a clene sheep.   shiten: defiled with excrement.
Wel oghte a preest ensample for to yive,   505   yive: give.
By his clennesse, how that his sheep sholde lyve.
He sette nat his benefice to hyre
And leet his sheep encombred in the myre   leet: left. encombred: stuck.
And ran to Londoun unto Seinte Poules
To seken hym a chaunterie for soules,   510
Or with a bretherhed to been withholde;
But dwelte at hoom, and kepte wel his folde,
So that the wolf ne made it nat myscarie;   myscarie: come to harm.
He was a shepherde and noght a mercenarie.
And though he hooly were and vertuous,   515
He was to synful men nat despitous,   despitous: pitiless, hateful.
Ne of his speche daungerous ne digne,   daungerous: severe, arrogant.
      digne: haughty.

---

481. In his emphasis on the Gospel (l. 498) and on Christ and the Apostles (l. 527), the Parson resembles Wyclif and his followers.

486. Wyclif protested against excommunication for non-payment of tithes.

507. Absenteeism was far too common in the latter part of the 14th century.

510. It was customary for people to establish endowments (chaunteries) for the daily masses to be sung for the repose of a soul.

511. Or to be retained (withholde) by a guild (bretherhed) to act as their chaplain.

514. mercenarie: Priests who made their living entirely by saying mass were given the title "chappelain mercenaire."

But in his techyng discreet and benygne.　　　　　　benygne: benign.
To drawen folk to hevene by fairnesse,
By good ensample, this was his bisynesse.　　520　bisynesse: endeavor.
But it were any persone obstinat,
What so he were, of heigh or lowe estat,
Hym wolde he snybben sharply for the nonys.　　　snybben: rebuke. for the nonys: on
A bettre preest I trowe that nowher noon ys.　　　　the occasion.
He waited after no pompe and reverence,　　525　waited after: looked for.
Ne maked him a spiced conscience,
But Cristes loore and his apostles twelve　　　　　loore: teaching, doctrine.
He taughte, but first he folwed it hymselve.
　　With hym ther was a Plowman, was his
　　　　　brother,
That hadde ylad of dong ful many a fother;　　530　ylad: carried (in a cart). fother: load.
A trewe swynkere and a good was he,　　　　　　swynkere: worker.
Lyvynge in pees and parfit charitee.
God loved he best with al his hoole herte
At alle tymes, thogh him gamed or smerte,
And thanne his neighebor right as hymselve.　　535
He wolde thresshe, and therto dyke and delve,　　　dyke: make ditches. delve: dig.
For Cristes sake, for every povre wight,
Withouten hire, if it lay in his myght.
His tithes payde he ful faire and wel,
Bothe of his propre swynk and his catel.　　540　propre: own. swynk: work. catel:
In a tabard he rood upon a mere.　　　　　　　　goods. tabard: smock, loose coat.
　　Ther was also a Reve, and a Millere,
A Somnour, and a Pardoner also,
A Maunciple, and myself—ther were namo.　　　　namo: no more.
　　The Millere was a stout carl for the nones;　545　stout: strong. carl: man. for the
Ful byg he was of brawn, and eek of bones.　　　　nones: exceedingly.
That proved wel, for over al ther he cam,　　　　proved: proved to be true. over al
At wrastlynge he wolde have alwey the ram.　　　　ther: wherever.
He was short-sholdred, brood, a thikke knarre;　　knarre: stout, sturdy fellow.
Ther was no dore that he nolde heve of harre, 550　nolde: (ne wolde) would not. of: off.
Or breke it at a rennyng with his heed.　　　　　harre: hinge. rennyng: running.
His berd as any sowe or fox was reed,
And therto brood, as though it were a spade.
Upon the cop right of his nose he hade　　　　　cop: tip.
A werte, and theron stood a tuft of herys,　　555　werte: wart. herys: hairs.
Reed as the bristles of a sowes erys;　　　　　　erys: ears.
His nosethirles blake were and wyde.　　　　　　nosethirles: nostrils.
A swerd and a bokeler bar he by his syde.　　　　bokeler: buckler, shield.
His mouth as greet was as a greet forneys.　　　　forneys: furnace.

---

525. He demanded no reverence.
526. spiced: seasoned, hence highly refined, over-scrupulous.
534. thogh him gamed or smerte: in pleasure or pain, under all circumstances.
541. mere: mare. The mare was a humble mount.
548. The ram was a common prize for wrestling.

He was a janglere and a goliardeys,   560
And that was moost of synne and harlotries.
Wel koude he stelen corn and tollen thries;
And yet he hadde a thombe of gold, pardee.
A whit cote and a blew hood wered he.
A baggepipe wel koude he blowe and sowne,   565
And therwithal he broghte us out of towne.

   A gentil Maunciple was ther of a temple,
Of which achatours myghte take exemple
For to be wise in byynge of vitaille;
For wheither that he payde or took by taille,   570
Algate he wayted so in his achaat
That he was ay biforn and in good staat.
Now is nat that of God a ful fair grace
That swich a lewed mannes wit shal pace
The wisdom of an heep of lerned men?   575
Of maistres hadde he mo than thries ten,
That weren of lawe expert and curious,
Of whiche ther were a dozeyne in that hous
Worthy to been stywardes of rente and lond
Of any lord that is in Engelond,   580
To make hym lyve by his propre good
In honour dettelees (but if he were wood),
Or lyve as scarsly as hym list desire;
And able for to helpen al a shire
In any caas that myghte falle or happe;   585
And yet this Manciple sette hir aller cappe.

   The Reve was a sclendre colerik man.
His berd was shave as ny as ever he kan;
His heer was by his erys ful round yshorn;
His top was dokked lyk a preest biforn.   590
Ful longe were his legges and ful lene,
Ylyk a staf, ther was no calf ysene.
Wel koude he kepe a gerner and a bynne;
Ther was noon auditour koude on him wynne.
Wel wiste he by the droghte and by the reyn   595
The yeldynge of his seed and of his greyn.
His lordes sheep, his neet, his dayerye,
His swyn, his hors, his stoor, and his pultrye
Was hoolly in this Reves governynge,

harlotries: ribald jests.
tollen: take toll. thries: thrice.
pardee: *pardieu*, certainly.
wered: wore.
sowne: sound, play upon.

which: whom. achatours: purchasers.
vitaille: victuals, provisions.
by taille: by tally, on credit.
algate: always. wayted: watched.
  achaat: purchase. was biforn: had
  the advantage.
lewed: ignorant, unlearned. pace: sur-
  pass.
mo: more. thries: thrice.
curious: careful, diligent; skilful.

rente: income.

propre: own. good: possessions.
dettelees: debtless. but if: unless.
  wood: mad. scarsly: frugally. hym
  list: it pleased him.
caas: mischance. falle: befall.
sette hir aller cappe: made fools of
  them all.
ny: nigh, close.
erys: ears. yshorn: shorn.
his top: the hair of his crown.
  dokked: docked, cut short.
ylyk: like. ysene: seen.
gerner: granary.

wiste: knew.

neet: neat, cattle. dayerye: dairy herd.
hors: horses. stoor: livestock.
hoolly: wholly.

560. janglere: a teller of dirty stories. goliardeys: coarse buffoon.
563. The reference is to the old proverb, "An honest miller has a golden thumb." The Miller was honest as millers go.
567. Maunciple: steward of an inn or college. temple: inn of court, where law was studied.
579. stywardes: stewards. A steward was the chief manager of an estate.
581. To make him live upon his own income.
587. Reve: an official accountant and overseer on an estate or manor. colerik: choleric (see note for line 333, above); hence, hot-tempered.
589. The Reve's close-cropped hair was a sign of his servile station.

And by his covenant yaf the rekenynge, 600
Syn that his lord was twenty yeer of age.
Ther koude no man brynge hym in arrerage.
Ther nas baillif, ne hierde, nor oother hyne,
That he ne knew his sleighte and his covyne;
They were adrad of hym as of the deeth. 605
His wonyng was ful faire upon an heeth;
With grene trees shadwed was his place.
He koude bettre than his lord purchace.
Ful riche he was astored pryvely:
His lord wel koude he plesen subtilly, 610
To yeve and lene hym of his owene good,
And have a thank, and yet a cote and hood.
In youthe he hadde lerned a good myster:
He was a wel good wrighte, a carpenter.
This Reve sat upon a ful good stot, 615
That was al pomely grey and highte Scot.
A long surcote of pers upon he hade,
And by his syde he baar a rusty blade.
Of Northfolk was this Reve of which I telle,
Biside a toun men clepen Baldeswelle. 620
Tukked he was as is a frere aboute,
And evere he rood the hyndreste of oure route.
    A Somonour was ther with us in that place,
That hadde a fyr-reed cherubynnes face,
For saucefleem he was, with eyen narwe. 625
As hoot he was and lecherous as a sparwe,
With scalled browes blake and piled berd.
Of his visage children were aferd.
Ther nas quyk-silver, lytarge, ne brymstoon,
Boras, ceruce, ne oille of tartre noon, 630
Ne oynement that wolde clense and byte,
That hym myghte helpen of his whelkes white,
Nor of the knobbes sittynge on his chekes.
Wel loved he garlek, oynons, and eek lekes,
And for to drynke strong wyn, reed as blood; 635
Thanne wolde he speke and crye as he were
            wood.
And whan that he wel dronken hadde the wyn,

yaf: gave.
syn: since.
arrerage: arrears.
nas: (ne was) was not.
covyne: deceitfulness.
the deeth: the Black Death; the plague. wonyng: dwelling.

purchace: acquire (property).
astored: provided, stored. pryvely: secretly.
yeve: give. lene: loan. good: goods.

myster: occupation.
wrighte: workman.
stot: stallion.
highte: was called.
surcote: surcoat, outer coat. pers: bluish cloth.

clepen: call.

route: company.

narwe: narrow.

scalled: scabby; having the scall.
piled: deprived of hair.
nas: was not. lytarge: litharge, an oxide of lead. ceruce: white lead.

helpen: cure. whelkes: pimples.

wood: mad.

---

603. hierde: herdsman, shepherd. hyne: hind, servant, farm laborer.
616. pomely: dappled, marked with round spots like an apple.
620. Baldeswelle: Bawdswell, in the northern part of Norfolk.
623. Somonour: A summoner (or apparitor) was an officer who cited delinquents to appear before the ecclesiastical court.
624. Cherubim (of the second order of angels) were depicted with flaming red faces in medieval manuscripts and wall paintings.
625. saucefleem: having pimples or eruptions (Lat. "salsum phlegma"). eyen narwe: His eyes are almost closed by the puffiness of his cheeks and the corrugation and swelling of his eyelids
626. Sparrows have long been associated with lechery and Venus.

Thanne wolde he speke no word but Latyn.

A fewe termes hadde he, two or thre,   termes: technical law terms.

That he had lerned out of some decree—   640

No wonder is, he herde it al the day;

And eek ye knowen wel how that a jay

Kan clepen "Watte" as wel as kan the pope.   clepen: call.

But whoso koude in oother thyng hym grope,   grope: grope, test, search out.

Thanne hadde he spent al his philosophie; 645

Ay *"Questio quid iuris"* wolde he crie.

He was a gentil harlot and a kynde;   harlot: low fellow, rascal, thief.

A bettre felawe sholde men noght fynde.

He wolde suffre for a quart of wyn   suffre: permit.

A good felawe to have his concubyn   650 his: i.e., the good felawe's.

A twelf month, and excuse hym atte fulle;

Ful prively a fynch eek koude he pulle.

And if he foond owher a good felawe,   owher: anywhere.

He wolde techen him to have noon awe

In swich caas of the ercedekenes curs, 655 ercedekenes: archdeacon's.

But if a mannes soul were in his purs;   but if: unless.

For in his purs he sholde ypunysshed be.

"Purs is the ercedekenes helle," seyde he.

But wel I woot he lyed right in dede;   woot: know.

Of cursyng oghte ech gilty man him drede, 660 cursyng: excommunication.

For curs wol slee right as assoillyng savith, slee: slay. assoillyng: absolving, abso-

And also war hym of a *Significavit*.   lution.

In daunger hadde he at his owene gyse   daunger: power. at his owene gyse:

The yonge girles of the diocise,   as he pleased. girles: prostitutes.

And knew hir conseil, and was al hir reed. 665 conseil: secrets. reed: (source of) ad-

A gerland hadde he set upon his heed   vice.

As greet as it were for an ale-stake.

A bokeler hadde he maad hym of a cake.   bokeler: shield. cake: a round, flat

   With hym ther rood a gentil Pardoner   loaf of bread.

Of Rouncivale, his freend and his compeer, 670 compeer: comrade.

That streight was comen fro the court of Rome.

Ful loude he soong "Com hider, love, to me!"

This Somonour bar to hym a stif burdoun;   bar: carried. stif: strong; loud; stiff.

Was nevere trompe of half so greet a soun.

---

643. "Watte": Jays were taught to cry "Watte" (Walter) just as parrots now cry "Poll."

646. *Questio quid iuris:* the opening words of a writ sometimes used as a summons.

652. To pluck the feathers from a finch is an obscene expression meaning to seduce a girl.

662. *Significavit:* "Significavit nobis venerabilis pater" were the opening words of a writ remanding to prison an excommunicated person.

666–67. The sign for a medieval alehouse was a garland of leaves hung from a pole (alestake) over the door.

669. Pardoner: pardoner, seller of indulgences.

670. Rouncivale: the hospital of the Blessed Mary of Rouncivalle, near Charing Cross; this was a cell (subordinate house) of the convent of Our Lady of Roncesvalles in Navarre.

671. court of Rome: the papal Curia Romana.

672. "Com hider, love, to me!": a popular love song.

673. burdoun: ground melody, bass; pilgrim's staff; club.

This Pardoner hadde heer as yelow as wex,   675
But smothe it heeng as dooth a strike of flex;   strike: hank.
By ounces henge his lokkes that he hadde,   ounces: ounces; i.e., thin strands.
And therwith he his shuldres overspradde;
But thynne it lay, by colpons oon and oon.   thynne: thin. colpons: bunches.
But hood, for jolitee, wered he noon,   680 wered: wore.
For it was trussed up in his walet.   trussed: packed.
Hym thoughte he rood al of the newe jet;   hym thoughte: it seemed to him. jet:
Dischevelee, save his cappe, he rood al bare.   fashion. dischevelee: disheveled,
Swiche glarynge eyen hadde he as an hare.   with loose or disordered hair.
A vernycle hadde he sowed upon his cappe.   685 glarynge: staring.
His walet biforn hym in his lappe,   walet: wallet.
Bretful of pardoun, comen from Rome al hoot.   bretful: brimful.
A voys he hadde as smal as hath a goot.   smal: high pitched.
No berd hadde he, ne nevere sholde have;
As smothe it was as it were late shave.   690 late: recently. shave: shaved.
I trowe he were a geldyng or a mare.   trowe: believe.
But of his craft, fro Berwyk into Ware,   into: into.
Ne was ther swich another pardoner.
For in his male he hadde a pilwe-beer,   male: bag, wallet. pilwe-beer: pillow-
Which that he seyde was Oure Lady veyl: 695 case. Lady: Lady's.
He seyde he hadde a gobet of the seyl   gobet: piece, fragment.
That Seint Peter hadde, whan that he wente
Upon the see, till Jhesu Crist hym hente.   hente: caught hold of.
He hadde a croys of latoun ful of stones,   croys: cross. latoun: a brasslike alloy.
And in a glas he hadde pigges bones.   700
But with thise relikes, whan that he fond
A povre person dwellyng upon lond,   povre: poor. person: parson. upon
Upon a day he gat hym moore moneye   lond: in the country.
Than that the person gat in monthes tweye;   tweye: two.
And thus, with feyned flaterye and japes,   705 japes: jests.
He made the person and the peple his apes.
But trewely to tellen atte laste,
He was in chirche a noble ecclesiaste.   ecclesiaste: ecclesiastic, minister.
Wel koude he rede a lessoun or a storie,
But alderbest he song an offertorie;   710 alderbest: best of all.
For wel he wiste, whan that song was songe,   wiste: knew.
He moste preche and wel affile his tonge   affile: file, polish, make smooth.
To wynne silver, as he ful wel koude;
Therefore he song the murierly and loude.
   Now have I toold you soothly, in a clause,   715 in a clause: briefly.
Th'estaat, th'array, the nombre, and eek the
      cause

---

685. vernycle: vernicle; a small copy of the handkerchief of St. Veronica. St. Veronica is said to have lent Christ her handkerchief as he was bearing his cross to Calvary, and so it received the imprint of his face.

686. walet: pronounced with stress on second syllable.

692. Berwyk, Ware: Berwick, near the Scottish border; Ware, in Hertfordshire, just north of London, or, for greater range, the less known Ware in Kent near the Strait of Dover.

Why that assembled was this compaignye
In Southwerk at this gentil hostelrye
That highte the Tabard, faste by the Belle.   highte: was called.
But now is tyme to yow for to telle   720
How that we baren us that ilke nyght,   baren us: conducted ourselves.
Whan we were in that hostelrie alyght;   ilke: same. alyght: alighted.
And after wol I telle of our viage   viage: journey.
And al the remenant of oure pilgrimage.   remenant: remainder, rest.
But first I pray yow, of youre curteisye,   725
That ye n'arette it nat my vileynye,   arette: impute, ascribe. vileynye:
Thogh that I pleynly speke in this mateere,   boorishness.
To telle yow hir wordes and hir cheere,   cheere: manner.
Ne thogh I speke hir wordes proprely.   proprely: exactly, literally.
For this ye knowen al so wel as I,   730
Whoso shal telle a tale after a man,
He moot reherce as ny as evere he kan   moot: must. ny: nearly.
Everich a word, if it be in his charge,   everich a: every. charge: power.
Al speke he never so rudeliche and large,   al: although. large: freely, broadly.
Or ellis he moot telle his tale untrewe,   735 moot: must.
Or feyne thyng, or fynde wordes newe.   feyne: invent.
He may nat spare, althogh he were his brother;
He moot as wel seye o word as another.   o: one.
Crist spak hymself ful brode in holy writ,   brode: outspokenly.
And wel ye woot no vileynye is it.   740 woot: know.
Eek Plato seith, whoso kan hym rede,
The wordes moote be cosyn to the dede.   moote: must.
Also I prey yow to foryeve it me,   foryeve: forgive.
Al have I nat set folk in hir degree   al: although. hir: their.
Here in this tale, as that they sholde stonde.   745
My wit is short, ye may wel understonde.
   Greet cheere made oure Hoost us everichon,   everichon: everyone.
And to the soper sette he us anon.   anon: immediately.
He served us with vitaille at the beste;   vitaille: victuals, food.
Strong was the wyn, and wel to drynke us   us leste: it pleased us.
     leste.   750
A semely man oure Hooste was withalle   semely: seemly, comely; pleasing.
For to been a marchal in an halle.
A large man he was with eyen stepe—   stepe: protruding.
A fairer burgeys was ther noon in Chepe—   burgeys: burgess; citizen.
Boold of his speche, and wys, and wel
     ytaught,   755
And of manhod hym lakkede right naught.   hym lakkede: he lacked.
Eek therto he was right a myrie man,   myrie: merry.
And after soper pleyen he bigan,   pleyen: to be playful.
And spak of myrthe amonges othere thynges,
Whan that we hadde maad our rekenynges,   760

---

719. the Belle: either an inn, or a licensed brothel owned by the Mayor of London.
754. Chepe: Cheapside, one of the principal London streets.

And seyde thus: "Now, lordynges, trewely,
Ye been to me right welcome, hertely;
For by my trouthe, if that I shal nat lye,
I saugh nat this yeer so myrie a compaignye
Atones in this herberwe as is now.   765   atones: at once. herberwe: inn.
Fayn wolde I doon yow myrthe, wiste I how.   doon: cause (to have). wiste: if I knew.
And of a myrthe I am right now bythoght,   bythoght: mindful.
To doon yow ese, and it shal coste noght.
  Ye goon to Caunterbury—God yow speede,
The blisful martir quite yow youre meede!   770   quite: repay. meede: meed, reward.
And wel I woot, as ye goon by the weye,
Ye shapen yow to talen and to pleye;   ye shapen yow: you intend. talen: tell
For trewely, confort ne myrthe is noon   tales.
To ride by the weye doumb as a stoon;
And therfore wol I maken yow disport,   775   disport: sport, pleasure.
As I seyde erst, and doon yow som confort.   erst: earlier.
And if yow liketh alle by oon assent
For to stonden at my juggement,
And for to werken as I shal yow seye,
To-morwe, whan ye riden by the weye,   780
Now, by my fader soule that is deed,
But ye be myrie, I wol yeve yow myn heed!   but: unless. heed: head.
Hoold up youre hondes, withouten moore
      speche."
  Oure conseil was nat longe for to seche.   conseil: decision. seche: seek.
Us thoughte it was noght worth to make it   us thoughte: it seemed to us.
      wys,   785
And graunted hym withouten moore avys,   avys: consideration.
And bad him seye his voirdit as hym leste.   voirdit: verdict.
"Lordynges," quod he, "now herkneth for the
      beste;
But taak it nought, I prey yow, in desdeyn.
This is the poynt, to speken short and pleyn,   790
That ech of yow, to shorte with oure weye,   to shorte with our weye: to shorten
In this viage shal telle tales tweye   our way with.
To Caunterbury-ward, I mene it so,
And homward he shal tellen othere two,
Of aventures that whilom han bifalle.   795   whilom: formerly, once.
And which of yow that bereth hym best of alle,
That is to seyn, that telleth in this caas   caas: affair.
Tales of best sentence and moost solaas,
Shal have a soper at oure aller cost   oure aller: of us all.
Heere in this place, sittynge by this post,   800
Whan that we come agayn fro Caunterbury.
And for to make yow the moore mury,

---

785. to make it wys: to make it a matter of wisdom, to hold off and deliberate.
798. sentence: sense, meaning, instruction (Lat. "sententia"). solaas: solace, amusement, enter-
tainment.

I wol myself goodly with yow ryde,

Right at myn owene cost, and be youre gyde;

And whoso wole my juggement withseye   805

Shal paye al that we spende by the weye.

And if ye vouche sauf that it be so,

Tel me anon, withouten wordes mo,

And I wol erly shape me therfore."

   This thyng was graunted, and oure othes swore   810

With ful glad herte, and preyden hym also

That he wolde vouche sauf for to do so,

And that he wolde been oure governour,

And of our tales juge and reportour,

And sette a soper at a certeyn pris,   815

And we wol reuled been at his devys

In heigh and lough; and thus by oon assent

We been acorded to his juggement.

And therupon the wyn was fet anon;

We dronken, and to reste wente echon,   820

Withouten any lenger taryynge.

   Amorwe, whan that day bigan to sprynge,

Up roos oure Hoost, and was oure aller cok,

And gadrede us togidre in a flok,

And forth we riden a litel moore than paas   825

Unto the Wateryng of Seint Thomas;

And there oure Hoost bigan his hors areste

And seyde, "Lordynges, herkneth, if yow leste.

Ye woot youre forward, and I it yow recorde.

If even-song and morwe-song accorde,   830

Lat se now who shal telle the firste tale.

As evere mote I drynke wyn or ale,

Whoso be rebel to my juggement

Shal paye for al that by the wey is spent.

Now draweth cut, er that we ferrer twynne;   835

He which that hath the shorteste shal bigynne.

Sire Knyght," quod he, "my mayster and my lord,

Now draweth cut, for that is myn accord.

Cometh neer," quod he, "my lady Prioresse.

And ye, sire Clerk, lat be youre shame-fastnesse,   840

Ne studieth noght; ley hond to, every man!"

Anon to drawen every wight bigan,

And shortly for to tellen as it was,

Were it by aventure, or sort, or cas,

The sothe is this, the cut fil to the Knyght,   845

Of which ful blithe and glad was every wyght,

---

goodly: gladly.

vouche sauf: vouchsafe, grant.
anon: immediately.
shape: prepare. therfore: for that purpose.
swore: sworn.

reportour: i.e., umpire.
pris: price.
devys: devising, direction, will.

fet: fetched.
echon: each one.

amorwe: on the morrow, in the morning. oure aller: of us all.

riden: rode. paas: foot-pace.

woot: know. forward: promise, agreement. recorde: recall.

cut: lot. ferrer: further. twynne: proceed.

shamefastnesse: shyness.

studieth: study, deliberate.
wight: man.

sort: destiny. cas: chance.
sothe: truth. fil: fell.
blithe: blithe, happy.

---

826. **Wateryng of Seint Thomas:** a brook at the second milestone from London.

And telle he moste his tale, as was resoun,   moste: must. resoun: i.e., agreeable to
By forward and by composicioun,   reason. forward: promise. compo-
As ye han herd; what nedeth wordes mo?   sicioun: agreement.
And whan this goode man saugh that it was
     so,   850
As he that wys was and obedient
To kepe his forward by his free assent,
He seyde, "Syn I shal bigynne the game,   syn: since.
What, welcome be the cut, a Goddes name!   a Goddes name: in God's name.
Now lat us ryde, and herkneth what I seye."   855
And with that word we ryden forth oure weye,   ryden: rode.
And he bigan with right a myrie cheere   right a: a right. cheere: look; manner.
His tale anon, and seyde as ye may heere.

Heere bigynneth the
Knyghtes tale.

Iamque domos patrias, Scithice post aspera gentis
Prelia, laurigero, &c.

Whilom, as olde stories tellen us,   whilom: once, formerly.
Ther was a duc that highte Theseus;   860   highte: was called.
Of Atthenes he was lord and governour,
And in his tyme swich a conquerour,
That gretter was ther noon under the sonne.
Ful many a riche contree hadde he wonne;
What with his wysdom and his chivalrye,   865   chivalrye: knightly prowess.
He conquered al the regne of Femenye,   regne: kingdom, realm. Femenye: the
That whilom was ycleped Scithia,   country of the Amazons.
And weddede the queene Ypolita,
And broghte hire hoom with hym in his contree
With muchel glorie and greet solempnitee,   870
And eek hir yonge suster Emelye.
And thus with victorie and with melodye
Lete I this noble duc to Atthenes ryde,
And al his hoost in armes hym bisyde.
And certes, if it nere to long to heere,   875   certes: certainly. nere: (ne were) were
I wolde have toold yow fully the manere   not.
How wonnen was the regne of Femenye
By Theseus and by his chivalrye;   chivalrye: host of knights.
And of the grete bataille for the nones   for the nones: for that purpose.
Bitwixen Atthenes and Amazones;   880

---

the Knyghtes tale. The Knight's Tale is a redaction of Boccaccio's *Il Teseida* (1339–40). In condensing this long pseudo-epic, Chaucer unified the plot by emphasizing the conflict between Palamon and Arcite and intensifying the personalities of these two heroes; and he has given his poem philosophical depths undreamed of by Boccaccio.

Head verse, *Iamque domos . . . &c.*: "And now to his native land, after fierce battle with the Scythian people, in a laureled, etc." These lines (xii.519–20) introduce the final episode of Statius' *Thebaid*, echoed in the Knight's Tale, ll. 859–1004.

And how asseged was Ypolita,

asseged: besieged.

The faire, hardy queene of Scithia;

And of the feste that was at hir weddynge,

feste: feast, merriment.

And of the tempest at hir hoom-comynge;

But al that thyng I moot as now forbere.   885

moot: must.

I have, God woot, a large feeld to ere,

ere: plough.

And wayke been the oxen in my plough.

wayke: weak.

The remenant of the tale is long ynough.

I wol nat letten eek noon of this route;

letten: hinder. route: company.

Lat every felawe telle his tale aboute,   890

lat: let. aboute: in turn.

And lat se now who shal the soper wynne;

And ther I lefte, I wol ayeyn bigynne.

ther: where.

   This duc, of whom I make mencioun,

Whan he was come almost to the toun,

In al his wele and in his mooste pride,   895

wele: success, happiness.

He was war, as he caste his eye aside,

Where that ther kneled in the heighe weye

A compaignye of ladyes, tweye and tweye,

tweye and tweye: two by two.

Ech after oother, clad in clothes blake;

But swich a cry and swich a wo they make   900

That in this world nys creature lyvynge

nys: (ne is) is not.

That herde swich another waymentynge;

waymentynge: lamenting.

And of this cry they nolde nevere stenten

nolde: (ne wolde) would not.

Til they the reynes of his brydel henten.

   stenten: cease. henten: seized.

   "What folk been ye, that at myn hom-
                  comynge   905

Perturben so my feste with criynge?"

Quod Theseus. "Have ye so greet envye

Of myn honour, that thus compleyne and crye?

Or who hath yow mysboden or offended?

mysboden: insulted, injured.

And telleth me if it may been amended,   910

And why that ye been clothed thus in blak."

   The eldeste lady of hem alle spak,

Whan she hadde swowned with a deedly cheere,

deedly cheere: lifeless appearance.

That it was routhe for to seen and heere.

routhe: a pity, a sad thing.

She seyde, "Lord, to whom Fortune hath
                  yiven   915

yiven: given.

Victorie, and as a conqueror to lyven,

Nat greveth us youre glorie and youre honour,

But we biseken mercy and socour.

biseken: beseech. socour: succor,

Have mercy on oure wo and oure distresse!

   help.

Som drope of pitee, thurgh thy gentillesse,   920

Upon us wrecched wommen lat thou falle.

For, certes, lord, ther is noon of us alle,

That she ne hath been a duchesse or a queene.

Now be we caytyves, as it is wel seene,

caytyves: wretches.

Thanked be Fortune and hir false wheel,   925

---

925. Fortune was pictured as turning a wheel to which men were bound, some falling, some rising. See pp. 208 and 209.

That noon estaat assureth to be weel.

weel: well.

Now certes, lord, to abiden youre presence,
Here in this temple of the goddesse Clemence
We have been waitynge al this fourtenyght.

fourtenyght: fourteen nights, a fort-

Now help us, lord, sith it is in thy might.   930

night. sith: since.

    I, wrecche, which that wepe and waille thus,
Was whilom wyf to kyng Cappaneus,
That starf at Thebes—cursed be that day!—

starf: died.

And alle we that been in this array

array: plight.

And maken al this lamentacioun,   935
We losten alle oure housbondes at that toun,
Whil that the seege theraboute lay.
And yet now the olde Creon, weylaway!
That lord is now of Thebes the citee,
Fulfild of ire and of iniquitee,   940

fulfild: full.

He, for despit and for his tyrannye,

despit: malice, spite.

To do the dede bodyes vileynye

vileynye: outrage.

Of alle oure lordes whiche that been slawe,

slawe: slain.

Hath alle the bodyes on an heep ydrawe,

ydrawe: dragged.

And wol nat suffren hem, by noon assent,   945
Neither to been yburyed nor ybrent,

ybrent: burned.

But maketh houndes ete hem in despit."
    And with that word, withouten moore respit,
They fillen gruf and criden pitously,

gruf: face downward, groveling.

"Have on us wrecched wommen som mercy,   950
And lat oure sorwe synken in thyn herte."
    This gentil duc doun from his courser sterte

sterte: leaped.

With herte pitous, whan he herde hem speke.

pitous: pitying, compassionate.

Hym thoughte that his herte wolde breke,

hym thoughte: it seemed to him.

Whan he saugh hem so pitous and so maat,   955

pitous: pitiable. maat: dejected.

That whilom weren of so greet estaat;
And in his armes he hem alle up hente,

hente: took.

And hem conforteth in full good entente,
And swoor his ooth, as he was trewe knyght,
He wolde doon so ferforthly his myght   960
Upon the tiraunt Creon hem to wreke,

wreke: avenge.

That al the peple of Grece sholde speke
How Creon was of Theseus yserved
As he that hadde his deeth ful wel deserved.
And right anoon, withouten moore abood,   965

abood: delay.

His baner he desplayeth, and forth rood
To Thebes-ward, and al his hoost biside.

biside: alongside.

No neer Atthenes wolde he go ne ride,

neer: nearer. go: walk.

Ne take his ese fully half a day,
But onward on his wey that nyght he lay,   970
And sente anon Ypolita the queene,

---

960. He would exert his strength to such an extent.

And Emelye, hir yonge suster sheene,
    sheene: bright, fair.
Unto the toun of Atthenes to dwelle,
And forth he rit; ther is namoore to telle.
    rit: (rideth) rides.
  The rede statue of Mars, with spere and
    statue: image.
      targe,   975 targe: shield.
So shyneth in his white baner large,
That alle the feeldes glyteren up and doun;
And by his baner born is his penoun
    penoun: pennon, pennant.
Of gold ful riche, in which ther was ybete
    ybete: embroidered.
The Mynotaur, which that he wan in Crete. 980 wan: conquered.
Thus rit this duc, thus rit this conquerour,
And in his hoost of chivalrye the flour,
Til that he cam to Thebes and alighte
    alighte: alighted.
Faire in a feeld, ther as he thoughte to fighte.
But shortly for to speken of this thyng, 985
With Creon, which that was of Thebes kyng,
He faught, and slough hym manly as a knyght
    slough: slew. manly: manfully.
In pleyn bataille, and putte the folk to flight;
    pleyn: open.
And by assaut he wan the citee after,
And rente adoun bothe wall and sparre and
    sparre: wooden beam.
      rafter;   990
And to the ladyes he restored agayn
The bones of hir freendes that were slayn,
    freendes: beloved kinsmen.
To doon obsequies, as was tho the gyse.
    tho: then. gyse: custom.
But it were al to long for to devyse
    devyse: tell, describe.
The grete clamour and the waymentynge 995
That the ladyes made at the brennynge
    brennynge: burning.
Of the bodies, and the grete honour
That Theseus, the noble conquerour,
Doth to the ladyes, whan they from hym wente;
But shortly for to telle is myn entente. 1000
  Whan that this worthy duc, this Theseus,
Hath Creon slayn, and wonne Thebes thus,
Stille in that feeld he took al nyght his reste,
And dide with al the contree as hym leste.
  To ransake in the taas of the bodies dede, 1005 taas: pile, heap.
Hem for to strepe of harneys and of wede,
    harneys: armor. wede: clothing.
The pilours diden bisynesse and cure
    pilours: pillagers. cure: care.
After the bataille and disconfiture.
And so bifel that in the taas they founde,
Thurgh-girt with many a grevous blody
    thurgh-girt: pierced through.
      wounde,   1010
Two yonge knyghtes liggynge by and by,
    liggynge: lying. by and by: side by side.
Bothe in oon armes, wroght ful richely,
Of whiche two Arcita highte that oon,
And that oother knyght highte Palamon.

1012. in oon armes: having identical coats of arms.

Nat fully quyke, ne fully dede they were,　　1015　quyke: alive.
But by hir cote-armures and by hir gere　　　　gere: accoutrements.
The heraudes knewe hem best in special
As they that weren of the blood roial
Of Thebes, and of sustren two yborn.　　　sustren: sisters.
Out of the taas the pilours han hem torn,　　1020
And han hem caried softe unto the tente
Of Theseus; and he ful soone hem sente
To Atthenes, to dwellen in prisoun
Perpetuelly,—he nolde no raunsoun.　　　nolde: would not (have).
And whan this worthy duc hath thus ydon,　　1025
He took his hoost, and hom he rit anon
With laurer crowned as a conquerour;　　laurer: laurel.
And ther he lyveth in joye and in honour
Terme of his lyf; what nedeth wordes mo?
And in a tour, in angwissh and in wo,　　1030　tour: tower.
Dwellen this Palamon and eek Arcite
For everemoore; ther may no gold hem quite.　　quite: ransom, set free.
　　This passeth yeer by yeer and day by day,　　this: thus.
Till it fil ones, in a morwe of May,　　fil: befell, happened. morwe: morning.
That Emelye, that fairer was to sene　　1035
Than is the lilie upon his stalke grene,　　his: its.
And fressher than the May with floures newe—
For with the rose colour stroof hir hewe,　　stroof: strove, vied.
I noot which was the fairer of hem two—　　noot: (ne woot) know not.
Er it were day, as was hir wone to do,　　1040　wone: wont, custom.
She was arisen and al redy dight;　　dight: arrayed.
For May wole have no slogardie a-nyght.　　slogardie: slothfulness, laziness.
The sesoun priketh every gentil herte,
And maketh it out of his slep to sterte,　　sterte: start.
And seith "Arys, and do thyn observaunce."　　1045
This maketh Emelye have remembraunce
To doon honour to May, and for to ryse.
Yclothed was she fressh, for to devyse:
Hir yelow heer was broyded in a tresse　　broyded: braided.
Bihynde hir bak, a yerde long, I gesse.　　1050
And in the gardyn, at the sonne upriste,　　the sonne upriste: the sun's uprising.
She walketh up and doun, and as hir liste　　hir liste: it pleased her.
She gadereth floures, party white and rede,　　party: parti-colored.
To make a subtil gerland for hir hede;　　subtil: cunningly woven.
And as an aungel hevenysshly she song.　　1055
The grete tour, that was so thikke and strong,

1016. cote-armures: coat armor is a vest embroidered with heraldic devices and worn by a knight over his armor.

Emilia in the Garden: The fundamental situation in the Knight's Tale is depicted in this illustration for the fifteenth-century translation of Boccaccio's *Teseida* prepared for René d'Anjou. Palamone and Arcita, in prison, see Emilia in the garden (ll. 1033–1122). She is making her garland (l. 1054) and they are behind the barred window (ll. 1075–76), but—apparently weary of roaming—she has decided to sit down.

Which of the castel was the chief dongeoun,
(Ther as the knyghtes weren in prisoun
Of which I tolde yow and tellen shal)
Was evene joynant to the gardyn wal   1060   evene joynant: just adjoining.
Ther as this Emelye hadde hir pleyynge.   pleyynge: recreation.
Bright was the sonne and cleer that mor-
         wenynge,
And Palamon, this woful prisoner,
As was his wone, by leve of his gayler,
Was risen and romed in a chambre an heigh, 1065
In which he al the noble citee seigh,   seigh: saw.
And eek the gardyn, ful of braunches grene,
Ther as this fresshe Emelye the shene
Was in hir walk, and romed up and doun.
This sorweful prisoner, this Palamoun,   1070
Goth in the chambre romyng to and fro,
And to hymself compleynyng of his wo
That he was born, ful ofte he seyde, "Allas!"
And so bifel, by aventure or cas,
That thurgh a wyndow, thikke of many a
         barre   1075
Of iren greet and square as any sparre,   sparre: wooden beam.
He cast his eye upon Emelya,
And therwithal he bleynte and cride, "A!"   bleynte: winced.
As though he stongen were unto the herte.
And with that cry Arcite anon up sterte,   1080
And seyde, "Cosyn myn, what eyleth thee,
That art so pale and deedly on to see?   deedly . . . see: deathlike to behold.
Why cridestow? who hath thee doon offence?   offence: injury.
For Goddes love, take al in pacience
Oure prisoun, for it may noon oother be.   1085
Fortune hath yeven us this adversitee.
Som wikke aspect or disposicioun   wikke: wicked; evil.
Of Saturne, by som constellacioun,
Hath yeven us this, although we hadde it sworn;   although . . . sworn: although we had
So stood the hevene whan that we were born. 1090   sworn to the contrary.
We moste endure it; this is the short and playn."
    This Palamon answerde and seide agayn,   agayn: in reply.
"Cosyn, for sothe, of this opinioun
Thow hast a veyn ymaginacioun.   veyn ymaginacioun: foolish or false
This prison caused me not to crye,   1095   notion.
But I was hurt right now thurghout myn eye
Into myn herte, that wol my bane be.   my bane: cause of my death.
The fairnesse of that lady that I see

1087. aspect: situation, in relation to another planet; the visual angular distance between two planets. disposicioun: position.

1088. constellacioun: configuration of planets. On Saturn as a planet of evil influence, see ll. 2453 ff., below.

Yond in the gardyn romen to and fro   yond: yonder.
Is cause of al my criyng and my wo.   1100
I noot wher she be womman or goddesse,   wher: whether.
But Venus is it soothly, as I gesse."
And therwithal on knees doun he fil,
And seide: "Venus, if it be thy wil
Yow in this gardyn thus to transfigure   1105
Bifore me, sorweful, wrecched creature,
Out of this prisoun help that we may scapen.   scapen: escape.
And if so be my destynee be shapen
By eterne word to dyen in prisoun,
Of oure lynage have som compassioun,   1110
That is so lowe ybroght by tirannye."
And with that word Arcite gan espye   gan: did.
Wher as this lady romed to and fro,
And with that sighte hir beautee hurte hym so,
That, if that Palamon was wounded sore,   1115
Arcite is hurt as muche as he, or moore.
And with a sigh he seyde pitously:
"The fresshe beautee sleeth me sodeynly   sleeth: slayeth.
Of hire that rometh in the yonder place,
And but I have hir mercy and hir grace,   1120
That I may seen hire at the leeste weye,   at the leeste weye: at least.
I nam but deed; ther nis namoore to seye."   I nam but deed: I am not but (no bet-
    This Palamon, whan he tho wordes herde,   ter than) dead. tho: those.
Dispitously he looked and answerde,   dispitously: angrily.
"Wheither seistow this in ernest or in pley?"   1125
    "Nay," quod Arcite, "in ernest, by my fey!   fey: faith.
God help me so, me list ful yvele pleye."
    This Palamon gan knytte his browes tweye.
"It were to thee," quod he, "no greet honour
For to be fals, ne for to be traitour   1130
To me, that am thy cosyn, and thy brother
Ysworn ful depe, and ech of us til oother,   til: to.
That nevere, for to dyen in the peyne,
Til that the deeth departe shal us tweyne,   departe: part. tweyne: two.
Neither of us in love to hyndre oother,   1135
Ne in noon other cas, my leeve brother;   leeve: dear.
But that thou sholdest trewely forthre me   forthre: assist.
In every cas, as I shal forthre thee,—
This was thyn ooth, and myn also, certeyn;
I woot right wel, thou darst it nat withseyn.   1140   withseyn: deny.
Thus artow of my counseil, out of doute,   counseil: secret counsel. out of
And now thow woldest falsly been aboute   doute: beyond doubt.

1127. So help me God, I have little desire to jest.
1132. ysworn ful depe: i.e., by solemn oath of brotherhood (see Shipman's Tale, ll. 41–42; Friar's Tale, ll. 1404–05; Pardoner's Tale, ll. 696–704).
1133. for to dyen in the peyne: though we had to die by torture.

To love my lady, whom I love and serve,
And evere shal til that myn herte sterve.   sterve: die.
Now certes, false Arcite, thow shalt nat so. 1145
I loved hire first, and tolde thee my wo
As to my counseil and my brother sworn
To forthre me, as I have toold biforn.
For which thou art ybounden as a knyght
To helpe me, if it lay in thy myght,   1150
Or elles artow fals, I dar wel seyn."
    This Arcite ful proudly spak ageyn:
"Thow shalt," quod he, "be rather fals than I; rather: sooner.
But thou art fals, I telle thee outrely,   outrely: plainly.
For paramour I loved hire first er thow.   1155
What wiltow seyen? Thou woost nat yet now
Wheither she be a womman or goddesse!
Thyn is affeccioun of holynesse,
And myn is love, as to a creature;
For which I tolde thee myn aventure   1160
As to my cosyn and my brother sworn.
I pose that thow lovedest hire biforn;   I pose: I suppose, grant for the sake
Wostow nat wel the olde clerkes sawe,   of argument. wostow: knowest thou.
That 'Who shal yeve a lovere any lawe?'
Love is a gretter lawe, by my pan,   1165 pan: brain-pan, skull.
Than may be yeve to any erthely man;
And therfore positif lawe and swich decree
Is broken al day for love in ech degree.   in ech degree: in every way.
A man moot nedes love, maugree his heed.
He may nat fleen it, thogh he sholde be deed, 1170 fleen: flee, escape.
Al be she mayde, wydwe, or elles wyf.
And eek it is nat likly al thy lyf
To stonden in hir grace; namoore shal I;
For wel thou woost thyselven, verraily,   woost: knowest.
That thou and I be dampned to prisoun   1175 dampned: condemned.
Perpetuelly; us gayneth no raunsoun.   gayneth: avails.
We stryve as dide the houndes for the boon;   boon: bone.
They foughte al day, and yet hir part was noon. part: share.
Ther cam a kyte, whil they were so wrothe,   kyte: kite (bird).
That bar awey the boon bitwixe hem bothe.   1180
And therfore, at the kynges court, my brother,
Ech man for hymself, ther is noon oother.
Love, if thee list, for I love and ay shal;
And soothly, leve brother, this is al.   leve: dear.
Here in this prisoun moote we endure,   1185 endure: remain.
And everich of us take his aventure."   everich: every one; each.
    Greet was the strif and long bitwix hem
            tweye,

___

1155. for paramour: as far as passion is concerned.
1167. positif lawe: law resting solely upon man's decree (as opposed to natural law).
1169. maugree his heed: in spite of his resistance.

If that I hadde leyser for to seye,   **leyser:** leisure, opportunity.
But to th'effect. It happed on a day,   **effect:** outcome, upshot.
To telle it yow as shortly as I may,   1190
A worthy duc that highte Perotheus,
That felawe was unto duc Theseus   **felawe:** companion, comrade.
Syn thilke day that they were children lite,   **lite:** little.
Was come to Atthenes his felawe to visite,
And for to pleye as he was wont to do;   1195
For in this world he loved no man so,
And he loved hym als tendrely agayn.
So wel they lovede, as olde bookes sayn,
That whan that oon was deed, soothly to telle,   **deed:** dead.
His felawe wente and soughte hym doun in
         helle,—   1200
But of that storie list me nat to write.
Duc Perotheus loved wel Arcite,
And hadde hym knowe at Thebes yeer by yere,   **knowe:** known. **by:** i.e., after.
And finally at requeste and prayere
Of Perotheus, withouten any raunsoun,   1205
Duc Theseus hym leet out of prisoun
Frely to goon wher that hym liste over al,
In swich a gyse as I you tellen shal.   **gyse:** manner.
   This was the forward, pleynly for t'endite,   **forward:** agreement. **endite:** write.
Bitwixen Theseus and hym Arcite: 1210
That if so were that Arcite were yfounde
Evere in his lif, by day or nyght, o stounde   **o:** one. **stounde:** moment.
In any contree of this Theseus,
And he were caught, it was acorded thus,
That with a swerd he sholde lese his heed.   1215 **lese:** lose.
Ther nas noon oother remedye ne reed;   **reed:** counsel.
But taketh his leve, and homward he him
         spedde.
Lat hym be war! his nekke lith to wedde.   **lith to wedde:** i.e., as a pledge;
   How greet a sorwe suffreth now Arcite!   hence, lies in jeopardy.
The deeth he feeleth thurgh his herte smyte; 1220
He wepeth, wayleth, crieth pitously;
To sleen hymself he waiteth prively.   **sleen:** slay.
He seyde, "Allas the day that I was born!
Now is my prisoun worse than biforn;
Now is me shape eternally to dwelle   1225 **shape:** destined.
Noght in purgatorie, but in helle.
Allas, that evere knew I Perotheus!
For elles hadde I dwelled with Theseus,
Yfetered in his prisoun everemo.
Thanne hadde I been in blisse, and nat in wo. 1230
Oonly the sight of hire whom that I serve,
Though that I nevere hir grace may deserve,
Wolde have suffised right ynough for me.

1222. He watches secretly for a chance to kill himself.

O deere cosyn Palamon," quod he,
"Thyn is the victorie of this aventure.   1235
Ful blisfully in prison maistow dure,—   dure: remain.
In prison? certes nay, but in paradys!   certes: certainly.
Wel hath Fortune yturned thee the dys,   dys: dice.
That hast the sight of hire, and I th'absence.
For possible is, syn thou hast hir presence,   1240
And art a knyght, a worthy and an able,
That by som cas, syn Fortune is chaungeable,
Thow mayst to thy desir somtyme atteyne.   atteyne: attain.
But I, that am exiled and bareyne   bareyne: destitute.
Of alle grace, and in so greet despeir,   1245
That ther nys erthe, water, fir, ne eir,
Ne creature that of hem maked is,
That may me helpe or doon confort in this,
Wel oughte I sterve in wanhope and distresse.   sterve: die. wanhope: despair.
Farwel my lif, my lust, and my gladnesse!   1250 lust: joy.
   Allas, why pleynen folk so in commune   in commune: commonly, generally.
On purveiaunce of God, or of Fortune,   purveiaunce: providence.
That yeveth hem ful ofte in many a gyse
Wel bettre than they kan hemself devyse?
Som man desireth for to have richesse,   1255
That cause is of his mordre or greet siknesse;
And som man wolde out of his prisoun fayn,   wolde: would be. fayn: gladly.
That in his hous is of his meynee slayn.   meynee: household, menials.
Infinite harmes been in this matere.
We woot nat what thing that we prayen   woot: know.
        heere: 1260
We faren as he that dronke is as a mous.   faren: behave, act.
A dronke man woot wel he hath an hous,
But he noot which the righte wey is thider,
And to a dronke man the wey is slider.   slider: slippery.
And certes, in this world so faren we;   1265
We seken faste after felicitee,
But we goon wrong ful often, trewely.
Thus may we seyen alle, and namely I,   namely: especially.
That wende and hadde a greet opinioun   wende: weened, thought.
That if I myghte escapen from prisoun,   1270
Thanne hadde I been in joye and perfit heele,   heele: happiness.
Ther now I am exiled fro my wele.   ther: whereas.
Syn that I may nat seen you, Emelye,
I nam but deed; ther nys no remedye."   nys: (ne is) is not.
   Upon that oother syde Palamon,   1275
Whan that he wiste Arcite was agon,   agon: gone.
Swich sorwe he maketh that the grete tour
Resouneth of his yowlyng and clamour.

1251. pleynen: complain, lament.

The pure fettres of his shynes grete   pure: very. of: on. **shynes grete:**
Weren of his bittre, salte teeres wete.   1280 swollen shins.
"Allas," quod he, "Arcita, cosyn myn,
Of al oure strif, God woot, the fruyt is thyn.
Thow walkest now in Thebes at thy large,
And of my wo thow yevest litel charge.   charge: consideration.
Thou mayst, syn thou hast wisdom and man-
      hede,   1285
Assemblen alle the folk of oure kynrede,
And make a werre so sharp on this citee,   werre: war.
That by som aventure or som tretee
Thow mayst have hire to lady and to wyf
For whom that I moste nedes lese my lyf.   1290 lese: lose.
For, as by wey of possibilitee,
Sith thou art at thy large, of prisoun free,   sith: since. **at thy large:** at large.
And art a lord, greet is thyn avauntage
Moore than is myn, that sterve here in a cage.   sterve: die. **cage:** prison.
For I moot wepe and waille, whil I lyve,   1295
With al the wo that prison may me yive,
And eek with peyne that love me yeveth also,
That doubleth al my torment and my wo."
Therwith the fyr of jalousie up sterte
Withinne his brest, and hente him by the   hente: seized.
      herte   1300
So woodly that he lyk was to biholde   woodly: madly.
The boxtree or the asshen dede and colde.   asshen: ashes.
    Thanne seyde he, "O crueel goddes that
      governe
This world with byndying of youre word eterne,
And writen in the table of atthamaunt   1305 atthamaunt: adamant.
Youre parlement and youre eterne graunt,   parlement: i.e., decisions. **graunt:** de-
What is mankynde moore unto you holde   cree.
Than is the sheep that rouketh in the folde?   rouketh: cowers.
For slayn is man right as another beest,
And dwelleth eek in prison and arreest,   1310 prison: captivity. **arreest:** detention.
And hath siknesse and greet adversitee,
And ofte tymes giltelees, pardee.   pardee: *pardieu,* certainly.
    What governance is in this prescience
That giltelees tormenteth innocence?
And yet encresseth this al my penaunce,   1315 penaunce: suffering.
That man is bounden to his observaunce,
For Goddes sake, to letten of his wille,   to letten of his wille: to refrain from
Ther as a beest may al his lust fulfille.   his desire.

1301–02. lyk the boxtree: i.e., pale.
1307. How is mankind more beholden, or obligated, to you.
1313. What kind of controlling (or determining) influence is there in this foreknowledge (i.e., providence).
1316. observaunce: i.e., of his religious duty.

And whan a beest is deed he hath no peyne;
But after his deeth man moot wepe and
        pleyne,   1320 **pleyne:** complain, lament.
Though in this world he have care and wo.
Withouten doute it may stonden so.   **stonden:** be.
The answere of this lete I to dyvynys,   **lete:** leave. **dyvynys:** theologians.
But wel I woot that in this world greet pyne ys.   **pyne:** suffering.
Allas, I se a serpent or a theef,   1325
That many a trewe man hath doon mescheef,   **mescheef:** injury.
Goon at his large, and where hym list may
        turne.
But I moot been in prisoun thurgh Saturne,
And eek thurgh Juno, jalous and eek wood,
That hath destroyed wel ny al the blood   1330
Of Thebes with his waste walles wyde;   **waste:** devastated.
And Venus sleeth me on that oother syde   **sleeth:** slayeth.
For jalousie and fere of hym Arcite."
   Now wol I stynte of Palamon a lite,   **stynte:** cease (to tell). **lite:** little.
And lete hym in his prisoun stille dwelle,   1335
And of Arcita forth I wol yow telle.
   The somer passeth, and the nyghtes longe
Encressen double wise the peynes stronge
Bothe of the lovere and the prisoner.
I noot which hath the wofuller myster.   1340 **myster:** occupation.
For, shortly for to seyn, this Palamoun
Perpetuelly is dampned to prisoun,   **dampned:** condemned.
In cheynes and in fettres to been deed;
And Arcite is exiled upon his heed   **upon his heed:** on pain of losing his
For evermo, as out of that contree,   1345 head.
Ne nevere mo ne shal his lady see.
   Yow loveres axe I now this questioun,   **axe:** ask.
Who hath the worse, Arcite or Palamoun?
That oon may seen his lady day by day,
But in prison moot he dwelle alway;   1350
That oother wher hym list may ride or go,   **go:** walk.
But seen his lady shal he nevere mo.
Now demeth as yow list, ye that kan,
For I wol telle forth as I bigan.

         EXPLICIT PRIMA PARS.
      SEQUITUR PARS SECUNDA.

   Whan that Arcite to Thebes comen was,   1355
Ful ofte a day he swelte and seyde "Allas!"   **swelte:** swooned.
For seen his lady shal he nevere mo.
And shortly to concluden al his wo,
So muche sorwe hadde nevere creature

1347. **questioun:** There follows a typical love-question of the sort popular in courts of love.

That is, or shal, whil that the world may
        dure.   1360   **dure:** last, endure.
His sleep, his mete, his drynke, is hym biraft,   **mete:** food. **biraft:** taken away from.
That lene he wex and drye as is a shaft;   **wex:** grew, became. **shaft:** i.e., of an ar-
His eyen holwe, and grisly to biholde,   row. **holwe:** hollow. **grisly:** horrible.
His hewe falow and pale as asshen colde,   **falow:** faded.
And solitarie he was and evere allone,   1365
And wailynge al the nyght, makynge his mone;
And if he herde song or instrument,
Thanne wolde he wepe, he myghte nat be stent.   **stent:** stopped.
So feble eek were his spiritz, and so lowe,
And chaunged so, that no man koude knowe 1370
His speche nor his voys, though men it herde.
And in his geere for al the world he ferde,   **geere:** behavior. **ferde:** fared.
Nat oonly lik the loveris maladye
Of Hereos, but rather lyk manye,   **manye:** mania.
Engendred of humour malencolyk,   1375 **engendred:** caused.
Biforen, in his celle fantastik.
And shortly, turned was al up so doun
Bothe habit and eek disposicioun   **habit:** bodily condition.
Of hym, this woful lovere daun Arcite.   **daun:** lord.
    What sholde I al day of his wo endite? 1380 **what:** why. **endite:** write.
Whan he endured hadde a yeer or two
This cruel torment and this peyne and wo,
At Thebes, in his contree, as I seyde,
Upon a nyght in sleep as he hym leyde,
Hym thoughte how that the wynged god
        Mercurie   1385
Biforn hym stood and bad hym to be murye.   **murye:** merry, glad.
His slepy yerde in hond he bar uprighte;   **slepy yerde:** sleep-bringing rod, ca-
An hat he wered upon his heres brighte.   duceus. **heres:** hairs; i.e., hair.
Arrayed was this god, as he took keep,   **he:** i.e., Arcite. **keep:** notice.
As he was whan that Argus took his sleep; 1390
And seyde hym thus: "To Atthenes shaltow   **shaltow:** you shall.
        wende,
Ther is thee shapen of thy wo an ende."   **shapen:** destined.
And with that word Arcite wook and sterte.   **sterte:** gave a start.
"Now trewely, how sore that me smerte,"   **me smerte:** it may hurt me.
Quod he, "to Atthenes right now wol I fare, 1395
Ne for the drede of deeth shal I nat spare   **spare to see:** refrain from seeing.
To see my lady, that I love and serve.

1374. **Hereos:** a form of erotic hysteria.

1375. See note for l. 333 above.

1376. **celle fantastik:** The brain was divided into three cells, the front one assigned to fantasy, the middle one to reason, the back one to memory. Mania was a disease of the front cell, melancholy of the middle cell. The description of Arcite's love-sickness (ll. 1355–76) is medically accurate according to medieval treatises.

1390. **Argus:** the hundred-eyed monster put to sleep by Mercury.

In hire presence I recche nat to sterve."
  And with that word he caughte a greet mirour,

recche . . . sterve: care not if I die.

And saugh that chaunged was al his colour, 1400
And saugh his visage al in another kynde.
And right anon it ran hym in his mynde,
That, sith his face was so disfigured
Of maladye the which he hadde endured,
He myghte wel, if that he bar hym lowe, 1405

lowe: humbly.

Lyve in Atthenes everemoore unknowe,

unknowe: unknown.

And seen his lady wel ny day by day.
And right anon he chaunged his array,
And cladde hym as a povre laborer,
And al allone, save oonly a squier 1410
That knew his privetee and al his cas,

privetee: private affairs.

Which was disgised povrely as he was,
To Atthenes is he goon the nexte way.

nexte: nearest, shortest.

And to the court he wente upon a day,
And at the gate he profreth his servyse 1415
To drugge and drawe, what so men wol devyse.

drugge: drudge. drawe: carry. devyse: order.

And shortly of this matere for to seyn,
He fil in office with a chamberleyn

office: employment.

The which that dwellyng was with Emelye;
For he was wys and koude soone espye 1420

espye: discover.

Of every servant which that serveth here.

here: her.

Wel koude he hewen wode, and water bere,
For he was yong and myghty for the nones,

for the nones: for the purpose.

And therto he was strong and big of bones
To doon that any wight kan hym devyse. 1425

that: that which, what.

A yeer or two he was in this servyse,
Page of the chambre of Emelye the brighte;
And Philostrate he seyde that he highte.
But half so wel biloved a man as he
Ne was ther nevere in court of his degree; 1430
He was so gentil of condicioun

condicioun: disposition.

That thurghout al the court was his renoun.
They seiden that it were a charitee
That Theseus wolde enhauncen his degree,

enhauncen his degree: raise his rank.

And putten hym in worshipful servyse, 1435
Ther as he myghte his vertu excercise.
And thus withinne a while his name is spronge,

spronge: gone abroad, become famous.

Bothe of his dedes and his goode tonge,
That Theseus hath taken hym so neer,
That of his chambre he made hym a squier, 1440
And gaf hym gold to mayntene his degree.
And eek men broghte hym out of his contree,
From yeer to yeer, ful pryvely his rente;

rente: income.

But honestly and slyly he it spente,

honestly and slyly: suitably and prudently.

That no man wondred how that he it hadde. 1445

And thre yeer in this wise his lif he ladde,   ladde: led.
And bar hym so, in pees and eek in werre,
Ther was no man that Theseus hath derre.   hath derre: holds more dearly.
And in this blisse lete I now Arcite,   lete: leave.
And speke I wole of Palamon a lite.   1450
    In derknesse and horrible and strong prisoun
This seven yeer hath seten Palamoun   seten: dwelt.
Forpyned, what for wo and for distresse.   forpyned: wasted by suffering.
Who feeleth double soor and hevynesse   soor: misery.
But Palamon, that love destreyneth so   1455   destreyneth: distresses, torments.
That wood out of his wit he goth for wo?
And eek therto he is a prisoner
Perpetuelly, nat oonly for a yer.
    Who koude ryme in Englyssh proprely
His martirdom? for sothe it am nat I;   1460
Therfore I passe as lightly as I may.
    It fel that in the seventhe yeer, of May   fel: befell.
The thridde nyght, (as olde bookes seyn,
That al this storie tellen moore pleyn)   pleyn: fully.
Were it by aventure or destynee—   1465
As, whan a thyng is shapen, it shal be—
That soone after the mydnyght Palamoun,
By helpyng of a freend, brak his prisoun   brak: broke, escaped from.
And fleeth the citee faste as he may go.
For he hadde yeve his gailler drynke so   1470
Of a clarree maad of a certeyn wyn,   clarree: a mixed drink of wine, honey,
With nercotikes and opie of Thebes fyn,   and spices.
That al that nyght, thogh that men wolde him   men: one.
      shake,
The gailler sleep, he myghte nat awake;   sleep: slept.
And thus he fleeth as faste as evere he may. 1475
The nyght was short and faste by the day,
That nedes cost he moot hymselven hyde;   nedes cost: of necessity.
And til a grove faste ther bisyde   til: to.
With dredeful foot thanne stalketh Palamon.   dredeful: full of fear.
For, shortly, this was his opinion,   1480
That in that grove he wolde hym hyde al day,
And in the nyght thanne wolde he take his way
To Thebes-ward, his freendes for to preye
On Theseus to helpe him to werreye;   werreye: make war.
And shortly, outher he wolde lese his lif,   1485   outher: either. lese: lose.
Or wynnen Emelye unto his wyf.
This is th'effect and his entente pleyn.   effect: purport. pleyn: full.
    Now wol I turne to Arcite ageyn,
That litel wiste how ny that was his care,   ny: near. care: woe; misfortune.
Til that Fortune had broght him in the snare. 1490

1472. opie . . . fyn: Fine opium came from Egyptian Thebes. Possibly that city is here confused
with Grecian Thebes.

The bisy larke, messager of day,
Salueth in hir song the morwe gray,   salueth: salutes, greets. **morwe**: morn-
And firy Phebus riseth up so bright   ing.
That al the orient laugheth of the light,
And with his stremes dryeth in the greves   1495 stremes: beams. **greves**: bushes.
The silver dropes hangynge on the leves.
And Arcita, that in the court roial
With Theseus is squier principal,
Is risen and looketh on the myrie day.
And for to doon his observaunce to May,   1500
Remembrynge on the poynt of his desir,   poynt: aim.
He on a courser, startlynge as the fir,   startlynge: leaping. **fir**: fire.
Is riden into the feeldes hym to pleye,
Out of the court, were it a myle or tweye;
And to the grove of which that I yow tolde   1505
By aventure his wey he gan to holde,
To maken hym a gerland of the greves   greves: sprays.
Were it of wodebynde or hawethorn leves,   wodebynde: woodbine.
And loude he song ayeyn the sonne shene: ayeyn: in. **shene**: bright, shining.
"May, with alle thy floures and thy grene,   1510
Welcome be thou, faire, fresshe May,
In hope that I som grene gete may."
And from his courser, with a lusty herte,
Into the grove ful hastily he sterte,   sterte: sprang, leaped.
And in a path he rometh up and doun,   1515
Ther as by aventure this Palamoun
Was in a bussh, that no man myghte hym se,
For soore afered of his deeth was he.   afered: afraid.
No thyng ne knew he that it was Arcite;   no thyng: not at all.
God woot he wolde have trowed it ful lite. 1520 trowed: believed.
But sooth is seyd, gon sithen many yeres,   gon sithen many yeres: many years
That "feeld hath eyen and the wode hath eres."   ago.
It is ful fair a man to bere hym evene,   evene: evenly, calmly.
For al day meeteth men at unset stevene.   unset stevene: unappointed time.
Ful litel woot Arcite of his felawe,   1525
That was so ny to herknen al his sawe,   ny: near. **sawe**: speech.
For in the bussh he sitteth now ful stille.
   Whan that Arcite hadde romed al his fille,
And songen al the roundel lustily,   roundel: roundelay.
Into a studie he fil sodeynly,   1530 studie: meditation.
As doon thise loveres in hir queynte geres,   geres: ways of behavior.
Now in the crope, now doun in the breres,   crope: top (of a tree). **breres**: briers.
Now up, now doun, as boket in a welle.
Right as the Friday, soothly for to telle,
Now it shyneth, now it reyneth faste,   1535
Right so kan geery Venus overcaste   geery: changeable.
The hertes of hir folk; right as hir day

1531. **thise loveres**: lovers in general.

Is gereful, right so chaungeth she array.
Selde is the Friday al the wike ylike.
  Whan that Arcite had songe, he gan to
          sike,   1540 sike: sigh.
And sette hym doun withouten any moore.
"Allas," quod he, "that day that I was bore!   bore: born.
How longe, Juno, thurgh thy crueltee,
Woltow werreyen Thebes the citee?   woltow: will you. werreyen: war
Allas, ybroght is to confusioun   1545   against.
The blood roial of Cadme and Amphioun,—
Of Cadmus, which that was the firste man
That Thebes bulte, or first the toun bigan,
And of the citee first was crowned kyng.
Of his lynage am I and his ofspryng   1550
By verray ligne, as of the stok roial,   verray ligne: true descent.
And now I am so caytyf and so thral,   caytyf: captive, wretched. thral: en-
That he that is my mortal enemy,   slaved.
I serve hym as his squier povrely.   povrely: in lowly guise.
And yet doth Juno me wel moore shame,   1555
For I dar noght biknowe myn owene name;   biknowe: acknowledge.
But ther as I was wont to highte Arcite,   highte: be called.
Now highte I Philostrate, noght worth a myte.   highte: am called.
Allas, thou felle Mars! allas, Juno!   felle: fierce.
Thus hath youre ire oure lynage al fordo,   1560 lynage: lineage, family.
Save oonly me and wrecched Palamoun,   fordo: destroyed.
That Theseus martireth in prisoun.
And over al this, to sleen me outrely,   outrely: utterly.
Love hath his firy dart so brennyngly
Ystiked thurgh my trewe, careful herte,   1565 ystiked: stabbed. careful: sorrowful.
That shapen was my deeth erst than my sherte.   erst than: before.
Ye sleen me with youre eyen, Emelye!   sleen: slay.
Ye been the cause wherfore that I dye.
Of al the remenant of myn oother care   care: woe; distress.
Ne sette I nat the mountance of a tare,   1570 mountance: amount.
So that I koude doon aught to youre plesaunce."
And with that word he fil doun in a traunce
A long tyme, and afterward he up sterte.
  This Palamoun, that thoughte that thurgh his
          herte
He felte a coold swerd sodeynliche glyde,   1575
For ire he quook, no lenger wolde he byde.   quook: quaked.
And whan that he had herd Arcites tale,
As he were wood, with face deed and pale,
He sterte hym up out of the buskes thikke,   buskes: bushes.
And seide: "Arcite, false traytour wikke,   1580 wikke: wicked.
Now artow hent, that lovest my lady so,
For whom that I have al this peyne and wo,

1539. This saying means that Friday is seldom like the rest of the week.

And art my blood, and to my counseil sworn,   counseil: secret counsel.
As I ful ofte have told thee heerbiforn,
And hast byjaped here duc Theseus,   1585 byjaped: tricked.
And falsely chaunged hast thy name thus!
I wol be deed, or elles thou shalt dye.   be deed: die.
Thou shalt nat love my lady Emelye,
But I wol love hire oonly and namo;   namo: no one else.
For I am Palamon, thy mortal foo.   1590
And though that I no wepene have in this place, wepene: weapon.
But out of prison am astert by grace,   astert: escaped.
I drede noght that outher thou shalt dye,   drede: doubt. outher: either.
Or thou ne shalt nat loven Emelye.
Chees which thou wolt, or thou shalt nat   chees: choose. wolt: will.
    asterte!"   1595 asterte: escape.
  This Arcite, with ful despitous herte,   despitous: hateful.
Whan he hym knew, and hadde his tale herd,
As fiers as leon pulled out his swerd,
And seyde thus: "By God that sit above,   sit: (sitteth) sits.
Nere it that thou art sik and wood for love,   1600 nere it: (ne were it) were it not.
And eek that thow no wepne hast in this place,
Thou sholdest nevere out of this grove pace,
That thou ne sholdest dyen of myn hond.
For I defye the seuretee and the bond   defye: disavow.
Which that thou seist that I have maad to
    thee.   1605
What, verray fool, thynk wel that love is free,
And I wol love hire maugree al thy myght!   maugree: in spite of.
But for as muche thou art a worthy knyght;
And wilnest to darreyne hire by bataille,   darreyne hire: decide the right to her.
Have heer my trouthe, tomorwe I wol nat   trouthe: troth, promise.
    faille,   1610
Withoute wityng of any oother wight,
That heere I wol be founden, as a knyght,
And bryngen harneys right ynough for thee;   harneys: armor; equipment.
And chees the beste, and leve the worste for
    me.
And mete and drynke this nyght wol I   mete: food.
    brynge   1615
Ynough for thee, and clothes for thy beddynge.
And if so be that thou my lady wynne,
And slee me in this wode ther I am inne,   ther: where.
Thow mayst wel have thy lady as for me."
  This Palamon answerde, "I graunte it
    thee."   1620
And thus they been departed til amorwe,   departed: parted. amorwe: the next
Whan ech of hem had leyd his feith to borwe.   morning. to borwe: for a pledge.
  O Cupide, out of alle charitee!
O regne, that wolt no felawe have with thee!   regne: rule. felawe: associate.
Ful sooth is seyed that love ne lordshipe   1625

Wol noght, his thankes, have no felaweshipe.   his thankes: willingly.
Wel fynden that Arcite and Palamoun.
Arcite is riden anon unto the toun,
And on the morwe, er it were dayes light,
Ful prively two harneys hath he dight,   1630   dight: prepared.
Bothe suffisaunt and mete to darreyne   mete: suitable. darreyne: decide.
The bataille in the feeld bitwix hem tweyne;   tweyne: two.
And on his hors, allone as he was born,
He carieth al this harneys hym biforn.
And in the grove, at tyme and place yset,   1635
This Arcite and this Palamon been met.
To chaungen gan the colour in hir face
Right as the hunters in the regne of Trace,   hunters: hunter's. regne: realm.
That stondeth at the gappe with a spere,   Trace: Thrace.
Whan hunted is the leon or the bere,   1640   gappe: opening in the forest.
And hereth hym come russhyng in the greves,   greves: bushes.
And breketh bothe bowes and the leves,
And thynketh, "Heere cometh my mortal
         enemy!
Withoute faille, he moot be deed, or I;
For outher I moot sleen hym at the gappe,   1645   outher: either.
Or he moot sleen me, if that me myshappe,"—
So ferden they in chaungyng of hir hewe,
As fer as everich of hem oother knewe.
    Ther nas no "good day," ne no saluyng,   saluyng: saluting, greeting.
But streight, withouten word or rehersyng,   1650
Everich of hem heelp for to armen other   heelp: helped.
As freendly as he were his owene brother;
And after that, with sharpe speres stronge
They foynen ech at other wonder longe.   foynen: thrust.
Thou myghtest wene that this Palamon   1655   wene: ween, suppose.
In his fightyng were a wood leon,
And as a crueel tigre was Arcite;
As wilde bores gonne they to smyte,   gonne they to: they did.
That frothen whit as foom for ire wood.
Up to the ancle foghte they in hir blood.   1660
And in this wise I lete hem fightyng dwelle,   dwelle: remain.
And forth I wole of Theseus yow telle.
    The destinee, ministre general,   ministre: agent.
That executeth in the world over al   over al: everywhere.
The purveiaunce that God hath seyn biforn,   1665   purveiaunce: providence.
So strong it is that, though the world had sworn
The contrarie of a thyng by ye or nay,
Yet somtyme it shal fallen on a day   fallen: befall.
That falleth nat eft withinne a thousand yeer.   eft: again.
For certeinly, oure appetites heer,   1670   appetites: desires.
Be it of werre, or pees, or hate, or love,
Al is this ruled by the sighte above.   sighte: foresight.
    This mene I now by myghty Theseus,

That for to hunten is so desirus,
And namely at the grete hert in May,   1675   namely: especially. **hert**: hart.
That in his bed ther daweth hym no day   daweth: dawns.
That he nys clad, and redy for to ryde
With hunte and horn and houndes hym bisyde.   hunte: huntsman.
For in his huntyng hath he swich delit
That it is al his joye and appetit   1680
To been hymself the grete hertes bane,   bane: slayer.
For after Mars he serveth now Dyane.   **Mars, Dyane**: the deities of war and
    Cleer was the day, as I have told er this,   hunting respectively.
And Theseus with alle joye and blis,
With his Ypolita, the faire queene,   1685
And Emelye, clothed al in grene,
On huntyng be they riden roially.
And to the grove that stood ful faste by,
In which ther was an hert, as men hym tolde,
Duc Theseus the streighte wey hath holde.   1690   holde: held.
And to the launde he rideth hym ful right,   launde: glade, forest-clearing (used for
For thider was the hert wont have his flight,   hunting-ground).
And over a brook, and so forth on his weye.
This duc wol han a cours at hym or tweye   a cours: a run.
With houndes swiche as that hym list
        comaunde.   1695
    And whan this duc was come unto the
        launde,
Under the sonne he looketh, and anon
He was war of Arcite and Palamon,
That foughten breme, as it were boles two.   breme: furiously. **boles**: bulls.
The brighte swerdes wenten to and fro   1700
So hidously that with the leeste strook
It seemed as it wolde felle an ook.
But what they were, no thyng he ne woot.
This duc his courser with his spores smoot,   spores: spurs.
And at a stert he was bitwix hem two,   1705   at a stert: with a bound.
And pulled out a swerd, and cride, "Ho!
Namoore, up peyne of lesyng of youre heed!   up: upon.
By myghty Mars, he shal anon be deed
That smyteth any strook that I may seen.
But telleth me what myster men ye been,   1710   what myster men: what kind of men.
That been so hardy for to fighten here
Withouten juge or oother officere,
As it were in a lystes roially."
    This Palamon answerde hastily
And seyde, "Sire, what nedeth wordes mo?   1715
We have the deeth disserved bothe two.
Two woful wrecches been we, two caytyves,   caytyves: miserable persons.
That been encombred of oure owene lyves;

1697. **under the sonne**: against the sun.

And as thou art a rightful lord and juge,
Ne yif us neither mercy ne refuge,   1720   yif: give.
But slee me first, for seinte charitee!   seinte: holy.
But slee my felawe eek as wel as me;
Or slee hym first, for though thow knowest it
        lite,
This is thy mortal foo, this is Arcite,
That fro thy lond is banysshed on his heed,   1725   on his heed: on pain of losing his
For which he hath deserved to be deed.   head.
For this is he that cam unto thy gate
And seyde that he highte Philostrate.
Thus hath he japed thee ful many a yer,   japed: tricked.
And thou hast maked hym thy chief squier;   1730
And this is he that loveth Emelye.
For sith the day is come that I shal dye,
I make pleynly my confessioun   pleynly: openly, fully.
That I am thilke woful Palamoun   confessioun: admission.
That hath thy prisoun broken wikkedly.   1735
I am thy mortal foo, and it am I
That loveth so hoote Emelye the brighte
That I wol dye present in hir sighte.   present: at once.
Wherfore I axe deeth and my juwise;   axe: ask for. juwise: sentence.
But slee my felawe in the same wise,   1740
For bothe have we deserved to be slayn."
   This worthy duc answerde anon agayn,
And seyde, "This is a short conclusioun.   short conclusioun: prompt decision.
Youre owene mouth, by youre confessioun,
Hath dampned yow, and I wol it recorde;   1745   recorde: declare as (my) verdict.
It nedeth noght to pyne yow with the corde.   to pyne with the corde: i.e., to force
Ye shal be deed, by myghty Mars the rede!"   confession by torture.
The queene anon, for verray wommanhede,
Gan for to wepe, and so dide Emelye,
And alle the ladyes in the compaignye.   1750
Greet pitee was it, as it thoughte hem alle,
That evere swich a chaunce sholde falle;   falle: befall.
For gentil men they were of greet estaat,
And no thyng but for love was this debaat;   debaat: fighting.
And sawe hir blody woundes wyde and
        soore,   1755
And alle cryden, bothe lasse and moore,   lasse: less.
"Have mercy, Lord, upon us wommen alle!"
And on hir bare knees adoun they falle,
And wolde have kist his feet ther as he stood;
Til at the laste aslaked was his mood,   1760   aslaked: subsided.
For pitee renneth soone in gentil herte.
And though he first for ire quook and sterte,   quook: quaked. sterte: started.
He hath considered shortly, in a clause,   in a clause: in a few words.
The trespas of hem bothe, and eek the cause,
And although that his ire hir gilt accused,   1765   hir gilt accused: accused them.

Yet in his resoun he hem bothe excused,
As thus: he thoghte wel that every man
Wol helpe hymself in love, if that he kan,
And eek delivere hymself out of prisoun.
And eek his herte had compassioun   1770
Of wommen, for they wepen evere in oon;   evere in oon: continually.
And in his gentil herte he thoughte anon,
And softe unto hymself he seyde, "Fy
Upon a lord that wol have no mercy,
But been a leon, bothe in word and dede,   1775
To hem that been in repentaunce and drede,
As wel as to a proud despitous man   despitous: hateful.
That wol mayntene that he first bigan.
That lord hath litel of discrecioun,
That in swich cas kan no divisioun,   1780   kan: knows. divisioun: distinction.
But weyeth pride and humblesse after oon."   after oon: according to one standard.
And shortly, whan his ire is thus agoon,   agoon: passed away.
He gan to looken up with eyen lighte,
And spak thise same wordes al on highte: on highte: aloud.
    "The god of love, a, benedicitee!   1785
How myghty and how greet a lord is he!
Agayns his myght ther gayneth none obstacles.   gayneth: prevails.
He may be cleped a god for his miracles;
For he kan maken, at his owene gyse,   at . . . gyse: as he pleases.
Of everich herte as that hym list devyse.   1790
Lo here this Arcite and this Palamoun,
That quitly weren out of my prisoun,   quitly: freely.
And myghte han lyved in Thebes roially,
And witen I am hir mortal enemy,   witen: know.
And that hir deeth lyth in my myght also;   1795
And yet hath love, maugree hir eyen two,
Broght hem hyder bothe for to dye.
Now looketh, is nat that an heigh folye?
Who may been a fool but if he love?
Bihoold, for Goddes sake that sit above,   1800   sit: (sitteth) sits.
Se how they blede! be they noght wel arrayed?
Thus hath hir lord, the god of love, ypayed
Hir wages and hir fees for hir servyse!
And yet they wenen for to be ful wyse   wenen: suppose (themselves).
That serven love, for aught that may bifalle.   1805
But this is yet the beste game of alle,
That she for whom they have this jolitee   jolitee: passion.
Kan hem therfore as muche thank as me.   kan hem thank: owes them thanks.
She woot namoore of al this hoote fare,   fare: activity.
By God, than woot a cokkow or an hare!   1810
But all moot ben assayed, hoot and coold;   assayed: experienced.

1785. benedicitee!: see Basic Glossary.
1796. maugree hir eyen two: in spite of all they could do.

A man moot been a fool, or yong or oold,
I woot it by myself ful yore agon,   yore agon: long ago.
For in my tyme a servant was I oon.   servant: lover.
And therfore, syn I knowe of loves peyne, 1815
And woot how soore it kan a man distreyne, distreyne: distress, torment.
As he that hath ben caught ofte in his laas, laas: snare.
I yow foryeve al hoolly this trespaas, hoolly: wholly.
At requeste of the queene, that kneleth here,
And eek of Emelye, my suster dere. 1820
And ye shul bothe anon unto me swere
That nevere mo ye shal my contree dere, dere: harm.
Ne make werre upon me nyght nor day,
But been my freendes in al that ye may.
I yow foryeve this trespas every del." 1825 del: bit.
And they hym sworen his axyng faire and wel, axyng: request.
And hym of lordshipe and of mercy preyde,
And he hem graunteth grace, and thus he
        seyde:
"To speke of roial lynage and richesse,
Though that she were a queene or a
        princesse, 1830
Ech of you bothe is worthy, doutelees,
To wedden whan tyme is, but nathelees
I speke as for my suster Emelye,
For whom ye have this strif and jalousye.
Ye woot yourself she may nat wedden two 1835
Atones, though ye fighten everemo. atones: at the same time.
That oon of you, al be hym looth or lief, al be hym looth or lief: whether he
He moot go pipen in an yvy leef;   like it or not.
This is to seyn, she may nat now have bothe,
Al be ye never so jalous ne so wrothe. 1840 wrothe: angry.
And forthy I yow putte in this degree, forthy: therefore. degree: position.
That ech of yow shal have his destynee
As hym is shape, and herkneth in what wyse; shape: determined.
Lo here youre ende of that I shall devyse. ende: ultimate fate.
   My wyl is this, for plat conclusioun, 1845 plat: blunt, plain.
Withouten any replicacioun,— replicacioun: reply.
If that you liketh, take it for the beste:
That everich of you shal goon where hym leste everich: everyone; each.
Frely, withouten raunson or daunger; daunger: liability.
And this day fifty wykes, fer ne ner, 1850 fer ne ner: neither later nor sooner.
Everich of you shal brynge an hundred knyghtes
Armed for lystes up at alle rightes, rightes: points.
Al redy to darreyne hire by bataille. darreyne hire: decide the right to her.
And this bihote I yow withouten faille, bihote: promise.
Upon my trouthe, and as I am a knyght, 1855

1827. of lordshipe: i.e., to be their lord.
1838. He may as well go whistle.

That wheither of yow bothe that hath myght,— wheither: whichever.
This is to seyn, that wheither he or thou wheither: whether.
May with his hundred, as I spak of now,
Sleen his contrarie, or out of listes dryve, sleen: slay. contrarie: opponent.
Thanne shal I yeve Emelye to wyve 1860
To whom that Fortune yeveth so fair a grace. whom that: him whom. grace: fortune.
The lystes shal I maken in this place,
And God so wisly on my soule rewe,
As I shal evene juge been and trewe. evene: impartial.
Ye shul noon oother ende with me maken, 1865 ende: agreement.
That oon of yow ne shal be deed or taken.
And if yow thynketh this is wel ysayd, yow thinketh: it seems to you.
Sey youre avys, and holdeth you apayd. avys: opinion. apayd: content.
This is youre ende and youre conclusioun."
    Who looketh lightly now but Palamoun? 1870
Who spryngeth up for joye but Arcite?
Who koude telle, or who koude it endite,
The joye that is maked in the place
Whan Theseus hath doon so fair a grace?
But doun on knees wente every maner wight, 1875
And thonken hym with al hir herte and myght,
And namely the Thebans often sithe. namely: especially. sithe: times.
And thus with good hope and with herte blithe blithe: glad.
They taken hir leve, and homward gonne they gonne: did.
      ride
To Thebesward, with olde walles wyde. 1880

      EXPLICIT SECUNDA PARS.
      SEQUITUR PARS TERCIA.

    I trowe men wolde deme it necligence
If I foryete to tellen the dispence foryete: forget. dispence: expenditure.
Of Theseus, that gooth so bisily
To maken up the listes roially,
That swich a noble theatre as it was, 1885
I dar wel seyn in this world ther nas.
The circuit a myle was aboute,
Walled of stoon, and dyched al withoute.
Round was the shap, in maner of compas, compas: circle.
Ful of degrees, the heighte of sixty pas, 1890 degrees: steps, tiers. pas: paces.
That whan a man was set on o degree,
He letted nat his felawe for to see. letted: hindered.
    Estward ther stood a gate of marbul whit,
Westward right swich another in the opposit.
And shortly to concluden, swich a place 1895
Was noon in erthe, as in so litel space;

1863–64. God . . . been: God have pity on my soul as surely as I shall be impartial judge.
1896. as in so litel space: (constructed) in so short a time.

For in the lond ther was no crafty man
That geometrie or ars-metrik kan,   ars-metrik: art or science of measur-
Ne portreyour, ne kerver of ymages,   ing and calculating. kan: knows.
That Theseus ne yaf him mete and wages,   1900
The theatre for to maken and devyse.   devyse: construct.
And for to doon his ryte and sacrifise,
He estward hath, upon the gate above,
In worship of Venus, goddesse of love,
Doon make an auter and an oratorie;   1905 auter: altar.
And on the gate westward, in memorie
Of Mars, he maked hath right swich another,
That coste largely of gold a fother.   fother: load.
And northward, in a touret on the wal,
Of alabastre whit and reed coral,   1910
An oratorie, riche for to see,
In worship of Dyane of chastitee,
Hath Theseus doon wrought in noble wyse.
   But yet hadde I forgeten to devyse
The noble kervyng and the portreitures,   1915
The shap, the contenance, and the figures,
That weren in thise oratories thre.
   First in the temple of Venus maystow se
Wroght on the wal, ful pitous to biholde,
The broken slepes, and the sikes colde,   1920 sikes: sighs. colde: anguished.
The sacred teeris, and the waymentynge,   waymentynge: lamenting.
The firy strokes of the desirynge
That loves servantz in this lyf enduren;
The othes that hir covenantz assuren;
Plesance and Hope, Desir, Foolhardynesse,   1925
Beautee and Youthe, Baudrye, Richesse,   Baudrye: gaiety; ? matchmaking.
Charmes and Force, Lesynges, Flaterye,   Lesynges: deceits.
Despense, Bisynesse, and Jalousye,   Despense: expense.
That wered of yelowe gooldes a gerland,   gooldes: marigolds.
And a cokkow sittyng on hir hand;   1930
Festes, instrumentz, caroles, daunces,   caroles: dances, accompanied by
Lust and Array, and alle the circumstaunces   song. Lust: pleasure.
Of love, which that I rekned and rekne shal,
By ordre weren peynted on the wal,
And mo than I kan make of mencioun.   1935 make of mencioun: make mention of.
For soothly al the mount of Citheroun,
Ther Venus hath hir principal dwellynge,
Was shewed on the wal in portreyynge,
With al the gardyn and the lustynesse.
Nat was foryeten the porter, Ydelnesse,   1940 foryeten: forgotten.
Ne Narcisus the faire of yore agon,   yore agon: long ago.
Ne yet the folye of kyng Salomon,   folye: lechery.
Ne yet the grete strength of Ercules—
Th'enchauntementz of Medea and Circes—

Ne of Turnus, with the hardy fiers corage,   1945
The riche Cresus, kaytyf in servage.   kaytyf: wretched. **servage**: bondage.
Thus may ye seen that wisdom ne richesse,
Beautee ne sleighte, strengthe, hardynesse,   sleighte: skill. **hardynesse**: boldness.
Ne may with Venus holde champartie,   champartie: partnership in power.
For as hir list the world than may she gye. 1950 gye: guide, govern.
Lo, al thise folk so caught were in hir las,   las: snare.
Til they for wo ful ofte seyde "Allas!"
Suffiseth here ensamples oon or two,
And though I koude rekene a thousand mo.
   The statue of Venus, glorious for to see, 1955
Was naked, fletynge in the large see,   fletynge: swimming.
And fro the navele doun al covered was
With wawes grene, and bright as any glas.   wawes: waves.
A citole in hir right hand hadde she,   citole: a kind of harp or zither.
And on hir heed, ful semely for to se,   1960
A rose gerland, fressh and wel smellynge;
Above hir heed hir dowves flikerynge.
Biforn hire stood hir sone Cupido;
Upon his shuldres wynges hadde he two,
And blynd he was, as it is often seene;   1965
A bowe he bar and arwes brighte and kene. bar: carried.
   Why sholde I nat as wel eek telle yow al
The portreiture that was upon the wal
Withinne the temple of myghty Mars the rede?
Al peynted was the wal, in lengthe and
       brede,   1970 brede: breadth.
Lyk to the estres of the grisly place   estres: interior.
That highte the grete temple of Mars in Trace,
In thilke colde, frosty regioun
Ther as Mars hath his sovereyn mansioun.
   First on the wal was peynted a forest,   1975
In which ther dwelleth neither man ne best,
With knotty, knarry, bareyne trees olde,   knarry: gnarled.
Of stubbes sharpe and hidouse to biholde,
In which ther ran a rumbel in a swough,   swough: noise (of wind); blast.
As though a storm sholde bresten every   bresten: break.
       bough.   1980
And dounward from an hille, under a bente,   under a bente: beside an open field.
Ther stood the temple of Mars armypotente,
Wroght al of burned steel, of which the entree burned: burnished.
Was long and streit, and gastly for to see.   streit: narrow.
And therout came a rage and swich a veze 1985 rage: i.e., of wind. **veze**: blast.
That it made al the gate for to rese.   rese: shake.
The northren lyght in at the dores shoon,
For wyndow on the wal ne was ther noon,
Thurgh which men myghten any light discerne.

1945. The love of Turnus for Lavinia eventually led to his death in battle with Aeneas.

The dore was al of adamant eterne,   1990
Yclenched overthwart and endelong
  overthwart and endelong: crosswise
   and lengthwise.
With iren tough; and for to make it strong,
Every pyler, the temple to sustene,
Was tonne greet, of iren bright and shene.
  tonne greet: as thick as a tun or cask.
    Ther saugh I first the derke ymaginyng   1995
Of Felonye, and al the compassyng;
  compassyng: conspiring.
The crueel Ire, reed as any gleede;
  gleede: live coal.
The pykepurs, and eek the pale Drede;
  pykepurs: pick-purse.
The smylere with the knyf under the cloke;
The shepne brennyng with the blake smoke;   2000   shepne: cowshed. brennyng: burning.
The tresoun of the mordryng in the bed;
The open werre, with woundes al bibled;
  bibled: stained with blood.
Contek, with blody knyf and sharp manace.
  Contek: conflict.
Al ful of chirkyng was that sory place.
  chirkyng: strident noises.
The sleere of hymself yet saugh I ther,—   2005   sleere: slayer.
His herte-blood hath bathed al his heer;
The nayl ydryven in the shode a-nyght;
  shode: parting of the hair; temple.
The colde deeth, with mouth gapyng upright.
Amyddes of the temple sat Meschaunce,
  Meschaunce: misfortune, disaster.
With disconfort and sory contenaunce.   2010   disconfort: discouraged.
Yet saugh I Woodnesse, laughyng in his rage,
  Woodnesse: madness.
Armed Compleint, Outhees, and fiers Outrage;
  Outhees: outcry.
The careyne in the bussh, with throte ycorve;
  careyne: corpse. ycorve: cut.
A thousand slayn, and nat of qualm ystorve;
  qualm: plague. ystorve: dead.
The tiraunt, with the pray by force yraft;   2015   pray: plunder. yraft: bereft, snatched
   away.
The toun destroyed, ther was no thyng laft.
Yet saugh I brent the shippes hoppesteres;
  shippes hoppesteres: dancing ships.
The hunte strangled with the wilde beres;
  hunte: hunter. with: by.
The sowe freten the child right in the cradel;
  freten: devour.
The cook yscalded, for al his longe ladel.   2020
Noght was forgeten by the infortune of Marte:
  forgeten: forgotten. by: of. infortune:
   malign influence.
The cartere overryden with his carte,
Under the wheel ful lowe he lay adoun.
Ther were also, of Martes divisioun,
The barbour, and the bocher, and the smyth, 2025
That forgeth sharpe swerdes on his styth.
  styth: anvil.
And al above, depeynted in a tour,
Saugh I Conquest, sittyng in greet honour,
With the sharpe swerd over his heed
Hangynge by a subtil twynes threed.   2030   subtil: thin.
Depeynted was the slaughtre of Julius,
Of grete Nero, and of Antonius;
Al be that thilke tyme they were unborn,
Yet was hir deeth depeynted ther-biforn
By manasynge of Mars, right by figure.   2035   manasynge: menace, threat.
So was it shewed in that portreiture,

2035. figure: a configuration of heavenly bodies; a diagram of the same.

As is depeynted in the sterres above   sterres: stars.
Who shal be slayn or elles deed for love.
Suffiseth oon ensample in stories olde;
I may nat rekene hem alle though I wolde. 2040
    The statue of Mars upon a carte stood
Armed, and looked grym as he were wood;
And over his heed ther shynen two figures   shynen: shone.
Of sterres, that been cleped in scriptures,
That oon Puella, that oother Rubeus— 2045
This god of armes was arrayed thus.
A wolf ther stood biforn hym at his feet
With eyen rede, and of a man he eet;   eet: ate.
With subtil pencel was depeynted this storie
In redoutynge of Mars and of his glorie. 2050 redoutynge: reverence.
    Now to the temple of Diane the chaste,
As shortly as I kan, I wol me haste,
To telle yow al the descripsioun.
Depeynted been the walles up and doun
Of huntyng and of shamefast chastitee. 2055 shamefast: modest.
Ther saw I how woful Calistopee,
Whan that Diane agreved was with here,   agreved: aggrieved, vexed.
Was turned from a womman til a bere,
And after was she maad the lode-sterre;   lode-sterre: lodestar, polestar.
Thus was it peynted, I kan sey yow no ferre. 2060 ferre: further.
Hir sone is eek a sterre, as men may see.
Ther saw I Dane, yturned til a tree,—
I mene nat the goddesse Diane,
But Penneus doghter, which that highte Dane.
Ther saw I Attheon an hert ymaked, 2065 Attheon: Actaeon.
For vengeaunce that he saw Diane al naked;
I saugh how that his houndes have hym caught
And freeten hym, for that they knewe hym   freeten: devoured.
        naught.
Yet peynted was a litel forther moor
How Atthalante hunted the wilde boor, 2070 Atthalante: Atalanta of Arcadia.
And Meleagre, and many another mo,
For which Diane wroghte hym care and wo.
Ther saugh I many another wonder storie,
The which me list nat drawen to memorie.   drawen to memorie: remember.
    This goddesse on an hert ful hye seet, 2075 seet: sat.
With smale houndes al aboute hir feet;
And undernethe hir feet she hadde a moone,—
Wexynge it was and sholde wanye soone.

2043, 2045. figures, Puella, Rubeus: configurations used in divination, here signifying the astro-
logical influence of Mars.
2062. Dane: Daphne, changed by her father into a laurel so that she might escape the love of
Apollo.
2071. Meleagre: Meleager of Calydon, who fell in love with Atalanta while they hunted the boar
sent by Diana to ravage Calydon.

In gaude grene hir statue clothed was,

gaude grene: a yellowish green ma-

With bowe in honde, and arwes in a cas,   2080   terial. cas: quiver.

Hir eyen caste she ful lowe adoun,

Ther Pluto hath his derke regioun.

A womman travaillyng was hire biforn;

travaillyng: laboring, in labor.

But for hir child so longe was unborn,

for: because.

Ful pitously Lucyna gan she calle,   2085

And seyde, "Help, for thou mayst best of alle!"

Wel koude he peynte lifly that it wroghte;

lifly: in a lifelike manner.

With many a floryn he the hewes boghte.

   Now been thise lystes maad, and Theseus,

That at his grete cost arrayed thus   2090

The temples and the theatre every del,

del: bit.

Whan it was doon, hym lyked wonder wel.

hym lyked: pleased him.

But stynte I wol of Theseus a lite,

stynte: cease (to tell).

And speke of Palamon and of Arcite.

   The day approcheth of hir retournynge,   2095

That everich sholde an hundred knyghtes brynge

The bataille to darreyne, as I yow tolde.

darreyne: decide.

And til Atthenes, hir covenant for to holde,

Hath everich of hem broght an hundred

       knyghtes,

Wel armed for the werre at alle rightes.   2100   rightes: points.

And sikerly ther trowed many a man

sikerly: surely.

That nevere, sithen that the world bigan,

As for to speke of knyghthod of hir hond,

of hir hond: of the deeds of their

As fer as God hath maked see and lond,

hand.

Nas of so fewe so noble a compaignye.   2105

For every wight that loved chivalrye,

And wolde, his thankes, han a passant name,

his thankes: gladly. passant: surpass-

Hath preyed that he myghte been of that game;

ing.

And wel was hym that therto chosen was.

For if ther fille tomorwe swich a cas,   2110   fille: befell.

Ye knowen wel that every lusty knyght

That loveth paramours and hath his myght,

paramours: passionately.

Were it in Engelond or elleswhere,

They wolde, hir thankes, wilnen to be there,—

wilnen: like.

To fighte for a lady, benedicitee!   2115

It were a lusty sighte for to see.

   And right so ferden they with Palamon.

With hym ther wenten knyghtes many oon;

Som wol ben armed in an haubergeoun,

haubergeoun: hauberk, coat of mail.

And in a brestplate and a light gypoun;   2120   gypoun: tunic (worn under hauberk).

And some wol have a paire plates large;

paire: set of.

And som wol have a Pruce sheeld or a targe;

Pruce: Prussian. targe: shield.

Som wol ben armed on his legges weel,

2085. Lucyna: Lucina (goddess of childbirth), a title of Diana.

And have an ax, and som a mace of steel—
Ther nys no newe gyse that it nas old.   2125
Armed were they, as I have yow told,
Everych after his opinioun.
   Ther maystow seen, comynge with Palamoun,
Lygurge hymself, the grete kyng of Trace.
Blak was his berd, and manly was his face;   2130
The cercles of his eyen in his heed,   cercles: irises.
They gloweden bitwixen yelow and reed,
And lik a grifphon looked he aboute,
With kempe heres on his browes stoute;   kempe: shaggy.
His lymes grete, his brawnes harde and   lymes: limbs. brawnes: muscles.
       stronge,   2135
His shuldres brode, his armes rounde and longe;
And as the gyse was in his contree,
Ful hye upon a chaar of gold stood he,   chaar: chariot.
With foure white boles in the trays.   boles: bulls. trays: traces.
In stede of cote-armure over his harnays,   2140 harnays: armor.
With nayles yelewe and brighte as any gold,
He hadde a beres skyn, col-blak for old.   for old: with age.
His longe heer was kembed bihynde his bak;
As any ravenes fethere it shoon for blak;   for: very.
A wrethe of gold, arm greet, of huge wighte, 2145 arm greet: as thick as an arm. wighte:
Upon his heed, set ful of stones brighte,   weight.
Of fyne rubyes and of dyamauntz.
Aboute his chaar ther wenten white alauntz,   alauntz: huge wolf-hounds.
Twenty and mo, as grete as any steer,
To hunten at the leoun or the deer,   2150
And folwed hym with mosel faste ybounde,   mosel: muzzle.
Colered of gold, and tourettes fyled rounde.   colered: having collars. tourettes:
An hundred lordes hadde he in his route,   leash-rings. route: retinue.
Armed ful wel, with hertes sterne and stoute.
   With Arcita, in stories as men fynde,   2155
The grete Emetreus, the kyng of Inde,
Upon a steede bay trapped in steel,
Covered in clooth of gold, dyapred weel,   dyapred: decorated with diamond-
Cam ridynge lyk the god of armes, Mars.   shaped fretwork.
His cote-armure was of clooth of Tars   2160
Couched with perles white and rounde and   couched: set.
       grete;
His sadel was of brend gold newe ybete;   brend: refined, pure. ybete: beaten,
A mantelet upon his shulder hangynge,   hammered; decorated.
Bret-ful of rubyes rede as fyr sparklynge;   bret-ful: brimful.
His crispe heer lyk rynges was yronne,   2165 crispe: curly. yronne: clustered.

2125. "There is no new fashion that has not been old."
2140. cote-armure: see note for l. 1016.
2160. Tars: probably Tarsia in Chinese Turkestan, although Chaucer and his audience may have
associated the rich silk with Tartary.

And that was yelow, and glitred as the sonne.
His nose was heigh, his eyen bright citryn,   citryn: citron-colored.
His lippes rounde, his colour was sangwyn; sangwyn: blood-red.
A fewe frakenes in his face yspreynd,   frakenes: freckles. yspreynd:
Bitwixen yelow and somdel blak ymeynd; 2170 sprinkled. ymeynd: mingled.
And as a leon he his lookyng caste.
Of fyve and twenty yeer his age I caste.   caste: conjecture.
His berd was wel bigonne for to sprynge;
His voys was as a trompe thonderynge.
Upon his heed he wered of laurer grene 2175
A gerland, fressh and lusty for to sene.
Upon his hand he bar for his deduyt   deduyt: delight.
An egle tame, as any lilye whyt.
An hundred lordes hadde he with hym there,
Al armed, save hir heddes, in al hir gere, 2180
Ful richely in alle maner thynges.
For trusteth wel that dukes, erles, kynges
Were gadered in this noble compaignye,
For love and for encrees of chivalrye.   chivalrye: chivalrous glory.
Aboute this kyng ther ran on every part 2185 part: side.
Ful many a tame leon and leopart.
And in this wise thise lordes, alle and some,
Been on the Sonday to the citee come
Aboute pryme, and in the toun alight.   pryme: 9 A.M. or earlier.
 This Theseus, this duc, this worthy
    knyght,   2190
Whan he had broght hem into his citee,
And inned hem, everich at his degree,   inned: lodged. at: according to.
He festeth hem, and dooth so greet labour
To esen hem and doon hem al honour,
That yet men wenen that no mannes wit 2195 wenen: think.
Of noon estaat ne koude amenden it.   amenden: improve upon.
 The mynstralcye, the service at the feeste,
The grete yiftes to the meeste and leeste, yiftes: gifts. meeste: most, highest.
The riche array of Theseus paleys,
Ne who sat first ne last upon the deys, 2200
What ladyes fairest been or best daunsynge,
Or which of hem kan [chaunten] best and synge,
Ne who moost felyngly speketh of love;
What haukes sitten on the perche above,
What houndes liggen on the floor adoun,— 2205 liggen: lie.
Of al this make I now no mencioun,
But al th'effect, that thynketh me the beste. thynketh me: seems to me.
Now cometh the point, and herkneth if yow
   leste.
 The Sonday nyght, er day bigan to sprynge,

2168. his colour was sangwyn: see note for l. 333, above.
2202. chaunten: O' reads dauncen; Manly suggests the emendation.

Whan Palamon the larke herde synge,   2210
(Although it nere nat day by houres two,
Yet song the larke) and Palamon right tho
With hooly herte and with an heigh corage,
He roos to wenden on his pilgrymage
Unto the blisful Citherea benigne,—   2215
I mene Venus, honurable and digne.   digne: worthy.
And in hir houre he walketh forth a pas   a pas: at a footpace.
Unto the lystes ther hire temple was,
And doun he kneleth, and with humble cheere
And herte soor, he seyde as ye shal heere: 2220
   "Faireste of faire, O lady myn, Venus,
Doughter to Jove, and spouse to Vulcanus,
Thow gladere of the mount of Citheron,
For thilke love thow haddest to Adoon,   Adoon: Adonis.
Have pitee of my bittre teeris smerte,   2225
And taak myn humble preyere at thyn herte.
Allas! I ne have no langage to telle
Th'effectes ne the tormentz of myn helle;
Myn herte may myne harmes nat biwreye;   harmes: sufferings. biwreye: reveal.
I am so confus that I kan noght seye   2230
But, 'Mercy, lady bright, that knowest weele
My thought, and seest what harmes that I
            feele!'
Considere al this and rewe upon my soore,   rewe: have pity. soore: misery.
As wisly as I shal for everemoore,   wisly: surely.
Emforth my myght, thy trewe servant be,   2235 emforth: to the extent of.
And holden werre alwey with chastitee.
That make I myn avow, so ye me helpe!   avow: vow.
I kepe noght of armes for to yelpe,   kepe: care. yelpe: boast.
Ne I ne axe nat tomorwe to have victorie,   axe: ask.
Ne renoun in this cas, ne veyne glorie   2240
Of pris of armes blowen up and doun;   pris: renown, honor.
But I wolde have fully possessioun
Of Emelye, and dye in thy servyse.
Fynd thow the manere hou, and in what wyse:
I recche nat but it may bettre be   2245 recche: care.
To have victorie of hem, or they of me,
So that I have my lady in myne armes.
For though so be that Mars is god of armes,
Youre vertu is so greet in hevene above   vertu: power.
That if yow list, I shal wel have my love.   2250
Thy temple wol I worshipe everemo,
And on thyn auter, where I ride or go,   auter: altar. where: whether.
I wol doon sacrifice and fires beete.   beete: kindle.
And if ye wol nat so, my lady sweete,

2217. hir houre: The twenty-third hour after sunrise on Sunday is assigned, astrologically, to
Venus; the first hour of Monday (l. 2273) to the Moon; the fourth (l. 2367) to Mars.

Thanne preye I thee, tomorwe with a spere   2255
That Arcita me thurgh the herte bere.   bere: pierce.
Thanne rekke I noght, whan I have lost my lyf,
Though that Arcita wynne hire to his wyf.
This is th'effect and ende of my preyere:
Yif me my love, thow blisful lady deere."   2260   yif: give.
    Whan the orison was doon of Palamon,   orison: prayer.
His sacrifice he dide, and that anon,
Ful pitously, with alle circumstaunces,
Al telle I noght as now his observaunces;
But atte laste the statue of Venus shook,   2265
And made a signe, wherby that he took
That his preyere accepted was that day.
For thogh the signe shewed a delay,
Yet wiste he wel that graunted was his boone;   boone: request.
And with glad herte he wente hym hoom ful
      soone.   2270
    The thridde houre inequal that Palamon
Bigan to Venus temple for to gon,
Up roos the sonne, and up roos Emelye,
And to the temple of Dyane gan hye.   gan hye: hastened.
Hir maydens, that she thider with hire ladde, 2275 ladde: led.
Ful redily with hem the fyr they hadde,
Th'encens, the clothes, and the remenant al   clothes: hangings.
That to the sacrifice longen shal;   longen: belong.
The hornes fulle of meeth, as was the gyse: meeth: mead, a drink made from fer-
Ther lakked noght to doon hir sacrifise.   2280   mented honey.
Smokynge the temple, ful of clothes faire,
This Emelye, with herte debonaire,
Hir body wessh with water of a welle.   wessh: washed.
But hou she dide hir ryte I dar nat telle,
But it be any thing in general;   2285
And yet it were a game to heeren al.   game: pleasure.
To hym that meneth wel it were no charge;   it . . . charge: it wouldn't matter.
But it is good a man been at his large.   at his large: free (to speak or be
Hir brighte heer was kembd, untressed al;   silent). untressed: loose.
A coroune of a grene ook cerial   2290
Upon hir heed was set ful fair and meete.
Two fyres on the auter gan she beete,
And dide hir thynges, as men may biholde
In Stace of Thebes and thise bookes olde.
Whan kyndled was the fyr, with pitous
      cheere   2295

2271. houre inequal: Astrological hours were reckoned twelve from sunrise to sunset, twelve from sunset to sunrise; hence the hours of the day were unequal to the hours of the night (except just at the equinoxes).

2290. ook cerial: *Quercus Cerris,* an oak of southern Europe.

2294. Stace: Statius, the late-Roman author of the *Thebaid.*

Unto Dyane she spak as ye may heere:
　"O chaste goddesse of the wodes grene,
To whom bothe hevene and erthe and see is sene,　sene: visible.
Queene of the regne of Pluto derk and lowe,　regne: realm.
Goddesse of maydens, that myn herte hast
　　　　knowe　　　　　　　　　　　　　　2300
Ful many a yeer, and woost what I desire,　woost: knowest.
As keepe me fro thy vengeaunce and thyn ire,　as keepe: please keep.
That Attheon aboughte cruelly.　aboughte: suffered.
Chaste goddesse, wel wostow that I
Desire to ben a mayden al my lyf,　　　　　2305
Ne nevere wol I be no love ne wyf.　wol be: desire to be.
I am, thow woost, yet of thy compaignye,
A mayde, and love huntynge and venerye,　venerye: the chase.
And for to walken in the wodes wilde,
And noght to ben a wyf and be with childe.　2310
Noght wol I knowe compaignye of man.
Now help me, lady, sith ye may and kan,
For tho thre formes that thou hast in thee.　thre formes: i.e., Luna, Diana, and
And Palamon, that hath swich love to me,　　Proserpina.
And eek Arcite, that loveth me so soore,　2315
(This grace I preye thee withoute moore)
As sende love and pees bitwixe hem two,
And fro me turne awey hir hertes so
That al hire hoote love and hir desir,
And al hir bisy torment, and hir fir　　　2320　bisy: severe.
Be queynt, or turned in another place.　queynt: quenched.
And if so be thou wolt nat do me grace,　wolt: will.
Or if my destynee be shapen so
That I shal nedes have oon of hem two,
As sende me hym that moost desireth me.　2325
Bihoold, goddesse of clene chastitee,
The bittre teeris that on my chekes falle.
Syn thou art mayde and kepere of us alle,　kepere: guardian.
My maydenhede thou kepe and wel conserve,
And whil I lyve, a mayde I wol thee serve."　2330
　The fires brenne upon the auter cleere,　cleere: brightly.
While Emelye was thus in hir preyere.
But sodeynly she saugh a sighte queynte,　queynte: strange.
For right anon oon of the fyres queynte,　queynte: was quenched.
And quyked agayn, and after that anon　2335　quyked: became alive, burst into
That oother fyr was queynt and al agon;　　flame. agon: gone.
And as it queynte it made a whistelynge,
As doon thise wete brondes in hir brennynge,　brondes: firebrands.
And at the brondes ende out ran anon
As it were blody dropes many oon;　　　　2340

────────

2303. See ll. 2065–68, above.

For which so soore agast was Emelye
That she was wel ny mad, and gan to crye,
For she ne wiste what it signyfied;
But oonly for the feere thus hath she cried,
And weep that it was pitee for to heere.   2345   weep: wept.
And therwithal Dyane gan appeere,
With bowe in honde, right as an hunteresse,
And seyde, "Doghter, stynt thyn hevynesse.   stynt: cease. hevynesse: sorrow.
Among the goddes hye it is affermed,
And by eterne word writen and confermed,   2350
Thou shalt ben wedded unto oon of tho   tho: those.
That han for thee so muche care and wo;
But unto which of hem I may nat telle.
Farwel, for I ne may no lenger dwelle.
The fires which that on myn auter brenne   2355
Shulle thee declaren, er that thou go henne,   henne: hence.
Thyn aventure of love, as in this cas."
And with that word, the arwes in the caas
Of the goddesse clateren faste and rynge,
And forth she wente, and made a
            vanysshynge;   2360
For which this Emelye astoned was,   astoned: stunned.
And seyde, "What amounteth this, allas?
I putte me in thy proteccioun,
Dyane, and in thy disposicioun."
And hoom she goth anon the nexte weye.   2365   nexte: nearest, shortest.
This is th'effect; ther is namoore to seye.   effect: upshot.
    The nexte houre of Mars folwynge this,
Arcite unto the temple walked is
Of fierse Mars, to doon his sacrifise,
With alle the rytes of his payen wyse.   2370   payen: pagan.
With pitous herte and heigh devocioun,
Right thus to Mars he seyde his orisoun.   orisoun: prayer.
    "O strong god, that in the regnes colde   regnes: kingdoms.
Of Trace honoured art and lord yholde,   yholde: esteemed to be.
And hast in every regne and every lond   2375
Of armes al the brydel in thyn hond,
And hem fortunest as thee lyst devyse,   hem fortunest: controls their destinies.
Accepte of me my pitous sacrifise.
If so be that my youthe may deserve,
And that my myght be worthy for to serve   2380
Thy godhede, that I may been oon of thyne,
Thanne preye I thee to rewe upon my pyne.   rewe: have pity. pyne: suffering.
For thilke peyne, and thilke hoote fir
In which thow whilom brendest for desir,
Whan that thow usedest the beautee   2385   usedest: enjoyed.
Of faire, yonge, fresshe Venus free,
And haddest hire in armes at thy wille—
Although thee ones on a tyme mysfille,   mysfille: it went amiss with.

Whan Vulcanus hadde caught thee in his las,   las: net.
And foond thee liggynge by his wyf, allas!— 2390 liggynge: lying.
For thilke sorwe that was in thyn herte,
Have routhe as wel upon my peynes smerte.   routhe: pity.
I am yong and unkonnynge, as thow woost,   unkonnynge: unskilful.
And, as I trowe, with love offended moost   offended: assailed; wounded.
That evere was any lyves creature;   2395 lyves: living.
For she that dooth me al this wo endure
Ne reccheth nevere wher I synke or fleete.   wher: whether. fleete: swim.
And wel I woot, er she me mercy heete,   heete: promise.
I moot with strengthe wynne hire in the place,   place: i.e., lists.
And, wel I woot, withouten help or grace   2400
Of thee, ne may my strengthe noght availle.
Thanne help me, lord, tomorwe in my bataille,
For thilke fyr that whilom brente thee,   brente: burned.
As wel as thilke fyr now brenneth me,
And do that I tomorwe have victorie.   2405
Myn be the travaille, and thyn be the glorie!   travaille: labor.
Thy sovereyn temple wol I moost honouren
Of any place, and alwey moost labouren
In thy plesaunce and in thy craftes stronge,
And in thy temple I wol my baner honge   2410 honge: hang.
And alle the armes of my compaignye;
And everemo, unto that day I dye,
Eterne fir I wol bifore thee fynde.   fynde: provide.
And eek to this avow I wol me bynde:
My beerd, myn heer, that hongeth long
        adoun,   2415
That nevere yet ne felte offensioun   offensioun: injury.
Of rasour nor of shere, I wol thee yive,
And ben thy trewe servant whil I lyve.
Now, lord, have routhe upon my sorwes soore;   routhe: pity.
Yif me the victorie, I aske thee namoore."   2420 yif: give.
    The preyere stynt of Arcita the stronge,   stynt: being ended.
The rynges on the temple dore that honge,
And eek the dores, clatereden ful faste,
Of which Arcita somwhat hym agaste.   hym agaste: took fright.
The fyres brenden upon the auter brighte,   2425
That it gan al the temple for to lighte;
A sweete smel anon the ground up yaf,
And Arcita anon his hand up haf,   haf: lifted.
And moore encens into the fyr he caste,
With othere rytes mo; and atte laste   2430
The statue of Mars bigan his hauberk rynge;   hauberk: armor for breast and back.
And with that soun he herde a murmurynge
Ful lowe and dym, and seyde thus, "Victorie!"

———

2389. Vulcan caught Mars lying with Venus.

For which he yaf to Mars honour and glorie.
And thus with joye and hope wel to fare   2435
Arcite anon unto his in is fare,   in: lodging. **fare:** gone.
As fayn as fowel is of the brighte sonne.   fowel: bird.
  And right anon swich strif ther is bigonne,
For thilke grauntyng, in the hevene above,
Bitwixe Venus, the goddesse of love,   2440
And Mars, the stierne god armypotente,
That Juppiter was bisy it to stente;
Til that the pale Saturnus the colde,
That knew so manye of aventures olde,
Foond in his olde experience an art   2445
That he ful soone hath plesed every part.   part: side.
As sooth is seyd, elde hath greet avantage;   elde: old age.
In elde is bothe wysdom and usage;   usage: experience.
Men may the olde atrenne, and noght atrede.   atrenne: outrun. **atrede:** outwit.
Saturne anon, to stynten strif and drede,   2450
Al be it that it is agayn his kynde,   agayn his kynde: against his nature.
Of al this strif he gan remedie fynde.
  "My deere doghter Venus," quod Saturne,   doghter: i.e., female descendant.
"My cours, that hath so wyde for to turne,
Hath moore power than woot any man.   2455
Myn is the drenchyng in the see so wan;   drenchyng: drowning.
Myn is the prison in the derke cote;   prison: imprisonment. **cote:** shed, hut.
Myn is the stranglyng and hangyng by the throte,
The murmure and the cherles rebellyng,
The groynynge, and the pryvee empoyson-   groynynge: grumbling.
       yng;   2460
I do vengeance and pleyn correccioun,   pleyn: full. **correccioun:** punishment.
Whil I dwelle in the signe of the leoun.   leoun: i.e., in the zodiac.
Myn is the ruyne of the hye halles,
The fallynge of the toures and of the walles
Upon the mynour or the carpenter.   2465
I slow Sampsoun, shakynge the piler;   slow: slew.
And myne be the maladyes colde,
The derke tresons, and the castes olde;   castes: plots.
My lookyng is the fader of pestilence.   lookyng: aspect.
Now weep namoore, I shal doon diligence   2470
That Palamon, that is thyn owene knyght,
Shal have his lady, as thou hast him hight.   hight: promised.
Though Mars shal helpe his knyght, yet nathelees
Bitwixe yow ther moot be some tyme pees,
Al be ye noght of o compleccioun,   2475 compleccioun: temperament.
That causeth al day swich divisioun.

2443. the colde: baleful; dominated by "cold" quality; see General Prologue, l. 420, note.
2454. The course or orbit of Saturn was the largest known in the Middle Ages.
2459. Perhaps this line refers to the Peasants' (**cherles**) Revolt (1381).
2462. Saturn is most malefic in Leo.

I am thyn aiel, redy at thy wille;   aiel: grandfather.
Weep now namoore, I wol thy lust fulfille."   lust: desire.
   Now wol I stynten of the goddes above,
Of Mars, and of Venus, goddesse of love,   2480
And telle yow as pleynly as I kan
The grete effect, for which that I bygan.   grete effect: culminating action.

EXPLICIT TERCIA PARS.
SEQUITUR PARS QUARTA.

   Greet was the feeste in Atthenes that day,
And eek the lusty seson of that May
Made every wight to been in swich plesaunce   2485
That al that Monday justen they and daunce,   justen: joust.
And spenden it in Venus heigh servyse.
And by the cause that they sholde ryse
Eerly, for to seen the grete fight,
Unto hir reste wenten they at nyght.   2490
And on the morwe, whan the day gan sprynge,
Of hors and harneys noyse and claterynge   harneys: arms.
Ther was in hostelryes al aboute;
And to the paleys rood ther many a route
Of lordes upon steedes and palfreys.   2495
Ther maystow seen devisynge of harneys   devisynge: fashioning.
So unkouth and so riche, and wroght so weel   unkouth: curious.
Of goldsmythrye, of browdynge, and of steel;   browdynge: embroidery.
The sheeldes brighte, testeres, and trappures,   testeres: head-pieces. trappures:
Gold-hewen helmes, hauberkes, cote-armures; 2500   trappings.
Lordes in paramentz on hir courseres,   paramentz: decorated robes.
Knyghtes of retenue, and eek squieres
Nailynge the speres, and helmes bokelynge;
Giggynge of sheeldes, with layneres lacynge   giggynge: fitting the arm-strap to a
(There as nede is they weren no thyng ydel); 2505   shield. layneres: thongs.
The fomy steedes on the golden brydel
Gnawynge, and faste the armurers also
With fyle and hamer prikynge to and fro;   prikynge: spurring; riding quickly.
Yemen on foote, and communes many oon   communes: common soldiers.
With shorte staves, thikke as they may goon; 2510
Pypes, trompes, nakers, clariounes,   nakers: kettle-drums.
That in the bataille blowen blody sounes;
The paleys ful of peple up and doun,
Heere thre, ther ten, holdynge hir questioun,   questioun: discussion.
Dyvynynge of thise Thebane knyghtes two.   2515   dyvynynge: guessing.
Somme seyden thus, somme seyde, "It shal be
      so";
Somme helden with hym with the blake berd,
Somme with the balled, somme with the thikke   balled: bald.
      herd;   herd: haired.
Somme seyde he looked grymme, and he wolde   he: that fellow.
      fighte:—

"He hath a sparth of twenty pound of
       wighte."   2520

sparth: battle-axe.

Thus was the halle ful of divynynge,

divynynge: guessing, opinion.

Longe after that the sonne gan to sprynge.
    The grete Theseus, that of his sleep awaked
With mynstralcie and noyse that was maked,
Heeld yet the chambre of his paleys riche,   2525
Til that the Thebane knyghtes, bothe yliche

yliche: equally.

Honured, were into the paleys fet.

fet: summoned.

Duc Theseus is at a wyndow set,
Arrayed right as he were a god in trone.

trone: throne.

The peple preesseth thiderward ful soone   2530
Hym for to seen, and doon heigh reverence,
And eek to herkne his heste and his sentence.

heste: command.

An heraud on a scaffold made an "Oo!"
Til al the noyse of the peple was ydo,

ydo: done, ended.

And whan he saugh the peple of noyse al
       stille,   2535
Thus shewed he the myghty dukes wille:
    "The lord hath of his heigh discrecioun
Considered that it were destruccioun
To gentil blood to fighten in the gyse
Of mortal bataille now in this emprise.   2540

emprise: enterprise, undertaking.

Wherfore, to shapen that they shal nat dye,

shapen: bring it about.

He wol his firste purpos modifye.
No man therfore, up peyne of los of lyf,

up: upon.

No maner shot, ne polax, ne short knyf

shot: arrow, dart, missile.

Into the lystes sende, or thider brynge;   2545
Ne short swerd, for to stoke with poynt bitynge,

stoke: stab.

No man ne drawe, ne bere it by his syde.
Ne no man shal unto his felawe ryde

felawe: adversary.

But o cours, with a sharpe ygrounde spere;
Foyne, if hym list, on foote, hymself to were.   2550

foyne: let him thrust. were: defend.

And he that is at meschief shal be take

at meschief: in distress.

And noght slayn, but he broght unto the stake
That shal ben ordeyned on either syde;

ordeyned: set up.

But thider he shal by force, and there abyde.

by force: perforce.

And if so falle the chieftayn be take   2555

falle: befall.

On outher syde, or elles sleen his make,

sleen: slay. make: match, opponent.

No lenger shal the turneiynge laste.
God spede you! gooth forth, and ley on faste!
With long swerd and with mace fighteth youre
       fille.
Gooth now youre wey, this is the lordes
       wille."   2560
    The voys of people touchede the hevene,
So loude cride they with murie stevene,

stevene: voice.

"God save swich a lord, that is so good,
He wilneth no destruccion of blood!"

wilneth: desires.

Up goon the trompes and the melodye,   2565
And to the lystes rit the compaignye,   rit: rides.
By ordinance, thurghout the citee large,
Hanged with clooth of gold, and nat with sarge.   sarge: serge.
    Ful lik a lord this noble duc gan ryde,
Thise two Thebans upon either syde;   2570
And after rood the queene, and Emelye,
And after that another compaignye
Of oon and oother, after hir degree.   after: according to.
And thus they passen thurghout the citee,
And to the lystes come they by tyme.   2575 by tyme: early.
It nas nat of the day yet fully pryme   pryme: 9 A.M. or earlier.
Whan set was Theseus ful riche and hye,
Ypolita the queene, and Emelye,
And othere ladys in degrees aboute.   degrees: tiers.
Unto the setes preesseth al the route.   2580
And westward, thurgh the gates under Marte,
Arcite, and eek the hondred of his parte,
With baner reed is entred right anon;
And in that selve moment Palamon   selve: same.
Is under Venus, estward in the place,   2585
With baner whyt, and hardy chiere and face.
In al the world, to seken up and doun,
So evene, withouten variacioun,   evene: equal.
Ther nere swiche compaignyes tweye;
For ther was noon so wys that koude seye   2590
That any hadde of oother avauntage
Of worthynesse, ne of estaat, ne age,
So evene were they chosen, for to gesse.
And in two renges faire they hem dresse.   renges: ranks. dresse: set in order.
Whan that hir names rad were everichon,   2595 rad: read.
That in hir nombre gyle were ther noon,   that: so that. gyle: deceit.
Tho were the gates shet, and cried was loude:
"Do now youre devoir, yonge knyghtes proude!"   devoir: duty.
    The heraudes lefte hir prikyng up and doun;   prikyng: spurring.
Now ryngen trompes loude and clarioun.   2600
Ther is namoore to seyn, but west and est
In goon the speres ful sadly in th'arest;   sadly: firmly. in th'arest: into the rest
In gooth the sharpe spore into the syde.   (for charging).
Ther seen men who kan juste and who kan ryde;
Ther shyveren shaftes upon sheeldes thikke; 2605
He feeleth thurgh the herte-spoon the prikke.
Up spryngen speres twenty foot on highte;   on highte: on high.
Out goon the swerdes as the silver brighte;
The helmes they tohewen and toshrede;
Out brest the blood with stierne stremes rede; 2610 brest: bursts. stierne: violent.

2606. herte-spoon: the spoon-shaped depression at the end of the breast-bone.
2609. tohewen and toshrede: hew to pieces and cut into shreds.

With myghty maces the bones they tobreste. tobreste: smash in pieces.
He thurgh the thikkeste of the throng gan
          threste;
Ther stomblen steedes stronge, and doun gooth
          al;
He rolleth under foot as dooth a bal;
He foyneth on his feet with his tronchoun, 2615 foyneth: thrusts. tronchoun: broken
And he hym hurtleth with his hors adoun;   shaft of a spear.
He thurgh the body is hurt and sithen ytake, sithen: afterwards.
Maugree his heed, and broght unto the stake:
As forward was, right there he moste abyde. forward: agreement.
Another lad is on that oother syde. 2620 lad is: is led.
And som tyme dooth hem Theseus to reste, dooth: causes.
Hem to refresshe and drynken, if hem leste.
Ful ofte a day han thise Thebanes two a day: that day.
Togydre ymet, and wroght his felawe wo;
Unhorsed hath ech oother of hem tweye. 2625 tweye: twice.
Ther nas no tygre in the vale of Galgopheye,
Whan that hir whelp is stole whan it is lite,
So crueel on the hunte as is Arcite on the hunte: toward the hunter.
For jelous herte upon this Palamon. upon: toward.
Ne in Belmarye ther nys so fel leon, 2630
That hunted is, or for his hunger wood, wood: raging.
Ne of his praye desireth so the blood,
As Palamon to sleen his foo Arcite.
The jelous strokes on hir helmes byte; jelous: furious.
Out renneth blood on bothe hir sydes rede. 2635
    Som tyme an ende ther is of every dede.
For er the sonne unto the reste wente,
The stronge kyng Emetreus gan hente
This Palamon, as he faught with Arcite,
And made his swerd depe in his flessh to
          byte; 2640
And by the force of twenty is he take,
Unyolden, and ydrawen to the stake. unyolden: without yielding.
And in the rescus of this Palamoun rescus: rescue, aid.
The stronge kyng Lygurge is born adoun,
And kyng Emetreus, for al his strengthe, 2645
Is born out of his sadel a swerdes lengthe,
So hitte him Palamoun er he were take;
But al for noght, he was broght to the stake.
His hardy herte myghte hym helpe naught:
He moste abyde, whan that he was caught, 2650
By force and eek by composicioun. composicioun: agreement.
    Who sorweth now but woful Palamoun,
That moot namoore goon agayn to fighte?
And whan that Theseus hadde seyn this sighte,

2618. maugree his heed: in spite of his resistance.

Unto the folk that foghten thus echon   2655
He cryde, "Hoo! namoore, for it is doon!
I wol be trewe juge, and nat partie.   partie: partisan.
Arcite of Thebes shal have Emelie,
That by his fortune hath hire faire ywonne."
Anon ther is a noyse of peple bigonne   2660
For joye of this, so loude and heighe withalle,
It semed that the lystes sholde falle.
    What kan now faire Venus doon above?
What seith she now? What dooth this queene of
        love,
But wepeth so, for wantynge of hir wille,   2665
Til that hir teeres in the lystes fille?
She seyde, "I am ashamed, doutelees."   ashamed: disgraced.
    Saturnus seyde, "Doghter, hoold thy pees!
Mars hath his wille, his knyght hath al his
        boone.   boone: request.
And, by myn heed, thow shalt been esed   esed: compensated.
        soone."   2670
    The trompours, with the loude mynstralcie,   trompours: trumpeters.
The heraudes, that ful loude yelle and crie,
Been in hire wele for joye of daun Arcite.   been in hire wele: are merry.
But herkneth me, and stynteth noyse a lite,
Which a myracle ther bifel anon.   2675   which a: how great a.
    This fierse Arcite hath of his helm ydon,   fierse: bold. of ydon: taken off, doffed.
And on a courser, for to shewe his face,
He priketh endelong the large place   endelong: through the length of.
Lokynge upward upon this Emelye;
And she agayn hym caste a freendlich eye   2680   agayn: toward.
(For wommen, as to speken in comune,   in comune: generally.
They folwen al the favour of Fortune)
And was al his chiere, as in his herte.   chiere: joy.
    Out of the ground a furie infernal sterte,
From Pluto sent at requeste of Saturne,   2685
For which his hors for fere gan to turne,
And leep aside, and foundred as he leep;   leep: leapt. foundred: stumbled.
And er that Arcite may taken keep,
He pighte hym on the pomel of his heed,   pighte: pitched. pomel: top.
That in the place he lay as he were deed,   2690
His brest tobrosten with his sadel-bowe.   tobrosten: broken in two; crushed.
As blak he lay as any cole or crowe,
So was the blood yronnen in his face.   yronnen: coagulated.
Anon he was yborn out of the place,   yborn: carried.
With herte soor, to Theseus paleys.   2695
Tho was he korven out of his harneys,   tho: then. korven: cut. harneys: armor.
And in a bed ybrought ful faire and blyve;   blyve: quickly.
For he was yet in memorie and alyve,   in memorie: conscious.
And alwey criynge after Emelye.
    Duc Theseus, with al his compaignye,   2700

Is comen hoom to Atthenes his citee,
With alle blisse and greet solempnitee.
Al be it that this aventure was falle,
He nolde noght disconforten hem alle.   disconforten: dishearten.
Men seyde eek that Arcite shal nat dye;   2705
He shal been heeled of his maladye.   heeled: healed.
And of another thyng they weren as fayn,
That of hem alle was ther noon yslayn,
Al were they soore yhurt, and namely oon,
That with a spere was thirled his brest boon. 2710 thirled: pierced.
To othere woundes and to broken armes
Somme hadden salves, and somme hadden
      charmes;
Fermacies of herbes, and eek save   fermacies: medicines. **save:** a decoc-
They dronken, for they wolde hir lymes have.   tion of herbs.
For which this noble duc, as he wel kan,   2715
Conforteth and honoureth every man,
And made revel al the longe nyght
Unto the straunge lordes, as was right.   straunge: foreign.
Ne ther was holden no disconfitynge   disconfitynge: defeat in battle.
But as a justes, or a tourneiynge;   2720
For soothly ther was no disconfiture.
For fallyng nys nat but an aventure,
Ne to be lad by force unto the stake   lad: led.
Unyolden, and with twenty knyghtes take,   unyolden: without having yielded.
O persone allone, withouten mo,   2725
And haryed forth by arme, foot, and too,   haryed: dragged, pulled violently.
And eke his steede dryven forth with staves
With footmen, bothe yemen and eek knaves,—   knaves: servants.
It nas arretted hym no vileynye;   arretted: imputed.
Ther may no man clepen it cowardye.   2730   vileynye: disgrace.
For which anon duc Theseus leet crye,   leet crye: caused to be proclaimed.
To stynten alle rancour and envye,   envye: enmity.
The gree as wel of o syde as of oother,   gree: victory.
And eyther syde ylik as ootheres brother;   ylik: alike, equal.
And yaf hem yiftes after hir degree,   2735 yiftes: gifts.
And fully heeld a feeste dayes three,
And conveyed the kynges worthily
Out of his toun a journee largely.   journee: day's journey. **largely:** fully.
And hoom wente every man the righte way.   righte: direct.
Ther was namoore but "Fare wel, have good
      day!"   2740
Of this bataille I wol namoore endite,
But speke of Palamon and of Arcite.
    Swelleth the brest of Arcite, and the soore
Encreesseth at his herte moore and moore.
The clothered blood, for any lechecraft,   2745 clothered: clotted.

2714. **lymes:** a limb was any organ, part, or member of the body.

Corrupteth, and is in his bouk ylaft,   bouk: trunk. ylaft: left.
That neither veyne-blood, ne ventusynge,
Ne drynke of herbes may ben his helpynge.
The vertu expulsif, or animal,
Fro thilke vertu cleped natural   2750
Ne may the venym voyden ne expelle.
The pipes of his longes gonne to swelle,   longes: lungs.
And every lacerte in his brest adoun   lacerte: muscle.
Is shent with venym and corrupcioun.   shent: infected.
Hym gayneth neither, for to gete his lif,   2755 gayneth: helps.
Vomyt upward, ne dounward laxatif.
Al is tobrosten thilke regioun;   tobrosten: shattered.
Nature hath no dominacioun.
And certeinly, ther Nature wol nat wirche,   wirche: work.
Fare wel phisik! go ber the man to chirche!   2760 phisik: medical science.
This al and som, that Arcita moot dye;   this: this is.
For which he sendeth after Emelye,
And Palamon, that was his cosyn deere.
Thanne seyde he thus, as ye shal after heere:
"Naught may the woful spirit in myn herte   2765
Declare o point of alle my sorwes smerte
To yow, my lady, that I love moost;
But I biquethe the servyce of my goost   goost: spirit.
To yow aboven every creature,
Syn that my lyf may no lenger dure.   2770 dure: last.
Allas, the wo! allas, the peynes stronge,
That I for yow have suffred, and so longe!
Allas, the deeth! allas, myn Emelye!
Allas, departynge of oure compaignye!   departynge: separation.
Allas, myn hertes queene! allas, my wyf!   2775
Myn hertes lady, endere of my lyf!
What is this world? what asketh men to have?   men: one.
Now with his love, now in his colde grave
Allone, withouten any compaignye.
Fare wel, my sweete foo, myn Emelye!   2780
And softe taak me in youre armes tweye,
For love of God, and herkneth what I seye.
    I have heer with my cosyn Palamon
Had strif and rancour many a day agon
For love of yow, and for my jalousye.   2785
And Juppiter so wys my soule gye,   wys: surely. gye: guide.
To speken of a servaunt proprely,   servaunt: lover.
With circumstances alle trewely—
That is to seyen, trouthe, honour, knyghthede,

2747. That neither bloodletting nor cupping.
2749–51. In terms of medieval physiology, the "animal virtue" of Arcite's body was unable to re-
move or expel the poison from the "natural virtue," which controlled breathing.
2788. Faithfully in every respect.

Wysdom, humblesse, estaat, and heigh
    kynrede, 2790
Fredom, and al that longeth to that art—
So Juppiter have of my soule part,
As in this world right now ne knowe I non
So worthy to ben loved as Palamon,
That serveth yow, and wol doon al his lyf. 2795
And if that evere ye shul ben a wyf,
Foryet nat Palamon, the gentil man."
And with that word his speche faille gan,
For from his feet up to his brest was come
The coold of deeth, that hadde hym over-
    come, 2800
And yet mooreover, for in his armes two
The vital strengthe is lost and al ago.
Oonly the intellect, withouten moore,
That dwelled in his herte syk and soore,
Gan faillen whan the herte felte deeth. 2805
Dusked his eyen two, and failled breeth,
But on his lady yet caste he his eye;
His laste word was, "Mercy, Emelye!"
His spirit chaunged hous and wente ther
As I cam nevere, I kan nat tellen wher. 2810
Therfore I stynte, I nam no divinistre;
Of soules fynde I nat in this registre,
Ne me ne list thilke opinions to telle
Of hem, though that they writen wher they
    dwelle.
Arcite is coold, ther Mars his soule gye! 2815
Now wol I speken forth of Emelye.

    Shrighte Emelye, and howleth Palamon,
And Theseus his suster took anon
Swownynge, and baar hire fro the corps away.
What helpeth it to tarien forth the day 2820
To tellen how she weep bothe eve and morwe?
For in swich cas wommen have swich sorwe,
Whan that hir housbondes ben from hem ago,
That for the moore part they sorwen so,
Or ellis fallen in swich a maladye, 2825
That at the laste certeinly they dye.

    Infinite been the sorwes and the teeres
Of olde folk, and folk of tendre yeeres,
In al the toun for deeth of this Theban.
For hym ther wepeth bothe child and man; 2830
So greet wepyng was ther noon, certayn,

Glosses (right column):

humblesse: humility.
kynrede: kindred.
fredom: generosity.

ago: gone.

dusked: grew dim.

ther as: where.

divinistre: diviner.
registre: written record.

ther: i.e., may. gye: protect.

shrighte: shrieked.

tarien: delay, waste.
weep: wept.

ago: gone.

2792. of my soule part: interest in, concern for, my soul.
2801. yet mooreover: there is yet more to be said.
2803–5. oonly the intellect gan failen whan: the intellect failed only when.

Whan Ector was ybroght, al fressh yslayn,
To Troye. Allas, the pitee that was ther,
Cracchynge of chekes, rentynge eek of heer.　　cracchynge: scratching. **rentynge:**
"Why woldestow be deed," thise wommen　　　　rending, tearing.
　　　　　crye,　　　　　　　　　　　　　2835
"And haddest gold ynough, and Emelye?"
　　No man myghte gladen Theseus,
Savynge his olde fader Egeus,
That knew this worldes transmutacioun,
As he hadde seyn it up and doun,　　　　　2840
Joye after wo, and wo after gladnesse,
And shewed hem ensample and liknesse.　　liknesse: parable.
　　"Right as ther dyed nevere man," quod he,
"That he ne lyvede in erthe in som degree,
Right so ther lyvede never man," he seyde,　2845
"In al this world, that som tyme he ne deyde.
This world nys but a thurghfare ful of wo,
And we been pilgrymes, passynge to and fro.
Deeth is an ende of every worldly soore."　　soore: pain, sorrow, misery.
And over al this yet seyde he muchel moore　2850
To this effect, ful wisely to enhorte　　　　enhorte: exhort.
The peple that they sholde hem reconforte.　hem reconforte: recover their spirits.
　　Duc Theseus, with al his bisy cure,　　　bisy: diligent. **cure:** care.
Caste now wher that the sepulture　　　　　caste: considered. **sepulture:** i.e.,
Of goode Arcite may best ymaked be,　　　2855　funeral.
And eek moost honurable in his degree.　　　in his degree: according to his rank.
And at the laste he took conclusioun
That ther as first Arcite and Palamoun
Hadden for love the bataille hem bitwene,
That in the selve grove, swoote and grene,　2860　selve: same. **swoote:** sweet.
Ther as he hadde his amorouse desires,
His compleynte, and for love his hoote fires,
He wolde make a fyr in which the office
Funeral he myghte al accomplice.
And leet anon comande to hakke and hewe　2865　leet comande: had men commanded.
The okes olde, and leye hem on a rewe　　　rewe: row.
In colpons wel arrayed for to brenne.　　　colpons: pieces, chunks.
His officers with swifte feet they renne　　　renne: run.
And ryde anon at his comandement.
And after this, Theseus hath ysent　　　　2870
After a beere, and it al over spradde　　　beere: bier.
With clooth of gold, the richeste that he hadde.
And of the same suyte he cladde Arcite;　　suyte: material.
Upon his hondes his gloves white,
Eek on his heed a coroune of laurer grene,　2875
And in his hond a swerd ful bright and kene.
He leyde hym, bare the visage, on the beere;
Therwith he weep that pitee was to heere.　weep: wept.
And for the peple sholde seen hym alle,　　for: so that.

Whan it was day, he broghte hym to the
      halle,   2880
That roreth of the criyng and the soun.
  Tho cam this woful Theban Palamoun,
With flotery berd and ruggy, asshy heeres,   flotery: fluttering. **ruggy**: rough.
In clothes blake, ydropped al with teeres;
And, passynge othere of wepynge, Emelye,   2885
The rewefulleste of al the compaignye.
In as muche as the servyce sholde be
The moore noble and riche in his degree,   in his degree: according to his rank.
Duc Theseus leet forth thre steedes brynge,   leet brynge: caused to be brought.
That trapped were in steel al gliterynge,   2890
And covered with the armes of daun Arcite.   armes: coat of arms.
Upon thise steedes, grete and white,
Ther seten folk, of whiche oon baar his sheeld,   seten: sat.
Another his spere up on his hondes heeld,
The thridde baar with hym his bowe Turkeys 2895 Turkeys: Turkish.
(Of brend gold was the caas and eek the   brend: refined, pure.
      harneys);   harneys: fittings.
And riden forth a paas with sorweful cheere   riden: rode.
Toward the grove, as ye shul after heere.
The nobleste of the Grekes that ther were
Upon hir shuldres caryeden the beere,   2900
With slakke paas, and eyen rede and wete,   slakke: slow.
Thurghout the citee by the maister strete,
That sprad was al with blak, and wonder hye
Right of the same is the strete ywrye.   ywrye: covered.
Upon the right hond wente olde Egeus,   2905
And on that oother syde duc Theseus,
With vessels in hir hand of gold ful fyn,
Al ful of hony, milk, and blood, and wyn;
Eek Palamon, with ful greet compaignye;
And after that cam woful Emelye,   2910
With fyr in honde, as was that tyme the gyse,
To do the office of funeral servyse.
  Heigh labour and ful greet apparaillynge   apparaillynge: preparation.
Was at the service and the fyr-makynge,
That with his grene top the hevene raughte; 2915 raughte: reached.
And twenty fadme of brede the armes straughte,   brede: breadth. **straughte**: stretched.
This is to seyn, the bowes weren so brode.   bowes: boughs.
Of stree first ther was leyd many a lode.   stree: straw.
But how the fyr was maked upon highte,   upon highte: on high.
Ne eek the names how the trees highte,   2920 highte: were called.
As ook, firre, birch, aspe, alder, holm, popler,   holm: holm-oak.
Wylugh, elm, plane, assh, box, chasteyn, lynde,   wylugh: willow. **chasteyn**: chestnut.
      laurer,
Mapul, thorn, bech, hasel, ew, whippeltree,—   whippeltree: cornel-tree.
How they weren feld, shal nat be toold for me;
Ne hou the goddes ronnen up and doun,   2925 ronnen: ran.

Disherited of hire habitacioun,
In whiche they woneden in reste and pees,   woneden: dwelt.
Nymphes, fawnes, and amadrides;   fawnes: fauns. amadrides: hama-
Ne hou the beestes and the briddes alle   dryads.
Fledden for fere, whan the wode was falle;   2930 falle: felled.
Ne how the ground agast was of the light,
That was nat wont to seen the sonne bright;
Ne how the fyr was couched first with stree,   couched: laid.
And thanne with drye stikkes cloven a thre,   a: in.
And thanne with grene wode and spicerye,   2935 spicerye: spices.
And thanne with clooth of gold and with perrye,   perrye: precious stones; jewelry.
And gerlandes, hangynge with ful many a flour;
The mirre, th'encens, with al so greet odour;
Ne how Arcite lay among al this,
Ne what richesse aboute his body is;   2940
Ne how that Emelye, as was the gyse,
Putte in the fyr of funeral servyse;
Ne how she swowned whan men made the fyr,
Ne what she spak, ne what was hir desir;
Ne what jeweles men in the fyre caste,   2945
Whan that the fyr was greet and brente faste;
Ne how somme caste hir sheeld, and somme hir
        spere,
And of hire vestimentz, whiche that they were,   were: wore.
And coppes fulle of milk, and wyn, and blood,
Into the fyr, that brente as it were wood;   2950
Ne how the Grekes, with an huge route,
Thries riden al the fyr aboute   thries: thrice. riden: rode.
Upon the left hand, with a loud shoutynge,
And thries with hir speres claterynge;
And thries how the ladyes gonne crye;   2955
And how that lad was homward Emelye;   lad: led.
Ne how Arcite is brent to asshen colde;
Ne how that lyche-wake was yholde   lyche-wake: wake over a corpse.
Al thilke nyght; ne how the Grekes pleye   yholde: held.
The wake-pleyes, ne kepe I nat to seye;   2960 wake-pleyes: funeral games. kepe:
Who wrastleth best naked with oille enoynt.   care. enoynt: anointed.
Ne who that baar hym best in no disjoynt.   disjoynt: dilemma.
I wol nat tellen how they alle goon
Hoom til Atthenes, whan the pley is doon;
But shortly to the point thanne wol I wende,   2965
And maken of my longe tale an ende.
   By processe and by lengthe of certeyn yeres,   by processe: in the course.
Al stynted is the moornynge and the teres   certeyn: a certain number of.
Of Grekes, by oon general assent.
Thanne semed me ther was a parlement   2970 parlement: deliberation.
At Atthenes, upon certein pointz and caas;   caas: matters.
Among the whiche pointz yspoken was,
To have with certein contrees alliaunce,

And have fully of Thebans obeisaunce.   obeisaunce: submission.
For which this noble Theseus anon   2975
Leet senden after gentil Palamon,   leet senden: i.e., sent.
Unwist of hym what was the cause and why;
But in his blake clothes sorwefully
He cam at his comandement in hye.   in hye: in haste.
Tho sente Theseus for Emelye.   2980
Whan they were set, and hust was al the place, hust: hushed.
And Theseus abiden hath a space   a space: a while.
Er any word cam fram his wise brest,
His eyen sette he ther as was his lest,   lest: pleasure.
And with a sad visage he siked stille,   2985 siked stille: sighed softly.
And after that right thus he seyde his wille:
 "The Firste Moevere of the cause above,
Whan he first made the faire cheyne of love,
Greet was th'effect, and heigh was his entente.
Wel wiste he why, and what therof he mente; 2990
For with that faire cheyne of love he bond   bond: joined together.
The fyr, the eyr, the water, and the lond
In certeyn boundes, that they may nat flee.
That same Prince and that Moevere—quod he—
Hath stablissed in this wrecched world adoun 2995 adoun: below.
Certeyne dayes and duracioun
To al that is engendred in this place,
Over the whiche day they may nat pace,
Al mowe they yet tho dayes abregge.   mowe: may. abregge: shorten.
Ther nedeth noon auctoritee t'allegge.   3000
For it is preeved by experience,
But that me list declaren my sentence.
Thanne may men wel by this ordre discerne
That thilke Moevere stable is and eterne. stable: unchangeable. eterne: eternal.
Wel may men knowe, but it be a fool,   3005
That every part dirryveth from his hool;
For nature hath nat taken his bigynnyng
Of no partie or cantel of a thyng,   partie: part. cantel: portion.
But of a thyng that parfit is and stable,
Descendynge so til it be corrumpable. 3010 corrumpable: corruptible.
And therefore, for his wise purveiaunce,   purveiaunce: providence.
He hath so wel biset his ordinaunce,   biset: planned.
That speces of thynges and progressiouns
Shullen enduren by successiouns,   enduren: live.
And nat eterne, withouten any lye.   3015
This maystow understonde and seen at eye. at eye: manifestly.
 Loo the ook, that hath so long a norisshynge
Fro the tyme that it first bigynneth sprynge,
And hath so long a lif, as ye may see,

2992. The four elements.

Yet at the laste wasted is the tree.   3020
   Considereth eek how that the harde stoon
Under oure feet, on which we trede and goon,
Yet wasteth it as it lyth by the weye.
The brode ryver somtyme wexeth dreye;   **wexeth: becomes.**
The grete tounes se we wane and wende.   3025 **wende: pass away.**
Thanne ye se that al this thyng hath ende.
   Of man and womman seen we wel also
That nedes, in oon of thise termes two,
This is to seyn, in youthe or elles age,
He moot be deed, the kyng as shal a page;   3030
Som in his bed, som in the depe see,
Som in the large feeld, as ye may see;
Ther helpeth noght, al goth that ilke weye.
Thanne may I seyn that al this thyng moot deye.
   What maketh this but Juppiter, the kyng,   3035
That is prince and cause of alle thyng,
Convertynge al unto his propre welle
From which it is dirryved, sooth to telle?
And heer-agayns no creature on lyve,   **on lyve: alive.**
Of no degree, availleth for to stryve.   3040
   Thanne is it wysdom, as it thynketh me,   **thynketh me: seems to me.**
To maken vertu of necessitee,
And take it weel that we may nat eschue,   **it that: that which.**
And namely that to us alle is due.
And whoso gruccheth ought, he dooth folye, 3045 **gruccheth: murmurs. ought: at all.**
And rebel is to hym that al may gye.   **gye: govern.**
And certeinly a man hath moost honour
To dyen in his excellence and flour,
Whan he is siker of his goode name;   **siker: sure.**
Thanne hath he doon his freend, ne hym, no **hym: himself.**
       shame.   3050
And gladder oghte his freend been of his deeth,
Whan with honour is yolden up his breeth,   **yolden: yielded.**
Than whan his name apalled is for age,   **apalled: dimmed.**
For al forgeten is his vassellage.   **vassellage: prowess.**
Thanne is it best, as for a worthy fame,   3055
To dyen whan that he is best of name.
   The contrarie of al this is wilfulnesse.
Why grucchen we, why have we hevynesse,   **hevynesse: sorrow.**
That goode Arcite, of chivalrie flour,
Departed is with duetee and honour   3060 **duetee: due respect.**
Out of this foule prisoun of this lyf?
Why grucchen heere his cosyn and his wyf
Of his welfare, that loveth hem so weel?
Kan he hem thank? Nay, God woot, never a
       deel,

3037. Causing everything to return to its own source.

That both his soule and eek hemself offende, 3065 hemself: themselves.
And yet they mowe hir lustes nat amende. hir lustes: their desires. **amende:**
    What may I conclude of this longe serye, change. **serye:** process.
But after wo I rede us to be merye, rede: advise, counsel.
And thanken Juppiter of al his grace?
And er we departen from this place   3070
I rede we make of sorwes two
O parfit joye, lastynge everemo. o: one.
And looketh now, wher moost sorwe is herinne,
Ther wol I first amenden and bigynne.
    Suster,—quod he—this is my fulle assent, 3075 assent: opinion.
With all th'avys heere of my parlement, avys: advice.
That gentil Palamon, youre owene knyght,
That serveth yow with wille, herte, and myght,
And ever hath doon syn ye first hym knewe,
That ye shul of youre grace upon hym rewe, 3080 rewe: have pity.
And taken hym for housbonde and for lord.
Lene me youre hond, for this is oure accord. lene: give. **accord:** agreement.
Lat se now of youre wommanly pitee.
He is a kynges brother sone, pardee; brother: brother's. **pardee:** *pardieu,*
And though he were a povre bacheler,   3085 certainly.
Syn he hath served yow so many a yeer,
And had for yow so greet adversitee,
It moste been considered, leeveth me; leeveth: believe.
For gentil mercy oghte to passen right." passen: surpass, transcend.
    Thanne seyde he thus to Palamon the
        knight: 3090
"I trowe ther nedeth litel sermonyng
To make yow assente to this thyng.
Com neer, and taak youre lady by the hond."
Bitwixen hem was maad anon the bond
That highte matrimoigne or mariage,   3095
By al the conseil and the baronage. conseil: council.
And thus with alle blisse and melodye
Hath Palamon ywedded Emelye.
And God, that al this world hath wroght,
Sende hym his love that hath it deere hym that: to him (whatever man) who.
      aboght;   3100 deere: dearly.
For now is Palamon in alle wele,
Lyvynge in blisse, in richesse, and in heele, heele: happiness, prosperity.
And Emelye hym loveth so tendrely,
And he hire serveth so gentilly,
That nevere was ther no word hem bitwene 3105
Of jalousie or any oother teene. teene: vexation.
Thus endeth Palamon and Emelye;
And God save al this faire compaignye! Amen.

      Heere is ended
      the Knyghtes tale.

Heere folwen the wordes
bitwene the Hoost and
the Millere

Whan that the Knyght had thus his tale
    ytoold,
In al the route nas ther yong ne oold   3110   route: company.
That he ne seyde it was a noble storie,
And worthy for to drawen to memorie;   drawen to memorie: remember.
And namely the gentils everichon.   namely: especially.
Oure Hooste lough and swoor, "So moot I gon,   lough: laughed. so moot I: as I hope
This gooth aright; unbokeled is the male.   3115   to. male: bag.
Lat se now who shal telle another tale;
For trewely the game is wel bigonne.
Now telleth ye, sir Monk, if that ye konne   konne: know.
Somwhat to quite with the Knyghtes tale."   to quite with: with which to match.
The Millere, that for dronken was al pale,   3120   for dronken: because of being drunk.
So that unnethe upon his hors he sat,   unnethe: hardly.
He nolde avalen neither hood ne hat,   avalen: doff, take off.
Ne abyde no man for his curteisie,   abyde: wait for.
But in Pilates voys he gan to crie,
And swoor, "By armes, and by blood and   armes: (Christ's) arms.
    bones,   3125
I kan a noble tale for the nones,   kan: know.
With which I wol now quite the Knyghtes
    tale."
Oure Hooste saugh that he was dronke of ale,
And seyde, "Abyd, Robyn, my leeve brother;   leeve: dear.
Som bettre man shal telle us first another.   3130
Abyd, and lat us werken thriftily."   thriftily: properly.
    "By Goddes soule," quod he, "that wol nat I;
For I wol speke, or elles go my wey."
Oure Hoost answerde, "Tel on, a devel wey!   a devel wey!: what the devil! etc.
Thou art a fool; thy wit is overcome."   3135
    "Now herkneth," quod the Millere, "alle and
    some!
But first I make a protestacioun
That I am dronke, I knowe it by my soun;   soun: sound (of his voice).
And therfore if that I mysspeke or seye,   seye: i.e., missay.
Wyte it the ale of Southwerk, I you preye.   3140   wyte it: blame it on.
For I wol telle a legende and a lyf
Bothe of a carpenter and of his wyf,
How that a clerk hath set the wrightes cappe."

3113. gentils: those of gentle birth; the well-bred.
3124. Pilates voys: a high, falsetto voice, like that used by the Subdeacon of the Mass in singing Pilate's words.
3143. set the wrightes cappe: made a fool of the carpenter.

The Reve answerde and seyde, "Stynt thy
    clappe!

clappe: noise, chatter.

Lat be thy lewed dronken harlotrye.   3145

lewed: low, vulgar. harlotrye: ribaldry.

It is a synne and eek a greet folye
To apeyren any man, or hym defame,

apeyren: impair, injure.

And eek to bryngen wyves in swich fame.
Thou mayst ynogh of othere thynges seyn."
    This dronke Millere spak ful soone
    ageyn   3150

ageyn: in reply.

And seyde, "Leve brother Osewold,
Who hath no wyf, he is no cokewold.

cokewold: cuckold.

But I sey nat therfore that thou art oon;
Ther been ful goode wyves many oon,
And evere a thousand goode ayeyns oon

ayeyns: to.

    badde.   3155
That knowestow wel thyself, but if thou
    madde.

madde: are mad.

Why artow angry with my tale now?
I have a wyf, pardee, as wel as thow;

pardee: *pardieu,* certainly.

Yet nolde I, for the oxen in my plogh,
Take upon me moore than ynogh,   3160
As demen of myself that I were oon;
I wol bileve wel that I am noon.
An housbonde shal nat been inquisityf
Of Goddes pryvetee, nor of his wyf.

pryvetee: private affairs (for wife: private parts). foyson: plenty.

So he may fynde Goddes foyson there,   3165
Of the remenant nedeth nat enquere."
    What sholde I moore seyn, but this Millere
He nolde his wordes for no man forbere,

forbere: spare.

But tolde his cherles tale in his manere.

cherles: churl's, rough person's.

M'athynketh that I shal reherce it heere.   3170

m'athynketh: I regret. shal: must.

And therfore every gentil wight I preye,
Demeth nat, for Goddes love, that I seye
Of yvel entente, but for I moot reherce
Hir tales alle, be they bettre or werse,
Or elles falsen som of my mateere.   3175
And therfore, whoso list it nat yheere,

list: desires. yheere: to hear.

Turne over the leef and chese another tale;

chese: choose.

For he shal fynde ynowe, grete and smale,
Of storial thyng that toucheth gentillesse,

storial: historical.

And eek moralitee and hoolynesse.   3180
Blameth nat me if that ye chese amys.
The Millere is a cherl, ye knowe wel this;
So was the Reve eek and othere mo,
And harlotrie they tolden bothe two.

harlotrie: wickedness, ribaldry.

Avyseth yow, and put me out of blame;   3185

avyseth yow: take thought.

And eek men shal nat maken ernest of
    game.

ernest of game: seriousness out of sport.

Heere bigynneth the
Millere his tale.

Whilom ther was dwellynge in Oxenford   Oxenford: Oxford.
A riche gnof, that gestes heeld to bord,   gnof: lout, churl.
And of his craft he was a carpenter.
With hym ther was dwellynge a poure scoler, 3190
Hadde lerned art, but al his fantasye   hadde: (who) had. fantasye: desire.
Was turned for to lerne astrologye,
And koude a certeyn of conclusiouns,
To demen by interrogaciouns,
If that men asked hym in certein houres   3195
Whan that men sholde have droghte or elles
      shoures,
Or if men asked hym what sholde bifalle
Of every thyng; I may nat rekene hem alle.
    This clerk was cleped hende Nicholas.
Of deerne love he koude and of solas;   3200 deerne: secret. solas: pleasure.
And therto he was sleigh and ful privee,   sleigh: sly, crafty.
And lyk a mayden meke for to see.   for to see: to look at.
A chambre hadde he in that hostelrye   hostelrye: lodging house.
Allone, withouten any compaignye,
Ful fetisly ydight with herbes swoote;   3205 fetisly: neatly, handsomely.
And he hymself as sweete as is the roote   ydight: arrayed. swoote: sweet.
Of lycorys, or any cetewale.   cetewale: zedoary, a plant related to
His *Almageste,* and bookes grete and smale,   ginger.
His astrelabie, longynge for his art,   longynge for: belonging to. art: i.e.,
His augrym stones layen faire apart,   3210 astronomy.
On shelves couched at his beddes heed;   couched: set.
His presse ycovered with a faldyng reed;   faldyng: coarse woolen cloth.
And al above ther lay a gay sautrie,
On which he made a-nyghtes melodie
So swetely that all the chambre rong;   3215
And *Angelus ad virginem* he song;
And after that he song *The Kynges Noote.*   *The Kynges Noote:* an unidentified
    medieval song or hymn.

---

the Millere his tale. The Miller's Tale has its roots in the brilliant tradition of the French fabliaux, brief verse narratives with simple, direct plots, stock characters (the loose wife, the duped priest, the clever student, etc.), and broad rapid comic effect. Chaucer's poem develops the genre with careful attention to the rounding of the personalities of the characters, the presentation of realistic setting and atmosphere, and the interweaving of such motifs as religion, music, and fire.

3191. **art:** the subject matter of the "seven arts" of the medieval curriculum.

3193–94. He knew a certain number of propositions to decide questions by.

3199. For the epithet **hende,** so often applied to Nicholas, see Basic Glossary.

3208. *Almageste:* the famous astronomical treatise by Ptolemy.

3209. **astrelabie:** astrolabe, an instrument used for observation of heavenly bodies.

3210. **augrym stones:** marked counters used for calculations on a ruled table, the medieval "line abacus."

3212. **presse:** a large clothes cupboard, with shelves.

3213. **sautrie:** psaltery, a medieval stringed instrument played like a harp.

3216. *Angelus ad virginem:* a medieval anthem on the Annunciation.

Ful often blessed was his myrie throte.
And thus this sweete clerk his tyme spente
After his freends fyndyng and his rente.   3220 after: according to. fynding: provision.
      rente: income. newe: newly.
  This carpenter hadde wedded newe a wyf,
Which that he lovede moore than his lyf;
Of eighteteene yeer she was of age.
Jalous he was, and heeld hir narwe in cage,   heeld hire narwe in cage: kept her
For she was yong and wilde and he was old, 3225 closely confined.
And demed hymself been lik a cokewold.   been lik: likely to be made.
He knew nat Catoun, for his wit was rude,   rude: uneducated.
That bad men sholde wedde his simylitude.   bad: bade. simylitude: counterpart.
Men sholde wedden after hire estaat,
For youthe and elde is often at debaat.   3230 elde: old age. debaat: conflict.
But sith that he was fallen in the snare,
He moste endure, as oother folk, his care.   care: woe; misfortune.
  Fair was this yonge wyf, and therwithal
As any wezele hir body gent and smal.   gent: slender, graceful.
A ceynt she werede, barred al of silk,   3235 ceynt: cincture, sash.
A barmclooth as whit as morne milk   barmclooth: apron. morne: morning.
Upon hir lendes, ful of many a goore.   lendes: loins.
Whit was hir smok, and broyden al bifoore   smok: smock; chemise. broyden: em-
And eek bihynde, on hir coler aboute,   broidered. coler: collar.
Of col-blak silk, withinne and eek withoute. 3240
The tapes of hir white voluper   voluper: cap.
Were of the same suyte of hir coler;   suyte: material.
Hir filet brood of silk, and set ful hye.
And sikerly she hadde a likerous eye;   likerous: lecherous.
Ful smale ypulled were hire browes two, 3245 ypulled: plucked.
And tho were bent, and blake as any sloo.   tho: those.
She was ful moore blisful on to see
Than is the newe pere-jonette tree,   pere-jonette: early pear.
And softer than the wolle is of a wether.   wether: ram.
And by hir girdel heeng a purs of lether, 3250 girdel: belt.
Tasseled with silk, and perled with latoun.   perled: studded. latoun: an alloy re-
In al this world, to seken up and doun,   sembling brass.
There nys no man so wys that koude thenche thenche: imagine.
So gay a popelote or swich a wenche.   popelote: doll.
Ful brighter was the shynyng of hir hewe 3255 hewe: complexion.
Than in the Tour the noble yforged newe.
But of hir song, it was as loude and yerne   of: as for. yerne: eager, lively.

3227. **Catoun:** Dionysius Cato, supposed author of a collection of Latin maxims studied in medieval schools.
3228. **men:** man, one (indefinite singular; "man" with unstressed vowel).
3229. **after hire estaat:** according to their rank or condition.
3237. **goore:** gore; a wedge-shaped section of a garment (wider at the bottom than the top); or a skirt or petticoat.
3246. **sloo:** sloe; the fruit of the blackthorn, which is purplish or bluish black.
3256. **Tour:** the Tower of London, where gold nobles and other coins were minted. From 1389 to 1391 Chaucer had charge of the upkeep of the Tower.

As any swalwe sittynge on a berne.   berne: barn.
Therto she koude skippe and make game,
As any kyde or calf folwynge his dame.   3260 dame: dam, mother.
Hir mouth was sweete as bragot or the meeth,
Or hoord of apples leyd in hey or heeth.   heeth: heather.
Wynsynge she was, as is a joly colt,   wynsynge: skittish. joly: gay, wanton.
Long as a mast, and upright as a bolt.   upright: straight.
A brooch she baar upon hir lowe coler,   3265 baar: wore.
As brood as is the boos of a bokeler.
Hir shoes were laced on hir legges hye.
She was a prymerole, a piggesnye,   prymerole: primrose. piggesnye:
For any lord to leggen in his bedde,   cuckoo-flower. leggen: lay.
Or yet for any good yeman to wedde.   3270

   Now, sire, and eft, sire, so bifel the cas,   eft: again.
That on a day this hende Nicholas
Fil with this yonge wyf to rage and pleye,   rage: behave wantonly.
Whil that hir housbonde was at Oseneye,
As clerkes ben ful subtile and ful queynte;   3275 queynte: clever, crafty.
And prively he caughte hire by the queynte,   queynte: genitals.
And seyde, "Ywis, but if ich have my wille,   ich: I.
For deerne love of thee, lemman, I spille."   deerne: secret. lemman: sweetheart.
And heeld hire harde by the haunchebones,   spille: perish.
And seyde, "Lemman, love me al atones,   3280 atones: at once.
Or I wol dyen, also God me save!"
And she sproong as a colt dooth in the trave,
And with hir heed she wryed faste awey;   wryed: twisted.
She seyde, "I wol nat kisse thee, by my fey!   fey: faith.
Why, lat be! Quod ich, 'Lat be,' Nicholas,   3285 quod ich: I said.
Or I wol crie, 'Out!' 'Harrow!' and 'Allas!'   Out!: alas! Harrow!: help!, a cry of
Do wey youre handes, for youre curteisye!"   distress.

   This Nicholas gan mercy for to crye,
And spak so faire, and profred him so faste,   faste: eagerly; vigorously.
That she hir love hym graunted atte laste,   3290
And swoor hir ooth, by Seint Thomas of Kent,
That she wolde been at his comandement,
Whan that she may hir leyser wel espie.   leyser: opportunity.
"Myn housbonde is so ful of jalousie
That but ye wayte wel and been privee,   3295
I woot right wel I nam but deed," quod she.
"Ye moste been ful deerne, as in this cas."

   "Nay, therof care thee noght," quod Nicholas.
"A clerk hadde litherly biset his whyle,   litherly biset his whyle: ill used his
But if he koude a carpenter bigyle."   3300 time.

3261. **bragot:** a drink made of honey and ale fermented together. **meeth:** a drink made of fermented honey.
3264. **bolt:** bolt or arrow (of a crossbow).
3266. **boos:** boss, the protuberance in the center of a shield.
3282. **trave:** wooden frame for holding horses, at a smith's forge.

And thus they been accorded and ysworn
To wayte a tyme, as I have told biforn.

Whan Nicholas had doon thus everideel,   *everideel: fully.*
And thakked hire aboute the lendes weel,   *thakked: patted, stroked. lendes:*
He kiste hire sweete and taketh his sawtrie, 3305 *loins; buttocks.*
And pleyeth faste, and maketh melodie.   *faste: vigorously.*

Thanne fil it thus, that to the paryssh chirche,   *fil: befell.*
Cristes owene werkes for to wirche,   *wirche: work, perform.*
This goode wyf went on an haliday.
Hir forheed shoon as bright as any day, 3310
So was it wasshen whan she leet hir werk.   *leet: left off.*
Now was ther of that chirche a parissh clerk,
The which that was ycleped Absolon.
Crul was his heer, and as the gold it shoon,   *crul: curly.*
And strouted as a fanne large and brode; 3315 *strouted: spread out.*
Ful streight and evene lay his joly shode.   *shode: part.*
His rode was reed, his eyen greye as goos.   *rode: complexion.*
With Poules wyndow corven on his shoos,
In hoses rede he wente fetisly.   *fetisly: neatly, handsomely.*
Yclad he was ful smal and proprely 3320 *smal: tightly.*
Al in a kirtel of a lyght waget;   *kirtel: long coat. waget: sky blue.*
Ful faire and thikke been the poyntes set.   *poyntes: laces with tagged ends.*
And therupon he hadde a gay surplys   *surplys: loose robe.*
As whit as is the blosme upon the rys.   *rys: twig, small branch.*
A myrie child he was, so God me save. 3325 *child: youth.*
Wel koude he laten blood and clippe and shave,
And maken a chartre of lond or acquitaunce.   *chartre . . . acquitaunce: deed or quit-*
In twenty manere koude he trippe and daunce   *claim deed.*
After the scole of Oxenforde tho,
And with his legges casten to and fro, 3330 *casten: leap, prance.*
And pleyen songes on a smal rubible;   *rubible: medieval fiddle.*
Therto he song som tyme a loud quynyble;   *quynyble: very high-pitched part.*
And as wel koude he pleye on a giterne.   *giterne: guitar.*
In al the toun nas brewhous ne taverne
That he ne visited with his solas, 3335 *solas: entertainment.*
Ther any gaylard tappestere was.   *gaylard: lively. tappestere: barmaid.*
But sooth to seyn, he was somdeel squaymous *squaymous: squeamish, fastidious.*
Of fartyng, and of speche daungerous.   *daungerous: fastidious.*

This Absolon, that jolif was and gay,
Gooth with a sencer on the haliday, 3340 *sencer: censer.*
Sensynge the wyves of the parisshe faste;   *faste: diligently.*
And many a lovely look on hem he caste,   *lovely: amorous.*
And namely on this carpenteris wyf.

3312. **parissh clerk**: a person in minor orders who assisted in church services.
3318. **Poules wyndow**: His shoes had open-work designs like the tracery of a window—perhaps the rose window—of old St. Paul's Cathedral, London.
3329. **scole**: discipline (cf. General Prologue, l. 125), as if in the curriculum then **(tho)**.
3339. Absolon appears to be **jolif** in every sense of this epithet; see Basic Glossary.

To looke on hire hym thoughte a myrie lyf,
She was so propre and sweete and likerous.   3345   propre: well made. **likerous:** appetizing.
I dar wel seyn, if she hadde been a mous,
And he a cat, he wolde hire hente anon.   hente: seize.
This parissh clerk, this joly Absolon,
Hath in his herte swich a love-longynge
That of no wyf took he noon offrynge;   3350
For curteisie, he seyde, he wolde noon.
     The moone, whan it was nyght, ful brighte
         shoon,
And Absolon his gyterne hath ytake,
For paramours he thoghte for to wake.   paramours: love-making, wenching.
And forth he gooth, jolif and amorous,   3355   wake: stay awake.
Til he cam to the carpenteres hous
A litel after cokkes hadde ycrowe,
And dressed hym up by a shot-wyndowe   dressed hym up: took up his station.
That was upon the carpenteris wal.
He syngeth in his voys gentil and smal,   3360   smal: high.
"Now, deere lady, if thy wille be,
I praye yow that ye wole rewe on me,"   rewe: have pity.
Ful wel acordaunt to his gyternynge.   acordaunt to: harmonizing with.
This carpenter awook, and herde him synge.
And spak unto his wyf, and seyde anon,   3365
"What! Alison! herestow nat Absolon,   herestow nat: don't you hear.
That chaunteth thus under oure boures wal?"   boures: bed-chamber's.
And she answerde hir housbonde therwithal,
"Yis, God woot, John, I heere it every deel."   deel: bit.
     This passeth forth; what wol ye bet than   bet: better.
         weel?   3370
Fro day to day this joly Absolon
So woweth hire that hym is wo bigon.   woweth: woos.
He waketh al the nyght and al the day;
He kembeth his lokkes brode, and made hym   kembeth: combs.
         gay;
He woweth hire by meenes and brocage,   3375   meenes and brocage: go-betweens and mediation.
And swoor he wolde been hir owene page;
He syngeth, brokkynge as a nyghtyngale;   brokkynge: quavering.
He sente hire pyment, meeth, and spiced ale,   pyment: spiced wine. **meeth:** mead.
And wafres, pipyng hoot out of the gleede;   gleede: live coal.
And, for she was of towne, he profred   for: because.
         meede.   3380   meede: reward (money).
For som folk wol ben wonnen for richesse,   for: by.
And somme for strokes, and somme for gentil-   strokes: blows.
         lesse.
     Somtyme, to shewe his lightnesse and mais-   lightnesse: agility. **maistrye:** skill.
         trye,

3358. shot-wyndowe: a hinged window, casement.

He pleyeth Herodes upon a scaffold hye.
But what availleth hym as in this cas?   3385
She loveth so this hende Nicholas
That Absolon may blowe the bukkes horn;
He ne hadde for his labour but a scorn.
And thus she maketh Absolon hire ape,
And al his ernest turneth til a jape.   3390   jape: jest.
Ful sooth is this proverbe, it is no lye,
Men seyn right thus, "Alwey the nye slye
Maketh the ferre leeve to be looth."   looth: unwanted.
For though that Absolon be wood or wrooth,   wrooth: wroth, angry.
By cause that he fer was from hire sight,   3395
This nye Nicholas stood in his light.
   Now ber thee wel, thou hende Nicholas,
For Absolon may waille and synge "Allas."
And so bifel it on a Saterday,
This carpenter was goon til Osenay;   3400
And hende Nicholas and Alisoun
Acorded been to this conclusioun,
That Nicholas shal shapen hem a wyle   wyle: wile, stratagem.
This sely jalous housbonde to bigyle;
And if so be the game wente aright,   3405
She sholde slepen in his arm al nyght,
For this was his desir and hire also.   hire: hers.
And right anon, withouten wordes mo,
This Nicholas no lenger wolde tarie,
But dooth ful softe unto his chambre carie   3410
Bothe mete and drynke for a day or tweye,
And to hire housbonde bad hire for to seye,
If that he axed after Nicholas,   axed: asked.
She sholde seye she nyste where he was,   nyste: (ne wiste) knew not.
Of al that day she saugh hym nat with eye; 3415 of: during.
She trowed that he was in maladye,
For for no cry hir mayde koude hym calle,
He nolde answere for nothyng that myghte falle. falle: befall.
   This passeth forth al thilke Saterday,
That Nicholas stille in his chambre lay,   3420
And eet and sleep, or dide what hym leste,   eet: ate. sleep: slept.
Til Sonday, that the sonne gooth to reste.   that: when.
This sely carpenter hath greet merveyle
Of Nicholas, or what thyng myghte hym eyle, eyle: ail.

3384. I.e., he took the part of Herod in a mystery play.
3387. There is no hope for him.
3392–93. the nye slye, the ferre leeve: the near sly one, the distant dear one.
3400. Osenay: Oseney, near Oxford, where there was an abbey of Augustinian canons; see ll. 3274 and 3657–70.
3404. In the course of the tale carpenter John rings the changes on the various meanings of the epithet sely: see Basic Glossary.

And seyde, "I am adrad, by Seint Thomas,   3425
It stondeth nat aright with Nicholas.
God shilde that he deyde sodeynly!   shilde: forbid.
This world is now ful tikel, sikerly.   tikel: uncertain.
I saugh to-day a cors yborn to chirche   cors: corpse. yborn: carried.
That now, on Monday last, I saugh hym
     wirche.   3430   wirche: work.
    "Go up," quod he unto his knave anoon,   knave: servant.
"Clepe at his dore, or knokke with a stoon.
Looke how it is, and tel me boldely."   boldely: immediately.
    This knave gooth hym up ful sturdily,
And at the chambre dore whil that he stood, 3435
He cride and knokked as that he were wood,
"What! how! what do ye, maister Nicholay?
How may ye slepen al the longe day?"
    But al for noght, he herde nat a word.
An hole he foond, ful lowe upon a bord,   3440
Ther as the cat was wont in for to crepe,   in crepe: creep in.
And at that hole he looked in ful depe,
And at the laste he hadde of hym a sight.
This Nicholas sat evere capyng upright,   capyng upright: gaping upward.
As he had kiked on the newe moone.   3445   kiked: gazed.
Adoun he gooth, and tolde his maister soone
In what array he saugh this ilke man.   array: condition.
    This carpenter to blessen hym bigan,   blessen hym: cross himself.
And seyde, "Help us, Seinte Frydeswyde!
A man woot litel what hym shal bityde.   3450
This man is falle, with his astromye,
In som woodnesse or in som agonye.   woodnesse: madness.
I thoghte ay wel how that it sholde be!
Men sholde nat knowe of Goddes pryvetee.   pryvetee: private affairs.
Ye, blessed be alwey, a lewed man   3455   lewed: unlearned, ignorant.
That noght but oonly his bileve kan!   bileve: Creed.
So ferde another clerk with astromye;   ferde: fared.
He walked in the feeldes, for to prye   prye: pry, peer, spy.
Upon the sterres, what ther sholde bifalle,
Til he was in a marle-pit yfalle;   3460
He saugh nat that. But yet, by Seint Thomas,
Me reweth soore of hende Nicholas.   me reweth: I am sorry.
He shal be rated of his studiyng,   rated: berated, scolded.
If that I may, by Jhesus, hevene kyng!
Get me a staf, that I may underspore,   3465

3449. **Seinte Frydeswyde:** There was a priory of St. Frideswide at Oxford. She was patron saint of city and university.
3451. **astromye:** astronomy (here and in l. 3457) and Noah (ll. 3818 and 3834) are hard words for carpenter John.
3457. **another clerk:** Thales (according to Plato).
3465. **underspore:** thrust under and pry up (to lift the door off its hinges).

Whil that thou, Robyn, hevest up the dore.
He shal out of his studiyng, as I gesse"—
And to the chambre dore he gan hym dresse.   dresse: direct.
His knave was a strong carl for the nones,   carl: man, fellow.
And by the haspe he haaf it up atones;   3470   haaf: heaved. atones: at one stroke.
Into the floor the dore fil anon.
This Nicholas sat ay as stille as stoon,
And evere caped upward into the eir.
This carpenter wende he were in despeir,   wende: weened, thought.
And hente hym by the sholdres myghtily,   3475
And shook hym harde, and cride spitously,   spitously: vehemently.
"What! Nicholay! what, how! what, looke
       adoun!
Awak, and thenk on Cristes passioun!
I crouche thee from elves and fro wightes."   wightes: creatures.
Therwith the nyght-spel seyde he anon-   anon-rightes: immediately.
       rightes   3480
On foure halves of the hous aboute,   halves: sides.
And on the thresshfold of the dore withoute:
"Jhesu Crist and Seinte Benedight,
Blesse this hous from every wikked wight,   blesse: deliver.
For nyghtes verye, the white *pater-noster!*   3485   verye: evil spirits (?).
Where wentestow, Seinte Petres soster?"   wentestow: have you gone.
    And atte laste this hende Nicholas
Gan for to sike soore, and seyde, "Allas!   sike: sigh.
Shall al the world be lost eftsoones now?"   eftsoones: a second time.
    This carpenter answerde, "What seystow?   3490
What! thynk on God, as we doon, men that
       swynke."   swynke: labor, toil.
    This Nicholas answerde, "Fecche me drynke,
And after wol I speke in pryvetee   pryvetee: secrecy.
Of certeyn thyng that toucheth me and thee.
I wol telle it noon oother man, certeyn."   3495
    This carpenter goth doun, and comth ageyn,   ageyn: back.
And broghte of myghty ale a large quart;
And whan that ech of hem had dronke his part,
This Nicholas his dore faste shette,
And doun the carpenter by hym he sette,   3500
And seyde, "John, myn hooste, lief and deere,   lief: beloved.
Thou shalt upon thy trouthe swere me heere   trouthe: honor.
That to no wight thou shalt this conseil wreye;   conseil: secret. wreye: betray, dis-
For it is Cristes conseil that I seye,   close.
And if thou telle it man, thou art forlore;   3505   man: to any man. forlore: utterly lost.
For this vengeaunce thou shalt han therfore,

3469. See General Prologue, ll. 545 and 550.
3479. crouche: protect by marking with the sign of the Cross.
3480. nyght-spel: a charm said at night to keep off evil spirits; the sense of the verses (ll. 3483–86) is **not** wholly clear.

That if thou wreye me, thou shalt be wood."
"Nay, Crist forbede it, for his hooly blood!"
Quod tho this sely man, "I nam no labbe;   labbe: blabber, tell-tale.
Ne, though I seye, I nam nat lief to gabbe.   3510 lief: desirous. gabbe: talk indiscreetly.
Sey what thou wolt, I shal it nevere telle
To child ne wyf, by hym that harwed helle!"
    "Now John," quod Nicholas, "I wol nat lye;
I have yfounde in myn astrologye,
As I have looked in the moone bright,   3515
That now a Monday next, at quarter nyght,
Shal falle a reyn, and that so wilde and wood,   wood: furious.
That half so greet was nevere Noees flood.
This world," he seyde, "in lasse than in an hour lasse: less.
Shal al be dreynt, so hidous is the shour.   3520 dreynt: drowned.
Thus shal mankynde drenche, and lese hir lyf." drenche: drown. lese: lose.
    This carpenter answerde, "Allas, my wyf!
And shal she drenche? allas, myn Alisoun!"
For sorwe of this he fil almoost adoun,
And seyde, "Is ther no remedie in this cas?" 3525
    "Why, yis, for Gode," quod hende Nicholas, for: before.
"If thou wolt werken after loore and reed.   loore and reed: learning and counsel.
Thou mayst nat werken after thyn owene heed; heed: head.
For thus seith Salomon, that was ful trewe,
'Werk al by conseil, and thou shalt nat rewe.' 3530 rewe: be sorry.
And if thou werken wolt by good conseil,
I undertake, withouten mast or seyl,
Yet shal I saven hire and thee and me.
Hastow nat herd hou saved was Noe,
Whan that oure Lord hadde warned hym bi-
        forn   3535
That al the world with water sholde be lorn?" lorn: laid waste.
    "Yis," quod this Carpenter, "ful yoore ago." yoore ago: long ago.
    Hastou nat herd," quod Nicholas, "also
The sorwe of Noe with his felaweshipe,
Er that he myghte gete his wyf to shipe?   3540
Hym hadde levere, I dar wel undertake,   hym hadde levere: he had rather.
At thilke tyme, than alle his wetheres blake wetheres: rams.
That she hadde had a ship hirself allone.
And therfore, woostou what is best to doone?
This asketh haste, and of an hastif thyng   3545
Men may nat preche or maken tariyng.
    Anon go gete us faste into this in   in: lodging, dwelling.
A knedyng trogh, or ellis a kymelyn,   kymelyn: shallow tub.

3512. hym: Christ; the carpenter may have seen a mystery play of the Harrowing of Hell, describing the descent of Christ into hell in order to release the souls of the patriarchs.
3516. at quarter nyght: at the end of the first quarter of the night; about 9 P.M.
3539. sorwe: the trouble endured by Noah and his company, in the mystery play, because of the conduct of Noah's wife.

For ech of us, but looke that they be large,
  looke: see, make sure.

In which we mowe swymme as in a barge, 3550
  swymme: float. **barge:** boat.

And han therinne vitaille suffisant
  vitaille: victuals, provisions.

But for a day,—fy on the remenant!

The water shal aslake and goon away
  aslake: diminish, recede.

Aboute pryme upon the nexte day.

But Robyn may nat wite of this, thy knave, 3555

Ne eek thy mayde Gille I may nat save;

Axe nat why, for though thou aske me,

I wol nat tellen Goddes pryvetee.

Suffiseth thee, but if thy wittes madde,
  suffiseth thee: be content. **madde:** are

To han as greet a grace as Noe hadde. 3560
  mad.

Thy wyf shal I wel saven, out of doute.
  out of doute: beyond doubt.

Go now thy wey, and speed thee heeraboute.

 But whan thou hast, for hire and thee and me,

Ygeten us thise knedyng tubbes thre,

Thanne shaltow hange hem in the roof ful
   hye, 3565
  shaltow: you shall.

That no man of oure purveiaunce espye.
  purveiaunce: provision.

And whan thou thus hast doon, as I have seyd,

And hast oure vitaille faire in hem yleyd,

And eek an ax, to smyte the corde atwo,
  atwo: in two.

Whan that the water comth, that we may go, 3570

And breke an hole an heigh, upon the gable,

Unto the gardyn-ward, over the stable,
  unto the gardyn-ward: towards the

That we may frely passen forth oure way,
  garden.

Whan that the grete shour is goon away,

Thanne shaltou swymme as myrie, I under-
  myrie: merrily.
   take, 3575

As dooth the white doke after his drake.
  his: its.

Thanne wol I clepe, 'How, Alison! how, John!

Be myrie, for the flood wol passe anon.'

And thou wolt seyn, 'Hayl, maister Nicholay!

Good morwe, I se thee wel, for it is day.' 3580

And thanne shul we be lordes al oure lyf

Of al the world, as Noe and his wyf.

 But of o thyng I warne thee ful right:

Be wel avysed on that ilke nyght

That we ben entred into shippes bord, 3585
  that: when. into shippes bord: on

That noon of us ne speke nat a word,
  board.

Ne clepe, ne crie, but be in his preyere;

For it is Goddes owene heeste deere.
  heeste: command.

 Thy wyf and thou moote hange fer atwynne;
  atwynne: apart.

For that bitwixe yow shal be no synne, 3590

Namoore in lookyng than ther shal in deede,

This ordinance is seyd. Go, God thee speede!

Tomorwe at nyght, whan men ben alle aslepe,

Into oure knedyng-tubbes wol we crepe,

And sitten there, abidying Goddes grace. 3595

Go now thy wey, I have no lenger space
To make of this no lenger sermonyng.
Men seyn thus: 'Sende the wise, and sey no
        thyng:'
Thou art so wys, it needeth thee nat teche.
Go, save oure lyf, and that I the biseche."   3600
    This sely carpenter goth forth his wey.
Ful ofte he seyde "Allas and weylawey,"
And to his wyf he tolde his pryvetee,
And she was war, and knew it bet than he,   bet: better.
What al this queynte cast was for to seye.   3605
But nathelees she ferde as she wolde deye,   as: as if.
And seyde, "Allas! go forth thy wey anon,
Help us to scape, or we been dede echon!
I am thy trewe, verray wedded wyf;
Go, deere spouse, and help to save our lyf."   3610
    Lo, which a greet thyng is affeccioun!   affeccioun: emotion, excitement.
Men may dyen of ymaginacioun,
So depe may impressioun be take.   take: taken.
This sely carpenter bigynneth quake;
Hym thynketh verraily that he may see   3615
Noees flood come walwynge as the see
To drenchen Alisoun, his hony deere.   drenchen: drown.
He wepeth, weyleth, maketh sory cheere;
He siketh with ful many a sory swogh,   siketh: sighs. swogh: sigh.
And gooth and geteth hym a knedyng trogh,   3620
And after that a tubbe and a kymelyn,
And pryvely he sente hem to his in,
And heng hem in the roof in pryvetee.
His owene hand he made laddres thre,   his: i.e., with his.
To clymben by the ronges and the stalkes   3625   stalkes: uprights.
Unto the tubbes hangynge in the balkes,   balkes: beams.
And hem vitailled, bothe trogh and tubbe,   vitailled: provisioned.
With breed and chese, and good ale in a jubbe,   jubbe: vessel, jug.
Suffisynge right ynogh as for a day.
But er that he hadde maad al this array,   3630   array: arrangement.
He sente his knave, and eek his wenche also,   knave: servant.
Upon his nede to London for to go.   nede: business.
And on the Monday, whan it drow to nyght,   drow to: drew near.
He shette his dore withoute candel-lyght,
And dressed alle thyng as it sholde be.   3635   dressed: prepared.
And shortly, up they clomben alle thre;   clomben: climbed.
They seten stille wel a furlong way.   seten: sat.
    "Now, *Pater-noster*, clom!" seyde Nicholay,

3605. What all this ingenious plan was about.
3637. a furlong way: the time required to walk a furlong; about two and one-half minutes.
3638. *Pater-noster*, clom: say a Paternoster, and then mum's the word.

And "Clom," quod John, and "Clom," seyde Ali-
    soun.
This carpenter seyde his devocioun,   3640
And stille he sit, and biddeth his preyere,   sit: (sitteth) sits. biddeth: offers.
Awaitynge on the reyn, if he it heere.
    The dede sleep, for wery bisynesse,
Fil on this carpenter right, as I gesse,
Aboute corfew-tyme, or litel moore;   3645   corfew-tyme: eight or nine o'clock.
For travaille of his goost he groneth soore,
And eft he routeth, for his heed myslay.   eft: presently. routeth: snores.
Doun of the laddre stalketh Nicholay,   of. off.
And Alisoun ful softe adoun she spedde;
Withouten wordes mo they goon to bedde,   3650
Ther as the carpenter is wont to lye.
Ther was the revel and the melodye;
And thus lith Alison and Nicholas,
In bisynesse of myrthe and in solas,   solas: delight.
Til that the belle of laudes gan to rynge,   3655
And freres in the chauncel gonne synge.
    This parissh clerk, this amorous Absolon,
That is for love alwey so wo bigon,
Upon the Monday was at Oseneye
With compaignye, hym to disporte and
    pleye,   3660
And axed upon cas a cloisterer   upon cas: by chance.
Ful prively after John the carpenter;
And he drough hym apart out of the chirche,   drough: drew.
And seyde, "I noot: I saugh hym heere nat wirche   wirche: work.
Syn Saterday; I trowe that he be went   3665
For tymber, ther oure abbot hath hym sent;
For he is wont for tymber for to go,
And dwellen at the grange a day or two;   grange: farmhouse (of the monastery).
Or elles he is at his hous, certeyn.
Where that he be, I kan nat soothly seyn."   3670
    This Absolon ful joly was and light,   joly: amorous. light: wanton.
And thoghte, "Now is tyme to wake al nyght;   wake: stay awake.
For sikirly I saugh hym nat stirynge
Aboute his dore, syn day bigan to sprynge.
    So moot I thryve, I shal, at cokkes crowe,   3675
Ful pryvely knokken at his wyndowe
That stant ful lowe upon his boures wal.   stant: stands. boures: chamber's.
To Alison now wol I tellen al
My love-longynge, for yet I shal nat mysse
That at the leeste wey I shal hire kisse.   3680   at the leeste wey: at least.
Som maner confort shal I have, parfay.   parfay: by my faith.

3646. for travaille of his goost: because of trouble of spirit.
3655. It is early morning, perhaps four o'clock.

My mouth hath icched al this longe day;
That is a signe of kissyng atte leeste.
Al nyght me mette eek I was at a feeste.   me mette: I dreamed.
Therfore I wol go slepe an houre or tweye,   3685
And al the nyght thanne wol I wake and pleye."
    Whan that the firste cok hath crowe, anon
Up rist this joly lovere Absolon,   rist: (riseth) rises.
And hym arraieth gay, at poynt-devys.   at poynt-devys: to perfection.
But first he cheweth greyn and lycorys,   3690
To smellen sweete, er he hadde kembd his heer.
Under his tonge a trewe-love he beer,   beer: bore.
For therby wende he to ben gracious.   wende: expected. gracious: pleasing,
He rometh to the carpenteres hous,   attractive.
And stille he stant under the shot-
        wyndowe—   3695
Unto his brest it raughte, it was so lowe—   raughte: reached.
And softe he cougheth with a semy soun: semy soun: half-sound.
"What do ye, hony-comb, sweete Alisoun,
My faire bryd, my sweete cynamome?   bryd: sweetheart.
Awaketh, lemman myn, and speketh to me! 3700   lemman: sweetheart.
Wel litel thynken ye upon my wo,
That for youre love I swete ther I go.   swete: sweat. ther: wherever.
No wonder is thogh that I swelte and swete;   swelte: swelter.
I moorne as dooth a lamb after the tete.   moorne: yearn. tete: teat.
Ywis, lemman, I have swich love-longynge, 3705
That lik a turtel trewe is my moornynge.   turtel: turtle-dove.
I may nat ete na moore than a mayde."
    "Go fro the wyndow, Jakke fool," she sayde;
"As help me God, it wol nat be 'com pa me.'   com pa me: come kiss me.
I love another—and elles I were to blame— 3710
Wel bet than thee, by Jhesu, Absolon.   bet: better.
Go forth thy wey, or I wol caste a ston,
And lat me slepe, a twenty devel wey!"
    "Allas," quod Absolon, "and weylawey,
That trewe love was evere so yvel biset!   3715   yvel biset: ill treated.
Thanne kys me, syn it may be no bet,
For Jhesus love, and for the love of me."
    "Wiltow thanne go thy wey therwith?" quod
        she.
    "Ye, certes, lemman," quod this Absolon.
    "Thanne make thee redy," quod she, "I come
        anon."   3720
And unto Nicholas she seyde stille,
"Now hust, and thou shalt laughen al thy fille."
    This Absolon doun sette hym on his knees

3690. greyn: grain of paradise (cardamom), a common aphrodisiac in the Middle Ages.
3692. trewe-love: a leaf of herb-paris, evidently supposed to bring luck in love.

And seyde, "I am a lord at alle degrees;
For after this I hope ther cometh moore.   3725
Lemman, thy grace, and sweete bryd, thyn
      oore!"   oore: favor, mercy.
  The wyndow she undoth, and that in haste.
"Have do," quod she, "com of, and speed the   do: done. of: off.
      faste,
Lest that oure neighebores thee espie."
  This Absolon gan wype his mouth ful drie.   3730
Derk was the nyght as pich, or as the cole,
And at the wyndow out she putte hir hole,
And Absolon, hym fil no bet ne wers,
But with his mouth he kiste hir naked ers   ers: arse.
Ful savourly, er he were war of this.   3735   savourly: with relish.
Abak he stirte, and thoughte it was amys,
For wel he wiste a womman hath no berd.
He felte a thyng al rough and long yherd,   yherd: haired.
And seyde, "Fy! allas! what have I do?"
  "Tehee!" quod she, and clapte the wyndow
      to,   3740
And Absolon gooth forth a sory pas.   a sory pas: with mournful step.
  "A berd! a berd!" quod hende Nicholas,
"By Goddes corpus, this goth faire and weel."   corpus: body.
  This sely Absolon herde every deel,
And on his lippe he gan for anger byte,   3745
And to hymself he seyde, "I shal thee quyte."   quyte: repay.
  Who rubbeth now, who froteth now his lippes   froteth: rubs.
With dust, with sond, with straw, with clooth,
      with chippes,
But Absolon, that seith ful ofte, "Allas!"
"My soule bitake I unto Sathanas,   3750   bitake: consign.
But me were levere than al this toun," quod he,   me were levere: I had rather.
"Of this despit awroken for to be.   despit: insult. awroken: avenged.
Allas," quod he, "allas, I ne hadde ybleynt!"   ybleynt: abstained.
His hoote love was coold and al yqueynt;   yqueynt: quenched.
For fro that tyme that he hadde kist hir ers, 3755
Of paramours he sette nat a kers;   paramours: wenches. kers: cress.
For he was heeled of his maladie.   heeled: healed.
Ful ofte paramours he gan deffie,   gan deffie: repudiated.
And weep as dooth a child that is ybete.   weep: wept.
A softe paas he wente over the strete   3760
Until a smyth men clepen daun Gerveys,   until: unto.
That in his forge smythed plough harneys;   harneys: fittings.
He sharpeth shaar and kultour bisily.   shaar: plowshare.
This Absolon knokketh al esily,   esily: softly.

3724. lord at alle degrees: master at every stage (of love).
3742. N.b. that "to make someone's beard" means to make a fool of him, to deceive him.
3763. kultour: colter, iron blade fixed in front of shaar.

And seyde, "Undo, Gerveys, and that anon." 3765
   "What, who artow?" "It am I, Absolon."
"What, Absolon! what, Cristes sweete tree!   tree: Cross.
Why rise ye so rathe? ey, benedicitee!   rathe: early.
What eyleth yow? Som gay gerl, God it woot,
Hath broght yow thus upon the viritoot.   3770 viritoot: frisk, whirl.
By Seinte Note, ye woot wel what I mene."   Seinte Note: St. Neot.
   This Absolon ne roghte nat a bene   roghte: recked, cared.
Of al his pley; no word agayn he yaf;
He hadde moore tow on his distaf   tow: flax.
Than Gerveys knew, and seyde, "Freend so
         deere,   3775
That hoote kultour in the chymenee heere,   chymenee: forge.
As lene it me, I have therwith to doone,   as lene: (please) lend.
And I wol brynge it thee agayn ful soone."
   Gerveys answerde, "Certes, were it gold,
Or in a poke nobles alle untold,   3780 poke: bag. untold: uncounted, count-
Thou sholdest have, as I am trewe smyth.   less.
Ey, Cristes foo! what wol ye do therwith?"
   "Therof," quod Absolon, "be as be may.
I shal wel telle it thee to-morwe day"—
And caughte the kultour by the colde stele. 3785 stele: handle.
Ful softe out at the dore he gan to stele,
And wente unto the carpenteris wal.
He cogheth first, and knokketh therwithal
Upon the wyndowe, right as he dide er.   er: before.
   This Alison answerde, "Who is ther   3790
That knokketh so? I warante it a theef."
   "Why, nay," quod he, "God woot, my sweete
         leef,   leef: beloved.
I am thyn Absolon, my deerelyng.
Of gold," quod he, "I have thee broght a ryng.
My mooder yaf it me, so God me save;   3795
Ful fyn it is, and therto wel ygrave.   ygrave: engraved.
This wol I yeve thee, if thou me kisse."
   This Nicholas was risen for to pisse,
And thoughte he wolde amenden al the jape;   amenden: improve on.
He sholde kisse his ers ere that he scape. 3800 He: i.e., Absolon.
And up the wyndowe dide he hastily,   up dide: opened.
And out his ers he putteth pryvely
Over the buttok, to the haunche-bon;
And therwith spak this clerk, this Absolon,
"Spek, sweete bryd, I noot nat where thou
         art."   3805
   This Nicholas anon leet fle a fart,   fle: fly.

_____

3768. benedicitee!: see Basic Glossary.

As greet as it had been a thonder-dent,   thonder-dent: thunder-blast.
That with the strook he was almoost yblent;   yblent: blinded.
And he was redy with his iren hoot,
And Nicholas in the ers he smoot.   3810
    Of gooth the skyn an hande-brede aboute,   of: off. hande-brede: hand's breadth.
The hoote kultour brende so his toute,   brende: burned. toute: buttocks.
That for the smert he wende for to dye.   wende: expected.
As he were wood, for wo he gan to crye,
"Help! water! water! help, for Goddes
       herte!"   3815
    This carpenter out of his slomber sterte,
And herde oon crien "Water" as he were wood,
And thoughte, "Allas, now comth Nowelis
       flood!"
He sit hym up withouten wordes mo,   sit: (sitteth) sits.
And with his ax he smoot the corde atwo,   3820 atwo: in two.
And doun gooth al; he foond neither to selle,   foond: tried.
Ne breed ne ale, til he cam to the celle   celle: sill, flooring.
Upon the floor, and ther aswowne he lay.   floor: earth, ground. aswowne: in a
    Up stirte hire Alison and Nicholay,   swowne. stirte hire: started.
And criden, "Out!" and "Harrow!" in the
       strete.   3825
The neighebores, bothe smale and grete,
In ronnen for to gauren on this man,   ronnen: ran. gauren: gaze, stare.
That aswowne lay, bothe pale and wan,
For with the fal he brosten hadde his arm.   brosten: broken.
But stonde he moste unto his owene harm;   3830 stonde unto: accept responsibility for.
For whan he spak, he was anon bore doun
With hende Nicholas and Alisoun.   with: by.
They tolden every man that he was wood,
He was agast so of Nowelis flood
Thurgh fantasie, that of his vanytee   3835 vanytee: folly.
He hadde yboght hym knedying tubbes thre,
And hadde hem hanged in the roof above;
And that he preyed hem, for Goddes love,
To sitten in the roof, *par compaignye.*   *par:* for.
    The folk gan laughen at his fantasye;   3840
Into the roof they kiken and they cape,   kiken: gaze. cape: gape.
And turned al his harm unto a jape.
For what so that this carpenter answerde,
It was for noght, no man his reson herde.
With othes grete he was so sworn adoun   3845
That he was holde wood in al the toun;
For every clerk anonright heeld with oother.
They seyde, "The man is wood, my leeve   leeve: dear.
       brother";
And every wight gan laughen at this stryf.
Thus swyved was the carpenteris wyf,   3850 swyved: slept with.

For al his kepyng and his jalousye;
And Absolon hath kist hir nether eye;   nether: lower.
And Nicholas is scalded in the towte.
This tale is doon, and God save al the rowte! rowte: company.

Heere endeth the
Millere his tale.

The prologe of the
Reves tale.

Whan folk hadde laughen at this nyce cas 3855 nyce: ludicrous.
Of Absolon and hende Nicholas,
Diverse folk diversely they seyde,
But for the moore part they loughe and pleyde. loughe: laughed.
Ne at this tale I saugh no man hym greve, hym greve: become angry.
But it were oonly Osewold the Reve. 3860
By cause he was of carpenteris craft,
A litel ire is in his herte ylaft;   ylaft: left.
He gan to grucche, and blamed it a lite. grucche: murmur, grumble.
 "So theek," quod he, "ful wel koude I thee
   quite
With bleryng of a proud milleres eye, 3865
If that me liste speke of ribaudye.   ribaudye: ribaldry, ribald jesting.
But ik am oold, me list not pley for age; ik: I.
Gras tyme is doon, my fodder is now forage; forage: winter food (as hay).
This white top writeth myne olde yeris;
Myn herte is also mowled as myne heris, 3870 mowled: grown moldy; decayed.
But if I fare as dooth an open-ers: heris: hairs.
That ilke fruyt is ever lenger the wers, ever lenger: the longer it lasts.
Til it be roten in mullok or in stree. mullok: heap of refuse. stree: straw.
We olde men, I drede, so fare we:
Til we be roten, kan we nat be rype; 3875
We hoppen alwey whil that the world wol pype. hoppen: hop; dance.
For in oure wyl ther stiketh evere a nayl,
To have an hoor heed and a grene tayl, hoor: hoar.
As hath a leek; for thogh oure myght be goon,
Oure wyl desireth folie evere in oon. 3880 folie: lechery. evere in oon: inces-
For whan we may nat doon, than wol we speke; santly.

3864. so theek: (*for* so thee ik) as I hope to prosper.
3865. With (a tale of the) hoodwinking of a proud miller.
3868. I have left the pasture for the stable.
3869. My white hair declares my old age.
3871. open-ers: fruit of the medlar tree; it is inedible until decayed.
3877. For our desire has a cross, a burden.

Yet in oure asshen olde is fyr yreke.

    Foure gleedes han we, which I shal devyse,—

Avauntyng, liyng, anger, coveitise;

This foure sparkles longen unto eelde.   **3885**

Oure olde lemes mowe wel been unweelde,

But wyl ne shal nat faillen, that is sooth.

And yet ik have alwey a coltes tooth,

As many a yeer as it is passed henne

Syn that my tappe of lif bigan to renne.   **3890**

For sikerly, whan I was bore, anon

Deeth drough the tappe of lyf and leet it gon;

And ever sithe hath so the tappe yronne

Til that almoost al empty is the tonne.

The streem of lyf now droppeth on the

    chymbe.   **3895**

The sely tonge may wel rynge and chymbe

Of wrecchednesse that passed is ful yoore;

With olde folk, save dotage, is namoore!"

    Whan that oure Hoost hadde herd this ser-

        monyng,

He gan to speke as lordly as a kyng.   **3900**

He seide, "What amounteth al this wit?

What shul we speke alday of holy writ?

The devel made a reve for to preche,

Or of a soutere a shipman or a leche.

Sey forth thy tale, and tarie nat the tyme   **3905**

Lo Depeford! and it is half-wey pryme.

Lo Grenewych, ther many a shrewe is inne!

It were al tyme thy tale to bigynne."

    "Now, sires," quod this Osewold the Reve,

"I pray yow alle that ye nat yow greve,   **3910**

Thogh I answere, and somdeel sette his howve;

For leveful is with force force of-showve.

    This dronke Millere hath ytoold us heer

How that bigyled was a carpenteer,

Peraventure in scorn, for I am oon.   **3915**

And, by youre leve, I shal hym quite anoon;

Right in his cherles termes wol I speke.

---

yreke: raked together; covered up.

gleedes: live coals; fires.

avauntyng: boasting. **coveitise:** avarice.

lemes: limbs; flames. **unweelde:** (unwieldy) hard to move; weak; impotent.

henne: hence.

renne: run.

drough: drew.

chymbe: the rim of the "tonne."

tonge: tongue (of a man; of a bell).

yoore: for a long time.

what shul: why must.

soutere: cobbler. **leche:** physician.

tarie: delay, waste.

half-wey pryme: 7:30 A.M.

shrewe: scoundrel.

al: altogether.

leveful: lawful. **of-showve:** shove off, repel.

3885. **longen unto eelde:** belong to old age.

3886. **lemes:** A limb was any organ, part, or member of the body.

3888. **coltes tooth:** i.e., youthful desires, lascivious appetites.

3889. **as . . . as:** in spite of the fact that.

3890. **tappe:** tap of a tun or cask of wine.

3891. **bore:** born (i.e., the Reeve); bored (i.e., the figurative tun).

3906. **Depeford:** Deptford, about four miles from Southwark.

3907. **Grenewych:** Greenwich, near Deptford; Chaucer lived here probably from around 1385 to 1391.

3911. **sette his howve:** set his hood (awry); make a fool of him.

I pray to God his nekke mote to-breke;   to-breke: break.
He kan wel in myn eye seen a stalke,
But in his owene he kan nat seen a balke.   3920 balke: balk, beam.

Heere bigynneth the
Reves tale.

At Trumpyngtoun, nat fer fro Cantebrigge,
Ther gooth a brook, and over that a brigge,
Upon the whiche brook ther stant a melle;   melle: mill.
And this is verray sooth that I yow telle:
A millere was ther dwellyng many a day.   3925
As any pecok he was proud and gay.
Pipen he koude and fisshe, and nettes beete,   pipen: play the bagpipe.
And turne coppes, and wel wrastle and sheete; turne coppes: carouse. sheete: shoot.
Ay by his belt he baar a long panade,   panade: cutlass.
And of a swerd ful trenchant was the blade. 3930 trenchant: cutting, sharp.
A joly poppere baar he in his pouche;   joly poppere: short dagger.
Ther was no man, for peril, dorste hym touche.
A Sheffeld thwitel baar he in his hose.   thwitel: large knife.
Round was his face, and camuse was his nose; camuse: flat, snub.
As piled as an ape was his skulle.   3935 piled: bald.
He was a market betere atte fulle.   atte fulle: fully.
Ther dorste no wight hand upon hym legge,   legge: lay.
That he ne swoor he sholde anon abegge.   abegge: pay a penalty, be punished.
A theef he was forsothe of corn and mele,
And that a sly, and usaunt for to stele.   3940 usaunt: accustomed.
His name was hoten deynous Symkyn.   hoten: called. deynous: disdainful.
A wyf he hadde, comen of noble kyn;
The person of the toun hir fader was.
With hire he yaf ful many a panne of bras,   panne: penny. of: i.e., alloyed with (?).
For that Symkyn sholde in his blood allye. 3945 allye: ally; alloy.
She was yfostred in a nonnerye;   yfostred: brought up; educated.
For Symkyn wolde no wyf, as he sayde,
But she were wel ynorissed and a mayde,   ynorissed: nurtured.
To saven his estaat of yemanrye.
And she was proud, and peert as is a pye. 3950 pye: magpie.
A ful fair sighte was it upon hem two;

3920. See Matthew vii.3.
the Reves tale. The Reeve's Tale is in the fabliau tradition; see the footnote at the beginning of the Miller's Tale.
3921. Trumpington is about a mile and a half south of Cambridge.
3927. nettes beete: repair fishing nets.
3936. market betere: a quarrelsome frequenter of markets.
3943. person: parson, priest. Since she was his illegitimate daughter, the parson paid a generous dowry in order to get her married.
3945. in his blood allye: marry into his family (with pun on "allaie" meaning "alloy").
3949. To preserve his dignity as small landowner.

On halidayes biforn hire wolde he go
With his tipet wounde aboute his heed,   tipet: scarf.
And she cam after in a gyte of reed;   gyte: gown.
And Symkyn hadde hosen of the same.   3955
Ther dorste no wight clepen hire but "dame";   dame: lady.
Was noon so hardy that wente by the weye
That with hire dorste rage or ones pleye,   rage: behave wantonly.
But if he wolde be slayn of Symkyn   but if: unless.
With panade, or with knyf, or boydekyn.   3960 boydekyn: dagger.
For jalous folk been perilous everemo;
Algate they wolde hire wyves wenden so.   algate: at any rate. wenden: should
And eek, for she was somdel smoterlich,   think. smoterlich: besmirched.
She was as digne as water in a dich,   digne: disdainful, scornful.
And ful of hoker and of bisemare.   3965 hoker: derision. bisemare: scorn.
Hir thoughte that a lady sholde hir spare,
What for hir kynrede and hir nortelrye   nortelrye: education.
That she hadde lerned in the nonnerye.
    A doghter hadde they bitwix hem two
Of twenty yeer, withouten any mo,   3970
Savyng a child that was of half yeer age;
In cradel it lay and was a propre page.   a propre page: a fine boy.
This wenche thikke and wel ygrowen was,
With camuse nose, and eyen greye as glas,
With buttokes brode, and brestes rounde and
          hye;   3975
But right fair was hir heer, I wol nat lye.
    The person of the toun, for she was feir,   for: because.
In purpos was to maken hir his heir,
Bothe of his catel and his mesuage,   catel: property. mesuage: dwelling.
And straunge he made it of hir mariage.   3980   house.
His purpos was for to bistowe hire hye
Into som worthy blood of auncetrye;   auncetrye: lineage.
For holy chirches good moot been despended   good: goods, property, wealth.
On holy chirches blood, that is descended.   descended: inherited; degenerated.
Therefore he wolde his holy blood honoure, 3985
Though that he holy chirche sholde devoure.
    Greet soken hath this millere, out of doute,
With whete and malt of al the land aboute;
And nameliche ther was a greet collegge
Men clepen the Scoler Halle at Cantebregge; 3990

3966. It seemed to her that a lady ought to treat her gently, leniently.
3980. And he made difficulties about her marriage.
3987. soken: resort of people to his mill to have their grain ground.
3989. collegge: an endowed establishment for a body of scholars together with its residents.
3990. Scoler Halle: King's Hall, founded by Edward III in 1337, for thirty-two scholars who had to be at least fourteen years of age on admission. Documents refer to King's Hall as "Aulam Scolarium Regis," "collegium scolarium," and "la Salle des Escoliers." Most MSS read soler halle, but four unrelated MSS, each associated with East Anglia—the hinterland of Cambridge—read Scoler halle. See D. S. Brewer, *Chaucer Review*, 5 (1971), 311–17.

Ther was hir whete and eek hir malt ygrounde.
And on a day it happed, in a stounde,
— *in a stounde: at a time, once.*
Sik lay the maunciple on a maladye;
— *maunciple: steward. on: of.*
Men wenden wisly that he sholde dye.
— *wenden: expected. wisly: surely.*
For which this millere stal bothe mele and
corn   3995
— *stal: stole.*
An hundred tyme moore than biforn;
For therbiforn he stal but curteisly,
But now he was a theef outrageously,
For which the wardeyn chidde and made fare.
— *fare: fuss, to-do.*
But therof sette the millere nat a tare;   4000
— *sette: cared.*
He craked boost, and swoor it was nat so.
— *craked boost: threatened; blustered.*
    Thanne were ther yonge povre scolers two,
That dwelten in the halle of which I seye.
Testyf they were, and lusty for to pleye,
— *testyf: headstrong.*
And, oonly for hire myrthe and reverye,   4005
— *reverye: wildness.*
Upon the wardeyn bisily they crye
To yeve hem leve, but a litel stounde,
— *stounde: time, while.*
To go to mille and seen hir corn ygrounde;
And hardily they dorste leye hir nekke
— *hardily: with confidence. leye: wager.*
The millere sholde nat stele hem half a
pekke   4010
Of corn by sleighte, ne by force hem reve;
— *reve: rob.*
And at the laste the wardeyn yaf hem leve.
John highte that oon, and Aleyn highte that
oother;
— *highte: was called.*
Of oon toun were they born, that highte
Strother,
Fer in the north, I kan nat telle where.   4015
    This Aleyn maketh redy al his gere,
And on an hors the sak he caste anon.
Forth goth Aleyn the clerk, and also John,
With good swerd and with bokeler by hir syde.
John knew the wey—hym nedede
no gyde—   4020
— *hym nedede: i.e., he needed.*
And at the mille the sak adoun he layth.
Aleyn spak first, "Al hayl, Symond, in fayth!
How fares thy faire doghter and thy wyf?"
— *fares: fare (N).*
    "Aleyn, welcome," quod Symkyn, "by my lyf!
And John also, how now, what do ye here?" 4025
    "By God," quod John, "Symond, nede has na
peere.
— *nede: necessity. has: (N). na: no (N). peere: equal.*
Hym boes serve hymself that has na swayn,
— *boes: (it) behooves (N). swayn: servant-lad.*

4014. **Strother:** a place supposedly in Northumbria.
4023. In the speech of Aleyn and John, Chaucer has made use of enough Northern forms to achieve a comic dialectal effect: for example, long **a** for the usual long **o** (**gas, swa, ham**); present indicative in **-es** or **-s**; **til** for **to**; and such words as **boes, lathe,** and **fonne.** A large proportion of these Northernisms are marked (N) in the glossarial notes.

Or elles he is a fool, as clerkes sayn.
Oure manciple, I hope he wil be deed,   *hope: expect.*
Swa werkes ay the wanges in his heed; 4030 *swa: so (N). werkes: ache (N).*
And forthy is I come, and eek Alayn,   *wanges: molar teeth (N). forthy:*
To grynde oure corn and carie it ham agayn;   *therefore. is: am (N). ham: home (N).*
I pray yow spede us heythen that ye may."   *heythen: hence (N).*
   "It shal be doon," quod Symkyn, "by my fay! *fay: faith.*
What wol ye doon whil that it is in hande?" 4035 *in hande: in process.*
   "By God, right by the hoper wil I stande,"
Quod John, "and se how gates the corn gas in. *how gates: how (N). gas: goes (N).*
Yet saw I nevere, by my fader kyn,   *fader: father's.*
How that the hoper wagges til and fra."   *til and fra: to and fro (N).*
   Aleyn answerde, "John, and wiltow swa? 4040 *swa: so (N).*
Thanne wil I by bynethe, by my croun,
And se how that the mele falles doun
Into the trough; that sal be my disport.   *sal: shall (N).*
For John, in faith, I may been of youre sort;
I is as ille a millere as ar ye." 4045 *is: (N). ille: bad (N). ar: (N).*
   This millere smyled of hir nycetee, *of: at. nycetee: simplicity.*
And thoghte, "Al this nys doon but for a wyle. *wyle: crafty trick.*
They wene that no man may hem bigyle, *wene: think.*
But by my thrift, yet shal I blere hir eye, *blere hir eye: hoodwink them.*
For al the sleighte in hir philosophye. 4050 *sleighte: craftiness.*
The moore queynte crekes that they make, *queynte: sly. crekes: tricks.*
The moore wol I stele whan I take.
In stede of flour yet wol I yeve hem bren. *bren: bran.*
'The grettest clerkes been noght wisest men,'
As whilom to the wolf thus spak the mare. 4055
Of al hir art counte I noght a tare."
   Out at the dore he gooth ful pryvely,
Whan that he saugh his tyme, softely.
He looketh up and doun til he hath founde
The clerkes hors, ther as it stood ybounde 4060 *ther as: where.*
Bihynde the mille, under a leefsel; *leefsel: leafy arbor.*
And to the hors he goth hym faire and wel;
He strepeth of the bridel right anon. *strepeth of: strips off.*
And whan the hors was laus, he gynneth gon *laus: loose. gynneth gon: starts to go;*
Toward the fen, ther wilde mares renne, 4065 *dashes.*
And forth with "Wehee," thurgh thikke and
     thenne. *thenne: thin.*
   This millere gooth agayn, no word he seyde,
But dooth his note, and with the clerkes pleyde, *note: task.*
Til that hir corn was faire and wel ygrounde.
And whan the mele is sakked and ybounde, 4070
This John goth out and fynt his hors away, *fynt: (findeth) finds.*

4033. I pray you that you may speed us hence as fast as you can.
4054–55. In the fable the wolf was kicked by a mare while trying to read on her foot the price of her foal.

And gan to crye, "Harrow and weylaway!   gan to crye: cried.
Oure hors is lorn, Alayn, for Goddes banes,   lorn: lost. banes: bones (N).
Step on thy feet! Com of, man, al at anes!   at anes: at once (N).
Allas, our wardeyn has his palfrey lorn."   4075
This Aleyn al forgat, bothe mele and corn;
Al was out of his mynde his housbondrye.   housbondrye: thrifty management.
"What, whilk way is he gane?" he gan to crye.   whilk: which (N). gane: gone (N).

    The wyf cam lepyng inward with a ren.   ren: run.
She seyde, "Allas! youre hors goth to the fen 4080
With wilde mares, as faste as he may go.
Unthank come on his hand that boond hym so,   unthank: a curse.
And he that bettre sholde have knyt the reyne!"   knyt: knotted.

    "Allas," quod John, "Aleyn, for Cristes peyne,
Lay doun thy swerd, and I wil myn alswa.   4085   alswa: also (N).
I is ful wight, God waat, as is a raa;   wight: swift. waat: knows (N). raa:
By Goddes herte, he sal nat scape us bathe!   roe (N). sal: shall (N). bathe: both
Why ne had thow pit the capul in the lathe?   (N).
Il hail! by God, Aleyn, thou is a fonne!"   il hail: bad luck (N). fonne: fool (N).

    This sely clerkes han ful faste yronne   4090
Toward the fen, bothe Aleyn and eek John.

    And whan the millere saugh that they were
        gon,
He half a busshel of hir flour hath take,   take: taken.
And bad his wyf go knede it in a cake.   cake: a flat, round loaf of bread.
He seyde, "I trowe the clerkes were aferd.   4095   aferd: afraid (of what he might do).
Yet kan a millere make a clerkes berd,   make a berd: deceive.
For al his art; ye, lat hem goon hir weye!   art: learning. ye: yea.
Lo, wher he gooth! ye, lat the children pleye.
They gete hym nat so lightly, by my croun."   lightly; easily; quickly.

    Thise sely clerkes rennen up and doun   4100
With "Keep! keep!" "Stand! stand!" "Jossa!"
        "Warderere!"
"Ga whistle thou, and I sal kepe hym here!"   ga: go (N).
But shortly, til that it was verray nyght,
They koude nat, though they dide al hir myght,
Hir capul cacche, he ran alwey so faste,   4105
Til in a dich they caughte hym at the laste.

    Wery and weet, as beest is in the reyn,   weet: wet.
Comth sely John, and with him comth Aleyn.
"Allas," quod John, "the day that I was born!
Now are we dryven til hethyng and til scorn. 4110   til hethyng: into contempt (N).
Oure corn is stoln, men wil us fooles calle,
Bathe the wardeyn and oure felawes alle,   bathe: both (N). felawes: fellows of
And namely the millere, weylaway!"   their college. namely: especially.

    Thus pleyneth John as he gooth by the way

4088. Why didn't you put the horse in the barn? (N).
4101. keep!: watch!, wait! jossa: down here! warderere: watch out behind!

Toward the mille, and Bayard in his hond. 4115 Bayard: the horse. hond: i.e., posses-
The millere sittyng by the fyr he fond,   sion.
For it was nyght, and ferther myghte they noght;
But for the love of God they hym bisoght
Of herberwe and of ese, as for hir peny.   herberwe: harbor, shelter.
  The millere seide agayn, "If ther be eny, 4120 agayn: in reply.
Swich as it is, yet shal ye have youre part.
Myn hous is streit, but ye han lerned art;   streit: narrow, small. art: dialectic.
Ye kan by argumentes make a place
A myle brood of twenty foot of space.
Lat se now if this place may suffise,   4125
Or make it rowm with speche, as is youre gise."   rowm: roomy, spacious. gise: custom.
  "Now, Symond," seyde this John, "by Seint
        Cutberd,
Ay is thou myrie, and that is faire answerd.
I have herd seye, 'Men sal taa of twa thynges   sal taa: (N). twa: two (N).
Slyk as he fyndes, or taa slyk as he brynges.' 4130 slyk: such (N).
But specially I pray thee, hooste deere,
Get us som mete and drynk, and make us   make us cheere: treat us hospitably.
        cheere,
And we wil payen trewely atte fulle.
With empty hand men may na haukes tulle;   na haukes tulle: lure no hawks.
Lo, here oure silver, redy for to spende."   4135
  This millere into toun his doghter sende   sende: sent.
For ale and breed, and rosted hem a goos,
And boond hire hors, it sholde namoore go loos;
And in his owene chambre hem made a bed,
With sheetes and with chalons faire yspred, 4140 chalons: bedspreads of figured woolen
Noght from his owene bed ten foot or twelve.   material.
His doghter hadde a bed, al by hirselve,
Right in the same chambre by and by.   by and by: alongside.
It myghte be no bet, and cause why?   cause: the reason.
Ther was no roumer herberwe in the place.   4145 roumer: roomier, larger.
They soupen and they speke, hem to solace,   soupen: sup. solace: entertain.
And drynken evere strong ale atte beste.   atte beste: in the best way.
Aboute mydnyght wente they to reste.
  Wel hath this millere vernysshed his heed;   vernysshed: varnished (with ale).
Ful pale he was for dronken, and nat reed. 4150 for dronken: because of being drunk.
He yexeth, and he speketh thurgh the nose   yexeth: belches.
As he were on the quakke, or on the pose.   on the quakke: hoarse. on the pose:
To bedde he goth, and with hym goth his wyf.   had a cold in the head.
As any jay she light was and jolyf,   light: frivolous.
So was hir joly whistle wel ywet.   4155
The cradel at hir beddes feet is set,

_____

4119. as for hir peny: in return for their money. The gates of Scoler Hall have closed for the night.
4127. Seint Cutberd: St. Cuthbert, a Northumbrian bishop of the seventh century, was reputed as
a young man to lie all night in freezing water, engaged in prayer.
4129–30. A man must take what he finds or what he brings.

To rokken, and to yeve the child to sowke. sowke: suck.
And whan that dronken al was in the crowke, crowke: jar, pitcher.
To bedde wente the doghter right anon;
To bedde goth Aleyn and also John. 4160
    Ther nas na moore,—hem nedede no dwale. dwale: sleeping potion.
This millere hath so wisly bibbed ale wisly: surely. bibbed: imbibed.
That as an hors he fnorteth in his sleep, fnorteth: snorts, snores.
Ne of his tayl bihynde he took no keep.
His wyf bar hym a burdon, a ful strong; 4165 burdon: bass accompaniment.
Men myghte hir rowtyng heren a furlong; rowtyng: snoring.
The wenche rowteth eek, *par compaignye*. *par:* for.
    Aleyn the clerk, that herde this melodye,
He poked John, and seyde, "Slepestow?
Herdestow evere slyk a sang er now? 4170 slyk: such (N).
Lo, swilk a complyn is ymel hem alle, swilk: such (N). ymel: among (N).
A wilde fyr on thair bodyes falle!
Wha herkned evere slyk a ferly thyng? ferly: terrifying.
Ye, they sal have the flour of il endyng. flour: flower, prize. endyng: outcome.
This lange nyght ther tydes me na reste; 4175 tydes: betides, comes to. na: no (N).
But yet, na force, al sal be for the beste. na force: no matter.
For, John," seyde he, "als evere moot I thryve,
If that I may, yon wenche wil I swyve. swyve: lie with.
Som esement has lawe yshapen us; esement: redress. yshapen: provided.
For, John, ther is a lawe that says thus, 4180
That gif a man in a point be agreved, gif: if (N).
That in another he sal be releved.
Oure corn is stolen, soothly, it is na nay, it is na nay: there's no denying it.
And we han had an ille fit this day; ille fit: bad time, hard luck (N).
And syn I sal have naan amendement 4185 naan: no (N).
Agayn my los, I will have esement. agayn: in return for.
By Goddes saule, it sal naan other be!" saule: soul (N).
    This John answerde, "Alayn, avyse thee! avyse thee: take thought.
The millere is a perilous man," he seyde,
"And gif that he out of his sleep abreyde, 4190 abreyde: start, awake.
He myghte doon us bathe a vileynye." bathe: both (N).
    Aleyn answerde, "I counte hym nat a flye."
And up he rist, and by the wenche he crepte. rist: (riseth) rises.
This wenche lay uprighte, and faste slepte, uprighte: on her back.
Til he so ny was, er she myghte espie, 4195 espie: notice.
That it had been to late for to crie, to: too.
And shortly for to seyn, they were at oon. at oon: at one, in accord.
Now pley, Aleyn, for I wol speke of John.

4166. **a furlong:** an eighth of a mile.
4171. **complyn:** Although the reading of O′ was **couplyng** (copulation; or perhaps collaboration), a few MSS read **complyn;** that Chaucer intended to compare the snoring of Symkyn and his family to the "night song" of the Church, is suggested by the extensive parody of the language, prayers, and themes of the Compline liturgy through actions and words in the Tale. (See R. M. Correale, *Chaucer Review*, 1 (1967), 161–66.
4172. **wilde fyr:** a very painful skin disease, also called "the fire of hell."

This John lith stille a furlong wey or two,

   lith: (lieth) lies.

And to hymself he maketh routhe and wo.

   4200 routhe: lamentation.

"Allas!" quod he, "this is a wikked jape;

   jape: joke.

Now may I seyn that I is but an ape.

Yet has my felawe somwhat for his harm;

He has the milleris doghter in his arm.

He auntred hym, and has his nedes sped,

   4205 auntred hym: ventured. sped: pro-
      vided for.

And I lye as a draf-sak in my bed;

And when this jape is tald another day,

   tald: told (N).

I sal been halde a daf, a cokenay!

   halde: held (N). daf: fool.

I wil arise and auntre it, by my fayth!

   auntre: venture.

'Unhardy is unseely,' thus men sayth."

   4210 unseely: unsuccessful, unfortunate.

And up he roos, and softely he wente

Unto the cradel, and in his hand it hente,

   hente: took.

And baar it softe unto his beddes feet.

    Soone after this the wyf hir rowtyng leet,

   rowtyng: snoring. leet: left off.

And gan awake, and wente hire out to pisse,

   4215

And cam agayn, and gan hir cradel mysse,

And groped heer and ther, but she foond noon.

"Allas!" quod she, "I hadde almoost mysgoon;

I hadde almoost goon to the clerkes bed.

Ey, benedicite! thanne had I foule ysped."

   4220 ysped: sped.

And forth she gooth til she the cradel fond.

She gropeth alwey forther with hir hond,

   alwey: progressively.

And foond the bed, and thoghte noght but good,

Bycause that the cradel by it stood,

And nyste wher she was, for it was derk;

   4225 nyste: (ne wiste) knew not.

But faire and wel she creep in to the clerk,

   creep: crept.

And lyth ful stille, and wolde have caught a sleep.

   caught a: gone to.

Withinne a while this John the clerk up leep,

   leep: leaped.

And on this goode wyf he leyth on soore.

So myrie a fit ne hadde she nat ful yoore;

   4230 myrie fit: good time. yoore: for a long
      time.

He priketh harde and depe as he were mad.

    This joly lyf han thise two clerkes lad

Til that the thridde cok bigan to synge.

    Aleyn wax wery in the dawenynge,

   wax: grew.

For he had swonken al the longe nyght,

   4235 swonken: toiled.

And seyde, "Farewel, Malyne, sweete wight!

The day is come, I may no lenger byde;

   byde: abide, remain.

But evermo, wher so I go or ryde,

   wher so: wheresover. go: walk.

I is thyn awen clerk, swa have I seel!"

   is: (N). awen: own (N). swa: so (N).
      seel: bliss (N). lemman: lover,

    "Now, deere lemman," quod she, "go,
      farewel!

   4240 sweetheart.

But er thow go, o thyng I wol thee telle:

4199. **a furlong wey:** the time required to walk one furlong; about two and one-half minutes.
4206. **draf-sak:** sack full of draff or refuse.
4208. **cokenay:** cock's egg, effeminate youth.
4233. **the thridde cok:** the cock crowing at dawn.

Whan that thou wendest homward by the melle,   melle: mill.
Right at the entree of the dore bihynde
Thou shalt a cake of half a busshel fynde   cake: loaf of bread.
That was ymaked of thyn owene mele,   4245 mele: meal.
Which that I heelp my sire for to stele.   heelp: helped.
And, goode lemman, God thee save and kepe!"
And with that word almoost she gan to wepe.
    Aleyn up rist, and thoughte, "Er that it dawe,   rist: rises. dawe: dawn, grow light.
I wol go crepen in by my felawe";   4250
And fond the cradel with his hand anon.
"By God," thoughte he, "al wrang I have   wrang: wrong (N).
    mysgon.
Myn heed is toty of my swynk tonyght,   toty: dizzy. swynk: labor.
That maketh me that I go nat aright.   aright: straight.
I woot wel by the cradel I have mysgo;   4255
Heere lyth the millere and his wyf also."
And forth he goth, a twenty devel way,
Unto the bed ther as the millere lay.
He wende have cropen by his felawe John,   wende: expected to. cropen: crept.
And by the millere in he creep anon,   4260 creep: crept.
And caughte hym by the nekke, and softe he
    spak.
He seyde, "Thou John, thou swynes-heed, awak,
For Cristes saule, and heer a noble game.   heer: hear.
For by that lord that called is Seint Jame,
As I have thries in this shorte nyght   4265 thries: thrice.
Swyved the milleres doghter bolt upright,   swyved: lain with.
Whil thow hast, as a coward, been agast."   agast: afraid.
    "Ye, false harlot," quod the millere, "hast?   harlot: rogue.
A, false traitour! false clerk!" quod he,
"Thow shalt be deed, by Goddes dignitee!   4270
Who dorste be so bold to disparage   disparage: defile.
My doghter, that is come of swich lynage?"
And by the throte-bolle he caught Alayn,   throte-bolle: Adam's apple.
And he hente hym despitously agayn,   despitously: furiously. agayn: in re-
And on the nose he smoot hym with his fest.   4275 turn.
Doun ran the blody streem upon his brest;
And in the floor, with nose and mouth tobroke,   tobroke: crushed.
They walwe as doon two pigges in a poke;   poke: sack.
And up they goon, and doun agayn anon,
Til that the millere sporned at a stoon,   4280 sporned at: stumbled over.
And doun he fil bakward upon his wyf,
That wiste no thyng of this nyce stryf;   nyce: foolish.
For she was falle aslepe a lite wight   lite wight: little while.
With John the clerk, that waked hadde al nyght,
And with the fal out of hir sleep she breyde.   4285 breyde: started, awoke.

4257. a twenty devel way: to the devils; to utter destruction.
4266. bolt: straight as an arrow. upright: flat on her back.

"Help! holy cros of Bromeholm," she seyde,
"*In manus tuas!* Lord, to thee I calle!
Awak, Symond! the feend is on me falle.
Myn herte is broken; help! I nam but ded!   nam but: am as good as.
Ther lyth oon upon my wombe and on myn   wombe: belly.
       heed.   4290
Help, Symkyn, for the false clerkes fighte!"
    This John sterte up as faste as ever he myghte,
And graspeth by the walles to and fro,   graspeth: gropes.
To fynde a staf; and she sterte up also,
And knew the estres bet than dide this John,   4295   estres: room.
And by the wal a staf she foond anon,
And saugh a litel shymeryng of a light,
For at an hole in shoon the moone bright;
And by that light she saugh hem bothe two,
But sikerly she nyste who was who,   4300
But as she saugh a whit thyng in hir eye.   but as: except that. in: with.
And whan she gan this white thyng espye,
She wende the clerk hadde wered a volupeer,   wende: thought. **volupeer**: night-cap.
And with the staf she drow ay neer and neer,   neer: nearer.
And wende han hit this Aleyn at the fulle,   4305   wende han: expected to have. **at the**
And smoot the millere on the pyled skulle,   fulle: squarely. pyled: bald.
That doun he gooth, and cride, "Harrow! I   that: so that. harrow!: help!
       dye!"
Thise clerkes beete hym weel and lete hym lye;
And greythen hem, and took hir hors anon,   greythen: get ready.
And eek hire mele, and on hir wey they gon.   4310
And at the mille yet they tooke hir cake
Of half a busshel flour, ful wel ybake.   ybake: baked.
    Thus is the proude millere wel ybete,   ybete: beaten.
And hath ylost the gryndyng of the whete,
And payed for the soper everydel   4315   everydel: fully.
Of Aleyn and of John, that bette hym wel.   bette: beat.
His wyf is swyved, and his doghter als.   als: also.
Lo, swich it is a millere to be fals!   swich it is: such a thing it is for.
And therfore this proverbe is seyd ful sooth,
"Hym thar nat wene wel that yvele dooth";   4320
A gylour shal hymself bigyled be.   gylour: beguiler, trickster.
And God, that sitteth heighe in magestee,
Save al this compaignye, grete and smale!
Thus have I quyt the Millere in my tale.   quyt: requited, repaid.

      Heere is ended the
       Reves tale.

4286. A supposed piece of the true Cross, brought to Bromholm in Norfolk in 1223, was reputed to free the obsessed from demons, to cure the sick, and to raise the dead.
4287. *In manus tuas,* [*Domine, commendo spiritum meum*]: "Into thy hands, O Lord, I commend my spirit"—a common religious formula. See Luke xxiii.46.
4320. "He must not expect good who does evil."

The prologe of the
Cokes tale.

The Cook of Londoun, whil the Reve spak, 4325
For joye him thoughte he clawed him on the
    bak.   clawed: scratched, rubbed.
"Ha! ha!" quod he, "for Cristes passion,
This millere hadde a sharp conclusion
Upon his argument of herbergage!   herbergage: lodging.
Wel seyde Salomon in his langage,   4330
'Ne bryng nat every man into thyn hous';
For herberwynge by nyghte is perilous.
Wel oghte a man avysed for to be   avysed for to be: to consider.
Whom that he broghte into his pryvetee.   pryvetee: privacy.
I pray to God, so yeve me sorwe and care,   4335
If evere, sitthe I highte Hogge of Ware,
Herde I a millere bettre yset a-werk.   yset a-werk: fooled.
He hadde a jape of malice in the derk.   hadde: i.e., experienced. jape: joke,
But God forbede that we stynte heere;   trick.
And therfore, if ye vouche sauf to heere   4340
A tale of me, that am a povre man,
I wol yow telle, as wel as evere I kan,
A litel jape that fil in oure citee."   fil: befell, happened.
   Oure Hoost answerde and seide, "I graunte it
      thee.
Now telle on, Roger, looke that it be good;   4345
For many a pastee hastow laten blood,   laten blood: drained off the gravy.
And many a Jakke of Dovere hastow soold   Jakke of Dovere: (?) an old meat pie.
That hath been twies hoot and twies coold.
Of many a pilgrym hastow Cristes curs,
For of thy percely yet they fare the wors,   4350 percely: parsley.
That they han eten with thy stubbel goos;   stubbel goos: an old goose fatted on
For in thy shoppe is many a flye loos.   stubble.
Now telle on, gentil Roger by thy name.
But yet I pray thee, be nat wroth for game;
A man may seye ful sooth in game and pley." 4355
   "Thou seist ful sooth," quod Roger, "by my
      fey!
But 'sooth pley, quaad pley,' as the Flemyng
      seith.
And therfore, Herry Bailly, by thy feith,   departen: separate.
Be thou nat wrooth, er we departen heer,
Though that my tale be of an hostileer.   4360 hostileer: innkeeper.
But nathelees I wol nat telle it yit;

4325. For two portraits of **The Cook of Londoun** see p. 479.
4326. It seemed to the Cook, because of his joy, that the Reve rubbed him on the back.
4331–32. See Ecclesiasticus xi.31.
4357. A true jest is a bad jest.

But er we parte, ywis, thou shalt be quit."
And therwithal he lough and made cheere,
And seyde his tale, as ye shul after heere.

lough: laughed. **cheere:** *good cheer.*

Heere bigynneth the
Cookes tale.

A prentys whilom dwelled in oure citee, 4365
And of a craft of vitailliers was hee.
Gaillard he was as goldfynch in the shawe,
Broun as a berye, a propre short felawe,
With lokkes blake, ykembd ful fetisly.
Dauncen he koude so wel and jolily 4370
That he was cleped Perkyn Revelour.
He was as ful of love and paramour
As is the hyve ful of hony sweete:
Wel was the wenche with hym myghte meete.
At every bridale wolde he synge and hoppe; 4375
He loved bet the taverne than the shoppe.
For whan ther any ridyng was in Chepe,
Out of the shoppe thider wolde he lepe—
Til that he hadde al the sighte yseyn,
And daunced wel, he wolde nat come
          ayeyn— 4380
And gadered hym a meynee of his sort
To hoppe and synge and maken swich disport;
And ther they setten stevene for to meete,
To pleyen at the dys in swich a streete.
For in the toune nas ther no prentys 4385
That fairer koude caste a paire of dys
Than Perkyn koude, and therto he was free
Of his dispense, in place of pryvetee.
That fond his maister wel in his chaffare;
For often tyme he foond his box ful bare. 4390
For sikerly a prentys revelour
That haunteth dys, riot, or paramour,
His maister shal it in his shoppe abye,
Al have he no part of the mynstralcye.
For thefte and riot, they been convertible, 4395
Al konne he pleye on gyterne or ribible.
Revel and trouthe, as in a lowe degree,
They been ful wrothe al day, as men may see.

prentys: apprentice.
vitailliers: victuallers.
gaillard: gay. **shawe:** *wood, grove.*
propre: handsome.
fetisly: neatly.

paramour: sexual love.

wel: lucky.
hoppe: dance.

ridyng: procession; jousting.

ayeyn: back.
meynee: company.

setten stevene: made an appointment.
dys: dice.

dispense: spending. **pryvetee:** *privacy.*
wel: easily. **chaffare:** *business.*

paramour: wenching.
abye: pay for, buy dearly.

convertible: interchangeable.
ribible: fiddle.

4377. **Chepe:** Cheapside, one of the principal streets of London, a favorite scene of festivals and processions.
4392. **riot:** wanton living; debauchery.
4397–98. Reveling and honesty, in a man of low rank, are always angry (i.e., incompatible) with each other.

This joly prentys with his maister bood,   **bood:** stayed.
Til he were ny out of his prentishood,   4400
Al were he snybbed bothe erly and late,   **snybbed:** snubbed; chided, rebuked.
And somtyme lad with revel to Newegate.
But atte laste his maister hym bithoghte,   **hym bithoghte:** remembered.
Upon a day, whan he his papir soghte,
Of a proverbe that seith this same word,   4405
"Wel bet is roten appul out of hoord
Than that it rotie al the remenaunt."   **rotie:** cause to rot.
So fareth it by a riotous servaunt;
It is ful lasse harm to lete hym pace,   **pace:** depart.
Than he shende alle the servantz in the   **shende:** spoil.
    place.   4410
Therfore his maister yaf hym acquitance,
And bad hym go, with sorwe and with mes-
    chance!
And thus this joly prentys hadde his leve.
Now lat hym riote al the nyght or leve.   **leve:** leave off.
And for ther is no theef withoute a lowke,   4415   **lowke:** confederate.
That helpeth hym to wasten and to sowke   **sowke:** cheat, embezzle.
Of that he brybe kan or borwe may,   **that:** that which. **brybe:** steal.
Anon he sente his bed and his array   **array:** gear; clothing.
Unto a compeer of his owene sort,   **compeer:** comrade.
That lovede dys, and revel, and disport,   4420
And hadde a wyf that heeld for contenance   **heeld:** kept. **contenance:** appearance.
A shoppe, and swyved for hir sustenance.   **swyved:** copulated.

The wordes of the Hoost
to the compaignye.

  Oure Hooste saugh wel that the brighte sonne
The ark of his artificial day hath ronne   **ark:** arc.
The ferthe part, and half an houre and moore,
And though he were nat depe ystert in loore,
He wiste it was the eightetethe day   5   **eightetethe:** eighteenth.
Of Aprill, that is messager to May;   **messager:** forerunner, harbinger.
And saw wel that the shadwe of every tree
Was as in lengthe the same quantitee
That was the body erect that caused it.
And therfore, by the shadwe he took his wit   10   **wit:** judgment.

4402. City minstrels accompanied criminals to prison.
4404. Probably when the apprentice wished release from his apprenticeship.
4422. It is impossible to say whether the rest of this poem was lost or never written. No analogue has been discovered, perhaps because the fragment is so brief or because it starts a true story of London life.
2. **artificial day:** from sunrise to sunset (the natural day is 24 hours).
4. And though he had not rushed deeply into learning.

That Phebus, which that shoon so clere and
      brighte,
Degrees was fyve and fourty clombe on highte;   was clombe: had climbed.
And for that day, as in that latitude,
It was ten at the clokke, he gan conclude,
And sodeynly he plighte his hors aboute.   15   plighte: pulled.
   "Lordynges," quod he, "I warne yow, al this
      route,   route: company.
The fourthe party of this day is gon.   party: part.
Now, for the love of God and of Seint John,
Leseth no tyme, as ferforth as ye may.   ferforth: far.
Lordynges, the tyme wasteth nyght and day,   20
And steleth from us, what pryvely slepynge,   what: what with. pryvely: secretly.
And what thurgh necligence in oure wakynge,
As dooth the streem that turneth nevere agayn,   agayn: back.
Descendynge fro the montaigne into playn.
Wel kan Senec and many a philosophre   25
Biwaillen tyme moore than gold in cofre;
For 'Los of catel may recovered be,   catel: chattels; goods.
But los of tyme shendeth us,' quod he.   shendeth: ruins.
It wol nat come agayn, withouten drede,   drede: doubt.
Namoore than wole Malkynes maydenhede,   30
Whan she hath lost it in hir wantownesse.
Lat us nat mowlen thus in ydelnesse.   mowlen: grow moldy.
   "Sire Man of Lawe," quod he, "so have ye
      blis,
Telle us a tale anon, as forward is.   forward: agreement.
Ye been submytted, thurgh youre free assent,   35
To stonden in this cas at my juggement.   cas: case (at law).
Acquiteth yow now of youre biheeste;   acquiteth yow: make good. biheeste:
Thanne have ye do youre devoir atte leeste."   promise. devoir: duty.
   "Hooste," quod he, "*depardieux,* ich assente;   *depardieux:* in God's name. ich: I.
To breke forward is nat myn entente.   40
Biheste is dette, and I wole holde fayn
Al my biheste, I kan no bettre sayn.
For swich lawe as a man yeveth another wight,
He sholde hymselven usen it, by right;
Thus wole oure text. But nathelees, certeyn,   45   oure text: a legal textbook.
I kan right now no thrifty tale seyn   thrifty: profitable.
That Chaucer, thogh he kan but lewedly   lewedly: ignorantly.
On metres and on rymyng craftily,
[Nath] seyd hem in swich Englissh as he kan
Of olde tyme, as knoweth many a man;   50
And if he have nat seyd hem, leve brother,   leve: dear.
In o book, he hath seyd hem in another.
For he hath toold of loveris up and doun

---

30. **Malkyn:** proverbial name for a wanton woman.
34–45. Both the Host and the Man of Law here use legal terminology.

Mo than Ovide made of mencioun
In his Episteles, that been ful olde.   55
What sholde I tellen hem, syn they been tolde?
   In youthe he made of Ceys and Alcione,
And sitthen hath he spoken of everichone,
Thise noble wyves and thise loveris eke.
Whoso that wole his large volume seke,   60
Cleped the Seintes Legende of Cupide,
Ther may he seen the large woundes wyde
Of Lucresse, and of Babilan Tesbee;
The swerd of Dido for the false Enee;
The tree of Phillis for hire Demophon;   65
The pleinte of Dianire and of Hermyon,
Of Adriane, and of Isiphilee;
The bareyne yle stondynge in the see;
The dreynte Leandre for his Erro;
The teeris of Eleyne, and eek the wo   70
Of Brixseyde, and of the, Ladomya;
The crueltee of the, queene Medea,
The litel children hangyng by the hals,
For thy Jason, that was of love so fals!
O Ypermystra, Penelopee, Alceste,   75
Youre wifhod he comendeth with the beste!
   But certeinly no word ne writeth he
Of thilke wikke ensample of Canacee,
That loved hir owene brother synfully
(Of swiche cursed stories I sey 'Fy!');   80
Or ellis of Tyro Appollonius,
How that the cursed kyng Antiochus
Birafte his doghter of hir maydenhede,
That is so horrible a tale for to rede,
Whan he hir threw upon the pavement.   85
And therfore he, of ful avysement,
Nolde nevere write in none of his sermons
Of swiche unkynde abhominacions,
Ne I wol noon reherce, if that I may.
   But of my tale how shal I doon this day?   90
Me were looth be likned, doutelees,
To Muses that men clepe Pierides—
Methamorphosios woot what I mene;

Glosses:

of mencioun: mention of.

what: why.

sitthen: since then.
wyves: women.

seke: search through.

dreynte: drowned. **Erro**: Hero.

the: thee.

hals: neck.

wifhod: womanhood.

birafte: robbed.

avysement: deliberation.
sermons: writings.
unkynde: unnatural.
if that I may: so far as it is in my
    power; if I can help it.
me were looth: I should be displeased
    to be.

---

55. Episteles: the *Heroides,* a series of twenty-one verse epistles, fourteen of which were purportedly written by heroines listed below (ll. 64–75, omitting Alceste).

57. Ceys and Alcione: a story from Ovid's *Metamorphoses,* briefly retold by Chaucer in *The Book of the Duchess.*

61. *The Legend of Good Women,* in which appear the stories of seven of these women.

78–85. These stories were told by John Gower in his *Confessio Amantis.*

92. Pierides: (1) the nine Muses, daughters of Pieros of Macedonia; (2) the daughters of King Pieros of Emathia, who gave them the names of the nine Muses; Ovid (*Metamorphoses* V) tells how they contended with the Muses and were changed into magpies.

But nathelees, I recche noght a bene   bene: bean.
Though I come after hym with hawebake.   95 hawebake: baked haws; meager fare.
I speke in prose, and lat him rymes make."
And with that word he, with a sobre cheere,
Bigan his tale, as ye shal after heere.

The prologe of the
Mannes tale of Lawe.

O hateful harm, condicion of poverte!   harm: misfortune.
With thurst, with cold, with hunger so con-
        foundid!   100
To asken help thee shameth in thyn herte;
If thou noon aske, with nede artow so woundid
That verray nede unwrappeth al thy wounde hid!
Maugree thyn heed, thou most for indigence
Or stele, or begge, or borwe thy despence!   105 despence: means of sustenance.

Thow blamest Crist, and seist ful bitterly,
He mysdeparteth richesse temporal;   mysdeparteth: distributes wrongly.
Thy neighebor thou wytest synfully,   wytest: blamest.
And seist thou hast to lite, and he hath al.   to: too. lite: little.
"Parfay," seistow, "somtyme he rekene shal,   110 parfay: by my faith.
Whan that his tayl shal brennen in the gleede,   gleede: live coals.
For he noght helpeth needfulle in hir neede."   needfulle: the needy.

  Herkne what is the sentence of the wise: sentence: maxim.
"Bet is to dyen than have indigence";
"Thy selve neighebor wol thee despise."   115 selve: very.
If thou be povre, farwel thy reverence!
Yet of the wise man take this sentence:
"Alle the dayes of povre men been wikke."   wikke: evil.
Be war, therfore, er thou come to that prikke!   prikke: point.

If thou be povre, thy brother hateth thee,   120
And alle thy freendes fleen from thee, allas!
O riche marchauntz, ful of wele been yee,   wele: weal, well-being.
O noble, o prudent folk, as is this cas!
Youre bagges been nat filled with ambes as,
But with sys cynk, that renneth for youre
        chaunce;   125
At Cristemasse myrie may ye daunce!

---

96. The Man of Law was first assigned the prose *Melibee*, now assigned to Chaucer.
104. maugree thyn heed: in spite of your resistance.
124–25. ambes as: double ace, a losing cast in the medieval dice game called hazard.   sys cynk: six-five, a winning cast.   chaunce: the caster's throw which he tries to match, as in craps.

Ye seken lond and see for youre wynnynges;   seken: search through.
As wise folk ye knowen al th'estaat   estaat: estate, condition.
Of regnes; ye been fadres of tidynges   regnes: realms, kingdoms.
And tales, bothe of pees and of debaat.   130 debaat: conflict, war.
I were right now of tales desolaat,   desolaat: destitute.
Nere that a marchant, goon is many a yeere,   nere: were it not.
Me taughte a tale, which that ye shal heere.

Heere bigynneth the Man of Lawe his tale.

In Surrye whilom dwelte a compaignye   Surrye: Syria.
Of chapmen riche, and therto sadde and   chapmen: merchants. sadde: trust-
    trewe,   135 worthy.
That wyde-where senten hir spicerye,   wyde-where: far and wide.
Clothes of gold, and satyns riche of hewe.
Hir chaffare was so thrifty and so newe   chaffare: merchandise.
That every wight hath deyntee to chaffare   deyntee: pleasure. chaffare: trade.
With hem, and eek to sellen hem hire ware.   140

Now fil it that the maistres of that sort   fil it: it befell. sort: company.
Han shapen hem to Rome for to wende;   han shapen hem: planned.
Were it for chapmanhod or for disport,   chapmanhod: business. disport:
Noon oother message wolde they thider sende,   pleasure. message: messengers.
But comen hemself to Rome, this is the ende; 145 comen: came. ende: sum total.
And in swich place as thoughte hem avantage
For hire entente, they take hir herbergage.   herbergage: lodging.

Sojourned han thise marchantz in that toun
A certein tyme, as fil to hire plesance.
But so bifel that th'excellent renoun   150
Of the Emperoures doghter, dame Custance,
Reported was, with every circumstance,   with every circumstance: in full detail.
Unto thise Surryen marchantz in swich wyse,
Fro day to day, as I shal yow devyse.

This was the commune voys of every man: 155
"Oure Emperour of Rome—God hym see!—   see: behold, protect.
A doghter hath that, syn the world bigan,
To rekene as wel hir goodnesse as beautee,
Nas nevere swich another as is she.
I pray to God in honour hir susteene,   160
And wolde she were of al Europe the queene.

---

the Man of Lawe his tale. The Man of Law's Tale is a Christian romance based on an episode recounted by Nicholas Trevet in *Les Cronicles* (completed c. 1334). Chaucer intensified his poem by the addition of moving prayers and auctorial apostrophes and comments.
138. thrifty: i.e., profitable to the buyer.

"In hire is heigh beautee, withoute pride,
Youthe, withoute grenehede or folye;

To alle hire werkes vertu is hir gyde;
Humblesse hath slayn in hir al tirannye.   165
She is mirour of alle curteisye;
Hir herte is verray chambre of holynesse,
Hir hand, ministre of fredam for almesse."

And al this voys was sooth, as God is trewe.
But now to purpos lat us turne agayn.   170
Thise marchantz han doon fraught hir shippes
          newe,

doon fraught: caused to be loaded.

And whan they han this blisful mayden sayn,
Hoom to Surrye been they went ful fayn,

blisful: excellent. sayn: seen.

And doon hir nedes as they han doon yoore,
And lyven in wele; I kan sey yow namoore.   175

nedes: business. yoore: formerly.

Now fil it that thise marchantz stode in grace
Of hym that was the Sowdan of Surrye;

Sowdan: Sultan.

For whan they cam from any strange place,
He wolde, of his benigne curteisye,
Make hem good cheere, and bisily espye   180
Tidynges of sondry regnes, for to leere

espye: inquire about.
regnes: realms. leere: learn.

The wondres that they myghte seen or heere.

Amonges othere thynges, specially,
Thise marchantz han hym told of dame Cus-
          tance
So greet noblesse in ernest, ceriously,   185

ceriously: in detail.

That this Sowdan hath caught so greet plesance
To han hir figure in his remembrance;
And al his lust and al his bisy cure

lust: desire. cure: care, endeavor.

Was for to love hire while his lyf may dure.

dure: last.

Paraventure in thilke large book   190
Which that men clepe the hevene ywriten was
With sterres, whan that he his birthe took,
That he for love sholde han his deeth, allas!
For in the sterres, clerer than is glas,
Is writen, God woot, whoso koude it rede,   195

whoso: (for) whoever.

The deeth of every man, withouten drede.

drede: doubt.

In sterres, many a wynter therbiforn,
Was writen the deeth of Ector, Achilles,
Of Pompei, Julius, er they were born;

---

168. Her hand, servant of liberality in almsgiving.
180. make hem good cheere: receive them hospitably.
187. I.e., to imagine her, to think about her.

The strif of Thebes; and of Hercules,   200
Of Sampson, Turnus, and of Socrates
The deeth; but mennes wittes been so dulle
That no wight kan wel rede it atte fulle.   atte fulle: fully.

   This Sowdan for his privee conseil sente,
And, shortly of this matere for to pace,   205 of: from. pace: pass.
He hath to hem declared his entente,
And seyde hem, certein, but he myghte have
          grace
To han Custance withinne a litel space,   space: time.
He nas but deed; and charged hem in hye   in hye: in haste.
To shapen for his lyf som remedye.   210

   Diverse men diverse thynges seyden;
They argumenten, casten up and doun;   casten: deliberate.
Many a subtil reson forth they leyden;
They speken of magyk and abusioun.   abusioun: deception.
But finally, as in conclusioun,   215
They kan nat seen in that noon avantage,
Ne in noon oother wey, save mariage.

Thanne sawe they therinne swich difficultee
By wey of reson, for to speke al playn,   by wey of: according to.
By cause that ther was swich diversitee   220
Bitwene hir bothe lawes, that they sayn   lawes: religions.
They trowe, "that no Cristen prince wolde fayn   fayn: willingly.
Wedden his child under oure lawe sweete
That us was taught by Mahoun, oure prophete."   Mahoun: Mahomet.

   And he answerde, "Rather than I lese   225 lese: lose.
Custance, I wol be cristned, doutelees.
I moot been hires, I may noon oother chese.   chese: choose.
I pray yow hold youre argumentz in pees;
Saveth my lyf, and beth noght recchelees   recchelees to geten: careless about
To geten hire that hath my lyf in cure;   230 winning. in cure: in her power.
For in this wo I may nat longe endure."

   What nedeth gretter dilatacioun?   dilatacioun: diffuseness.
I seye, by tretys and embassadrie,
And by the popes mediacioun,
And al the chirche, and al the chivalrie,   235 chivalrie: nobility.
That in destruccioun of mawmettrie,   mawmettrie: Mohammedanism;
And in encrees of Cristes lawe deere,   idolatry.
They been acorded, so as ye shal heere:

How that the Sowdan and his baronage
And alle his lieges sholde ycristned be,   240 lieges: subjects.

And he shal han Custance in mariage,
And certein gold, I noot what quantitee;   certein: a certain amount of.
And heer-to founden sufficient seuretee.   founden: (was) furnished.
This same accord was sworn on either syde;
Now, faire Custance, almyghty God thee
      gyde!   245   gyde: keep.

Now wolde som men waiten, as I gesse,   waiten: expect.
That I sholde tellen al the purveiance   purveiance: provision.
That th'Emperour, of his grete noblesse,
Hath shapen for his doghter, dame Custance.
Wel may men knowen that so greet ordinance 250 ordinance: provision.
May no man tellen in a litel clause
As was arrayed for so heigh a cause.   arrayed: arranged. cause: affair.

Bisshopes been shapen with hire for to wende, shapen: appointed.
Lordes, ladies, knyghtes of renoun,
And oother folk ynowe, this is th'ende;   255   th'ende: the upshot.
And notified is thurghout the toun
That every wight, with greet devocioun,
Sholde preyen Crist that he this mariage
Receyve in gree, and spede this viage.   gree: favor.

The day is comen of hir departynge;   260
I seye, the woful day fatal is come,
That ther may be no lenger tariynge,
But forthward they hem dressen, alle and some. forthward: forward. hem dressen: pre-
Custance, that was with sorwe al overcome,   pare (to go).
Ful pale arist, and dresseth hire to wende; 265 arist: (ariseth) arises. dresseth hire:
For wel she seeth ther is noon oother ende.   prepares herself.

Allas! what wonder is it thogh she wepte,
That shal be sent to strange nacioun
Fro freendes that so tendrely hir kepte,   kepte: took care of.
And to be bounden under subjeccioun   270
Of oon, she knoweth nat his condicioun?   condicioun: character.
Housbondes been alle goode, and han ben
      yoore;   yoore: for a long time.
That knowen wyves; I dar sey yow na moore.

"Fader," she seyde, "thy wrecched child Cus-
      tance,
Thy yonge doghter fostred up so softe,   275 softe: tenderly.
And ye, my moder, my soverayn pleasance
Over alle thyng, out-taken Crist on-lofte,   out-taken: except. on-lofte: above.
Custance youre child hir recomandeth ofte   hir: herself.
Unto youre grace, for I shal to Surrye,
Ne shal I nevere seen yow moore with eye.   280

"Allas! unto the Barbre nacioun   Barbre: heathen, Saracen.
I moste anon, syn that it is youre wille;   moste: must go.
But Crist, that starf for our redempcioun   starf: died.
So yeve me grace his heestes to fulfille!   heestes: commandments.
I, wrecche womman, no fors though I spille!   285   wrecche: wretched. **no fors**: no matter. spille: am destroyed.
Wommen are born to thraldom and penance,
And to been under mannes governance."

    I trowe at Troye, whan Pirrus brak the wal   brak: broke.
Or Ilion brende, at Thebes the citee,   or: ere, before.
N'at Rome, for the harm thurgh Hanybal   290
That Romayns hath venquysshed tymes thre,
Nas herd swich tendre wepyng for pitee
As in the chambre was for hir departynge;
But forth she moot, wher-so she wepe or synge.   moot: is to go. **wher-so**: whether.

    O firste moevyng! cruel firmament,   295
With thy diurnal sweigh that crowdest ay
And hurlest al from est til occident
That naturelly wolde holde another way,
Thy crowdyng set the hevene in swich array   array: arrangement.
At the bigynnyng of this fiers viage,   300   fiers: dangerous.
That cruel Mars hath slayn this mariage.

Infortunat ascendent tortuous,
Of which the lord is helplees falle, allas,
Out of his angle into the derkest hous!
O Mars, o atazir, as in this cas!   305   **as in this cas**: in this situation.
O fieble moone, unhappy been thy paas!   **been thy paas**: are thy steps (is your course).
Thou knyttest thee ther thou art nat receyved;
Ther thou were wel, fro thennes artow weyved.   wel: well situated. **weyved**: forced.

Imprudent Emperour of Rome, allas!
Was ther no philosophre in al thy toun?   310   philosophre: astrologer.
Is no tyme bet than oother in swich cas?   cas: situation.
Of viage is ther noon eleccioun,
Namely to folk of heigh condicioun?   condicioun: station.
Nat whan a roote is of a burthe yknowe?
Allas, we been to lewed or to slowe!   315   **to lewed**: too ignorant. **slowe**: slothful.

---

295. **firste moevyng**: Primum Mobile, the outermost concentric sphere of the Ptolemaic universe, beyond the sphere of the fixed stars, and those of the seven planets. Its motion or sway (**sweigh**, l. 296) pushes (cf. **crowdest**, l. 296) everything with it from east to west, and was thus responsible for the unfortunate position of Mars at the time of the voyage and marriage of Constance.

302–5. Mars (305) was the lord (303) of (had a dominant influence over) his angle (304) or house, Aries, a sign of the zodiac called **tortuous** (302) because it ascends most obliquely. The **derkest hous** (304) is the most unfavorable position; **atazir** (305) is an Arabic astrological term meaning influence.

307. **knyttest thee**: joinest thyself (art in conjunction). **nat receyved**: in unfavorable position.

312. **eleccioun**: an astrological term meaning the choice of a time favorable for an undertaking.

314. **roote**: the planetary positions in the heavens at the moment of a person's birth.

To ship is brought this woful faire mayde
Solempnely, with every circumstance.
"Now Jhesu Crist be with yow alle!" she sayde;
Ther nys namoore, but "Farewel, faire Cus-
      tance!"
She peyneth hire to make good contenance;   320   make good contenance: appear com-
And forth I lete hir saille in this manere,   posed.
And turne I wol agayn to my matere.

The moder of the Sowdan, welle of vices,
Espied hath hir sones pleyn entente,   espied: discovered. pleyn: full.
How he wol lete his olde sacrifices;   325   lete: forsake.
And right anon she for hir conseil sente,
And they been come to knowe what she mente.   mente: purposed.
And whan assembled was this folk in-feere,   in-feere: together.
She sette hir doun, and seyde as ye shal heere.

"Lordes," quod she, "ye knowen every-
      chon,   330
How that my sone in point is for to lete
The holy lawes of our Alkaron,   Alkaron: Koran.
Yeven by Goddes message Makomete.   message: messenger.
But oon avow to grete God I heete,
The lyf shal rather out of my body sterte   335   rather: sooner. sterte: go.
Or Makometes lawe out of myn herte!   or: ere, before.

"What sholde us tyden of this newe lawe   tyden: befall. of: from.
But thraldom to oure bodies and penance,
And afterward in helle to be drawe,   drawe: brought.
For we reneyed Mahoun oure creance?   340   for: because. reneyed: denied.
But, lordes, wol ye maken assurance,   creance: faith.
As I shal seyn, assentynge to my loore,   loore: advice.
And I shal make us sauf for everemoore?"   and: if. sauf: secure.

They sworen and assenten, every man,
To lyve with hire and dye, and by hir stonde,   345
And everich, in the beste wise he kan,
To strengthen hire shal alle his frendes fonde;   fonde: seek.
And she hath this emprise ytake on honde,   emprise: enterprise. on honde: in
Which ye shal heren that I shal devyse,   hand.
And to hem alle she spak right in this wyse: 350

"We shul first feyne us cristendom to take,—
Coold water shal nat greve us but a lite!
And I shal swich a feeste and revel make
That, as I trowe, I shal the Sowdan quite.

---

317. with every circumstance: with careful attention to propriety.
334. oon avow heete: make one vow.

For thogh his wyf be cristned never so white, 355
She shal have nede to wasshe awey the rede,
Thogh she a font-ful water with hire lede."   lede: may bring.

O Sowdanesse, roote of iniquitee!
Virago, thou Semyrame the secounde!
O serpent under femynynytee,   360
Lik to the serpent depe in helle ybounde!
O feyned womman, al that may confounde   feyned: deceiving, hypocritical.
Vertu and innocence, thurgh thy malice,
Is bred in thee, as nest of every vice!

O Sathan, envious syn thilke day   365
That thou were chaced from oure heritage,   chaced from: deprived of.
Wel knowestow to wommen the olde way!   way: path.
Thou madest Eva brynge us in servage;   servage: servitude.
Thou wolt fordoon this Cristen mariage.   fordoon: destroy.
Thyn instrument so, weylawey the while!   370
Makestow of wommen, whan thou wolt bigile.

This Sowdanesse, whom I thus blame and
      warye,   warye: curse.
Leet prively hir conseil goon hire way.   leet: caused.
What sholde I in this tale lenger tarye?   what: why.
She rideth to the Sowdan on a day,   375
And seyde hym that she wolde reneye hir lay,   reneye: renounce. lay: creed.
And cristendom of preestes handes fonge,   fonge: accept.
Repentynge hire she hethen was so longe;

Bisechynge hym to doon hire that honour,
That she moste han the Cristen folk to   moste: might.
      feeste,—   380
"To plesen hem I wol do my labour."
The Sowdan seith, "I wol doon at youre heste";   doon . . . heste: carry out your order.
And knelynge thanketh hire of that requeste.
So glad he was, he nyste what to seye.   nyste: (ne wiste) knew not.
She kiste hir sone, and hom she gooth hir
      weye.   385

      Explicit prima pars.
      Sequitur pars secunda.

Arryved been this Cristen folk to londe
In Surrye, with a greet solempne route,   route: company.
And hastily this Sowdan sente his sonde,   sonde: messenger.
First to his moder, and al the regne aboute,

---

359. Semyrame: Semiramis, who, by Chaucer's time, had become a type of vicious pagan woman-hood.

360. According to medieval belief, the serpent who tempted Eve had a woman's face.

And seyde his wyf was comen, out of doute,   390
And preyde hire for to ryde agayn the queene,   agayn: toward; i.e., to meet.
The honour of his regne to sustene.

Greet was the prees, and riche was th'array   prees: press, crowd.
Of Surryens and Romayns met yfeere;   yfeere: together.
The moder of the Sowdan, riche and gay,   395
Receyveth hire with also glad a cheere   also: as. cheere: spirit.
As any moder myghte hir doghter deere,
And to the nexte citee ther bisyde
A softe paas solempnely they ryde.   softe: gentle, slow.

Noght trowe I the triumphe of Julius,   400
Of which that Lucan maketh swich a boost,
Was roialler ne moore curius   curius: splendid.
Than was th'assemblee of this blisful hoost.   blisful: illustrious.
But this scorpion, this wikked goost,   goost: spirit.
The Sowdanesse, for al hire flaterynge,   405
Caste under this ful mortally to stynge.   caste: contrived.

The Sowdan comth hymself soone after this
So roially, that wonder is to telle;
He welcometh hire with alle joye and blis,
And thus in myrthe and joye I lete hem
      dwelle;   410
The fruyt of this matere is that I telle.   fruyt: essential part. that: that which.
Whan tyme cam, men thoughte it for the beste
That revel stynte, and men go to hir reste.

The tyme cam, this olde Sowdanesse
Ordeyned hath this feeste of which I tolde,   415   ordeyned: arranged.
And to the feeste Cristen folk hem dresse   hem dresse: direct themselves, go.
In general, ye, bothe yonge and olde.
Heere may men feeste and roialtee biholde,   roialtee: splendor.
And deyntees mo than I kan yow devyse;
But al to deere they boghte it er they ryse.   420   to: too. ryse: rose.

O sodeyn wo, that evere art successour
To worldly blisse, spreynd with bitternesse!   spreynd: sprinkled.
The ende of the joye of oure worldly labour!
Wo occupieth the fyn of oure gladnesse.   occupieth: dwells in. fyn: end.
Herke this conseil for thy sikernesse: 425   sikernesse: security.
Upon thy glade day have in thy mynde
The unwar wo or harm that comth bihynde.   unwar: unexpected.

For shortly for to tellen, at o word,   at: in.
The Sowdan and the Cristen everichone   Cristen: Christians.
Been al tohewe and stiked at the bord,   430   tohewe: hewn in pieces. stiked:
But it were oonly dame Custance allone.   stabbed. bord: table. but: except.

This olde Sowdanesse, cursed crone,
Hath with hir freendes doon this cursed dede,
For she hirself wolde al the contree lede.   lede: govern.

Ne ther nas Surryen noon that was converted, 435
That of the conseil of the Sowdan woot,
That he nas al tohewe er he asterted.   asterted: escaped.
And Custance han they take anon, foot-hoot,   foot-hoot: hastily.
And in a ship al steerelees, God woot,   steerelees: rudderless.
They han hir set, and bidde hir lerne saille   440
Out of Surrye agaynward to Itaille.   agaynward: back.

A certein tresor that she thider ladde,   ladde: brought.
And, sooth to seyn, vitaille gret plentee   vitaille: victuals, provisions.
They han hir yeven, and clothes eek she hadde,
And forth she saileth in the salte see.   445
O my Custance, ful of benignytee,
O Emperours yonge doghter deere,
He that is lord of Fortune be thy steere!   steere: rudder; steersman, guide.

She blesseth hire, and with ful pitous voys   blesseth hire: crosses herself.
Unto the croys of Crist thus seyde she: 450
"O cleere, o weleful auter, holy croys,   cleere: shining. weleful: blessed.
Reed of the Lambes blood ful of pitee,   auter: altar. reed: red. of: from.
That wessh the world fro the olde iniquitee, wessh: washed.
Me fro the feend and fro his clawes kepe,
That day that I shal drenchen in the depe. 455 drenchen: drown.

Victorious tree, proteccioun of trewe,   trewe: the faithful.
That oonly worthy were for to bere
The Kyng of Hevene with his woundes newe,
The white Lamb, that hurt was with a spere,
Flemere of feendes out of hym and here   460 flemere: one who puts to flight.
On which thy lymes feithfully extenden,
Me kepe, and yeve me myght my lyf t'amenden."

   Yeres and dayes fleet this creature   fleet: (floateth) floats, drifts.
Thurghout the See of Grece unto the Strayte
Of Marrok, as it was hir aventure.   465 aventure: destiny.
On many a sory meel now may she bayte;   bayte: feed.
After hir deeth ful often may she wayte,   after wayte: expect.
Er that the wilde wawes wol hir dryve   wawes: waves.
Unto the place ther she shal arryve.

460–61. Expeller of fiends from those over whom your arms, in accordance with Christian rite, extend (i.e., in blessing; making the sign of the Cross was central to the rite of exorcism).
464–65. See . . . Marrok: Mediterranean to the Strait of Morocco, i.e., of Gibraltar.

Men myghten asken why she was nat slayn 470
Eek at the feeste? who myghte hir body save?
And I answere to that demande agayn,   agayn: in reply.
Who saved Danyel in the horrible cave
Ther every wight save he, maister and knave,
Was with the leon frete er he asterte?   475   with: by. frete: devoured. asterte:
No wight but God, that he bar in his herte.   might escape. bar: bore.

God liste to shewe his wonderful myracle
In hire, for we sholde seen his myghty werkis;   for: in order that.
Crist, which that is to every harm triacle,   triacle: sovereign remedy.
By certein meenes ofte, as knowen clerkis,   480
Dooth thyng for certein ende that ful derk is
To mannes wit, that for oure ignorance
Ne konne noght knowe his prudent purveiance.   purveiance: providence.

Now sith she was nat at the feeste yslawe,   yslawe: slain.
Who kepte hire fro the drenchyng in the see? 485   drenchyng: drowning.
Who kepte Jonas in the fisshes mawe   mawe: maw, stomach.
Til he was spouted up at Nynyvee?
Wel may men knowe it was no wight but he
That kepte the peple Ebrayk from hir drench-
      ynge,
With drye feet thurghout the see passynge.   490

Who bad the foure spiritz of tempest
That power han t'anoyen lond and see,   anoyen: disturb.
Bothe north and south, and also west and est,
"Anoyeth neither see, ne land, ne tree"?
Soothly, the comandour of that was he   495
That fro the tempest ay this womman kepte
As wel whan she wook as whan she slepte.   wook: was awake.

Where myghte this womman mete and drynke   where: from what source. mete: food.
      have
Thre yeer and moore? how lasteth hir vitaille?
Who fedde the Egipcien Marie in the cave,   500
Or in desert? No wight but Crist, sanz faille.   sanz faille: without fail, certainly.
Fyve thousand folk it was as greet mervaille
With loves fyve and fisshes two to feede.   loves: loaves.
God sente his foyson at hir grete neede.   foyson: bounty.

470–504. Skeat suggests that such passages as this, not found in Trevet, may have been added by Chaucer in revision.

491–94. See Revelation vii.1–3.

500. St. Mary the Egyptian, after spending her youth in debauchery, lived forty-seven years alone in the wilderness.

She dryveth forth into oure occian   505
Thurghout oure wilde see, til at the laste   oure see: the North Sea.
Under an hoold that nempnen I ne kan,   hoold: stronghold, castle. nempnen:
Fer in Northhumberlond the wawe hir caste,   name. wawe: wave.
And in the sond hir ship stiked so faste   sond: sand. stiked: stuck.
That thennes wolde it noght of al a tyde;   510 of: during. al a: a whole.
The wyl of Crist was that she sholde abyde.

The constable of the castel doun is fare   constable: governor. is fare: went.
To seen this wrak, and al the ship he soghte,   soghte: searched through.
And foond this wery womman ful of care;
He foond also the tresor that she broghte.   515
In hir langage mercy she bisoghte,
The lyf out of hir body for to twynne,   twynne: separate.
Hir to delivere of wo that she was inne.

A maner Latyn corrupt was hir speche,
But algates therby was she understonde.   520 algates: nevertheless.
This constable, whan hym liste no longer seche,   seche: search.
This woful womman broghte he to the londe.
She kneleth doun and thanketh Goddes sonde;   sonde: gifts (what He sent).
But what she was she wolde no man seye,   seye: tell.
For foul ne fair, thogh that she sholde deye. 525

She seyde she was so mazed in the see   mazed: bewildered.
That she forgat hir mynde, by hir trouthe.   forgat hir mynde: lost her memory.
The constable hath of hire so greet pitee,
And eek his wyf, that they wepen for routhe.   routhe: pity.
She was so diligent, withouten slouthe,   530 slouthe: sloth.
To serve and plese everich in that place,   everich: everyone.
That alle hir loven that looken on hir face.

This constable and dame Hermengyld, his wyf,
Were payens, and that contree everywhere;   payens: pagans. that contree: the peo-
But Hermengyld loved hire right as hir lyf,   535   ple of that country.
And Custance hath so longe sojourned there,
In orisons, with many a bitter teere,
Til Jhesu hath converted thurgh his grace
Dame Hermengyld, constablesse of that place.   constablesse: constable's wife.

In al that lond no Cristen dorste route;   540 route: assemble in a company.
Alle Cristen folk been fled fro that contree
Thurgh payens, that conquereden al aboute   thurgh: because of.
The plages of the north, by land and see.   plages: regions.
To Walys fledde the Cristianytee   Walys: Wales. Cristianytee: Christian
Of olde Britons dwellyng in this ile;   545   group.
Ther was hir refut for the meene while.   refut: place of refuge.

---

508. Northhumberlond: an English kingdom bordering north of the River Humber.

But yet nere Cristen Britons so exiled
That ther nere somme that in hir privetee   nere: were not. in hir privetee: in
Honoured Crist and hethen folk bigiled,   secret.
And ny the castel swiche ther dwelten three.   550
That oon of hem was blynd and myghte nat see,
But it were with thilke eyen of his mynde
With whiche men seen, after that they been
        blynde.

Bright was the sonne as in that someres day,
For which the constable and his wyf also   555
And Custance han ytake the righte way   righte: straight.
Toward the see a furlong wey or two,
To pleyen and to romen to and fro;
And in hir walk this blynde man they mette,
Croked and oold, with eyen faste yshette.   560   yshette: shut.

"In name of Crist," cride this blinde Britoun,
"Dame Hermengyld, yif me my sighte agayn!"
This lady weex affrayed of the soun,   weex: became.
Lest that hir housbonde, shortly for to sayn,
Wolde hire for Jhesu Cristes love han slayn,   565   Cristes love: her love for Christ.
Til Custance made hir boold, and bad hir
        wirche   wirche: work, perform.
The wyl of Crist, as doghter of his chirche.

The constable weex abasshed of that sight,   weex abasshed: became upset.
And seide, "What amounteth al this fare?"   amounteth: means. fare: business.
Custance answerde, "Sire, it is Cristes myght, 570
That helpeth folk out of the feendes snare."
And so ferforth she gan oure lay declare   ferforth: far. lay: doctrine.
That she the constable, er that it was eve,
Converteth, and on Crist made hym bileve.

This constable was nothyng lord of this place 575   nothyng: not at all.
Of which I speke, ther he Custance fond,
But kepte it strongly many wyntres space
Under Alla, kyng of al Northhumberlond,
That was ful wys, and worthy of his hond   worthy of his hond: valiant in deeds.
Agayn the Scottes, as men may wel heere;   580
But turne I wol agayn to my matere.

Sathan, that evere us waiteth to bigile,   waiteth: lies in wait.
Saugh of Custance al hir perfeccioun,
And caste anon how he myghte quite hir while,   caste: plotted. quite hir while: repay
And made a yong knyght that dwelte in that   her time, i.e., her trouble.
        toun   585

---

557. a furlong wey: the time needed to walk one furlong; about two and one-half minutes.

Love hire so hote, of foul affeccioun,
That verraily hym thoughte he sholde spille,   spille: perish.
But he of hire myghte ones have his wille.

He woweth hire, but it availleth noght;   woweth: woos.
She wolde do no synne, by no weye.   590
And for despit he compassed in his thoght   compassed: planned.
To maken hire on shameful deeth to deye.
He wayteth whan the constable was aweye,   wayteth: watches. whan: i.e., until.
And pryvely upon a nyght he crepte
In Hermengyldes chambre, whil she slepte.   595

    Wery, forwaked in hir orisouns,   forwaked: exhausted by staying awake.
Slepeth Custance, and Hermengyld also.
This knyght, thurgh Sathanas temptaciouns,
Al softely is to the bed ygo,   ygo: gone.
And kitte the throte of Hermengyld atwo,   600 kitte: cut. atwo: in two.
And leyde the blody knyf by dame Custance,
And wente his wey, ther God yeve hym mes-   ther: i.e., may. meschance: disaster.
    chance!

Soone after cometh this constable hom agayn,
And eek Alla, that kyng was of that lond,
And saw his wyf despitously yslayn,   605 despitously: cruelly.
For which ful ofte he weep and wrong his   weep: wept.
    hond,
And in the bed the blody knyf he fond
By Dame Custance. Allas! what myghte she
    seye?
For verray wo hir wit was al aweye.   aweye: gone.

    To kyng Alla was told al this meschance,   610
And eek the tyme, and where, and in what wise
That in a ship was founden this Custance,
As heer-biforn that ye han herd devyse.
The kynges herte of pitee gan agryse,   agryse: feel deep compassion.
Whan he saw so benigne a creature   615
Falle in disese and in mysaventure.   disese: distress. mysaventure: mis-
    fortune.

For as the lomb toward his deeth is broght,   lomb: lamb.
So stant this innocent bifore the kyng.   stant: (standeth) stands.
This false knyght, that hath this tresoun wroght,
Bereth hire on hond that she hath doon this   bereth on hond: asserts.
    thyng.   620
But nathelees, ther was greet moornyng
Among the peple, and seyn they kan nat gesse   seyn: (they) say. gesse: believe.
That she had doon so greet a wikkednesse;

For they han seyn hire evere so vertuous,   seyn: seen.
And lovyng Hermengyld right as hir lyf.   625

Of this baar witnesse everich in that hous,
Save he that Hermengyld slow with his knyf.   slow: slew.
This gentil kyng hath caught a gret motyf
Of this witnesse, and thoghte he wolde enquere   witnesse: testimony (cf. 1.626).
Depper in this, a trouthe for to lere.   630   lere: learn.

   Allas! Custance, thou hast no champioun,
Ne fighte kanstow noght, so weylaway!   kanstow: canst thou.
But he that starf for our redempcioun,   starf: died.
And boond Sathan (and yet lyth ther he lay),   lyth ther: (Satan) lies where.
So be thy stronge champion this day!   635
For, but if Crist open miracle kithe,   kithe: may show.
Withouten gilt thou shalt be slayn as swithe.   as swithe: as quickly as possible, im-
                                                   mediately.

She sette hire doun on knees, and thus she
      sayde:
"Immortal God, that savedest Susanne
Fro false blame, and thou, merciful mayde,   640
Marie I meene, doghter to Seint Anne,
Bifore whos child angeles synge Osanne,
If I be giltlees of this felonye,
My socour be, for ellis shal I dye!"   socour: succor, help.

   Have ye nat seyn somtyme a pale face,   645
Among a prees, of hym that hath be lad   prees: press, crowd. be lad: been led.
Toward his deeth, wher as hym gat no grace,
And swich a colour in his face hath had,
Men myghte knowe his face that was bistad,   bistad: in distress.
Amonges alle the faces in that route?   650
So stant Custance, and looketh hire aboute.

   O queenes, lyvynge in prosperitee,
Duchesses, and ye ladies everichone,
Haveth som routhe on hir adversitee!
An Emperoures doghter stant allone;   655
She hath no wight to whom to make hir mone.
O blood roial, that stondest in this drede,   drede: peril.
Fer been thy freendes at thy grete nede!

   This Alla kyng hath swich compassioun,
As gentil herte is fulfild of pitee,   660 fulfild: full.
That from his eyen ran the water doun.
"Now hastily do fecche a book," quod he,   do fecche: have fetched.
"And if this knyght wol sweren how that she
This womman slow, yet wol we us avyse   slow: slew. us avyse: consider.

628–29. caught a gret motyf of: was greatly moved by.
639. Susanne: The two elders falsely accused Susanna of adultery (see the apocryphal book of Susanna; or, in the Vulgate, Daniel xiii).

Whom that we wole that shal been oure jus-
     tise.”   665

A Britoun book, written with Evaungiles,
Was fet, and on this book he swoor anoon   fet: fetched.
She gilty was, and in the meene whiles
An hand hym smoot upon the nekke-boon,
That doun he fil atones as a stoon,   670   atones: at one stroke.
And bothe his eyen broste out of his face   broste: burst.
In sighte of everybody in that place.

A voys was herd in general audience,
And seyde, “Thou hast desclaundred, giltelees,   desclaundred: slandered.
The doghter of holy chirche in heigh pres-   heigh: i.e., of God.
     ence;   675
Thus hastou doon, and yet I holde my pees!”
Of this mervaille agast was al the prees;
As mazed folk they stoden everichone,   mazed: bewildered.
For drede of wreche, save Custance allone.   wreche: vengeance.

Greet was the drede and eek the repentance 680
Of hem that hadden wrong suspecioun
Upon this sely innocent, Custance;   sely: holy.
And for this miracle, in conclusioun,
And by Custances mediacioun,
The kyng—and many another in that place— 685
Converted was, thanked be Cristes grace!

This false knyght was slayn for his untrouthe
By juggement of ·Alla hastily;   hastily: in a short time.
And yet Custance hadde of his deeth greet
     routhe.
And after this Jhesus, of his mercy.   690
Made Alla wedden ful solempnely
This holy mayden, that is so bright and sheene; sheene: shining.
And thus hath Crist ymaad Custance a queene.

But who was woful, if I shal nat lye,
Of this weddyng but Donegild, and namo, 695 namo: no one else.
The kynges mooder, ful of tirannye?
Hir thoughte hir cursed herte brast atwo.   hir thoughte: it seemed to her. brast:
She wolde noght hir sone had doon so;   would burst: atwo: in two.
Hir thoughte a despit that he sholde take   despit: outrage.
So strange a creature unto his make.   700 strange: foreign, strange. make: mate,
                                         wife.

---

666. A copy of the Gospels in British or Welsh.
673. in general audience: in the hearing of everyone present.

Me list nat of the chaf, ne of the stree,   stree: straw.
Maken so long a tale as of the corn.   corn: grain, kernel.
What sholde I tellen of the roialtee   what: why. roialtee: splendor.
At mariage, or which cours goth biforn;
Who bloweth in a trumpe or in an horn?   705
The fruyt of every tale is for to seye;   fruyt: essential part.
They ete, and drynke, and daunce, and synge,
      and pleye.

They goon to bedde, as it was skile and right;   skile: the proper thing.
For though that wyves be ful holy thynges,
They moste take in pacience at nyght   710
Swiche manere necessaries as been plesynges
To folk that han ywedded hem with rynges,
And leye a lite hir holynesse aside,
As for the tyme,—it may noon oother bitide.

On hire he gat a knave child anon,   715 gat: begot. knave: male.
And to a bisshop, and his constable eke,
He took his wyf to kepe, whan he is gon
To Scotland-ward, his foomen for to seke.
Now faire Custance, that is so humble and meke,
So longe is goon with childe, til that stille   720 stille: constantly.
She halt hir chambre, abidyng Cristes wille.   halt: (holdeth) remains in.

The tyme is come a knave child she beer;   beer: bore.
Mauricius at the fontstoon they hym calle.   fontstoon: baptismal font.
This constable dooth forth come a messageer,   dooth: causes.
And wroot unto his kyng, that cleped was
      Alle,   725
How that this blisful tidyng is bifalle,   tidyng: event.
And othere tidynges speedful for to seye.   speedful: advantageous.
He tath the lettre, and forth he goth his weye.   tath: (taketh) takes.

This messager, to doon his avantage,   doon his avantage: better himself.
Unto the kynges moder rideth swithe,   730 swithe: rapidly.
And salueth hire ful faire in his langage: salueth: greets.
"Madame," quod he, "ye may be glad and blithe;
And thanketh God an hundred thousand sithe!   thanketh: thank (imperative). sithe:
My lady queene hath child, withouten doute,   times.
To joye and blisse of al this regne aboute.   735

Lo, here the lettres seled of this thyng,   lettres: letter.
That I moot bere with al the haste I may.
If ye wol aught unto youre sone the kyng,
I am youre servant, bothe nyght and day."
Donegild answerde, "As now at this tyme,
      nay;   740

But here al nyght I wol thou take thy reste.
Tomorwe wol I seye thee what me leste."

This messager drank sadly ale and wyn,   sadly: unstintingly.
And stolen were his lettres pryvely
Out of his box, whil he sleep as a swyn;   745 sleep: slept.
And countrefeted was ful subtilly   countrefeted: forged.
Another lettre, wroght ful synfully,
Unto the kyng direct, of this mateere,   direct: directed.
Frô his constable, as ye shal after heere.

The lettre spak the queene delivered was   750 spak: said.
Of so horrible a feendly creature
That in the castel noon so hardy [nas]
That any while dorste ther endure.   endure: stay.
The moder was an elf, by aventure   elf: a supernatural being having magi-
Ycomen, by charmes or by sorcerie,   755   cal powers.
And every wight hateth hir compaignye.

Wo was this kyng whan he this lettre had
    sayn,   sayn: seen.
But to no wight he tolde his sorwes soore,
But of his owene hand he wroot agayn,   agayn: in reply.
"Welcome the sonde of Crist for everemoore 760 the sonde: the "sending" (i.e., what
To me that am now lerned in his loore!   He sends). loore: doctrine.
Lord, welcome be thy lust and thy plesaunce;   lust: desire.
My lust I putte al in thyn ordinaunce.   ordinaunce: governance.

Kepeth this child, al be it foul or feir,   kepeth: take care of (imperative).
And eek my wyf, unto myn hom-comynge.   765
Crist, whan hym list, may sende me an heir
Moore agreable than this to my likynge."
This lettre he seleth, pryvely wepynge,
Which to the messager was take soone,   take: given.
And forth he goth; ther is na moore to doone. 770

O messager, fulfild of dronkenesse,—
Strong is thy breeth, thy lymes faltren ay,   lymes: limbs. faltren: falter, are un-
And thou biwreyest alle secreenesse.   steady. biwreyest: divulge.
Thy mynde is lorn, thou janglest as a jay,   lorn: lost. janglest: chatter.
Thy face is turned in a new array.   775 array: appearance.
Ther dronkenesse regneth in any route,
Ther is no conseil hid, withouten doute.

O Donegild, I ne have noon Englissh digne   digne: suitable.
Unto thy malice and thy tirannye!
And therfore to the feend I thee resigne;   780

---

752. nas: the reading of one late MS; all others read **was**. It seems likely that this uncharac-
teristic rime was due to scribal carelessness in O'.

Lat hym enditen of thy traitorie!
Fy, mannysh, fy!—o nay, by God, I lye—   mannysh: manlike (i.e., unwomanly).
Fy, feendlych spirit, for I dar wel telle,
Thogh thou heere walke, thy spirit is in helle!

This messager comth fro the kyng agayn,   785
And at the kynges modres court he lighte,   lighte: alighted.
And she was of this messager ful fayn,   fayn: solicitous.
And plesed hym in al that ever she myghte.
He drank, and wel his girdel underpighte;   underpighte: propped up.
He slepeth, and he fnorteth in his gyse   790 fnorteth: snores. gyse: usual manner.
Al nyght, til the sonne gan aryse.

Eft were his lettres stolen everychon,   eft: again.
And countrefeted lettres in this wyse:
"The king comandeth his constable anon,
Up peyne of hangyng, and on heigh juyse,   795 up: on. heigh juyse: severe judgment.
That he ne sholde suffren in no wyse
Custance in-with his regne for t'abyde   in-with: within. regne: kingdom.
Thre dayes and a quarter of a tyde;   a: one.

"But in the same ship as he hire fond,
Hire, and hir yonge sone, and al hir geere,   800
He sholde putte, and crowde hir fro the lond,   crowde: push.
And charge hire that she never eft come there."   eft: again.
O my Custance, wel may thy goost have feere,   goost: spirit.
And, slepyng, in thy dreem been in penance,   penance: suffering, pain.
Whan Donegild cast al this ordinance.   805 cast: plotted. ordinance: plan.

This messager on morwe, whan he wook,
Unto the castel halt the nexte way,   halt: holds. nexte: nearest.
And to the constable he the lettre took;
And whan that he this pitous lettre say,   say: saw.
Ful ofte he seyde, "Allas! and weylaway!"   810
"Lord Crist," quod he, "how may this world
        endure,
So ful of synne is many a creature?

"O myghty God, if that it be thy wille,
Sith thou art rightful juge, how may it be   rightful: just.
That thou wolt suffren innocentz to spille,   815 spille: perish.
And wikked folk regne in prosperitee?
O goode Custance, allas! so wo is me
That I moot be thy tormentour, or deye   tormentour: executioner.
On shames deeth; ther is noon oother weye."   on shames deeth: in a death of shame.

Wepen bothe yonge and olde in al that   wepen: wept.
        place   820
Whan that the kyng this cursed lettre sente,

And Custance, with a dedly pale face,
The ferthe day toward hir ship she wente.   ferthe: fourth.
But nathelees she taketh in good entente   in good entente: with good will.
The wyl of Crist, and knelyng on the stronde, 825   stronde: strand, shore.
She seyde, "Lord, ay welcome be thy sonde!   thy sonde: what you send.

    "He that me kepte fro the false blame
While I was on the lond amonges yow,
He kan me kepe from harm and eek fro shame
In salte see, althogh I se noght how.   830
As strong as evere he was, he is yet now.
In hym triste I, and in his moder deere,   triste: trust.
That is to me my sayl and eek my steere."   steere: rudder.

Hir litel child lay wepyng in hir arm,
And knelyng, pitously to hym she seyde,   835
"Pees, litel sone, I wol do thee noon harm."
With that hir coverchief of hir hed she breyde,   of: off. breyde: pulled.
And over his litel eyen she it leyde,
And in hir arm she lulleth it ful faste,   faste: tenderly.
And into hevene hir eyen up she caste.   840

    "Moder," quod she, "and mayde bright,
            Marie,
Sooth is that thurgh wommans eggement   eggement: egging, instigation.
Mankynde was lorn, and damned ay to dye,   lorn: lost.
For which thy child was on a croys yrent.   yrent: torn.
Thy blisful eyen sawe al his torment;   845
Thanne is ther no comparison bitwene
Thy wo and any wo man may sustene.   sustene: endure.

"Thow saw thy child yslayn bifore thyne eyen,
And yet now lyveth my litel child, parfay!   parfay: by my faith.
Now, lady bright, to whom alle woful cryen,   850
Thow glorie of wommanhod, thow faire may,   may: maiden.
Thow haven of refut, brighte sterre of day,   refut: refuge.
Rewe on my child, that of thy gentillesse,   rewe: have pity. that: thou who.
Rewest on every reweful in distresse.

    "O litel child, allas! what is thy gilt,   855
That nevere wroghtest synne as yet, pardee?
Why wil thyn harde fader han thee spilt?   spilt: destroyed.
O mercy, deere constable," quod she,
"As lat my litel child dwelle here with thee;   as lat: pray let.
And if thou darst nat saven hym, for blame,   860   blame: fear of doing wrong.
So kys hym ones in his fadres name!"

Therwith she looketh bakward to the londe,
And seyde, "Farewel, housbonde routhelees!"   routhelees: pitiless.

And up she rist, and walketh doun the stronde — rist: (riseth) rises.
Toward the ship; hir folweth al the prees;   865
And evere she prayeth hir child to holde his
      pees;
And taketh hir leve, and with an holy entente — entente: heart.
She blesseth hire, and into ship she wente. — blesseth hire: crosses herself.

Vitailled was the ship, it is no drede, — it is no drede: assuredly.
Habundantly for hire ful longe space,   870 — space: time.
And othere necessaries that sholde nede — nede: be necessary.
She hadde ynogh, heryed be Goddes grace! — heryed: praised.
For wynd and weder almyghty God purchace, — God purchace: may God provide.
And brynge hir hom! I kan no bettre seye,
But in the see she dryveth forth hir weye.   875 — dryveth forth: pursues.

EXPLICIT SECUNDA PARS.
SEQUITUR PARS TERCIA.

Alla the kyng comth hom soone after this
Unto his castel, of the which I tolde,
And asketh where his wyf and his child is.
The constable gan aboute his herte colde, — colde: grow cold, be chilled.
And pleynly al the manere he hym tolde   880 — pleynly: fully.
As ye han herd—I kan telle it no bettre—
And sheweth the kyng his seel, and his lettre,

And seyde, "Lord, as ye comanded me
Up peyne of deeth, so have I doon, certein." — up: upon.
This messager tormented was til he   885 — tormented: put to torture.
Moste biknowe and tellen, plat and pleyn, — moste: had to. biknowe: make known.
Fro nyght to nyght, in what place he had leyn; — plat: flatly. pleyn: fully.
And thus, by wit and subtil enquerynge,
Ymagined was by whom this harm gan sprynge. — ymagined: conjectured.

The hand was knowe that the lettre wroot,   890
And al the venym of this cursed dede,
But in what wise, certeinly, I noot.
Th'effect is this, that Alla, out of drede, — effect: upshot. out of drede: assuredly.
His moder slow—that may men pleynly rede— — slow: slew.
For that she traitour was to hire ligeance.   895 — ligeance: allegiance.
Thus endeth olde Donegild, with meschance! — with meschance!: a curse upon her!

The sorwe that this Alla nyght and day
Maketh for his wyf, and for his child also,
Ther is no tonge that it telle may.
But now wol I unto Custance go,   900
That fleteth in the see, in peyne and wo, — fleteth: drifts.
Fyve yeer and moore, as liked Cristes sonde, — sonde: dispensation.
Er that hir ship approched unto londe.

Under an hethen castel, atte laste,
Of which the name in my text noght I fynde,   905
Custance, and eek hir child, the see up caste.
Almyghty God, that saveth al mankynde,
Have on Custance and on hir child som mynde,
That fallen is in hethen hand eft soone,
In point to spille, as I shal telle yow soone.   910

eft soone: again.

in point to spille: on the point of perishing.

Doun fro the castel comth ther many a wight
To gauren on this ship and on Custance.
But shortly, from the castel, on a nyght,
The lordes styward—God yeve hym mes-
        chance!—
A theef, that hadde reneyed oure creance,   915
Cam into ship allone, and seyde he sholde
Hir lemman be, wher-so she wolde or nolde.

gauren: gaze; stare.

*theef: villain. reneyed: renounced.
creance: faith, religion.*

lemman: lover.

Wo was this wrecched womman tho bigon;
Hir child cride, and she cride pitously.
But blisful Marie heelp hire right anon;   920
For with hir struglyng wel and myghtily
The theef fil overbord al sodeynly,
And in the see he dreynte for vengeance;
And thus hath Crist unwemmed kept Custance.

wo was bigon: was overcome with grief.

heelp: helped.

dreynte: drowned.

unwemmed: unspotted.

O foule lust of luxurie, lo, thyn ende!   925
Nat oonly that thou fayntest mannes mynde,
But verraily thou wolt his body shende.
Th'ende of thy werk, or of thy lustes blynde,
Is compleynyng. How many oon may men fynde
That noght for werk somtyme, but for th'en-
        tente   930
To doon this synne, been outher slayn or shente!

luxurie: lechery.

fayntest: enfeeble.

shende: ruin.

compleynyng: lamentation. oon: a one.

werk: deed.

shente: ruined.

How may this wayke womman han this
        strengthe
Hir to defende agayn this renegat?
O Golias, unmesurable of lengthe,
How myghte David make thee so maat,   935
So yong and of armure so desolat?
How dorste he looke upon thy dredful face?
Wel may men seen, it was but Goddes grace.

wayke: weak.

renegat: renegade.

Golias: Goliath.

maat: defeated utterly.

desolat: lacking.

Who yaf Judith corage or hardynesse
To sleen hym Olofernus in his tente,   940
And to deliveren out of wrecchednesse

hardynesse: boldness.

---

923. vengeance: retributive punishment.

The peple of God? I sey, for this entente,
That right as God spirit of vigour sente
To hem, and saved hem out of meschance,
So sente he myght and vigour to Custance.   945

   Forth gooth hir ship thurghout the narwe
          mouth
Of Jubaltare and Septe, dryvyng ay
Somtyme west, and somtyme north and south,
And somtyme est, ful many a wery day,
Til Cristes moder—blessed be she ay!—   950
Hath shapen, thurgh hir endelees goodnesse,   shapen: planned.
To make an ende of al hir hevynesse.

   Now lat us stynte of Custance but a throwe,   throwe: while.
And speke we of the Romayn Emperour,
That out of Surrye hath by lettres knowe   955
The slaughtre of cristen folk, and dishonour
Doon to his doghter by a fals traytour,
I mene the cursed wikked Sowdanesse
That at the feeste leet sleen bothe moore and   leet sleen: caused to be slain.
          lesse.

For which this Emperour hath sent anon   960
His senatour, with roial ordinance,   ordinance: command.
And othere lordes, God woot, many oon,
On Surryens to taken heigh vengeance.
They brennen, sleen, and brynge hem to mes-
          chance
Ful many a day; but shortly, this is th'ende,   965   ende: upshot.
Homward to Rome they shapen hem to wende.   shapen hem: prepare themselves.

   This senatour repaireth with victorie   repaireth: returns.
To Rome-ward, saillynge ful roially,
And mette the ship dryvynge, as seith the storie,
In which Custance sit ful pitously.   970   sit: (sitteth) sits.
Nothyng ne knew he what she was, ne why
She was in swich array, ne she nyl seye   array: state. nyl: (ne wyl) will not.
Of hire estaat, althogh she sholde deye.   sholde: might.

He bryngeth hire to Rome, and to his wyf
He yaf hire, and hir yonge sone also;   975
And with the senatour she ladde hir lyf.
Thus kan Oure Lady bryngen out of wo
Woful Custance, and many another mo.
And longe tyme dwelled she in that place,
In holy werkes evere, as was hir grace.   980

---

947. Jubaltare: Gibraltar. Septe: the African promontory opposite Gibraltar.

The senatoures wyf hir aunte was,
But for al that she knew hir never the moore.
I wol no lenger taryen in this cas,
But to kyng Alla, which I spak of yoore,   yoore: before.
That for his wyf wepeth and siketh soore,   985 siketh: sighs.
I wol retourne, and lete I wol Custance   lete: leave.
Under the senatoures governance.

   Kyng Alla, which that hadde his moder slayn,
Upon a day fil in swich repentance
That, if I shortly tellen shal and playn,   990
To Rome he comth to receyven his penance;
And putte hym in the Popes ordinance   ordinance: governance, control.
In heigh and logh, and Jhesu Crist bisoghte
Foryeve his wikked werkes that he wroghte.

   The fame anon thurgh Rome toun is born, 995 fame: rumor.
How Alla kyng shal comen in pilgrymage,
By herbergeours that wenten hym biforn;   herbergeours: harbingers; providers of
For which the senatour, as was usage,   lodgings.
Rood hym agayns, and many of his lynage,   agayns: to meet.
As wel to shewen his heighe magnificence   1000
As to doon any kyng a reverence.

   Greet cheere dooth this noble senatour   cheere: hospitality, kindness.
To kyng Alla, and he to hym also;
Everich of hem dooth oother greet honour.
And so bifel that in a day or two   1005
This senatour is to kyng Alla go
To feste, and shortly, if I shall nat lye,
Custances sone wente in his compaignye.

   Som men wolde seyn at requeste of Cus-
      tance
This senatour hath lad this child to feeste;   1010
I may nat tellen every circumstance,—
Be as be may, ther was he at the leeste.
But sooth is this that at his modres heeste   heeste: behest.
Biforn Alla, duryng the metes space,   metes space: time of the repast.
The child stood, lookyng in the kynges face. 1015

   This Alla kyng hath of this child greet wonder,
And to the senatour he seyde anon,
"Whos is that faire child that stondeth yonder?"
"I noot," quod he, "by God, and by Seint John!
A moder he hath, but fader hath he non   1020
That I of woot"—and shortly, in a stounde,   stounde: a short time.
He tolde Alla how that this child was founde.

"But God wot," quod this senatour also,
"So vertuous a lyvere in my lyf
Ne saw I nevere as she, ne herde of mo,   1025   as: such as.
Of worldly wommen, mayde, ne of wyf.   worldly: in the world; secular.
I dar wel seyn hir hadde levere a knyf   hir hadde levere: she had rather.
Thurghout hir brest, than ben a womman wikke;   wikke: wicked.
There is no man koude brynge hire to that
       prikke."   prikke: point.

   Now was this child as lyk unto Custance   1030
As possible is a creature to be.
This Alla hath the face in remembrance
Of dame Custance, and ther on mused he
If that the childes moder were aught she   aught: a whit, at all.
That is his wyf, and pryvely he sighte,   1035   sighte: sighed.
And spedde hym fro the table that he myghte.   that: as well as, as fast as.

"Parfay," thoghte he, "fantome is in myn heed!   fantome: phantom, illusion.
I oghte deme, of skilful jugement,   of: by. skilful: discerning.
That in the salte see my wyf is deed."
And afterward he made his argument: 1040   made his argument: reasoned.
"What woot I if that Crist have hider sent   what: how.
My wyf by see, as wel as he hir sente
To my contree fro thennes that she wente?"

And after noon, hom with the senatour
Goth Alla, for to seen this wonder chaunce.   1045   wonder: wondrous. chaunce: possi-
This senatour dooth Alla greet honour,   bility.
And hastifly he sente after Custaunce.
But trusteth wel, hir liste nat to daunce,
Whan that she wiste wherfore was that sonde;   sonde: sending.
Unnethe upon hir feet she myghte stonde.   1050   unnethe: scarcely.

   Whan Alla saugh his wyf, faire he hir grette,   grette: greeted.
And weep, that it was routhe for to see;   weep: wept.
For at the firste look he on hir sette,
He knew wel verraily that it was she.
And she, for sorwe, as doumb stant as a tree, 1055 stant: (standeth) stands.
So was hir herte shet in hir distresse,   shet: shut, closed.
Whan she remembered his unkyndenesse.

Twies she swowneth in his owene sighte;
He weep, and hym excused pitously.
"Now God," quod he, "and his halwes   halwes: saints.
       brighte   1060
So wisly on my soule as have mercy,   wisly: surely.
That of youre harm as giltelees am I   harm: suffering.

1049. wherfore was that sonde: why she was sent for.
1061–62. as have mercy, that: have mercy, as that.

As is Maurice my sone, so lyk youre face;
Elles the feend me fecche out of this place!"

Long was the sobbyng and the bitter
        peyne,   1065
Er that hir woful hertes myghte cesse;   cesse: become tranquil.
Greet was the pitee for to heere hem pleyne,   pleyne: complain, lament.
Thurgh whiche pleintes gan hir wo encresse.
I pray yow al my labour to relesse;
I may nat tell hir wo until to-morwe,   1070
I am so wery for to speke of sorwe.

But finally, whan that the sooth is wist
That Alla giltelees was of hir wo,
I trowe an hundred tymes been they kist,
And swich a blisse is ther bitwix hem two   1075
That, save the joye that lasteth everemo,
Ther is noon lyk that any creature
Hath seyn or shal, whil that the world may dure.   dure: endure, last.

Tho preyde she hir housbond mekely,
In relief of hir longe, pitous pyne,   1080 pyne: suffering.
That he wolde preye hir fader specially
That of his magestee he wolde enclyne   enclyne: be willing.
To vouche sauf som day with hym to dyne.
She preyde hym eek he sholde by no weye   weye: means.
Unto hir fader no word of hire seye.   1085

Som men wolde seyn how that the child
        Maurice
Dooth this message unto this Emperour;   dooth: delivers.
But, as I gesse, Alla was nat so nyce   nyce: foolish.
To hym that was of so sovereyn honour
As he that is of Cristen folk the flour,   1090 as he that: as one who. flour: flower.
Sente any child, but it is bet to deeme   sente: that he would send.
He wente hymself, and so it may wel seeme.

This Emperour hath graunted gentilly   graunted: agreed.
To come to dyner, as he hym bisoughte;
And wel rede I he looked bisily   1095 bisily: intently.
Upon this child, and on his doghter thoghte.
Alla goth to his in, and as hym oghte,   in: lodging.
Arrayed for this feste in every wise   arrayed: arranged.
As ferforth as his konnyng may suffise.   as ferforth as: insofar as. konnyng:
                                         ability.

The morwe cam, and Alla gan hym dresse, 1100 hym dresse: prepare himself.
And eek his wyf, this Emperour to meete;
And forth they ryde in joye and in gladnesse.   ryde: rode.

And whan she saugh hir fader in the strete,
She lighte doun, and falleth hym to feete.   lighte: alighted. hym to: at his.
"Fader," quod she, "youre yonge child Cus-
    tance   1105
Is now ful clene out of youre remembrance.

I am youre doghter Custance," quod she,
"That whilom ye han sent unto Surrye.
It am I, fader, that in the salte see
Was put allone and dampned for to dye.   1110   dampned: condemned.
Now, goode fader, mercy I yow crye!
Sende me namoore unto noon hethenesse,   hethenesse: realm of the heathen.
But thonketh my lord heere of his kyndenesse."   of: for.

  Who kan the pitous joye tellen al
Bitwixe hem thre, syn they been thus ymette? 1115
But of my tale make an ende I shal;
The day goth faste, I wol no lenger lette.   lette: delay.
This glade folk to dyner they hem sette;
In joye and blisse at mete I lete hem dwelle
A thousand fold wel moore than I kan telle.   1120   moore: greater.

  This child Maurice was sithen Emperour   sithen: afterwards.
Maad by the Pope, and lyved cristenly;
To Cristes chirche he dide greet honour.
But I lete al this storie passen by;
Of Custance is my tale specially.   1125
In the olde Romayn gestes may men fynde   gestes: histories.
Maurices lyf; I bere it noght in mynde.

  This kyng Alla, whan he his tyme say,   say: saw.
With his Custance, his holy wyf so sweete,
To Engelond been they come the righte way, 1130   righte: direct.
Wher as they lyve in joye and in quiete.
But litel while it lasteth, I yow heete,   heete: assure.
Joye of this world, for tyme wol nat abyde;
Fro day to nyght it changeth as the tyde.   tyde: tide.

Who lyved euere in swich delit a day   1135   a: one.
That hym ne moeved outher conscience,
Or ire, or talent, or som kynnes affray,   talent: lust. kynnes affray: kind of fear.
Envye, or pride, or passion, or offence?   offence: injury.
I ne seye but for this ende this sentence,   sentence: opinion.
That litel while in joye or in plesance   1140
Lasteth the blisse of Alla with Custance.

1126–27. Like the story of Constance, **Maurices lyf** is found in the section of Trevet's *Les Cronicles* entitled "Les gestes des apostles, emperours, et rois."

For Deeth, that taketh of heigh and logh his
        rente,   *of: from.*
Whan passed was a yeer, evene as I gesse,   *rente: tribute.*
Out of this world this kyng Alla he hente,   *evene: exactly.*
For whom Custance hath ful greet hevynesse. 1145   *he: i.e., Death.*
Now lat us prayen God his soule blesse!
And dame Custance, finally to seye,
Toward the toun of Rome goth hir weye.

   To Rome is come this holy creature,
And fyndeth hire freendes hoole and sounde; 1150
Now is she scaped al hir aventure.   *is scaped: has escaped.*
And whan that she hir fader hath yfounde,
Doun on hir knees falleth she to grounde;
Wepynge for tendrenesse in herte blithe,
She heryeth God an hundred thousand sithe. 1155 *heryeth: praises. sithe: times.*

   In vertu and in holy almes-dede   *almes-dede: deeds of mercy.*
They lyven alle, and nevere asonder wende;
Til deeth departeth hem, this lyf they lede.   *departeth: separates.*
And fareth now wel! my tale is at an ende.
Now Jhesu Crist, that of his myght may
        sende   1160
Joye after wo, governe us in his grace,
And kepe us alle that been in this place! Amen.

Heere endeth the tale of the Man of Lawe.

   Owre Hoost upon his stiropes stood anon,
And seyde, "Goode men, herkeneth everych on!
This was a thrifty tale for the nones!   1165 *thrifty: profitable.* **for the nones:** *for*
Sir Parisshe Prest," quod he, "for Goddes bones,   *the occasion.*
Telle us a tale, as was thi forward yore.   *forward: promise.* **yore:** *before.*
I se wel that ye lerned men in lore
Can muche good, by Goddes dignitee!"   *can: know.*
   The Parson him answerde, "Benedicite!   1170
What eyleth the man, so synfully to swere?"   *eyleth: makes.*
Oure Host answerde, "O Jankin, be ye there?

1163–90. These lines are found in only thirty-four manuscripts. Apparently they were originally written with the Wife of Bath as interrupter and as teller of the story of the monk and the merchant's wife (eventually the Shipman's Tale). According to this theory, line 1179 was later rewritten to designate a pilgrim beginning with an "S" (twenty-seven manuscripts read "Squyer"; six read "Somnour"; one reads "Shipman"). Robinson prints "Shipman," but he believes that Chaucer "meant to cancel" the link (p. 6) and accordingly encloses it in square brackets. Robinson states (p. 889) that Chaucer "never made a final arrangement of what he had written" and therefore follows the "arrangement of the best MSS., with all its imperfections," i.e., the Ellesmere order, in which the Man of Law's Tale is followed by the Wife of Bath's Tale. See the section "The Order of the Tales" (pp. xxxv–xxxvii, above).

1172. **Jankin:** a derisive name for a priest, often referred to as Sir John.

I smelle a Lollere in the wynd," quod he.
"Now! goode men," quod oure Hoste, "herken-
      eth me;
Abydeth, for Goddes digne passioun,   1175 digne: noble.
For we shal han a predicacioun;   predicacioun: preaching, sermon.
This Lollere heer wil prechen us somwhat."
   "Nay, by my fader soule, that shal he nat!"   fader: father's.
Seyde the Shipman; "heer shal he nat preche;
He shal no gospel glosen here ne teche.   1180 glosen: gloss, explain.
We leven alle in the grete God," quod he;   leven: believe.
"He wolde sowen som difficultee,
Or springen cokkel in our clene corn.   springen: sow. cokkel: tares.
And therfore, Hoost, I warne thee biforn,   corn: grain.
My joly body shal a tale telle,   1185
And I shal clynken you so mery a belle,
That I shal waken al this compaignie.
But it shal not ben of philosophie,
Ne phislyas, ne termes queinte of lawe.
Ther is but litel Latyn in my mawe!"   1190 mawe: maw, belly.

Heere bigynneth the Shipmannes tale.

   A marchant whilom dwelled at Seint-Denys,
That riche was, for which men helde hym wys.
A wyf he hadde of excellent beautee;
And compaignable and revelous was she,   revelous: merry-making.
Which is a thyng that causeth more dispence   5 dispence: expenditure.
Than worth is al the cheere and reverence   cheere: attention.
That men hem doon at festes and at daunces.
Swiche salutaciouns and contenaunces   contenaunces: gestures, behavior.
Passen as dooth a shadwe upon the wal;
But wo is hym that payen moot for al!   *1200 moot: must.
The sely housbonde, algate he moot paye,   sely: wretched. algate: at all times.
He moot us clothe, and he moot us arraye,
Al for his owene worship richely,   worship: honor.

1173. **Lollere:** a contemptuous term, like Lollard, for the followers of John Wyclif; the Wyclifites opposed swearing.

1189. **phislyas:** This strange word may echo the physicians mentioned in the Tale of Melibee, originally assigned to the Man of Law; Melibee has also "philosophie," "termes queinte of lawe," "Latyn," and "lore" (l. 1168).

the Shipmannes tale. The Shipman's Tale may be Chaucer's earliest fabliau (for the genre see the first note on the Miller's Tale). Its closest analogues are Boccaccio, *Decamerone* viii.1 and the redaction of it by Giovanni Sercambi of Lucca, *Novelle,* no. 32. Chaucer fleshed out the characters and created a realistic setting which is clearly French, as indicated by the places and by oaths and other expressions.

1. **Seint-Denys:** St.-Denis-sur-Seine, eight miles north of Paris.

11—19. Chaucer transferred this tale from the Wife of Bath to the Shipman without revising these lines, which reflect her personality.

In which array we daunce jolily.
And if that he noght may, par aventure,   15
Or ellis list no swich dispence endure,   *list: desires.*
But thynketh it is wasted and ylost,
Thanne moot another payen for oure cost,
Or lene us gold, and that is perilous.   *lene: lend.*
    This noble marchant heeld a worthy
        hous,   *1210
For which he hadde alday so greet repair   *alday: constantly. repair: resort, re-*
For his largesse, and for his wyf was fair,   *pairing (of people). for: because*
That wonder is; but herkneth to my tale.   *(of). largesse: liberality.*
Amonges alle his gestes, grete and smale,
Ther was a monk, a fair man and a bold—   25
I trowe a thritty wynter he was old—   *thritty: thirty.*
That evere in oon was drawyng to that place.   *evere in oon: at all times. drawyng:*
This yonge monk, that was so fair of face,   *resorting.*
Aqueynted was so with the goode man,
Sith that hir firste knoweliche bigan,   *1220 *knoweliche: acquaintance, friendship.*
That in his hous as famulier was he
As it is possible any freend to be.
    And for as muchel as this goode man,
And eek this monk, of which that I bigan,
Were bothe two yborn in o village,   35 *o: one.*
The monk hym claymeth as for cosynage;   *cosynage: cousinhood; kinship.*
And he agayn, he seith nat ones nay,   *agayn: in return.*
But was as glad therof as fowel of day;   *fowel: bird.*
For to his herte it was a greet plesaunce.
Thus been they knyt with eterne alliaunce,   *1230
And ech of hem gan oother for t'assure
Of bretherhede, whil that hir lyf may dure.
    Free was daun John, and namely of dispence,   *daun: lord, sir (title of respect).*
As in that hous, and ful of diligence   *as in: in.*
To doon plesaunce, and also greet costage.   45 *doon costage: spend money.*
He nat forgat to yeve the leeste page
In al that hous; but after hir degree,   *after: according to.*
He yaf the lord, and sitthe al his meynee,   *sitthe: afterwards. meynee: household.*
Whan that he cam, som manere honest thyng;   *honest: befitting.*
For which they were as glad of his comyng   *1240
As fowel is fayn whan that the sonne up riseth.
Na moore of this as now, for it suffiseth.
    But so bifel, this marchant on a day
Shoop hym to make redy his array   *shoop hym: prepared. array: clothing;*
Toward the toun of Brugges for to fare,   55 *equipment.*
To byen there a porcioun of ware;   *byen: buy. ware: merchandise.*
For which he hath to Parys sent anon
A messager, and preyed hath daun John
That he sholde come to Seint-Denys and pleye

41–42. See Knight's Tale, l. 1132 and footnote.

With hym and with his wyf a day or tweye,   *1250
Er he to Brugges wente, in alle wise.

    This noble monk, of which I yow devyse,
Hath of his abbot, as hym list, licence,
By cause he was a man of heigh prudence,
And eek an officer, out for to ryde,   65
To seen hir graunges and hir bernes wyde,
And unto Seint-Denys he comth anon.
Who was so welcome as my lord daun John,
Oure deere cosyn, ful of curteisye?
With hym broghte he a jubbe of malvesye,   *1260
And eek another, ful of fyn vernage,
And volatyl, as ay was his usage.
And thus I lete hem ete and drynke and pleye,
This marchant and this monk, a day or tweye.

    The thridde day, this marchant up ariseth,   75
And on his nedes sadly hym avyseth,
And up into his countour-hous goth he
To rekene with hymselve, wel may be,
Of thilke yeer how that it with hym stood,
And how that he despended hadde his good, *1270
And if that he encressed were or noon.
His bookes and his bagges many oon
He leyth biforn hym on his countyng-bord.
Ful riche was his tresor and his hord,
For which ful faste his countour-dore he
      shette;   85
And eek he nolde that no man sholde hym lette
Of his acountes, for the meene tyme;
And thus he sit til it was passed pryme.

    Daun John was risen in the morwe also,
And in the gardyn walketh to and fro,   *1280
And hath his thynges seyd ful curteisly.

    This goode wyf cam walkyng pryvely
Into the gardyn, ther he walketh softe,
And hym salueth, as she hath doon ofte.
A mayde child cam in hir compaignye,   95
Which as hir list she may governe and gye,
For yet under the yerde was the mayde.
"O deere cosyn myn, daun John," she sayde,
"What eyleth yow so rathe for to ryse?"
    "Nece," quod he, "it oghte ynough
      suffise   *1290
Fyve houres for to slepe upon a nyght,

in alle wise: by all means.

licence: leave.

out ryde: ride abroad.

wyde: spread over a large region; far asunder.

jubbe: jug. **malvesye:** malmsey wine.

vernage: a white wine of Italy.

volatyl: wildfowl.

despended: spent. **good:** money.

encressed: more prosperous.

lette: hinder.

sit: sits. **passed pryme:** past nine o'clock.

his thynges seyd: read his Breviary.

salueth: salutes, greets.

gye: guide.

the yerde: the rod (of authority).

eyleth: makes. **rathe:** early.

nece: a term meaning female relative as well as niece; here a term of intimacy.

---

65. I.e., he was an outrider, an officer who rode about inspecting the estates, granges, and barns of a monastery.

76. And seriously takes thought on his necessary business.

77. **countour-hous:** countinghouse, a room or building in which accounts are kept.

But it were for an old apalled wight,   apalled: grown tired.
As been thise wedded men, that lye and dare   dare: cower.
As in a forme sit a wery hare,   forme: burrow.
Were al forstraught with houndes grete and   were: that is. forstraught: distraught.
      smale.   105
But deere nece, why be ye so pale?
I trowe, certes, that oure goode man
Hath yow laboured sith the nyght bigan,
That yow were nede to resten hastily."   hastily: soon.
And with that word he lough ful myrily,   *1300 lough: laughed.
And of his owene thought he wex al reed.   wex: waxed, grew.
    This faire wyf gan for to shake hir heed
And seyde thus, "Ye, God woot al," quod she.
"Nay, cosyn myn, it stant nat so with me;   stant: (standeth) stands.
For, by that God that yaf me soule and lyf, 115
In al the reawme of France is ther no wyf   reawme: realm.
That lasse lust hath to that sory pley.   lasse: less.
For I may synge 'Allas and weylawey
That I was born,' but to no wight," quod she,
"Dar I nat telle how it stant with me.   *1310
Wherfore I thynke out of this land to wende,
Or elles of myself to make an ende,
So ful am I of drede and eek of care."   drede: anxiety.
    This monk bigan upon this wyf to stare,
And seyde, "Allas, my nece, God forbede 125
That ye, for any sorwe or any drede,
Fordo yourself; but telleth me youre grief.   fordo: kill. grief: trouble.
Paraventure I may, in youre meschief,   meschief: distress.
Conseille or helpe; and therfore telleth me
Al youre anoy, for it shal been secree.   *1320 anoy: annoyance.
For on my *portehors* I make an oth   *portehors:* portas, portable breviary.
That nevere in my lyf, for lief ne loth,   for lief ne loth: i.e., for weal nor woe.
Ne shal I of no conseil yow biwreye."   conseil: confidence. biwreye: betray.
    "The same agayn to yow," quod she, "I seye.
By God and by this *portehors* I swere, 135
Though men me wolde al into pieces tere,
Ne shal I nevere, for to gon to helle,   for to gon: though I had to go.
Biwreye a word of thyng that ye me telle,
Nat for no cosynage ne alliance,
But verraily, for love and affiance."   *1330 affiance: faith, trust.
Thus been they sworn, and heerupon they kiste,
And ech of hem tolde oother what hem liste.
    "Cosyn," quod she, "if that I hadde a space,   a space: an opportunity.

131, 135. My assumption that Don John and the wife use the French pronunciation of *portehors* (Middle English, **porthors**) makes unnecessary the emendations offered by some scribes and editors for the purpose of adding a syllable to each of these lines. The tale has many French touches (including the phrase in line 214); these are the only occurrences of the word in Chaucer.
139. Not for any cousinhood or relationship by marriage.

As I have noon, and namely in this place,
Thanne wolde I telle a legende of my lyf,   145
What I have suffred sith I was a wyf
With myn housbonde, al be he youre cosyn."
   "Nay," quod this monk, "by God and Seint
        Martyn,
He is na more cosyn unto me
Than is this leef that hangeth on the tree!   *1340
I clepe hym so, by Seint Denys of Fraunce,
To have the moore cause of aqueyntaunce   cause of: occasion for.
Of yow, which I have loved specially
Aboven alle wommen, sikerly.
This swere I yow on my professioun.   155 professioun: oath made on becoming
Telleth youre grief, lest that he come adoun;   a monk.
And hasteth yow, and goth awey anon."
   "My deere love," quod she, "O my daun John,
Ful lief were me this conseil for to hyde,   lief: desirous. conseil: private matter.
But out it moot, I may namoore abyde.   *1350
Myn housbonde is to me the worste man
That evere was sith that the world bigan.
But sith I am a wyf, it sit nat me   sit: (sitteth) is fitting for, befits.
To tellen no wight of oure privetee,   privetee: private affairs.
Neither abedde, ne in noon oother place;   165
God shilde I sholde it tellen, for his grace!   shilde: forbid.
A wyf ne shal nat seyn of hir housbonde
But al honour, as I kan understonde;
Save unto yow thus muche I tellen shal:
As help me God, he is noght worth at al   *1360
In no degree the value of a flye.   in no degree: in no way.
But yet me greveth moost his nygardye.   nygardye: niggardliness.
And wel ye woot that wommen naturelly
Desiren thynges sixe as wel as I:
They wolde that hir housbondes sholde be   175
Hardy, and wise, and riche, and therto free,   free: liberal, generous.
And buxom unto his wyf, and fressh abedde.   buxom: obedient, submissive, humble,
But by that ilke Lord that for us bledde,   gracious, helpful.
For his honour, myself for to arraye,
A Sonday next I moste nedes paye   *1370 a: on.
An hundred frankes, or ellis am I lorn.   lorn: lost, ruined.
Yet were me levere that I were unborn
Than me were doon a sclaundre or vileynye;   vileynye: dishonor, disgrace.
And if myn housbonde eek myghte it espye,   espye: discover.
I nere but lost; and therfore I yow preye,   185
Lene me this somme, or ellis moot I deye.   lene: lend.
Daun John, I seye, lene me thise hundred
        frankes.
Pardee, I wol nat faille yow my thankes,
If that yow list to doon that I yow praye.
For at a certeyn day I wol yow paye,   *1380

And doon to yow what plesance and service
That I may doon, right as yow list devise.
And but I do, God take on me vengeance
As foul as evere hadde Genylon of France."

This gentil monk answerde in this manere: 195
"Now trewely, myn owene lady deere,
I have," quod he, "on yow so greet a routhe
That I yow swere, and plighte yow my trouthe,   plighte: pledge.
That whan youre housbond is to Flaundres fare,   fare: gone.
I wol delyvere yow out of this care;   *1390 care: distress.
For I wol brynge yow an hundred frankes."
And with that word he caughte hire by the
          flankes,
And hire embraceth harde, and kiste hire ofte.
"Gooth now youre wey," quod he, "al stille and
          softe,
And lat us dyne as soone as that ye may;   205
For by my chilyndre it is pryme of day.   chilyndre: a portable sun dial in the
Goth now, and beeth as trewe as I shal be."   shape of a cylinder.
   "Now elles God forbede, sire," quod she;   elles: otherwise.
And forth she goth as jolif as a pye,   pye: magpie.
And bad the cookes that they sholde hem
          hye,   *1400 hye: hasten, hie.
So that men myghte dyne, and that anon.
Up to hir housbonde is this wyf ygon,
And knokketh at his countour boldely.   countour: countinghouse.
   "Qui la?" quod he. "Peter! it am I,"   Peter!: by St. Peter!
Quod she; "what, sire, how longe wol ye faste? 215
How longe tyme wol ye rekene and caste   caste: add up, calculate.
Youre sommes, and youre bookes, and youre
          thynges?
The devel have part on alle swiche rekenynges!
Ye have ynough, pardee, of Goddes sonde;   sonde: sending, gifts.
Come doun to-day, and lat youre bagges
          stonde.   *1410
Ne be ye nat ashamed that daun John
Shal fasting al this day alenge goon?   alenge: miserable, sad.
What! lat us heere a masse, and go we dyne."
   "Wyf," quod this man, "litel kanstow devyne   kanstow: canst thou.
The curious bisynesse that we have.   225 curious: involving elaborate care.
For of us chapmen, also God me save,   chapmen: merchants.
And by that lord that clepid is Seint Yve,
Scarsly amonges twelve tweye shul thryve
Continuelly, lastyng unto oure age.   age: old age.
We may wel make chiere and good visage,   *1420 make chiere: assume an expression.

---

194. Genylon: Ganelon, who betrayed Charlemagne's army at Roncesvalles; it was said that for
punishment he was torn to death by wild horses.
214. Qui la?: Who's there?

And dryve forth the world as it may be,   dryve forth: pursue, make the most of.
And kepen oure estaat in pryvetee,
Til we be dede, or elles that we pleye   pleye: pretend.
A pilgrymage, or goon out of the weye.
And therfore have I gret necessitee   235
Upon this queynte world t'avyse me;   queynte: strange, queer. t'avyse me:
For everemoore we mote stonde in drede   to take thought. drede: peril.
Of hap and fortune in oure chapmanhede.   chapmanhede: trading, bargaining.
      To Flaundres wol I go to-morwe at day,
And come agayn, as soone as evere I may.   *1430
For which, my deere wyf, I thee biseke,
As be to every wight buxom and meke,   buxom: gracious, obedient.
And for to kepe oure good be curious,   curious: careful.
And honestly governe wel oure hous.   honestly: honorably.
Thou hast ynough, in every maner wise,   245
That to a thrifty houshold may suffise.
Thee lakketh noon array ne no vitaille;   array: equipment.
Of silver in thy purs shaltow nat faille."
And with that word his countour-dore he shette,
And doun he goth, no lenger wolde he lette. *1440 lette: delay.
But hastily a masse was ther seyd,
And spedily the tables were yleyd,   yleyd: set up.
And to the dyner faste they hem spedde,
And richely this monk the chapman fedde.
      At after-dyner daun John sobrely   255   sobrely: gravely.
This chapman took apart, and prively
He seyde hym thus: "Cosyn, it standeth so,
That wel I se to Brugges wol ye go.
God and Seint Austyn spede yow and gyde!   gyde: keep.
I prey yow, cosyn, wisely that ye ryde.   *1450
Governeth yow also of youre diete
Atemprely, and namely in this hete.   atemprely: with moderation.
Bitwix us two nedeth no strange fare;   strange fare: distant behavior.
Farewel, cosyn; God shilde yow fro care!
And if that any thyng by day or nyght,   265
If it lye in my power and my myght,
That ye me wol comande in any wise,
It shal be doon, right as ye wol devyse.
      O thyng, er that ye goon, if it may be,
I wolde prey yow; for to lene me   *1460 lene: lend.
An hundred frankes, for a wyke or tweye,   wyke: week.
For certein beestes that I moste beye,   beye: buy.
To store with a place that is oures.   to store with: with which to store.
God help me so, I wolde it were youres!
I shal nat faille surely of my day,   275   of: i.e., to repay on.
Nat for a thousand frankes, a mile way.
But lat this thyng be secree, I yow preye,

—————
276. a mile way: the time required to walk one mile; about twenty minutes.

For yet to-nyght thise beestes moot I beye.
And fare now wel, myn owene cosyn deere;
Graunt mercy of youre cost and of youre
    cheere."   *1470
    This noble marchant gentilly anon
Answerde and seyde, "O cosyn myn, daun John,
Now sikerly this is a smal requeste.
My gold is youres, whan that it yow leste,
And nat oonly my gold, but my chaffare.   285
Take what yow list, God shilde that ye spare.
    But o thyng is, ye knowe it wel ynow,
Of chapmen, that hir moneye is hir plow.
We may creaunce whil we have a name;
But goldlees for to be, it is no game.   *1480
Pay it agayn whan it lyth in youre ese;
After my myght ful fayn wolde I yow plese."
    Thise hundred frankes he fette forth anon,
And prively he took hem to daun John.
No wight in al this world wiste of this lone,   295
Savyng this marchant and daun John allone.
They drynke, and speke, and rome a while and
    pleye,
Til that daun John rideth to his abbeye.
    The morwe cam, and forth this marchant
    rideth
To Flaundres-ward; his prentys wel hym
    gydeth,   *1490
Til he came into Brugges murily.
Now goth this marchant faste and bisily
Aboute his nede, and byeth and creaunceth.
He neither pleyeth at the dees ne daunceth,
But as a marchaunt, shortly for to telle,   305
He let his lyf, and there I lete hym dwelle.
    The Sonday next the marchant was agon,
To Seint-Denys ycomen is daun John,
With crowne and berd al fressh and newe
    yshave.
In al the hous ther nas so litel a knave,   *1500
Ne no wight elles, that he nas ful fayn
That my lord daun John was come agayn.
And shortly to the point right for to gon,
This faire wyf acorded with daun John
That for thise hundred frankes he sholde al
    nyght   315
Have hire in his armes bolt upright;
And this acord parfourned was in dede.
In myrthe al nyght a bisy lyf they lede

cost: outlay of money.
cheere: kindness, friendliness.
gentilly: courteously.

chaffare: goods, merchandise.
shilde: forbid. spare: refrain.

creaunce: obtain credit, borrow money. game: sport, fun.

after: according to.
fette: brought out.
took: gave.
lone: loan.

rome: roam, wander.

creaunceth: borrows on credit.
dees: dice.

let: (leadeth) leads.
next: next after.

yshave: shaven.
knave: servant-lad, page.
fayn: pleased, delighted.

right: straight.
acorded: agreed.

bolt: straight as an arrow. upright: face up, flat on her back.

---

280. **graunt mercy of:** many thanks for.

Til it was day, that daun John wente his way,
And bad the meynee "Farewel, have good
              day!"   *1510
For noon of hem, ne no wight in the toun,
Hath of daun John right no suspecioun.
And forth he rydeth hoom to his abbeye,
Or where hym list; namoore of hym I seye.
    This marchant, whan that ended was the
              faire,   325
To Seint-Denys he gan for to repaire,
And with his wyf he maketh feste and cheere,
And telleth hire that chaffare is so deere
That nedes moste he make a chevyssaunce;
For he was bounden in a reconyssaunce   *1520
To paye twenty thousand sheeld anon.
For which this marchant is to Parys gon
To borwe of certeine freendes that he hadde
A certeyn frankes; and somme with him he
              ladde.
And whan that he was come into the toun,   335
For greet chiertee and greet affeccioun,
Unto daun John he first goth, hym to pleye;
Nat for to axe or borwe of hym moneye,
But for to wite and seen of his welfare,
And for to tellen hym of his chaffare,   *1530
As freendes doon whan they been met yfeere.
Daun John hym maketh feste and murye
              cheere,
And he hym tolde agayn, ful specially,
How he hadde wel yboght and graciously,
Thanked be God, al hool his marchandise;   345
Save that he moste, in alle maner wise,
Maken a chevyssaunce, as for his beste,
And thanne he sholde been in joye and reste.
    Daun John answerde, "Certes, I am fayn
That ye in heele ar comen hom agayn.   *1540
And if that I were riche, as have I blisse,
Of twenty thousand sheeld sholde ye nat mysse,
For ye so kyndely this oother day
Lente me gold; and as I kan and may,
I thanke yow, by God and by Seint Jame!   355
But nathelees, I took unto oure dame,
Youre wyf, at hom, the same gold agayn
Upon youre bench; she woot it wel, certayn,
By certeyn tokenes that I kan yow telle.
Now, by youre leve, I may no lenger
              dwelle;   *1550

that: so that.
meynee: household.

right no: no . . . at all.

faire: business.
repaire: go home.
maketh . . . cheere: makes merry.
chaffare: merchandise.
make a chevyssaunce: borrow money.
reconyssaunce: recognizance, legal
  obligation.

certeyn: certain number of.
ladde: carried.

chiertee: love.
pleye: amuse, divert.

wite: know.

chaffare: bargaining, business.
yfeere: together.

agayn: in turn.
graciously: favorably.

in . . . wise: by all means.
for his beste: for his best interests.

heele: well-being, prosperity.
have I: I may have.
mysse: want.

took: gave.
agayn: back again.

---

331. **sheeld:** shields, French gold coins (*écus*).

Oure abbot wol out of this toun anon,
And in his compaignye moot I gon.
Grete wel oure dame, myn owene nece sweete,   grete: greet. nece: niece; here a term
And fare wel, deere cosyn, til we meete!"   of intimacy.
    This marchant, which that was ful war and
        wys,   365
Creanced hath, and payd eek in Parys   creanced: borrowed.
To certeyn Lumbardes, redy in hir hond,   redy: i.e., with cash.
The somme of gold, and gat of hem his bond;   bond: contract.
And hoom he gooth, murye as a papejay,   papejay: parrot, green woodpecker.
For wel he knew he stood in swich array   *1560 array: condition, state.
That nedes moste he wynne in that viage   viage: journey.
A thousand frankes aboven al his costage.   costage: costs, expenses.
    His wyf ful redy mette hym atte gate,
As she was wont of old usage algate,   algate: on all occasions.
And al that nyght in myrthe they bisette;   375 bisette: spent.
For he was riche and cleerly out of dette.   cleerly: entirely.
Whan it was day, this marchant gan embrace
His wyf al newe, and kiste hire on hir face,
And up he goth and maketh it ful tough.   tough: vigorous.
    "Namoore," quod she, "by God, ye have
        ynough!"   *1570
And wantownly agayn with hym she pleyde,
Til atte laste that this marchant seyde:
"By God," quod he, "I am a litel wroth
With yow, my wyf, although it be me looth.   it be me looth: I don't like it.
And woot ye why? by God, as that I gesse   385
That ye han maad a manere straungenesse   straungenesse: estrangement.
Bitwixen me and my cosyn daun John.
Ye sholde han warned me, er I had gon,
That he yow hadde an hundred frankes payed,
By redy token; and heeld hym yvele
        apayed,   *1580
For that I to hym spak of chevyssaunce;
Me semed so, as by his contenaunce.
But nathelees, by God, oure hevene kyng,
I thoughte nat to axe of hym no thyng.
I prey thee, wyf, ne do namoore so;   395
Telle me alwey, er that I fro thee go,
If any dettour hath in myn absence
Ypayed thee, lest thurgh thy necligence
I myghte hym axe a thing that he hath payed."
    This wyf was nat afered nor affrayed,   *1590 affrayed: frightened.
But boldely she seyde, and that anon:
"Marie! I deffye the false monk, daun John!   Marie!: an oath by the Virgin.
I kepe nat of his tokenes never a del;   kepe: care, reck.

---

367. Many Lombards were international bankers.
390. With handy evidence; and felt himself ill treated.

He took me certeyn gold, this woot I wel,—   took: gave. **certeyn:** a certain amount
What! yvel thedam on his monkes snowte!   405   of. **thedam:** success.
For, God it woot, I wende, withouten doute,   **wende:** supposed, thought.
That he hadde yeve it me bycause of yow,
To doon therwith myn honour and my prow,   **doon:** accomplish. **prow:** profit.
For cosynage, and eek for bele cheere   **cosynage:** cousinhood; kinship.
That he hath had ful ofte tymes heere.   *1600
But sith I se I stonde in this disjoynt,   **disjoynt:** dilemma, fix.
I wol answere yow shortly to the poynt.
Ye han mo slakker dettours than am I!
For I wol paye yow wel and redily
Fro day to day, and if so be I faille,   415
I am youre wyf; score it upon my taille,   **taille:** tally; tail.
And I shal paye as soone as ever I may.
For by my trouthe, I have on myn array,
And nat on wast, bistowed every del;   **wast:** wastefulness.
And for I have bistowed it so wel   *1610
For youre honour, for Goddes sake, I seye,
As be nat wrooth, but lat us laughe and pleye.   **as be:** be.
Ye shal my joly body have to wedde;   **to wedde:** as pledge.
By God, I wol nat paye yow but abedde!
Forgyve it me, myn owene spouse deere;   425
Turne hiderward, and maketh bettre cheere."
   This marchant saugh ther was no remedye,
And for to chide it nere but folye,
Sith that the thyng may nat amended be.
"Now wyf," he seyde, "and I foryeve it
      thee;   *1620
But, by thy lyf, ne be namoore so large.   **large:** wasteful, lavish.
Keep bet thy good, this yeve I thee in charge."   **good:** money.
Thus endeth my tale, and God us sende
Taillynge ynough unto oure lyves ende.

Heere endeth the Shipmannes tale.

*Bihoold the murie wordes of
the Hoost to the Shipman
and to the Lady Prioresse.*

   "Wel seyd, by *corpus dominus*," quod oure
      Hoost,   435
"Now longe moote thou saille by the cost,   **cost:** coast.
Sire gentil maister, gentil maryneer!

---

409. bele cheere: good cheer, food and drink, hospitality.
416. score it upon my taille: score it upon my tally, charge it to my account.
435. *corpus dominus*: the Host's blunder for "Corpus Domini," the body of the Lord.

God yeve the monk a thousand last quade yeer!
A ha! felawes! beth ware of swich a jape!
The monk putte in the mannes hood an
        ape,   *1630
And in his wyves eek, by Seint Austyn!
Draweth no monkes moore in to youre in.
    But now passe over, and lat us seke aboute:
Who shal now telle first of al this route
Another tale?" and with that word he sayde,   445
As curteisly as it had been a mayde,
"My lady Prioresse, by youre leve,
So that I wiste I sholde yow nat greve,
I wolde demen that ye tellen sholde
A tale next, if so were that ye wolde.   *1640
Now wol ye vouche sauf, my lady deere?"
    "Gladly," quod she, and seyde as ye shal
        heere.

a thousand . . . yeer: a thousand cartloads of bad years.

in: dwelling.

route: company.

as it: as if he.

so that: provided that.

Explicit.

The prologe of the Prioresses tale.

Domine dominus noster.

    "O Lord, oure Lord, thy name how merveillous
Is in this large world ysprad," quod she;
"For nat oonly thy laude precious   455
Parfourned is by men of dignitee,
But by the mouth of children thy bountee
Parfourned is, for on the brest soukynge
Somtyme shewen they thyn heriynge.

Wherfore in laude, as I best kan or may,   *1650
Of thee and of the white lilye flour
Which that the bar, and is a mayde alway,
To telle a storie I wol do my labour;
Nat that I may encreessen hir honour,
For she hirself is honour and the roote   465
Of bountee, next hir Sone, and soules boote.

ysprad: spread.

laude: praise.
parfourned: performed.
bountee: praise.
soukynge: sucking.
heriynge: praise.

the: thee. bar: bore.

bountee: goodness. boote: salvation.

440–41. The monk made dupes of the man and his wife, by St. Augustine!
446. *Domine dominus noster:* the opening of Psalms viii.1 (Vulgate, 2); see the following note.
453–87. This **prologe** contains many ideas and expressions drawn from the Bible, the services of the church, and religious poetry, including the *Paradiso* of Dante. For example, the first stanza paraphrases verses 1–2 (Vulgate, 3–4) of Psalms viii, the opening psalm of Matins in the Little Office of the Blessed Virgin.
461, 468. The white lily and the burning bush unconsumed were common symbols of Mary's perpetual virginity.

O moder Mayde! o mayde Moder free!

free: gracious, bountiful.

O bussh unbrent, brennynge in Moyses sighte,

unbrent: unburned.

That ravysedest doun fro the Deitee,

ravysedest: didst draw (down).

Thurgh thyn humblesse, the Goost that in
th'alighte, *1660

in th'alighte: in thee alighted.

Of whos vertu, whan he thyn herte lighte,

*lighte: lightened, made happy; illu-
minated.* **sapience:** *wisdom (Christ).*

Conceyved was the Fadres sapience,

Help me to telle it in thy reverence!

Lady, thy bountee, thy magnificence,

Thy vertu, and thy grete humylitee, 475

Ther may no tonge expresse in no science;

in: with. **science:** *mastery of learning.*

For somtyme, Lady, er men praye to thee,

Thou goost biforn of thy benyngnytee,

And getest us the light, of thy prayere,

of: by means of.

To gyden us unto thy Sone so deere. *1670

My konnyng is so wayk, o blisful Queene,

konnyng: skill. **wayk:** *weak.*

For to declare thy grete worthynesse

That I ne may the weighte nat susteene;

But as a child of twelf month oold, or lesse,

That kan unnethe any word expresse, 485

unnethe: hardly.

Right so fare I, and therfore I yow preye,

Gydeth my song that I shal of yow seye."

gydeth: direct (imperative). **song:**
poem.

Explicit.

*Heere bigynneth the
Prioresses tale.*

Ther was in Asye, in a greet citee,

Amonges Cristene folk, a Jewerye,

Jewerye: Jews' quarter, Jewry.

Sustened by a lord of that contree *1680

For foule usure and lucre of vileynye,

lucre of vileynye: vile gain.

Hateful to Christ and to his compaignye;

his compaignye: i.e., Christians.

And thurgh this strete men myghte ride or
wende,

wende: walk.

For it was free and open at eyther ende.

A litel scole of Cristen folk ther stood 495

scole: school.

Doun at the ferther ende, in which ther were

Children an heep, ycomen of Cristen blood,

heep: crowd. **ycomen:** *come.*

That lerned in that scole yeer by yere

Swich manere doctrine as men used there,

manere doctrine: kind of training.

---

the Prioresses tale. The Prioress's Tale is a miracle of the Virgin which exists in many forms;
somewhat similar is the story of Hugh of Lincoln, mentioned in line 684.

491. foule usure: Usury was forbidden to Christians.

This is to seyn, to syngen and to rede,   *1690
As smale children doon in hire childhede.   childhede: childhood.

Among thise children was a wydwes sone,
A litel clergeon, seven yeer of age,   clergeon: pupil.
That day by day to scole was his wone,   to: (to go) to. wone: custom.
And eek also, where as he saugh th'ymage   505
Of Cristes mooder, hadde he in usage,
As hym was taught, to knele adoun and seye
His *Ave Marie,* as he goth by the weye.

Thus hath this wydwe hir litel sone ytaught
Oure blisful Lady, Cristes mooder deere,   *1700
To worshipe ay, and he forgat it naught,
For sely child wol alwey soone leere.   sely: good. leere: learn.
But ay, whan I remembre on this mateere,
Seint Nicholas stant evere in my presence,
For he so yong to Crist dide reverence.   515 for: because.

This litel child, his litel book lernynge,
As he sat in the scole at his prymer,
He *Alma redemptoris* herde synge,
As children lerned hire antiphoner;
And as he dorste, he drough hym ner and ner,   drough hym: approached. ner: nearer.
And herkned ay the wordes and the note,   *1711 note: music.
Til he the firste vers koude al by rote.   koude: knew.

Nat wiste he what this Latyn was to seye,   was to seye: meant.
For he so yong and tendre was of age.
But on a day his felawe gan he preye   525
T'expounden hym this song in his langage,
Or telle hym why this song was in usage;
This preyde he hym to construe and declare   construe: translate. declare: explain.
Ful often tyme upon his knowes bare.   knowes: knees.

His felawe, which that elder was than he,   *1720
Answerde hym thus: "This song, I have herd
      seye,
Was maked of our blisful Lady free,   of: concerning; for. free: gracious,
Hire to salue, and eek hire for to preye   bountiful.
To been oure help and socour whan we deye.   socour: succor, help.

----

505. th'ymage: Images of the Virgin were frequent along medieval streets.

514. **Seint Nicholas:** As an infant St. Nicholas is said to have sucked only once on Wednesdays and Fridays (Breviarium Romanum, December 6). He was the patron of schoolboys.

517. **prymer:** This probably included the alphabet, Pater Noster, Ave Maria, Creed, and Confession.

519. **antiphoner:** antiphonary, anthem book. The Alma Redemptoris Mater (Bountiful Mother of the Redeemer) is an anthem.

533. To greet her, and also to pray her.

I kan namoore expounde in this mateere;   535   kan: know.
I lerne song, I kan but smal grammeere."

  "And is this song maked in reverence
Of Cristes mooder?" seyde this innocent.
"Now, certes, I wol do my diligence   diligence: i.e., utmost.
To konne it al er Cristemasse be went.   *1730
Though that I for my prymer shal be shent,   shent: scolded.
And shal be beten thries in an houre,   thries: thrice.
I wol it konne Oure Lady for to honoure!"   konne: learn.

His felawe taughte hym homward prively,
Fro day to day, til he koude it by rote,   545   koude: knew.
And thanne he song it wel and boldely,   boldely: vigorously.
Fro word to word, accordynge with the note.   note: music.
Twies a day it passed thurgh his throte,
To scoleward and homward whan he wente;
On Cristes moder set was his entente.   *1740   entente: heart.

  As I have seyd, thurghout the Juerye,
This litel child, as he cam to and fro,
Ful murily wolde he synge and crye
O Alma redemptoris everemo.
The swetnesse his herte perced so   555
Of Cristes moder that, to hire to preye,
He kan nat stynte of syngyng by the weye.   stynte of: stop.

  Oure firste foo, the serpent Sathanas,   Sathanas: Satan.
That hath in Jewes herte his waspes nest,
Up swal, and seide, "O Hebrayk peple,   up swal: swelled up.
      allas!   *1750
Is this to yow a thyng that is honest,   honest: honorable.
That swich a boy shal walken as hym lest
In youre despit, and synge of swich sentence   in youre despit: in contempt of you.
Which is agayn oure lawes reverence?"   sentence: subject.

Fro thennes forth the Jewes han conspired   565
This innocent out of this world to chace.
An homycide therto han they hired,
That in an aleye hadde a privee place;
And as the child gan forby for to pace,   forby for to pace: to go by.
This cursed Jew hym hente, and heeld hym
      faste,   *1760
And kitte his throte, and in a pit hym caste.   kitte: cut.

I seye that in a wardrobe they hym threwe   wardrobe: privy.
Where as thise Jewes purgen hire entraille.
O cursed folk of Herodes al newe,   Herodes al newe: new (i.e., modern)
What may youre yvel entente yow availle?   575   Herods.

Mordre wol out, certeyn, it wol nat faille,
And namely ther as th'onour of God shal sprede;
The blood out crieth on youre cursed dede.

O martir, sowded to virginitee,   sowded: consolidated.
Now maystow syngen, folwynge evere in   evere in oon: continually.
     oon   *1770
The white Lamb celestial—quod she—
Of which the grete evaungelist, Seint John,
In Pathmos wroot, which seith that they that
     gon
Biforn this Lamb, and synge a song al newe,
That nevere, flesshly, wommen they ne knewe. 585 flesshly: carnally.

This povre wydwe awaiteth al that nyght
After hir litel child, but he cam noght;
For which, as soone as it was dayes lyght,
With face pale of drede and bisy thoght,   thoght: anxiety.
She hath at scole and elleswhere hym soght, *1780
Til finally she gan so fer espie   gan so fer espie: learned this much.
That he last seyn was in the Jewerie.   seyn: seen.

With modres pitee in hir brest enclosed,
She goth, as she were half out of hir mynde,
To every place where she hath supposed   595
By liklihede hir litel child to fynde;
And evere on Cristes moder meeke and kynde
She cride, and atte laste thus she wroghte,   wroghte: did.
Among the cursed Jewes she hym soghte.

She frayneth and she preyeth pitously   *1790 frayneth: asks.
To every Jew that dwelte in thilke place,
To telle hire if hir child wente oght forby.   oght: at all. forby: by.
They seyde "Nay"; but Jhesu, of his grace,
Yaf in hir thought, inwith a litel space,   inwith: within. space: time.
That in that place after hir sone she cryde, 605 that: so that.
Wher he was casten in a pit bisyde.   where bisyde: near where.

580–85. See Revelation xiv.3,4.

583. Pathmos: St. John is believed to have written the Apocalypse, or Book of Revelation, on the Aegean island of Patmos.

This illustration, made in England about 1380, is a composite of several episodes from an analogue of the Prioress's Tale, which shows slight variations from Chaucer's version. In the upper right the Jew entices the boy into his house (not into an alley; cf. ll. 567–700); in the center he cuts the boy's throat; and on the left throws him into "a gonge-put" (the pit of a privy; cf. ll. 571–73). At the lower right the mother complains to the mayor (cf. ll. 614–16, where the "Cristene folk" send for the "provost"). In the lower left the Bishop has already removed from the boy's throat a lily flower with golden letters reading "Alma Redemptoris Mater"—the title and first words of the anthem the boy had sung (cf. the Abbot who removed the "greyn"; ll. 670–71). Now the Bishop starts the opening antiphon of the Requiem Mass: "Requiem aeternam dona eis, Domine, et lux perpetua luceat eis" ("Eternal rest give to them, O Lord, and let light everlasting shine on them"). Thereupon the corpse arises and, as is fitting in a miracle of the Virgin, sings from her Office the "Salve sancta parens" ("Hail, holy Mother").

O grete God, that parfournest thy laude
By mouth of innocentz, lo here thy myght!
This gemme of chastite, this emeraude,
And eek of martirdom the ruby bright,   *1800
Ther he with throte ykorven lay upright,
He *Alma redemptoris* gan to synge
So loude that al the place gan to rynge.

parfournest: bringest to pass. laude:
praise. lo: behold.

ykorven: carved, cut. upright: face up.

The Cristene folk that thurgh the strete wente
In coomen for to wondre upon this thyng,   615
And hastily they for the provost sente;
He cam anon withouten tariyng,
And herieth Crist that is of hevene kyng,
And eek his moder, honour of mankynde,
And after that the Jewes leet he bynde.   *1810

coomen: came.
provost: chief magistrate.

herieth: praises.

leet he bynde: he had bound.

This child with pitous lamentacioun
Up taken was, syngynge his song alway,
And with honour of greet processioun
They carien hym unto the nexte abbay.
His moder swownynge by his beere lay;   625
Unnethe myghte the peple that was theere
This newe Rachel brynge fro his beere.

beere: bier.
unnethe: hardly.

With torment and with shameful deeth echon
This provost dooth thise Jewes for to sterve
That of this mordre wiste, and that anon.   *1820
He nolde no swich cursednesse observe.
"Yvele shal have that yvele wol deserve";
Therfore with wilde hors he dide hem drawe,
And after that he heng hem by the lawe.

dooth for to sterve: causes to die.

observe: countenance.

hors: horses.

Upon this beere ay lith this innocent   635
Biforn the chief auter, whil the masse laste;
And after that, the abbot with his covent
Han sped hem for to burien hym ful faste;
And whan they holy water on hym caste,
Yet spak this child, whan spreynd was holy
        water,   *1830
And song *O Alma redemptoris mater!*

lith: lies.
auter: altar. laste: lasted.
covent: i.e., the group of monks com-
    prising the convent.

spreynd: sprinkled.

This abbot, which that was an holy man,
As monkes been, or elles oghte be,
This yonge child to conjure he bigan,
And seyde, "O deere child, I halsen thee,   645
In vertu of the hooly Trinitee,

conjure: implore.

halsen: adjure, entreat.

---

627. newe Rachel: second Rachel; see Matthew ii.18.

Tel me what is thy cause for to synge,
Sith that thy throte is kut to my semynge?"   to my semynge: as it seems to me.

"My throte is kut unto my nekke boon,"
Seyde this child, "and, as by wey of kynde, *1840   as by wey of kynde: in the course of
I sholde have dyed, ye, longe tyme agon.   nature.
But Jesu Crist, as ye in bookes fynde,
Wil that his glorie laste and be in mynde,   wil: wills, desires.
And for the worship of his Moder deere
Yet may I synge *O Alma* loude and cleere.   655

"This welle of mercy, Cristes moder sweete,
I loved alwey, as after my konnynge;   konnynge: knowledge, learning.
And whan that I my lyf sholde forlete,   forlete: yield up.
To me she cam, and bad me for to synge
This antheme, verraily in my deyynge,   *1850   in: during.
As ye han herd, and whan that I hadde songe,
Me thoughte she leyde a greyn upon my tonge.   greyn: grain of paradise (cardamom).

"Wherfore I synge, and synge moot certeyn,
In honour of that blisful Mayden free,
Til fro my tonge of taken is the greyn;   665   of: off.
And after that thus seyde she to me:
'My litel child, now wol I fecche thee,
Whan that the greyn is fro thy tonge ytake.
Be nat agast, I wol thee nat forsake.' "

This holy monk, this abbot, hym meene I, *1860
His tonge out caughte, and took awey the greyn,
And he yaf up the goost ful softely.
And whan this abbot hadde this wonder seyn,   seyn: seen.
His salte teeris trikled doun as reyn,
And gruf he fil at plat upon the grounde,   675   gruf: face downward; groveling. **plat:**
And stille he lay as he had been ybounde.   flat.

The covent eek lay on the pavement   covent: see l. 637.
Wepynge, and herying Cristes moder deere,   herying: praising.
And after that they ryse, and forth been went,   ryse: rose.
And tooken awey this martir from his
            beere;   *1870
And in a tombe of marbul stones cleere   cleere: bright, splendid, noble.
Enclosen they this litel body sweete.
Ther he is now, God leve us for to meete!   ther: where. leve: grant.

O yonge Hugh of Lyncoln, slayn also
With cursed Jewes, as it is notable,   685   with: by.

---

684. **Hugh of Lyncoln:** supposed to have been similarly murdered in 1255.

For it is but a litel while ago,
Preye eek for us, we synful folk unstable,
That, of his mercy, God so merciable
On us his grete mercy multiplie,
For reverence of his moder Marie. Amen.   *1880

Heere is ended the Prioresses tale.

Bihoold the murye wordes
of the Hoost to Chaucer.

Whan seyd was al this miracle, every man
As sobre was that wonder was to se,
Til that oure hooste japen tho bigan,   japen: joke.
And thanne at erst he looked upon me,   at erst: for the first time.
And seyde thus, "What man artow?" quod he; 695
"Thou lookest as thou woldest fynde an hare,
For evere upon the ground I se thee stare.

"Approche neer, and looke up murily.
Now war yow, sires, and lat this man have place!
He in the waast is shape as wel as I;   *1890   waast: waist.
This were a popet in an arm t'enbrace   popet: puppet, doll.
For any womman, smal and fair of face.
He semeth elvyssh by his contenaunce,   elvyssh: like an otherworld creature.
For unto no wight dooth he daliaunce.   dooth he daliaunce: he chats, talks, is
                                                             sociable.

"Sey now somewhat, syn oother folk han
          sayd;   705
Telle us a tale of myrthe, and that anon."
"Hoost," quod I, "ne beth nat yvele apayd,   yvele apayd: ill pleased.
For oother tale certes kan I noon,   kan: know.
But of a rym I lerned longe agoon."
"Ye, that is good," quod he; "now shul we   ye: yea.
          heere   *1900
Som deyntee thyng, me thynketh by his cheere."   deyntee: delightful. cheere: behavior.

Explicit.

Heere bigynneth Chaucers
tale of Thopas.

Listeth, lordes, in good entent,
And I wol telle verrayment   verrayment: verily, truly.
   Of myrthe and of solas;   solas: delight.

Al of a knyght was fair and gent
In bataille and in tourneyment,
   His name was sire Thopas.

Yborn he was in fer contree,
In Flaundres, al biyonde the see,
   At Poperyng, in the place.
His fader was a man ful free,
And lord he was of that contree,
   As it was Goddes grace.

Sire Thopas wax a doghty swayn;
Whit was his face as payndemayn,
   His lippes rede as rose;
His rode is lyk scarlet in grayn,
And I yow telle in good certayn,
   He hadde a semely nose.

His heer, his berd was lyk saffroun,
That to his girdel raughte adoun;
   His shoon of cordewane.
Of Brugges were his hosen broun,
His robe was of syklatoun,
   That coste many a jane.

He koude hunte at wilde deer,
And ride an haukyng for river
   With grey goshauk on honde;
Therto he was a good archeer;
Of wrastlyng was ther noon his peer,
   Ther any ram shal stonde.

Ful many a mayde, bright in bour,
They moorne for hym paramour,
   Whan hem were bet to slepe;
But he was chaast and no lechour,
And sweete as is the brembul flour
   That bereth the rede hepe.

And so bifel upon a day,
For sothe, as I yow telle may,
   Sire Thopas wolde out ride.
He worth upon his steede gray,

---

715 gent: genteel; graceful, shapely.

Thopas: The topaz was a symbol of chastity.
fer: far.

*1910 place: market-place?
free: noble.

doghty: doughty, bold; doughy.
725 payndemayn: very fine white bread.

rode: complexion. **scarlet in grayn:** cloth fast-dyed with scarlet.

*1920
raughte: reached.
cordewane: Cordovan leather.

735 jane: silver half-penny of Genoa.

deer: animals.
river: waterfowl.
goshauk: a hawk for yeomen.

*1930
ther: where. ram: as a wrestling prize.

moorne: yearn. **paramour:** for sexual love. bet: better.

745

brembul flour: bramble-flower, dog-rose. hepe: hip of the dog-rose.

*1940
worth upon: (became on) got on.

---

720. Poperinge is sixty miles east of Dover; its lord was the abbot of St. Bertin.

724. wax: grew into. swayn: man (of low degree).

730. saffroun: saffron, a deep orange powder used as a stimulant, and as a coloring and flavoring for pies, meats, and confectionery.

734. syklatoun: a costly cloth from the East, of scarlet silk embroidered with gold.

And in his hand a launcegay,   launcegay: a light, slender lance.
  A long swerd by his side.

He priketh thurgh a fair forest,   priketh: spurs, rides.
Therinne is many a wilde best,   755
  Ye, bothe bukke and hare;
And as he priketh north and est,
I telle it yow, hym hadde almest   hym: to him.
  Bitid a sory care.   bitid: happened. sory care: grievous
                                trouble.

Ther spryngen herbes grete and smale, *1950
The lycorys and the cetewale,   cetewale: zedoary, related to ginger.
  And many a clowe-gylofre;   clowe-gylofre: clove.
And notemuge to putte in ale,   notemuge: nutmeg.
Wheither it be moyste or stale,   moyste: new and watery. stale: old,
  Or for to leye in cofre.   765   clear, and strong.

The briddes synge, it is no nay,
The sparhauk and the papejay,   papejay: parrot.
  That joye it was to heere;
The thrustelcok made eek his lay,   thrustelcock: male thrush.
The wodedowve upon the spray   *1960 wodedowve: wood-pigeon.
  She sang ful loude and cleere.

Sire Thopas fil in love-longynge,   fil: fell.
Al whan he herde the thrustel synge,
  And pryked as he were wood.   wood: mad.
His faire steede in his prikynge   775
So swatte that men myghte him wrynge; swatte: sweated.
  His sydes were al blood.

Sire Thopas eek so wery was
For prikyng on the softe gras,
  So fiers was his corage,   *1970
That doun he leyde him in the plas   plas: place.
To make his steede som solas,   solas: refreshment.
  And yaf hym good forage.   forage: dry fodder.

"O Seinte Marie, benedicite!
What eyleth this love at me   785 eyleth at me: has against me.
  To bynde me so soore?
Me dremed al this nyght, pardee,
An elf-queene shal my lemman be   lemman: sweetheart; concubine.
  And slepe under my goore.   goore: gore or gusset; garment.

"An elf-queene wol I love, ywis,   *1980
For in this world no womman is
  Worthy to be my make   make: mate.
      In towne:

Alle othere wommen I forsake,
And to an elf-queene I me take   795
  By dale and eek by downe!"
                                                  downe: hill.

Into his sadel he clamb anon,   clamb: climbed.
And priketh over stile and stoon
  An elf-queene for t'espye,   espye: look for.
Til he so longe hath riden and goon   *1990
That he foond, in a pryve woon,   pryve: privy, secret. woon: retreat,
  The contree of Fairye   place of shelter. Fairye: supernat-
        So wilde;   ural creatures.
For in that contree was ther noon   804
  Neither wyf ne childe,   806

Til that ther cam a greet geaunt,
His name was sire Olifaunt,   Olifaunt: Elephant.
  A perilous man of dede.
He seyde, "Child, by Termagaunt!   *2000   child: sir. Termagaunt: supposedly a
But if thou prike out of myn haunt,   god or idol of the Saracens.
  Anon I sle thy steede   sle: shall slay.
        With mace.
  Heere is the queene of Fayerye,
With harpe and pipe and symphonye,   815   symphonye: a kind of drum.
  Dwellynge in this place."

The child seyde, "Also moote I thee,   child: young knight. also . . . thee: as
Tomorwe wol I meete thee,   I may prosper.
  Whan I have myn armoure;
  And yet I hope, *par ma fay,*   *2010   *par ma fay:* by my faith.
That thou shalt with this launcegay
  Abyen it ful soure.   abyen: pay for; suffer. soure: bitterly.
        Thy mawe   mawe: stomach.
Shal I percen, if I may,
Er it be fully pryme of day,   825
  For heere thow shalt be slawe."   slawe: slain.

Sire Thopas drow abak ful faste;
This geant at hym stones caste
  Out of a fel staf-slynge.   fel: deadly; terrible. staf-slynge: sling-
But faire escapeth child Thopas,   *2020   shot.
And al it was thurgh Goddes gras,   gras: grace.
  And thurgh his fair berynge.   berynge: bearing, behavior.

Yet listeth, lordes, to my tale
Murier than the nightyngale;

---

805. The line usually printed by editors ("That to him durst ride or goon") is found in few manu-
scripts and seems to be a scribal addition to regularize the stanza.

I wol yow rowne
How sir Thopas, with sydes smale,
Prikyng over hill and dale,
   Is comen agayn to towne.

835 rowne: whisper; tell.

His myrie men comanded he
To make hym bothe game and glee,
   For nedes moste he fighte
With a geaunt with hevedes three,
For paramour and jolitee
   Of oon that shoon ful brighte.

*2030 myrie men: merry men, companions
in arms. glee: music, entertainment.

hevedes: heads.
paramour: sexual love.

"Do come," he seyde, "my mynstrales,
And geestours for to tellen tales,
   Anon in myn armynge,
Of romances that been roiales,
Of popes and of cardinales,
   And eek of love-likynge."

845 do come: summon.
geestours: storytellers.
in: during.

*2040

They fette hym first the sweete wyn,
And mede eek in a mazelyn,
   And roial spicerye
Of gyngebreed that was ful fyn,
And lycorys, and eek comyn,
   With sugre that is trye.

fette: fetched.
mede: mead, a drink fermented from
   honey. mazelyn: a maple bowl.
gyngebreed: preserved ginger.
855 comyn: cummin (a condiment).
trye: excellent, choice.

He dide next his white leere,
Of clooth of lake fyn and cleere,
   A breech and eek a sherte;
And next his sherte an aketoun,
And over that an haubergeoun
   For percynge of his herte;

dide: put. leere: loins.
lake: fine linen.
breech: underpants.
*2050 aketoun: padded jacket or tunic.
haubergeoun: coat of chain mail.
for: to prevent.

And over that a fyn hawberk,
Was al ywroght of Jewes werk,
   Ful strong it was of plate;
And over that his cote-armour
As whit as is a lilye flour,
   In which he wol debate.

hawberk: mail plates for breast and
   back.
865
cote-armour: garment decorated with
   heraldic arms.
debate: fight.

His sheeld was al of gold so reed,
And therinne was a bores heed,
   A charbocle bisyde;
And there he swoor on ale and breed
How that the geaunt shal be deed,
   Bityde what bityde!

*2060 bores heed: i.e., as a heraldic bear-
ing.

---

835. Rather than admit prolonged stresses on the first two words of this line, a fifteenth-century
scribe, who had a number of followers, started the line with the words "For now."
871. charbocle: the eight-rayed heraldic bearing representing the precious stone, carbuncle.

His jambeux were of quyrboilly,   875 jambeux: leggings, leg-armor.
His swerdes shethe of yvory,   quyrboilly: boiled leather.
  His helm of latoun bright;   latoun: a brass-like alloy.
His sadel was of rewel boon,   rewel boon: whale ivory.
His brydel as the sonne shoon,
  Or as the moone light.   *2070

His spere was of fyn ciprees,
That bodeth werre, and nothyng pees,
  The heed ful sharpe ygrounde;
His steede was al dappull gray,
It gooth an ambil in the way   885
  Ful softely and rounde   rounde: easily.
      In londe.   in londe: in the country.
  Loo, lordes myne, here is a fit!   fit: canto.
If ye wol any moore of it,
  To telle it wol I fonde.   *2080 fonde: try.

Now holde youre mouth, *par charitee*,
Bothe knyght and lady free,   free: noble.
  And herkneth to my spelle;   spelle: tale.
Of bataille and of chivalry,
And of ladyes love-drury   895 love-drury: passionate love.
  Anon I wol yow telle.

Men speken of romances of prys,   prys: excellence; renown.
Of Horn child and of Ypotys,
  Of Beves and sir Gy,
Of sir Lybeux and Pleyndamour,—   *2090
But sir Thopas, he bereth the flour
  Of roial chivalry!

His goode steede al he bistrood,
And forth upon his wey he glood   glood: glided.
  As sparcle out of the bronde;   905 bronde: firebrand; torch.
Upon his creest he bar a tour,   tour: tower.
And therinne stiked a lilie flour,   stiked: stuck, fixed.
  God shilde his cors fro shonde!   cors: body. **shonde**: shame; harm.

And for he was a knyght auntrous,   auntrous: adventurous.
He nolde slepen in noon hous,   *2100
  But liggen in his hoode;   liggen: lie.
His brighte helm was his wonger,   wonger: pillow.
And by hym baiteth his dextrer   baiteth: grazes. **dextrer**: war-horse.
  Of herbes fyne and goode.

---

891. **Now holde**: Here begins the second canto (**fit**) as is indicated by line 888.
898–900. Here are listed the heroes of some of the rimed romances that Chaucer parodies.

Hymself drank water of the well,   915
As dide the knyght sire Percyvell
  So worly under wede,   worly: worthy. wede: armor, mail.
Til on a day—

Heere the Hoost stynteth
Chaucer of his tale of   stynteth: stops.
Thopas.

"Namoore of this, for Goddes dignitee,"
Quod oure Hooste, "for thou makest me   *2110
So wery of thy verray lewednesse   lewednesse: ignorance.
That, also wisly God my soule blesse,   wisly: surely.
Myne eres aken of thy drasty speche.   drasty: filthy.
Now swich a rym the devel I biteche!   biteche: consign to.
This may wel be rym dogerel," quod he.   925
  "Why so?" quod I, "why wiltow lette me   lette: hinder, obstruct.
Moore of my tale than another man,
Syn that it is the beste rym I kan?"   kan: know.
  "By God," quod he, "for pleynly, at o word,
Thy drasty rymyng is nat worth a toord!   *2120
Thou doost noght elles but despendest tyme.   despendest: spend; waste.
Sire, at o word, thou shalt no lenger ryme.
Lat se wher thou kanst tellen aught in geeste,
Or telle in prose somwhat, at the leeste,
In which ther be som murthe or som doc-   doctryne: instruction.
      tryne."   935
  "Gladly," quod I, "by Goddes sweete pyne!   pyne: suffering.
I wol yow telle a litel thyng in prose
That oghte liken yow, as I suppose,   liken: please.
Or elles, certes, ye been to daungerous.   daungerous: hard to please.
It is a moral tale vertuous,   *2130
Al be it told somtyme in sondry wyse
Of sondry folk, as I shal yow devyse.
  As thus: ye woot that every Evaungelist,
That telleth us the peyne of Jhesu Crist,
Ne seith nat alle thyng as his felawe dooth;   945
But nathelees hir sentence is al sooth.
And alle acorden as in hire sentence,   sentence: meaning.
Al be ther in hir tellyng difference.
For somme of hem seyn moore, and somme seyn
      lesse,
Whan they his pitous passioun expresse—   *2140
I meene of Mark, Mathew, Luk, and John—

---

933. in geeste: (perhaps) in couplets or assonance, as in *chansons de geste*.

But doutelees hir sentence is al oon.   oon: the same.
Therfore, lordynges alle, I yow biseche,
If that yow thynke I varie as in my speche,
As thus, though that I telle somwhat moore   955
Of proverbes than ye han herd bifoore
Comprehended in this litel tretys heere,
To enforce with th' effect of my mateere.
And though I nat the same wordes seye
As ye han herd, yet to yow alle I preye   *2150
Blameth me nat; for, as in my sentence,
Shul ye nowher fynden difference
Fro the sentence of this tretys lite
After the which this murye tale I write.
And therfore herkneth what that I shal seye, 965
And lat me tellen al my tale, I preye."

Explicit.

Heere bigynneth Chaucers tale of Melibee.

A yong man called Melibeus, myghty and riche, bigat upon his wyf, that called was Prudence, a doghter which that called was Sophie./

Upon a day bifel that he for his desport is went into the feeldes hym to pleye./ His wyf and eek his doghter hath he left inwith his hous, of which the dores weren faste yshette./ Thre of his olde foes han it espyed, and setten laddres to the walles of his hous, and by wyndowes been entred, [*2160] and betten his wyf, and wounded his doghter with fyve mortal woundes in fyve sondry places,—/ this is to seyn, in hir feet, in hir handes, in hir erys, in hir nose, and in hir mouth,—and leften hire for deed, and wenten awey./

Whan Melibeus retourned was in to his hous, and saugh al this meschief, he, lyk a mad man, rentynge his clothes, gan to wepe and crye./

---

958. To support the significance of my matter with.

Chaucers Tale of Melibee. Chaucer based this allegorical tale on a French version (by Renaud de Louens, a Dominican friar) of the Latin *Book of Consolation and Counsel* by the thirteenth-century Italian judge, Albertano of Brescia. In these popular writings, the ideal of settling disputes through arbitration rather than fighting is supported by some two hundred maxims and quotations, classical and Christian. Because of the importance of this feature, the ultimate sources of the quotations, when definitely known, are generally indicated in the notes. It will be seen that Solomon is sometimes credited with verses from the Ecclesiasticus, by Jesus son of Sirach, and that Seneca's name is attached to the sayings of Publilius Syrus and to the anonymous *De Moribus*. The Bible (and Apocrypha) are cited in the Authorized Version; references to the Latin Vulgate Bible are given when different and when the Authorized Version lacks the parallel passages. The Vulgate of course offers a text closer to Albertano, Renaud, and Chaucer.

968. desport: pleasure, recreation.

969. inwith: within.   yshette: shut.

971. betten: beat.

972. erys: ears.

973. saugh: saw.   meschief: harm; evil.   rentynge: tearing.

Prudence, his wyf, as ferforth as she dorste, bisoughte hym of his wepyng for to stynte;/ but nat forthy he gan to crye and wepen evere lenger the moore. [975]

This noble wyf Prudence remembred hire upon the sentence of Ovide, in his book that cleped is the Remedie of Love, where as he seith/ "He is a fool that destourbeth the moder to wepen in the deth of hir child, til she have wept hir fille as for a certein tyme;/ and thanne shal man doon his diligence with amyable wordes hire to reconforte, and preyen hire of hir wepyng for to stynte."/ For which resoun this noble wyf Prudence suffred hir housbonde for to wepe and crye as for a certein space;/ and whan she saugh hir tyme, she seyde hym in this wise: "Allas, my lord," quod she, "why make ye youreself for to be lyk a fool? [*2170] For sothe it aperteneth nat to a wys man to maken swich a sorwe./ Youre doghter, with the grace of God, shal warisshe and escape./ And, al were it so that she right now were deed, ye ne oughte nat, as for hir deth, youreself to destroye./ Senek seith: 'The wise man shal nat take to greet disconfort for the deth of his children;/ but, certes, he sholde suffren it in pacience as wel as he abideth the deth of his owene propre persone.' " [985]

This Melibeus answerde anon, and seyde, "What man," quod he, "sholde of his wepyng stynte that hath so greet a cause for to wepe?/ Jhesu Crist, oure Lord, hymself wepte for the deth of Lazarus hys freend."/

Prudence answerde: "Certes, wel I woot attempree wepyng is no thyng defended to hym that sorweful is, amonges folk in sorwe, but it is rather graunted hym to wepe./ The Apostle Paul unto the Romayns writeth, 'Man shal rejoyse with hem that maken joye, and wepen with swich folk as wepen.'/ But though attempree wepyng be graunted, outrageous wepyng certes is defended. [*2180] Mesure of wepyng sholde be considered, after the loore that techeth us Senek:/ 'Whan that thy frend is deed,' quod he, 'lat nat thyne eyen to moyste been of teeris, ne to

---

974. **as ferforth:** as much. **dorste:** dared. **stynte:** cease.
975. **nat forthy:** nevertheless.
976. **remembred hire upon:** recalled. **sentence:** saying. **Ovide:** see Ovid, *Remedia Amoris* 127–30.
977. **destourbeth to wepen in:** hinders from weeping over.
978. **doon his diligence:** exert himself to the utmost. **reconforte:** comfort.
980. **tyme:** right moment, opportunity.
981. **aperteneth:** befits.
982. **warisshe:** recover. **escape:** recover.
983. **al were it so that:** even though. **deed:** dead.
984. **Senek:** see Seneca, *Epistolae* 74.§ 30. **to greet:** too great. **disconfort:** suffering.
985. **abideth:** awaits.
986. **stynte:** stop.
987. See John xi.35.
988. **attempree:** moderate. **no thyng defended:** not at all forbidden. **graunted:** permitted.
989. **Paul:** see Romans xii.15.
990. **outrageous:** excessive.
991. **mesure of:** moderation in. **after:** according to. **loore:** doctrine. **Senek:** see *Epistolae* 63.§§ 1, 11.
992. **to moyste:** too moist.
The Attack on Prudence and Sophie: This miniature, found at the beginning of a fifteenth-century text of Chaucer's source for the Tale of Melibee, presents the opening event which sets the tale in motion, so to speak. Simplifying details of the text ("eschielles aus murs," "les fenestres") and disregarding principles of architecture, the artist has produced a vivid and fantastic setting for the three-man attack on Prudence and Sophie, who is being wounded before our very eyes. (See lines 967–972.)

muche drye; although the teeris come to thyne eyen, lat hem nat falle;/ and whan thou hast forgoon thy freend, do diligence to gete another freend; and this is moore wysdom than for to wepe for thy freend which that thou hast lorn, for therinne is no boote.'/ And therfore, if ye governe yow by sapience, put awey sorwe out of youre herte./ Remembre yow that Jhesus Syrak seith, 'A man that is joyous and glad in herte, it hym conserveth florisshynge in his age; but soothly sorweful herte maketh his bones drye.' [995] He seith eek thus, that sorwe in herte sleeth ful many a man./ Salomon seith that right as moththes in the shepes flees anoyeth to the clothes, and the smale wormes to the tree, right so anoyeth sorwe to the herte./ Wherfore us oghte, as wel in the deth of oure children as in the losse of oure goodes temporels, have pacience./ Remembre yow upon the pacient Job. Whan he hadde lost his children and his temporel substance, and in his body endured and receyved ful many a grevous tribulacion, yet seyde he thus:/ 'Oure Lord hath yeven it me; oure Lord hath biraft it me; right so as oure Lord hath wold, right so it is doon; blessed be the name of oure Lord!' " [*2190]

To thise forseide thynges answerde Melibeus unto his wyf Prudence: "Alle thy wordes," quod he, "been sothe, and therto profitable; but trewely myn herte is troubled with this sorwe so grevously that I noot what to doone."/

"Lat calle," quod Prudence, "thy trewe freendes alle, and thy lynage whiche that been wise. Telleth youre cas, and herkneth what they seye in conseillyng, and yow governe after hire sentence./ Salomon seith, 'Werke alle thy thynges by conseil, and thou shalt never repente.' "/

Thanne, by the conseil of his wyf Prudence, this Melibeus leet callen a greet congregacion of folk;/ as surgiens, phisiciens, olde folk and yonge, and somme of his olde enemys reconsiled as by hir semblaunt to his love and into his grace; [1005] and therwithal ther coomen somme of his neighebores that diden hym reverence moore for drede than for love, as it happeth ofte./ Ther coomen also ful many subtile flatereres, and wise advocatz lerned in the lawe./

And whan this folk togidre assembled weren, this Melibeus in sorweful wise shewed hem his cas./ And by the manere of his speche it semed that in herte he baar a cruel ire, redy to doon vengeaunce upon his foes, and sodeynly desired that the werre sholde bigynne;/ but nathelees, yet axed he hire conseil upon this matere.

---

993. forgoon: lost. do diligence: make an effort. lorn: lost. boote: help; use.
994. sapience: wisdom.
995. Jhesus Syrak: see Proverbs xvii.22. conserveth: keeps
996. He: see Ecclesiasticus (The Wisdom of Jesus the Son of Sirach) xxx.23 (Vulgate 25). sleeth: (slayeth) slays.
997. Salomon: see Vulgate, Proverbs xxv.20. shepes flees: sheep's fleece. anoyeth: is harmful.
998. us oghte: it would become us.
999. Job: see Job i.21. substance: goods. tribulacion: affliction.
1000. biraft it: taken it away (from). wold: willed.
1001. doone: do.
1002. lynage: kinsmen. cas: case, situation. sentence: opinion.
1003. Salomon: see pseudo-Bede, Liber Proverbiorum. werk: do.
1004. leet callen: summoned.
1005. reconsiled: brought back. semblaunt: appearance.
1009. baar: bore. werre: war.
1010. axed: asked.

[*2200] A surgien, by licence and assent of swiche as weren wise, up roos, and unto Melibeus seyde as ye may heere:/

"Sire," quod he, "as to us surgiens aperteneth that we do to every wight the beste that we kan, where as we been withholde, and to oure pacientz that we do no damage;/ wherfore it happeth many tyme and ofte that whan twey men han everich wounded oother, oon same surgien heeleth hem bothe;/ wherfore unto oure art it is nat pertinent to norice werre ne parties to supporte./ But certes, as to the warisshynge of youre doghter, al be it so that she perilously be wounded, we shullen do so ententif bisynesse fro day to nyght that with the grace of God she shal be hool and sound as soone as is possible." [1015]

Almoost right in the same wise the phisiciens answerden, save that they seyden a fewe woordes moore:/ that right as maladies been cured by hir contraries, right so shal men warisshe werre by vengeaunce./

His neighbores ful of envye, his feyned freendes that semeden reconsiled, and his flatereres/ maden semblant of wepyng, and empeired and agregged muchel of this matere in preisynge gretly Melibee of myght, of power, of richesse, and of freendes, despisynge the power of his adversaries,/ and seiden outrely that he anon sholde wreken hym on his foes, and bigynne werre. [*2210]

Up roos thanne an advocat that was wys, by leve and by conseil of othere that were wise, and seide:/ "Lordynges, the nede for the which we been assembled in this place is ful hevy thyng and an heigh matere,/ by cause of the wrong and of the wikkednesse that hath be doon, and eek by resoun of the grete damages that in tyme comynge been possible to fallen for the same cause,/ and eek by resoun of the grete richesse and power of the parties bothe;/ for the whiche resouns it were a ful greet peril to erren in this matere. [1025] Wherfore, Melibeus, this is oure sentence: we conseille yow aboven alle thyng that right anon thou do thy diligence in kepynge of thy propre persone in swich a wise that thou ne wante noon espie ne wacche, thy body for to save./ And after that, we conseille that in thyn hous thou sette sufficeant garnisoun so that they may as wel thy body as thyn hous defende./ But certes, for to moeve werre, ne sodeynly for to doon vengeaunce, we may nat demen in so litel tyme that it were profitable./ Wherfore we axen leyser and espace

---

1011. roos: rose.
1012. aperteneth: belongs the duty. where as: where. withholde: retained.
1013. everich: each. heeleth: heals.
1014. norice: nourish, foment. to supporte parties: i.e., to take sides.
1015. warisshynge: healing. al be it so that: although. do so ententif bisynesse: devote ourselves so attentively. hool: whole.
1017. contraries: opposites. warisshe: cure.
1018. envye: enmity. feyned: pretended. semeden: seemed.
1019. maden semblant: assumed looks. empeired and agregged of: made worse and more difficult. of: for. despisynge: disparaging.
1020. outrely: straight out. wreken hym: revenge himself. werre: war.
1022. nede: business. hevy: weighty of import.
1023. fallen: befall, occur.
1026. kepynge: guarding. espie: spy. wacche: sentinel.
1027. garnisoun: garrison.
1028. moeve: stir up, commence. sodeynly: without delay. demen: decide.
1029. leyser: leisure. espace: time.

to have deliberacion in this cas to deme./ For the commune proverbe seith thus: 'He that soone deemeth, soone shal repente.' [*2220] And eek men seyn that thilke juge is wys that soone understondeth a matere and juggeth by leyser;/ for al be it so that alle tariyng be anoyful, algates it is nat to repreve in yevynge of juggement ne in vengeance takyng, whan it is sufficeant and resonable./ And that shewed oure Lord Jhesu Crist by ensample; for whan that the womman that was taken in avoutrye was broght in his presence to knowen what sholde be doon with hir per-sone, al be it that he wiste wel hymself what that he wolde answere, yet ne wolde he nat answere sodeynly, but he wolde have deliberacion, and in the ground he wroot twies./ And by thise causes we axen deliberacioun, and we shal thanne, by the grace of God, conseille thee thyng that shal be profitable./

Up stirten thanne the yonge folk atones, and the mooste partie of that com-paignye han scorned this olde wise man, and bigonnen to make noyse, and seyden that [1035] right so as, whil that iren is hoot, men sholden smyte, right so sholde men wreken hir wronges whil that they been fresshe and newe; and with loud voys they criden "Werre! werre!"/

Up roos tho oon of thise olde wise, and with his hand made contenaunce that men sholde holden hem stille and yeven hym audience./ "Lordynges," quod he, "ther is ful many a man that crieth 'Werre! werre!' that woot ful litel what werre amounteth./ Werre at his bigynnyng hath so greet an entryng and so large, that every wight may entre whan hym liketh, and lightly fynde werre;/ but certes what ende that shal therof bifalle, it is nat light to knowe. [*2230] For soothly, whan that werre is ones bigonne, ther is ful many a child unborn of his moder that shal sterve yong by cause of thilke werre, or elles lyve in sorwe and dye in wrecchednesse./ And therfore, er that any werre be bigonne, men moste have gret conseil and gret deliberacion."/ And whan this olde man wende to enforcen his tale by resons, wel ny alle atones bigonne they to rise for to breken his tale, and beden hym ful ofte his wordes for to abregge./ For soothly, he that precheth to hem that listen nat heeren his wordes, his sermon hem anoyeth./ For Jhesus Syrak seith that "musik in wepynge is anoyous thyng"; this is to seyn: as much availleth to speken bifore folk to which his speche anoyeth, as it is to synge bifoorn hym that wepeth. [1045] And

---

1030. **proverbe**: see Publilius Syrus, *Sententiae* 32.

1031. **by leyser**: with full deliberation.

1032. **al be it so that**: although. **algates**: nevertheless. **to repreve**: to be reproved.

1033. **avoutrye**: adultery. **wroot**: wrote. **twies**: twice.

1034. **by thise causes**: for these reasons. **axen**: ask for.

1035. **stirten**: started. **atones**: at once. **mooste partie**: chief part.

1036. **hoot**: hot. **wreken**: avenge.

1037. **made contenaunce**: indicated.

1038. **amounteth**: amounts to, means.

1039. **entryng**: place of entrance. **lightly**: easily.

1040. **light**: easy.

1043. **wende**: thought. **enforcen**: strengthen, support. **tale**: discourse. **atones**: at once. **beden**: bade, told. **abregge**: abridge.

1044. **listen**: wish.

1045. **Jhesus Syrak**: see Ecclesiasticus xxii.6. **in wepynge**: i.e., at a time of mourning. **anoyous**: disturbing.

whan this wise man saugh that hym wanted audience, al shamefast he sette hym doun agayn./ For Salomon seith: "Ther as thou ne mayst have non audience, enforce thee nat to speke."/ "I see wel," quod this wise man, "that the commune proverbe is sooth, that 'good conseil wanteth whan it is moost nede.' "/

Yet hadde this Melibeus in his conseil many folk that prively in his eere conseilled hym certeyn thyng, and conseilled hym the contrarie in general audience./

Whan Melibeus hadde herd that the gretteste partie of his conseil were accorded that he sholde make werre, anon he consented to hir conseilyng, and fully affermed hire sentence. [*2240] Thanne dame Prudence, whan that she saugh how that hir housbonde shoop hym for to wreke hym on his foes, and to bigynne werre, she in ful humble wise, whan she saugh hir tyme, seide hym thise wordes:/ "My lord," quod she, "I yow biseche as hertely as I dar and kan, ne haste yow nat to faste, and for alle gerdons, as yeveth me audience./ For Piers Alfonce seith, 'Whoso that dooth to thee outher good or harm, haste thee nat to quiten it; for in this wise thy freend wol abyde, and thyn enemy shal the lenger lyve in drede.'/ The proverbe seith, 'He hasteth wel that wisely kan abyde,' and in wikked haste is no profit."/

This Melibee answerde unto his wyf Prudence: "I purpose nat," quod he, "to werke by thy conseil, for many causes and resouns. For certes, every wight wolde holde me thanne a fool; [1055] this is to seyn, if I, for thy conseillyng, wolde chaunge thynges that been ordeyned and affermed by so manye wyse./ Secoundly, I seye that alle wommen been wikke, and noon good of hem alle. For 'of a thousand men,' seith Salomon, 'I foond o good man, but certes, of alle wommen, good womman foond I nevere.'/ And also, certes, if I governed me by thy conseil, it sholde seme that I hadde yeve to thee over me the maistrie; and Goddes forbode that it so weere!/ For Jhesus Syrak seith that 'if the wyf have maistrie, she is contrarious to hir housbonde.'/ And Salomon seith: 'Nevere in thy lyf to thy wyf, ne to thy child, ne to thy freend, ne yeve no power over thyself; for bettre it were that thy children aske of thy persone thynges that hem nedeth, than thou see thyself in the handes of thy children.' [*2250] And also if I wolde werke by thy conseillyng, certes, my conseil moste som tyme be secree, til it were tyme that it moste be

---

1046. wanted: lacked. shamefast: ashamed.

1047. Salomon: see Vulgate, Ecclesiasticus xxxii.6. ther as: where. enforce thee: endeavor.

1048. proverbe: see Publilius Syrus, Sententiae 594. wanteth: is lacking. nede: needful.

1049. in general audience: in the hearing of all.

1050. partie: part.

1051. shoop hym: prepared. wreke hym: avenge himself. saugh: saw. tyme: right moment, opportunity.

1052. hertely: earnestly. to: too. for alle gerdons: for all rewards; ? as you hope to prosper. as yeveth: (please) give.

1053. Piers Alfonce: see Petrus Alfonsi, Disciplina Clericalis ex. xxiv. outher: either. harm: evil. quiten: requite, repay. abyde: wait, be patient.

1056. for: because of. ordeyned: arranged, established. affermed: confirmed.

1057. wikke: wicked. noon good of: no good one among. Salomon: see Ecclesiastes vii.28 (Vulgate 29). o: one.

1058. Goddes forbode: (God's prohibition) God forbid.

1059. Jhesus Syrak: see Vulgate, Ecclesiasticus xxv.30.

1060. Salomon: see Ecclesiasticus xxxiii.19–21 (Vulgate 20–22). hem nedeth: i.e., they need.

1061. moste: must.

knowe, and this ne may noght be./ [*Car il est escript, 'La genglerie des femmes ne puet riens celer fors ce qu'elle ne scet.'/ Après, le philosophe dit, 'En mauvais conseil les femmes vainquent les hommes.' Pour ces raisons je ne doy point user de ton conseil.*]"/

Whanne dame Prudence, ful debonairly and with gret pacience, hadde herd al that hir housbonde liked for to seye, thanne axed she of hym licence for to speke, and seyde in this wise:/ "My lord," quod she, "as to youre firste resoun, certes it may lightly been answered. For I seye that it is no folie to chaunge conseil whan the thyng is chaunged, or elles whan the thyng semeth ootherweyes than it was biforn. [1065] And mooreover, I seye that though ye han sworn and bihight to perfourne youre emprise, and nathelees ye weyve to perfourne thilke same emprise by juste cause, men sholde nat seyn therfore that ye were a liere ne forsworn./ For the book seith that 'the wise man maketh no lesyng whan he turneth his corage to the bettre.'/ And al be it so that youre emprise be establissed and ordeyned by gret multitude of folk, yet thar ye nat accomplice thilke ordinaunce, but yow like./ For the trouthe of thynges and the profit ben rather founde in fewe folk that ben wise and ful of reson, than by gret multitude of folk ther every man crieth and clatereth what that hym liketh. Soothly swich multitude is nat honest./

And to the seconde resoun, where as ye seyn that alle wommen been wikke; save youre grace, certes ye despise alle wommen in this wyse, and 'he that al despiseth, al displeseth,' as seith the book. [*2260] And Senec seith that 'whoso wole have sapience shal no man dispreyse, but he shal gladly teche the science that he kan withoute presumpcion or pride;/ and swiche thynges as he noght ne kan, he shal nat ben ashamed to lerne hem, and enquere of lasse folk than hymself.'/ And, sire, that ther hath been ful many a good womman, may lightly be preved./ For certes, sire, oure Lord Jhesu Crist wolde nevere have descended to be born of a womman, if alle wommen hadde been wikke./ And after that, for the grete bountee that is in wommen, oure Lord Jhesu Crist, whan he was risen fro deeth to lyf, appeered rather to a womman than to his Apostles. [1075] And though that Salomon seith that he ne foond nevere womman good, it folweth nat therfore that alle wommen ben wikke./ For though that he ne foond no good womman, certes, many another man hath founde many a womman ful good and trewe./ Or elles, par aventure, the

---

1062–63. For it is written, 'The chattering of women can hide nothing except what she does not know.' Furthermore, the philosopher says, 'In bad advice women outdo men.' For these reasons I must not use your advice." (Of the French passages not represented in Chaucer's text, this one and two later ones [1433–34, 1664] are necessary to the sense.)

1064. debonairly: graciously.

1065. lightly: easily. conseil: plan. thyng: affair. ootherweyes: otherwise.

1066. bihight: promised. perfourne: carry out. emprise: enterprise, undertaking. weyve to perfourne: refrain from carrying out. liere: liar.

1067. book: see Seneca, *De Beneficiis* iv.38.1. lesyng: lie, falsehood. turneth his corage: changes his mind.

1068. al be it so that: although. establissed: set up. ordeyned: arranged, established. thar: need. thilke ordinaunce: that plan, that arrangement.

1070. save youre grace: i.e., by your leave. despise: disparage.

1071. sapience: wisdom. no man dispreyse: disparage no man. gladly: willingly. science: knowledge. kan: knows.

1072. noght ne kan: knows not. lasse: lesser.

1073. lightly: easily.

1075. bountee: goodness. rather: sooner.

entente of Salomon was this, that, as in sovereyn bountee, he foond no womman;/ this is to seyn, that ther is no wight that hath sovereyn bountee save God allone, as he hymself recordeth in hys Evaungelie./ For ther nys no creature so good that hym ne wanteth somwhat of the perfeccioun of God, that is his makere. [*2270]

Youre thridde reson is this: ye seyn that if ye governe yow by my conseil, it sholde seme that ye hadde yeve me the maistrie and the lordshipe over youre persone./ Sire, save youre grace, it is nat so. For if so were that no man sholde be conseiled but oonly of hem that hadde lordshipe and maistrie of his persone, men wolde nat be conseilled so ofte./ For soothly thilke man that asketh conseil of a purpos, yet hath he free choys wheither he wole werke by that conseil or noon./ And as to youre fourthe reson, ther ye seyn that the janglerie of wommen kan hide thynges that they woot nat, as who seith that a womman kan nat hide that she woot;/ sire, thise wordes been understonde of wommen that ben jangleresses and wikked; [1085] of whiche wommen men seyn that thre thynges dryven a man out of his hous,—that is to seyn, smoke, droppyng of reyn, and wikked wyves;/ and of swiche wommen seith Salomon that 'it were bettre dwelle in desert than with a womman that is riotous.'/ And sire, by youre leve, that am nat I;/ for ye han ful ofte assayed my grete silence and my grete pacience, and eek how wel that I kan hyde and hele thynges that men oghte secreely to hyde./ And soothly, as to youre fifthe reson, where as ye seyn that in wikked conseil wommen venquisshe men, God woot, thilke reson stant heere in no stede. [*2280] For understond now, ye asken conseil to do wikkednesse;/ and if ye wole werke wikkednesse, and youre wif restreyneth thilke wikked purpos, and overcometh yow by reson and by good conseil,/ certes youre wyf oghte rather to be preised than yblamed./ Thus sholde ye understonde the philosophre that seith, 'In wikked conseil wommen venquisshen hir housbondes.'/ And ther as ye blamen alle wommen and hir resons, I shal shewe by manye ensamples that many a womman hath ben ful good, and yet ben, and hir conseils holsom and profitable. [1095] Eek som men han seyd that the conseilyng of wommen is outher to deere, or elles to litel of pris./ But al be it so that ful many a womman is badde, and hir conseil vile and noght worth, yet han men founde ful many a good womman, and ful discrete and wise in conseilynge./ Lo, Jacob, by conseil of his moder Rebekka, wan the benysoun of Ysaak his fader, and the lordshipe over alle his brethren./ Judith, by hir good conseil, delivered the citee of Bethulie, in which she dwelled, out of the handes of Olofernus, that hadde it biseged and wolde it al destroye./ Abygail delivered Nabal hir housbonde fro David

---

1078. **entente:** meaning. **sovereyn:** supreme. **bountee:** goodness.
1079. **Evaungelie:** Gospel revelation; see Matthew xix.17; Luke xviii.19.
1080. **wanteth:** lacks.
1083. **of:** about. **noon:** not.
1084. **ther:** where. **janglerie:** gossip. **woot:** know.
1085. **jangleresses:** talkative women.
1086. **men:** see St. Jerome, *Epistola adversus Jovinianum* I.28. **droppying:** dripping. **reyn:** rain.
1087. **Salomon:** see Proverbs xxi.9. **riotous:** wanton, dissolute.
1089. **assayed:** tested. **hele:** conceal.
1090. **venquisshe:** surpass. **stant:** (standeth) stands. **stede:** avail.
1095. **yet ben:** still are. **holsom:** beneficial.
1096. **outher:** either. **to deere:** too dear. **pris:** value.
1097. **al be it so that:** although. **noght:** not, not at all. **worth:** of value.
1098. See Genesis xxvii. **wan:** won. **benysoun:** blessing.

the kyng, that wolde have slayn hym, and apaysed the ire of the kyng by hir wit and by hir good conseillyng. [*2290] Hester, by hir good conseil, enhaunced gretly the peple of God in the regne of Assuerus the kyng./ And the same bountee in good conseillyng of many a good womman may men telle./ And mooreover, whan that oure Lord hadde creat Adam, oure forme fader, he seyde in this wise:/ 'It is nat good to be a man allone; make we to hym an help semblable to hymself.'/ Heere may ye se that if that wommen were nat goode, and hir conseil goode and profitable, [1105] oure Lord God of hevene wolde neither han wroght hem, ne called hem help of man, but rather confusioun of man./ And ther seyde oones a clerk in two vers, 'What is bettre than gold? Jaspre. What is bettre than jaspre? Wisdom./ And what is bettre than wisdom? Womman. And what it bettre than a good womman? Nothyng.'/ And, sire, by manye othere resons may ye seen that manye wommen ben goode, and hir conseil good and profitable./ And therfore, sire, if ye wol truste to my conseil, I shal restore yow youre doghter hool and sound. [*2300] And eek I wol do to yow so muche that ye shul have honour in this cause."/

Whan Melibee hadde herd the wordes of his wyf Prudence, he seyde thus:/ "I se wel that the word of Salomon is sooth. He seith that 'wordes that ben spoken discreetly by ordinaunce been honycombes, for they yeve swetnesse to the soule and holsomnesse to the body.'/ And, wyf, by cause of thy sweete wordes, and eek for I have assayed and preved thy grete sapience and thy grete trouthe, I wol governe me by thy conseil in alle thyng."/

"Now, sire," quod dame Prudence, "and syn ye vouche sauf to been governed by my conseil, I wol enforme yow how ye shal governe yourself in chesynge of youre conseillours. [1115] Ye shal first in alle youre werkes mekely biseken to the heighe God that he wol be youre conseillour;/ and shapeth yow to swich entente that he yeve yow conseil and confort, as taughte Thobie his sone:/ 'At alle tymes thou shalt blesse God, and praye hym to dresse thy weyes, and looke that alle thy conseils ben in hym for everemoore.'/ Seint Jame eek seith: 'If any of yow have nede of sapience, axe it of God.'/ And afterward thanne shal ye take conseil in youreself, and examyne wel youre thoghtes of swich thynges as yow thynketh that

---

1099. See Judith, xi–xiii.

1100. See I Samuel xxv. **apaysed:** appeased. **wit:** intelligence, judgment.

1101. See Esther vii. **enhaunced:** enhanced the fortune of.

1102. **bountee:** excellence.

1103. **creat:** created. **forme:** first.

1104. **to be a man:** for a man to be. **help:** helper. **semblable:** similar.

1106. **confusioun:** ruin.

1107. **vers:** verses.

1111. **to:** for.

1113. **Salomon:** see Proverbs xvi.24. **by ordinaunce:** i.e., well ordered, well arranged. **holsomnesse:** health.

1114. **for:** because. **assayed:** tried. **preved:** tested. **sapience:** wisdom. **trouthe:** loyalty.

1115. **chesynge:** choosing.

1116. **werkes:** actions. **biseken to:** beseech.

1117. **shapeth yow:** dispose yourself. **to switch entente:** to the end. **Thobie:** see Tobit iv.19 (Vulgate 20).

1118. **to dresse thy weyes:** to direct your way. **looke:** make sure. **conseils:** deliberations. **ben in:** i.e., remain true to.

1119. **Seint Jame:** see James i.5.

1120. **take conseil:** deliberate. **of:** concerning.

is best for youre profit. [*2310] And thanne shal ye dryve fro youre herte thre thynges that been contrariouse to good conseil;/ that is to seyn, ire, coveitise, and hastynesse./

First, he that axeth conseil of hymself, certes he moste ben withouten ire, for many causes./ The firste is this: he that hath greet ire and wrathe in hymself, he weneth alwey that he may do thyng that he may nat do./ And secoundly, he that is irous and wroth, he ne may nat wel deme; [1125] and he that may nat wel deme, may nat wel conseille./ The thridde is this, that he that is irous and wroth, as seith Senec, ne may nat speke but blameful thynges,/ and with his viciouse wordes he stireth oother folk to angre and to ire./ And eek, sire, ye moste dryve coveitise out of youre herte./ For the Apostle seith that coveitise is the roote of alle harmes. [*2320] And trust wel that a coveitous man ne kan nat deme ne thynke, but oonly to fulfille the ende of his coveitise;/ and certes, that ne may nevere been accompliced; for evere the moore habundaunce that he hath of richesse, the moore he desireth./ And, sire, ye moste also dryve out of youre herte hastifnesse; for certes,/ ye may nat deeme for the best a sodeyn thought that falleth in youre herte, but ye moste avyse yow on it ful ofte./ For, as ye herde here biforn, the commune proverbe is this, that 'he that soone deemeth, soone repenteth.' [1135] Sire, ye be nat alwey in lyk disposicioun;/ for certes, somthyng that somtyme semeth to yow that it is good for to do, another tyme it semeth to yow the contrarie./

When ye han taken conseil in youreself, and han deemed by good deliberacion swich thyng as you semeth best,/ thanne rede I yow that ye kepe it secree./ Biwrey nat youre conseil to no persone, but if so be that ye wenen sikerly that thurgh youre biwreyyng youre condicioun shal be to yow the moore profitable. [*2330] For Jhesus Syrak seith, 'Neither to thy foo, ne to thy frend, discovere nat thy secree ne thy folie;/ for they wol yeve yow audience and lookynge and supportacioun in thy presence, and scorne thee in thyn absence.'/ Another clerk seith that 'scarsly shaltou fynden any persone that may kepe conseil secrely.'/ The book seith, 'Whil that thou kepest thy conseil in thyn herte, thou kepest it in thy prison;/ and whan thou biwreyest thy conseil to any wight, he holdeth thee in his snare.' [1145] And therfore yow is bettre to hide youre conseil in youre herte than praye

---

1122. hastynesse: undue haste, rashness.
1123. causes: reasons.
1125. irous: angry. deme: judge.
1127. Senec: see Publilius Syrus, *Sententiae* 281. blameful: reprehensible, sinful.
1128. stireth: stirs, moves.
1129. moste: must.
1130. Apostle: see I Timothy vi.10. harmes: evils.
1132. accompliced: accomplished.
1134. avyse: take thought.
1135. proverbe: see Publilius Syrus, *Sententiae* 32. deemeth: judges.
1136. lyk disposicioun: the same frame of mind.
1138. deemed: decided.
1139. rede: advise.
1140. biwrey: reveal. conseil: decision, plan. biwreyyng: confiding.
1141. Jhesus Syrak: see Ecclesiasticus xix.8, 9. discovere: reveal. folie: wrongdoing, crime.
1142. supportacioun: support.
1145. biwreyest: divulge.
1146. yow is: for you it is.

him to whom ye han biwreyed youre conseil that he wol kepen it cloos and stille./ For Seneca seith: 'If so be that thou ne mayst nat thyn owene conseil hyde, how darstou prayen any oother wight thy conseil secrely to kepe?'/ But nathelees, if thou wene sikerly that thy biwreiyng of thy conseil to a persone wol make thy condicion to stonden in the bettre plyt, thanne shaltou telle hym thy conseil in this wise./ First thou shalt make no semblant wheither thee were levere pees or werre, or this or that, ne shewe hym nat thy wille and thyn entente./ For trust wel that comunely thise conseillours ben flatereres, [*2340] namely the conseillours of grete lordes;/ for they enforcen hem alwey rather to speke plesante wordes, enclynynge to the lordes lust, than wordes that been trewe or profitable./ And therfore men seyn that the riche man hath selde good conseil, but if he have it of himself./

And after that thou shalt considere thy freendes and thyne enemys./ And as touchynge thy freendes, thou shalt considere which of hem been moost feithful and moost wise and eldest and most approved in conseillyng; [1155] and of hem shalt thou aske thy conseil, as the caas requireth./ I seye that first ye shul clepe to youre conseil youre freendes that ben trewe./ For Salomon seith that 'right as the herte of a man deliteth in savour that is soote, right so the conseil of trewe freendes yeveth swetnesse to the soule.'/ He seith also, 'Ther may no thyng be likned to the trewe freend;/for certes gold ne silver ben nat so muche worth as the goode wyl of a trewe freend.' [*2350] And eek he seith that 'a trewe freend is a strong defense; who so that it fyndeth, certes he fyndeth a gret tresor.'/ Thanne shul ye eek considere if that youre trewe freendes been discrete and wise. For the book seith, 'Axe alwey thy conseil of hem that been wise.'/ And by this same reson shul ye clepen to youre conseil of youre freendes that ben of age, swiche as han seyn and been expert in manye thynges and been approved in conseillynges./ For the book seith that 'in olde men is the sapience, and in longe tyme the prudence.'/ And Tullius seith that 'grete thynges ne ben nat ay accompliced by strengthe, ne by delivernesse of body, but by good conseil, by auctoritee of persones, and by science; the whiche thre thynges ne been nat fieble by age, but certes they enforcen and encreescen day by day.' [1165]

And thanne shal ye kepe this for a general reule: First shal ye clepe to youre

---

1147. Seneca: see pseudo-Seneca, *De Moribus* sent. 16; although this anonymous work is erroneously attributed to Seneca in most manuscripts, and never to St. Martin of Braga or Dumium, it has been erroneously published as Martin's along with his genuine writings.
darstou: darest thou.

1148. biwreiyng: confiding.   plyt: plight, state.

1149. make no semblant: have no expression suggesting.

1152. enforcen hem: endeavor.   lust: desire.

1153. selde: seldom.

1157. clepe: call.

1158. Salomon: see Proverbs xxvii.9.   soote: sweet.

1159. He: see Ecclesiasticus vi.15.

1161. he: see Ecclesiasticus vi.14.

1162. book: see Tobit iv.18 (Vulgate 19).

1163. reson: reasoning.   of youre: i.e., some of your, those of your.   of age: i.e., old enough.
seyn: seen.   expert: experienced.   approved: proven, tried.

1164. book: see Job xii.12.

1165. Tullius: see Cicero, *De Senectute* vi.17.   delivernesse: dexterity.   science: knowledge.
fieble: feeble, weak.   by: because of.   enforcen: grow stronger.   encreescen: increase.

conseil a fewe of youre freendes that ben especiale;/ for Salomon seith, 'Manye freendes have thou, but among a thousand chese thee oon to be thy conseillour.'/ For al be it so that thou first ne telle thy conseil but to a fewe, thou mayst afterward telle it to mo folk if it be nede./ But looke alwey that thy conseillours have thilke thre condiciouns that I have seyd bifore, that is to seye, that they be trewe, wise, and of old experience./ And werk nat alwey in every nede by oon counseillour allone; for somtyme bihooveth it to be conseiled by manye. [*2360] For Salomon seith, 'Salvacion of thynges is where as ther ben manye conseillours.'/

Now, sith that I have told yow of which folk ye sholde be counseilled, now wol I teche yow which conseil ye oghte eschewe./ First, ye shul eschue the conseillyng of fooles; for Salomon seith, 'Take no conseil of a fool, for he ne kan nat conseille but after his owene lust and his affeccioun.'/ The book seith that 'the propretee of a fool is this: he troweth lightly harm of every wight, and lightly troweth alle bountee in hymself.'/

Thou shalt eek eschue the conseillyng of alle flaterers, swiche as enforcen hem rather to preise youre persone by flaterye than for to telle yow the soothfastnesse of thynges. [1175] Wherfore Tullius seith, 'Among alle the pestilences that been in frendshipe the gretteste is flaterie.' And therfore is it moore nede that thou eschue and drede flaterers than any oother peple./ The book seith, 'Thou shalt rather drede and flee fro the sweete wordes of flaterynge preiseres than fro the egre wordes of thy freend that seith thee thy sothes.'/ Salomon seith that 'the wordes of a flaterere is a snare to cacche innocentz.'/ He seith also that 'he that speketh to his freend wordes of swetnesse and of plesaunce, setteth a net biforn his feet to cacche hym.'/ And therfore seith Tullius, 'Enclyne nat thyne eres to flatereres, ne take no conseil of wordes of flaterye.' [*2370] And Caton seith, 'Avyse thee wel, and eschue wordes of swetnesse and of plesaunce.'/

And eek thou shalt eschue the conseillyng of thyne olde enemys that ben reconsiled./ The book seith that 'no wight retourneth saufly into the grace of his olde enemy.'/ And Isope seith, 'Ne trust nat to hem to whiche thou hast had som tyme werre or enmytee, ne telle hem nat thy conseil.'/ And Seneca telleth the cause why: 'It may nat be,' seith he, 'that where as greet fyr hath longe tyme endured, that ther

---

1167. Salomon: see Ecclesiasticus vi.6.

1168. al be it so that: although. conseil: decision.

1169. looke: make sure. condiciouns: qualities.

1170. werk: act.

1171. Salomon: see Proverbs xi.14.

1172. of: by. eschewe: avoid.

1173. Salomon: see Ecclesiasticus viii.17 (Vulgate 20). affeccioun: inclination.

1174. book: see Cicero, *Disputationes Tusculanae* iii.30.73. propretee: property, distinctive quality. lightly: readily. harm: evil. bountee: goodness.

1175. eschue: avoid, shun. enforcen hem: endeavor. soothfastnesse: truth.

1176. Tullius: see Cicero, *De Amicitia* xxv.91. pestilences: plagues, curses.

1177. preiseres: praisers. egre: sharp. sothes: truths.

1178–79. Salomon; He: see Proverbs xxix.5.

1180. Tullius: see Cicero, *De Officiis* i.26.91.

1181. Caton: see Dionysius Cato, *Disticha* iii.4.

1183. the book: see Publilius Syrus, *Sententiae* 91. saufly: safely.

1185. Seneca: see Publilius Syrus, *Sententiae* 389. cause: reason.

ne dwelleth som vapour of warmnesse.' [1185] And therfore seith Salomon, 'In thyn olde foo trust nevere.'/ For sikerly, though thyn enemy be reconsiled, and maketh thee cheere of humylitee, and louteth to thee with his heed, ne trust hym nevere./ For certes he maketh thilke feyned humilitee moore for his profit than for any love of thy persone, by cause that he deemeth to have victorie over thy persone by swich feyned contenance, the which victorie he myghte nat have by strif or werre./ And Peter Alfonce seith, 'Make no felawshipe with thyne olde enemys; for if thou do hem bountee, they wol perverten it into wikkednesse.'/ And eek thou most eschue the conseillyng of hem that ben thy servantz and beren thee gret reverence, for peraventure they seyn it moore for drede than for love. [*2380] And therfore seith a philosophre in this wise: 'Ther is no wight parfitly trewe to hym that he to soore dredeth.'/ And Tullius seith, 'Ther nys no myght so gret of any emperour that longe may endure, but if he have moore love of the peple than drede.'/ Thou shalt also eschue the conseiling of folk that been dronkelewe, for they ne kan no conseil hyde./ For Salomon seith, 'Ther is no privetee ther as regneth dronke-nesse.'/ Ye shal also han in suspect the conseillyng of swich folk as conseille yow a thyng prively, and conseille yow the contrarie openly. [1195] For Cassidorie seith that 'it is a manere sleighte to hyndre, whan he sheweth to doon a thyng openly and werketh prively the contrarie.'/ Thou shalt also have in suspect the conseillyng of wikked folk. For the book seith, 'The conseillyng of wikked folk is alwey ful of fraude.'/ And David seith, 'Blisful is that man that hath nat folwed the conseilyng of shrewes.'/ Thou shalt also eschue the conseillyng of yong folk, for hir conseil is nat rype./

Now, sire, sith I have shewed yow of which folk ye shul take youre conseil, and of which folk ye shul folwe the conseil, [*2390] now wol I teche yow how ye shal examyne youre conseil, after the doctrine of Tullius./ In the examynynge thanne of youre conseillour ye shul considere many thynges.

Alderfirst thou shalt considere that in thilke thyng that thou purposest, and upon what thyng thou wolt have conseil, that verray trouthe be seyd and conserved; this is to seyn, telle trewely thy tale./ For he that seith fals may nat wel be conseiled in that cas of which he lieth./ And after this thou shalt considere the thynges that acorden to that thou purposest for to do by thy conseillours, if resoun accorde

---

1186. **Salomon:** see Ecclesiasticus xii.10.
1187. **maketh cheere:** assumes an expression.　**louteth:** bows down.　**heed:** head.
1188. **contenance:** appearance.
1189. **Peter Alfonce:** see Petrus Alphonsus, *Disciplina Clericalis* iv.4.
1191. **to soore:** too sorely, too greatly.
1192. **Tullius:** cf. *De Officiis* ii.7.　**of the peple:** from the people.
1193. **eschue:** avoid.　**dronkelewe:** addicted to drink.
1194. **Salomon:** see Proverbs xxxi.4.　**privetee:** secrecy.
1195. **han in suspect:** be suspicious of.
1196. **Cassidorie:** see Cassiodorus, *Variae* x.18.　**a manere sleighte:** a kind of trick.　**sheweth:** pretends.
1197. **the book:** see Proverbs xii.5.
1198. **David:** see Psalms i.1.　**shrewes:** scoundrels.
1201. **Tullius:** see *De Officiis* ii.5.18, for the basis of 1201–10.
1203. **alderfirst:** first of all.　**verray:** exact, actual.　**conserved:** preserved.
1204. **cas:** matter.
1205. **by:** with the advice of.

therto; [1205] and eek if thy myght may atteine therto; and if the moore part and the bettre part of thy conseillours acorde therto, or no./. Thanne shaltou considere what thyng shal folwe of that conseillyng, as hate, pees, werre, grace, profit, or damage, and many othere thynges./ And in alle thise thynges thou shalt chese the beste, and weyve alle othere thynges./ Thanne shaltow considere of what roote is engendred the matere of thy conseil, and what fruyt it may conceyve and engendre./ Thou shalt eek considere alle thise causes, fro whennes they ben sprongen. [*2400]

And whan ye have examyned youre conseil, as I have seyd, and which partie is the bettre and moore profitable, and han approved it by manye wise folk and olde,/ thanne shaltou considere if thou mayst parforme it and maken of it a good ende./ For resoun wol nat that any man sholde bigynne a thyng, but if he myghte parforme it as hym oghte;/ ne no wight sholde take upon hym so hevy a charge that he myghte nat bere it./ For the proverbe seith, 'He that to muche embraceth, distreyneth litel.' [1215] And Catoun seith, 'Assay to do swich thyng as thou hast power to doon, lest that the charge oppresse thee so soore that thee bihoveth to weyve thyng that thou hast bigonne.'/ And if so be that thou be in doute wheither thou mayst parfourne a thing or noon, chese rather to suffre than bigynne./ And Peter Alphonce seith, 'If thou hast myght to doon a thyng of which thou most repente, it is bettre "nay" than "ye." '/ This is to seyn, that thee is bettre to holde thy tonge stille than for to speke./ Thanne may ye understonde by strenger resons that if thou hast power to parforme a werk of which thou shalt repente, thanne is it bettre that thou suffre than bigynne. [*2410] Wel seyn they that defenden every wight to assaye a thyng of which he is in doute wheither he may parforme it or no./ And after, whan ye have examyned youre conseil, as I have seyd biforn, and knowen wel that ye may parforme youre emprise, conferme it thanne sadly til it be at an ende./

Now is it resoun and tyme that I shewe yow whanne and wherfore that ye may chaunge youre conseil withouten youre repreve./ Soothly, a man may chaungen his purpos and his conseil if the cause cesseth, or whan a newe caas bitideth./ For the lawe seith that 'upon thynges that newely bityden bihoveth newe conseil.' [1225] And Seneca seith, 'If thy conseil is come to the eeris of thyn enemy, chaunge thy conseil.'/ Thou mayst also chaunge thy conseil if so be that thou fynde that by

---

1207. **of:** from.
1208. **chese:** choose. **weyve:** waive, reject.
1209. **matere:** substance. **engendre:** produce.
1211. **partie:** course, proposal.
1212. **parforme it:** carry it out.
1214. **charge:** burden.
1215. **to:** too. **distreyneth:** retains.
1216. **Catoun:** see Dionysius Cato, *Disticha* iii.14. **assay:** attempt. **soore:** i.e., much. **weyve:** abandon.
1217. **or noon:** or not. **suffre:** endure, wait patiently.
1218. **Peter Alphonce:** see Petrus Alphonsi, *Disciplina Clericalis* ex. iv. **most:** might.
1220. **suffre:** endure, wait patiently.
1221. **defenden:** forbid.
1222. **conseil:** decision, plan. **emprise:** enterprise. **conferme:** promote. **sadly:** steadfastly.
1223. **repreve:** reproach.
1224. **cesseth:** ceases to be. **caas:** situation. **bitideth:** occurs.
1225. **bihoveth:** is needed.

errour, or by oother cause, harm or damage may bityde./ Also if thy conseil be dishonest, or elles cometh of dishonest cause, chaunge thy conseil./ For the lawes seyn that 'alle bihestes that ben dishoneste ben of no value';/ and eek if it so be that it be inpossible, or may nat goodly be parformed or kept. [*2420]

And take this for a general reule, that every conseil that is affermed so strongly that it may nat be chaunged for no condicioun that may bityde, I seye that thilke conseil is wikked."/

This Melibeus, whan he hadde herd the doctrine of his wyf dame Prudence, answerde in this wise: "Dame," quod he, "as yet into this tyme ye han wel and covenably taught me as in general, how I shal governe me in the chesynge and in the withholdyng of my conseillours./ But now wolde I fayn that ye wolde condescende in especial,/ and telle me how liketh yow, or what semeth yow, by oure conseillours that we han chosen in oure present nede." [1235]

"My lord," quod she, "I biseke yow in al humblesse that ye wol nat wilfully replie agayn my resons, ne distempre youre herte, thogh I speke thyng that yow displese./ For God woot that, as in myn entent, I speke it for youre beste, for youre honour, and for youre profite eke./ And soothly, I hope that youre benygnytee wol taken it in pacience./ Trusteth me wel," quod she, "that youre conseil as in this caas ne sholde nat, as to speke properly, be called a conseillyng, but a mocioun or a moevyng of folye,/ in which conseil ye han erred in many a sondry wise. [*2430]

First and forward, ye han erred in the assemblyng of youre conseillours./ For ye sholde first have cleped a fewe folk to youre conseil, and after ye myghte han shewed it to mo folk, if it hadde been nede./ But certes, ye han sodeynly cleped to youre conseil a gret multitude of peple, ful chargeant and ful anoyous for to heere./ Also ye han erred, for theras ye sholde oonly have cleped to youre conseil youre trewe frendes olde and wise,/ ye han ycleped straunge folk, yong folk, false flatereres, and enemys reconsiled, and folk that doon yow reverence withouten love. [1245] And eek also ye have erred, for ye han broght with yow to youre conseil ire, coveitise, and hastifnesse,/ the whiche thre thinges ben contrariouse to every conseil honest and profitable;/ the whiche thre thinges ye han nat anientissed or destroyed hem, neither in youreself, ne in youre conseillours, as ye oghte./ Ye han erred also, for ye han shewed to youre conseillours youre talent and youre affeccioun to make werre anon, and for to do vengeance./ They han espied by youre wordes to what thyng ye ben enclyned; [*2440] and therfore han they conseilled yow rather to youre talent than to youre profit./ Ye han erred also, for it semeth

---

1227. harm: evil.
1229. bihestes: promises.
1230. may nat goodly: can hardly.
1231. affermed: established. condicioun: circumstance.
1233. convenably: suitably. chesynge: choosing. withholdynge: retaining.
1234. condescende: descend. in especial: to a special point, to a particular matter.
1236. agayn: against. resons: statements, remarks. distempre: disturb.
1238. youre benygnytee: your graciousness, your gracious self.
1239. of folye: i.e., foolish.
1242. cleped: called. after: afterwards.
1243. chargeant: burdensome.
1246. hastifnesse: rashness, impetuosity.
1248. anientissed: annihilated.
1249. talent: desire. affeccioun: inclination.

that yow suffiseth to han ben conseilled by thise conseillours oonly, and with litel avys,/ whereas in so gret and so heigh a nede it hadde been necessarie mo conseillours and moore deliberacion to parforme youre emprise./ Ye han erred also, for ye han nat examyned youre conseil in the forseyde manere, ne in due manere, as the caas requireth./ Ye han erred also, for ye han maked no division bitwixe youre conseillours; this is to seyn, bitwixe youre trewe freendes and youre feyned conseillours; [1255] ne ye han nat knowe the wil of youre trewe freendes olde and wise;/ but ye han cast alle hire wordes in an hochepot, and enclyned youre herte to the moore part and to the gretter nombre, and there ben ye condescended./ And sith ye woot wel that men shal alwey fynde a gretter nombre of fooles than of wise men,/ and therfore the conseils that ben at congregaciouns and multitudes of folk, there as men take moore reward to the nombre than to the sapience of persones,/ ye se wel that in swiche conseillynges fooles han the maistrie." [*2450]

Melibeus answerde agayn, and seyde, "I graunte wel that I have erred;/ but there as thou hast toold me heerbiforn that he nys nat to blame that chaungeth his conseillours in certein caas and for certeine juste causes,/ I am al redy to chaunge my conseillours right as thow wolt devyse./ The proverbe seith that 'for to do synne is mannyssh, but certes for to persevere longe in synne is werk of the devel.' "/

To this sentence answered anon dame Prudence, and seyde: [1265] "Examineth," quod she, "youre conseil, and lat us see the whiche of hem han spoken most resonably, and taught yow best conseil./ And for as muche as that the examynacion is necessarie, lat us bigynne at the surgiens and at the phisiciens, that first speeken in this matere./ I sey yow that the surgiens and phisiciens han seyd yow in youre conseil discreetly, as hem oughte;/ and in hir speche seyden ful wisely that to the office of hem aperteneth to doon to every wight honour and profit, and no wight to anoye;/ and after hir craft to doon gret diligence unto the cure of hem which that they han in hir governaunce. [*2460] And, sire, right as they han answered wisely and discreetly,/ right so rede I that they be heighly and sovereynly gerdoned for hir noble speche;/ and eek for they shullen do the moore ententif bisynesse in the curacion of thy doghter deere./ For al be it so that they ben youre freendes, therfore shal ye nat suffren that they serve yow for noght,/ but ye oghte the rather gerdone hem and shewe hem youre largesse. [1275] And as touchynge the proposi-

1252. yow suffiseth: it suffices you. avys: time spent in consultation.
1253. it . . . necessarie: i.e., there were needed. emprise: undertaking, task.
1254. conseil: decision, plan.
1255. division: distinction. feyned: pretended, false.
1257. hochepot: stew, hodgepodge. moore part: greater part, majority. there ben ye condescended: to that you have agreed, conceded, yielded.
1259. reward: regard, heed.
1261. wel: readily.
1262. caas: cases, situations.
1264. mannyssh: human. persevere: continue.
1267. speeken: spoke.
1268. yow: to you.
1269. to the office of hem aperteneth: it is a proper part of their duty.
1270. craft: skill. cure: treatment. governaunce: care.
1272. rede: counsel. gerdoned: rewarded.
1273. for: so that. do . . . bisynesse in: devote themselves the more attentively to. curacion: curing.
1275. gerdone: reward. largesse: generosity.

cioun which that the phisiciens encreesceden in this caas, this is to seyn,/ that in maladies that oon contrarie is warisshed by another contrarie;/ I wolde fayn knowe how ye understande thilke text, and what is youre sentence."/

"Certes," quod Melibeus, "I understonde it in this wise:/ that right as they han doon me a contrarie, right so sholde I doon hem another. [*2470] For right as they han venged hem on me and doon me wrong, right so shal I venge me upon hem and doon hem wrong;/ and thanne have I cured oon contrarie by another."/

"Lo, lo," quod dame Prudence, "how lightly is every man enclined to his owene desir and to his owene plesaunce!/ Certes," quod she, "the wordes of the phisiciens ne sholde nat han been understonden in that wise./ For certes, wikkednesse is nat contrarie to wikkednesse, ne vengeance to vengeaunce, ne wrong to wrong, but they been semblable. [1285] And therfore o vengeaunce is nat warisshed by another vengeaunce, ne o wrong by another wrong,/ but everich of hem encreesceth and aggreggeth oother./ But certes, the wordes of the phisiciens sholde ben understonde in this wise,/ for good and wikkednesse been two contraries, and pees and werre, vengeaunce and suffraunce, discord and accord, and many othere thynges:/ But certes, wikkednesse shal be warisshed by goodnesse, discord by accord, werre by pees, and so forth of othere thynges. [*2480] And heerto accordeth Seint Paul the Apostle in manye places./ He seith: 'Ne yeldeth nat harm for harm, ne wikked speche for wikked speche;/ but do wel to hym that dooth thee harm, and blesse hym that seith to thee harm.'/ And in manye othere places he amonesteth pees and accord./

But now wol I speke to yow of the conseil which that was yeven to yow by the men of lawe and the wise folk, [1295] that seyden alle by oon accord, as ye han herd bifore,/ that over alle thyngs ye shal do youre diligence to kepen youre persone and to warnestore youre hous;/ and seyden also that in this caas ye oghten for to werke ful avysely and with greet deliberacioun./

And, sire, as to the firste point, that toucheth to the kepyng of youre persone,/ ye shul understonde that he that hath werre shal everemoore devoutly and mekely preyen, biforn alle thyngs, [*2490] that Jhesus Crist of his mercy wol han hym in his proteccion and ben his sovereyn helpyng at his nede./ For certes, in this world

---

1276. encreesceden: developed, promoted.
1277. warisshed: cured.
1278. understande: interpret.   sentence: opinion.
1280. contrarie: hostile act.
1281. venged hem: avenged themselves.
1283. lightly: readily.
1285. semblable: similar.
1286. warisshed: cured.
1287. aggreggeth: aggravates.
1289. good: goodness.   suffraunce: forbearance.
1291. accordeth: agrees.   Seint Paul: see Romans xii.17.
1292. yeldeth: render.   harm: evil.
1294. amonesteth: admonishes, inculcates.
1296. by: with.
1297. over: above.   kepen: protect.   warnestore: fortify.
1298. avysely: prudently.
1300. biforn: above.

ther is no wight that may be conseilled ne kept sufficeantly withouten the kepyng of oure Lord Jhesu Crist./ To this sentence accordeth the prophete David, that seith,/ 'If God ne kepe the citee, in ydel waketh he that it kepeth.'/ Now, sire, thanne shul ye committe the kepyng of youre persone to youre trewe freendes, that been approved and yknowe, [1305] and of hem shul ye axen help youre persone for to kepe. For Catoun seith: 'If thou hast nede of help, axe it of thy freendes;/ for ther nys noon so good a phisicien as thy trewe freend.'/ And after this thanne shul ye kepe yow fro alle straunge folk, and fro lyeres, and have alwey in suspect hire compaignye./ For Piers Alfonce seith, 'Ne taak no compaignye by the weye of a straunge man, but if so be that thou have knowe hym of a lenger tyme./ And if so be that he falle into thy compaignye paraventure, withouten thyn assent, [*2500] enquere thanne as subtilly as thou mayst of his conversacion, and of his lyf bifore, and feyne thy wey; sey that thou wolt go thider as thou wolt nat go;/ and if he bereth a spere, hoold thee on the right syde, and if he bere a swerd, hoold thee on the left syde.'/ And after this than shal ye kepe yow wisely from all swich manere peple as I have seyd bifore, and hem and hir conseil eschewe./ And after this thanne shul ye kepe yow in swich manere/ that, for any presumpcion of youre strengthe, that ye ne dispise nat, ne accompte nat the myght of youre adversarie so litel, that ye lete the kepyng of youre persone for youre presumpcioun; [1315] for every wys man dredeth his enemy./ And Salomon seith: 'Weleful is he that of alle hath drede;/ for certes, he that thurgh the hardynesse of his herte, and thurgh the hardynesse of hymself, hath to gret presumpcioun, hym shal yvel bityde.'/ Thanne shul ye everemoore contrewayte embusshementz and alle espialle./ For Senec seith that 'the wise man that dredeth harmes, escheweth harmes, [*2510] ne he ne falleth into perils that perils escheweth.'/ And al be it so that it seme that thou art in siker place, yet shaltow alwey do thy diligence in kepynge of thy persone;/ this is to seyn, ne be nat necligent to kepe thy persone, nat oonly fro thy grettest enemys, but fro thy leeste enemy./ Senek seith: 'A man that is well avysed, he dredeth his leste enemy.'/ Ovyde seith that 'the litel wesele wol slee the grete bole and the wilde hert.' [1325] And the book seith, 'A litel thorn may prikke a

---

1302. **kept:** protected. **kepyng:** protection.

1303. **sentence:** opinion. **David:** see Psalms cxxvii.1 (Vulgate cxxvi.1).

1304. **in ydel:** in vain. **waketh:** stays awake, watches, guards.

1306. **Catoun:** see *Disticha* iv.13.

1308. **have in suspect:** hold in suspicion. **compaignye:** companionship, fellowship.

1309. **Piers Alfonce:** see *Disciplina Clericalis* ex. xvii. **by the weye:** along the road.

1311. **conversacion:** manner of living. **feyne thy wey:** conceal your route (by feigning another).

1313. **eschewe:** shun.

1315. **for:** by reason of. **accompte:** account, consider. **lete:** neglect. **kepyng:** defense. **for:** because of.

1317. **Salomon:** see Proverbs xxviii:14. **weleful:** happy.

1318. **hardynesse:** rashness. **to gret:** too great.

1319. **contrewayte:** watch against. **embusshementz:** ambushes. **espialle:** companies of spies.

1320. **Senec:** see Publilius Syrus, *Sententiae* 607.

1321. **ne he ne falleth:** nor does he fall. **that:** who. **escheweth:** avoids.

1322. **al be it so that:** although. **siker:** secure. **do . . . of:** endeavor to protect.

1324. **Senek:** see Publilius Syrus, *Sententiae* 255. **well avysed:** well informed, prudent.

1325. **Ovyde:** see *Remedia Amoris* 421–22. **bole:** bull.

kyng ful soore, and an hound wol holde the wilde boor.'/ But nathelees, I sey nat thou shalt be so coward that thou doute ther wher as is no drede./ The book seith that 'somme folk have gret lust to deceyve, but yet they dreden hem to be deceyved.'/ Yet shaltou drede to been empoisoned, and kepe the from the compaignye of scorneres./ For the book seith, 'With scorneres make no compaignye, but flee hire wordes as venym.' [*2520]

Now, as to the seconde point, where as youre wise conseillours conseilled yow to warnestoore youre hous with gret diligence,/ I wolde fayn knowe how that ye understonde thilke wordes and what is youre sentence."/

Melibeus answerde, and seyde, "Certes, I understande it in this wise: That I shal warnestoore myn hous with toures, swiche as han castelles and othere manere edifices, and armure, and artelries;/ by whiche thynges I may my persone and myn hous so kepen and defenden that myne enemys shul been in drede myn hous for to approche."/

To this sentence answerde anon Prudence: "Warnestooryng," quod she, "of heighe toures and of grete edifices apperteyneth somtyme to pride. [1335] And eek men make heighe toures, and grete edifices with grete costages and with gret travaille; and whan that they been accompliced, yet be they nat worth a stree, but if they be defended by trewe freendes that been olde and wise./ And understonde wel that the gretteste and the strongeste garnysoun that a riche man may have, as wel to kepen his persone as his goodes, is/ that he be biloved with his subgetz and with his neighebores./ For thus seith Tullius, that 'ther is a manere garnysoun that no man may venquysse ne discomfite, and that is/ a lord to be biloved of his citezeins and of his peple.' [*2530]

Now, sire, as to the thridde point, where as youre olde and wise conseillours seiden that yow ne oghte nat sodeynly ne hastily proceden in this nede,/ but that yow oghte purveyen and apparailen yow in this caas with greet diligence and greet deliberacioun;/ trewely, I trowe that they seyden right wisely and right sooth./ For Tullius seith: 'In every nede, er thou bigynne it, apparaile thee with greet diligence.'/ Thanne seye I that in vengeance-takyng, in werre, in bataille, and in warnestooryng, [1345] er thow bigynne, I rede that thou apparaile thee therto, and do it with greet deliberacion./ For Tullius seith that 'longe apparailynge biforn the bataille maketh

---

1326. **soore:** sorely. **boor:** boar.
1327. **coward:** cowardly. **doute:** fear. **drede:** danger.
1328. **book:** see Seneca, *Epistolae* iii.§3. **lust:** desire.
1329. **compaignye:** fellowship.
1331. **warnestoore:** fortify.
1332. **understonde:** interpret. **sentence:** opinion.
1333. **han castelles:** castles have. **armure:** military equipment. **artelries:** ballistic engines.
1335. **apperteyneth:** is related.
1336. **costages:** expenditures. **travaille:** labor. **stree:** straw.
1337. **garnysoun:** protection.
1338. **with:** by.
1339. **Tullius:** see Seneca, *De Clementia* i.19,6. **discomfite:** overcome.
1341. **hastily:** precipitately.
1342. **purveyen:** provide. **apparailen:** prepare.
1344. **Tullius:** see Cicero, *De Officiis* i.21,73.
1346. **rede:** counsel.
1347. **Tullius:** see Publilius Syrus, *Sententiae* 125. **apparailynge:** preparation.

short victorie.'/ And Cassidorus seith, 'The garnysoun is stronger, whan it is longe tyme avysed.'/

But now lat us speken of the conseil that was accorded by youre neighebores, swiche as doon yow reverence withouten love,/ youre olde enemys reconsiled, youre flaterers, [*2540] that conseilled yow certeyne thynges prively, and openly conseilleden yow the contrarie;/ the yonge folk also, that conseilleden yow to venge yow, and make werre anon./ And certes, sire, as I have seyd biforn, ye han greetly erred to han cleped swich manere folk to youre conseil,/ which conseillours been ynogh repreved by the resons aforeseyd.

But nathelees, lat us now descende to the special. Ye shuln first procede after the doctrine of Tullius. [1355] Certes, the trouthe of this matere, or of this conseil, nedeth nat diligently enquere;/ for it is wel wist whiche they been that han doon to yow this trespas and vileynye,/ and how manye trespassours, and in what manere they han to yow doon al this wrong and al this vileynye./

And after this, thanne shul ye examyne the seconde condicion which that the same Tullius addeth in this matere./ For Tullius put a thyng which that he clepeth 'consentynge'; this is to seyn, [*2550] who been they, and whiche been they and how manye, that consenten to thy conseil in thy wilfulnesse to do hastif vengeance./ And lat us considere also who been they, and how manye been they, and whiche been they, that consenteden to youre adversaries./ And certes, as to the firste poynt, it is wel knowen whiche folk been they that consenteden to youre hastif wilfulnesse;/ for trewely, alle tho that conseilleden yow to maken sodeyn werre ne been nat youre freendes./ Lat us now considere whiche been they that ye holde so greetly youre freendes as to youre persone. [1365] For al be it so that ye be myghty and riche, certes ye ne been but allone,/ for certes ye ne han no child but a doghter,/ ne ye ne han bretheren, ne cosyns germayns, ne noon oother neigh kynrede,/ wherfore that youre enemys for drede sholde stinte to plede with yow, or destroye youre persone./ Ye knowen also that youre richesses mooten be dispended in diverse parties, [*2560] and whan that every wight hath his part, they ne wollen take but litel reward to venge thy deeth./ But thyne enemys been thre, and they han manye children, bretheren, cosyns, and oother ny kynrede./ And though so were that thou haddest slayn of hem two or three, yet dwellen ther ynowe to wreken hir deeth and to sle thy persone./ And though so be that youre kynrede be moore siker and stedefast than the kyn of youre adversarie,/ yet nathelees youre kynrede nys

---

1347. **short:** quick.
1348. **Cassidorus:** see *Variae* i.17.   **avysed:** considered.
1352. **venge yow:** avenge yourself.
1354. **repreved:** reproached.
1355. **special:** particular.   **Tullius:** see *De Officiis* ii.5.
1356. **nedeth nat:** it is not necessary.   **enquere:** to inquire into.
1360. **put:** (putteth) puts.
1361. **whiche:** what sort.   **consenten to:** accord with.   **hastif:** rash.
1362. **consenteden to:** accorded with.
1368. **cosyns germayns:** first cousins.   **neigh:** close.
1369. **wherfore that:** i.e., because of whom.   **stinte:** cease.
1370. **mooten:** must.   **dispended:** distributed.   **parties:** parts.
1371. **reward:** regard.   **venge:** avenge.
1373. **ynowe:** enough.   **wreken:** avenge.
1374. **siker:** dependable.

but a fer kynrede; they been but litel syb to yow, [1375] and the kyn of youre enemys been ny syb to hem. And certes, as in that, hir condicioun is bet than youres.

Thanne lat us considere also if the conseillyng of hem that conseileden yow to taken sodeyn vengeaunce, wheither it accorde to resoun./ And certes, ye knowe wel 'nay.'/ For, as by right and resoun, ther may no man taken vengeance on no wight but the juge that hath the jurisdiccioun of it,/ whan it is graunted hym to take thilke vengeance hastily or attemprely, as the lawe requireth. [*2570]

And yet mooreover of thilke word that Tullius clepeth 'consentynge':/ thou shalt considere if thy myght and thy power may consente and suffise to thy wilful-nesse and to thy conseillours./ And certes thou mayst wel seyn that 'nay.'/ For sikerly, as for to speke proprely, we may do no thyng, but oonly swich thyng as we may do rightfully./ And certes rightfully ne mowe ye take no vengeance, as of youre propre auctoritee. [1385] Thanne mowe ye seen that youre power ne con-senteth nat, ne accordeth nat, with youre wilfulnesse./

Lat us now examyne the thridde point, that Tullius clepeth 'consequent.'/ Thou shalt understande that the vengeance that thou purposest for to take is the conse-quent;/ and therof folweth another vengeaunce, peril, and werre, and othere damages withoute nombre, of whiche we be nat war, as at this tyme./

And as touchynge the fourthe point, that Tullius clepeth 'engendrynge,' [*2580] thou shalt considere that this wrong which that is doon to thee is engendred of the hate of thyne enemys,/ and of the vengeance-takynge upon that wolde engendre another vengeance, and muchel sorwe and wastynge of richesses, as I seyde./

Now, sire, as to the point that Tullius clepeth 'causes,' which that is the laste point,/ thou shalt understonde that the wrong that thou hast receyved hath certeine causes,/ whiche that clerkes clepen *Oriens* and *Efficiens,* and *Causa longinqua* and *Causa propinqua,* this is to seyn, the fer cause and the ny cause. [1395] The fer cause is almyghty God, that is cause of alle thynges./ The neer cause is thy thre enemys./ The cause accidental was hate./ The cause material been the fyve woundes of thy doghter./ The cause formal is the manere of hir werkynge that broghten laddres and clomben in at thy wyndowes. [*2590] The cause final was for to sle thy doghter. It letted nat in as muche as in hem was./ But for to speke of the fer cause, as to what ende they shul come, or what shal finally bityde of hem in this cas, ne kan I nat deeme but by conjectynge and by supposynge./ For we

---

1375. **fer:** far, distant.   **litel syb:** slightly related.

1376. **ny syb:** closely related.   **condicioun:** situation.

1380. **hastily:** violently.   **attemprely:** with restraint.

1382. **consente:** be consistent with, accord with.

1383. **seyn that 'nay':** say 'no'.

1385. **propre:** own.

1387. **consequent:** consequence, result.

1389. **another:** additional.   **werre:** war.   **war:** aware.

1391. **engendred of:** engendered by.

1392. **and . . . that:** and that avenging that.   **another:** further.

1395. **fer:** far, remote, ultimate.   **ny:** near, immediate, proximate.

1400. **hir werkynge:** their action.   **clomben:** climbed.

1401. **it letted . . . was:** as far as concerned them it did not tarry; for them it did not remain, continue.

1402. **come to:** attain to, reach.   **bityde of:** happen to, become of.   **conjectynge:** conjecture.

shul suppose that they shul come to a wikked ende,/ by cause that the Book of Decrees seith, 'Seelden, or with greet peyne, been causes ybroght to good ende whan they been baddely bigonne.'/

Now, sire, if men wolde axe me why that God suffred men to do yow this vileynye, certes, I kan nat wel answere, as for no soothfastnesse. [1405] For the apostle seith that 'the sciences and the juggementz of oure Lord God almyghty been ful depe;/ ther may no man comprehende ne serchen hem suffisantly.'/ Nathelees, by certeyne presumpciouns and conjectynges, I holde and bileeve/ that God, which that is ful of justice and of rightwisnesse, hath suffred this bityde by juste cause resonable./

Thy name is Melibee, this is to seyn, 'a man that drynketh hony.' [*2600] Thou hast ydronke so muchel hony of sweete temporel richesses, and delices and honours of this world,/ that thou art dronken, and hast forgeten Jhesu Crist thy creatour./ Thou ne hast nat doon to hym swich honour and reverence as thee oughte,/ ne thou ne hast nat wel ytaken kepe to the wordes of Ovide, that seith,/ 'Under the hony of the goodes of the body is hyd the venym that sleeth the soule.' [1415] And Salomon seith, 'If thou hast founden hony, ete of it that suffiseth;/ for if thou ete of it out of mesure, thou shalt spewe,' and be needy and povre./ And peraventure Crist hath thee in despit, and hath turned awey fro thee his face and his eeris of misericorde;/ and also he hath suffred that thou hast been punysshed in the manere that thow hast ytrespassed./ Thou hast doon synne agayn oure Lord Crist; [*2610] for certes, the three enemys of mankynde, that is to seyn, the flessh, the feend, and the world,/ thou hast suffred hem entre in to thyn herte wilfully by the wyndowes of thy body,/ and hast nat defended thyself suffisantly agayns hire assautes and hire temptaciouns, so that they han wounded thy soule in fyve places;/ this is to seyn, the dedly synnes that been entred into thyn herte by thy fyve wittes./ And in the same manere oure Lord Crist hath wold and suffred that thy three enemys been entred into thyn house by the wyndowes, [1425] and han ywounded thy doghter in the forseyde manere."/

"Certes," quod Melibee, "I se wel that ye enforce yow muchel by wordes to overcome me in swich manere that I shal nat venge me of myne enemys,/ shewynge me the perils and the yveles that myghten falle of this vengeance./ But whoso wolde

---

1404. **Book of Decrees:** see *Decretum Gratiani,* Pars ii, causa i, qu. 1, c. 25. **seelden:** seldom.

1405. **as for no soothfastnesse:** i.e., because of no certainty.

1406. **sciences:** knowledge.

1407. **serchen:** examine.

1409. **rightwisnesse:** righteousness. **bityde:** to happen.

1411. **delices:** pleasures.

1412. **dronken:** drunk.

1414. **kepe:** heed. **Ovide:** see *Amores* i.8,104.

1415. **goodes of the body:** see Parson's Tale, 452.

1416. **Salomon:** see Proverbs xxv:16. **that:** that which.

1417. **out of mesure:** beyond all bounds, excessively. **spewe:** vomit.

1418. **despit:** contempt. **eeris:** ears. **misericorde:** mercy.

1419. **suffred:** allowed.

1424. **wittes:** senses.

1425. **wold:** willed. **suffred:** permitted.

1427. **enforce yow:** endeavor.

1428. **falle of:** happen as a result of.

considere in alle vengeances the perils and yveles that myghte sewe of vengeance-takynge,/ a man wolde nevere take vengeance, and that were harm; [*2620] for by the vengeance-takynge been the wikked men dissevered fro the goode men,/ and they that han wil to do wikkednesse restreyne hir wikked purpos, whan they seen the punyssynge and the chastisynge of trespassours."/

[*Ad ce respont Dame Prudence: "Certes," dist elle, "je vous ottroye que de venge vient moult de biens,/ mais faire vengence n'appartient pas a un chascun fors seulement aus juges et a ceulx qui ont la juridicion sur les malfaiteurs.*]/ And yet seye I moore, that right as a singuler persone synneth in takynge vengeance of another man, [1435] right so synneth the juge if he do no vengeance of hem that it han disserved./ For Senec seith thus: 'That maister,' he seith, 'is good that proveth shrewes.'/ And as Cassidore seith, 'A man dredeth to do outrages whan he woot and knoweth that it displeseth to the juges and the sovereyns.'/ And another seith, 'The juge that dredeth to do right, maketh men shrewes.'/ And Seint Paul the Apostle seith in his Epistle, whan he writeth unto the Romayns, that 'the juges beren nat the spere withouten cause, [*2630] but they beren it to punysshe the shrewes and mysdoers, and for to defende the goode men./ If ye wol thanne take vengeance of youre enemys, ye shul retourne or have youre recours to the juge that hath the jurisdiccion upon hem,/ and he shal punysshe hem as the lawe axeth and requireth."/

"A!" quod Melibee, "this vengeance liketh me no thyng./ I bithenke me now and take heede how Fortune hath norisshed me fro my childhode, and hath holpen me to passe many a strong paas. [1445] Now wol I assayen hire, trowynge, with Goddes help, that she shal helpe me my shame for to venge."/

"Certes," quod Prudence, "if ye wol werke by my conseil, ye shul nat assaye Fortune by no wey,/ ne ye shul nat lene or bowe unto hire, after the word of Senec;/ for 'thynges that been folily doon, and that been in hope of Fortune, shullen nevere come to good ende.'/ And, as the same Senec seith, 'The moore cleer

---

1429. **sewe of:** ensue from, result from.

1430. **were:** would be. **harm:** pity.

1431. **dissevered:** divided.

1433–34. And to this dame Prudence replied, "Certainly," she said, "I grant you that from vengeance comes much good; but to do vengeance does not belong to anyone except only to judges and to those who have jurisdiction over evil-doers. (See 1062–63, note, above.)

1435. **singuler:** private (i.e., not holding office).

1436. **disserved:** deserved.

1437. **Senec:** cf. pseudo-Seneca, *De Moribus* v. **proveth:** makes trial of, tests. **shrewes:** scoundrels.

1438. **Cassidore:** see Cassiodorus, *Variae* i.4.

1439. **another:** see Publilius Syrus, *Sententiae* 528.

1440. **Seint Paul:** see Romans xiii.4.

1442. **of:** on. **retourne:** return (to the judge).

1444. **liketh:** please.

1445. **bithenke me:** consider. **norisshed:** cherished. **holpen:** helped. **passe:** go through. **strong paas:** critical situation.

1446. **assayen:** call upon.

1447. **nat by no wey:** by no means, not at all.

1448. **lene:** bend. **Senec:** see Publilius Syrus, *Sententiae* 320.

1449. **folily:** foolishly. **in hope of:** with trust in.

1450. **Senec:** see Publilius Syrus, *Sententiae* 189. **cleer:** bright.

and the moore shynyng that Fortune is, the moore brotil and the sonner broken she is.' [*2640] Trusteth nat in hire, for she nys nat stedefast ne stable;/ for whan thow trowest to be moost seur or siker of hir help, she wol faile thee and deceyve thee./ And where as ye seyn that Fortune hath norisshed yow fro youre childhode,/ I seye that in so muchel shul ye the lasse truste in hire and in hir wit./ For Senec seith, 'What man that is norisshed by Fortune, she maketh hym to greet a fool.' [1455]

Now thanne, syn ye desire and axe vengeance, and the vengeance that is doon after the lawe and bifore the juge ne liketh yow nat,/ and the vengeance that is doon in hope of Fortune is perilous and uncertein,/ thanne have ye noon oother remedie but for to have youre recours unto the sovereyn Juge that vengeth alle vileynyes and wronges./ And he shal venge yow after that hymself witnesseth, where as he seith,/ 'Leveth the vengeance to me, and I shal do it.' " [*2650]

Melibee answerde, "If I ne venge me nat of the vileynye that men han doon to me,/ I somne or warne hem that han doon to me that vileynye, and alle othere, to do me another vileynye./ For it is writen, 'If thou take no vengeance of an old vileynye, thou somnest thyne adversaries to do thee a newe vileynye.'/ And also for my suffrance men wolden do me so muchel vileynye that I myghte neither bere it ne sustene,/ and so sholde I been put and holden overlowe. [1465] For men seyn, 'In muchel suffrynge shul manye thynges falle unto thee whiche thou shalt nat mowe suffre.' "/

"Certes," quod Prudence, "I graunte yow that over-muchel suffraunce is nat good./ But yet ne folweth it nat therof that every persone to whom men doon vileynye take of it vengeance;/ for that aperteneth and longeth al oonly to the juges, for they shul venge the vileynyes and injuries./ And therfore tho two auc-toritees that ye han seyd above been oonly understonden in the juges. [*2660] For whan they suffren over-muchel the wronges and vileynyes to be doon withouten punysshynge,/ they somne nat a man al oonly for to do newe wronges, but they comanden it./ Also a wys man seith that 'the juge that correcteth nat the synnere comandeth and biddeth hym do synne.'/ And the juges and sovereyns myghten in hir land so muchel suffre of the shrewes and mysdoers/ that they sholden, by swich

---

1450. **brotil:** brittle. **sonner:** sooner; more readily.
1452. **seur or siker:** sure or certain.
1454. **lasse:** less. **wit:** wisdom.
1455. **Senec:** see Publilius Syrus, *Sententiae* 172. **to greet:** too great.
1456. **after:** according to.
1459. **after that:** as. **witnesseth:** testifies.
1460. See Romans xii.19. **do:** inflict.
1462. **somne:** summon, call upon. **warne:** notify.
1463. See Publilius Syrus, *Sententiae* 645.
1464. **suffrance:** long-suffering, patient endurance. **sustene:** endure.
1465. **holden:** held. **overlowe:** too low, exceedingly contemptible.
1466. See Publilius Syrus, *Sententiae* 487. **falle:** befall, happen. **mowe suffre:** be able to en-dure.
1469. **aperteneth to:** belongs to, is the duty of. **longeth:** belongs. **al oonly:** exclusively.
1470. **tho:** those. **auctoritees:** statements. **seyd:** mentioned. **in:** with regard to, in connection with.
1473. **wys man:** see Caecilius Balbus, *De Nugis Philosophorum* no. xli.4.
1474. **suffre:** allow, tolerate.
1475. **they:** the villains and evil-doers.

suffrance, by proces of tyme wexen of swich power and myght that they sholden putte out the juges and the sovereyns from hir places, [1475] and atte laste maken hem lesen hire lordshipes./

But lat us now putte that ye have leve to venge yow./ I seye ye be nat of myght and power as now to venge yow;/ for if ye wol maken comparisoun unto the myght of youre adversaries, ye shul fynde in manye thynges that I have shewed yow er this that hire condicion is bettre than youres./ And therfore seye I that it is good as now that ye suffre and be pacient. [*2670]

Forthermoore, ye knowen wel that after the comune sawe, 'it is a woodnesse a man to stryve with a strenger or a moore myghty man than he is hymself;/ and for to stryve with a man of evene strengthe, that is to seyn, with as strong a man as he is, it is peril;/ and for to stryve with a weyker man, it is folye.'/ And therfore sholde a man flee stryvynge as muchel as he myghte./ For Salomon seith, 'It is a greet worshipe to a man to kepen hym fro noyse and stryf.' [1485] And if it so bifalle or happe that a man of gretter myght and strengthe than thou art do thee grevaunce,/ studie and bisye thee rather to stille the same grevaunce than for to venge thee./ For Senec seith that 'he putteth hym in greet peril that stryveth with a gretter man than he is hymself.'/ And Catoun seith, 'If a man of hyer estaat or degree, or moore myghty than thou, do thee anoy or grevaunce, suffre hym;/ for he that ones hath greved thee, may another tyme releeve thee and helpe.'

Yet sette I cas, ye have bothe myght and licence for to venge yow, [*2680] I seye that ther be ful manye thynges that shul restreyne yow of vengeance-takynge,/ and make yow for to enclyne to suffre, and for to han pacience in the wronges that han been doon to yow.

First and foreward, if ye wole, considere the defautes that been in youre owene persone,/ for which defautes God hath suffred yow have this tribulacioun, as I have seyd yow heer-biforn. [1495] For the poete seith that 'we oghte paciently taken the tribulacions that comen to us, whan that we thynken and consideren that we han disserved to have hem.'/ And Seint Gregorie seith that 'whan a man considereth wel the nombre of his defautes and of his synnes,/ the peynes and the tribulaciouns that he suffreth semen the lesse unto hym;/ and in as muche as hym thynketh his synnes moore hevy and grevous,/ in so muche semeth his peyne the lighter and the esier unto hym.' [*2690] Also ye owen to enclyne and bowe youre herte to take

---

1475. **wexen of:** grow to.
1476. **lesen:** lose. **lordshipes:** sovereignties.
1477. **putte:** suppose.
1478. **as now:** as of now.
1481. **sawe:** saying. **woodnesse a:** madness for a. **stryve:** contend.
1484. **flee:** avoid.
1485. **Salomon:** see Proverbs xx.3. **worshipe:** honor. **noyse:** contention.
1486. **grevaunce:** injury.
1487. **stille:** allay.
1488. **Senec:** see Publilius Syrus, *Sententiae* 483.
1489. **Catoun:** see Dionysius Cato, *Disticha* iv.39.
1490. **greved:** injured. **releeve:** assist.
1491. **yet:** again. **sette I cas:** (if) I suppose.
1492. **of:** from.
1494. **foreward:** foremost. **if ye wole:** if you will, if you please. **defautes:** defects, faults.
1498. **semen:** seem.
1501. **owen:** ought. **take:** adopt, have recourse to.

the pacience of oure Lord Jhesu Crist, as seith Seint Peter in his Epistles./ 'Jhesu Crist,' he seith, 'hath suffred for us and yeven ensample to every man to folwe and sewe hym;/ for he dide nevere synne, ne nevere cam ther a vileyns word out of his mouth./ Whan men cursed hym, he cursed hem noght; and whan men betten hym, he manaced hem noght.'/ Also the grete pacience which seintes that been in Paradys han had in tribulaciouns that they han ysuffred, withouten hir desert or gilt, [1505] oghte muchel stiren yow to pacience./ Forthermoore ye sholde enforce yow to have pacience,/ consideringe that the tribulaciouns of this world but litel while endure, and soone passed been and goon,/ and the joye that a man seketh to have by pacience in tribulaciouns is perdurable, after that the Apostle seith in his epistle./ 'The joye of God,' he seith, 'is perdurable,' that is to seyn, everelastynge. [*2700] Also troweth and bileveth stedefastly that he nys nat wel ynorisshed, ne wel ytaught, that kan nat have pacience, or wol nat receyve pacience./ For Salomon seith that 'the doctrine and the wit of a man is knowen by pacience.'/ And in another place he seith that 'he that is pacient governeth hym by greet prudence.'/ And the same Salomon seith, 'The angry and wrathful man maketh noyses, and the pacient man attempreth hem and stilleth.'/ He seith also, 'It is moore worth to be pacient than for to be right strong; [1515] and he that may have the lordshipe of his owene herte is moore to preyse than he that by his force or strengthe taketh grete citees.'/ And therfore seith Seint Jame in his Epistle that pacience is a greet vertu of perfeccioun."

"Certes," quod Melibee, "I graunte yow, dame Prudence, that pacience is a greet vertu of perfeccioun;/ but every man may nat have the perfeccioun that ye seken;/ ne I am nat of the nombre of right parfite men, [*2710] for myn herte may nevere be in pees unto the tyme it be venged./ And al be it so that it was greet peril to myne enemys to do me a vileynye in takynge vengeance upon me,/ yet tooken they noon heede of the peril, but fulfilleden hir wikked wyl and hir corage./ And therfore me thynketh men oghten nat repreve me, though I putte me in a litel peril for to venge me,/ and though I do a greet excesse, that is to seyn, that I venge oon outrage by another." [1525]

1501. **Seint Peter:** see I Peter ii. 21–23.

1502. **sewe:** follow, imitate.

1503. **vileyns:** villainous.

1504. **betten:** beat.   **manaced:** menaced, threatened.

1506. **stiren:** stir, move.

1507. **enforce yow:** endeavor.

1508. **goon:** gone.

1509. **after that:** according to what.   **Apostle:** see II Corinthians iv.17.

1511. **troweth:** trust.   **ynorisshed:** brought up.

1512. **Salomon:** see Vulgate, Proverbs xix.11.   **doctrine:** knowledge, learning.   **wit:** wisdom.

1513. See Vulgate, Proverbs xiv.29.

1514. **Salomon:** see Proverbs xv.18.   **noyses:** contentions, brawls.   **attempreth:** moderates, restrains.   **stilleth:** quiets.

1515. See Proverbs xvi.32.

1516. **to preyse:** to be praised.

1517. **Seint Jame:** see James i.4.

1521. **unto:** until.   **venged:** avenged.

1522. **al be it so that:** although.

1523. **wyl:** intention; desire.   **corage:** desire.

1524. **repreve:** reproach.

1525. **outrage:** deed of violence.

"A," quod dame Prudence, "ye seyn youre wyl and as yow liketh,/ but in no caas of the world a man sholde nat doon outrage ne excesse for to vengen hym./ For Cassidore seith that 'as yvele dooth he that vengeth hym by outrage as he that dooth the outrage.'/ And therfore ye shul venge yow after the ordre of right, that is to seyn, by the lawe, and nat by excesse ne by outrage./ And also, if ye wol venge yow of the outrage of youre adversaries in oother manere than right comandeth, ye synnen. [*2720] And therfore seith Senec that 'a man shal nevere venge shrewednesse by shrewednesse.'/ And if ye seye that right axeth a man to defende violence by violence, and fightyng by fightyng,/ certes ye seye sooth, whan the defense is doon anon withouten intervalle or withouten tariyng or delay,/ for to defenden hym and nat for to vengen hym./ And it bihoveth that a man putte swich attemperance in his deffense [1535] that men have no cause ne matere to repreven hym that defendeth hym of excesse and outrage, for ellis were it agayn resoun./ Pardee, ye knowe wel that ye maken no defense as now for to defende yow, but for to venge yow;/ and so seweth it that ye han no wyl to do youre dede attemprely./ And therfore me thynketh that pacience is good; for Salomon seith that 'he that is nat pacient shal have greet harm.' "/

"Certes," quod Melibee, "I graunte yow that whan a man is inpacient and wrooth, of that that toucheth hym nat and that aperteneth nat unto hym, though it harme hym, it is no wonder. [*2730] For the lawe seith that 'he is coupable that entremetteth hym or medleth with swych thyng as aperteneth nat unto hym.'/ And Salomon seith that 'he that entremetteth hym of the noyse or strif of another man is lyk to hym that taketh an hound by the eris.'/ For right as he that taketh a straunge hound by the eris is outherwhile biten with the hound,/ right in the same wise is it resoun that he have harm that by his inpacience medleth hym of the noyse of another man, wheras it aperteneth nat unto hym./ But ye knowe wel that this dede, that is to seyn, my grief and my disese, toucheth me right ny. [1545] And therfore, though I be wrooth and inpacient, it is no merveille./ And, savynge your grace, I kan nat seen that it myghte greetly harme me though I tooke vengeaunce./ For I am richer and moore myghty than myne enemys been;/ and wel knowen ye that by moneye and by havynge grete possessions been alle the thynges of this

---

1526. seyn: state.
1527. of: in. doon outrage: exercise violence. excesse: outrageous act.
1528. Cassidore: see *Variae* i.30.
1529. after the ordre of: according to.
1531. Senec: see pseudo-Seneca, *De Moribus* vi. shrewednesse: evil.
1532. axeth: requires. defende: protect himself against.
1535. attemperance: moderation.
1536. matere: reason. repreven: reproach. of: against. agayn: against.
1538. seweth it: it follows. wyl: desire. attemprely: moderately.
1539. Salomon: see Proverbs xix.19. harm: injury.
1540. of that that: in a matter that. aperteneth unto: concerns.
1541. coupable: culpable, guilty. that entremetteth hym: who interferes. aperteneth unto: concerns.
1542. Salomon: see Proverbs xxvi.17. of: with. noyse: contention. eris: ears.
1543. right: just. outherwhile: sometimes. with: by.
1544. wheras: when.
1545. grief: injury, damage. disese: misfortune. right ny: very closely.

world governed./ And Salomon seith that 'alle thynges obeyen to moneye.' "
[*2740]

When Prudence hadde herd hir housbonde avanten hym of his richesse and of
his moneye, dispreisynge the power of his adversaries, she spak, and seyde in this
wise:/ "Certes, deere sire, I graunte yow that ye been riche and myghty,/ and that
the richesses been goode to hem that han wel ygeten hem and that wel konne usen
hem./ For right as the body of a man may nat lyve withoute the soule, namoore
may it lyve withoute temporel goodes./ And by richesses may a man gete hym
grete freendes. [1555] And therfore seith Pamphilles: 'If a net-herdes doghter,' he
seith, 'be riche, she may chesen of a thousand men which she wol take to hir
housbonde;/ for, of a thousand men, oon wol nat forsaken hire ne refusen hire.'/
And this Pamphilles seith also: 'If thow be right happy—that is to seyn, if thou
be right riche—thou shalt fynde a greet nombre of felawes and freendes./ And if
thy fortune change that thou wexe poore, farewel freendshipe and felaweshipe;/ for
thou shalt be allone withouten any compaignye, but if it be the compaignye of
poore folk.' [*2750] And yet seith this Pamphilles moreover that 'they that been
thralle and bonde of lynage shullen been maad worthy and noble by the richesses.'/

And right so as by richesses ther comen manye goodes, right so by poverte come
ther manye harmes and yveles./ For greet poverte constreyneth a man to do manye
yveles./ And therfore clepeth Cassidore poverte the moder of ruyne,/ that is to
seyn, the moder of overthrowynge or fallynge doun. [1565] And therfore seith Piers
Alfonce: 'Oon of the gretteste adversitees of this world is/ whan a free man by
kynde or of burthe is constreyned by poverte to eten the almesse of his enemy,'/
and the same seith Innocent in oon of his bookes. He seith that 'sorweful and mys-
happy is the condicioun of a poore beggere;/ for if he axe nat his mete, he dyeth
for hunger;/ and if he axe, he dyeth for shame; and algates necessitee constreyneth
hym to axe.' [*2760] And therfore seith Salomon that 'bettre is to dye than for to
have swich poverte.'/ And as the same Salomon seith, 'Bettre it is to dye of bitter

---

1550. **Salomon:** see Ecclesiastes x.19.

1551. **avanten hym:** boast. **dispreisynge:** disparaging.

1553. **wel ygeten:** properly acquired.

1556. **Pamphilles:** the hero of a twelfth-century poetic dialogue; see *Pamphilus de Amore* 53–54.
net-herdes: neatherd's, cowherd's. **to:** for.

1557. **oon wol nat:** not one will. **forsaken:** reject.

1558. **Pamphilles:** see Ovid, *Tristia* i.9.5–6. **felawes:** comrades.

1559. **that:** so that. **wexe:** become.

1561. **Pamphilles:** see Petrus Alfonsi, *Disciplina Clericalis* ex. iv. **thralle:** enslaved. **bonde:**
in bondage. **of lynage:** i.e., by birth.

1564. **Cassidore:** see *Variae* ii.13.

1565. **overthrowynge:** overturning, destruction. **fallynge doun:** misfortune.

1566. **Piers Alfonce:** see *Disciplina Clericalis* ex.ii.

1567. **free man by kynde or of burthe:** i.e., of gentle birth. **kynde:** nature. **eten the almesse:**
live on the charity.

1568. **Innocent:** see Innocent III, *De Contemptu Mundi* i.16. **myshappy:** unhappy.

1569. **axe:** beg for. **mete:** food.

1570. **algates:** in any case.

1571. **Salomon:** see Ecclesiasticus xl.28 (Vulgate 29).

1572. **Salomon:** see Ecclesiasticus xxx.17.

deeth than for to lyven in swich wise.'/ By thise resons that I have seid unto yow, and by manye othere resons that I koude seye,/ I graunte yow that richesses been goode to hem that geten hem wel, and to hem that wel usen tho richesses./ And therfore wol I shewe yow how ye shul have yow and how ye shul bere yow in gaderynge of richesses, and in what manere ye shul usen hem. [1575]

First, ye shul geten hem withouten greet desir, by good leiser, sokyngly and nat over-hastily./ For a man that is to desirynge to gete richesses abandoneth hym first to thefte, and to alle othere yveles;/ and therfore seith Salomon, 'He that hasteth hym to bisily to wexe riche shal be noon innocent.'/ He seith also that 'the richesse that hastily cometh to a man, soone and lightly gooth and passeth from a man;/ but that richesse that cometh litel and litel, wexeth alwey and multiplieth.' [*2770]

And, sire, ye shul geten richesses by youre wit and by youre travaille unto youre profit;/ and that withouten wrong or harm doynge to any oother persone./ For the lawe seith that 'ther maketh no man himselven riche, if he do harm to another wight.'/ This is to seyn, that nature defendeth and forbedeth by right that no man make hymself riche unto the harm of another persone./ And Tullius seith that 'no sorwe, ne no drede of deeth, ne no thyng that may falle unto a man, [1585] is so muchel agayns nature as a man to encresse his owene profit to the harm of another man./

And though the grete men and the myghty men geten richesses moore lightly than thou,/ yet shaltou nat be ydel ne slow to do thy profit, for thou shalt in alle wise flee ydelnesse.'/ For Salomon seith that 'ydelnesse techeth a man to do manye yveles.'/ And the same Salomon seith that 'he that travailleth and bisieth hym to tilien his land, shal ete breed; [*2780] but he that is ydel and casteth hym to no bisynesse ne occupacioun, shal falle into poverte, and dye for hunger.'/ And he that is ydel and slow kan nevere fynde covenable tyme for to do his profit./ For ther is a versifiour seith that 'the ydel man excuseth hym in wynter by cause of the grete coold, and in somer by enchesoun of the heete.'/ For thise causes seith Caton, 'Waketh and enclyneth yow nat over-muchel for to slepe, for over-muchel reste

---

1573. **by:** for.

1574. **geten wel:** acquire properly.

1575. **how ye shul have yow:** how you ought to comport yourself, behave yourself. **bere yow:** conduct yourself.

1576. **by good leiser:** with full deliberation. **sokyngly:** (soakingly) slowly, gradually.

1577. **to desirynge:** too desirous.

1578. **Salomon:** see Proverbs xxviii.20. **to bisily:** too intently. **wexe:** grow, become. **noon:** no.

1579. **He:** see Proverbs xiii.11. **lightly:** easily.

1580. **and:** by. **wexeth:** increases.

1581. **wit:** intelligence. **travaille:** labor. **unto:** for.

1584. **defendeth:** prohibits.

1585. **Tullius:** see *De Officiis* iii.5.21. **falle:** befall, happen.

1586. **encresse:** increase.

1588. **slow:** slothful. **do:** make, procure. **in alle wise:** in every way.

1589. **Salomon:** see Ecclesiasticus xxxiii.27 (Vulgate 29).

1590. **Salomon:** see Proverbs xxviii.19. **tilien:** till.

1591. **casteth hym:** sets himself, devotes himself.

1592. **slow:** slothful. **covenable:** suitable.

1593. **enchesoun:** reason.

1594. **Caton:** see *Disticha* i.2. **waketh:** stay awake.

norissheth and causeth manye vices.'/ And therfore seith Seint Jerome, 'Dooth somme goode dedes that the devel, which is oure enemy, ne fynde yow nat unocupied.' [1595] For the devel ne taketh nat lightly unto his werkynge swiche as he fyndeth occupied in goode werkes./ Thanne thus in getynge richesses, ye mosten flee ydelnesse./

And afterward, ye shul use the richesses which ye have geten by youre wit and by youre travaille,/ in swich a manere that men holde yow nat to scars, ne to sparynge, ne to fool-large, that is to seyn, over-large a spendere./ For right as men blamen an avaricious man by cause of his scarsitee and chyncherie, [*2790] in the same wise is he to blame that spendeth over-largely./ And therfore seith Caton: 'Use,' he seith, 'thy richesses that thou hast geten/ in swich a manere that men have no matere ne cause to calle thee neither wrecche ne chynche;/ for it is greet shame to a man to have a poore herte and a riche purs.'/ He seith also: 'The goodes that thou hast ygeten, use hem by mesure,' that is to seyn, spende mesurably; [1605] for they that folily wasten and despenden the goodes that they han,/ whan they han namoore propre of hir owene, they shapen hem to take the goodes of another man./

I seye thanne that ye shul flee avarice; / usynge youre richesses in swich manere that men seye nat that youre richesses been yburyed,/ but that ye have hem in youre myght and in youre weeldynge. [*2800] For a wys man repreveth the avaricious man, and seith thus in two vers:/ 'Wherto and why burieth a man his goodes by his grete avarice, and knoweth wel that nedes moste he dye?/ For deeth is the ende of every man as in this present lyf.'/ And for what cause or enchesoun joyneth he hym or knytteth he hym so faste unto his goodes/ that alle hise wittes mowen nat disseveren hym or departen hym from his goodes, [1615] and knoweth wel, or oghte knowe, that whan he is deed he shal no thyng bere with hym out of this world?/ And therfore seith Seint Austyn that 'the avaricious man is likned unto helle,/ that the moore it swolweth, the moore desir it hath to swolwe and devoure.'/ And as wel as ye wolde eschewe to be called an avaricious man or chynche,/ as wel sholde ye kepe yow and governe yow in swich a wise that men calle yow nat

---

1595. Seint Jerome: see *Epistolae* cxxv.11.
1596. lightly: easily.   werkynge: work; i.e., employ, service.
1599. to scars: too stingy.   fool-large: foolishly prodigal, wasteful.   over-large: over-liberal.
1600. scarsitee: stinginess.   chyncherie: miserliness.
1602. Caton: see *Disticha* iv.16.
1603. matere: reason.   wrecche: niggard.   chynche: miser.
1604. poore: paltry.
1605. He: see *Disticha* iii.21. by mesure: in moderation.
1606. despenden: squander.
1607. propre: belonging to themselves.   shapen hem: dispose themselves.
1608. seye: say.
1610. weeldynge: (wielding) power.
1611. repreveth: reproves.   vers: verses.
1612. wherto: wherefore.   by: through.
1614. enchesoun: reason.   faste: securely.
1615. disseveren: separate.   departen: part.
1616. deed: dead.
1618. swolweth: swallows.
1619. as wel: as much.   chynche: miser.
1620. as wel: so much.

fool-large. [*2810] Therfore seith Tullius: 'The goodes,' he seith, 'of thyn hous sholde nat been hid ne kept so cloos, but that they myghte been opened by pitee and debonairetee;'/ that is to seyn, to yeven hem part that han greet nede;/ 'ne thy goodes sholden nat been so open to be every mannes goodes.'/

Afterward, in getynge of youre richesses and in usynge hem, ye shul alwey have thre thynges in youre herte,/ that is to seyn, oure Lord God, conscience, and good name. [1625]

First, ye shul have God in youre herte,/ and for no richesse ye shullen do no thyng which may in any manere displese God, that is youre creatour and makere./ For after the word of Salomon, 'It is bettre to have a litel good with the love of God,/ than to have muchel good and tresour, and lese the love of his Lord God./ And the prophete seith that 'bettre it is to been a good man and have litel good and tresour, [*2820] than to been holden a shrewe and have grete richesses.'/

And yet seye I ferthermoore, that ye sholde alwey doon youre bisynesse to gete yow richesses,/ so that ye gete hem with good conscience./ And th'apostle seith that 'ther nys thyng in this world of which we sholden have so greet joye as whan oure conscience bereth us good witnesse.'/ And the wise man seith, 'The substance of a man is ful good, whan synne is nat in mannes conscience.' [1635]

Afterward, in getynge of youre richesses and in usynge of hem,/ yow moste have greet bisynesse and greet diligence that youre goode name be alwey kept and conserved./ For Salomon seith that 'bettre it is and moore it availleth a man to have a good name, than for to have grete richesses.'/ And therfore he seith in another place, 'Do greet diligence,' seith Salomon, 'in kepyng of thy freend and of thy goode name;/ for it shal lenger abide with thee than any tresour, be it never so precious.' [*2830] And certes he sholde nat be called a gentil man that after God and good conscience, alle thynges left, ne dooth his diligence and bisynesse to kepen his goode name./ And Cassidore seith that 'it is signe of a gentil herte, whan a man loveth and desireth to have a good name.'/ And therfore seith Seint Austyn that 'ther been two thynges that arn necessarie and nedefulle,/ and that is good conscience and good loos;/ that is to seyn, good conscience to thyn owene persone inward, and good loos for thy neighebor outward.' [1645] And he that trusteth hym so muchel in his goode conscience/ that he displeseth, and setteth at noght his goode

---

1620. **fool-large:** foolishly wasteful.

1621. **Tullius:** see *De Officiis* ii.15.55. **kept so cloos:** guarded so closely. **debonairetee:** mercy.

1628 **after:** according to. **Salomon:** see Proverbs xv.16. **a litel good:** a few goods.

1630. **prophete:** see Psalms xxxvi.16.

1631. **been holden:** be considered. **shrewe:** scoundrel.

1632. **doon youre bisynesse:** make an effort.

1633. **so that:** so long as.

1634. **apostle:** see II Corinthians i.12. **so:** such.

1635. **wise man:** see Ecclesiasticus xiii.30. **substance:** property, wealth.

1637. **bisynesse:** earnestness. **conserved:** preserved.

1638. **Salomon:** see Proverbs xxii.1. **availleth:** is helpful to.

1639. **do greet diligence:** make a great effort. **Salomon:** see Ecclesiasticus xli.12 (Vulgate 15).

1641. **after:** in accord with. **alle thynges left:** i.e., all (other) things put aside.

1642. **Cassidore:** see *Variae* i.4.

1643. **Seint Austyn:** see St. Augustine, *Sermo* ccclv.1.

1644. **loos:** reputation.

1646. **trusteth hym so muchel:** trusts so much.

name or loos, and rekketh noght though he kepe nat his goode name, nys but a cruel cherl./

Sire, now have I shewed yow how ye shul do in getynge richesses, and how ye shullen usen hem,/ and I se wel that for the trust that ye han in youre richesses ye wole moeve werre and bataille./ I conseille yow that ye bigynne no werre in trust of youre richesses, for they ne suffisen noght werres to mayntene. [*2840] And therfore seith a philosophre, 'That man that desireth and wole algates han werre, shal nevere have suffisaunce;/ for the richer that he is, the gretter despenses moste he make, if he wol have worship and victorie.'/ And Salomon seith that 'the gretter richesses that a man hath, the mo despendours he hath.'/

And, deere sire, al be it so that for youre richesses ye mowe have muchel folk,/ yet bihoveth it nat, ne it is nat good, to bigynne werre, whereas ye mowe in oother manere have pees unto youre worshipe and profit. [1655] For the victorie of batailles that been in this world lyth nat in greet nombre or multitude of peple, ne in the vertu of man,/ but it lith in the wyl and in the hand of oure Lord God Almyghty./ And therfore Judas Machabeus, which was Goddes knyght,/ whan he sholde fighte agayn his adversarie that hadde a gretter nombre and a gretter multitude of folk and strenger than was the peple of Machabee,/ yet he reconforted his litel compaignye, and seyde right in this wise: [*2850] 'Als lightly,' quod he, 'may oure Lord God Almyghty yeve victorie to fewe folk as to many folk;/ for the victorie of a bataile cometh nat by the grete nombre of peple,/ but it cometh from oure Lord God of hevene.'/

And, deere sire, for as muchel as ther is no man certein if it be worthy that God yeve hym victorie, [*ne plus qu'il est certain s'il est digne de l'amour de Dieu*], or naught, after that Salomon seith;/ therfore every man sholde greetly drede werres to bigynne. [1665] And by cause that in batailles fallen manye perils,/ and happeth oother while that as soone is the grete man slayn as the litel man;/ and as it is writen in the seconde Book of Kynges, 'The dedes of batailles been aventurouse and nothyng certeyne,/ for as lightly is oon hurt with a spere as another';/ and for ther is gret peril in werre; therfore sholde a man flee and eschue werre, in as muchel

---

1647. cruel: severe, unfeeling.

1649. moeve: stir up, begin.

1650. in trust: because of faith.

1651. algates: under all circumstances. **suffisaunce:** sufficient wealth.

1652. despenses: expenditures.

1653. Salomon: see Ecclesiastes v.11 (Vulgate 10). **despendours:** wasters.

1654. al be it so that: although. **for:** because of.

1655. whereas: when. **worshipe:** honor.

1658. Judas Machabeus: see I Maccabees iii.18–19.

1660. reconforted: inspired with fresh courage.

1661. als lightly: as easily.

1664. worthy: appropriate. *ne plus . . . Dieu:* any more than he is certain whether he is worthy of the love of God. (See 1062–63, note, above.) **naught:** not. **after that:** according to what. Salomon: see Vulgate, Ecclesiastes ix.1.

1666. fallen: occur.

1667. happeth: it happens. **oother while:** sometimes.

1668. seconde Book of Kynges: see II Samuel (Vulgate, Liber Secundus Regum) xi.25. **dedes:** outcomes. **aventurouse:** governed by chance.

1669. lightly: readily.

as a man may goodly. [*2860] For Salomon seith, 'He that loveth peril shal falle in peril.' "/

After that Dame Prudence hadde spoken in this manere, Melibee answerde, and seyde:/ "I see wel, dame Prudence, that by youre faire wordes, and by youre resons that ye han shewed me, that the werre liketh yow no thyng;/ but I have nat yet herd youre conseil, how I shal do in this nede."/

"Certes," quod she, "I conseile yow that ye accorde with youre adversaries and that ye have pees with hem. [1675] For Seint Jame seith in his Epistles that 'by concord and pees the smale richesses wexen grete,/ and by debaat and discord the grete richesses fallen doun.'/ And ye knowen wel that oon of the gretteste and moost sovereyn thyng that is in this world is unitee and pees./ And therfore seyde oure Lord Jhesu Crist to his apostles in this wise:/ 'Wel happy and blessed been they that loven and purchacen pees, for they been called children of God.' " [*2870]

"A," quod Melibee, "now se I wel that ye loven nat myn honour ne my worshipe./ Ye knowen wel that myne adversaries han bigonnen this debaat and brige by hire outrage,/ and ye se wel that they ne requeren ne preyen me nat of pees, ne they asken nat to be reconsiled./ Wol ye thanne that I go and meke me and obeye me to hem, and crie hem mercy?/ For sothe, that were nat my worship. [1685] For right as men seyn that 'over-greet homlynesse engendreth dispreisynge,' so fareth it by to greet humylitee or mekenesse."/

Thanne bigan dame Prudence to maken semblant of wrathe, and seyde:/ "Certes, sire, sauf youre grace, I love youre honour and youre profit as I do myn owene, and evere have doon;/ ne ye, ne noon oother, seyn nevere the contrarie./ And yet if I hadde seyd that ye shold han purchaced the pees and the reconsiliacioun, I ne hadde nat muchel mystaken me, ne seyd amys. [*2880] For the wise man seith, 'The dissensioun bigynneth by another man, and the reconsilyng bigynneth by thyself.'/ And the prophete seith, 'Flee shrewednesse and do goodnesse;/ seke pees and folwe it, as muchel as in thee is.'/ Yet seye I nat that ye shul rather pursue to youre adversaries for pees than they shuln to yow./ For I knowe wel that ye been

---

1670. may goodly: can with propriety; possibly can.
1671. Salomon: see Ecclesiasticus iii.26 (Vulgate 27).
1676. Seint Jame: see Seneca, *Epistolae* 94.46. wexen: grow.
1677. debaat: strife. fallen doun: decrease.
1679. Crist: see Matthew v.9.
1680. purchacen: bring about.
1681. worshipe: renown.
1682. brige: contention.
1683. requeren: request.
1684. meke me: humble myself.
1685. my worship: to my honor.
1686. homlynesse: familiarity. dispreisynge: contempt. by: with. to greet: too great.
1687. maken semblant: make a pretence.
1688. sauf: saving.
1689. seyn: saw.
1690. purchaced: brought about. mystaken me: done wrong.
1691. wise man: see pseudo-Seneca, *De Moribus* iii. by: with.
1692. prophete: see Psalms xxxiii.15 (Vulgate xxxiv.15). shrewednesse: evil.
1694. rather: sooner. pursue to: sue.

so hardherted that ye wol do no thyng for me. [1695] And Salomon seith that 'he that hath over-hard an herte, atte laste he shal myshappe and mystyde.' "/

Whanne Melibee hadde herd dame Prudence make semblant of wrathe, he seyde in this wise:/ "Dame, I pray yow that ye be nat displesed of thynges that I seye,/ for ye knowe wel that I am angry and wrooth, and that is no wonder;/ and they that been wrothe witen nat wel what they don, ne what they seyn. [*2890] Therfore the prophete seith that 'troubled eyen han no cleer sighte.'/ But seyeth and conseileth me as yow liketh, for I am redy to do right as ye wol desire;/ and if ye repreve me of my folye, I am the moore holden to love yow and to preise yow./ For Salomon seith that 'he that repreveth hym that dooth folye,/ he shal fynde gretter grace than he that deceyveth hym by sweete wordes.' " [1705]

Thanne seide dame Prudence, "I make no semblant of wrathe ne of anger, but for youre grete profit./ For Salomon seith, 'He is moore worth that repreveth or chideth a fool for his folye, shewynge hym semblant of wrathe,/ than he that supporteth hym and preiseth hym in his mysdoynge, and laugheth at his folye.'/ And this same Salomon seith afterward that 'by the sorweful visage of a man,' that is to seyn by the sory and hevy contenaunce of a man,/ 'the fool correcteth and amendeth hymself.' " [*2900]

Thanne seyde Melibee, "I shal nat konne answere to so manye faire resons as ye putten to me and shewen./ Seyeth shortly youre wil and youre conseil, and I am al redy to fulfille and parfourne it."/

Thanne dame Prudence discovered al hir wyl to hym, and seyde,/ "I conseille yow," quod she, "aboven alle thynges, that ye make pees bitwene God and yow;/ and beth reconsiled unto hym and to his grace. [1715] For, as I have seyd yow heer biforn, God hath suffred yow to have this tribulacioun and disese for youre synnes./ And if ye do as I sey yow, God wol sende youre adversaries unto yow,/ and maken hem falle at youre feet, redy to do youre wyl and youre comandementz./ For Salomon seith, 'Whan the condicioun of man is plesaunt and likynge to God,/ he chaungeth the hertes of the mannes adversaries and constreyneth hem to biseken hym of pees and of grace.' [*2910] And I prey yow lat me speke with youre adversaries in privee place,/ for they shal nat knowe that it be of youre wyl or youre assent./ And thanne, whan I knowe hir wil and hire entente, I may conseille yow the moore seurely."/

1696. Salomon: see Proverbs xxviii.14. myshappe and mystyde: have mishap and misfortune.
1697. make semblant: make a pretence.
1700. witen: know. seyn: say.
1702. seyeth: say. as yow liketh: what pleases you.
1703. repreve: reprove. holden: bound.
1704. Salomon: see Proverbs xxviii.23.
1706. make no semblant: make no pretence.
1707. Salomon: cf. Vulgate, Ecclesiastes vii.4–6.
1709. Salomon: see Vulgate, Ecclesiastes vii.4.
1711. konne: know how to.
1713. discovered: revealed.
1716. disese: misfortune.
1719. Salomon: see Proverbs xvi.7. condicioun: morals, ways. likynge: pleasing.
1720. biseken of: beseech for. grace: favor.
1722. for: so that. of: with.
1723. seurely: surely, infallibly.

"Dame," quod Melibee, "dooth youre wil and youre likynge;/ for I putte me hoolly in youre disposicioun and ordinaunce." [1725]

Thanne dame Prudence, whan she saugh the goode wyl of hir housbonde, she delibered and took avys in hirself,/ thinkinge how she myghte brynge this nede unto a good conclusioun and to a good ende./ And whan she saugh hir tyme, she sente for thise adversaries to come unto hire into a pryvee place,/ and shewed wisely unto hem the grete goodes that comen of pees,/ and the grete harmes and perils that been in werre; [*2920] and seyde to hem in a goodly manere how that hem oughten have greet repentaunce/ of the injurie and wrong that they hadden doon to Melibee hir lord, and unto hire, and to hire doghter./

And whan they herden the goodliche wordes of dame Prudence,/ they weren so surprised and ravysshed, and hadden so greet joye of hire that wonder was to telle./ "A, lady," quod they, "ye han shewed unto us the blessynge of swetnesse, after the sawe of David the prophete; [1735] for the reconsilynge which we been nat worthy to have in no manere,/ but we oghte requeren it with greet contricioun and humylitee,/ ye of youre grete goodnesse have presented unto us./ Now se we wel that the science and the konnynge of Salomon is ful trewe./ For he seith that 'sweete wordes multiplien and encreescen freendes, and maken shrewes to be debonaire and meeke.' [*2930]

"Certes," quod they, "we putten oure dede and al oure matere and cause al hoolly in youre goode wyl/ and been redy to obeye to the speche and comandement of my lord Melibee./ And therfore, deere and benygne lady, we preyen yow and biseke yow as mekely as we konne and mowen,/ that it like unto youre grete goodnesse to fulfille in dede youre goodliche wordes./ For we consideren and knowelichen that we han offended and greved my lord Melibee out of mesure, [1745] so forth that we be nat of power to maken his amendes./ And therfore we oblige and bynde us and oure freendes for to do al his wyl and his comandementz./ But peraventure he hath swich hevynesse and swich wrathe to us-ward, by cause of oure offense,/ that he wole enjoyne us swich a peyne as we mowe nat bere ne sustene./ And therfore, noble lady, we biseke to youre wommanly pitee [*2940]

1725. hoolly: wholly. disposicioun: rule. ordinaunce: control.
1726. delibered: deliberated. took avys: pondered.
1727. nede: difficult situation.
1728. tyme: right moment, opportunity.
1729. goodes: benefits. of: from.
1731. goodly: kindly.
1733. goodliche: gracious.
1734. ravysshed: delighted, entranced.
1735. sawe: saying. David: see Vulgate, Psalms xx.4.
1736. reconsilynge: reconciliation.
1737. requeren: request.
1739. Salomon: see Vulgate, Ecclesiasticus vi.5.
1740. shrewes: scoundrels. debonaire: merciful.
1741. dede: action, conduct. matere: affair, business. hoolly: wholly.
1744. fulfille: carry out.
1745. consideren: deem. knowelichen: acknowledge, confess.
1746. so forferth: so far. his amendes: amends to him.
1748. hevynesse: rancor. to us-ward: toward us.
1749. peyne: penalty, punishment.
1750. biseke to: beseech.

to taken swich avysement in this nede that we, ne oure freendes, be nat desherited ne destroyed thurgh oure folye."/

"Certes," quod Prudence, "it is an hard thyng and right perilous/ that a man putte hym al outrely in the arbitracioun and juggement, and in the myght and power of his enemys./ For Salomon seith, 'Leeveth me, and yeveth credence to that I shal seyn: I seye,' quod he, 'ye peple, folk and governours of holy chirche,/ to thy sone, to thy wyf, to thy freend, ne to thy brother, [1755] ne yeve thou nevere myght ne maistrie of thy body whil thou lyvest.'/ Now sithen he defendeth that man sholde nat yeve to his brother ne to his freend the myght of his body,/ by a strenger resoun he defendeth and forbedeth a man to yeve hymself to his enemy./ And nathelees I conseille you that ye mystruste nat my lord,/ for I woot wel and knowe verraily that he is debonaire and meeke, large, curteys, [*2950] and nothyng desirous ne coveitous of good ne richesse./ For ther nys nothyng in this world that he desireth, save oonly worshipe and honour./ Forthermoore I knowe wel and am right seur that he shal nothyng doon in this nede withouten my conseil;/ and I shal so werken in this cause that, by the grace of oure Lord God, ye shul been reconsiled unto us."/

Thanne seyden they with o voys, "Worshipful lady, we putten us and oure goodes al fully in youre wil and disposicioun, [1765] and been redy to come, what day that it like unto youre noblesse to lymyte us or assigne us,/ for to maken oure obligacioun and boond as strong as it liketh unto youre goodnesse,/ that we mowe fulfille the wille of yow and of my lord Melibee."/

Whan dame Prudence hadde herd the answeres of thise men, she bad hem go agayn prively;/ and she retourned to hir lord Melibee, and tolde hym how she foond his adversaries ful repentant, [*2960] knowelechynge ful lowely hir synnes and trespas, and how they were redy to suffren all peyne,/ requirynge and preiynge hym of mercy and pitee./

Thanne seyde Melibee: "He is wel worthy to have pardoun and foryifnesse of his synne, that excuseth nat his synne,/ but knowelecheth and repenteth hym, axinge indulgence./ For Senec seith, 'There is the remissioun and foryifnesse, where as the

---

1751. **taken avysement:** take thought, take counsel. **nede:** difficult situation. **desherited:** dispossessed.

1753. **putte:** should put. **outrely:** utterly.

1754. **Salomon:** see Ecclesiasticus xxxiii.18–19 (Vulgate 19–20). **leeveth:** believe. **that:** that which, what.

1756. **of:** over.

1757. **defendeth that man sholde nat yeve:** forbids that a man should give. **myght of:** power over.

1758. **defendeth:** forbids.

1760. **debonaire:** merciful. **large:** generous.

1761. **good:** goods.

1763. **seur:** sure. **nede:** situation.

1764. **cause:** matter.

1765. **o:** one. **putten in youre wil and disposicioun:** submit to your will and discretion.

1766. **lymyte us:** appoint for us.

1767. **it liketh unto:** pleases.

1771. **knowelechynge:** acknowledging, confessing. **lowely:** humbly. **peyne:** penalty, punishment.

1772. **requirynge:** requesting.

1773. **excuseth:** makes excuses for.

1775–76. **Senec:** see pseudo-Seneca, *De Moribus* iii. **remissioun:** pardon. **where as:** where.

confessioun is'; [1775] for confessioun is neighebor to innocence./ And he seith in another place, 'He is worthy to have remissioun and foryifnesse that hath shame of his synne and knowlecheth it.' And therfore I assente and conferme me to have pees;/ but it is good that we do it nat withouten the assent and wyl of oure freendes."/

Thanne was Prudence right glad and joyeful, and seyde;/ "Certes, sire," quod she, "ye han wel and goodly answered; [*2970] for right as by the conseil, assent, and help of youre frendes ye han been stired to venge yow and make werre,/ right so withouten hire conseil shul ye nat accorde yow ne have pees with youre adversaries./ For the lawe seith: 'Ther nys no thyng so good by wey of kynde as a thyng to be unbounde by hym that it was ybounde.' "/

And thanne dame Prudence, withouten delay or tariynge, sente anon hir messages for hir kyn, and for hire olde freendes which that were trewe and wise,/ and tolde hem by ordre in the presence of Melibee al this matere as it is above expressed and declared, [1785] and preyde hem that they wolde yeven hire avys and conseil what best were to do in this nede.

And whan Melibees freendes hadde taken hire avys and deliberacioun of the forseide matere,/ and hadden examyned it by greet bisynesse and greet diligence,/ they yave ful conseil for to have pees and reste,/ and that Melibee sholde receyve with good herte his adversaries to foryifnesse and mercy. [*2980]

And whan dame Prudence hadde herd the assent of hir lord Melibee, and the conseil of his freendes/ accorde with hire wille and hire entencioun,/ she was wonderly glad in hire herte, and seyde:/ "Ther is an old proverbe," quod she, "seith that 'the goodnesse that thou mayst do this day, do it,/ and abide nat ne delaye it nat til tomorwe.' [1795] And therfore I conseille that ye sende youre messages, swiche as been discrete and wise,/ unto youre adversaries, tellynge hem on youre bihalve/ that if they wol trete of pees and of accord,/ that they shape hem withouten delay or tariyng to come unto us."/ Which thyng parfourned was in dede. [*2990]

And whanne thise trespassours and repentynge folk of hire folies, that is to seyn, the adversaries of Melibee,/ hadden herd what thise messagers seyden unto hem,/

1777. another place: see Publilius Syrus, *Sententiae* 489, and pseudo-Seneca as above. conferme me: resolve.
1781. right: just. stired: stirred, moved.
1782. accorde yow: become reconciled.
1783. lawe: see Justinian, *Digesta* I.17.35. by wey of kynde: by nature, naturally. that: i.e., by whom.
1784. messages: messengers. kyn: kindred, relatives.
1785. by: in.
1786. avys: advice.
1787. taken avys: taken thought.
1788. bisynesse: care, pains.
1789. yave conseil: gave consent, agreement. reste: tranquility.
1795. abide: wait.
1796. messages: messengers.
1797. bihalve: behalf.
1799. shape hem: prepare.
1800. parfourned: performed, carried out.
1801. repentynge folk: folk repenting.

they weren right glad and joyeful, and answereden ful mekely and benignely,/ yeldynge graces and thankynges to hire lord Melibee and to al his compaignye;/ and shopen hem withouten delay to go with the messagers, and obeye to the comandement of hire lord Melibee. [1805] And right anon they tooken hire wey to the court of Melibee,/ and tooken with hem somme of hire trewe freendes to make feith for hem and for to been hire borwes./

And whan they were come to the presence of Melibee, he seyde hem thise wordes:/ "It standeth thus," quod Melibee, "and sooth it is, that ye,/ causelees and withouten skile and resoun, [*3000] han doon grete injuries and wronges to me and to my wyf Prudence, and to my doghter also./ For ye han entred into myn house by violence,/ and have doon swich outrage that alle men knowen wel that ye have deserved the deeth./ And therfore wol I knowe and wite of yow/ wheither ye wol putte the punysshynge and the chastisynge and the vengeance of this outrage in the wil of me and of my wyf Prudence, or ye wol nat?" [1815]

Thanne the wiseste of hem thre answerde for hem alle, and seyde,/ "Sire," quod he, "we knowen wel that we been unworthy to comen unto the court of so greet a lord and so worthy as ye been./ For we han so gretly mystaken us, and han offended and agilt in swich a wise agayn youre heigh lordshipe,/ that trewely we han deserved the deeth./ But yet, for the grete goodnesse and debonairetee that al the world witnesseth of youre persone, [*3010] we submitten us to the excellence and benignitee of youre gracious lordshipe,/ and ben redy to obeye to alle youre comandementz;/ bisekynge yow that of youre merciable pitee ye wol considere oure grete repentaunce and lowe submissioun,/ and graunten us foryevenesse of oure outrageous trespas and offense./ For wel we knowe that youre liberal grace and mercy strecchen ferther into goodnesse than doon oure outrageouse giltes and trespas into wikkednesse, [1825] al be it that cursedly and dampnablely we han agilt agayn youre heigh lordshipe."/

Thanne Melibee took hem up fro the ground ful benignely,/ and receyved hire obligaciouns and hir boondes by hire othes upon hire plegges and borwes,/ and assigned hem a certeyn day to retourne unto his court,/ for to accepte and receyve the sentence and jugement that Melibee wolde comande to be doon on hem by the causes aforeseyd. [*3020] Whiche thynges ordeyned, every man retourned to his hous./

And whan that dame Prudence saugh hir tyme, she freyned and axed hir lord Melibee/ what vengeance he thoughte to taken of his adversaries./

1804. yeldynge graces: giving thanks.
1805. shopen hem: prepared.
1807. make feith: give surety. borwes: pledges.
1810. skile: cause.
1815. putte: i.e., submit. in the wil: to the will.
1818. mystaken us: transgressed. agilt: been guilty. agayn: against.
1820. debonairetee: mercy. of: concerning.
1823. lowe: humble.
1825. strecchen: stretch, reach. giltes: sins.
1826. agilt: been guilty. agayn: against.
1828. boondes: promises. othes: oaths. plegges: pledges (i.e., sureties). borwes: sureties.
1831. ordeyned: ordered, arranged.
1832. tyme: right moment, opportunity. freyned: inquired.

To which Melibee answerde, and seyde: "Certes," quod he, "I thynke and purpose me fully/ to desherite hem of al that evere they han, and for to putte hem in exil for evere." [1835]

"Certes," quod dame Prudence, "this were a cruel sentence and muchel agayn resoun./ For ye been riche ynough, and han no nede of oother mennes good;/ and ye myghte lightly in this wise gete yow a coveitous name,/ which is a vicious thyng, and oghte been eschewed of every good man./ For after the sawe of the word of the Apostle, 'Coveitise is roote of alle harmes.' [*3030] And therfore it were bettre for yow to lese so muchel good of youre owene, than for to take of hire good in this manere;/ for bettre it is to lese good with worshipe, than it is to wynne good with vileynye and shame./ And every man oghte to do his diligence and his bisynesse to geten hym a good name./ And yet shal he nat oonly bisie hym in kepynge of his good name,/ but he shal also enforcen hym alwey to do somthyng by which he may renovelle his good name. [1845] For it is writen that 'the olde good loos or good name of a man is soone goon and passed, whan it is nat newed ne renovelled.'/

And as touchynge that ye seyn ye wol exile youre adversaries,/ that thynketh me muchel agayn resoun and out of mesure,/ considered the power that they han yeven yow upon hemself./ And it is writen that 'he is worthy to lesen his privilege, that mysuseth the myght and the power that is yeven hym.' [*3040] And I sette cas ye myghte enjoyne hem that peyne by right and by lawe,/ which I trowe ye mowe nat do,/ I seye ye mighte nat putten it to execucioun peraventure,/ and thanne were it likely to retourne to the werre as it was biforn./ And therfore, if ye wole that men do yow obeisance, ye moste deme moore curteisly; [1855] this is to seyn, ye moste yeve moore esy sentences and jugementz./ For it is writen that 'he that moost curteisly commandeth, to hym men moost obeyen.'/ And therfore I prey yow that in this necessitee and in this nede ye caste yow to overcome youre herte./ For Senec seith that 'he that overcometh his herte, overcometh twies.'/ And Tullius seith: 'Ther is no thyng so commendable in a greet lord [*3050] as whan he is debonaire and meeke, and appeseth him lightly.'/

1835. desherite: dispossess.
1837. good: goods.
1838. lightly: easily.   coveitous name: reputation for covetousness.
1840. after the sawe of the word: according to the saying in the message.   Apostle: see I Timothy vi.10.   harmes: evils.
1841. lese: lose.   so muchel: i.e., that much.
1842. worshipe: honor.
1843. do his diligence and his bisynesse: make every effort and exertion.
1845. enforcen hym: endeavor.   renovelle: renew, i.e., add to.
1846. loos: reputation.   goon: gone.
1848. out of mesure: beyond all bounds, excessive.
1849. considered: considering.
1851. I sette cas: if I suppose.   enjoyne: impose on.   peyne: penalty, punishment.
1854. were it: it were, it would mean.
1855. do obeisance: do homage.   moste: must.   curteisly: mercifully.
1857. writen: see Seneca, De Clementia i.24.1.   moost: most.
1858. caste yow: decide.
1859. Senec: see Publilius Syrus, Sententiae 64.   twies: twice.
1860. Tullius: see De Officiis i.25.88.
1861. debonaire: merciful.   appeseth him: grows calm.   lightly: readily.

And I prey yow that ye wol forbere now to do vengeance,/ in swich a manere that youre good name may be kept and conserved,/ and that men mowe have cause and matiere to preyse yow of pitee and of mercy,/ and that ye have no cause to repente yow of thyng that ye doon. [1865] For Senec seith, 'He overcometh in an yvel manere that repenteth hym of his victorie.'/ Wherfore I pray yow, lat mercy be in youre herte,/ to th' effect and entente that God Almighty have mercy on yow in his laste jugement./ For Seint Jame seith in his Epistle: 'Jugement withoute mercy shal be doon to hym that hath no mercy of another wight.'/

Whanne Melibee hadde herd the grete skiles and resons of dame Prudence, and hir wise informaciouns and techynges, [*3060] his herte gan enclyne to the wil of his wif, considerynge hir trewe entente,/ and conformed hym anon, and assented fully to werken after hir conseil;/ and thonked God, of whom procedeth al vertu and al goodnesse, that hym sente a wyf of so greet discrecioun./

And whan the day came that his adversaries sholde appieren in his presence,/ he spak to hem ful goodly, and seyde in this wise: [1875] "Al be it so that of youre pride and heigh presumpcioun and folie, and of youre necligence and unkonnynge,/ ye have mysborn yow and trespassed unto me,/ yet for as muche as I see and biholde youre grete humylitee,/ and that ye been sory and repentant of youre giltes,/ it constreyneth me to do yow grace and mercy. [*3070] Wherfore I receyve yow to my grace,/ and foryeve yow outrely alle the offenses, injuries, and wronges that ye have doon agayn me and myne,/ to this effect and to this ende that God of his endelees mercy/ wole at the tyme of oure diynge foryeven us oure giltes that we han trespassed to hym in this wrecched world./ For doutelees, if we be sory and repentant of the synnes and giltes which we han trespassed in the sighte of oure Lord God, [1885] he is so free and so merciable/ that he wole foryeven us oure giltes,/ and bryngen us to the blisse that nevere hath ende. Amen.

Heere is ended Chaucers tale of Melibee
and of Dame Prudence.

1863. conserved: preserved.
1864. matiere: reason.   of: on account of (your).
1866. Senec: see Publilius Syrus, *Sententiae* 366.
1868. effect: end.   entente: intent, purpose.
1869. Seint Jame: see James ii.13.   doon: given.   of: on.
1870. skiles: arguments.
1871. enclyne to: to favor.
1872. werken after: act according to.
1873. of whom: from whom.
1876. unkonnynge: ignorance.
1877. mysborn yow: misbehaved, conducted yourselves badly.
1879. giltes: sins.
1880. it constreyneth me: I am constrained.   do: grant, show.
1882. outrely: utterly.
1884. diynge: dying.   giltes: sins.   to: against.
1886. free: generous.   merciable: merciful.

The murye wordes of
the Hoost to the Monk.

Whan ended was my tale of Melibee,
And of Prudence and hire benignytee,   *3080 benignytee: graciousness.
Oure Hooste seyde, "As I am feithful man,
And by that precious corpus Madrian,
I hadde levere than a barel ale
That Goodelief, my wyf, hadde herd this tale!
For she nys no thyng of swich pacience   1895
As was this Melibeus wyf Prudence.
By Goddes bones! whan I bete my knaves,   knaves: servant-lads.
She bryngeth me the grete clobbed staves,   clobbed: club-shaped.
And crieth, 'Slee the dogges everichoon,
And brek hem, bothe bak and every boon!'   *3090
   And if that any neighebor of myne
Wol nat in chirche to my wyf enclyne,   enclyne: bow.
Or be so hardy to hire to trespace,   trespace: do offence.
Whan she comth hoom she rampeth in my face,   rampeth: ramps; rages.
And crieth, 'False coward, wrek thy wyf!   1905 wrek: avenge.
By corpus bones, I wol have thy knyf,
And thou shalt have my distaf and go spynne!'
Fro day to nyght right thus she wol bigynne.   day: daybreak.
'Allas!' she seith, 'that evere I was shape   shape: destined.
To wedden a milksop, or a coward ape,   *3100
That wol been overlad with every wight!   overlad: overborne, brow-beaten.
Thou darst nat stonden by thy wyves right!'
   This is my lif, but if that I wol fighte;
And out at dore anon I moot me dighte,   me dighte: hasten.
Or elles I am but lost, but if that I   1915
Be lik a wilde leoun, fool-hardy.
I woot wel she wol do me slee som day   do me slee: cause me to slay.
Som neighebor, and thanne go my way;   go my way: depart, flee.
For I am perilous with knyf in honde,
Al be it that I dar nat hire withstonde,   *3110
For she is big in armes, by my feith:
That shal he fynde that hire mysdooth or seith.
But lat us passe awey fro this mateere.
   My lord, the Monk," quod he, "be myrie of
       cheere,
For ye shul telle a tale trewely.   1925
Lo, Rouchestre stant heer faste by!   Rouchestre: Rochester, 30 miles from
          Southwark.

1891. Upon my faith as a Christian.
1892. corpus Madrian: the body of St. Mathurin (?). The Host's blunders are sometimes puzzling.
1906. Here the Host attributes a blundering oath to his wife.
The Wheel of Fortune: At Rochester—with its imposing Monastic Cathedral, a Benedictine foundation—the Monk begins his account of the tragic falls brought to great men by Fortune. There still remains on the north wall of the choir about half of a thirteenth-century painting of Fortune, her wheel, and her victims. A regal figure is seated luxuriously at the top; and other men and their garments are degraded according to their positions on the wheel. See lines 2397–98 and 2445–46 below, and Knight's Tale, 925–26.

Ryde forth, myn owene lord, brek nat oure game.
But, by my trouthe, I knowe nat youre name.
Wher shal I calle yow my lord daun John,   daun: sir (from Latin *dominus*).
Or daun Thomas, or elles daun Albon?   *3120
Of what hous be ye, by youre fader kyn?   hous: religious establishment. fader:
I vow to God, thou hast a ful fair skyn;   father's.
It is a gentil pasture ther thow goost.
Thou art nat lyk a penant or a goost: penant: penitent. goost: ghost.
Upon my feith, thou art som officer,   1935
Som worthy sexteyn, or som celerer,
For by my fader soule, as to my doom,   doom: judgment.
Thou art a maister whan thou art at hoom;
No povre cloystrer, ne no novys,
But a governour, wily and wys,   *3130
And therwithal of brawnes and of bones,   brawnes: muscles.
A wel farynge persone for the nones.   wel farynge: handsome.
I pray to God, yeve hym confisioun
That first thee broghte unto religioun!   unto religioun: to monastic life.
Thou woldest han been a tredefowel aright. 1945 tredefowel: treader (copulator) of
Haddestow as greet a leeve, as thou hast   fowls. leeve: permission.
          myght,
To parfourne al thy lust in engendrure,   lust: desire. engendrure: engender-
Thou haddest bigeten ful many a creature.   ing, procreation.
Allas, why werestow so wyd a cope?
God yeve me sorwe, but, and I were a pope, *3140
Nat oonly thou, but every myghty man,
Though he were shorn ful hye upon his pan,   pan: brain-pan, skull.
Sholde have a wyf; for al the world is lorn!   lorn: ruined, desolate.
Religioun hath take up al the corn   corn: best portion.
Of tredyng, and we borel men been shrympes.   borel men: laymen.
Of fieble trees ther comen wrecched ympes. 1956 wrecched ympes: poor grafts, weakly
This maketh that oure heires been so sklendre   shoots. sklendre: thin, weak.
And feble that they may nat wel engendre.
This maketh that oure wyves wole assaye   assaye: try.
Religious folk, for they mowe bettre paye   *3150
Of Venus paiementz than mowe we;
God woot, no lussheburghes payen ye!
But be nat wrooth, my lord, though that I pleye.   wrooth: wroth, angry.
Ful ofte in game a sooth I have herd seye!"   sooth: truth.
    This worthy Monk took al in pacience,   1965
And seyde, "I wol doon al my diligence,
As fer as sowneth into honestee,   sowneth into: is consonant with.
To telle yow a tale, or two, or three.
And if yow list to herkne hiderward,

1936. sexteyn: sacristan of the monastery, in charge of its sacred vessels, vestments, relics, and the like. celerer: cellarer, in charge of cellar, kitchen, food, and drink.
1962. lussheburghes: spurious, light coins imported into England from Luxemburg.
1966. doon al my diligence: exert myself to the utmost.

I wol yow seyn the lyf of Seint Edward; *3160
Or ellis, first, tragedies wol I telle,
Of whiche I have an hundred in my celle.
Tragedie is to seyn a certeyn storie,
As olde bookes maken us memorie,   memorie: remembrance.
Of hym that stood in greet prosperitee, 1975
And is yfallen out of heigh degree
Into myserie, and endeth wrecchedly.
And they ben versified communely
Of six feet, which men clepen *exametron*. *exametron:* hexameter.
In prose eek been endited many oon, *3170 endited: written, composed.
And eek in meetre, in many a sondry wyse.
Lo, this declaryng oghte ynogh suffise.   declaryng: explanation.
    Now herkneth, if yow liketh for to heere.
But first I yow biseeke in this mateere,
Though I by ordre telle nat thise thynges, 1985 ordre: i.e., chronological order.
Be it of popes, emperours, or kynges,
After hir ages, as men writen fynde,   after: according to. ages: eras.
But tellen hem som bifore and som bihynde,
As it now cometh to my remembraunce,
Have me excused of myn ignoraunce." *3180

                Explicit.

               *Heere bigynneth the
               Monkes tale De Casibus
               Virorum Illustrium.*

    I wol biwaille, in manere of tragedie,
The harm of hem that stoode in heigh degree, harm: misfortune. degree: station,
And fillen so that ther nas no remedie   estate, rank. fillen: fell.
To brynge hem out of hire adversitee.
For certein, whan that Fortune list to flee, 1995
Ther may no man the cours of hire withholde. withholde: keep in check, stay.
Lat no man truste on blynd prosperitee;
Be war by thise ensamples trewe and olde.   be war: take warning. ensamples: ex-
                          amples.

1970. **Seint Edward:** probably Edward the Confessor.
1973–77. See second note below, and Chaucer's *Boece* II.pr. 2, 67–72.
1986. See, for example, the long section of Trevet's *Les Cronicles* entitled "Les gestes des apostles, emperours, et rois."
De Casibus Virorum Illustrium. This title is the same as that of Boccaccio's *Falls of Illustrious Men,* the book which gave Chaucer the basic plan for his collection of tragic falls, though not the material of the tragedies themselves. Lines 1973–77 of the introductory link, the first stanza of the Tale, and its final lines (2761–66) in the story of Croesus, are based on *De Consolatione Philosophiae* by *Boethius* (ii, pr. 2; iii, pr. 5) and the commentary thereon by Nicholas Trevet, and set the prevailing tone of the poem. Another important influence is that of Jean de Meun's comments on Fortune found between lines 4837 and 6894 of *Le Roman de la Rose.*

Lucifer

At Lucifer, though he an angel were,
And nat a man, at hym I wol bigynne.   *3190
For though Fortune may noon angel dere,   noon: no. dere: harm.
From heigh degree yet fel he for his synne
Doun into helle, where as he yet is inne.
O Lucifer, brightest of angels alle,
Now artow Sathanas, that mayst nat twynne   2005 twynne: escape.
Out of miserie, in which thou art falle.

Adam

Lo Adam, in the feeld of Damyssene,
With Goddes owene fynger wroght was he,
And nat bigeten of mannes sperme unclene,   bigeten: begotten.
And welte al paradys savynge o tree.   *3200 welte: (wielded) had as his own. o:
Hadde nevere worldly man so heigh degree   one. worldly: earthly, on earth.
As Adam, til he for mysgovernaunce   mysgovernaunce: misconduct.
Was dryve out of his hye prosperitee
To labour, and to helle, and to meschaunce.   meschaunce: disaster.

Sampson

Lo Sampsoun, which that was annunciat   2015 which that: who (i.e., whose birth).
By th' angel, longe er his nativitee,   annunciat: announced.
And was to God Almyghty consecrat,   consecrat: consecrated.
And stood in noblesse whil he myghte see.   whil: as long as (see l. 2070).
Was nevere swich another as was he,
To speke of strengthe, and therwith   to speke of: with regard to.
          hardynesse;   *3210 hardynesse: courage, boldness.
But to his wyves tolde he his secree,   secree: secret.
Thurgh which he slow hymself for   slow: slew.
          wrecchednesse.

Sampsoun, this noble almyghty champioun,
Withouten wepen, save his handes tweye,   wepen: weapon.
He slow and al torente the leoun,   2025 al torente: rent all in pieces.
Toward his weddyng walkynge by the weye.   toward: on his way to.
His false wyf koude hym so plese and preye
Til she his conseil knew; and she, untrewe,   conseil: secret.
Unto his foos his conseil gan biwreye,   gan biwreye: betrayed, revealed.
And hym forsook, and took another newe. *3220

Thre hundred foxes took Sampson for ire,
And alle hir tayles he togydre bond,   bond: bound.

Lucifer: "light-bearer," the name of the morning-star; it was applied to the rebel archangel because of the words of Isaiah (xiv.12): "How art thou fallen from heaven, O Lucifer, son of the morning!"
2007. Damyssene: of Damascus. Adam was said to have been created in a field where Damascus afterwards stood.

And sette the foxes tayles alle on fire,
For he on every tayl had knyt a brond;   knyt: tied. brond: firebrand.
And they brende alle the cornes in that lond, 2035   brende: burned. cornes: grain crops.
And alle hire olyveres, and vynes eke.   olyveres: olive-trees.
A thousand men he slow eek with his hond,   slow: slew.
And hadde no wepen but an asses cheke.   cheke: jawbone.

Whan they were slayn, so thursted hym that he
Was wel ny lorn, for which he gan to preye *3230 lorn: lost.
That God wolde on his peyne have some pitee,
And sende hym drynke, or elles moste he deye;   moste: must.
And of this asses cheke, that was dreye,   dreye: dry.
Out of a wang-tooth sprang anon a welle,   wang-tooth: molar tooth. welle: spring.
Of which he drank ynogh, shortly to seye; 2045
Thus heelp hym God, as *Judicum* can telle.   heelp: helped.

By verray force at Gazan, on a nyght,   verray: sheer. Gazan: Gaza.
Maugree Philistiens of that citee,   maugree: in spite of.
The gates of the toun he hath up plyght,   up plyght: heaved up (off their hinges).
And on his bak ycaried hem hath hee   *3240 ycaried: carried.
Hye on an hill whereas men myghte hem see.   whereas: where.
O noble, almyghty Sampsoun, lief and deere,   lief: beloved.
Had thou nat toold to wommen thy secree,
In al this world ne hadde been thy peere!   ne hadde been: there would not have
    been.

This Sampson nevere ciser drank ne wyn, 2055 ciser: strong drink.
Ne on his heed cam rasour noon ne sheere,   noon: no.
By precept of the messager divyn,   messager: angel.
For alle his strengthes in his heeres weere.   heeres: hair.
And fully twenty wynter, yeer by yeere,
He hadde of Israel the governaunce.   *3250
But soone shal he wepe many a teere,
For wommen shal hym bryngen to meschaunce! meschaunce: disaster.

Unto his lemman Dalida he tolde   lemman: mistress. Dalida: Delilah.
That in his heeris al his strengthe lay,
And falsly to his foomen she hym solde. 2065 solde: sold; betrayed.
And slepynge in hir barm, upon a day,   barm: lap; bosom.
She made to clippe or shere his heer away,   made: caused (a servant).
And made his foomen al this craft espyen;   craft: trickery. espyen: see, notice.
And whan that they hym foond in this array, foond: found. array: condition.
They bounde hym faste and putten out his   putten: put.
    eyen.   *3260

But er his heer was clipped or yshave,
Ther was no bond with which men myghte   bond: fetter, shackle.
    him bynde;

2046. *Judicum:* Liber Judicum, the Book of Judges, where (xiii–xvi) the story of Sampson is told.

But now is he in prison in a cave,   prison: captivity.
Where-as they made hym at the querne grynde.   querne: hand-mill.
O noble Sampsoun, strongest of mankynde, 2075
O whilom juge, in glorie and in richesse!   whilom: sometime.
Now maystow wepen with thyne eyen blynde,   wepen: weep.
Sith thou fro wele art falle in wrecchednesse.   wele: prosperity, happiness.

The ende of this caytyf was as I shal seye.   caytyf: captive; wretched person.
His foomen made a feeste upon a day,   *3270
And made hym as hire fool bifore hem pleye;
And this was in a temple of greet array.   array: splendor.
But atte laste he made a foul affray;   foul: horrible. affray: assault.
For he two pilers shook and made hem falle,
And doun fil temple and al, and ther it lay,— 2085
And slow hymself, and eek his foomen alle.   slow: slew.

This is to seyn, the prynces everichoon,
And eek thre thousand bodies, were ther slayn
With fallyng of the grete temple of stoon.
Of Sampson now wol I namoore sayn.   *3280
Beth war by this ensample oold and playn   beth war: take warning.
That no men telle hir conseil til hir wyves   til: to.
Of swich thyng as they wolde han secree fayn, fayn: eagerly, gladly.
If that it touche hir lymes or hir lyves.   lymes: limbs.

Hercules

Of Hercules, the sovereyn conquerour,   2095
Syngen his werkes laude and heigh renoun;   his werkes: his deeds', of his deeds.
For in his tyme of strengthe he was the flour.   laude: praise. flour: flower.
He slow, and rafte the skyn fro the leoun;
He of Centauros leyde the boost adoun;   boost: pride.
He Arpies slow, the crueel bryddes felle;   *3290 slow: slew. felle: terrible.
He golden apples rafte of the dragoun;   rafte of: stole from. dragoun: i.e.
He drow out Cerberus, the hound of helle;   Ladon. drow: drew, dragged.

He slow the crueel tyrant Busirus,
And made his hors to frete hym, flessh and bon; hors: horses. frete: devour.
He slow the firy serpent venymus;   2105
Of Acheloys two hornes he brak oon;   Acheloys: Achelous'. brak: broke.
And he slow Cacus in a cave of stoon;
He slow the geant Antheus the stronge;   Antheus: Antaeus.

2095–2110. These werkes are from Boethius (De Consolatione Philosophiae, iv, m. 7), whose list corresponds only in part with the traditional Twelve Labors.
2098. He slew and despoiled the (Nemean) lion of his skin.
2099. Centauros: i.e., he slew the Centaurs Pholus and Nessus.
2100. Arpies: Harpies, i.e., the Stymphalian birds.
2103. Busirus: the story of Busiris is here confused with that of Diomedes, King of Thrace.
2105. serpent: the Lernaean Hydra, fiery because Chaucer, misreading Virgil, applied "flammisque" to the Hydra rather than to the Chimaera (Aeneid vi.288).

He slow the grisly boor, and that anon;
And bar the hevene on his nekke longe. *3300

grisly: horrible. the boor: i.e., the Erymanthian boar. hevene: heavens. longe: for a long time.

Was nevere wight, sith that this world bigan,
That slow so manye monstres as dide he.
Thurghout this wyde world his name ran,
What for his strengthe and for his heigh bountee,
And every reawme wente he for to see. 2115
He was so stroong that no man myghte hym
        lette.
At bothe the worldes endes, seith Trophee,
In stede of boundes he a pileer sette.

slow: slew.
name: reputation.
bountee: strength, valor.
reawme: realm.
lette: hinder, prevent.
boundes: boundary markers.

A lemman hadde this noble champioun,
That highte Dianira, fressh as May; *3310
And as thise clerkes maken mencioun,
She hath hym sent a sherte, fressh and gay.
Allas! this sherte, allas and weylaway!
Envenymed was so subtilly withalle,
That er that he had wered it half a day, 2125
It made his flessh al from his bones falle.

lemman: sweetheart.
highte: was called. Dianira: Deianira.
clerkes: learned writers.

wered: worn.

But nathelees somme clerkes hire excusen
By oon that highte Nessus, that it maked.
Be as be may, I wol hire noght accusen;
But on his bak this sherte he wered al
        naked, *3320
Til that his flessh was for the venym blaked.
And whan he saugh noon oother remedye,
In hote coles he hath hymselven raked,
For with no venym deigned hym to dye.

by: on account of.

blaked: blackened.
saugh: saw.
raked: covered by raking.

Thus starf this worthy, myghty Hercules. 2135
Lo, who may truste on Fortune any throwe?
For hym that folweth al this world of prees,
Er he be war, is ofte yleyd ful lowe.
Ful wys is he that kan hymselven knowe!
Beth war, for whan that Fortune list to
        glose, *3330
Thanne waiteth she her man to overthrowe
By swich a wey as he wolde leest suppose.

starf: died.
throwe: space of time.
folweth: pursues; keeps up with.
    prees: difficulty, danger. war:
    aware. yleyd: laid.
beth war: beware.
glose: blandish, flatter, deceive.
waiteth: lies in wait, lurks in ambush.

Nabugodonosor

The myghty trone, the precious tresor,
The glorious ceptre, and roial magestee
That hadde the kyng Nabugodonosor 2145

trone: throne.
ceptre: scepter.

2117. Who **Trophee** was supposed to be is a mystery.
Nabugodonosor. For Nebuchadnezzar and Belshazzar, see Daniel i–v.

With tonge unnethe may discryved bee.　　　　　　unnethe: hardly. discryved: described.
He twies wan Jerusalem the citee;　　　　　　　　wan: won, conquered.
The vessel of the temple he with hym ladde.　　　the vessel: the vessels, the plate.
At Babiloigne was his sovereyn see,　　　　　　　　ladde: carried off. Babiloigne:
In which his glorie and his delit he hadde.　*3340　Babylon. see: royal seat, throne.

The faireste children of the blood roial　　　　　　children: youths.
Of Israel he leet do gelde anon,　　　　　　　　　leet do gelde: caused to be castrated.
And maked ech of hem to been his thral.　　　　thral: slave.
Amonges othere Daniel was oon,　　　　　　　　　othere: others.
That was the wiseste child of everychon;　2155　of everychon: of all.
For he the dremes of the kyng expowned,　　　　expowned: expounded, interpreted.
Whereas in Chaldeye clerk ne was ther noon
That wiste to what fyn his dremes sowned.　　　fyn: end, outcome. sowned: tended.

This proude kyng leet make a statue of gold,
Sixty cubites long and sevene in brede;　*3350　brede: breadth.
To which ymage bothe yong and old
Comanded he to loute, and have in drede,　　　　loute: bow. drede: awe.
Or in a fourneys, ful of flambes rede,
He shal be brent that wolde noght obeye.　　　　brent: burned.
But nevere wolde assente to that dede　2165
Daniel, ne his yonge felawes tweye.

This kyng of kynges proud was and elat;　　　　elat: haughty.
He wende that God, that sit in magestee,　　　　wende: thought. sit: (sitteth) sits.
Ne myghte hym nat bireve of his estat.　　　　　bireve: deprive.
But sodeynly he loste his dignytee,　*3360　dignytee: high office.
And lyk a beest hym semed for to be,
And eet hey as an oxe, and lay theroute　　　　　eet: ate. theroute: out of doors, in the
In reyn; with wilde beestes walked hee,　　　　　open.
Til certein tyme was ycome aboute.

And lik an egles fetheres wax his heres;　2175　wax: grew. heres: hair.
His nayles lyk a briddes clawes weere;　　　　　briddes: bird's.
Til God relessed hym a certeyn yeres,
And yaf hym wit, and thanne with many a teere
He thanked God, and evere his lyf in feere　　　in feere: afraid.
Was he to doon amys or moore trespace;　*3370　to doon: i.e., lest he do.
And til that tyme he leyd was on his beere,　　beere: bier.
He knew that God was ful of myght and grace.

Balthasar

His sone, which that highte Balthasar,
That heeld the regne after his fader day,　　　　regne: kingdom. fader: father's.
He by his fader koude noght be war,　2185　by: from the experience of. be war:
For proud he was of herte and of array;　　　　take warning. array: adornment.

2177. Until God revoked for him a certain number of years of punishment.

And eek an ydolastre was he ay.
His hye estat assured hym in pryde;
But Fortune caste hym doun, and ther he lay,
And sodeynly his regne gan divide.   *3380

A feeste he made unto his lordes alle,
Upon a tyme, and made hem blithe be;
And thanne his officeres gan he calle:
"Gooth, bryngeth forth the vessels," quod he,
"Whiche that my fader in his prosperitee   2195
Out of the temple of Jerusalem birafte;
And to oure hye goddes thanke we
Of honour that oure eldres with us lafte."

Hys wyf, his lordes, and his concubynes
Ay dronken, whil hire appetites laste,   *3390
Out of thise noble vessels sondry wynes.
And on a wal this kyng his eyen caste,
And saugh an hand, armlees, that wroot ful
       faste,
For feere of which he quook and siked soore.
This hand, that Balthasar so soore agaste,   2205
Wroot *Mane, techel, phares,* and namoore.

In all that land magicien was noon
That koude expounde what this lettre mente;
But Daniel expowned it anoon,
And seyde, "Kyng, God to thy fader lente   *3400
Glorie and honour, regne, tresor, rente;
And he was proud, and nothyng God ne dradde,
And therfore God greet wreche upon hym
       sente,
And hym birafte the regne that he hadde.

He was out cast of mannes compaignye;   2215
With asses was his habitacioun,
And eet hey as a beest in weet and drye,
Til that he knew, by grace and by resoun,
That God of hevene hath domynacioun
Over every regne and every creature;   *3410
And thanne hadde God of hym compassioun,
And hym restored his regne and his figure.

Eek thou, that art his sone, art proud also,
And knowest alle thise thynges verraily,
And art rebel to God, and art his fo.   2225
Thou drank eek of his vessels boldely;
Thy wyf eek, and thy wenches, synfully
Dronke of the same vessels sondry wynys;

---

ydolastre: idolater. ay: ever.
assured: confirmed.

gan divide: broke up.

blithe: merry.

birafte: carried off, stole.

of: for. eldres: ancestors. lafte: left.

dronken: drank. laste: lasted.

saugh: saw. wroot: wrote.

quook: quaked. siked: sighed.
agaste: terrified.

expounde: explain, make clear. lettre: writing.

regne: royal power. rente: revenue.
nothyng . . . dradde: feared God not at all. greet: great. wreche: vengeance.
birafte: deprived of. regne: kingdom.

out cast of: cast out from.

eet: ate. weet: rainy weather.

regne: kingdom.

figure: (human) form.

of: from. boldely: blasphemously.

dronke of: drank from. wynys: wines.

And heryest false goddes cursedly;
Therfore to thee yshapen ful greet pyne is. *3420

heryest: (thou) worshipest.
yshapen: decreed. pyne: punishment.

This hand was sent from God that on the wal
Wroot *Mane, techel, phares,* truste me;
Thy regne is doon, thou weyest noght at al.
Dyvyded is thy regne, and it shal be
To Medes and to Perses yeven," quod he. 2235
And thilke same nyght this kyng was slawe,
And Darius occupieth his degree,
Though he therto hadde neither right ne lawe.

regne: reign. weyest noght: art of no
  account.

Perses: Persians.
slawe: slain.
degree: station, position.
therto: in support of that.

Lordynges, ensample heerby may ye take
How that in lordshipe is no sikernesse; *3430
For whan Fortune wol a man forsake,
She bereth awey his regne and his richesse,
And eek his freendes, bothe moore and lesse.
For what man that hath freendes thurgh
      Fortune,
Mishap wol make hem enemys, I gesse; 2245
This proverbe is ful sooth and ful commune.

sikernesse: security, certainty.

regne: kingdom.

what: whatever.

mishap: misfortune.
commune: widely known.

Cenobia

Cenobia, of Palymerie queene,
As writen Persiens of hir noblesse,
So worthy was in armes and so keene,
That no wight passed hire in hardynesse, *3440
Ne in lynage, ne in oother gentillesse.
Of kynges blood of Perce is she descended.
I seye nat that she hadde moost fairnesse,
But of hir shap she myghte nat been amended.

writen: wrote.

passed: surpassed. hardynesse: valor.
gentillesse: nobility.
Perce: Persia.

shap: form, figure. amended: sur-
  passed.

From hire childhede I fynde that she fledde 2255
Office of wommen, and to wode she wente,
And many a wilde hertes blood she shedde
With arwes brode that she to hem sente.
She was so swift that she anon hem hente;
And whan that she was elder, she wolde
      kille *3450
Leouns, leopardes, and beres al torente,
And in hir armes weelde hem at hir wille.

office: function; duty. wode: wood.
hertes: hart's.

hente: caught.
elder: older.

torente: rend to pieces.
weelde: manage, handle.

She dorste wilde beestes dennes seke,
And rennen in the montaynes al the nyght,
And slepen under the bussh, and she koude
      eke 2265

rennen: run.
the bussh: the undergrowth.

Cenobia. Chaucer learned of Zenobia of Palmyra from Boccaccio's *Famous Women* (*De Claris Mulieribus*) xcviii.

Wrastlen, by verray force and verray myght,
With any yong man, were he never so wight.
Ther myghte no thyng in hir armes stonde.
She kepte hir maydenhod from every wight;
To no man deigned hire for to be bonde.   *3460

> verray: sheer.
> wight: powerful; agile.
> thyng: i.e., man or beast. in: grasped
> in. stonde: remain standing. wight:
> person. deigned hire: she deigned.
> bonde: married.

But atte laste hir freendes han hire maried
To Odenake, a prynce of that contree,
Al were it so that she hem longe taried.
And ye shal understande how that he
Hadde swiche fantasies as hadde she.   2275
But nathelees, whan they were knyt in-feere,
They lyved in joye and in felicitee;
For ech of hem hadde oother lief and deere.

> hem taried: kept them waiting.
> fantasies: inclinations.
> knyt: joined. in-feere: together.
> hadde oother: held the other. lief: be-
> loved.

Save o thyng, that she wolde nevere assente,
By no wey, that he sholde by hire lye   *3470
But ones, for it was hir pleyn entente
To have a child, the world to multiplye;
And also soone as that she myghte espye
That she was nat with childe with that dede,
Thanne wolde she suffre hym doon his
       fantasye   2285
Eft-soone, and nat but oones, out of drede.

> o: one.
> by no wey: by no means, not at all.
> ones: once. pleyn: candid; straight-
> forward.
> also: as. espye: discover.
> eft-soone: again. out of drede: with-
> out doubt.

And if she were with childe at thilke cast,
Namoore sholde he pleyen thilke game
Til fully fourty wikes weren past;
Thanne wolde she ones suffre hym do the
       same.   *3480
Al were this Odenake wilde or tame,
He gat namoore of hire, for thus she seyde,
It was to wyves lecherie and shame,
In oother cas, if that men with hem pleyde.

> at thilke cast: on that occasion.
> wilde: passionate.
> in oother cas: otherwise.

Two sones by this Odenake hadde she,   2295
The whiche she kepte in vertu and lettrure;
But now unto oure tale turne we.
I seye, so worshipful a creature,
And wys therwith, and large with mesure,
So penyble in the werre, and curteis eke,   *3490
Ne moore labour myghte in werre endure,
Was noon, though al this world men sholde seke.

> kepte: brought up. lettrure: learning.
> large: generous. mesure: moderation.
> penyble: hardworking.

2272. Odenake: Odenathus, the ruler of Palmyra.

2289. All MSS except two, which are very late, read **dayes** instead of **wikes**, which Boccaccio's text indicates to be the correct reading. Manly points out that " 'Forty weeks' is the common term for the period of gestation" (IV, 232, 510).

Hir riche array ne myghte nat be told,
As wel in vessel as in hire clothyng.   vessel: vessels, plate.
She was al clad in perree and in gold,   2305   perree: precious stones; jewelry.
And eek she lafte noght, for noon huntyng,   lafte: neglected.
To have of sondry tonges ful knowyng,   tonges: languages. knowyng: knowl-
Whan that she leyser hadde; and for to entende   edge. entende: endeavor.
To lerne bookes was al hir likyng,   likyng: delight.
How she in vertu myghte hir lyf dispende.   *3500 dispende: spend.

And shortly of this storie for to trete,
So doughty was hir housbonde and eek she,
That they conquered manye regnes grete
In the orient, with many a fair citee
Appertenant unto the magestee   2315   appertenant: belonging.
Of Rome, and with strong hond held hem ful
          faste,
Ne nevere myghte hir foomen doon hem flee,   doon: cause.
Ay whil that Odenakes dayes laste.   laste: lasted.

Hir batailles, whoso list hem for to rede,
Agayn Sapor the kyng and othere mo,   *3510
And how that al this proces fil in dede   proces: succession of events. fil: be-
Why she conquered, and what title had therto,   fell. why: because of which. therto:
And after, of hir meschief and hire wo,   i.e., to her conquests. meschief:
How that she was biseged and ytake,—   misfortune. ytake: taken, captured.
Lat hym unto my maister Petrak go,   2325
That writ ynough of this, I undertake.   writ: wrote.

Whan Odenake was deed, she myghtily   deed: dead.
The regnes heeld, and with hire propre hond   propre: own.
Agayn hir foos she faught so cruelly   agayn: against.
That ther nas kyng ne prynce in al that lond *3520
That he nas glad, if he that grace fond,
That she ne wolde upon his lond werreye.   werreye: make war.
With hire they maden alliance by bond
To been in pees, and lete hire ride and pleye.

The Emperour of Rome, Claudius   2335
Ne hym bifore, the Romayn Galien,
Ne dorste nevere been so corageus,
Ne noon Ermyn, ne noon Egipcien,   Ermyn: Armenian.

2306–10. Zenobia knew several languages and studied Greek and Roman literature under the
philosopher Longinus.
2320. **Sapor:** Shapur I, King of Persia.
2325. **Petrak:** Chaucer's source was Boccaccio rather than Petrarch.
2335, 2336, 2351: As Emperor of Rome, Claudius Gothicus (268–70) was preceded by Gallienus
(253–68) and followed by Aurelianus (270–75).

Ne Surrien, ne noon Arabyen,   **Surrien:** Syrian.
Withinne the feeld that dorste with hire   **feeld:** field of battle.
     fighte,   *3530
Lest that she wolde hem with hir handes slen,   **slen:** slay.
Or with hir meynee putten hem to flighte.   **meynee:** army.

In kynges habit wente hir sones two,   **habit:** raiment.
As heires of hir fadres regnes alle,
And Hermanno and Thymalao   2345
Hir names were, as Persiens hem calle.
But ay Fortune hath, in hire hony, galle;   **galle:** a bitter taste.
This myghty queene may no while endure.
Fortune out of hir regne made hire falle   **regne:** sovereignty.
To wrecchednesse and to mysaventure.   *3540 **mysaventure:** misfortune.

Aurelian, whan that the governaunce
Of Rome cam into his handes tweye,
He shoop upon this queene to doon   **shoop:** prepared.
     vengeaunce.
And with his legions he took his weye
Toward Cenobie, and, shortly for to seye,   2355
He made hire flee, and atte laste hire hente,   **hente:** captured.
And fettred hire, and eek hire children tweye,
And wan the land, and hoom to Rome he wente.   **wan:** won. **land:** country.

Amonges othere thynges that he wan,
Hir chaar, that was with gold wroght and   **chaar:** chariot.
     perree,   *3550 **perree:** precious stones; jewelry.
This grete Romayn, this Aurelian,
Hath with hym lad, for that men sholde it see.   **lad:** led. **for that:** in order that.
Biforen his triumphe walketh she,
With gilte cheynes on hire nekke hangynge.   **gilte:** gilded.
Corowned was she, as after hir degree,   2365 **as after hir degree:** as befitted her
And ful of perree charged hir clothynge.   station. **charged:** loaded.

Allas, Fortune! she that whilom was
Dredeful to kynges and to emperoures,
Now gaureth al the peple on hire, allas!   **gaureth:** stare.
And she that helmed was in starke   **helmed was:** wore a helmet. **starke:**
     stoures,   *3560 fierce. **stoures:** battles.
And wan by force townes stronge and toures,
Shal on hir heed now were a vitremyte;   **were:** wear. **vitremyte:** a headdress of
And she that bar the ceptre ful of floures   linen or light canvas. **ceptre:** scep-
Shal bere a distaf, hire cost for to quyte.   ter. **hire . . . quyte:** to pay her
    keep.

2373. **ful of floures:** ? ornamented with golden flowers (Baugh).

De Petro Rege Ispannie

O noble, O worthy Petro, glorie of
        Spayne,   2375
Whom Fortune heeld so heighe in magestee,
Wel oghten men thy pitous deeth complayne!
Out of thy land thy brother made thee flee,
And after, at a seege, by subtiltee,
Thou were bitraysed and lad unto his tente, *3570   bitraysed: deceived, tricked. **lad:** led.
Where as he with his owene hand slow thee,   slow: slew.
Succedynge in thy regne and in thy rente.   rente: revenue.

The feeld of snow, with th'egle of blak therinne,
Caught with the lymerod coloured as the gleede,   gleede: burning coal.
He brew this cursednesse and al this synne.   2385 brew: brewed.
The wikked nest was werker of this nede.   nede: violence.
Noght Charles Olyver, that took ay heede
Of trouthe and honour, but of Armorike
Genylon-Olyver, corrupt for meede,   corrupt: corrupted. **for meede:** through
Broghte this worthy kyng in swich a brike. *3580   bribery. **brike:** trap.

De Petro Rege de Cipro

O worthy Petro, kyng of Cipre, also,
That Alisandre wan by heigh maistrie,   maistrie: victory.
Ful many an hethen wroghtestow ful wo,   hethen: heathen.
Of which thyne owene liges hadde envie,   liges: lieges, vassals. **envie:** malice;
And for no thyng but for thy chivalrie   2395 hatred.
They in thy bed han slayn thee by the morwe.   by the morwe: at dawn.
Thus kan Fortune hir wheel governe and gye,   gye: guide.
And out of joye brynge men to sorwe.

De Barnabo de Lumbardia

Of Melan grete Barnabo Viscounte,
God of delit, and scourge of Lumbardye,   *3590

De Petro Rege Ispannie. King Pedro of Castile and Leon was assassinated in 1369 by his illegitimate half-brother, Don Enrique of Trastamare, who was aided by Bertrand du Guesclin, Oliver de Mauny, and others. Chaucer presumably heard about the murder from some such friend as Sir Guichard d'Angle, who was a partisan of Pedro. (Pedro's daughter, Costanza of Castile, in 1371 became the second duchess of John of Gaunt.) Lines 2383–84 allude to the heraldic arms of Bertrand du Guesclin; lines 2386–89, to Oliver de Mauny (**wikked nest** = *mau ni*).

2384. **lymerod:** a rod smeared with birdlime for catching birds.

2387. **Charles Olyver:** Charlemagne's Oliver, faithful friend of Roland.

2388. **Armorike:** Armorica (coastal Brittany and Normandy), the home of Oliver de Mauny.

2389. **Genylon-Olyver:** i.e., a traitor like Ganilon, who betrayed Roland.

De Petro Rege de Cipro. Pierre de Lusignan, King of Cyprus, had visited Edward III in 1363 to obtain support for his crusade (1365) against Alexandria (see General Prologue, note for lines 56–66); the account of his death (1369) Chaucer evidently based on Guillaume de Machaut's *La Prise d'Alexandrie.*

De Barnabo de Lumbardia. Chaucer had known Bernabò Visconti personally, for in 1378 he was sent by Richard II as emissary to this Lord of Milan. Chaucer shows knowledge of two later events, though not of their circumstances: in 1380 Bernabò's nephew, Gian Galeazzo Visconti, married (as his second wife) Caterina, daughter of Bernabò; and in 1385 Gian Galeazzo had Bernabò arrested and put in prison, where he died, presumably by poison.

Why sholde I nat thyn infortune acounte,   acounte: recount, relate.
Sith in estat thow clombe were so hye?
Thy brother sone, that was thy double allye,   brother: brother's. allye: relative.
For he thy nevew was, and sone-in-lawe,
Withinne his prisoun made thee to dye,—   2405
But why, ne how, noot I that thou were slawe.   slawe: slain.

De Hugelino Comite de Pize

Of the Erl Hugelyn of Pize the langour   langour: woeful plight.
Ther may no tonge telle for pitee.
But litel out of Pize stant a tour,   stant: (standeth) stands.   tour: tower.
In which tour in prisoun put was he,   *3600
And with hym been his litel children thre;
The eldest scarsly fyve yeer was of age.
Allas, Fortune! it was greet crueltee
Swiche briddes for to putte in swich a cage!   briddes: birds.

Dampned was he to dyen in that prisoun,   2415 dampned: condemned.
For Roger, which that bisshop was of Pize,
Hadde on hym maad a fals suggestioun,   suggestioun: charge, accusation.
Thurgh which the peple gan upon hym rise,   upon: against.
And putten hym to prisoun, in swich wise
As ye han herd, and mete and drynke he   mete: food.
       hadde   *3610
So smal, that wel unnethe it may suffise,   unnethe: scarcely.
And therwithal it was ful povre and badde.

And on a day bifil that in that hour
Whan that his mete wont was to be broght,
The gayler shette the dores of the tour.   2425 gayler: jailer.
He herde it wel, but he spak right noght,   right noght: not at all.
And in his herte anon ther fil a thoght   fil: fell, came.
That they for hunger wolde doon hym dyen.   doon: make.
"Allas!" quod he, "allas, that I was wroght!"
Therwith the teeris fillen from his eyen.   *3620 fillen: fell.

His yonge sone, that thre yeer was of age,
Unto hym seyde, "Fader, why do ye wepe?
Whanne wol the gayler bryngen oure potage?   potage: thick soup or stew.
Is ther no morsel breed that ye do kepe?   morsel breed: bite of bread.
I am so hungry that I may nat slepe.   2435
Now wolde God that I myghte slepen evere!
Thanne sholde nat hunger in my wombe crepe;   wombe: stomach.
Ther is no thyng, but breed, that me were levere."   me were levere: I'd rather have.

De Hugelino Comite de Pize. The stanzas on Count Ugolino della Gheradesca (c. 1230–1289) are based primarily on Dante's *Inferno,* xxxiii; but the variations suggest that Chaucer either wrote from memory or else had additional information.
2416. **Roger:** Ruggieri degli Ubaldini, Archbishop of Pisa (1278–1295).

Thus day by day this child bigan to crye,
Til in his fadres barm adoun it lay,   *3630   barm: lap.
And seyde, "Farewel, fader, I moot dye!"   moot: must.
And kiste his fader, and deyde the same day.
And whan the woful fader deed it say,   deed: dead. say: saw.
For wo his armes two he gan to byte,
And seyde, "Allas, Fortune, and weylaway!   2445
Thy false wheel my wo al may I wyte."   my . . . wyte: may I blame you for all
                                       my woe.

His children wende that it for hunger was
That he his armes gnow, and nat for wo,   gnow: gnawed.
And seyde, "Fader, do nat so, allas!
But rather ete the flessh upon us two.   *3640
Oure flessh thou yaf us, take oure flessh us fro,
And ete ynogh,"—right thus they to hym seyde,
And after that, withinne a day or two,
They leyde hem in his lappe adoun and deyde.

Hymself, despeired, eek for hunger starf;   2455   starf: died.
Thus ended is this myghty Erl of Pize.
From heigh estat Fortune awey hym carf.   carf: carved, cut.
Of this tragedie it oghte ynough suffise;
Whoso wol heere it in a lenger wise,
Redeth the grete poete of Ytaille   *3650   Ytaille: Italy.
That highte Dant, for he kan al devyse
Fro point to point, nat o word wol he faille.   faille: omit.

Nero

Although that Nero were as vicius
As any feend that lith ful lowe adoun,   lith: (lieth) lies.
Yet he, as telleth us Swetonius,   2465
This wyde world hadde in subjeccioun,
Bothe est and west, [south], and septemtrioun.   septemtrioun: north.
Of rubies, saphires, and of perles white   of: with.
Were alle his clothes brouded up and doun;   brouded: ornamented.
For he in gemmes greetly gan delite.   *3660

Moore delicat, moore pompous of array,   delicat: fond of luxury, sensual.
Moore proud was nevere emperour than he;
That ilke clooth that he hadde wered o day,   clooth: garment, robe.
After that tyme he nolde it nevere see.
Nettes of gold threed hadde he greet plentee   2475
To fisshe in Tybre, whan hym liste pleye.

Nero. Most of Chaucer's information about the Emperor Nero (A.D. 54–68) comes from Jean de Meun's passage on Fortune in *Le Roman de la Rose* (6183–6488).

2465. Swetonius: Book I of *The Lives of the Twelve Caesars* by Suetonius was an ultimate source for both Jean de Meun and Chaucer.

2467. [south] is Skeat's emendation. Hengwrt, Ellesmere, and related MSS read **north;** the rest omit.

His lustes were al lawe in his decree,   lustes: desires. **decree: code.**
For Fortune as his freend hym wolde obeye.

He Rome brende for his delicacie;   brende: burned. **delicacie:** pleasure,
The senatours he slow upon a day   *3670   gratification. **slow:** slew.
To heere how men wolde wepe and crye;
And slow his brother, and by his suster lay.
His moder made he in pitous array,   made in pitous array: brought to a
For he hire wombe slitte to biholde   pitiful state.
Where he conceyved was; so weilaway!   2485
That he so litel of his moder tolde.   tolde of: thought of, set store by.

No teere out of his eyen for that sighte
Ne cam, but seyde, "A fair womman was she!"   seyde: (he) said.
Greet wonder is how that he koude or myghte
Be domesman of hire dede beautee.   *3680   domesman: judge. **dede:** dead.
The wyn to bryngen hym comanded he,   comanded: commanded (a servant).
And drank anon,—noon oother wo he made.
Whan myght is joyned unto crueltee,
Allas, to depe wol the venym wade!   to: too. **wade:** penetrate.

In yowthe a maister hadde this emperour   2495   maister: i.e., Seneca.
To teche hym letterure and curteisye,   letterure: knowledge of books.
For of moralitee he was the flour,   flour: flower.
As in his tyme, but if bookes lye;
And whil this maister hadde of hym maistrye,
He maked hym so konnyng and so souple   *3690   konnyng: refined. **souple:** compliant.
That longe tyme it was er tirannye
Or any vice dorste on hym uncouple.   uncouple: let loose (as dogs for the
       chase).

This Seneca, of which that I devyse,
By cause Nero hadde of hym swich drede,
For he fro vices wolde hym ay chastise   2505   for.: because. **chastise fro:** warn
Discreetly, as by word and nat by dede,—   against.
"Sire," wolde he seyn, "an emperour moot nede   moot: must.
Be vertuous and hate tirannye—"
For which he in a bath made hym to blede   blede.: bleed.
On bothe his armes, til he moste dye.   *3700   moste: must.

This Nero hadde eek of acustumaunce   hadde of acustumaunce: was accus-
In youthe agayns his maister for to rise,   tomed. **agayns:** in the presence of.
Which afterward hym thoughte a greet
         grevaunce;
Therefore he made hym dyen in this wise.
But nathelees this Seneca the wise   2515
Chees in a bath to dye in this manere   chees: chose.
Rather than han another tormentise;   tormentise: torment, torture.
And thus hath Nero slayn his maister deere.

Now fil it so that Fortune liste no lenger
The hye pryde of Nero to cherice,   *3710
For though that he was strong, yet was she
    strenger.
She thoughte thus, "By God! I am to nyce
To sette a man that is fulfild of vice
In heigh degree, and emperour hym calle.
By God! out of his sete I wol hym trice;   2525
Whan he leest weneth, sonnest shal he falle."

The peple roos upon hym on a nyght
For his defaute, and whan he it espied,
Out of his dores anon he hath hym dight
Allone, and ther he wende han been allied,   *3720
He knokked faste, and ay the moore he cried,
The fastere shette they the dores alle.
Tho wiste he wel, he hadde himself mysgyed,
And wente his wey; no lenger dorste he calle.

The peple cried and rombled up and doun,   2535
That with his erys herde he how they seyde,
"Where is this false tiraunt, this Neroun?"
For fere almoost out of his wit he breyde,
And to his goddes pitously he preyde
For socour, but it myghte nat bityde.   *3730
For drede of this, hym thoughte that he deyde,
And ran into a gardyn hym to hyde.

And in this gardyn foond he cherles tweye
That seten by a fyr greet and reed.
And to thise cherles two he gan to preye   2545
To sleen hym, and to girden of his heed,
That to his body, whan that he were deed,
Were no despit ydoon for his defame.
Hymself he slow, he koude no bettre reed,
Of which Fortune lough, and hadde a
    game.   *3740

De Oloferno

   Was nevere capitayn under a kyng
That regnes mo putte in subjeccioun,
Ne strenger was in feeld of alle thyng,
As in his tyme, ne gretter of renoun,
Ne moore pompous in heigh presumpcioun   2555
Than Oloferne, which Fortune ay kiste

Glosses (right column):

fil: befell, happened.
cherice: cherish, favor.

strenger: stronger.

to nyce: too foolish.
fulfild: full.

sete: royal seat, throne. **trice:** pluck, snatch. **weneth:** expects. **sonnest:** soonest.

roos: rose.
defaute: wickedness.
hym dight: betaken himself, hastened.
wende han been allied: thought he had allies. **faste:** hard, vigorously.
shette: shut.
tho: then. **himself mysgyed:** misbehaved.

rombled: rumbled, made a tumult.
erys: ears.

breyde: started.

bityde: come.
deyde: would have died.

seten: sat. **greet:** great. **reed:** red.

sleen: slay. **girden of:** strike off.

despit: outrage. **ydoon:** done. **defame:** dishonor. **slow:** slew. **koude:** knew. **reed:** plan. **lough:** laughed. **hadde a game:** was amused, had sport.

regnes mo: more kingdoms.

De Oloferno. For Holofernes see the apocryphal Book of Judith.
2553. Nor was stronger in every respect on the field of battle.

So likerously, and ladde hym up and doun,   likerously: wantonly. **ladde**: led.
Til that his heed was of, er that he wiste.   of: off.

Nat oonly that this world hadde hym in awe
For lesynge of richesse or libertee,   *3750   for: for fear of. **lesynge**: losing.
But he made every man reneye his lawe.   reneye: renounce. **lawe**: faith, religion.
"Nabugodonosor was god," seyde he;
"Noon oother god sholde adoured be."
Agayns his heste no wight dorst trespace,   heste: behest; command.
Save in Bethulia, a strong citee,   2565
Where Eliachim a preest was of that place.

But tak kepe of the deth of Oloferne:
Amydde his hoost he dronke lay a-nyght,   hoost: army.
Withinne his tente, large as is a berne,   berne: barn.
And yet, for al his pompe and al his
      myght,   *3760
Judith, a womman, as he lay upright   upright: flat on his back, his face up-
Slepynge, his heed of smoot, and from his tente   wards. **of smoot**: smote off.
Ful pryvely she stal from every wight,   stal: stole.
And with his heed unto hir toun she wente.   heed: head.

De Rege Anthiocho illustri

What nedeth it of kyng Anthiochus   2575
To telle his hye roial magestee,
His hye pride, his werkes venymus?   werkes: deeds.
For swich another was ther noon as he.   noon: none.
Rede which that he was, in Machabee,   which: what kind (of man).
And rede the proude wordes that he seyde,   *3770
And why he fil fro heigh prosperitee,   fil: fell.
And in an hill how wrecchedly he deyde.   in: on. **deyde**: died.

Fortune hym hadde enhaunced so in pride   enhaunced: exalted.
That verraily he wende he myghte attayne   attayne unto: reach.
Unto the sterres upon every syde,   2585
And in balance weyen ech montayne,   in balance: in scales. **weyen**: weigh.
And alle the floodes of the see restrayne.
And Goddes peple hadde he moost in hate;   hadde . . . hate: he hated most.
Hem wolde he sleen in torment and in payne,   sleen: slay.
Wenynge that God ne myghte his pride   wenynge: believing.
      abate.   *3780   abate: destroy.

And for that Nichanore and Thymothee   for that: because.
With Jewes weren venquysshed myghtily,   with: by.
Unto the Jewes swich an hate hadde he
That he bad greithe his chaar ful hastily,   greithe: prepare. **chaar**: chariot.
And swoor, and seyde ful despitously   2595   despitously: angrily.

2575. The story of Antiochus IV, King of Syria (175–163 B.C.), is found in II Maccabees ix.

Unto Jerusalem he wolde eftsoone,
To wreken his ire on it ful cruelly;
But of his purpos he was let ful soone.

wolde: would go. eftsoone: immediately. wreken: wreak.

let: prevented.

God for his manace hym so soore smoot
With invisible wounde, ay incurable,   *3790
That in his guttes carf it so and boot
That his peynes weren importable.
And certeinly the wreche was resonable,
For many a mannes guttes dide he peyne.
But from his purpos cursed and dampnable,   2605
For al his smert, he wolde hym nat restreyne,

manace: threat. smoot: smote.

carf: cut. boot: bit.
importable: unbearable.
wreche: vengeance, retribution.
dide peyne: tortured.

smert: pain.

But bad anon apparaillen his hoost;
And sodeynly, er he was of it war,
God daunted al his pride and al his boost.
For he so soore fil out of his char   *3800
That it his limes and his skyn totar,
So that he neyther myghte go ne ryde,
But in a chayer men aboute hym bar,
Al forbrused, bothe bak and syde.

apparaillen: prepare. hoost: army.

daunted: laid low. boost: arrogance.
soore: violently. fil: fell. char: chariot.
limes: limbs. totar: tore to pieces.
go: walk.
chayer: sedan chair; litter. aboute hym
   bar: bore him about. forbrused:
   severely bruised.

The wreche of God hym smoot so cruelly   2615
That thurgh his body wikked wormes crepte,
And therwithal he stank so horribly
That noon of al his meynee that hym kepte,
Wheither so he wook, or ellis slepte,
Ne myghte noght the stynk of hym endure.   *3810
In this meschief he wayled and eek wepte,
And knew God lord of every creature.

wreche: vengeance. smoot: smote.
wikked: foul.

meynee: attendants. kepte: took care
   of. wook: was awake.

noght: not.
meschief: evil plight.
knew: acknowledged.

To al his hoost and to hymself also
Ful wlatsom was the stynk of his careyne;
No man ne myghte hym bere to ne fro.   2625
And in this stynk and this horrible peyne,
He starf ful wrecchedly in a monteyne.
Thus hath this robbour and this homycide,
That many a man made to wepe and pleyne,
Swich gerdoun as bilongeth unto pryde.   *3820

wlatsom: loathsome. careyne: carcass.

starf: died. in: on. monteyne: mountain.

pleyne: bewail.
gerdoun: reward.

De Alexandro

The storie of Alisaundre is so commune
That every wight that hath discrecioun
Hath herd somwhat or al of his fortune.
This wyde world, as in conclusioun,

commune: wide spread.
hath discrecioun: is grown up.

as in conclusion: finally.

De Alexandro. This treatment of Alexander the Great (356–323 B.C.) is so generalized and the medieval accounts are so many and **so commune** (l. 2631) that Chaucer seems to have written out of his head.

He wan by strengthe, or for his hye renoun   2635   wan: won.
They were glad for pees unto hym sende.
The pride of man and beest he leyde adoun,
Wherso he cam, unto the worldes ende.

Comparisoun myghte nevere yet ben
     maked
Bitwixe hym and another conquerour,   *3830
For al this world for drede of hym hath quaked,
He of knyghthod and of fredom flour;   fredom: nobility; generosity. flour:
Fortune hym made the heir of hire honour.   flower.
Save wyn and wommen, no thing myghte
     aswage   aswage: temper, soften.
His hye entente in armes and labour,   2645   entente: desire. labour: exertion.
So was he ful of leonyn corage.   corage: heart; courage.

What pris were it to hym, though I yow tolde   pris: praise.
Of Darius, and an hundred thousand mo
Of kynges, princes, dukes, erles bolde
Whiche he conquered, and broghte hem into
     wo?   *3840
I seye, as fer as man may ride or go,   go: walk.
The world was his,—what sholde I moore devyse? what: why. devyse: say.
For though I write or tolde yow everemo   write: should write.
Of his knyghthod, it myghte nat suffise.

Twelf yeer he regned, as seith Machabee.   2655   Machabee: see I Maccabees i.1–8.
Philippes sone of Macidoyne he was,   Philippes sone of Macidoyne: son of
That first was kyng in Grece the contree.   Philip of Macedonia.
O worthy, gentil Alisandre, allas,   gentil: noble.
That evere sholde fallen swich a cas!   fallen: befall. cas: misfortune.
Empoysoned of thyn owene folk thou   of: by.
     weere;   *3850   weere: were.
Thy sys Fortune hath turned into aas,
And for thee ne weep she never a teere.   weep: wept.

Who shal me yeve teeris to compleyne
The deeth of gentillesse and of franchise,   gentillesse: nobility of character. fran-
That al the world weelded in his demeyne,   2665   chise: magnanimity. weelded: held.
And yet hym thoughte it myghte nat suffise?   demeyne: rule.
So ful was his corage of heigh emprise.   emprise: chivalric ideals.
Allas! who shal me helpe to endite   endite: indict.
False Fortune, and poyson to despise,   despise: disparage, revile.
The whiche two of al this wo I wyte?   *3860   of: for. wyte: blame.

2636. for . . . sende: to send envoys unto him to request (or sue for) peace.
2661. Fortune has turned your sys (highest throw of a die) into aas (lowest); see Man of Law's Prologue, lines 124–25 and note.

De Julio Cesare

By wisdom, manhede, and by greet labour,
From humble bed to roial magestee | humble bed: lowly birth.
Up roos he Julius, the conquerour, | roos: rose.
That wan al th'occident by land and see, | wan: won.
By strengthe of hand, or elles by tretee, | 2675
And unto Rome made hem tributarie;
And sithe of Rome the emperour was he, | sithe: afterwards.
Til that Fortune weex his adversarie. | weex: grew, became.

O myghty Cesar, that in Thessalie
Agayn Pompeus, fader thyn in lawe, | *3870 — fader . . . lawe: thy father-in-law.
That of the orient hadde al the chivalrie | chivalrie: knights; armies.
As fer as that the day bigynneth dawe, | dawe: to dawn.
Thou thurgh thy knyghthod hast hem take and slawe, | knyghthod: host of knights. slawe: slain.
Save fewe folk that with Pompeus fledde,
Thurgh which thou puttest al th'orient in awe. | 2685
Thanke Fortune, that so wel thee spedde! | spedde: assisted.

But now a litel while I wol biwaille
This Pompeus, this noble governour | governour: ruler.
Of Rome, which that fleigh at this bataille. | fleigh: fled.
I seye, oon of his men, a fals traitour, | *3880
His heed of smoot, to wynnen hym favour | heed: head. of smoot: smote off. hym: for himself.
Of Julius, and hym the heed he broghte.
Allas, Pompeye, of th'orient conquerour,
That Fortune unto swich a fyn thee broghte! | fyn: end.

To Rome agayn repaireth Julius | 2695
With his triumphe, lauriat ful hye; | lauriat: crowned with laurel.
But on a tyme Brutus Cassius,
That evere hadde of his hye estaat envye,
Ful prively hath maad conspiracye
Agayns this Julius in subtil wise, | *3890
And caste the place in which he sholde dye | caste: decided upon.
With boydekyns, as I shal yow devyse. | boydekyns: daggers.

This Julius to the Capitolie wente
Upon a day, as he was wont to goon,

De Julio Cesare. This account of Julius Caesar (c. 100–44 B.C.) is full of generalities widely current in the Middle Ages; certain passages come ultimately from such writers as Lucan, Suetonius, and Valerius Maximus (see lines 2719–20).

2680. Pompey the Great was actually Caesar's son-in-law (Pompeius Rufus was the father-in-law).

2697. Chaucer was not the first writer to make one person out of Brutus and Cassius.

2703. Capitolie: Capitol, the Temple of Jupiter on the Tarpeian (later Capitoline) Hill of Rome, where some medieval writers placed the assassination of Caesar; this actually took place in the Curia of Pompey in the Campus Martius.

And in the Capitolie anon hym hente   2705
This false Brutus and his othere foon,   foon: foes.
And stiked hym with boydekyns anoon   stiked: stabbed.
With many a wounde, and thus they lete hym
       lye;
But nevere gronte he at no strook but oon,   gronte: groaned.
Or elles at two, but if his storie lye.   *3900

So manly was this Julius of herte,
And so wel lovede estatly honestee,   estatly: stately. honestee: decorum.
That though his deedly woundes soore smerte,   deedly: mortal. soore: sorely. smerte:
His mantel over his hipes caste he,   smarted.
For no man sholde seen his privetee;   2715   for: so that. privetee: private parts.
And as he lay a-dyyng in a traunce,
And wiste verraily that deed was he,   deed was: would die.
Of honestee yet hadde he remembraunce.

Lucan, to thee this storie I recomende,   recomende: submit.
And to Swetoun, and to Valerius also,   *3910
That of this storie writen word and ende,   writen: wrote. word: (ord) beginning.
How that to thise grete conqueroures two
Fortune was first freend, and sitthe foo.   sitthe: afterwards.
No man ne truste upon hire favour longe,   no man ne truste upon: let no man
But have hire in awayt for everemoo;   2725   trust in. in awayt: under
Witnesse on alle thise conqueroures stronge.   surveillance.

Cresus

This riche Cresus, whilom kyng of Lyde,   whilom: at one time.
Of which Cresus Cirus soore hym dradde,   hym dradde: was afraid.
Yet was he caught amyddes al his pryde,   amyddes: amidst, in the midst of.
And to be brent men to the fyr hym ladde.   *3920   brent: burned. ladde: led.
But swich a reyn doun fro the welkne shadde   welkne: welkin, sky. shadde: poured.
That slow the fyr, and made hym to escape;   slow: slew, quenched.
But to be war no grace yet he hadde,
Til Fortune on the galwes made hym gape.   galwes: gallows.

Whanne he escaped was, he kan nat stente   2735   stente: forbear.
For to bigynne a newe werre agayn.
He wende wel, for that Fortune hym sente   wende: surmised. for that: because.
Swich hap that he escaped thurgh the rayn,   hap: good luck. thurgh: by means of.
That of his foos he myghte nat be slayn;   of: by.
And eek a sweven upon a nyght he mette,   *3930   sweven: dream. mette: dreamed.
Of which he was so proud and eek so fayn   proud: pleased. fayn: joyful.
That in vengeance he al his herte sette.   in: upon.

Cresus. Most of Chaucer's information about Croesus, last King of Lydia (560–546 B.C.), comes from Jean de Meun's passage on Fortune in *Le Roman de la Rose* (6489–6634).
2728. Cirus: Cyrus the Great, King of Persia, who conquered Croesus.
2733. But still he did not have the fortune to be cautious.

Upon a tree he was, as that hym thoughte,   hym thoughte: it seemed to him.
Ther Juppiter hym wessh, bothe bak and syde,   ther: where. wessh: washed.
And Phebus eek a fair towaille hym broughte 2745   towaille: towel.
To drye hym with; and therfore wax his pryde,   wax: increased.
And to his doghter, that stood hym bisyde,
Which that he knew in heigh sentence habounde,   sentence: insight. habounde:
He bad hire telle hym what it signyfyde,   abounded.
And she his dreem bigan right thus
       expounde: *3940

"The tree," quod she, "the galwes is to meene,   is to meene: signifies.
And Juppiter bitokneth snow and reyn,
And Phebus, with his towaille so clene,
Tho been the sonne stremes for to seyn.   sonne: sun's. stremes: beams.
Thou shalt anhanged be, fader, certeyn;   2755 anhanged: hanged.
Reyn shal thee wasshe, and sonne shal thee
       drye."
Thus warned hym ful plat and ful pleyn   plat: flatly, bluntly.
His doghter, which that called was Phanye.   Phanye: Phania.

Anhanged was Cresus, the proude kyng;
His roial trone myghte hym nat availle.   *3950 trone: throne.
Tragediës noon oother maner thyng
Ne kan in syngyng crye ne biwaille   crye: lament.
But that Fortune alwey wole assaille
With unwar strook the regnes that been proude;   unwar: unexpected. regnes: reigns.
For whan men trusteth hire, thanne wol she
       faille,   2765
And covere hire brighte face with a clowde.

Explicit Tragedia.

*Heere stynteth the
Knyght the Monk
of his tale.*

*The prologe of the
Nonnes Preestes tale.*

"Ho!" quod the Knyght, "good sire, namoore
    of this!
That ye han seyd is right ynough, ywis,
And muchel moore; for litel hevynesse
Is right ynough to muche folk, I gesse.   *3960

I seye for me, it is a greet disese, disese: annoyance.
Whereas men han been in greet welthe and ese,
To heeren of hire sodeyn fal, allas!
And the contrarie is joye and greet solas, solas: delight.
As whan a man hath been in povre estaat, 2775
And clymbeth up and wexeth fortunat, wexeth: becomes.
And there abideth in prosperitee.
Swich thyng is gladsom, as it thynketh me,
And of swich thyng were goodly for to telle."
"Ye," quod oure Hooste, "by Seint Poules
        belle! *3970
Ye seye right sooth; this Monk he clappeth clappeth: rings, chatters.
        loude.
He spak how Fortune covered with a cloude
I noot nevere what; and also of a tragedie
Right now ye herde, and, pardee, no remedie
It is for to biwaille ne compleyne 2785
That that is doon, and als it is a peyne, that that: that which.
As ye han seyd, to heere of hevynesse.
    Sire Monk, namoore of this, so God yow
        blesse!
Youre tale anoyeth al this compaignye.
Swich talkyng is nat worth a boterflye, *3980
For therinne is ther no desport ne game. desport: sport.
Wherfore, sire Monk, daun Piers by youre name,
I pray yow hertely telle us somwhat elles;
For sikerly, nere clynkyng of youre belles, nere: were (it) not (for).
That on youre bridel hange on every syde, 2795
By hevene kyng, that for us alle dyde, hevene: heaven's. dyde: died.
I sholde er this han fallen doun for sleep,
Althogh the slough had never been so deep;
Thanne hadde your tale al be toold in veyn.
For certeinly, as that thise clerkes seyn, *3990
Whereas a man may have noon audience,
Noght helpeth it to tellen his sentence. sentence: matter.
And wel I woot the substance is in me, substance: meaning. is in: i.e.,
If any thyng shal wel reported be. reaches.
Sir, sey somwhat of huntyng, I yow preye." 2805
    "Nay," quod this Monk, "I have no lust to
        pleye.
Now lat another telle, as I have toold."
Thanne spak oure Hoost with rude speche and
        boold, boold: brazen.
And seyde unto the Nonnes Preest anon,
"Com neer, thou preest, com hyder, thou sir sir John: common epithet for a priest.
        John! *4000
Telle us swich thyng as may oure hertes glade. glade: gladden.
Be blithe, though thou ryde upon a jade.
What thogh thyn hors be bothe foul and lene?

If he wol serve thee, rekke nat a bene.
Looke that thyn herte be murie everemo."   2815
    "Yis, sir," quod he, "yis, Hoost, so moot I go,   go: walk.
But I be myrie, ywis I wol be blamed."
And right anon his tale he hath attamed,   attamed: broached, begun.
And thus he seyde unto us everichon,
This sweete preest, this goodly man sir
            John.   *4010

Explicit.

Heere bigynneth the Nonnes Preestes tale of the Cok and Hen, Chauntecleer and Pertelote.

A povre widwe, somdeel stape in age   stape: advanced.
Was whilom dwellyng in a narwe cotage,   narwe: narrow, small.
Biside a grove, stondyng in a dale.
This widwe, of which I telle yow my tale,
Syn thilke day that she was last a wyf,   2825
In pacience ladde a ful symple lyf,   ladde: led.
For litel was hir catel and hir rente.   catel: property, goods. rente: income
By housbondrie of swich as God hire sente
She foond hirself and eek hir doghtren two.   foond: provided for.
Thre large sowes hadde she, and namo,   *4020
Three keen, and eek a sheep that highte Malle.   keen: kine, cows.
Ful sooty was hire bour and eek hir halle,   bour: bower, inner apartment (of a
In which she eet ful many a sklendre meel.   castle). halle: banquet hall.
Of poynaunt sauce hir neded never a deel.
No deyntee morsel passed thurgh hir throte;   2835
Hir diete was accordant to hir cote.
Replleccioun ne made hire nevere sik;   replleccioun: overeating.
Attempree diete was al hir phisik,   attempree: temperate, moderate.
And exercise, and hertes suffisaunce.   suffisaunce: contentment.
The goute lette hire nothyng for to daunce,   *4030 lette: hindered.
N'apoplexie shente nat hir heed.   shente: injured.
No wyn ne drank she, neither whit ne reed;

---

the Nonnes Preestes tale. The Nuns' Priest's Tale takes off from the fable of the cock and fox by Marie de France, from the corresponding episode by Pierre de Saint Cloud in Branch II of the great composite collection of animal tales called the *Roman de Renart,* and from the corresponding episode by an unknown *clerc* of Troyes in Branch VI of *Renart le Contrefait;* before the end, the narrator's satiric eye has ranged multifariously over the human predicament.
2836. cote: shelter for domestic livestock. She ate what her cote provided—milk, smoked pork, etc.

Hir bord was served moost with whit and blak,
Milk and broun breed, in which she foond no
      lak,

foond no lak: found no fault.

Seynd bacoun, and somtyme an ey or tweye; 2845
For she was, as it were, a maner deye.

seynd bacoun: smoked pork. ey: egg.
deye: dairy-woman.

    A yeerd she hadde, enclosed al aboute
With stikkes, and a drye dych withoute,
In which she hadde a cok, heet Chauntecleer.
In al the land of crowyng nas his peer.   *4040
His voys was murier than the murie orgon
On masse-dayes that in the chirche gon.
Wel sikerer was his crowyng in his logge
Than is a clokke or any abbey orlogge.
By nature he knew ech ascencioun   2855
Of the equinoxial in thilke toun;
For whan degrees fiftene were ascended,
Thanne crew he, that it myghte nat been
      amended.
His coomb was redder than the fyn coral,
And batailled as it were a castel wal;   *4050
His byle was blak, and as the jeet it shoon;
Lyk asure were his legges and his toon;
His nayles whitter than the lylye flour,
And lyk the burned gold was his colour.

stikkes: stakes.

heet: named.

masse-dayes: feast days.

logge: lodge, resting-place.

that: in such a way that.
amended: surpassed.

batailled: battlemented, notched with
   indentations. jeet: jet.
asure: lapis lazuli. toon: toes.

burned: burnished.

    This gentil cok hadde in his governaunce   2865
Sevene hennes for to doon al his plesaunce,
Whiche were his sustres and his paramours,
And wonder lyk to hym, as of colours;
Of whiche the faireste hewed on hir throte
Was cleped faire damoysele Pertelote.   *4060
Curteys she was, discreet, and debonaire,
And compaignable, and bar hyrself so faire,
Syn thilke day that she was seven nyght oold,
That trewely she hath the herte in hoold
Of Chauntecleer, loken in every lith;   2875
He loved hire so that wel was hym therwith.
But swich a joye was it to here hem synge,
Whan that the brighte sonne gan to sprynge,
In sweete accord, "My lief is faren in londe!"
For thilke tyme, as I have understonde,   *4070
Beestes and briddes koude speke and synge.
    And so bifel that in a dawenynge,
As Chauntecleer among his wyves alle

gentil: high-born.

paramours: mistresses.
as of: in.

debonaire: (lit. "of good disposition")
   gracious.

hoold: grasp, possession.

loken in every lith: locked in every
   limb.

briddes: birds.
dawenynge: dawn.

2854. **orlogge:** horologe, clock; in Chaucer's time clocks were not noted for accuracy.
2856. **equinoxial:** the equinoctial circle, a great circle of the heavens in the plane of the earth's equator. According to the old astronomy it made a complete daily revolution, so that fifteen degrees would pass, or "ascend," every hour
2879. **"My lief is faren in londe!":** a song, "My love has departed to the country."
2882. When a dream occurred at dawn, medieval theory held that it was true.

Sat on his perche, that was in the halle,
And next hym sat this faire Pertelote,   2885
This Chauntecleer gan gronen in his throte,
As man that in his dreem is drecched soore.   drecched: troubled, frightened.
And whan that Pertelote thus herde hym roore,
She was agast, and seyde, "Herte deere,   agast: frightened.
What eyleth yow, to grone in this manere? *4080 eyleth: ails.
Ye been a verray sleper; fy, for shame!"   verray: real.
    And he answerde, and seyde thus: "Madame,
I pray yow that ye take it nat agrief.   agrief: in grief, amiss.
By God, me mette I was in swich meschief   me mette: I dreamed. meschief:
Right now, that yet myn herte is soore   trouble.
      afright.   2895
Now God," quod he, "my swevene recche aright,   swevene: dream.
And kepe my body out of foul prisoun!   prisoun: captivity.
Me mette how that I romed up and doun
Withinne our yeerd, wheer as I saugh a beest
Was lyk an hound, and wolde han maad   maad areest upon: seized.
      areest   *4090
Upon my body, and han had me deed.   had deed: killed.
His colour was bitwixe yelow and reed,
And tipped was his tayl and bothe his eeris   eeris: ears.
With blak, unlyk the remenant of his heeris;
His snowte smal, with glowynge eyen tweye. 2905 smal: narrow.
Yet of his look for feere almoost I deye;   yet: still; even now.
This caused me my gronyng, doutelees."
    "Avoy!" quod she, "fy on yow, hertelees!   hertelees: lacking in courage.
Allas!" quod she, "for, by that God above,
Now han ye lost myn herte and al my love. *4100
I kan nat love a coward, by my feith!
For certes, what so any womman seith,
We alle desiren, if it myghte bee,
To han housbondes hardy, wise, and free,   free: generous, gracious.
And secree, and no nygard, ne no fool, 2915 secree: discreet. nygard: miser.
Ne hym that is agast of every tool,   agast: terrified. tool: weapon.
Ne noon avauntour, by that God above!   avauntour: boaster.
How dorste ye seyn, for shame, unto youre love
That any thyng myghte make yow aferd?
Have ye no mannes herte, and han a berd? *4110
Allas! and konne ye been agast of swevenys?   swevenys: dreams.
Nothyng, God woot, but vanitee in sweven is.
Swevenes engendren of replecciouns,
And ofte of fume and of complecciouns,   fume: vapor rising from the stomach.

2896. **recche aright:** interpret favorably (i.e., make turn out favorably).
2920. **berd:** Alexander Nequam in his *De Naturis Rerum* (c. 1200) says that the wattles of cocks are commonly called beards ("vulgo dicuntur barbae").
2923. Dreams spring from excesses in eating.
2924. **complecciouns:** mixtures of humors in the system; on the humors, see note for General Prologue, l. 333.

Whan humours been to habundant in a
      wight.   2925

to: too.

Certes this dreem, which ye han met to-nyght,
Cometh of the greete superfluytee
Of youre rede colera, pardee,
Which causeth folk to dreden in hir dremes
Of arwes, and of fyr with rede lemes,   *4120
Of rede beestes, that they wol hem byte,
Of contek, and of whelpes, grete and lyte;
Right as the humour of malencolie
Causeth ful many a man in sleep to crie
For feere of blake beres, or boles blake,   2935
Or elles blake develes wole hem take.
Of othere humours koude I telle also
That werken many a man in sleep ful wo;
But I wol passe as lightly as I kan.
   Lo Catoun, which that was so wys a man, *4130
Seyde he nat thus, 'Ne do no fors of dremes'?
   Now sire," quod she, "whan we flee fro the
      bemes,
For Goddes love, as taak som laxatyf.
Up peril of my soule and of my lyf,
I conseille yow the beste, I wol nat lye,   2945
That bothe of colere and of malencolye
Ye purge yow; and for ye shal nat tarie,
Though in this toun is noon apothecarie,
I shal myself to herbes techen yow
That shul been for youre hele and for youre
      prow;   *4140
And in oure yerd tho herbes shal I fynde
The whiche han of hire propretee by kynde
To purge yow bynethe and eek above.
Foryet nat this, for Goddes owene love!
Ye been ful coleryk of compleccioun;   2955
Ware the sonne in his ascencioun
Ne fynde yow nat repleet of humours hote.
And if it do, I dar wel leye a grote,
That ye shul have a fevere terciane,
Or an agu, that may be youre bane.   *4150
A day or two ye shul have digestyves
Of wormes, er ye take youre laxatyves
Of lawriol, centaure, and fumetere,

met: dreamed. to-nyght: this past
  night.

lemes: flames.

contek: strife, conflict. whelpes: pups,
  cubs.

boles: bulls.

werken: cause.

flee: fly.

as: please.
up: upon.
the beste: for the best.

for: so that.

techen: direct.
hele: health.
prow: benefit.

by kynde: by nature, natural.

ware: beware.

leye: wager.

youre bane: cause of your death.

2941. ne do no fors of: attach no importance to; the quotation is from *Disticha* ii.31, attributed to
Dionysius Cato (see Miller's Tale, l. 3227 and note).
2952. Which have their natural property.
2958. grote: a silver coin, equivalent to several dollars.
2959. fevere terciane: a fever attributed to predominance of red and black bile.
2962. wormes: These were recommended by Dioscorides for tertian fever and other diseases.
2963–66. Here are listed various medicinal herbs, some laxative, some nauseating.

Or elles of ellebor, that groweth there,
Of katapuce, or of gaitrys beryis   2965
Of herbe yve, growyng in oure yerd, ther mery is;   ther mery is: where it is pleasant.
Pekke hem up right as they growe and ete hem in.
Be myrie, housbonde, for youre fader kyn!
Dredeth no dreem, I kan sey yow namoore."
     "Madame," quod he, "graunt mercy of youre   graunt mercy: many thanks.
          loore.   *4160   loore: learned advice.
But nathelees, as touchyng daun Catoun,
That hath of wisdom swich a greet renoun,
Though that he bad no dremes for to drede,
By God, men may in olde bookes rede
Of many a man moore of auctoritee   2975
Than evere Caton was, so moot I thee,   so . . . thee: as I may prosper.
That al the revers seyn of his sentence,
And han wel founden by experience
That dremes been significaciouns   been significaciouns: have signifi-
As wel of joye as of tribulaciouns   *4170   cance.
That folk enduren in this lif present.
Ther nedeth make of this noon argument;
The verray preeve sheweth it in dede.   verray preeve: actual experience.
    Oon of the gretteste auctour that men rede
Seith thus; that whilom two felawes wente   2985
On pilgrimage, in a ful good entente;   entente: faith, spirit.
And happed so, they coomen in a toun   coomen: came.
Wher as ther was swich congregacioun
Of peple, and eek so streit of herbergage,   so streit of herbergage: such scarcity
That they ne founde as much as a cotage   *4180   of lodgings.
In which they bothe myghte ylogged bee.   ylogged: lodged.
Wherfore they mosten of necessitee,
As for that nyght, departen compaignye;   departen: part.
And ech of hem gooth to his hostelrye,
And took his loggyng as it wolde falle.   2995
That oon of hem was logged in a stalle,

2968. **for youre fader kyn!**: a mild oath; it means "by your father's ancestry!"; cf. such lines as 2865, 3296.

2984. **oon . . . auctour**: i.e., one author of the greatest: Valerius Maximus, whom Chaucer thought to be the author of a splendid attack on women and marriage, the *Epistola Valerii* of Walter Map (see Wife of Bath's Prologue, line 671). The stories beginning at ll. 2985 and 3064 are found in the *De Factis Dictisque Memorabilibus* of Valerius Maximus.

A Medicinal Herb: Having interpreted Chauntecleer's dream as an indication of an excess of choler and melancholy in his system, Pertelote prescribes a regimen of medicinal herbs which, she tells him, have the property "To purge yow bynethe and eek above" (line 2953). Chaunte-cleer's terror of his dream is exceeded by his terror of this awful prospect and he devotes nearly two hundred lines to his "ensamples olde" in order to save himself from such a fate: "laxatyves . . . been venymes . . . ; I hem diffye, I love hem never a deel!" (lines 3154–56). The nature of Chauntecleer's horror is clarified by an early manuscript of the *Materia Medica* of Dioscorides (see General Prologue, line 430) which not only describes a double-acting herb (*thapsia*, unknown to Pertelote) but also depicts its curative powers. The text reads, in part, ". . . it [*thapsia*] is warm and cathartic; if taken mixed [with honey] it purges a man upward and downward. . . ." See Loren MacKinney, *Medical Illustrations in Medieval Manuscripts*, pp. 42–43 and Fig. 35. See Knight's Tale, lines 2755–56.

qui anguloſus ſunt ſup̄. qd ſuꝑ
mi albu̅ habet colore̅ . qui ꝑ cuiuſ
cidu . ſiccol̄ du . eſtonaꝗ ze ad
ceꝑ ꝓcui mul ſo ꝓ fleu̅ ma ꝑ iugu̅
uomenti; ſecludit̄ . ſed aligat̄ ce
pꝗ ni mul ſe aſſiduē te ci ꝑ ueni
aſ de obuleri . qua oſ ſo caſio neꝗ
ciſuꝗ ꝓſꝑerat . ſi gula exca re
ſar . bibe reta intra ꝑeduc̄l oꝑ neꝗ iuncta
ſcabie ſi plu̅ agineſ coll ſi alterū
elixa ze oſe fere catto omici ꝗ . fa
ce ſenouit . ſeu mang in ꝗ iuſ obſ
qned . cumoſ eſ ſaru ciꝑ ꝗ ꝗ ſꝓ
miſceat̄ & mala u̅ macrib; cal daꝗ.

PMH

d ette   ꝓ ſi ce dra pa ſ
Ⅱ arpſiꝗ . ſi ce ꝗꝗ d ſ ni no
Ⅱ tra poſt̄r.   ueneto ce lu ſclaſ .
Ⅱ ffi ra te x ſimil ſ fe ſu le . ſol ꝑe
ſim ch em er ꝑ ru ſ habet . ha ſ ꝑu ꝗ
ꝗ en uer flagh; ca ꝑo ꝓ ella ꝗ la ſi in
ꝗol ꝗharꝗ ſic ln crue ro flo reme ſ
l no er ſe m̄ latruſi mile ſ fe ſu le . ſ̄ꝗ
mino ꝑe ꝑa de x u illꝗ al bor ſi mo l ꝗ
coꝗ ugeta ſ ſ i habe de ui ꝗ ci dal no doſe .
ꝗuſ ra di ꝗe ꝗe cu cari ſic . ſo ſa ce ſ fer
l̄ beꝗra iꝗ ꝗꝗ . ſa ce t̄ꝗ quol nuno

l̄ co cou ceꝗ ſi ci ru a re o ſi ce ng ꝗ ſi er
ſou e ſe ꝗ e ge ner e ille cu humoſe e̅ mi ſe
ꝗ ni lax ſi mu l ln ca ru ca tu ꝑ illa ce
l ligat . qꝗ d oł ꝗ a de e coll i ce ꝗ e de ber
ꝗ ſi cu̅ fa ci eſ ſi c cru i de ſ ſ ꝑa di ce ꝗ ho ꝑ
cu̅ coꝗ ol ꝑ ſo . ꝗ coł ꝗa oł ꝑ ſo ꝗ e cu cari .
ze l nu a ro ꝑe nh ſi ſic c̄ a ri . ln ſo le ꝑo ri
cu̅ mul qꝗ ue ro fol ꝗo ueꝗ ꝑa re de e ce u
cari . ſe de ta qꝗ ſi cu cu ſ l e ru cꝗ ſi ſe ſ ſ ꝓ
no ueꝗ ſ qꝗ o ſe e fe de ꝗ ſ ſa ce t̄ il ru ꝗ ł ſ ſ
ꝗa rob; e mo ꝑle nu ſ ; ꝗ e cru ci ue ꝑo ſi c
cu̅ ni a co nu ſe ce n tu ce ſ ſu ſ humo ꝑo
t̄ . ꝗ ob ue ſo ci uſ cru i ſ cru a ue ꝗ ni e co
ue ꝗ i ant . m̄ a xi me il l o ce t̄ e ꝑo ſe
quo colligit̄ nol ꝗ e ꝓ ru e ne riuſ tra te
ꝗ cu̅ ꝗ ſi l ue ſo a ue ne riuſ ſi de u ꝗ qo cu̅ H
uſ a u iu e ru d l ne ꝑa re na ri . ꝗ ſa ce
re de mel uſ ꝑa ce ſi c ce ſꝑ ch ſ ſa ꝑꝑ ce ꝗ
ſa ce te . ꝗ i na ru qu in cre ꝗa t̄ . iu ſti
x e d caꝗ gꝗ e ꝗ ca tu ra ꝗ ce o . coꝗ ul ꝑ ſi
uſ ꝑa di ce ꝗ e ꝗ ſu cur e ꝗ la ce ti nu ſ in cu l
ſe coꝗ ce ꝑe ru ꝗ ; ſu ſi lu ſu l homi ni ſa ce
cu̅ t . ꝑa di ce ꝗ ueꝗ ꝑe ꝗ iu ꝗ obu l ꝗe e ꝗa n
cu̅ a ne ſi b; ꝗ . iu ꝗ da ne tu r ſu cu ſ ueꝗ ꝗ
ſu o obu l ꝗe a cci ꝑ u nt . la cri nu eꝗ
obu l uſ a cci ꝑu t . pluſ a ce ꝑu ꝗ ſi n
ꝑe fti ne e t̄ . puꝗ ꝑa ꝗo e ſ ſ a de e t̄ e l co
ce o ni n a ꝗo ri t̄ . o ꝑ ni a re ni ꝑe ꝑa ce to
la ri t̄ . a du r me ni ca ti t̄ qꝗ ꝗa ro ſu cꝗ ce ru
habe n; ſe d da ri t̄ . a u re te ꝑe ca aꝗ ni me yſ

Fer in a yeerd, with oxen of the plough;
That oother man was logged wel ynough,
As was his aventure or his fortune,
That us governeth alle as in commune.   *4190   as in commune: together.
   And so bifel that, longe er it were day,
This man mette in his bed, ther as he lay,   mette: dreamed.
How that his felawe gan upon hym calle,
And seyde, 'Allas! for in an oxes stalle
This nyght I shal be mordred ther I lye.   3005
Now help me, deere brother, or I dye.
In alle haste com to me!' he sayde.
This man out of his sleep for feere abrayde;   abrayde: started up.
But whan that he was wakened of his sleep,
He turned hym, and took of this no keep.   *4200   keep: heed, notice.
Hym thoughte his dreem nas but a vanitee.
Thus twies in his slepyng dremed hee;
And atte thridde tyme yet his felawe
Cam, as hym thoughte, and seide, 'I am now
           slawe.   slawe: slain.
Bihoold my bloody woundes depe and wyde! 3015
Arys up erly in the morwe tyde,   morwe tyde: morning time.
And at the west gate of the toun,' quod he,
'A carte ful of dong ther shaltow se,   shaltow: you shall.
In which my body is hid ful prively;
Do thilke carte arresten boldely.   *4210   do arresten: cause to be stopped.
My gold caused my mordre, sooth to sayn.'
And tolde hym every point how he was slayn,
With a ful pitous face, pale of hewe.
And truste wel, his dreem he foond ful trewe,
For on the morwe, as soone as it was day,   3025
To his felawes in he took the way;   in: inn, lodging.
And whan that he cam to this oxes stalle,
After his felawe he bigan to calle.
   The hostiler answerede hym anon,   hostiler: innkeeper.
And seyde, 'Sire, your felawe is agon.   *4220
As soone as day he wente out of the toun.'
   This man gan fallen in suspecioun,
Remembrynge on his dremes that he mette,
And forth he gooth—no lenger wolde he
           lette—   lette: delay.
Unto the west gate of the toun, and fond   3035
A dong-carte, wente as it were to donge lond,   wente: (which) went.
That was arrayed in the same wise   arrayed: arranged.
As ye han herd the dede man devyse.
And with an hardy herte he gan to crye
Vengeance and justice of this felonye.   *4230   of: for.
'My felawe mordred is this same nyght
And in this carte heere he lith gapyng upright.   upright: face up.
I crye out on the ministres,' quod he,   ministres: magistrates.

'That sholden kepe and reulen this citee.   kepe and reulen: preserve and rule.
Harrow! allas! heere lith my felawe slayn!'   **3045**
What sholde I moore unto this tale sayn?
The peple out sterte and caste the cart to
        grounde,
And in the myddel of the dong they founde
The dede man, that mordred was al newe.   *al newe: just newly.*
    O blisful God, that art so just and trewe,   *4240
Lo, how that thou biwreyest mordre alway!   *biwreyest: revealest.*
Mordre wol out, that se we day by day.
Mordre is so wlatsom and abhomynable   *wlatsom: disgusting, heinous.*
To God, that is so just and resonable,
That he ne wol nat suffre it heled be,   **3055**   *heled: concealed.*
Though it abyde a yeer, or two, or thre.
Mordre wol out, this is my conclusioun.
And right anon, ministres of that toun
Han hent the carter and so soore hym pyned,   *pyned: tortured.*
And eek the hostiler so soore engyned,   *4250   *engyned: tortured, racked.*
That they biknewe hire wikkednesse anon,   *biknewe: confessed.*
And were anhanged by the nekke-bon.   *anhanged: hanged.*
    Heere may men seen that dremes been to   *to drede: to be dreaded.*
        drede.
And certes in the same book I rede,
Right in the nexte chapitre after this—   **3065**
I gabbe nat, so have I joye or blis—   *gabbe: lie. so have I: as I hope for.*
Two men that wolde han passed over see,
For certeyn cause, into a fer contree,
If that the wynd ne hadde been contrarie,
That made hem in a citee for to tarie   *4260
That stood ful myrie upon an haven-syde;
But on a day, agayn the even-tyde,   *agayn: towards.*
The wynd gan chaunge, and blew right as hem
        leste.
Jolif and glad they wente unto hir reste,
And casten hem ful erly for to saille.   **3075**   *casten hem: intended.*
But herkneth! to that o man fil a greet mervaille:
That oon of hem, in slepyng as he lay,
Hym mette a wonder dreem agayn the day.   *agayn: towards.*
Hym thoughte a man stood by his beddes syde,
And hym comanded that he sholde abyde,   *4270
And seyde hym thus: "If thou tomorwe wende,
Thow shalt be dreynt; my tale is at an ende.'   *dreynt: drowned.*
He wook, and tolde his felawe what he mette,
And preyde hym his viage to lette;   *lette: give up.*
As for that day, he preyde hym to abyde.   **3085**
His felawe, that lay by his beddes syde,
Gan for to laughe, and scorned him ful faste.   *faste: hard, eagerly.*

3078. See footnote for line 2882 above.

'No dreem,' quod he, 'may so myn herte agaste   agaste: terrify.
That I wol lette for to do my thynges.
I sette nat a straw by thy dremynges,   *4280
For swevenes been but vanytees and japes.   japes: delusions.
Men dreme alday of owles and of apes,   alday: every day, all the time.
And of many a maze therwithal;   maze: delusion.
Men dreme of thyng that nevere was ne shal.   shal: shall be.
But sith I see that thou wolt heere abyde,   3095
And thus forslewthen wilfully thy tyde,   forslewthen: waste by sloth. tyde:
God woot, it reweth me; and have good day!'   time. reweth: sorrows.
And thus he took his leve, and wente his way.
But er that he hadde half his cours yseyled,   yseyled: sailed.
Noot I nat why, ne what myschaunce it   it eyled: ailed it.
      eyled,   *4290
But casuelly the shippes botme rente,   casuelly: accidentally. rente: split
And ship and man under the water wente   asunder.
In sighte of othere shippes it bisyde,   it bisyde: near it.
That with hem seyled at the same tyde.
And therfore, faire Pertelote so deere,   3105
By swiche ensamples olde maistow leere   leere: learn.
That no man sholde been to recchelees   recchelees: heedless.
Of dremes; for I seye thee, doutelees,
That many a dreem ful soore is for to drede.
   Lo, in the lyf of Seint Kenelm I rede,   *4300
That was Kenulphus sone, the noble kyng
Of Mercenrike, how Kenelm mette a thyng.
A lite er he was mordred, on a day,
His mordre in his avysioun he say.   say: saw.
His norice hym expowned every del   3115   norice: nurse.
His sweven, and bad hym for to kepe hym wel
For traisoun; but he nas but seven yeer old,   for traisoun: for fear of, to prevent
And therfore litel tale hath he told   treason.
Of any dreem, so holy was his herte.
By God! I hadde levere than my sherte   *4310
That ye hadde rad his legende, as have I.   rad: read.
   Dame Pertelote, I sey yow trewely,
Macrobeus, that writ the avisioun
In Affrike of the worthy Cipioun,
Affermeth dremes, and seith that they been   3125   affermeth: supports the validity of.
Warnynge of thynges that men after seen.   after: afterwards.
And forthermoore, I pray yow, looketh wel
In the olde testament, of Daniel,   of: concerning.
If he heeld dremes any vanitee.

3110. Seint Kenelm: a boy king of Mercia (Mercenrike), murdered c. 821, at the instigation of his aunt.
3114. avysioun: prophetic dream sent for warning.
3118–19. litel tale hath he told of: he held of little account.
3123. Macrobeus: the fourth-century commentator on Cicero's *Dream of Scipio* (Cipioun).
3128. Daniel vii.

Reed eek of Joseph, and ther shul ye see   *4320
Wher dremes be somtyme—I sey nat alle—   **wher:** whether.
Warnynge of thynges that shul after falle.
Looke of Egipte the kyng, daun Pharao,   **looke:** consider.
His bakere and his butiller also,
Wher they ne felte noon effect in dremes.   3135
Whoso wol seken actes of sondry remes   **actes:** histories. **remes:** realms.
May rede of dremes many a wonder thyng.
Lo Cresus, which that was of Lyde kyng,
Mette he nat that he sat upon a tree,
Which signified he sholde anhanged be?   *4330
Lo heere Andromacha, Ectores wyf,
That day that Ector sholde lese his lyf,   **sholde lese:** was to lose.
She dremed on the same nyght biforn
How that the lyf of Ector sholde be lorn,   **lorn:** lost, destroyed.
If thilke day he wente into bataille.   3145
She warned hym, but it myghte nat availle;
He wente for to fighte natheles,
But he was slayn anon of Achilles.
But thilke tale is al to longe to telle,
And eek it is ny day, I may nat dwelle.   *4340   **dwelle:** delay.
Shortly I seye, as for conclusioun,
That I shal han of this avisioun   **of:** from. **avisioun:** prophetic dream
Adversitee; and I seye forthermoor,   sent for warning.
That I ne telle of laxatyves no stoor,   **telle:** esteem. **stoor:** value.
For they been venymes, I woot it well;   3155   **venymes:** poisons.
I hem diffye, I love hem never a deel!   **diffye:** scorn; reject.
    Now let us speke of myrthe, and stynte al this.
Madame Pertelote, so have I blis,
Of o thyng God hath sent me large grace;   **large grace:** great good fortune.
For whan I se the beautee of youre face,   *4350
Ye been so scarlet reed aboute youre eyen,
It maketh al my drede for to dyen;
For al so siker as *In principio,*
Mulier est hominis confusio,—
Madame, the sentence of this Latyn is,   3165
'Womman is mannes joye and al his blis.'
For whan I feele a-nyght your softe syde,   **a-nyght:** in the night.
Al be it that I may nat on yow ryde,
For that oure perche is maad so narwe, allas!   **narwe:** narrow.

3130–35. Genesis xxxvii, xl, xli.
3135. Whether they foresaw in dreams any (future) effect or accomplishment.
3138. **Cresus:** see Monk's Tale, ll. 2727–60.
3141. **Andromacha:** Andromache's dream of the death of Hector is a medieval fabrication.
3163. For as sure as gospel truth. (See John i.1.)
3164. *Mulier . . . confusio:* "Woman is man's ruin," a common sentiment in medieval literature; cf. ll. 3256–59. Chauntecleer's interpretation of the passage enfolds an ironic truth from the medieval point of view: man's transitory mundane joy may be his only bliss and may lead to his eternal ruin.

I am so ful of joye and of solas,   *4360 solas: delight.
That I diffye bothe sweven and dreem."
And with that word he fley doun fro the beem,   fley: flew.
For it was day, and eke his hennes alle,
And with a chuk he gan hem for to calle,   chuk: cluck.
For he hadde founde a corn, lay in the yerd. 3175 corn: grain. lay: which lay.
Real he was, he was namoore aferd.   real: regal.
He fethered Pertelote twenty tyme,   fethered: covered with his wings.
And trad as ofte, er that it was pryme.   trad: copulated with. pryme: probably
He looketh as it were a grym leoun,   9 A.M.
And on his toos he rometh up and doun;   *4370
Hym deigned nat to sette his foot to grounde.
He chukketh, whan he hath a corn yfounde,
And to hym rennen thanne his wyves alle.
Thus roial, as a prince is in his halle,
Leve I this Chauntecleer in his pasture,   3185 pasture: eating area; domain.
And after wol I telle his aventure.
    Whan that the month in which the world
        bigan,
That highte March, whan God first maked man,
Was compleet, and passed were also,
Syn March [was gon], thritty dayes and   Syn March was gon: see footnote.
        two,   *4380
Bifel that Chauntecleer in al his pryde,
His sevene wyves walkynge by his syde,
Caste up his eyen to the brighte sonne,
That in the signe of Taurus hadde yronne
Twenty degrees and oon, and somwhat
        moore,   3195
And knew by kynde, and by noon oother loore, kynde: nature.
That it was pryme, and crew with blisful stevene. stevene: voice.
"The sonne," he seyde, "is clomben up on hevene is clomben: has climbed.
Fourty degrees and oon, and moore ywis.
Madame Pertelote, my worldes blis,   *4390
Herkneth thise blisful briddes how they synge,
And se the fresshe floures how they sprynge:
Ful is myn herte of revel and solas!"   revel: revelry.
But sodeynly hym fil a sorweful cas,
For evere the latter ende of joye is wo.   3205
God woot that worldly joye is soone ago;   ago: gone.
And if a rethor koude faire endite,   rethor: rhetorician; artificially elegant
He in a cronycle saufly myghte it write   writer. saufly: safely.

3187. According to medieval opinion, the world was created at the vernal equinox.
3190. Syn March was gon: O′ reads Syn March bigan; but since this clause makes no sense, I propose that Chaucer wrote Syn March was gon. The miswriting of was gon as bigan is not beyond the capabilities of the scribe of O′, who did not realize that the date was May 3 (see Robinson's note, and ll. 3191–99), and who may have been influenced by bigan in line 3187. Chaucer uses "ben gon" for the passage of time: see Man of Law's Tale, ll. 17 and 132, and Merchant's Tale, line 2140.
3194. Taurus: the second sign of the zodiac, right after Aries; see note for General Prologue, l. 7.

As for a sovereyn notabilitee.
Now every wys man, lat him herkne me;   *4400   herkne: harken to, listen to.
This storie is also trewe, I undertake,
As is the book of Launcelot de Lake,
That wommen holde in ful greet reverence.
Now wol I torne agayn to my sentence.   my sentence: the substance of my
    A col-fox, ful of sly iniquitee,   3215   poem. col-fox: coal fox, fox with
That in the grove hadde woned yeres three,   black tips. woned: lived, dwelt.
By heigh ymaginacioun forncast,
The same nyght thurghout the hegges brast   brast: burst.
Into the yerd ther Chauntecleer the faire
Was wont, and eek his wyves, to repaire;   *4410
And in a bed of wortes stille he lay,   wortes: cabbages.
Til it was passed undren of the day,   undren: mid-morning.
Waitynge his tyme on Chauntecleer to falle,
As gladly doon thise homycides alle   gladly: habitually.
That in await liggen to mordre men.   3225   await: wait. liggen: lie.
O false mordrour, lurkynge in thy den!
O newe Scariot, newe Genylon,
False dissymulour, o Greek Synon,
That broghtest Troye al outrely to sorwe!   outrely: utterly.
O Chauntecleer, acursed be that morwe   *4420
That thou into the yerd flaugh fro the bemes!   flaugh: flew.
Thou were ful wel ywarned by thy dremes
That thilke day was perilous to thee;
But what that God forwoot moot nedes bee,   forwoot: foreknows.
After the opinioun of certein clerkis.   3235
Witnesse on hym that any parfit clerk is,
That in scole is greet altercacioun   in scole: i.e., among scholastic phi-
In this matere, and greet disputisoun,   losophers and theologians.
And hath been of an hundred thousand men.
But I ne kan nat bulte it to the bren,   *4430   bulte it to the bren: bolt or sift it to
As kan the holy doctour Augustyn,   the bran.
Or Boece, or the Bisshop Bradwardyn,
Wheither that Goddes worthy forwityng   forwityng: foreknowledge.
Streyneth me nedely for to doon a thyng,—   streyneth: constrains. nedely: neces-
    sarily, of necessity.

3212. This is the book which had so affected Paolo and Francesca that she said to Dante, "That day we read no further in it" (see *Inferno* v.73–142); in his *Comento* Boccaccio declared that the *Lancelot* was "composed rather for approval than to accord with truth."

3217. Foreseen, or foretold, or imagined beforehand, by exalted imagination (i.e., in Chauntecleer's dream). Chauntecleer's was a "supercelestial" dream, a warning from God. See *Speculum*, 47 (1972), 666 and note 36.

3227. **Scariot:** Judas Iscariot. **Genylon:** the traitor in the *Chanson de Roland*.

3228. **Synon:** deviser of the Trojan horse, who deceived the Trojans by his false story about it, and then released the Greeks from it so that they could capture Troy.

3240–50. Bradwardine, of Oxford, who was Archbishop of Canterbury at his death in 1349, upheld foreordination and was opposed to free will (see ll. 3243–45). St. Augustine believed that free will was *granted* to man by God, to be used to the extent that God allowed (see ll. 3246–48). Boethius believed in conditional necessity, which can be crudely exemplified by such a statement as, "If God foreknows my deed, I must of necessity be going to do it; otherwise he couldn't foreknow it; but his foreknowing doesn't cause it" (see ll. 3249–50).

"Nedely" clepe I symple necessitee;   3245
Or elles, if free choys be graunted me
To do that same thyng, or do it noght,
Though God forwoot it er that I was wroght;   forwoot: foreknew.
Or if his wityng streyneth never a del
But by necessitee condicionel.   *4440
I wol nat han to do of swich matere;   of: with.
My tale is of a cok, as ye may heere,
That tok his conseil of his wyf, with sorwe,
To walken in the yerd upon that morwe
That he hadde met the dreem that I yow   met: dreamed.
      tolde.   3255
Wommennes conseils been ful ofte colde;   colde: baneful, fatal.
Wommannes conseil broghte us first to wo,
And made Adam fro Paradys to go,
Ther as he was ful myrie and wel at ese.
But for I noot to whom it myght displese,   *4450
If I conseil of wommen wolde blame,
Passe over, for I seyde it in my game.
Rede auctours, where they trete of swich matere,
And what they seyn of wommen ye may heere.
Thise been the cokkes wordes, and nat myne; 3265   cokkes: ?
I kan noon harm of no womman divyne.   harm: evil.
   Faire in the soond, to bathe hire myrily,   soond: sand.
Lith Pertelote, and alle hire sustres by,
Agayn the sonne, and Chauntecleer so free   agayn: in. free: noble.
Soong murier than the mermayde in the see; *4460 soong: sang.
For Phisiologus seith sikerly
How that they syngen wel and myrily.
And so bifel that, as he caste his eye
Among the wortes on a boterflye,   wortes: cabbages.
He was war of this fox, that lay ful lowe.   3275
Nothynge ne liste hym thanne for to crowe,
But cride anon, "Cok! cok!" and up he sterte
As man that was affrayed in his herte.   affrayed: frightened.
For naturelly a beest desireth flee
Fro his contrarie, if he may it see,   *4470 contrarie: enemy.
Though he never erst hadde seyn it with his eye.   erst: before.
   This Chauntecleer, whan he gan hym espye,

3245. **symple necessitee:** plain, ordinary necessity, as of cause and effect.

3250. **necessitee condicionel:** e.g., the sort of "necessity" found in such a conditional sentence as "If I see him standing, he must of necessity be standing."

3263. **auctours:** authors; several such authors—Valerius, Theophrastus, Jerome—are presented in the Wife of Bath's Prologue.

3266. **noon . . . no:** the double negative may be interpreted as an intensive negative, or as a positive. **divyne:** likewise has two possible meanings (verb and adjective). Thus the sentence can have four possible meanings.

3271. **Phisiologus:** the medieval Latin *Bestiary,* a book of fanciful zoology with allegorical interpretations; one chapter describes the Sirens—symbolic of sensual pleasures.

He wolde han fled, but that the fox anon   **wolde:** intended (to).
Seyde, "Gentil sire, allas! wher wol ye gon?
Be ye affrayed of me that am youre freend?   3285
Now, certes, I were worse than a feend,
If I to yow wolde harm or vileynye!
I am nat come youre conseil for t'espye,   **conseil:** private matters.
But trewely, the cause of my comynge   **cause:** purpose.
Was oonly for to herkne how that ye synge.   *4480
For trewely, ye have as myrie a stevene   **stevene:** voice.
As any aungel hath that is in hevene.
Therwith ye han in musyk moore feelynge
Than hadde Boece, or any that kan synge.
My lord youre fader—God his soule blesse!— 3295
And eek youre moder, of hire gentillesse,   **hire:** their.
Han in myn hous ybeen to my greet ese;
And certes, sire, ful fayn wolde I yow plese.
But for men speke of syngyng, I wol seye,   **for:** if.
So moote I brouke wel myne eyen tweye,   *4490   **brouke:** enjoy, use.
Save ye, I herde nevere man so synge
As dide youre fader in the morwenynge.
Certes, it was of herte, al that he song.   **of herte:** from the heart.
And for to make his voys the moore strong,
He wolde so peyne hym that with bothe his   **peyne hym:** strive.
       eyen   3305
He moste wynke, so loude he wolde cryen,   **wynke:** close his eyes.
And stonden on his tiptoon therwithal,
And strecche forth his nekke long and smal.   **smal:** slender.
And eek he was of swich discrecioun   **discrecioun:** discernment.
That ther nas no man in no regioun   *4500
That hym in song or wisdom myghte passe.
I have wel rad in 'Daun Burnel the Asse,'   **vers:** verses.
Among his vers, how that ther was a cok,   **for:** because.
For a preestes sone yaf hym a knok
Upon his leg whil he was yong and nyce,   3315   **he:** the son. **nyce:** foolish.
He made hym for to lese his benefice.   **he:** the cock (by letting him over-
But certeyn, ther nys no comparisoun   sleep).
Bitwixe the wisdom and discrecioun
Of youre fader and of his subtiltee.   **his:** i.e., the cock's. **subtiltee:** skill.
Now syngeth, sire, for seinte charitee;   *4510
Lat se, konne ye youre fader countrefete?"   **countrefete:** imitate.
     This Chauntecleer his wynges gan to bete,
As man that koude his traysoun nat espie,   **traysoun:** betrayal; treachery.
So was he ravysshed with his flaterie.
     Allas! ye lordes, many a fals flatour   3325   **flatour:** flatterer.
Is in youre courtes, and many a losengeour,   **losengeour:** deceiver.
That plesen yow wel moore, by my feith,

3294. **Boece:** Boethius had written a learned treatise, *De Musica.*
3312. **Daun Burnel the Asse:** This poem by Nigel Wireker has a similar story.

Than he that soothfastnesse unto yow seith.   soothfastnesse: truth.
Redeth Ecclesiaste of flaterye;
Beth war, ye lordes, of hir trecherye.   *4520
 This Chauntecleer stood hye upon his toos,
Strecchynge his nekke, and heeld his eyen cloos,
And gan to crowe loude for the nones.
And daun Russell the fox stirte up atones,   atones: at once.
And by the gargat hente Chauntecleer, 3335 gargat: throat.
And on his bak toward the wode hym beer,   beer: bore, carried.
For yet ne was ther no man that hym sewed. sewed: pursued, followed.
 O destinee, that mayst nat been eschewed! eschewed: escaped, avoided.
Allas, that Chauntecleer fleigh fro the bemes! fleigh: flew.
Allas, his wyf ne roghte nat of dremes! *4530 ne roghte nat of: didn't heed.
And on a Friday fil al this meschaunce.
 O Venus, that art goddesse of plesaunce,
Syn that thy servant was this Chauntecleer,
And in thy servyce dide al his poweer,
Moore for delit than world to multiplye, 3345 world to multiplye: to propagate the
Why woldestow suffre hym on thy day to dye?   species.
 O Gaufred, deere maister soverayn,
That whan thy worthy kyng Richard was slayn
With shot, compleynedest his deeth so soore, shot: by the shot of an arrow.
Why ne hadde I now thy sentence and thy   sentence: insight.
   loore   *4540
The Friday for to chide, as diden ye?
For on a Friday, soothly, slayn was he.
Thanne wolde I shewe yow how that I koude
   pleyne   pleyne: complain, lament.
For Chauntecleres drede and for his peyne. drede: peril.
 Certes, swich cry ne lamentacion, 3355
Was nevere of ladyes maad whan Ylion   Ylion: inner citadel of Troy.
Was wonne, and Pirrus with his streite swerd, streite swerd: drawn sword.
Whan he hadde hent kyng Priam by the berd,
And slayn hym, as seith us *Eneydos,*   *Eneydos: Aeneid,* ii, 533–58.
As maden alle the hennes in the clos, *4550
Whan they had seyn of Chauntecleer the sighte.
But sovereynly dame Pertelote shrighte, shrighte: shrieked.
Ful louder than dide Hasdrubales wyf,
Whan that hir housbonde hadde lost his lyf,
And that the Romayns hadde brend Cartage. 3365 brend: burned.

3329. Ecclesiaste: cf. Ecclesiasticus xii.10 ff. and xxvii.26.

3341. Friday (the day of Venus) is often considered a day of ill-luck; on Friday occurred the Expulsion, the Deluge, the Betrayal, the Crucifixion, and the wounding of Richard I.

3347. Gaufred: Geoffrey de Vinsauf, author of the standard rhetoric text used in medieval schools; he gives artificial rules, and then offers flamboyant illustrations of his own composition. Chaucer mimics the most famous of these, Geoffrey de Vinsauf's lamentation on the death of Richard the Lion-Hearted (ll. 3347–52), and then launches into an elaborate expansion of a simple statement in accordance with some of the rules set forth by Geoffrey, ll. 3355–73.

3360. clos: an enclosure near a building (e.g., the close of a monastery); a farmyard pen.

She was so ful of torment and of rage   rage: violent grief.
That wilfully into the fyr she sterte,   wilfully: deliberately. sterte: leaped.
And brende hirselven with a stedefast herte.
  O woful hennes, right so criden ye,
As, whan that Nero brende the citee   *4560
Of Rome, cryden senatoures wyves
For that hir husbondes losten alle hir lyves;
Withouten gilt this Nero hath hem slayn.   withouten gilt: unjustly.
Now wole I turne to my tale agayn.
  The sely wydwe and eek hir doghtres two   3375
Herden thise hennes crie and maken wo,   wo: lamentation.
And out at dores stirten they anon,
And syen the fox toward the grove gon,   syen: saw.
And bar upon his bak the cok away,
And cryden, "Out!" "Harrow!" and   out!: alas!
      "Weylaway!"   *4570
"Ha! ha!" "The fox!" and after hym they ran,
And eek with staves many another man.
Ran Colle oure dogge, and Talbot, and Gerland,
And Malkyn, with a dystaf in hir hand;
Ran cow and calf, and eek the verray
      hogges,   3385
So fered for the berkyng of the dogges   fered: frightened.
And shoutyng of the men and wommen eeke,
They ronne so hem thoughte hir herte breeke.
They yelleden as feendes doon in helle;   yelleden: yelled.
The dokes cryden as men wolde hem   men: man, one, someone.
      quelle;   *4580 quelle: kill.
The gees for feere flowen over the trees;   flowen: flew.
Out of the hyve cam the swarm of bees.
So hydous was the noyse, a, benedicitee!
Certes, he Jakke Straw and his meynee   meynee: followers.
Ne made nevere shoutes half so shrille,   3395
Whan that they wolden any Flemyng kille,
As thilke day was maad upon the fox.
Of bras they broghten bemes, and of box,   bemes: trumpets. box: boxwood.
Of horn, of boon, in whiche they blewe and   boon: bone.
      powped,
And therwithal they skriked and they   skriked: shrieked.
      howped.   *4590 howped: whooped.
It semed as that hevene sholde falle.
  Now, goode men, I prey yow herkneth alle:
Lo, how Fortune turneth sodeynly   turneth: overturns.
The hope and pryde eek of hir enemy!

3381. Ha! ha!: The regular shout for frightening away a marauding animal.
3388. They ran so (hard) it seemed to them their hearts would break.
3394. Jakke Straw: a leader of the Peasants' Revolt (1381); the Flemish quarter of London was one of the scenes of the bloody attack.

This cok, that lay upon the foxes bak,   3405
In al his drede unto the fox he spak,   drede: peril.
And seyde, "Sire, if that I were as ye,
Yet sholde I seyn, as wys God helpe me,   wys: surely.
'Turneth agayn, ye proude cherles alle!   agayn: back.
A verray pestilence upon yow falle!   *4600
Now I am come unto this wodes syde;
Maugree youre heed, the cok shal heere abyde.
I wol hym ete, in feith, and that anon!' "
    The fox answerde, "In feith, it shal be don."
And as he spak that word, al sodeynly   3415
This cok brak from his mouth delyverly,   brak: broke.
And heighe upon a tree he fleigh anon.   fleigh: flew.
And whan the fox saugh that he was gon,
    "Allas!" quod he, "O Chauntecleer, allas!
I have to yow," quod he, "ydoon trespas,   *4610   trespas: wrong.
In as muche as I maked yow aferd
Whan I yow hente and broghte out of the yerd.
But, sire, I dide it in no wikke entente.   wikke: wicked.
Com doun, and I shal telle yow what I mente;
I shal seye sooth to yow, God help me so!"   3425
    "Nay thanne," quod he, "I shrewe us bothe   shrewe: beshrew, curse.
        two.
And first I shrewe myself, both blood and bones,
If thou bigyle me any ofter than ones.
Thou shalt namoore, thurgh thy flaterye,
Do me to synge and wynke with myn eye;   *4620   do: cause.
For he that wynketh, whan he sholde see,
Al wilfully, God lat him nevere thee!"   thee: prosper.
    "Nay," quod the fox, "but God yeve hym
        meschaunce,
That is so undiscreet of governaunce   governaunce: self-control.
That jangleth whan he sholde holde his   jangleth: jangles, chatters.
        pees."   3435
    Lo, swich it is for to be recchelees   recchelees: reckless, careless.
And necligent, and truste on flaterye.
    But ye that holden this tale a folye,
As of a fox, or of a cok and hen,
Taketh the moralite, goode men.   *4630

3412. maugree youre heed: in spite of all you can do.

3416. delyverly: nimbly (with a pun on the idea of being set free?).

The Fox Chase: The heading in this fourteenth-century manuscript of the *Roman de Renart* says, "How R[enart] carries off a cock which he has seized in a farmyard with several hens. And a woman and villeins chase him with dogs and clubs, and the cock escapes by trickery." Except for the hens, this is an accurate description both of Pierre de St. Cloud's episode of the fox and cock, and also (omitting the dogs) of the illustration. We see a man with a stave (line 3382), a woman with a distaff (3384), and the cock just escaping (3416). The mock-heroic tone of the *Roman*—so influential on Chaucer—appears as early as the third line with its allusion to Paris and Helen (Elaine).

ui tant soit de mauuais mett
9 icome · R · emporte · j · coc que
il a pris en · i · part que plusieurs
gelines · Et une fame vilaine
le chacoient a chien et a baston
et le coc sen eschapu p baiat

gneurs oi aue3 maistrete
maint puj licrie ld iaote
ome paris rau clame
le mal quil en ot et laiaine
e tuttran qui la chieure filt

For Seint Paul seith that al that writen is,
To oure doctrine it is ywrite, ywis;   to oure doctrine: for teaching us.
Taketh the fruyt, and lat the chaf be stille.
Now, goode God, if that it be thy wille,
As seith my lord, so make us alle goode men, 3445 lord: bishop.
And brynge us to his heighe bliss! Amen.

Heere is ended the
Nonnes Preestes tale.

"Sire Nonnes Preest," oure Hooste seide
      anoon,
"I-blessed be thy breche, and every stoon!   breche: buttocks. stoon: testicle.
This was a murie tale of Chauntecleer.
But by my trouthe, if thou were seculer,   *4640 seculer: a layman.
Thou woldest ben a trede-foul aright.   trede-foul: a treader (copulator) of
For if thou have corage as thou hast myght,   fowls. aright: assuredly. corage: de-
Thee were nede of hennes, as I wene,   sire, ardor. thee: to thee.
Ya, moo than seven tymes seventene.
See, whiche braunes hath this gentil preest, 3455 whiche: what. braunes: muscles.
So gret a nekke, and swich a large breest!
He looketh as a sperhauk with his eyen;   sperhauk: sparrowhawk.
Him nedeth nat his colour for to dyen
With brasile, ne with greyn of Portyngale.
Now, sire, faire falle yow for youre tale!" *4650 falle: befall.
   And after that he, with ful merie cheere,
Seide unto another, as ye shuln heere.

The prologe of the
Wyves tale of Bathe.

"Experience, though noon auctoritee   auctoritee: authority; authoritative
Were in this world, is right ynogh for me   statement.
To speke of wo that is in mariage;
For, lordynges, sith I twelve yeer was of age,
Thonked be God that is eterne on lyve,   5 eterne: eternally. on lyve: alive.
Housbondes at chirche dore I have had fyve,—

3441–42. See Romans xv.4.

3444–46. That this benediction may echo an episcopal blessing is suggested by the presence of the following in the Benedictional of John Longlonde, Bishop of Lincoln (1521): "May almighty God have mercy on you and forgive you all your sins, deliver you from all evil, and preserve and confirm you in good, and bring you to life eternal." ("Miseriatur vestri omnipotens deus, et dimittat vobis omnia peccata vestra, liberet vos ab omni malo, conservet et confiremet in bono, et ad vitam perducat eternam.")

3447–62. These lines are found in only nine manuscripts and may have been cancelled by Chaucer when he wrote lines 1941–62 of the Monk's Prologue.

3459. brasile: a red dye-stuff obtained from brazil-wood. greyn of Portyngale: a crimson dye.

6. See General Prologue, l. 460, note. The Wife's preachment through line 162 is based on St. Jerome's thunderous Letter Against Jovinian, the fourth-century heretic, whose arguments the Wife uses to beat down Jerome's views and arguments. See also footnote 671, below.

If I so ofte myghte han wedded be,—
And alle were worthy men in hir degree.
But me was toold, certeyn, nat longe agon is,
That sith that Crist ne wente nevere but onis   10   onis: once.
To weddyng, in the Cane of Galilee,   Cane: Cana.
That by the same ensample taughte he me
That I ne sholde wedded be but ones.
Herke eek, lo, which a sharp word for the nones,   which: what.
Biside a welle, Jhesus, God and man,   15
Spak in repreeve of the Samaritan: repreeve: reproof, reproach.
'Thou hast yhad fyve housbondes,' quod he,
'And that ilke man that now hath thee
Is nat thyn housbonde,' thus he seyde, certeyn.
What that he mente therby, I kan nat seyn;   20
But that I axe, why that the fifthe man
Was noon housbonde to the Samaritan?
How manye myghte she have in mariage?
Yet herde I nevere tellen in myn age   age: life.
Upon this nombre diffinicioun.   25   diffinicioun: limitation.
Men may devyne and glosen, up and doun,   devyne: speculate. glosen: explain.
But wel I woot, expres, withoute lye,   expres: for certain.
God bad us for to wexe and multiplye;   wexe: increase.
That gentil text kan I wel understonde.
Eek wel I woot, he seyde myn housbonde   30
Sholde lete fader and mooder, and take to me.   lete: leave.
But of no nombre mencion made he,
Of bigamye, or of octogamye;   bigamye: two (successive) marriages.
Why sholde men thanne speke of it vileynye?
   Lo, here the wise kyng, daun Salomon;   35   daun: lord.
I trowe he hadde wyves mo than oon.
As wolde God it leveful were to me   leveful: permissible.
To be refresshed half so ofte as he!
Which yifte of God hadde he for alle his wyvys!   which: what a. yifte: gift.
No man hath swich that in this world alyve is.   40
God woot, this noble kyng, as to my wit,   wit: judgment; opinion.
The firste nyght had many a myrie fit   fit: bout.
With ech of hem, so wel was hym on lyve.   on lyve: during (his) life.
Yblessed be God that I have wedded fyve!
Of whiche I have pyked out the beste,   44a
Bothe of here nether purs and of here cheste.   nether: lower. cheste: strongbox.

---

7. I.e., if so many marriages could really be valid.

11. See John ii.1.

16. See John iv.5–19.

28. See Genesis i.28; cf. Nuns' Priest's Tale, l. 3345.

30–31. See Matthew xix.5.

36. See I Kings xi.3: "And he had seven hundred wives, princesses, and three hundred concubines."

44a–44f. These six lines were apparently added by Chaucer in revision.

Diverse scoles maken parfyt clerkes,
And diverse practyk in many sondry werkes
Maketh the werkman parfyt sekirly;   **sekirly:** certainly.
Of fyve husbondes scoleiyng am I.   44f **scoleiyng:** schooling.
Welcome the sixte, whan that evere he shal. 45 **sixte:** sixth. **shal:** shall (appear).
For sith I wol nat kepe me chaast in al,   **in al:** at all.
Whan myn housbonde is fro the world ygon,
Som Cristen man shal wedde me anon;
For thanne, th'apostle seith that I am free
To wedde, a Goddes half, where it liketh me. 50 **a Goddes half:** in God's name.
                                         liketh: pleases.
He seith that to be wedded is no synne;
Bet is to be wedded than to brynne.   **brynne:** burn.
What rekketh me, thogh folk seye vileynye   **what rekketh me:** what do I care.
Of shrewed Lameth and his bigamye?   **shrewed:** wicked, cursed.
I woot wel Abraham was an holy man,   55
And Jacob eek, as fer as evere I kan;
And ech of hem hadde wyves mo than two,
And many another holy man also.
Wher can ye seye, in any maner age,   **seye:** say.
That hye God defended mariage   60 **defended:** forbade.
By expres word? I pray yow, telleth me!   **expres:** clear. **telleth:** tell (imperative).
Or where comanded he virginitee?
I woot as wel as ye, it is no drede,   **it is no drede:** assuredly.
Th'apostel, whan he speketh of maydenhede, **maydenhede:** maidenhood, virginity.
He seyde that precept therof hadde he noon. 65
Men may conseille a womman to be oon,   **oon:** single.
But conseillyng is no comandement.
He putte it in oure owene juggement;
For hadde God comanded maydenhede,
Thanne hadde he dampned weddyng with the   **with the dede:** by that act.
     dede.   70
And certes, if ther were no seed ysowe,   **ysowe:** sown.
Virginitee, thanne wherof sholde it growe?
Poul dorste nat comanden, at the leeste,
A thyng of which his maister yaf noon heeste. **heeste:** commandment.
The dart is set up for virginitee: 75 **dart:** prize.
Cacche whoso may, who renneth best lat see. **cacche:** win.
  But this word is nat taken of every wight,   **taken of:** to be taken by.
But ther as God list gyve it of his myght.   **list:** pleases.
I woot wel that th'apostel was a mayde;   **mayde:** virgin.
But nathelees, thogh that he wroot and sayde 80 **wroot:** wrote.
He wolde that every wight were swich as he,

---

49. th'apostle: St. Paul; see I Corinthians vii.39.
51. See I Corinthians vii.28.
52. See I Corinthians vii.9.
54. Lameth: See Genesis iv.19–23.
65. See I Corinthians vii.25.
81. See I Corinthians vii.7.

Al nys but conseil to virginitee.
And for to been a wyf he yaf me leve
Of indulgence; so is it no repreve   repreve: shame.
To wedde me, if that my make dye,   85 to wedde me: for me to wed. make:
Withouten excepcion of bigamye.   mate.
Al were it good no womman for to touche,—
He mente as in his bed or in his couche;
For peril is bothe fyr and tow t'assemble: tow: flax.
Ye knowe what this ensample may resemble. 90 ensample: symbol. resemble: repre-
This is al and som, he heeld virginitee   sent.
Moore parfit than weddyng in freletee.   in freletee: through frailty.
Freletee clepe I, but if that he and she
Wolde leden al hir lyf in chastitee.   wolde: desired (to).
   I graunte it wel, I have noon envye,   95
Thogh maydenhede preferre bigamye.   preferre: excel. bigamye: remarriage.
It liketh hem to be clene in body and goost;
Of myn estaat ne wol I make no boost.
For wel ye knowe, a lord in his houshold,
He hath nat every vessel al of gold;   100
Somme been of tree, and doon hir lord servyse. tree: wood.
God clepeth folk to hym in sondry wyse,   clepeth: calls.
And everich hath of God a propre yifte,   propre: special. yifte: gift.
Som this, som that, as hym liketh shifte.   shifte: assign, distribute; ordain.
   Virginitee is greet perfeccion,   105
And continence eek with devocion,
But Crist, that of perfeccion is welle,   welle: source.
Bad nat every wight he sholde go selle
Al that he hadde, and gyve it to the poore
And in swich wise folwe hym and his foore. 110 foore: path; footsteps.
He spak to hem that wolde lyve parfitly;
And lordynges, by youre leve, that am nat I.
I wol bistowe the flour of al myn age   flour: flower; choice part; flourishing
In the actes and in fruyt of mariage.   time. fruyt: i.e., procreation.
   Telle me also, to what conclusion   115 conclusion: end, purpose.
Were membres maad of generacion,
And of so parfit wys a wright ywroght?
Trusteth right wel, they were nat maad for noght.
Glose whoso wole, and seye bothe up and doun, glose: explain.
That they were maked for purgacioun   120
Of uryne, and oure bothe thynges smale

---

84. See I Corinthians vii.6.
86. Without reservation on the score of two marriages.
87. See I Corinthians vii.1.
101. See II Timothy ii.20.
103. See I Corinthians vii.7.
105. See Revelation xiv.1–4.
107 ff. See Matthew xix.21.
117. And wrought by so perfectly wise a Creator (Jerome, i, c.36: "a conditore").

Was eek to knowe a female from a male,
And for noon oother cause,—sey ye no?   cause: purpose.
The experience woot wel it is noght so.
So that the clerkes be nat with me wrothe,   125
I sey this, that they maked ben for bothe,
That is to seye, for office, and for ese   office: natural function. ese: pleasure.
Of engendrure, ther we nat God displese.   engendrure: procreation. ther:
Why sholde men elles in hir bookes sette   whereby.
That man shal yelde to his wyf hir dette?   130   yelde: pay. dette: marital debt.
Now wherwith sholde he make his paiement,
If he ne used his sely instrument?
Thanne were they maad upon a creature
To purge uryne, and eek for engendrure.
    But I seye noght that every wight is holde,   135   holde: bound.
That hath swich harneys as I to yow tolde,   harneys: equipment.
To goon and usen hem in engendrure.
Thanne sholde men take of chastitee no cure.   cure: heed.
Crist was a mayde, and shapen as a man,   shapen: shaped.
And many a seint, sith that the world bigan;   140
Yet lyved they evere in parfit chastitee.
I nyl envye no virginitee.   nyl: will not.
Lat hem be breed of pured whete-seed,   breed: bread. pured: refined.
And lat us wyves hoten barly-breed;   hoten: be called.
And yet with barly-breed, Mark telle kan,   145
Oure Lord Jhesu refreshed many a man.
In swich estaat as God hath cleped us   estaat: estate; rank, condition.
I wol persevere; I nam nat precius.   precius: fastidious, over-nice.
In wyfhod wol I use myn instrument
As frely as my Makere hath it sent.   150   frely: generously; freely.
If I be daungerous, God yeve me sorwe!   daungerous: niggardly.
Myn housbonde shal it have bothe eve and
        morwe,
Whan that hym list come forth and paye his
        dette.
An housbonde wol I have, I wol nat lette,   lette: desist.
Which shal be bothe my dettour and my
        thral,   155   thral: thrall, slave.
And have his tribulacion withal
Upon his flessh, whil that I am his wyf.
I have the power durynge al my lyf
Upon his propre body, and nat he.   propre: own.
Right thus th' Apostle tolde it unto me;   160
And bad oure housbondes for to love us wel.

---

130. See I Corinthians vii.3.
145. See John vi.9.
156. See I Corinthians vii.28.
158. See I Corinthians vii.4.
161. See Ephesians v.25.

Al this sentence me liketh every del"—
    Up stirte the Pardoner, and that anon:
"Now, dame," quod he, "by God and by Seint
        John!
Ye been a noble prechour in this cas.   165   cas: question, problem.
I was aboute to wedde a wyf; allas!
What sholde I bye it on my flessh so deere?   what: why. bye: buy, pay for.
Yet hadde I levere wedde no wyf to-yeere!"   to-yeere: this year.
    "Abyde!" quod she, "my tale is nat bigonne.
Nay, thou shalt drynken of another tonne,   170   tonne: tun, cask.
Er that I go, shal savoure wors than ale.
And whan that I have toold thee forth my tale
Of tribulacion in mariage,
Of which I am expert in al myn age,   expert: experienced. age: life.
This is to seyn, myself have been the whippe,   175
Than maystow chese wheither thou wolt sippe
Of thilke tonne that I shal abroche.   abroche: broach, tap.
Be war of it, er thou to ny approche;   to ny: too nigh, too near.
For I shal telle ensamples mo than ten.
'Whoso that nyl be war by othere men,   180   nyl: (ne wyl) will not.
By hym shal othere men corrected be.'
Thise same wordes writeth Ptholomee;
Rede in his *Almageste,* and take it there."
    "Dame, I wolde praye yow, if youre wyl were,"
Seyde this Pardoner, "as ye bigan,   185
Telle forth youre tale, spareth for no man,
And teche us yonge men of youre praktike."   praktike: practice.
    "Gladly," quod she, "sith it may yow like;
But yet I praye to al this compaignye,
If that I speke after my fantasye,   190   fantasye: i.e., whim, caprice.
As taketh not agrief of that I seye;   as taketh: take. agrief: amiss.
For myn entente nys but for to pleye.
    Now, sire, thanne wol I telle yow forth my
        tale.—
As evere moote I drynken wyn or ale,
I shal seye sooth, tho housbondes that I
        hadde,   195
As thre of hem were goode, and two were badde.
The thre were goode men, and riche, and olde;
Unnethe myghte they the statut holde   holde: obey.
In which that they were bounden unto me.
Ye woot wel what I meene of this, pardee!   200
As help me God, I laughe whan I thynke
How pitously a-nyght I made hem swynke!   swynke: labor.
And, by my fey, I tolde of it no stoor.   tolde: accounted. stoor: value.
They had me yeven hir land and hir tresoor;   tresoor: treasure, wealth.

---

182. Ptholomee: This aphorism and that in lines 326–27, are found in a medieval preface to the
earliest Latin translation of Ptolemy's *Almagest.*

Me neded nat do lenger diligence 205
To wynne hir love, or doon hem reverence.
They loved me so wel, by God above,
That I ne tolde no deyntee of hir love!   tolde no deyntee of: set no store by.
A wys womman wol bisye hire evere in oon   bisye: bestir. evere in oon: always,
To gete hire love, ye, ther as she hath noon. 210   continually.
But sith I hadde hem hooly in myn hond,
And sith they hadde yeven me al hir lond,
What sholde I taken keep hem for to plese,   what: why. keep: care.
But it were for my profit and myn ese?
I sette hem so a-werke, by my fey, 215   sette a-werke: got into trouble; put
That many a nyght they songen 'weilawey!'   to work.
The bacon was nat fet for hem, I trowe,   fet: fetched.
That som men han in Essex at Dunmowe.
I governed hem so wel, after my lawe,
That ech of hem ful blisful was and fawe 220   fawe: glad, willing.
To brynge me gaye thynges fro the fayre.
They were ful glad whan I spak to hem faire;
For, God it woot, I chidde hem spitously.   spitously: spitefully.
   Now herkneth hou I baar me proprely,
Ye wise wyves, that kan understonde. 225
   Thus shulde ye speke and bere hem wrong on   bere . . . honde: accuse them falsely.
         honde;
For half so boldely kan ther no man   boldely: recklessly; brazenly.
Swere and lyen, as a womman kan.
I sey nat this by wyves that been wyse,   by: concerning.
But if it be whan they hem mysavyse. 230
A wys wyf, if that she kan hir good,   kan hir good: knows what's good for
Shal beren hym on honde the cow is wood,   her.
And take witnesse of hir owene mayde
Of hir assent; but herkneth how I sayde:
   'Sire olde kaynard, is this thyn array? 235   kaynard: sluggard. array: arrange-
Why is my neighbores wyf so gay?   ment; manner.
She is honoured over al ther she goth;
I sitte at hoom, I have no thrifty cloth.   thrifty: decent. cloth: clothing.
What dostow at my neighebores hous?   dostow: dost thou.
Is she so fair? Artow so amorous? 240
What rowne ye with oure mayde? Benedicite!   rowne: whisper.
Sire olde lecchour, lat thy japes be!   japes: jokes, tricks.
And if I have a gossib or a freend,
Withouten gilt, ye chiden as a feend,   withouten gilt: unjustly.
If that I walke or pleye unto his hous! 245
Thou comest hoom as dronken as a mous,

---

217. bacon: a flitch of bacon awarded annually at Dunmow to any couple who lived a year without quarreling or repenting of their union.

232. cow: chough. The allusion is to the bird that tells a jealous husband of his wife's infidelity; the wife persuades him that the bird is lying or mad.

243. gossib: fellow sponsor in baptism; spiritual relative; intimate friend.

And prechest on thy bench, with yvel preef!   with yvel preef: bad luck to you.
Thou seist to me it is a greet meschief   meschief: misfortune.
To wedde a povre womman, for costage;   costage: cost.
And if that she be riche, of heigh parage,   250 parage: birth, lineage.
Thanne seistow that it is a tormentrie
To soffre hire pride and hire malencolie.
And if that she be fair, thou verray knave,
Thou seyst that every holour wol hire have;   holour: lecher.
She may no while in chastitee abyde,   255
That is assailled upon ech a syde.   ech a: every.
   Thou seyst som folk desiren us for richesse,
Somme for oure shap, and somme for oure
         fairnesse,
And som for she kan outher synge or daunce,   outher: either.
And som for gentillesse and daliaunce;   260 daliaunce: amorous play.
Som for hir handes and hir armes smale:
Thus goth al to the devel, by thy tale.
Thou seyst men may nat kepe a castel wal,
It may so longe assailled been over al.   over al: everywhere.
   And if that she be foul, thou seist that she 265 foul: ugly.
Coveiteth every man that she may se,   coveiteth: lusts after.
For as a spaynel she wol on hym lepe,
Til that she fynde som man hire to chepe.   chepe: acquire.
Ne noon so grey goos goth ther in the lake
As, sëistow, wol been withoute make.   270 make: mate.
And seyst it is an hard thyng for to welde   welde: possess.
A thyng that no man wole, his thankes, helde.   his thankes: of his free will. helde:
Thus seistow, lorel, whan thow goost to bedde;   hold, retain. lorel: rogue.
And that no wys man nedeth for to wedde,
Ne no man that entendeth unto hevene.   275 entendeth: strives to go.
With wilde thonder-dynt and firy levene   dynt: stroke. levene: lightning.
Moote thy welked nekke be tobroke!   welked: withered. tobroke: broken.
   Thow seyst that droppyng houses, and eek   droppyng: leaky.
         smoke,
And chidyng wyves maken men to flee
Out of hir owene houses; a! benedicitee!   280
What eyleth swich an old man for to chide?
   Thow seyst we wyves wil oure vices hide   vices: vices, faults, blemishes.
Til we be fast, and thanne we wol hem   fast: securely wed.
         shewe,—
Wel may that be a proverbe of a shrewe!
   Thou seist that oxen, asses, hors, and
         houndes,   285 hors: horses.
They been assayed at diverse stoundes;   assayed: tested. stoundes: times.
Bacyns, lavours, er that men hem bye,   lavours: lavers, basins.
Spoones, stooles, and al swich housbondrye,   housbondrye: household goods.
And so been pottes, clothes, and array;   array: attire.
But folk of wyves maken noon assay,   290
Til they be wedded; olde dotard shrewe!   dotard: foolish.

And thanne, seistow, we wil oure vices shewe.
    Thou seist also that it displeseth me
But if that thou wolt preise my beautee,
And but thou poure alwey upon my face,   295 poure: gaze.
And clepe me "faire dame" in every place;
And but thou make a feeste on thilke day
That I was born, and make me fressh and gay;
And but thou do to my norice honour,   norice: nurse.
And to my chamberere withinne my bour,   300 chamberere: lady's maid. **bour:**
And to my fadres folk and his allyes,—   chamber, **allyes:** relatives.
Thus seistow, olde barel-ful of lyes!
    And yet of oure apprentice Janekyn,
For his crispe heer, shynynge as gold so fyn,   crispe: curly.
And for he squiereth me bothe up and doun, 305
Yet hastow caught a fals suspecioun.
I wil hym nat, thogh thou were deed tomorwe! wil: desire.
    But tel me this: why hydestow, with sorwe, with sorwe: bad luck to you!
The keyes of thy cheste awey fro me?
It is my good as wel as thyn, pardee!   310 good: property, goods.
What, wenestow make an ydiot of oure dame?   wenestow: to you think (to).
Now by that lord that called is Seint Jame,
Thou shalt nat bothe, thogh that thou were
        wood,
Be maister of my body and of my good;
That oon thou shalt forgo, maugree thyne
        eyen.   315
What helpeth it of me enquere and spyen?
I trowe thou woldest loke me in thy chiste!   loke: lock.
Thou sholdest seye, "Wyf, go wher thee liste;
Taak youre disport, I wol nat leve no talys.   disport: sport, amusement. **leve:** be-
I knowe yow for a trewe wyf, dame Alys."   320 lieve.
We love no man that taketh kep or charge   charge: concern.
Wher that we goon; we wol ben at oure large. large: liberty.
    Of alle men yblessed moot he be,
The wise astrologien, Daun Ptholome,
That seith this proverbe in his *Almageste*: 325
"Of alle men his wysdom is hyeste
That rekketh nat who hath the world in honde." in honde: in control.
By this proverbe thou shalt understonde,
Have thou ynogh, what thar thee rekke or care thar: need.
How myrily that othere folkes fare?   330
For, certes, olde dotard, by youre leve,
Ye shul have queynte right ynogh at eve.   queynte: genitals.
He is to greet a nygard that wil werne   nygard: miser. **werne:** forbid.
A man to lighte a candle at his lanterne;
He shal have never the lasse light, pardee. 335
Have thou ynogh, thee thar nat pleyne thee.   thee thar: you need.

---

315. maugree thyne eyen: in spite of all you can do.

Thou seyst also, that if we make us gay
With clothyng, and with precious array,
That it is peril of oure chastitee;
And yet, with sorwe! thou most enforce thee, 340   enforce thee: reinforce your position.
And seye thise wordes in the Apostles name:
"In habit maad with chastitee and shame
Ye wommen shul apparaille yow," quod he,
"And nat in tressed heer and gay perree,   tressed: braided. perree: jewelry, pre-
As perles, ne with gold, ne clothes riche." 345   cious stones.
After thy text, ne after thy rubriche,   rubriche: rubric.
I wol nat werke as muchel as a gnat.
   Thou seydest this, that I was lyk a cat;
For whoso wolde senge a cattes skyn,   senge: singe.
Thanne wolde the cat wel dwellen in his in; 350   in: dwelling.
And if the cattes skyn be slyk and gay,   slyk: sleek.
She wol nat dwelle in house half a day,
But forth she wole, er any day be dawed,   dawed: dawned.
To shewe hir skyn, and goon a-caterwawed.   a-caterwawed: a-caterwauling.
This is to seye, if I be gay, sire shrewe, 355
I wol renne out, my borel for to shewe.   borel: coarse woolen clothing.
   Sire olde fool, what helpeth thee t'espyen?
Thogh thou preye Argus with his hundred eyen
To be my warde-cors, as he kan best,   warde-cors: body-guard.
In feith, he shal nat kepe me but me lest; 360
Yet koude I make his berd, so moot I thee!   make his berd: deceive him.
   Thou seydest eek that ther been thynges thre,
The whiche thynges troublen al this erthe,
And that no wight may endure the ferthe.   ferthe: fourth.
O leeve sire shrewe, Jhesu shorte thy lyf! 365   shorte: shorten.
Yet prechestow and seyst an hateful wyf
Yrekened is for oon of thise meschances.   yrekened: accounted.
Been ther none othere resemblances
That ye may likne youre parables to,
But if a sely wyf be oon of tho? 370   sely: unfortunate. tho: those.
   Thou liknest eek wommanes love to helle,
To bareyne lond, ther water may nat dwelle.   bareyne: barren.
Thou liknest it also to wilde fyr;
The moore it brenneth, the moore it hath desir
To consume every thyng that brent wole be. 375
Thou seyest, right as wormes shende a tree,   shende: destroy.
Right so a wyf destroyeth hire housbonde;
This knowe they that been to wyves bonde.'   bonde: bound, enslaved.
   Lordynges, right thus, as ye have understonde,
Baar I stifly myne olde housbondes on honde 380   baar on honde: accused.

---

342 ff. See I Timothy ii.9.
358. Argus: a hundred-eyed monster set by Juno to guard Io, whom Jupiter loved and had changed into a heifer.
373. wilde fyr: Greek fire, a highly inflammable preparation used in warfare.

That thus they seyden in hir dronkenesse;
And al was fals, but that I took witnesse
On Janekyn, and on my nece also.
O Lord! the peyne I dide hem and the wo,
Ful giltelees, by Goddes sweete pyne!   385   pyne: pain, suffering.
For as an hors I koude byte and whyne.
I koude pleyne, and I was in the gilt,   in the gilt: guilty.
Or elles often tyme I hadde been spilt.   spilt: destroyed.
Whoso that first to mille comth, first grynt;   grynt: grinds.
I pleyned first, so was oure werre ystynt.   390   ystynt: stopped.
They were ful glad to excuse hem ful blyve   blyve: quickly.
Of thyng of which they nevere agilte hir lyve.   agilte: were guilty. hir lyve: in their
Of wenches wolde I beren hem on honde,   lives.
Whan that for syk they myghte unnethe stonde.   for syk: because of sickness.
        Yet tikled I his herte, for that he   395
Wende that I hadde of hym so greet chiertee!   chiertee: affection.
I swoor that al my walkynge out by nyghte
Was for t'espye wenches that he dighte;   dighte: lay with.
Under that colour hadde I many a myrthe.   colour: excuse, pretence.
For al swich wit it yeven us in oure birthe;   400
Deceite, wepyng, spynnyng God hath yive
To wommen kyndely, whil they may lyve.   kyndely: naturally, by nature.
And thus of o thyng I avaunte me,   avaunte me: boast.
Atte ende I hadde the bet in ech degree,   bet: better. in ech degree: in every
By sleighte, or force, or by some maner   way.
        thyng,   405
As by continuel murmur or grucchyng.   grucchyng: grumbling.
Namely abedde hadden they meschaunce: namely: especially.
Ther wolde I chide, and do hem no plesaunce;
I wolde no lenger in the bed abyde,
If that I felte his arm over my syde,   410
Til he had maad his raunson unto me;   maad his raunson: paid his penalty.
Thanne wolde I suffre hym do his nycetee.   nycetee: folly; lust.
And therfore every man this tale I telle,
Wynne whoso may, for al is for to selle;
With empty hand men may none haukes lure.   415
For wynnyng wolde I al his lust endure,   wynnyng: profit.
And make me a feyned appetit;
And yet in bacon hadde I nevere delit;   bacon: cured pork (i.e., old meat);
That made me that evere I wolde hem chide.   (here) old men.
For thogh the pope hadde seten hem biside,   420   seten: sat.
I wolde nat spare hem at hir owene bord;   bord: table, meals.
For, by my trouthe, I quitte hem word for word.   quitte: requited, repaid.
As helpe me verray God omnipotent,
Though I right now sholde make my testament,
I ne owe hem nat a word that it nys quit.   425
I broghte it so aboute by my wit
That they moste yeve it up, as for the beste,
Or elles hadde we nevere been in reste.

For thogh he looked as a wood leon,
Yet sholde he faille of his conclusion.   430   conclusion: purpose.
   Thanne wolde I seye, 'Goode lief, taak keep   lief: dear one.
How mekely looketh Wilkyn, oure sheep!
Com neer, my spouse, lat me ba thy cheke!   ba: kiss.
Ye sholde been al pacient and meke,
And han a sweete spiced conscience,   435   spiced conscience: scrupulous, fas-
Sith ye so preche of Jobes pacience.   tidious conscience.
Suffreth alwey, syn ye so wel kan preche;
And but ye do, certein we shal yow teche
That it is fair to have a wyf in pees.   fair: well.
Oon of us two moste bowen, doutelees;   440
And sith a man is moore resonable
Than womman is, ye moste been suffrable.   suffrable: patient.
What eyleth yow to grucche thus and grone?   grucche: grumble.
Is it for ye wolde have my queynte allone?   for: because. queynte: genitals.
Wy, taak it al! lo, have it every del!   445   allone: all to yourself.
Peter! I shrewe yow, but ye love it wel;   Peter!: by St. Peter! shrewe: curse.
For if I wolde selle my *bele chose,*   *bele chose:* (lit.) beautiful thing.
I koude walke as fressh as is a rose;
But I wol kepe it for youre owene tooth.   tooth: desires, appetites (? cf. line
Ye be to blame, by God! I sey yow sooth.'   450   602).
   Swiche manere wordes hadde we on honde.
Now wol I speken of my fourthe housbonde.
   My fourthe housbonde was a revelour;
This is to seyn, he hadde a paramour;   paramour: mistress.
And I was yong and ful of ragerye,   455   ragerye: wantonness, passion.
Stibourn and strong, and joly as a pye.   stibourn: untameable. pye: magpie.
How koude I daunce to an harpe smale,   smale: gracefully.
And synge, ywis, as any nyghtyngale,
Whan I had dronke a draughte of sweete wyn!
Metellius, the foule cherl, the swyn,   460
That with a staf birafte his wyf hir lyf,   birafte hir lyf: put to death.
For she drank wyn, thogh I hadde been his wyf,   for: because.
Ne sholde nat han daunted me fro drynke!   daunted: frightened.
And after wyn on Venus moste I thynke,
For al so siker as cold engendreth hayl,   465   al so siker as: as surely as.
A likerous mouth moste han a likerous tayl.   likerous: licentious, lecherous.
In womman vinolent is no defence,—   vinolent: addicted to drinking wine.
This knowen lecchours by experience.
   But, Lord Crist! whan that it remembreth me   it remembreth me: I remember.
Upon my yowthe, and on my jolitee,   470
It tikleth me aboute myn herte roote.   herte: heart's.
Unto this day it dooth myn herte boote   boote: good.
That I have had my world as in my tyme.
But age, allas! that al wole envenyme,

---

460. **Metellius:** This story comes from the collection of historical anecdotes compiled by the
Roman, Valerius Maximus.

Hath me biraft my beautee and my pith.   475   **me biraft:** robbed me of. **pith:** vigor.
Lat go, farewel! the devel go therwith!
The flour is goon, ther is namoore to telle;
The bren, as I best kan, now moste I selle;   **bren:** bran, husks.
But yet to be right myrie wol I fonde.   **fonde:** strive.
Now wol I tellen of my fourthe housbonde.   480

   I seye, I hadde in herte gret despit   **despit:** resentment.
That he of any oother had delit.
But he was quit, by God and by Seint Joce!   **quit:** paid back.
I made hym of the same wode a croce;   **croce:** staff (cf. ll. 454, 461).
Nat of my body, in no foul manere,   485
But certeinly, I made folk swich cheere   **made folk swich cheere:** treated folk
That in his owene grece I made hym frye   in such a way.
For angre, and for verray jalousye.
By God! in erthe I was his purgatorie,
For which I hope his soule be in glorie.   490
For, God it woot, he sat ful ofte and song,
Whan that his shoo ful bitterly hym wrong.   **wrong:** wrung, pinched.
Ther was no wight, save God and he, that wiste,
In many wise, how soore I hym twiste.   **soore:** sorely. **twiste:** tormented.
He deyde whan I cam fro Jerusalem,   495
And lith ygrave under the roode beem,   **ygrave:** buried.
Al is his tombe noght so curyus   **curyus:** elaborate.
As was the sepulcre of hym Daryus,
Which that Appelles wroghte subtilly;   **subtilly:** skilfully.
It nys but wast to burye hym preciously.   500   **wast:** waste. **preciously:** expensively.
Lat hym fare wel, God gyve his soul reste!
He is now in his grave and in his cheste.   **cheste:** coffin.

   Now of my fifthe housbonde wol I telle.
God lete his soule nevere come in helle!
And yet was he to me the mooste shrewe;   505   **mooste shrewe:** worst rascal.
That feele I on my ribbes al by rewe,   **by rewe:** in order, in a row.
And evere shal unto myn endyng day.
But in oure bed he was so fressh and gay,
And therwithal so wel koude he me glose,   **glose:** flatter, cajole.
Whan that he wolde han my *bele chose,*   510
That thogh he hadde me bete on every bon,   **bon:** bone.
He koude wynne agayn my love anon.
I trowe I loved hym best, for that he
Was of his love daungerous to me.   **daungerous:** niggardly.
We wommen han, if that I shal nat lye,   515
In this matere a queynte fantasye;
Wayte what thyng we may nat lightly have,   **wayte what:** whatever. **lightly:** easily.

---

483. Seint Joce: St. Judocus, a Breton saint.

496. roode beem: the beam, usually between the chancel and the nave, on which was placed a crucifix.

498. The tomb of Darius was described by Gautier de Chatillon, in his *Alexandreis,* as being particularly elaborate.

Therafter wol we crye al day and crave.   therafter: for that.
Forbede us thyng, and that desiren we;
Preesse on us faste, and thanne wol we fle.   520
With daunger oute we al oure chaffare;   oute: set forth.
Greet prees at market maketh deere ware,   prees: crowd.
And to greet cheep is holde at litel prys: prys: worth, esteem.
This knoweth every womman that is wys.
  My fifthe housbonde, God his soule blesse!   525
Which that I took for love, and no richesse,
He som tyme was a clerk of Oxenford,   Oxenford: Oxford.
And hadde left scole, and wente at hom to bord
With my gossib, dwellynge in oure toun;   gossib: intimate friend.
God have hir soule! hir name was Alisoun.   530
She knew myn herte, and eek my privetee,
Bet than oure parisshe preest, so moot I thee!
To hire biwreyed I my conseil al.   biwreyed: betrayed, revealed.
For hadde myn housbonde pissed on a wal,
Or doon a thyng that sholde han cost his lyf,   535
To hire, and to another worthy wyf,
And to my nece, which that I loved wel,
I wolde han toold his conseil every del.   conseil: secret.
And so I dide ful often, God it woot,
That made his face often reed and hoot   540
For verray shame, and blamed hymself for he   for: because.
Had toold to me so greet a pryvetee.
  And so bifel that ones in a Lente—
So often tymes I to my gossyb wente,
For evere yet I loved to be gay,   545
And for to walke in March, Averill, and May,
Fro hous to hous, to heere sondry tales—
That Jankyn clerk, and my gossyb dame Alys,
And I myself, into the feeldes wente.
Myn housbonde was at Londoun al that
      Lente;   550
I hadde the bettre leyser for to pleye,   leyser: opportunity.
And for to se, and eek for to be seye   seye: seen.
Of lusty folk. What wiste I wher my grace
Was shapen for to be, or in what place?
Therfore I made my visitaciouns   555
To vigilies and to processiouns,   vigilies: vigils.
To prechyng eek, and to thise pilgrimages,
To pleyes of myracles, and to mariages,
And wered upon my gaye scarlet gytes.   pleyes of myracles: miracle plays.
Thise wormes, ne thise motthes, ne thise   wered upon: wore. gytes: dresses,
      mytes,   560   gowns.

---

521. Grudgingly we set forth all we have to sell.
523. to greet cheep: too good a bargain, too low a price.
553–54. What . . . be: How did I know with whom my good fortune was destined to be.

Upon my peril, frete hem never a del;   frete: ate, consumed.
And wostow why? for they were used wel.
 Now wol I tellen forth what happed me.
I seye that in the feeldes walked we,
Til trewely we hadde swich daliance,   565
This clerk and I, that of my purveiance   of: because of. purveiance:
I spak to hym and seyde hym how that he,   providence, foresight.
If I were wydwe, sholde wedde me.
For certeinly, I sey for no bobance,   bobance: boast.
Yet was I nevere withouten purveiance   570
Of mariage, n'of othere thynges eek.
I holde a mouses herte nat worth a leek
That hath but oon hole for to sterte to,   sterte: start, run quickly.
And if that faille, thanne is al ydo.   ydo: done, finished.
 I bar hym on honde he hadde enchanted   bar hym on honde: persuaded him.
   me,—   575
My dame taughte me that soutiltee.   dame: mother.
And eek I seyde I mette of hym al nyght,   mette: dreamed.
He wolde han slayn me as I lay upright,   upright: face up.
And al my bed was ful of verray blood;
'But yet I hope that ye shal do me good,   580
For blood bitokeneth gold, as me was taught.'
And al was fals; I dremed of it right naught,
But as I folwed ay my dames loore,
As wel of that as of othere thynges moore.
 But now, sire, lat me se, what shal I seyn? 585
A ha! by God, I have my tale ageyn.
 Whan that my fourthe housbonde was on
   beere,   beere: bier.
I weep algate, and made sory cheere,   weep: wept. algate: unceasingly.
As wyves mooten, for it is usage,
And with my coverchief covered my visage, 590
But for that I was purveyed of a make,   purveyed of: provided with. make:
I wepte but smal, and that I undertake.   mate.
 To chirche was myn housbonde born a-morwe a-morwe: the next morning.
With neighebores, that for hym maden sorwe;
And Jankyn, oure clerk, was oon of tho. 595
As help me God! whan that I saw hym go
After the beere, me thoughte he hadde a paire
Of legges and of feet so clene and faire   clene: shapely.
That al myn herte I yaf unto his hoold.   hoold: possession.
He was, I trowe, twenty wynter oold,   600
And I was fourty, if I shal seye sooth;
But yet I hadde alwey a coltes tooth.   a coltes tooth: youthful desires, las-
Gat-tothed I was, and that bicam me weel; civious appetites.

---

565. daliance: mirth; playfulness; wanton behavior.
603. gat-tothed: with teeth set apart. This was believed to indicate a tendency toward luck, travel, boldness, falseness, gluttony, and lasciviousness.

I hadde the prente of seinte Venus seel.
As help me God! I was a lusty oon,   605
And faire, and riche, and yong, and wel bigon;
And trewely, as myne housbondes tolde me,
I hadde the beste *quoniam* myghte be.
For certes, I am al Venerien
In feelynge, and myn herte is Marcien.   610
Venus me yaf my lust, my likerousnesse,
And Mars yaf me my sturdy hardynesse;
Myn ascendent was Taur, and Mars therinne.
Allas! allas! that evere love was synne!
I folwed ay myn inclinacioun   615
By vertu of my constellacioun;
That made me I koude noght withdrawe
My chambre of Venus from a good felawe.
Yet have I Martes mark upon my face,
And also in another privee place.   620
For God so wysely be my savacioun,
I loved nevere by no discrecioun,
But evere folwede myn appetit,
Al were he short, long, blak or whit;
I took no kep, so that he liked me,   625
How poore he was, ne eek of what degree.
    What sholde I seye? but, at the monthes
                ende,
This joly clerk, Jankyn, that was so hende,
Hath wedded me with greet solempnytee;
And to hym yaf I al the lond and fee   630
That evere was me yeven therbifore.
But afterward repented me ful sore;
He nolde suffre nothyng of my list.
By God! he smoot me ones on the lyst,
For that I rente out of his book a leef,   635
That of the strook myn ere wax al deef.
Stibourn I was as is a leonesse,
And of my tonge a verray jangleresse,
And walke I wolde, as I had doon biforn,
From hous to hous, although he had it sworn;   640
For which he often tymes wolde preche,
And me of olde Romayn geestes teche;
How he Symplicius Gallus lefte his wyf,
And hire forsook for terme of al his lyf,

prente: print, impress; i.e., a birth-
mark.

wel bigon: well off; cheerful.

quoniam: genitals.

likerousnesse: lecherousness.

Martes mark: a birthmark from the in-
fluence of Mars.
wysely: surely.

liked: pleased.
degree: rank.

hende: pleasant, comely.

fee: property.

list: desire.
lyst: ear.

that: so that. wax: became.
stibourn: untameable.
jangleresse: nagging, chattering
  woman.
it: i.e., that I shouldn't.

609–610. Venerien . . . Marcien: The influence of the planets Venus and Mars is related to
much of the Wife of Bath's complex personality.

613. ascendent: the part of the zodiac arising above the horizon (at her birth).

616. constellacioun: configuration of planets (at her birth); horoscope.

642. olde Romayn geestes: stories of Roman history; these two anecdotes are from Valerius
Maximus.

Noght but for open-heveded he hir say
Lookynge out at his dore upon a day.
    Another Romayn tolde he me by name,
That, for his wyf was at a someres game
Withouten his wityng, he forsook hire eke.
And thanne wolde he upon his Bible seke
That ilke proverbe of Ecclesiaste
Where he comandeth, and forbedeth faste,
Man shal nat suffre his wyf go roule aboute.
Thanne wolde he seye right thus, withouten
        doute:
'Whoso that buyldeth his hous al of salwes,
And priketh his blynde hors over the falwes,
And suffreth his wyf to go seken halwes,
Is worthy to been hanged on the galwes!'
But al for noght, I sette noght an hawe
Of his proverbes n' of his olde sawe,
Ne I wolde nat of hym corrected be.
I hate hym that my vices telleth me,
And so doo mo, God woot, of us than I.
This made hym with me wood al outrely;
I nolde noght forbere hym in no cas.
    Now wol I seye yow sooth, by Seint Thomas,
Why that I rente out of his book a leef,
For which he smoot me so that I was deef.
    He hadde a book that gladly, nyght and day,
For his desport he wolde rede alway;
He cleped it Valerie and Theofraste,
At which book he lough alwey ful faste.
And eek ther was somtyme a clerk at Rome,
A cardinal, that highte Seint Jerome,
That made a book agayn Jovinian;
In which book eek ther was Tertulan,
Crisippus, Trotula, and Helowys,

645 open-heveded: bare-headed. **say:** saw.

someres game: midsummer revels.
wityng: knowledge.

650

faste: strictly.
roule: roam, gad.

655 salwes: willow-twigs, osiers.
priketh: spurs. **falwes:** fallow-ground.
halwes: shrines of saints.
galwes: gallows.
hawe: haw, fruit of the hawthorn.
660 sawe: saying.
of: by.

al outrely: completely.
665 forbere: tolerate. **in no cas:** not at all.

670 desport: amusement.

lough: laughed. **faste:** hard.

675

---

651. See Ecclesiasticus xxv.25.

655–58. This rimed proverb occurs elsewhere and is apparently rather ancient .

669–70. gladly wolde rede: liked to read.

671. **Valerie and Theofraste:** Jankyn's "book of wikked wyves" contained three anti-feminist, anti-matrimonial tracts which flourished in Chaucer's time as a part of the attempts of the Church to promote clerical celibacy and to encourage young men to embrace celibacy with eagerness and even thanksgiving. *The Advice of Valerius to Ruffinus the Philosopher not to Marry* (actually written by Walter Map, twelfth-century Archdeacon of Oxford) was thought to be the work of some ancient Roman, probably Valerius Maximus; anecdotes from this treatise are recounted by Dame Alice in ll. 715–16, 721–26, and 747–64. *The Little Golden Book of Theophrastus on Marriage* is a virulent attack on women which is echoed throughout ll. 236–307. These two treatises appear in medieval manuscripts along with anti-feminist excerpts from Jerome's *Letter against Jovinian,* echoed in ll. 727–46 and 782–83. Tertullian and Chrysippus are mentioned as anti-matrimonial writers by Jerome. To Trotula was attributed a famous medieval treatise on diseases of women and another on cosmetics. Eloise gave reasons for refusing to marry Abelard. The Book of Proverbs (*Liber Parabolarum*) is quoted in ll. 778–81 and 784–85. Ovid's *Art of Love* appears in one of the anti-feminist manuscripts still extant in British libraries and is echoed in ll. 733–36.

674. Nicholas Trevet, in *Les Cronicles,* refers to Jerome as "cardinal de Rome."

That was abbesse nat fer fro Parys;
And eek the Parables of Salomon,
Ovides Art, and bookes many on,   680 on: a one.
And alle thise were bounden in o volume.
And every nyght and day was his custume,
Whan he hadde leyser and vacacioun   vacacioun: spare time.
From oother worldly occupacioun,
To reden in this book of wikked wyves.   685
He knew of hem mo legendes and lyves
Than been of goode wyves in the Bible.
For trusteth wel, it is an impossible   an impossible: an impossibility (Latin,
That any clerk wol speke good of wyves,   *impossibile*: a term in medieval
But if it be of holy seintes lyves,   690 logic).
Ne of noon oother womman never the mo.
Who peyntede the leon? Tel me who!
By God! if wommen hadde writen stories,
As clerkes han withinne hire oratories,   oratories: closets for private devotions.
They wolde han writen of men moore
       wikkednesse   695
Than al the mark of Adam may redresse.
The children of Mercurie and of Venus
Been in hir wirkyng ful contrarius;   wirkyng: actions, doings.
Mercurie loveth wysdam and science,
And Venus loveth riot and dispence.   700 riot: wanton revelry. **dispence**: extrav-
And, for hir diverse disposicioun,   agance. **disposicioun**: position or
Ech falleth in otheres exaltacioun.   influence. **falleth**: loses influence.
And thus, God woot, Mercurie is desolat   desolat: destitute of influence.
In Pisces, wher Venus is exaltat;
And Venus falleth ther Mercurie is reysed.   705 reysed: raised.
Therfore no womman of no clerk is preysed.   of: by.
The clerk, whan he is old, and may noght do
Of Venus werkes worth his olde sho,
Thanne sit he doun, and writ in his dotage   writ: (writeth) writes.
That wommen kan nat kepe hir mariage!   710
   But now to purpos, why I tolde thee
That I was beten for a book, pardee!
Upon a nyght Jankyn, that was oure sire,   sire: husband.
Redde on his book, as he sat by the fire,
Of Eva first, that for hir wikkednesse   715
Was al mankynde broght to wrecchednesse,
For which that Jhesu Crist hymself was slayn,

---

692. In one of the *Fables* of Marie de France—No. 37, "Del leün e del vilein"—a peasant shows a lion a painting of a peasant killing a lion with an axe. The lion thereupon asks, "Who made this likeness here, a man or a lion? Tell me that much" (ll. 7–14). For Chaucer's knowledge of Marie's *Fables* see the first note on the Nuns' Priest's Tale.

696. **al the mark of Adam**: all [those in] the image of Adam.

697. Concerning those born under the influence of Venus see pages 270 and 271.

702. **exaltacioun**: the position of a planet in the zodiac where it was thought to exert its greatest influence.

That boghte us with his herte blood agayn.
    boghte agayn: redeemed.

Lo, heere expres of wommen may ye fynde,
    expres: explicitly.

That womman was the los of al mankynde.   720
    los: cause of the perdition.

    Tho redde he me how Sampson loste his heres:
    heres: hair.

Slepynge, his lemman kitte it with hir sheres;
    lemman: mistress. kitte: cut.

Thurgh which treson loste he bothe his eyen.

    Tho redde he me, if that I shal nat lyen,

Of Hercules and of his Dianyre,   725
    Dianyre: Deianira.

That caused hym to sette hymself afyre.

    No thyng forgat he the care and the wo

That Socrates hadde with his wyves two;

How Xantippa caste pisse upon his heed.

This sely man sat stille as he were deed;   730
    deed: dead.

He wiped his heed, namoore dorste he seyn,

But 'Er that thonder stynte, comth a reyn!'

    Of Phasipha, that was the queene of Crete,

For shrewednesse, hym thoughte the tale swete;
    shrewednesse: cursedness.

Fy! spek namoore—it is a grisly thyng—   735
    grisly: horrible.

Of hire horrible lust and hir likyng.

    Of Clitermystra, for hire lecherye,

That falsly made hire housbonde for to dye,

He redde it with ful good devocioun.

    He tolde me eek for what occasioun   740

Amphiorax at Thebes loste his lyf.

Myn housbonde hadde a legende of his wyf,

Eriphilem, that for an ouche of gold
    ouche: jeweled ornament.

Hath prively unto the Grekes told

Wher that hir housbonde hidde hym in a
        place,   745

For which he hadde at Thebes sory grace.
    sory grace: misfortune.

    Of Lyvia tolde he me, and of Lucye:

They bothe made hir housbondes for to dye;

That oon for love, that oother was for hate.

Lyvia hir housbonde, on an even late,   750
    even: evening.

---

733. Pasiphaë, in love with a bull, became the mother of the Minotaur.

737. **Clitermystra:** Clytemnestra, wife of Agamemnon.

741. Amphiaraus, a Grecian seer, was forced to fight against Thebes.

747. The wives of Drusus and Lucretius.

The Children of Venus: This representation of Venus and her children is in an English manuscript of about 1460 and accompanies the text of the *Boke off Astronomy and off phylosophye.* Although the representation of activities under the influence of the various planets goes back to late classical times, their assemblage in a composite picture appears to date from the late fourteenth century. Friday, the day of Venus (see Nuns' Priest's Tale, lines 3342–46) is named at the top, as are Taurus and Libra, her "mansions," the zodiacal signs in which her influence is most powerful. Her reddish brown hair is crowned with a garland of roses. Below the roses in her hand is the symbol for Libra, but below her mirror is a strange symbol (not that for Taurus) probably derived from the Netherlandish block-book which may have served as a model for the planets and their children in this manuscript. The composite scene shows characteristic diversions of the children of Venus, including drink, the bath, music, dance, and (under the rosetree) love; but the boys in front, who in the block-book sing from their sheet music, are strangely silent here, and one reader has suggested that they are playing a game. (See lines 697–700; Squire's Tale, 272; Franklin's Tale, 937.)

Empoysoned hath, for that she was his fo;
Lucia, likerous, loved hire housbonde so
That, for he sholde alwey upon hire thynke,
She yaf hym swich a manere love-drynke
That he was deed er it were by the morwe; 755 by the morwe: early in the morning.
And thus algates housbondes han sorwe.   algates: under all circumstances.
   Thanne tolde he me how oon Latumyus
Compleyned unto his felawe Arrius
That in his gardyn growed swich a tree
On which he seyde how that his wyves thre 760
Hanged hemself for herte despitus.   despitus: spiteful.
'O leeve brother,' quod this Arrius,
'Yif me a plante of thilke blissed tree,   plante: slip.
And in my gardyn planted shal it be.'
   Of latter date, of wyves hath he red   765 of latter date: recently, lately.
That somme han slayn hir housbondes in hir
       bed,
And lete hir lecchour dighte hire al the nyght, dighte: lie with.
Whan that the corps lay in the floor upright.   upright: face up.
And somme han dryve nayles in hir brayn,
Whil that they slepte, and thus they han hem
       slayn.   770
Somme han hem yeve poysoun in hire drynke.
He spak moore harm than herte may bithynke;   bithynke: think of.
And therwithal he knew of mo proverbes
Than in this world ther growen gras or herbes.
'Bet is,' quod he, 'thyn habitacioun   775
Be with a leon or a foul dragoun,
Than with a womman usynge for to chide.'   usynge: accustomed.
'Bet is,' quod he, 'hye in the roof abyde,
Than with an angry wyf doun in the hous;
They been so wikked and contrarious,   780
They haten that hir housbondes loven ay.'
He seyde, a 'womman cast hir shame away,   cast: (casteth) casts.
Whan she cast of hir smok'; and forthermo,   of: off. smok: smock, shift.
'A fair womman, but she be chaast also,
Is lyk a gold ryng in a sowes nose.'   785
Who wolde wene, or who wolde suppose,
The wo that in myn herte was, and pyne?   pyne: pain, torment.
   And whan I saugh he wolde nevere fyne   fyne: cease.
To reden on this cursed book al nyght,
Al sodeynly thre leves have I plyght   790 plyght: plucked, torn.
Out of his book, right as he radde, and eke   radde: read.
I with my fest so took hym on the cheke
That in oure fyr he fil bakward adoun.
And he up stirte as dooth a wood leoun,
And with his fest he smoot me on the heed,   795

---

781. They always hate what their husbands love.

That in the floor I lay as I were deed.
And whan he saugh how stille that I lay,
He was agast, and wolde han fled his way,
Til atte laste out of my swogh I breyde.
'O! hastow slayn me, false theef?' I seyde,   800
'And for my land thus hastow mordred me?
Er I be deed, yet wol I kisse thee.'

  And neer he cam, and kneled faire adoun,
And seyde, 'Deere suster Alisoun,
As help me God! I shal thee nevere smyte.   805
That I have doon, it is thyself to wyte.
Foryeve it me, and that I thee biseke!'
And yet eftsoones I hitte hym on the cheke,
And seyde, 'Theef, thus muchel am I wreke;
Now wol I dye, I may no lenger speke.'   810
But atte laste, with muchel care and wo,
We fille acorded by us selven two.
He yaf me al the bridel in myn hond,
To han the governance of hous and lond,
And of his tonge, and of his hond also;   815
And made hym brenne his book anon right tho.
And whan that I hadde geten unto me,
By maistrie, al the soveraynetee,
And that he seyde, 'Myn owene trewe wyf,
Do as thee lust the terme of al thy lyf;   820
Keep thyn honour, and keep eek myn estaat'—
After that day we hadden never debaat.
God helpe me so, I was to hym as kynde
As any wyf from Denmark unto Ynde,
And also trewe, and so was he to me.   825
I prey to God, that sit in magestee,
So blesse his soule for his mercy deere.
Now wol I seye my tale, if ye wol heere."

swogh: swoon. breyde: started,
awaked. theef: villain; thief.

that: what. wyte: blame.

eftsoones: again.
wreke: avenged.

thee lust: pleases you.

debaat: dispute.

Ynde: India.

Biholde the wordes bitwene the Somonour and the Frere.

  The Frere lough, when he hadde herd al this;
"Now dame," quod he, "so have I joye or
      blis,   830
This is a long preamble of a tale!"
And whan the Somonour herde the Frere gale,
"Lo," quod the Somonour, "Goddes armes two!
A frere wol entremette hym everemo.
Lo, goode men, a flye and eek a frere   835
Wol falle in every dyssh and mateere.

lough: laughed.

gale: cry out.

entremette: interfere, meddle.

What spekestow of preambulacioun?
What! amble, or trotte, or [pace], or go sit doun!   pace: walk. See footnote.
Thou lettest oure disport in this manere."   lettest: hinderest.
   "Ye, woltow so, sire Somonour?" quod the
      Frere;   840
"Now, by my feith, I shal, er that I go,
Telle of a somonour swich a tale or two,
That alle the folk shal laughen in this place."
   "Now elles, Frere, I bishrewe thy face,"   bishrewe: beshrew, curse.
Quod this Somonour, "and I bishrewe me,   845
But if I telle tales two or thre
Of freres, er I come to Sidyngborne,
That I shal make thyn herte for to morne,
For wel I woot thy pacience is gon."
   Oure Hooste cride "Pees! and that anon!"   850
And seyde, "Lat the womman telle hire tale.
Ye fare as folk that dronken ben of ale.
Do, dame, telle forth youre tale, and that is best."
   "Al redy, sire," quod she, "right as yow lest,
If I have licence of this worthy Frere."   855
   "Yis, dame," quod he, "tel forth, and I wol
      heere."

Heere endeth the Wyf of
Bathe hir prologe and
bigynneth hir tale.

   In th' olde dayes of the Kyng Arthour,
Of which that Britons speken greet honour,   which: whom.
Al was this land fulfild of fayerye.   fayerye: supernatural creatures.
The elf-queene, with hir joly compaignye,   860
Daunced ful ofte in many a grene mede.
This was the olde opinion, as I rede;
I speke of manye hundred yeres ago.
But now kan no man se none elves mo,
For now the grete charitee and prayeres   865
Of lymytours and othere holy freres,
That serchen every lond and every streem,
As thikke as motes in the sonne-beem,   serchen: visit, haunt.

---

837. preambulacioun: preambling (with pun on "preambulating" meaning "walk before").
838. pace: O' read pees. Koch's emendation pace is strongly suggested by preambulacioun and amble, or trotte.
847. Sidyngborne: Sittingbourne, about 40 miles from London and 16 from Canterbury.
hir tale. Study of the analogues of this tale—the *Weddynge of Sir Gawen and Dame Ragnell*, the *Marriage of Sir Gawaine*, and Gower's *Tale of Florent*—reveals the brilliance with which Chaucer completely transformed a traditional story for the glory of the Wife of Bath.
866. lymytours: friars licensed to hear confessions and preach in a certain area.

Blessynge halles, chambres, kichenes, boures,
Citees, burghes, castels, hye toures, 870
Thropes, bernes, shipnes, dayeryes—
This maketh that ther been no fayeryes.
For ther as wont to walken was an elf,
Ther walketh now the lymytour hymself
In undermeles and in morwenynges, 875
And seyth his matyns and his holy thynges
As he gooth in his lymytacioun.
Wommen may go saufly up and doun
In every bussh or under every tree;
Ther is noon oother incubus but he, 880
And he ne wol doon hem but dishonour.
　　And so bifel that this kyng Arthour
Hadde in his hous a lusty bacheler,
That on a day cam ridynge fro ryver;
And happed that, allone as he was born, 885
He saugh a mayde walkynge hym biforn,
Of which mayde anon, maugree hir heed,
By verray force, he rafte hire maydenhed;
For which oppressioun was swich clamour
And swich pursute unto the kyng Arthour, 890
That dampned was this knyght for to be deed,
By cours of lawe, and sholde han lost his heed—
Paraventure swich was the statut tho—
But that the queene and othere ladyes mo
So longe preyeden the kyng of grace, 895
Til he his lyf hym graunted in the place,
And yaf hym to the queene, al at hir wille,
To chese wheither she wolde hym save or spille.
　　The queene thanked the kyng with al hir
　　　　myght,
And after this thus spak she to the knyght, 900
Whan that she saugh hir tyme, upon a day:
"Thou standest yet," quod she, "in swich array
That of thy lyf yet hastow no suretee.
I grante thee lyf, if thou kanst tellen me
What thyng is it that wommen moost desiren. 905
Be war, and keep thy nekke-boon from iren!
And if thou kanst nat tellen it me anon,
Yet wol I yeve thee leve for to gon
A twelf-month and a day, to seche and lere
An answere suffisant in this matere; 910

Glosses:

boures: chambers for ladies.
burghes: boroughs.
thropes: villages. shipnes: cowsheds.
　dayeryes: dairies.

thynges: services, prayers.

bacheler: young knight.
ryver: hawking for waterfowl.
allone as he was born: utterly alone.

rafte: robbed. maydenhed: maiden-
　hood. oppressioun: rape.
pursute: suing.
dampned: condemned.
sholde han: would have.

of: for.

spille: put to death.

array: state.
suretee: surety, security.

seche: seek. lere: learn.

---

875. In later mornings and in very early mornings.
880. incubus: an evil spirit supposed to lie upon persons in their sleep, and to have intercourse with women; the incubus always caused conception, and the offspring were demon children.
881. ne . . . but: the double negative is ambiguous: no dishonor, *or* only dishonor.
887. maugree hir heed: in spite of her head, i.e., in spite of all she could do.

And suretee wol I han, er that thou pace,
Thy body for to yelden in this place."
    Wo was this knyght, and sorwefully he siketh;   siketh: sighs.
But what! he may nat do al as hym liketh.
And at the laste he chees hym for to wende,   915   chees: chose.
And come agayn, right at the yeres ende,
With swich answere as God wolde hym purveye;   purveye: provide.
And taketh his leve, and wendeth forth his weye.
    He seketh every hous and every place
Where as he hopeth for to fynde grace,   920
To lerne what thyng wommen loven moost;
But he ne koude arryven in no coost   coost: region.
Wher as he myghte fynde in this matere
Two creatures accordynge in-feere.   accordynge in-feere: agreeing together.
    Somme seyde wommen loven best richesse,   925
Somme seyde honour, somme seyde jolynesse,
Somme riche array, somme seyden lust abedde,
And oftetyme to be wydwe and wedde.   wydwe: widow.
Somme seyde that oure herte is moost esed
Whan that we been yflatered and yplesed.   930
He gooth ful ny the sothe, I wol nat lye.   ny: nigh, near. sothe: truth.
A man shal wynne us best with flaterye;
And with attendance, and with bisynesse,   attendance: attention. bisynesse: attentiveness. ylymed: caught (as with bird-lime).
Been we ylymed, bothe moore and lesse.
    And somme seyen that we loven best   935
For to be free, and do right as us lest,
And that no man repreve us of oure vice,   repreve: reprove, reproach.
But seye that we be wise, and no thyng nyce.   nyce: foolish.
For trewely ther is noon of us alle,
If any wight wol clawe us on the galle,   940   galle: sore spot.
That we nyl kike, for he seith us sooth.   nyl: will not. kike: kick.
Assay, and he shal fynde it that so dooth;   assay: try.
For, be we never so vicious withinne,
We wol been holden wise and clene of synne.
    And somme seyn that greet delit han we   945
For to been holden stable, and eek secree,   stable: trustworthy. secree: secret, able to keep secrets.
And in o purpos stedefastly to dwelle,
And nat biwreye thyng that men us telle.   biwreye: betray, make known.
But that tale is nat worth a rake-stele.   rake-stele: rake-handle.
Pardee, we wommen konne no thyng hele;   950   hele: conceal.
Witnesse on Myda,—wol ye heere the tale?
    Ovyde, amonges othere thynges smale,
Seyde Myda hadde, under his longe heres,

951. Myda: The villain of Ovid's story (*Metamorphoses* xi.174–93) was Midas's barber; apparently the Wife of Bath did not get the tale directly from Ovid.
954. Apollo had thus metamorphosed Midas's ears because Midas had judged Pan to be a better musician than Apollo.

Growynge upon his heed two asses eres,
The whiche vice he hydde, as he best myghte, 955   vice: blemish.
Ful subtilly from every mannes sighte,
That, save his wyf, ther wiste of it namo.
He loved hire moost, and trusted hire also;
He preyede hire that to no creature
She sholde tellen of his disfigure.   960   disfigure: disfigurement.
    She swoor him, "Nay," for al this world to
        wynne,
She nolde do that vileynye or synne,
To make hir housbonde han so foul a name.
She nolde nat telle it for hir owene shame.
But nathelees, hir thoughte that she dyde,   965   dyde: would die.
That she so longe sholde a conseil hyde;
Hir thoughte it swal so soore aboute hir herte   swal: swelled.
That nedely som word hire moste asterte;   nedely: of necessity. **asterte:** escape.
And sith she dorste telle it to no man,
Doun to a mareys faste by she ran—   970   mareys: marsh.
Til she cam there, hir herte was a-fyre—
And as a bitore bombleth in the myre,   bitore: bittern. **bombleth:** booms.
She leyde hir mouth unto the water doun:
"Biwreye me nat, thou water, with thy soun,"   biwreye: betray.
Quod she; "to thee I telle it and namo;   975
Myn housbonde hath longe asses erys two!
Now is myn herte al hool, now is it oute.   al hool: fully relieved.
I myghte no lenger kepe it, out of doute."
Heere may ye se, thogh we a tyme abyde,
Yet out it moot; we kan no conseil hyde.   980   conseil: secret.
The remenant of the tale if ye wol heere,
Redeth Ovyde, and ther ye may it leere.   leere: learn.
    This knyght, of which my tale is specially,
Whan that he saugh he myghte nat come therby,
This is to seye, what wommen love moost,   985
Withinne his brest ful sorweful was the goost.
But hoom he gooth, he myghte nat sojourne;   sojourne: delay.
The day was come that homward moste he
        tourne.
And in his wey it happed hym to ryde,
In al this care, under a forest syde,   990   under a forest syde: at the edge of a
Wher as he saugh upon a daunce go   forest.
Of ladyes foure and twenty, and yet mo;
Toward the whiche daunce he drow ful yerne,   drow: drew. **yerne:** eagerly.
In hope that som wysdom sholde he lerne.
But certeinly, er he cam fully there,   995
Vanysshed was this daunce, he nyste where.
No creature saugh he that bar lyf,
Save on the grene he saugh sittynge a wyf—   wyf: woman.
A fouler wight ther may no man devyse.

Agayn the knyght this olde wyf gan ryse,   1000   gan ryse agayn: rose to greet.
And seyde, "Sire knyght, heer forth ne lith no
       wey.
Tel me what that ye seken, by youre fey!
Paraventure it may the bettre be;
Thise olde folk kan muchel thyng," quod she.   kan: know.
   "My leeve moder," quod this knyght,
        "certeyn   1005
I nam but deed, but if that I kan seyn
What thyng it is that wommen moost desire.
Koude ye me wisse, I wolde wel quite youre   wisse: instruct.
   hire."   hire: payment.
   "Plight me thy trouthe here in myn hand,"   plight: pledge. trouthe: promise.
       quod she,
"The nexte thyng that I requere thee,   1010   requere: request.
Thou shalt it do, if it lye in thy myght.
And I wol telle it yow er it be nyght."
   "Have here my trouthe," quod the knyght,
       "I grante."
   "Thanne," quod she, "I dar me wel avante   avante: boast.
Thy lyf is sauf; for I wol stonde therby,   1015   sauf: safe, secure.
Upon my lyf, the queene wol seye as I.
Lat se which is the proudeste of hem alle,
That wereth on a coverchief or a calle,   wereth on: has on. calle: netted head-
That dar seye nay of that I shal thee teche.   dress.
Lat us go forth, withouten lenger speche."   1020
Tho rowned she a pistel in his ere,   rowned: whispered. pistel: message.
And bad hym to be glad, and have no fere.
   Whan they be comen to the court, this knyght
Seyde he had holde his day, as he hadde hight,   holde: kept. hight: promised.
And redy was his answere, as he sayde.   1025
Ful many a noble wyf, and many a mayde,
And many a wydwe, for that they been wise,   for that: because.
The queene hirself sittynge as justise,   justise: presiding judge.
Assembled been, his answere for to heere;
And afterward this knyght was bode appeere. 1030   bode: bidden.
   To every wight comanded was silence,
And that the knyght sholde telle in audience   in audience: in open hearing, publicly.
What thyng that worldly wommen loven best.
This knyght ne stood nat stille as doth a best,   best: beast.
But to his questioun anon answerde   1035
With manly voys, that al the court it herde:
   "My lige lady, generally," quod he,   generally: as a general principle;
"Wommen desiren to have sovereynetee   everywhere.
As wel over hir housbond as hir love,

1001. heer . . . wey: from here there lies no road.
1033. worldly: earthly; mortal; secular: of the world as distinct from the cloister; devoted to the
world and its pursuits.

And for to been in maistrie hym above.   1040   maistrie: mastery, domination.
This is youre mooste desir, thogh ye me kille.
Dooth as yow list; I am here at youre wille."
In al the court ne was ther wyf, ne mayde,
Ne wydwe, that contraried that he sayde,   contraried: contradicted.
But seyden he was worthy han his lyf.   1045   han: to have.
And with that word up stirte that olde wyf,   stirte: started, leapt.
Which that the knyght saugh sittynge on the
          grene;
"Mercy," quod she, "my sovereyn lady queene!
Er that youre court departe, do me right.
I taughte this answere unto the knyght;   1050
For which he plighte me his trouthe there,   plighte: pledged. trouthe: promise.
The firste thyng I wolde hym requere,   requere: request.
He wolde it do, if it lay in his myght.
Bifore the court thanne preye I thee, sir knyght,"
Quod she, "that thou me take unto thy wyf;   1055
For wel thou woost that I have kept thy lyf.   kept: saved.
If I seye fals, sey nay, upon thy fey!"
    This knyght answerde, "Allas! and weylawey!
I woot right wel that swich was my biheste.   biheste: behest, promise.
For Goddes love, as chees a newe requeste!   1060   as chees: choose.
Taak al my good, and lat my body go."   good: property, possessions.
    "Nay, thanne," quod she, "I shrewe us bothe   shrewe: beshrew, curse.
          two!
For thogh that I be foul, old, and poore,
I nolde for al the metal, ne for oore,   nolde for: would not want.
That under erthe is grave, or lith above,   1065   grave: buried.
But if thy wyf I were, and eek thy love."
    "My love?" quod he, "nay, my dampnacioun!
Allas! that any of my nacioun   nacioun: family.
Sholde evere so foule disparaged be!"   disparaged: degraded (for marrying
But al for noght; the ende is this, that he   1070   beneath his rank).
Constreyned was, he nedes moste hire wedde;
And taketh his olde wyf, and goth to bedde.
    Now wolden some men seye, paraventure,
That for my necligence I do no cure   do no cure: take no pains.
To tellen yow the joye and al th'array   1075   array: festivities.
That at the feeste was that ilke day.
To which thyng shortly answeren I shal:
I seye ther nas no joye ne feeste at al;
Ther nas but hevynesse and muche sorwe.
For prively he wedded hire on morwe,   1080
And al day after hidde hym as an owle,
So wo was hym, his wyf looked so foule.
    Greet was the wo the knyght hadde in his
          thoght,
Whan he was with his wyf abedde ybroght;
He walweth and he turneth to and fro.   1085   walweth: wallows, rolls, tosses.

His olde wyf lay smylynge everemo,
And seyde, "O deere housbonde, benedicitee!
Fareth every knyght thus with his wyf as ye?
Is this the lawe of kyng Arthures hous?
Is every knyght of his thus dangerous?   1090   dangerous: reluctant; niggardly.
I am youre owene love and youre wyf;
I am she which that saved hath youre lyf,
And, certes, yet ne dide I yow nevere unright;   unright: wrong, injury.
Why fare ye thus with me this firste nyght?
Ye faren lyk a man had lost his wit.   1095
What is my gilt? For Goddes love, tel it,   gilt: fault.
And it shal been amended, if I may."   amended: remedied.
    "Amended?" quod this knyght, "allas! nay, nay!
It wol nat been amended nevere mo.
Thou art so loothly, and so oold also,   1100
And therto comen of so lowe a kynde,   kynde: race, lineage.
That litel wonder is thogh I walwe and wynde.   wynde: turn about.
So wolde God myn herte wolde breste!"   breste: burst.
    "Is this," quod she, "the cause of youre unreste?"
    "Ye, certeinly," quod he, "no wonder is."   1105
    "Now, sire," quod she, "I koude amende al this,
If that me liste, er it were dayes thre,
So wel ye myghte bere yow unto me.   so: provided that.
    But, for ye speken of swich gentillesse
As is descended out of old richesse,   1110   old richesse: ancient (inherited)
That therfore sholden ye be gentil men,   wealth.
Swich arrogance is nat worth an hen.
Looke who that is moost vertuous alway,   looke who that: whoever.
Pryvee and apert, and moost entendeth ay   apert: openly. entendeth: strives.
To do the gentil dedes that he kan;   1115
Taak hym for the grettest gentil man.
Crist wole we clayme of hym oure gentillesse,   hym: Him.
Nat of oure eldres for hire old richesse.   eldres: ancestors.
For thogh they yeve us al hir heritage,
For which we clayme to been of heigh parage,   1120   parage: birth, lineage.
Yet may they nat biquethe, for no thyng,
To noon of us hir vertuous lyvyng,
That made hem gentil men ycalled be,
And bad us folwen hem in swich degree.   in swich degree: in such a manner.
    Wel kan the wise poete of Florence,   1125
That highte Dant, speken in this sentence.   in this sentence: on this subject.
Lo, in swich maner rym is Dantes tale:
'Ful selde up riseth by his branches smale   by . . . smale: i.e., from ancestors.

1128–30. See *Purgatorio* vii.121–23.

Prowesse of man, for God, of his prowesse,   prowesse: excellence, goodness.
Wole that of hym we clayme oure gentillesse'; 1130
For of oure eldres may we no thyng clayme
But temporel thyng, that man may hurte and
      mayme.
  Eek every wight woot this as wel as I,
If gentillesse were planted naturelly
Unto a certeyn lynage doun the lyne,   1135
Pryvee and apert, thanne wolde they nevere fyne   fyne: cease.
To doon of gentillesse the faire office;
They myghte do no vileynye or vice.
  Taak fyr, and ber it in the derkeste hous
Bitwix this and the mount of Kaukasous,   1140
And lat men shette the dores and go thenne;   thenne: thence.
Yet wole the fyr as faire lye and brenne   lye: blaze.
As twenty thousand men myghte it biholde;   as: as if.
His office naturel ay wol it holde,   office: function.
Up peril of my lyf, til that it dye.   1145   up: upon.
  Here may ye se wel how that genterye   genterye: gentility.
Is nat annexed to possessioun,   annexed to: connected with.
Sith folk ne doon hir operacioun
Alwey, as dooth the fyr, lo, in his kynde.   in his kynde: according to its nature.
For, God it woot, men may wel often fynde   1150
A lordes sone do shame and vileynye;
And he that wole han pris of his gentrye,   han pris of: be esteemed for.
For he was born of a gentil hous,
And hadde his eldres noble and vertuous,
And nyl hymselven do no gentil dedis,   1155   nyl: will not.
Ne folwen his gentil auncestre that deed is,   folwen: resemble.
He nys nat gentil, be he duc or erl;
For vileyns synful dedes make a cherl.   vileyns: villainous.
For gentillesse nys but renomee   renomee: renown.
Of thyne auncestres, for hire heigh bountee, 1160   bountee: goodness, virtue.
Which is a strange thyng to thy persone.   strange: extraneous.
Thy gentillesse cometh fro God allone.
Thanne comth oure verray gentillesse of grace;
It was no thyng biquethe us with oure place.   place: position, rank.
  Thenketh how noble, as seith Valerius,   1165
Was thilke Tullius Hostillius,
That out of poverte roos to heigh noblesse.   poverte: poverty.
Reedeth Senek, and redeth eek Boece;
Ther shul ye seen expres that no drede is   expres: clearly. drede: doubt.
That he is gentil that dooth gentil dedis.   1170
And therfore, leeve housbonde, I thus conclude:
Al were it that myne auncestres were rude,   rude: of humble birth.
Yet may the hye God, and so hope I,
Grante me grace to lyven vertuously.

1160, 1162. thyne, thy: any one's.

Thanne am I gentil, whan that I bigynne   1175
To lyven vertuously and weyve synne.

    weyve: waive; abandon.

   And ther as ye of poverte me repreeve,

    repreeve: reprove, reproach.

The hye God, on whom that we bileeve,
In wilful poverte chees to lyve his lyf.

    wilful: voluntary. chees: chose.

And certes every man, mayden, or wyf,   1180
May understonde that Jhesus, hevene kyng,

    hevene: heaven's.

Ne wolde nat chese a vicious lyvyng.

    chese: choose.

Glad poverte is an honest thyng, certeyn;
This wole Senec and othere clerkes seyn.
Whoso that halt hym payd of his poverte,   1185

    halt hym payd of: is satisfied with.

I holde hym riche, al hadde he nat a sherte.
He that coveiteth is a povre wight,
For he wolde han that is nat in his myght;
But he that noght hath, ne coveiteth to have,
Is riche, although ye holde hym but a knave. 1190
Verray poverte, it syngeth proprely;

    proprely: appropriately.

Juvenal seith of poverte myrily:
'The povre man, whan he goth by the weye,
Bifore the theves he may synge and pleye.'
Poverte is hateful good and, as I gesse,   1195
A ful greet bryngere out of bisynesse;
A greet amendere eek of sapience

    amendere: promoter. sapience: wis-
      dom.

To hym that taketh it in pacience.
Poverte is this, although it seme alenge,

    alenge: loathsome.

Possessioun that no wight wol chalenge.   1200
Poverte ful often, whan a man is lowe,
Maketh his God and eek hymself to knowe.
Poverte a spectacle is, as thynketh me,

    spectacle: spectacles, eye-glasses; or
      possibly a magic mirror or prism (cf.

Thurgh which he may his verray freendes see.

      Squire's Tale, ll. 132–36).

And therfore, sire, syn that I noght yow
      greve,   1205
Of my poverte namoore ye me repreve.
   Now, sire, of elde ye repreve me;

    elde: old age.

And certes, sire, thogh noon auctoritee
Were in no book, ye gentils of honour
Seyn that men sholde an old wight doon
      favour,   1210
And clepe hym fader, for youre gentillesse;
And auctours shal I fynden, as I gesse.

    auctours: authors; authorities.

   Now ther ye seye that I am foul and old,

    ther: whereas.

Than drede you noght to been a cokewold;

    cokewold: cuckold.

For filthe and eelde, also moot I thee,   1215
Been grete wardeyns upon chastitee.

    wardeyns upon: guardians of.

But nathelees, syn I knowe youre delit,

1196. A very great remover of anxiety.
1202. Makes the man know God and also himself.

I shal fulfille youre worldly appetit.

  Chese now," quod she, "oon of thise thynges
       tweye:

To han me foul and old til that I deye,   1220

And be to yow a trewe, humble wyf,

And nevere yow displese in al my lyf;

Or elles ye wol han me yong and fair,

And take youre aventure of the repair   aventure: chance. **repair:** resort, re-

That shal be to youre hous by cause of me,   1225   pairing.

Or in som oother place, may wel be.

Now chese yourselven, wheither that yow liketh."   wheither: which of the two.

  This knyght avyseth hym and sore siketh,   avyseth hym: deliberates. **siketh:**

But atte laste he seyde in this manere: sighs.

"My lady and my love, and wyf so deere,   1230

I put me in youre wise governance;

Cheseth youreself which may be moost plesance,

And moost honour to yow and me also.

I do no fors the wheither of the two;   do no fors: care not. **the wheither:**

For as yow liketh, it suffiseth me."   1235   which.

    "Thanne have I gete of yow maistrie," quod   gete: got.
      she,

  "Syn I may chese and governe as me lest?"

    "Ye, certes, wyf," quod he, "I holde it best."

    "Kys me," quod she, "we be no lenger
      wrothe;

For, by my trouthe, I wol be to yow bothe,   1240

This is to seyn, ye, bothe fair and good.

I prey to God that I moote sterven wood,   sterven wood: die mad.

But I to yow be also good and trewe

As evere was wyf, syn that the world was newe.

And but I be to-morn as fair to seene   1245 to-morn: tomorrow.

As any lady, emperice, or queene,

That is bitwixe the est and eek the west,

Do with my lyf and deth right as yow lest.

Cast up the curtyn, looke how that it is."

    And whan the knyght saugh verraily al
      this,   1250

That she so fair was, and so yong therto,

For joye he hente hire in his armes two,

His herte bathed in a bath of blisse.

A thousand tyme a-rewe he gan hir kisse,   a-rewe: in a row.

And she obeyed hym in every thyng   1255

That myghte do hym plesance or likyng.   plesance: pleasure, delight.

  And thus they lyve unto hir lyves ende

In parfit joye; and Jhesu Crist us sende

Housbondes meeke, yonge, and fressh abedde,

And grace t'overbyde hem that we wedde;   1260 overbyde: outlive, outlast.

And eek I praye Jhesu shorte hir lyves   shorte: shorten.

That noght wol be governed by hir wyves;
And olde and angry nygardes of dispence,   dispence: expenditure.
God sende hem soone verray pestilence!

Heere endeth the Wyves tale of Bathe.

The prologe of the Freres tale.

This worthy lymytour, this noble Frere,   1265
He made alwey a maner louryng chiere   louryng: louring, frowning. chiere:
Upon the Somonour, but for honestee   face, look. honestee: dignity.
No vileyns word as yet to hym spak he.   vileyns: villainous; rude.
But atte laste he seyde unto the wyf,
"Dame," quod he, "God yeve yow right good
       lyf!   1270
Ye han heer touched, also moot I thee,
In scole-matere greet difficultee.   scole-matere: matter for the schools,
Ye han seyd muche thyng right wel, I seye;   scholastic question.
But, dame, here as we ryde by the weye,
Us nedeth nat to speken but of game,   1275
And lete auctoritees, on Goddes name,   lete: let alone, leave.
To prechyng and to scoles of clergye.   clergye: learning.
But if it like to this compaignye,
I wol yow of a somonour telle a game.   game: amusing tale.
Pardee, ye may wel knowe by the name   1280
That of a somonour may no good be sayd;
I praye that noon of you be yvele apayd.   yvele apayd: ill pleased.
A somonour is a rennere up and doun   rennere: runner.
With mandementz for fornicacioun,   mandementz: summonses to the arch-
And is ybet at every townes ende."   1285   deacon's court. ybet: beaten.
  Oure Hoost tho spak, "A! sire, ye sholde be
     hende   hende: gentle.
And curteys, as a man of youre estaat;
In compaignye we wol no debaat.   debaat: quarreling.
Telleth youre tale, and lat the Somonour be."
   "Nay," quod the Somonour, "lat hym seye
     to me   1290
What so hym list; whan it comth to my lot,
By God! I shal hym quiten every grot.   every grot: every groat; thoroughly.
I shal hym tellen which a gret honour
It is to be a flaterynge lymytour;   flaterynge: flattering.
And of many another manere cryme   1295
Which nedeth nat rehercen at this tyme;
And his office I shal hym telle, ywis."   office: duty, function; office.

1276. auctoritees: texts, quotations; see l. 1208 and above.

Oure Hoost answerde, "Pees, namoore of
    this!"
And after this he seyde unto the Frere,
    "Tel forth youre tale, leeve maister deere." 1300

Heere bigynneth the
Freres tale.

Whilom ther was dwellynge in my contree	contree: district, area.
An erchedeken, a man of heigh degree,	
That boldely dide execucioun	boldely: vigorously.
In punysshynge of fornicacioun,	
Of wicchecraft, and eek of bawderye, 1305	bawderye: pandering.
Of diffamacioun, and avowtrye,	diffamacioun: act of defaming. avow-
Of chirche reves, and of testamentz,	trye: adultery. chirche reves:
Of contractes and of lakke of sacramentz,	church robbery.
Of usure, and of symonye also.	
But certes, lecchours dide he grettest wo; 1310	lecchours: lechers.
They sholde syngen if that they were hent;	hent: caught.
And smale tytheres were foule yshent,	yshent: put to shame, severely
If any persoun wolde upon hem pleyne.	blamed. persoun: parson, priest.
Ther myghte asterte hym no pecunyal peyne.	
For smale tithes and for smal offrynge 1315	smal(e): deficient.
He made the peple pitously to synge.	
For er the bisshop caughte hem with his hook,	
They weren in the erchedekenes book;	
And thanne hadde he, thurgh his jurisdiccioun,	
Power to doon on hem correccioun. 1320	correccioun: punishment.
He hadde a somonour redy to his hond;	
A slyer boy was noon in Engelond;	slyer: craftier. boy: rascal.
For subtilly he hadde his espiaille,	espiaille: body of spies.
That taughte hym wher hym myghte availle.	wher . . . availle: where there might
He koude spare of lecchours oon or two, 1325	be profit for him.
To techen hym to foure and twenty mo.	techen hym to: inform him of.

---

the Freres tale. For the Tales of the Friar and Summoner no sources are known; the several analogues serve to point up the brilliance of characterization, dialogue, and wit in each tale, of the interrelation of the two tales and their tellers. Both Manly and Robinson have pointed out northernisms and general northern complexion in each tale.

1302. erchedeken: archdeacon, the principal administrative assistant to a bishop; one of his functions was to hold the lowest ecclesiastical court, with the power of spiritual censure.

1307–8. testamentz . . . contractes: (abuses connected with) wills, marriage contracts.

1309. usure: usury, the loaning of money at interest. Usury was prohibited by Canon Law. symonye: simony, the buying or selling of ecclesiastical preferments, benefices, or emoluments.

1312. smale tytheres: payers of insufficient tithes.

1314. No pecuniary penalty (i.e., fine) might escape him.

1317. The bishop (whose pastoral staff is a crook) dealt with offenders who were contumacious to the archdeacon.

For thogh this somonour wood were as an hare,   wood: passionate.
To telle his harlotrye I wol nat spare;   harlotrye: wickedness.
For we been out of his correccioun.   correccioun: jurisdiction for punish-
They han of us no jurisdiccioun,   **1330**   ment of misconduct.
Ne nevere shullen, terme of alle hir lyves.—
  "Peter! so been wommen of the styves,"   Peter!: by Saint Peter!
Quod the Somonour, "yput out of my cure!"   cure: jurisdiction.
  "Pees! with myschance and with
    mysaventure!"
Thus seyde oure Hoost, "and lat hym telle his
    tale.   **1335**
Now telleth forth, thogh that the Somonour
    gale;   gale: yelp, make an outcry.
Ne spareth nat, myn owene maister deere."—
  This false theef, this somonour (quod the
    Frere)
Hadde alwey bawdes redy to his hond,   bawdes: procurers, go-betweens. **redy:**
As any hauk to lure in Engelond,   **1340**   ready (to come).
That tolde hym al the secree that they knewe;   secree: secrets.
For hire acqueyntance was nat come of newe.   of newe: newly, recently.
They weren his approwours prively.   approwours: agents.
He took hymself a greet profit therby;
His maister knew nat alwey what he wan.   **1345**
Withouten mandement a lewed man   mandement: summons. **lewed:** igno-
He koude somne, on peyne of Cristes curs,   rant. somne: summon. **Cristes curs:**
And they were glade for to fille his purs,   excommunication.
And make hym grete feestes atte nale.   atte nale: at the ale house.
And right as Judas hadde purses smale,   **1350**
And was a theef, right swich a theef was he;
His maister hadde but half his duetee.   his duetee: the sum due him.
He was, if I shal yeven hym his laude,   laude: praise.
A theef, and eek a somnour, and a baude.   baude: procurer, go-between.
He hadde eek wenches at his retenue,   **1355**   at his retenue: at his service.
That, wheither that sir Robert or sir Huwe,
Or Jakke, or Rauf, or whoso that it were
That lay by hem, they tolde it in his ere.
Thus was the wenche and he of oon assent;   was of oon assent: were accomplices.
And he wolde fecche a feyned mandement,   **1360**   feyned: false or forged.
And somne hem to chapitre bothe two,   chapitre: ecclesiastical court.
And pile the man, and lete the wenche go.   pile: plunder; despoil.

1327. Cf. the expression "mad as a March hare"—i.e., a hare in the breeding season.

1330. Each friar was under the jurisdiction of his order, which in turn was subject to the Papal See directly rather than through the episcopal hierarchy of archdiocese and diocese under which the Summoner flourished.

1332. styves: stews, brothels. These were licensed, and exempt from ecclesiastical control.

1340. as any hauk to lure: as any hawk is ready to come to lure. (A hawk returns to his master when shown the lure—usually an artificial bird.)

1350. Judas: see John xii.6.

1356. sir: a title usually given, by courtesy, to priests.

Thanne wolde he seye, "Freend, I shal for thy
    sake
Do striken hire out of oure lettres blake;   do hire: have her.
Thee thar namoore as in this cas travaille.   1365
I am thy freend, ther I thee may availle."   availle: help.
Certeyn he knew of briberyes mo   briberyes: swindlings.
Than possible is to telle in yeres two.
For in this world nys dogge for the bowe
That kan an hurt deer from an hool knowe 1370 hool: whole, well (unwounded).
Bet than this somnour knew a sly lecchour,
Or an avouter, or a paramour.   avouter: adulterer. paramour: loose
And for that was the fruyt of al his rente,   wench. for: because. fruyt: essen-
Therfore on it he sette al his entente.   tial part. rente: income. entente:
   And so bifel that ones on a day   1375 attention.
This somnour, evere waityng on his pray,   waityng on: watching for.
For to somne an old wydwe, a ribibe,
Feynynge a cause, for he wolde brybe,   brybe: practice extortion.
Happed that he saugh bifore hym ryde
A gay yeman, under a forest syde.   1380
A bowe he bar, and arwes brighte and kene;
He hadde upon a courtepy of grene,   hadde upon: had on. courtepy: short
An hat upon his heed with frenges blake.   coat; pea jacket.
   "Sire," quod this somnour, "hayl, and wel   wel atake!: well met!
    atake!"
"Welcome," quod he, "and every good
    felawe!   1385
Where rydestow, under this grene-wode shawe?" shawe: grove.
Seyde this yeman, "Wiltow fer to day?"   fer: (go) far.
   This somnour hym answerde and seyde,
    "Nay;
Here faste by," quod he, "is myn entente
To ryden, for to reysen up a rente   1390 reysen up: collect.
That longeth to my lordes duetee."   duetee: what is due.
   "Artow thanne a bailly?" "Ye," quod he.   bailly: bailiff, agent of a lord.
He dorste nat, for verray filthe and shame   for: because of.
Seye that he was a somonour, for the name.
   "Depardieux," quod this yeman, "deere   depardieux: in God's name.
    brother,   1395
Thou art a bailly, and I am another.
I am unknowen as in this contree;   contree: region.
Of thyn aqueyntance I wolde praye thee,
And eek of bretherhede, if that yow leste.
I have gold and silver in my cheste;   1400

1365. You need not exert yourself any more in this case.
1369. dogge for the bowe: dog trained to track game wounded by the bowmen.
1377. ribibe: an abusive term for an old woman (literally, a kind of fiddle).
1380. under a forest syde: cf. Wife of Bath's Tale, I. 990.

If that thee happe to comen in oure shire,
Al shal be thyn, right as thou wolt desire."
   "Grantmercy," quod this somonour, "by my   grantmercy: great thanks.
       feith!"
Everych in ootheres hand his trouthe leith,   everych: each. **trouthe**: troth, promise.
For to be sworn bretheren til they deye.   1405
In daliance they ryden forth and pleye.   in daliance: chatting.
   This somonour, which that was as ful of
       jangles,   jangles: noisy talk; disputes.
As ful of venym been thise waryangles,   venym: spite, virulence. **waryangles**:
And evere enqueryng upon every thyng,   shrikes, butcherbirds.
"Brother," quod he, "where is now youre
       dwellyng   1410
Another day if that I sholde yow seche?"   seche: seek.
This yeman hym answerde in softe speche,
   "Brother," quod he, "fer in the north contree,
Where-as I hope som tyme I shal thee see.
Er we departe, I shal thee so wel wisse   1415 wisse: direct.
That of myn hous ne shaltow nevere mysse."
   "Now, brother," quod this somonour, "I yow
       preye,
Teche me, whil that we ryden by the weye,
Syn that ye been a baillif as am I,
Som subtiltee, and tel me feithfully   1420 subtiltee: wily stratagem or trick.
In myn office how I may moost wynne;
And spareth nat for conscience ne synne,
But as my brother tel me, how do ye."
   "Now, by my trouthe, brother deere," seyde
       he,
"As I shal tellen thee a feithful tale,   1425
My wages been ful streite and ful smale.   streite: limited.
My lord is hard to me and daungerous,   daungerous: niggardly.
And myn office is ful laborous,
And therefore by extorcions I lyve.
For sothe, I take al that men wol me yive.   1430
Algate, by sleighte or by violence,   algate: in all ways.
Fro yeer to yeer I wynne al my dispence.   dispence: living.
I kan no bettre telle, feithfully."
   "Now certes," quod this Somonour, "so fare I.
I spare nat to taken, God it woot,   1435
But if it be to hevy or to hoot.   it: a thing. to: too.
What I may gete in conseil prively,   in conseil: secretly.
No maner conscience of that have I.
Nere myn extorcioun, I myghte nat lyven,   nere: were it not (for).
Ne of swiche japes wol I nat be shryven.   1440 japes: tricks.
Stomak ne conscience ne knowe I noon;   stomak: feelings.

1404–5. See Knight's Tale, l. 1132 and footnote.
1413. The North is traditionally associated with the infernal regions.

I shrewe thise shrifte-fadres everychon.
Wel be we met, by God and by Seint Jame!
But, leeve brother, tel me thanne thy name,"
Quod this somonour. In this meene while   1445
This yeman gan a litel for to smyle.
    "Brother," quod he, "wiltow that I thee telle?
I am a feend; my dwellyng is in helle,
And here I ryde aboute my purchasyng,
To wite wher men wol yeve me any thyng.   1450
My purchas is th'effect of al my rente.
Looke how thou rydest for the same entente,
To wynne good, thou rekkest nevere how;
Right so fare I, for ryde wolde I now
Unto the worldes ende for a preye."   1455
    "A!" quod this somonour, "benedicite! what
            sey ye?
I wende ye were a yeman trewely.
Ye han a mannes shap as wel as I;
Han ye a figure thanne determinat
In helle, ther ye been in youre estat?"   1460
    "Nay, certeinly," quod he, "ther have we
            noon;
But whan us liketh, we kan take us oon,
Or elles make yow seme we been shape.
Somtyme lyk a man, or lyk an ape,
Or lyk an angel kan I ryde or go.   1465
It is no wonder thyng thogh it be so;
A lousy jogelour kan deceyve thee,
And pardee, yet kan I moore craft than he."
    "Why," quod this somonour, "ryde ye thanne
            or goon
In sondry shap, and nat alwey in oon?"   1470
    "For we," quod he, "wol us swiche formes
            make
As moost able is oure preyes for to take."
    "What maketh yow to han al this labour?"
    "Ful many a cause, leeve sire somonour,"
Seyde this feend, "but alle thyng hath tyme.   1475
The day is short, and it is passed pryme,
And yet ne wan I nothyng in this day.
I wol entende to wynnyng, if I may,
And nat entende oure wittes to declare.
For, brother myn, thy wit is al to bare   1480
To understonde, althogh I tolde hem thee.

shrewe: beshrew, curse. shrifte-
fadres: confessors.

purchasyng: acquiring.

wite: know. wher: whether.

good: goods.

determinat: determinate, fixed.

estat: natural state.

go: walk.

lousy: infested with lice.
kan: know.

for: because.

preyes: prey.

passed pryme: past nine o'clock.
wan: won.
entende: attend.
entende: intend. declare: reveal.
bare: deficient.

1451. What I pick up is the sum and substance of all my income (cf. General Prologue, l. 256).
1463. Or else make it seem to you that we are shaped (have a certain shape).
1475. Here the fiend quotes Scripture: cf. Ecclesiastes iii.1.
1479. oure wittes: our ingenious plans or devices.

But, for thou axest why labouren we—
For somtyme we been Goddes instrumentz,
And meenes to doon his comandementz,
Whan that hym list, upon his creatures,   1485
In divers art and in diverse figures.
Withouten hym we have no myght, certayn,
If that hym list to stonde ther-agayn.
And somtyme, at oure prayere, han we leve
Oonly the body and nat the soule greve;   1490
Witnesse on Job, whom that we diden wo.
And somtyme han we myght of bothe two,
This is to seyn, of soule and body eke.
And somtyme be we suffred for to seke
Upon a man, and do his soule unreste,   1495
And nat his body, and al is for the beste.
Whan he withstandeth oure temptacioun,
It is a cause of his savacioun,
Al be it that it was nat oure entente
He sholde be sauf, but that we wolde hym
       hente.   1500
And somtyme be we servant unto man,
As to the erchebisshop Seint Dunstan,
And to the apostles servant eek was I."
    "Yet tel me," quod the somonour, "feithfully,
Make ye yow newe bodies thus alway   1505
Of elementz?" The feend answerde, "Nay.
Somtyme we feyne, and somtyme we aryse
With dede bodyes, in ful sondry wyse,
And speke as renably and faire and wel
As to the Phitonissa dide Samuel.   1510
(And yet wol som men seye it was nat he;
I do no fors of youre dyvynytee.)
But o thyng warne I thee, I wol nat jape,—
Thou wolt algates wite how we be shape;
Thou shalt herafterwardes, my brother
       deere,   1515
Come there thee nedeth nat of me to leere.
For thou shalt, by thyn owene experience,
Konne in a chayer rede of this sentence

for: because.

meenes: means, instruments.

art: ways. figures: shapes.

ther-agayn: against that.

seke upon: persecute, harass.
do unreste: disturb.

sauf: saved.

servant unto: subject to, in the service
of.

feyne: make a likeness.
wyse: manner.
renably: fluently, plainly.

jape: deceive.
algates: in any case.

leere: learn.

konne: know how to.

1502. St. Dunstan, the leading English saint until the canonization of St. Thomas; early lives of
St. Dunstan tell of demons in servitude to him; he was Archbishop of Canterbury from 961 until
his death in 988.

1503. Fiends are said to have been in the service of several of the apostles.

1510. the Phitonissa: the Witch of Endor; Saul's visit to her is recounted in I Samuel xxviii. It
was an elegant point of dispute (l. 1511) in medieval theological writings and schools, whether
the doom of Saul was prophesied by the spirit of Samuel or whether God sent a devil in the form
of Samuel.

1512. do no fors of: have no regard for.   dyvynytee: (the study of) divinity.

1518. chayer: (professorial) chair.   rede of: interpret; lecture about.   sentence: subject.

Bet than Virgile, while he was on lyve,   on lyve: alive.
Or Dant also. Now lat us ryde blyve,   1520   blyve: at once.
For I wol holde compaignye with thee
Til it be so that thou forsake me."
   "Nay," quod this somonour, "that shal nat
      bityde!
I am a yeman, knowen is ful wyde;
My trouthe wol I holde, as in this cas.   1525   trouthe: promise.
For though thou were the devel Sathanas,
My trouthe wol I holde to thee, my brother,
As I am sworn, and ech of us til oother,
For to be trewe brother in this cas;
And bothe we goon abouten oure purchas.   1530   purchas: business of acquisition.
Taak thou thy part, what that men wol thee yive,
And I shal myn; thus may we bothe lyve.
And if that any of us have moore than oother,
Lat hym be trewe, and parte it with his brother."   parte: divide, share.
   "I graunte," quod the devel, "by my fey." 1535   graunte: agree.
And with that word they ryden forth hir wey.   ryden: rode.
And right at the entryng of the townes ende,
To which this somonour shoop hym for to   shoop hym: intended.
      wende,
They saugh a cart that charged was with hey,   charged: loaded.
Which that a cartere droof forth in his wey. 1540   droof: drove.
Deep was the wey, for which the carte stood.   for: because of.
This cartere smoot, and cryde as he were wood,
"Hayt, Brok! hayt, Scot! what spare ye for the   hayt!: a country word for urging
      stones?   horses on.
The feend," quod he, "yow fecche, body and
      bones,
As ferforthly as evere were ye foled,   1545
So muche wo as I have with yow tholed!   tholed: suffered, endured.
The devel have al, bothe hors and cart and hey!"   hors: horses.
   This somonour seyde, "Heere shal we have a
      pley."   a pley: a game, sport.
And neer the feend he drough, as noght ne were,   neer: nearer. drough: drew.
Ful prively, and rowned in his ere: 1550   rowned: whispered.
"Herkne, my brother, herkne, by thy feith!
Herestow nat how that the cartere seith?   herestow: do you hear.
Hent it anon, for he hath yeve it thee,
Bothe hey and cart, and eek his caples thre."   caples: horses.
   "Nay," quod the devel, "God woot, never a
      del!   1555
It is nat his entente, trust me wel.
Axe hym thyself, if thou nat trowest me;   trowest: believe.
Or elles stynt a while, and thou shalt see."

1545. As sure as ever you were born.
1549. as noght ne were: as if there were nothing; i.e., in a casual manner.

This cartere thakketh his hors upon the
    croupe,
And they bigonne to drawen and to stoupe. 1560
"Heyt! now," quod he, "ther Jhesu Crist yow
    blesse,
And al his handwerk, bothe moore and lesse!
That was wel twight, myn owene lyard boy.
I pray God save thee, and Seinte Loy!
Now is my cart out of the slow, pardee!" 1565
    "Lo, brother," quod the feend, "what tolde I
    thee?
Heere may ye se, myn owene deere brother,
The carl spak oo thing, but he thoghte another.
Lat us go forth abouten oure viage;
Heere wynne I nothyng upon cariage." 1570
    Whan that they comen somwhat out of
    towne,
This somonour to his brother gan to rowne:
"Brother," quod he, "here woneth an old
    rebekke,
That hadde almoost as lief to lese hire nekke
As for to yeve a peny of hir good. 1575
I wole han twelf pens, though that she be wood,
Or I wol somoune hire unto oure office;
And yet, God wot, of hire knowe I no vice.
But for thou kanst nat, as in this contree,
Wynne thy cost, taak heer ensample of me." 1580
    This somonour clappeth at the wydwes gate.
"Com out," quod he, "thou olde virytrate!
I trowe thou hast som frere or preest with thee."
    "Who clappeth?" seyde this wyf, "benedicitee!
God save you, sire, what is youre sweete
    wille?" 1585
    "I have," quod he, "of somonce a bille;
Up peyne of cursyng, looke that thou be
To-morn bifore the erchedeknes knee,
T'answere to the court of certeyn thynges."
    "Now, Lord," quod she, "Crist Jhesu, kyng of
    kynges, 1590
So wisly helpe me, as I ne may.
I have been syk, and that ful many a day.
I may nat go so fer," quod she, "ne ryde,
But I be deed, so priketh it in my syde.
May I nat axe a libel, sire somonour, 1595

Glosses

thakketh: pats. hors: horses.
croupe: rump.
stoupe: strain forward.
ther: i.e., may.

handwerk: creatures.

twight: pulled, tugged. lyard: spotted
  with white or silver gray.

slow: slough.

carl: fellow.

viage: journey.

comen: came.

rowne: whisper.
woneth: dwells.

rebekke: woman (lit., fiddle).

hadde as lief: would as soon.

good: goods.

cost: expense money.
clappeth: knocks.
virytrate: hag.

somonce: summons. bille: formal
  document. up: upon. cursyng: ex-
  communication. to-morn: tomorrow.

wisly: certainly.

go: walk.
priketh: pains.

1562. moore and lesse: greater and smaller.
1564. Seinte Loy: the patron saint of carters.
1570. upon cariage: by exercising a landlord's claim upon the tenant's horses and cart (here figuratively).
1595. libel: written declaration of particulars.

And answere there by my procuratour
To swich thyng as men wole opposen me?"
 "Yis," quod this somonour, "pay anon, lat see,
Twelf pens to me, and I wol thee acquite.
I shal no profit han therby but lite;   1600
My maister hath the profit, and nat I.
Com of, and lat me ryden hastily;
Yif me twelf pens, I may no lenger tarye."
 "Twelf pens!" quod she, "now, lady Seinte
   Marie
So wisly help me out of care and synne,   1605
This wyde world thogh that I sholde wynne,
Ne have I nat twelf pens withinne myn hoold.
Ye knowen wel that I am povre and oold;
Kithe youre almesse on me povre wrecche."
 "Nay thanne," quod he, "the foule feend me
   fecche   1610
If I th'excuse, though thou shul be spilt!"
 "Allas!" quod she, "God woot, I have no gilt."
 "Pay me," quod he, "or by the sweete Seinte
   Anne,
As I wol bere awey thy newe panne
For dette which thou owest me of old.   1615
Whan that thou madest thyn housbonde
   cokewold,
I payde at hom for thy correccioun."
 "Thou lixt!" quod she, "by my savacioun,
Ne was I nevere er now, wydwe ne wyf,
Somoned unto youre court in al my lyf;   1620
Ne nevere I nas but of my body trewe!
Unto the devel blak and rough of hewe
Yeve I thy body and my panne also!"
 And whan the devel herde hire cursen so
Upon hir knees, he seyde in this manere,   1625
"Now, Mabely, myn owene moder deere,
Is this youre wyl in ernest that ye seye?"
 "The devel," quod she, "so fecche hym er he
   deye,
And panne and al, but he wol hym repente!"
 "Nay, olde stot, that is nat myn entente,"   1630
Quod this somonour, "for to repente me
For any thyng that I have had of thee.
I wolde I hadde thy smok and every clooth!"
 "Now, brother," quod the devel, "be nat
   wrooth;
Thy body and this panne been myne by right. 1635
Thou shalt with me to helle yet to-nyght,

procuratour: procurator, attorney.
opposen me: lay to my charge.

com of: come on!, hurry up!

yif: give.

wisly: surely.

hoold: grasp.

kithe: show. **almesse:** charity, pity.

spilt: destroyed, ruined.

panne: cloth; garment.

correccioun: punishment; fine.
lixt: liest.

stot: heifer (Yorkshire).

smok: smock; woman's undergarment.
 clooth: piece of clothing.

1606. sholde wynne: i.e., if I had them.

Where thou shalt knowen of oure privetee
Moore than a maister of dyvynytee."
And with that word this foule feend hym hente;
Body and soule he with the devel wente   1640
Where as that somonours han hir heritage.
And God, that maked after his ymage
Mankynde, save and gyde us, alle and some,   gyde: keep.
And leve thise somonours goode men bicome!   leve: allow.
    Lordynges, I koude han told yow—quod this
        Frere—   1645
Hadde I had leyser for this Somnour heere,
After the text of Crist, Poul, and John,
And of oure othere doctours many oon,
Swiche peynes that youre hertes myghte agryse,   agryse: shudder with dread.
Al be it so no tonge may devyse,   1650   devyse: describe.
Thogh that I myghte a thousand wynter telle
The peynes of thilke cursed hous of helle.
But for to kepe us fro that cursed place,
Waketh, and preyeth Jhesu for his grace   waketh: pass the night in prayer.
So kepe us fro the temptour Sathanas.   1655
Herketh this word! beth war, as in this cas:
"The leoun sit in his awayt alway   sit in his awayt: lies in wait or in am-
To sle the innocent, if that he may."   bush.
Disposeth ay youre hertes to withstonde
The feend, that yow wolde make thral and   thral: slave.
    bonde.   1660   bonde: vassal.
He may nat tempte yow over youre myght,
For Crist wol be youre champion and knyght.
And prayeth that this somonour hym repente
Of his mysdedes, er that the feend hym hente!

    Heere endeth the Freres Tale.

        The prologe of
      the Somonours tale.

    This Somonour in his stiropes hye stood;   1665
Upon this Frere his herte was so wood   wood: angry.
That lyk an aspen leef he quook for ire.   quook: quaked, trembled.
    "Lordynges," quod he, "but o thyng I desire;
I yow biseke that, of youre curteisye,
Syn ye han herd this false Frere lye,   1670
As suffreth me I may my tale telle.   suffreth: permit.
This Frere bosteth that he knoweth helle,
And God it woot, that it is litel wonder;

1646. Had I had opportunity so far as this Summoner here is concerned.
1657–58. See Psalms x.9.

Freres and feendes been but lyte asonder.

lyte: little.

For, pardee, ye han ofte tyme herd telle 1675
How that a frere ravysshed was to helle
In spirit ones by a visioun;

ones: once. by: in.

And as an angel ladde hym up and doun,
To shewen hym the peynes that ther were,
In al the place saugh he nat a frere; 1680
Of oother folk he saugh ynowe in wo.

ynowe: enough.

Unto this angel spak the frere tho:
    'Now, sire,' quod he, 'han freres swich a grace
That noon of hem shal come to this place?'
    'Yis,' quod this angel, 'many a millioun!' 1685
And unto Sathanas he ladde hym doun.
'And now hath Sathanas,' seith he, 'a tayl
Brodder than of a carryk is the sayl.

carryk: a large ship.

Hold up thy tayl, thou Sathanas!' quod he;
'Shewe forth thyn ers, and lat the frere se 1690

ers: arse.

Where is the nest of freres in this place!'
And er that half a furlong wey of space,

space: time.

Right so as bees out swarmen of an hyve,

out swarmen of: swarm out of.

Out of the develes ers they gonne dryve

gonne dryve: rushed.

Twenty thousand freres on a route, 1695
And thurghout helle swarmeden al aboute,
And comen agayn as faste as they may gon,

comen: came.

And in his ers they crepten everychon.
He clapte his tayl agayn and lay ful stille.
This frere, whan he looked hadde his fille 1700
Upon the tormentz of this sory place,
His spirit God restored, of his grace,
Unto his body agayn, and he awook.
But natheles, for fere yet he quook,
So was the develes ers ay in his mynde, 1705
That is his heritage of verray kynde.

of: by. kynde: nature.

God save yow alle, save this cursed Frere!
My prologe wol I ende in this manere."

1692. a furlong wey of space: a small amount of time (long enough to walk a furlong); about two and one-half minutes.

1707. save: a play on the two meanings "save" and "except."

Satan in Hell: The position of friars as described by the Summoner in his Prologue may be related to the iconological tradition of Satan defecating a man, which includes Giotto's painting of *The Last Judgment* in the Arena Chapel, Padua, and *The Last Judgment* by Giusto di Menabuoi in the Parish Church of Viboldone, near Milan. When Chaucer travelled from Genoa to Florence in 1373, the most famous sight to be seen in Pisa was the Camposanto, the burial ground with its more than fifty shiploads of earth from Jerusalem, its great rectangular cloister (415 by 171 feet), and its walls in the process of being covered with frescoes by Tuscan artists. The most magnificent of these—*The Triumph of Death,* and *The Last Judgment*—were already there, the work of Francesco Traini, the one great Pisan artist of the century. In *The Last Judgment,* at the center of Traini's Hell, is Satan, shown on the following page in a detail of the fresco.

Heere bigynneth the Somonour his tale.

Lordynges, ther is in Yorkshire, as I gesse,
A mersshy contree called Holdernesse,   1710
In which ther wente a lymytour aboute,
To preche, and eek to begge, it is no doute.
And so bifel that on a day this frere
Hadde preched at a chirche in his manere,
And specially, aboven every thyng,   1715
Excited he the peple in his prechyng
To trentals, and to yeve for Goddes sake,
Wherwith men myghte holy houses make,
Ther as divine service is honoured,
Nat ther as it is wasted and devoured,   1720
Ne ther it nedeth nat for to be yive,
As to possessioners, that mowen lyve,
Thanked be God, in wele and habundaunce.
"Trentals," seyde he, "deliveren from penaunce
Hir freendes soules, as wel olde as yonge,—   1725
Ye, whan that they been hastily ysonge,
Nat for to holde a preest joly and gay—
He syngeth nat but o masse in a day.
Delivereth out," quod he, "anon the soules!
Ful hard it is with flesshhook or with oules   1730
To been yclawed, or to brenne or bake.
Now spede yow hastily, for Cristes sake!"
And whan this frere had seyd al his entente,
With *qui cum patre* forth his wey he wente.
    Whan folk in chirche had yeve him what hem
        leste,   1735
He wente his way, no lenger wolde he reste.
With scrippe and tipped staf, ytukked hye,
In every hous he gan to poure and prye,
And beggeth mele and chese, or elles corn.
His felawe hadde a staf tipped with horn,   1740
A peyre of tables al of yvory,
And a poyntel polysshed fetisly,
And wroot the names alwey, as he stood,
Of alle folk that yaf hem any good,

excited: encouraged, exhorted.

holy houses: religious houses, convents.

wele: prosperity.

holde: detain.

flesshhook: implement for lifting meat from a pot. *oules:* awls, bodkins.

al his entente: all that was on his mind.

reste: remain.
scrippe: bag for alms. *tipped:* with a horn tip. *ytukked:* tucked up. *poure:* pore, gaze searchingly.

peyre: set. *tables:* writing tablets.
poyntel: stylus (writing instrument).
    fetisly: elegantly.
good: goods.

1710. **Holdernesse:** an extremely flat district in the southeast corner of Yorkshire.

1711. **lymytour:** see General Prologue, 1. 209 and note.

1717. **trentals:** offices of thirty masses for the benefit of souls in purgatory, usually sung on thirty consecutive days. This friar prefers that they be sung in one day (l. 1726).

1722. **possessioners:** the regular monastic orders and the beneficed clergy; in contrast to these, the friars were supposed to have no endowments and no private property, but to subsist entirely upon alms.

1734. *qui cum patre:* the opening of a formula for concluding prayers and sermons: "Qui cum Patre et Spiritu Sancto vivat et regnat per omnia secula seculorum."

1740. **felawe:** Friars went about in pairs.

Ascaunces that he wolde for hem preye.   1745 **ascaunces:** as if, pretending that.
"Yif us a busshel whete, malt, or reye,
A Goddes kechyl, or a trype of chese,   **trype:** morsel, small piece.
Or elles what yow lyst, we may nat chese;   **chese:** choose.
A Goddes halfpeny, or a masse peny,   **a masse peny:** an offering of money
Or yif us of youre brawn, if ye have eny;   1750 for a mass. **brawn:** meat.
A dagon of youre blanket, leeve dame,   **dagon:** a piece, scrap. **blanket:** un-
Oure suster deere,—lo! heere I write youre   dyed woolen cloth used for clothing.
      name,—
Bacon or beef, or swich thyng as ye fynde."
   A sturdy harlot wente hem ay bihynde,   **harlot:** servant, knave.
That was hir hostes man, and baar a sak,   1755 **hostes man:** servant to the guests at
And what men yaf hem, leyde it on his bak.   the convent.
And whan that he was out atte dore, anon
He planed awey the names everichon
That he biforn had writen in his tables;
He served hem with nyfles and with fables.   1760 **nyfles:** trifling or fictitious tales.
   "Nay, ther thou lixt, thou Somonour!" quod   **lixt:** liest.
      the Frere.
   "Pees," quod oure Hoost, "for Cristes moder
      deere!
Tel forth thy tale, and spare it nat at al."
   "So thryve I," quod this Somonour, "so I
      shal!"
   So longe he wente, hous by hous, til he   1765
Cam til an hous ther he was wont to be
Refresshed moore than in an hundred placis.
Syk lay the goode man whos the place is;
Bedred upon a couche lowe he lay.   **bedred:** bedridden.
"Deus hic!" quod he, "O Thomas, freend, good
      day!"   1770
Seyde this frere, curteisly and softe.
"Thomas," quod he, "God yelde yow! ful ofte   **yelde:** reward.
Have I upon this bench faren ful wel;   **faren:** fared.
Heere have I eten many a murye meel."
And fro the bench he droof awey the cat,   1775 **droof:** drove.
And leyde adoun his potente and his hat,   **potente:** staff.
And eek his scrippe, and sette hym softe adoun.
His felawe was go walked into toun   **go walked:** gone on a walk.
Forth with his knave, into that hostelrye
Where as he shoop hym thilke nyght to lye.   1780 **shoop hym:** intended.
   "O deere maister," quod this sike man,
"How han ye fare sith that March bigan?"   **fare:** fared.

1747. **a Goddess kechyl:** a little cake given as alms in the name, or for the sake, of God.
1758. The **tables** (line 1741) were coated with wax; the man wrote with the sharp end of the poyntel (1742), and with the flat end could smooth the writing away.
1770. *Deus hic!:* God be here!, formula of benediction on entering a house.
1782. **March:** It is presumably Lent.

I saw yow noght this fourtenyght or moore."

"God woot," quod he, "laboured I have ful soore,

And specially for thy savacion   1785

Have I seyd many a precious orison,

And for oure othere freendes, God hem blesse!

I have to day been at youre chirche at messe,

And seyd a sermon after my symple wit,

Nat al after the text of holy writ;   1790

For it is hard to yow, as I suppose,

And therfore wol I teche yow al the glose.

Glosyng is a glorious thyng, certeyn,

For lettre sleeth, so as we clerkes seyn.

There have I taught hem to be charitable,   1795

And spende hir good ther it is resonable;

And there I saugh oure dame,—a! where is she?"

    "Yond in the yerd I trowe that she be,"

Seyde this man, "and she wol come anon."

    "Ey, maister, welcome be ye, by Seint
        John!"   1800

Seyde this wyf, "how fare ye, hertely?"

    The frere ariseth up ful curteisly,

And hire embraceth in his armes narwe,

And kiste hire sweete, and chirketh as a sparwe

With his lippes: "Dame," quod he, "right
        wel,   1805

As he that is youre servant every del,

Thanked be God, that yow yaf soule and lyf!

Yet saugh I nat this day so fair a wyf

In al the chirche, God so save me!"

    "Ye, God amende defautes, sire," quod
        she.   1810

"Algates welcome be ye, by my fey!"

    "Graunt mercy, dame, this have I founde
        alwey.

But of youre grete goodnesse, by youre leve,

I wolde prey yow that ye nat yow greve,

I wol with Thomas speke a litel throwe.   1815

Thise curatz been ful necligent and slowe

To grope tendrely a conscience

In shrift; in prechyng is my diligence,

And studie in Petres wordes and in Poules.

I walke, and fisshe Cristen mennes soules,   1820

To yelden Jhesu Crist his propre rente;

To sprede his word is set al myn entente."

    "Now, by youre leve, o deere sire," quod she,

"Chideth him wel, for seinte Trinitee!

He is as angry as a pissemyre,   1825

---

fourtenyght: fourteen nights, a fort-night.

precious: of great spiritual worth.

messe: mass.

for: because. **to:** for.

glose: gloss, commentary (on the bib-lical text).

good: goods.

yond: yonder. **yerd:** yard, garden.

narwe: narrowly, closely.

amende defautes: forgive sins.

algates: at any rate.

graunt mercy: great thanks.

throwe: while, moment.

slowe: slothful, dilatory.

grope: examine, search out.

shrift: confession.

Cristen: Christian.

his propre rente: the tribute due him.

seinte: holy.

pissemyre: pismire, ant.

1794. **lettre sleeth:** II Corinthians iii.6, "the letter killeth, but the spirit giveth life."

Though that he have al that he kan desire,
Though I hym wrye a-nyght and make hym   wrye: cover.
       warm,
And on hym leye my leg outher myn arm,   outher: or.
He groneth lyk oure boor, lith in oure sty.   lith: (which) lies.
Oother disport right noon of hym have I;   1830   disport: sport, diversion.
I may nat plese hym in no maner cas."   in no maner cas: not at all.
     "O Thomas, *je vous dy,* Thomas! Thomas!   *je vous dy:* I tell you.
This maketh the feend; this moste ben amended.   this maketh: causes this.
Ire is a thyng that hye God defended,   defended: forbade, prohibited.
And therof wol I speke a word or two."   1835
     "Now, maister," quod the wyf, "er that I go,
What wol ye dyne? I wol go theraboute."   dyne: eat (for dinner).
     "Now, dame," quod he, "now *je vous dy sanz*   *je vous dy sanz doute:* I tell you with-
       doute,   out doubt.
Have I nat of a capon but the lyvere,
And of youre softe breed nat but a shyvere,   1840   shyvere: slice.
And after that a rosted pigges heed—
But that I nolde no beest for me were deed—
Thanne hadde I with yow homly suffisaunce.
I am a man of litel sustenaunce;
My spirit hath his fostryng in the Bible.   1845
The body is ay so redy and penyble   penyble: painstaking.
To wake, that my stomak is destroyed.   wake: stay awake to pass the night in
I prey yow, dame, ye be nat anoyed,   prayer. stomak: appetite.
Though I so freendly yow my conseil shewe.   conseil: private matters.
By God! I wolde nat telle it but a fewe."   1850   a fewe: to a few.
     "Now, sire," quod she, "but o word er I go.
My child is deed withinne thise wykes two,   wykes: weeks.
Soone after that ye wente out of this toun."
     "His deeth saugh I by revelacioun,"
Seide this frere, "at hom in oure dortour.   1855   dortour: dormitory.
I dar wel seyn that, er that half an hour   er that: i.e., within.
After his deeth, I saugh hym born to blisse   born: carried.
In myn avision, so God me wisse!   wisse: guide.
So dide oure sexteyn and oure fermerer,   fermerer: the friar in charge of the in-
That han been trewe freres fifty yeer;   1860   firmary.
They may now—God be thanked of his loone!—   loone: gift.
Maken hir jubilee and walke allone.
And up I roos, and al oure covent eke,   roos: arose. covent: convent; group
With many a teere trillyng on my cheke,   of friars. trillyng: trickling.
Withouten noyse or clateryng of belles;   1865
Te Deum was oure song, and nothyng elles,
Save that to Crist I seyde an orison,

1844–45. Compare General Prologue, ll. 435–38 and note.
1862. After serving fifty years in the convent, friars "made hir jubilee" and could go about alone.
1866. *Te Deum:* a song of thanksgiving, appropriate since the friar pretends that he saw the child's soul translated to paradise.

Thankynge hym of my revelacion. of: for.
For, sire and dame, trusteth me right wel,
Oure orisons been moore effectuel, 1870
And moore we seen of Cristes secree thynges,
Than burel folk, although they weren kynges. burel folk: laymen.
We lyve in poverte and in abstinence,
And burel folk in richesse and dispence dispence: expenditure.
Of mete and drynk, and in hir foul delit. 1875
We han this worldes lust al in despit. han in despit: despise.
Lazar and Dives lyveden diversly,
And divers gerdon hadden they therby. gerdon: guerdon, reward.
Whoso wol praye, he moot faste and be clene, clene: free from spiritual or moral pol-
And fatte his soule, and make his body lene. 1880 lution. fatte: nourish.
We fare as seith th'apostle; clooth and foode clooth: clothing.
Suffisen us, though they be nat ful goode.
The clennesse and the fastyng of us freres
Maketh that Crist accepteth oure prayeres.
    Lo, Moyses fourty dayes and fourty nyght 1885
Fasted, er that the heighe God of myght
Spak with hym in the mountayne of Synay. Synay: Sinai.
With empty wombe, fastynge many a day, wombe: stomach.
Receyved he the lawe that was writen
With Goddes fynger; and Elye, wel ye witen, 1890 Elye: Elijah.
In mount Oreb, er he hadde any speche
With hye God, that is oure lyves leche, leche: healer.
He fasted longe, and was in contemplaunce. contemplaunce: (a state of) contem-
    Aaron, that hadde the temple in governaunce, plation.
And eek the othere preestes everichon, 1895
Into the temple whan they sholde gon
To preye for the peple, and do servyse, do servyse: conduct worship.
They nolden drynken in no maner wyse
No drynke which that myghte hem dronke make,
But there in abstinence preye and wake, 1900 wake: pass the night in prayer.
Lest that they deyden. Taak heede what I seye!
But they be sobre that for the peple preye,
War that I seye—namoore, for it suffiseth. war: heed. that: what.
Oure Lord Jhesu, as holy writ devyseth, devyseth: tells.
Yaf us ensample of fastyng and prayeres. 1905
Therfore we mendynantz, we sely freres, mendynantz: mendicants. sely: holy,
Been wedded to poverte and continence, poor.
To charitee, humblesse, and abstinence,
To persecucioun for rightwisnesse,
To wepyng, misericorde, and clennesse. 1910 misericorde: mercy. clennesse: moral
purity.

1877. **Lazar:** Lazarus, the beggar; **Dives:** the rich man; see Luke xvi.19–31.
1881. **th'apostle:** see I Timothy vi.8.
1885. **Moyses:** see Exodus xxxiv.27–28.
1890. **Elye:** see I Kings xix.8.
1894. **Aaron:** see Leviticus x.8–9.

And therfore may ye se that oure prayeres—
I speke of us, we mendynantz, we freres—
Be to the hye God moore acceptable
Than youres, with youre feestes at the table.
Fro Paradys first, if I shal nat lye,   1915
Was man out chaced for his glotonye;   chaced: chased.
And chaast was man in Paradys, certeyn.   chaast: chaste.
     But herkne now, Thomas, what I shal seyn.
I ne have no text of it, as I suppose,
But I shal fynde it in a maner glose,   1920   in a maner glose: in some kind of
That specially oure sweete Lord Jhesus   comment on the text.
Spak this by freres, whan he seyde thus: by: concerning.
     'Blessed be they that povre in spirit been.'
And so forth al the gospel may ye seen,
Wher it be likker oure professioun,   1925
Or hirs that swymmen in possessioun.
Fy on hire pompe and on hire glotonye!
And for hir lewednesse I hem diffye.   lewednesse: ignorant behavior. diffye:
     Me thynketh they been lyk Jovinyan,   scorn.
Fat as a whale, and walkyng as a swan,   1930
Al vinolent as botel in the spence.
Hir preyere is of ful greet reverence,
Whan they for soules seye the psalm of Davit;
Lo, 'buf!' they seye, *cor meum eructavit!*
Who folweth Cristes gospel and his foore,   1935   foore: footsteps.
But we that humble been, and chaast, and poore,
Werkers of Goddes word, nat auditours?   auditours: listeners.
Therfore, right as an hauk up at a sours   at a sours: in the act of rising on the
Up springeth into th'eir, right so prayeres   wing.
Of charitable and chaste bisy freres   1940
Maken hir sours to Goddes eres two.
Thomas! Thomas! so moote I ryde or go,   go: walk.
And by that lord that clepid is Seint Yve,
Nere thou oure brother, sholdestou nat thryve.
In our chapitre praye we day and nyght   1945
To Crist, that he thee sende heele and myght heele: health.
Thy body for to weelden hastily."   weelden: have the use of.
     "God woot," quod he, "no thyng therof feele I!

1923. See Matthew v.3.
1925. Whether it be more like what we profess (i.e., our vow).
1926. possessioun: see footnote for line 1722, above.
1929. Jovinyan: Jovinian, the fourth-century heretic attacked by St. Jerome (see Wife of Bath's Prologue, ll. 673–75).
1931. vinolent: full of wine; addicted to drinking wine; tending to drunkenness. spence: buttery, store-room for wine and other provisions.
1934. *cor meum eructavit:* Psalm xlv.1 (xliv.2 in the Vulgate): *cor meum eructavit verbum bonum,* my heart hath uttered a good word. Here the Summoner takes *eructavit* in the literal sense of "belched."
1944. Friars were accustomed to grant "letters of fraternity" to generous laymen.

As help me Crist, as I in fewe yeres,
Have spended upon diverse manere freres   1950
Ful many a pound; yet fare I never the bet.
Certeyn, my good have I almoost biset.   good: goods. biset: spent.
Farwel, my gold, for it is al ago!"   ago: gone.
   The frere answerde, "O Thomas, dostow so?
What nedeth yow diverse freres seche?   1955 seche: seek.
What nedeth hym that hath a parfit leche   leche: physician.
To sechen othere leches in the toun?
Youre inconstance is youre confusioun.   confisioun: ruin.
Holde ye than me, or elles oure covent,   holde ye: do you hold the opinion
To praye for yow been insufficient?   1960   that. covent: convent.
Thomas, that jape nys nat worth a myte.   jape: foolish notion.
Youre maladye is for we han to lyte.   to lyte: too little.
A! yif that covent half a quarter otes!   yif: give. a quarter: a quarter of a
A! yif that covent foure and twenty grotes!   load; eight bushels.
A! yif that frere a peny, and lat hym go!   1965
Nay, nay, Thomas, it may no thyng be so!
What is a ferthyng worth parted in twelve?
Lo, ech thyng that is oned in himselve   oned: united.
Is moore strong than whan it is toscatered.   toscatered: scattered about.
Thomas, of me thou shalt nat been yflatered; 1970 of: by.
Thou woldest han oure labour al for noght.
The hye God, that al this world hath wroght,
Seith that the werkman worthy is his hire.
Thomas, noght of youre tresor I desire
As for myself, but that al oure covent   1975 that: because.
To praye for yow is ay so diligent,
And for to buylden Cristes owene chirche.
Thomas, if ye wol lernen for to wirche,   wirche: do something useful.
Of buyldynge up of chirches, may ye fynde
If it be good, in Thomas lyf of Inde.   1980 if: whether.
Ye lye heere ful of anger and of ire,
With which the devel set youre herte afire,   set: (setteth) sets.
And chiden heere the sely innocent,   sely: poor; good.
Youre wyf, that is so meke and pacient.
And therfore, Thomas, trowe me if thee
      leste,   1985
Ne stryve nat with thy wyf, as for thy beste;   as for thy beste: as will be best for
And bere this word awey now, by thy feith,   thee.
Touchynge swich thyng, lo, what the wise man
      seith:
'Withinne thyn hous ne be thou no leon;
To thy subgitz do noon oppression,   1990 subgitz: servants.
Ne make thyne aqueyntance nat for to flee.'

1980. St. Thomas the Apostle is said to have preached in India and built many churches.
1988. the wise man: i.e., Jesus the son of Sirach, writer or compiler of Ecclesiasticus, from which (iv.35) the next three lines are taken.

And, Thomas, yet eft-soones I charge thee,
Be war from ire that in thy bosom slepeth;
War fro the serpent that so slily crepeth
Under the gras, and styngeth subtilly.   1995
Be war, my sone, and herkne paciently,
That twenty thousand men han lost hir lyves
For stryvyng with hir lemmans and hir wyves.
Now sith ye han so holy, meke a wyf,
What nedeth yow, Thomas, to maken stryf? 2000
Ther nys, ywis, no serpent so cruel,
Whan man tret on his tayl, ne half so fel,
As womman is, whan she hath caught an ire;
Vengeance is thanne al that they desire.
Ire is a synne, oon of the grete of sevene, 2005
Abhomynable unto the God of hevene;
And to hymself it is destruccion.
This every lewed viker or person
Kan seye, how ire engendreth homicide.
Ire is, in sooth, executour of pride.   2010
I koude of ire seye so muche sorwe,
My tale sholde laste til to-morwe.
And therfore preye I God, bothe day and nyght,
An irous man, God sende hym litel myght!
It is greet harm and certes greet pitee   2015
To sette an irous man in heigh degree.
    Whilom ther was an irous potestat,
As seith Senek, that, durynge his estaat,
Upon a day out ryden knyghtes two,
And as Fortune wolde that it were so,   2020
That oon of hem cam hoom, that oother noght.
Anon the knyght bifore the juge is broght,
That seyde thus, 'Thou hast thy felawe slayn,
For which I deme thee to the deeth, certayn.'
And to another knyght comanded he,   2025
'Go lede hym to the deeth, I charge thee.'
And happed, as they wente by the weye
Toward the place ther he sholde deye,
The knyght cam which men wenden had be deed.
Thanne thoughte they it were the beste reed 2030
To lede hem bothe to the juge agayn.
They seiden, 'Lord, the knyght ne hath nat
    slayn
His felawe; heere he standeth hool alyve.'
'Ye shul be deed,' quod he, 'so moot I thryve!
This is to seyn, bothe oon, and two, and
    thre!'   2035
And to the firste knyght right thus spak he,

eft-soones: again.
from: of.

lemmans: mistresses.

man: one. **tret:** (treadeth) treads. **fel:** treacherous.

grete of sevene: chief of the seven deadly sins.

lewed: ignorant. **viker:** vicar. **person:** parson.

irous: given to anger, irascible.

potestat: potentate, magistrate.
estaat: term of office.
ryden: rode.

deme: sentence.

reed: plan.

hool: wholly.

2003. **hath caught an ire:** has become wrathful.

'I dampned thee; thou most algate be deed.   algate: in any event.
And thou also most nedes lese thyn heed,
For thou art cause why thy felawe deyth.'
And to the thridde knyght right thus he seith, 2040
'Thou hast nat doon that I comanded thee.'   that: that which.
And thus he dide doon sleen hem alle thre.   dide doon: caused to be.
  Irous Cambises was eek dronkelewe,   dronkelewe: addicted to drink.
And ay delited hym to been a shrewe.   shrewe: scoundrel.
And so bifel, a lord of his meynee,   2045 meynee: household; retinue.
That loved vertuous moralitee,
Seyde on a day bitwix hem two right thus:
  'A lord is lost, if he be vicius;
And dronkenesse is eek a foul record   record: reputation.
Of any man, and namely in a lord.   2050 namely: especially.
Ther is ful many an eye and many an ere
Awaityng on a lord, and he noot where.   awaityng on: watching.
For Goddes love, drynk moore attemprely!
Wyn maketh man to lesen wrecchedly
His mynde and eek his lymes everichon.'   2055 his lymes: i.e., the power of his limbs.
  'The revers shaltou se,' quod he, 'anon,
And preve it by thyn owene experience,
That wyn ne dooth to folk no swich offence.   offence: harm.
Ther is no wyn bireveth me my myght   bireveth: deprives.
Of hand ne foot, ne of myne eyen sight.'   2060
And for despit he drank ful muchel moore,   for despit: for resentment.
An hondred part, than he hadde don bifore;   part: times.
And right anon this irous, cursed wrecche
Leet this knyghtes sone bifore hym feeche,   leet fecche: cause to be fetched.
Comandynge hym he sholde bifore hym
          stonde.   2065
And sodeynly he took his bowe in honde,
And up the streng he pulled to his ere,
And with an arwe he slow the child right there.
'Now wheither have I a siker hand or noon?'   siker: sure, steady. or noon: or not.
Quod he; 'is al my myght and mynde agon?   2070
Hath wyn bireved me myn eyen sight?'   bireved me: robbed me of.
What sholde I telle th'answere of the knyght?   what: why.
His sone was slayn, ther is namoore to seye.
Beth war, therfore, with lordes how ye pleye.
Syngeth Placebo, and 'I shal, if I kan,'   2075
But if it be unto a povre man.
To a povre man men sholde his vices telle,
But nat to a lord, thogh he sholde go to helle.
  Lo irous Cirus, thilke Percien,
How he destroyed the ryver of Gysen,   2080
For that an hors of his was dreynt therinne,   for: because. dreynt: drowned.

2075. Placebo: I will please; "to sing Placebo" came to mean to be complaisant or to flatter.
2080. Gysen: the Gyndes, a tributary of the Tigris.

Whan that he wente Babiloyne to wynne.
He made that the ryver was so smal
That wommen myghte wade it over al.
Lo, what seyde he that so wel teche kan?   2085   he: Solomon (Proverbs xxii.24).
'Ne be no felawe to an irous man,
Ne with no wood man walke by the weye,
Lest thee repente'; I wol no ferther seye.
     Now, Thomas, leeve brother, leve thyn ire;
Thou shalt me fynde as just as is a squyre.   2090   squyre: (builder's) square.
Hoold nat the develes knyf ay at thyn herte—
Thyn angre dooth thee al to soore smerte—   dooth: causes. to soore: too sorely.
But shewe to me al thy confessioun."
     "Nay," quod the sike man, "by Seint Symoun!
I have be shryven this day at my curat.   2095   be shryven at: confessed to.
I have hym toold hoolly al myn estat;   estat: condition.
Nedeth namoore to speken of it," seith he,
"But if me list, of myn humylitee."
     "Yif me thanne of thy gold, to make oure
          cloystre,"
Quod he, "for many a muscle and many an   muscle: mussel.
          oystre,   2100
Whan othere men han ben ful wel at eyse,
Hath been oure foode, our cloystre for to reyse.   reyse: raise, build up.
And yet, God woot, unnethe the fundement   fundement: foundation.
Parfourned is, ne of our pavement   parfourned: completed.
Nys nat a tyle yet withinne oure wones.   2105   wones: habitation.
By God! we owen fourty pound for stones.
     Now help, Thomas, for hym that harwed   for: for the sake of.
          helle!
Or elles mote we oure bookes selle;
And if yow lakke oure predicacioun,   predicacioun: preaching, sermon.
Thanne goth the world al to destruccioun.   2110
For whoso fro this world wolde us bireve,   bireve: take away, snatch away.
So God me save, Thomas, by youre leve,
He wolde bireve out of this world the sonne.   sonne: sun.
For who kan teche and werchen as we konne?   werchen: work.
And that is nat of litel tyme," quod he,   2115   of: during.
"But syn Elye was, or Elise,
Han freres been, that fynde I of record,   of record: recorded in writing.
In charitee, ythanked be oure Lord!
Now Thomas, help, for seinte charitee!"   seinte: holy.
And doun anon he set hym on his knee.   2120
     This sike man wax wel ny wood for ire;   wax: became.
He wolde that the frere had been a-fire,
With his false dissimulacioun.

_____

2107. harwed helle: see Miller's Tale, l. 3512 and note.
2116. Elye: Elias, Elijah. Elise: Eliseus, Elisha. The Carmelites claimed that their order was
founded on Mt. Carmel by the prophet Elijah.

"Swich thyng as is in my possessioun,"
Quod he, "that may I yeve, and noon oother. 2125
Ye sey me thus, how that I am youre brother?"

    "Ye, certes," quod the frere, "trusteth wel.
I took oure dame oure lettre with oure seel."   took: gave.

    "Now wel," quod he, "and somwhat shal I yive
Unto youre holy covent whil I lyve;   2130
And in thyn hand thou shalt it have anon,
On this condicion, and oother noon,
That thou departe it so, my deere brother,   departe: divide into parts.
That every frere have as muche as oother.
This shaltou swere on thy professioun,   2135
Withouten fraude or cavillacioun."   cavillacioun: caviling, quibbling.

    "I swere it," quod this frere, "upon my feith!"
And therwithal his hand in his he leith,
"Lo, here my feith; in me shal be no lak."

    "Now thanne, put thyn hand doun by my
            bak,"   2140
Seyde this man, "and grope wel bihynde.
Bynethe my buttok there shaltow fynde
A thyng that I have hyd in pryvetee."

    "A!" thoghte this frere, "that shal go with me!"
And doun his hand he launcheth to the clifte, 2145   launcheth: thrusts. clifte: cleft.
In hope for to fynde there a yifte.   yifte: gift.
And whan this sike man felte this frere
Aboute his tuwel grope there and heere,   tuwel: hole.
Amydde his hand he leet the frere a fart:
Ther nys no capul, drawyng in a cart,   2150   capul: horse.
That myghte have lete a fart of swich a soun.

    The frere up stirte as dooth a wood leoun,—
"A! false cherl," quod he, "for Goddes bones!
This hastow for despit doon for the nones.   despit: anger. for the nones: on pur-
Thou shalt abye this fart, if that I may!"   2155   pose. abye: pay the penalty for.

    His meynee, which that herden this affray,   meynee: household, retinue. affray:
Cam lepyng in and chaced out the frere;   uproar.
And forth he gooth, with a ful angry cheere,
And fette his felawe, ther as lay his stoor.   fette: fetched. stoor: store; accumu-
He looked as it were a wilde boor;   2160   lated goods or money.
He grynte with his teeth, so was he wrooth.   grynte: ground, gnashed.
A sturdy paas doun to the court he gooth,   sturdy: furious. paas: pace.
Wher as ther woned a man of greet honour,   woned: dwelled.
To whom that he was alwey confessour.
This worthy man was lord of that village.   2165
This frere cam as he were in a rage,
Where as this lord sat etyng at his bord;

2126–28. See line 1944 and note.
2135. professioun: oath made on becoming a friar.
2162. the court: the manor-house with its court.

Unnethes myghte the frere speke a word,
Til atte laste he seyde, "God yow see!"   God yow see!: May God watch, pro-
   This lord gan looke, and seide,   tect, you.
        "Benedicitee!   2170
What, frere John, what maner world is this?
I se wel that som thyng ther is amys;
Ye looken as the wode were ful of thevys.   wode: woods.
Sit doun anon, and tel me what youre grief is,   grief: grievance.
And it shal been amended, if I may."   2175
   "I have," quod he, "had a despit to-day,   despit: insulting experience.
God yelde yow, adoun in youre village,   yelde: reward.
That in this world ther nys so povre a page   page: lad.
That he nolde have abhomynacioun   abhomynacioun: physical loathing,
Of that I have receyved in youre toun.   2180   nausea.
And yet ne greveth me nothyng so soore,
As that this olde cherl with lokkes hoore
Blasphemed hath oure hooly covent eke."
   "Now, maister," quod this lord, "I yow
       biseke,—"
   "No maister, sire," quod he, "but servitour, 2185
Thogh I have had in scole that honour.
God liketh nat that 'Raby' men us calle,
Neither in market ne in youre large halle."
   "No fors," quod he, "but tel me al youre grief."
   "Sire," quod this frere, "an odious
      meschief   2190   meschief: injury, wrong.
This day bityd is to myn ordre and me,   bityd is: has happened.
And so, *per consequens,* to ech degree   *per consequens:* consequently.
Of holy chirche, God amende it soone!"
   "Sire," quod the lord, "ye woot what is to
      doone.
Distempre yow noght, ye be my confessour;   2195
Ye been the salt of the erthe and the savour.
For Goddes love, youre pacience ye holde!
Tel me youre grief"; and he anon hym tolde,
As ye han herd biforn, ye woot wel what.
   The lady of the hous ay stille sat   2200
Til she had herd what the frere sayde.
"Ey, Goddes moder," quod she, "Blisful mayde!
Is ther aught elles? telle me feithfully."
   "Madame," quod he, "how thynketh yow   thynketh: does it seem (to).
      therby?"
   "How that me thynketh?" quod she, "so God
      me speede,   2205
I seye, a cherl hath doon a cherles dede.

2186. He had received the degree of Master of Divinity.
2187. See Matthew xxiii.7–8.
2192–93. ech degree of holy chirche: each grade of the ecclesiastical hierarchy.
2195. distempre yow noght: don't be upset.
2196. See Matthew v.13.

What shold I seye? God lat hym nevere thee!   thee: prosper.
His sike heed is ful of vanytee;   vanytee: foolishness.
I holde hym in a manere frenesye."   frenesye: frenzy.
   "Madame," quod he, "by God, I shal nat
       lye,   2210
But I on oother wise may be wreke,   wreke: avenged.
I shal diffame hym over al wher I speke,
The false blasphemour, that charged me
To parte that wol nat departed be,   that: that which. departed: divided.
To every man yliche, with meschaunce!"   2215 yliche: equally. with meschaunce!: a
   The lord sat stille as he were in a traunce,   curse upon him!
And in his herte he rolled up and doun,
"How hadde this cherl ymaginacioun
To shewe swich a probleme to the frere?   shewe: propose, propound.
Nevere erst er now herde I of swich matere. 2220 nevere erst: never before.
I trowe the devel putte it in his mynde.
In ars-metrik shal ther no man fynde,   ars-metrik: the art or science of meas-
Biforn this day, of swich a question.   uring and calculating.
Who sholde make a demonstracion
That every man sholde have ylyke his part   2225
As of a soun or savour of a fart?
O nyce, proude cherl, I shrewe his face!   nyce: foolish. shrewe: curse.
Lo, sires," quod the lord, "with harde grace!   with harde grace!: bad luck to him!
Who evere herde of swich a thyng er now?
To every man ylike, tel me how?   2230
It is an inpossible, it may nat be.   an inpossible: an impossibility (Latin,
Ey, nyce cherl, God lete him nevere thee!   *impossibile*: a term in medieval
The rumblyng of a fart, and every soun,   logic).
Nis but of eir reverberacioun,
And ther it wasteth lite and lite awey.   2235 lite and lite: little by little.
Ther nys no man kan deme, by my fey,
If that it were departed equally.
What, lo, my cherl, lo, yet how shrewedly   shrewedly: cursedly.
Unto my confessour to-day he spak!
I holde hym certeyn a demonyak!   2240 a demonyak: one possessed by a
Now ete youre mete, and lat the cherl go pleye;   demon.
Lat hym go hange hymself a devel weye!"   a devel weye: and go to the devil.

The wordes of the lordes Squier and his Kervere for departynge of the fart on twelve.

   Now stood the lordes squier at the bord,
That carf his mete, and herde word by word   carf: carved.
Of alle thyng of which I have yow sayd.   2245
"My lord," quod he, "be ye nat yvele apayd,   yvele apayd: displeased, resentful.
I koude telle, for a gowne-clooth,

To yow, sire frere, so ye be nat wrooth,
How that this fart sholde evene deled be   evene: in equal shares. deled: appor-
Among youre covent, if it liked me."   2250   tioned.
     "Tel," quod the lord, "and thou shalt have
          anon
A gowne-clooth, by God and by Seint John!"
     "My lord," quod he, "whan that the weder is   weder: weather.
          fair,
Withouten wynd or perturbynge of air,
Lat brynge a cartwheel heere into this halle; 2255
But looke that it have his spokes alle,—   his: its.
Twelve spokes hath a cartwheel comunly.
And bryng me thanne twelve freres, woot ye
          why?
For thrittene is a covent, as I gesse.
Youre confessour heere, for his worthynesse, 2260
Shal parfourne up the nombre of this covent.   parfourne up: complete.
Thanne shal they knele adoun, by oon assent,   by oon assent: of one mind.
And to every spokes ende, in this manere,
Ful sadly leye his nose shal a frere.   sadly: firmly.
Youre noble confessour—there God hym
          save!—   2265
Shal holde his nose upright under the nave.   nave: the central block of a wheel.
Thanne shal this cherl, with bely stif and toght   toght: taut.
As any tabour, hider been ybroght;
And sette hym on the wheel right of this cart,
Upon the nave, and make hym lete a fart.   2270
And ye shal seen, up peril of my lyf,   up: upon.
By preeve which that is demonstratif,   preeve: proof. demonstratif: based on
That equally the soun of it wol wende,   logic.
And eke the stynk, unto the spokes ende,
Save that this worthy man, youre confessour, 2275
By cause he is a man of greet honour,
Shal have the firste fruyt, as resoun is.   resoun: i.e., right, proper.
The noble usage of freres yet is this,
The worthy men of hem shul first be served;
And certeinly he hath it wel disserved.   2280
He hath to-day taught us so mucnel good
With prechyng in the pulpit ther he stood,
That I may vouche sauf, I sey for me,
He hadde the firste smel of fartes thre;
And so wolde al his covent hardily,   2285   hardily: certainly.
He bereth hym so faire and holily."
     The lord, the lady, and ech man, save the frere,
Seyde that Jankyn spak, in this matere,
As wel as Euclide or [as] Ptholomee.   as: see footnote.
Touchynge the cherl, they seyde, subtiltee   2290

2289. O' reads or Protholomee, which is an error for or Ptholomee (the scribe mistaking the
initial P for the abbreviation of pro); I insert as, following Skeat's emendation.

And heigh wit made hym speken as he spak;
He nys no fool, ne no demonyak.
And Jankyn hath ywonne a newe gowne.—
My tale is doon; we been almoost at towne.

Heere endeth the Somonours tale.

*Heere folweth the
prologe of the
Clerkes tale of Oxenford.*

"Sire Clerk of Oxenford," oure Hooste sayde,
"Ye ryde as coy and stille as dooth a mayde   coy: quiet; modest, shy.
Were newe spoused, sittynge at the bord;   spoused: espoused, wedded. bord:
This day ne herde I of youre tonge a word.   table.
I trowe ye studie aboute som sophyme;   5   studie: study, muse. sophyme: soph-
But Salomon seith 'every thyng hath tyme.'   ism; specious argument.
 For Goddes sake, as beth of bettre cheere!   as beth: be.
It is no tyme for to studien heere.
Telle us som myrie tale, by youre fey!   fey: faith.
For what man that is entred in a pley,   10   pley: game.
He nedes moot unto the pley assente.
But precheth nat, as freres doon in Lente,   Lente: see Summoner's Tale, l. 1782
To make us for oure olde synnes wepe,   and note.
Ne that thy tale make us nat to slepe.
 Telle us som murie thyng of aventures.   15
Youre termes, youre colours, and youre figures,
Keepe hem in stoor til so be ye endite
Heigh style, as whan that men to kynges write.
Spraketh so pleyn at this tyme, we yow preye,
That we may understonde what ye seye."   20
 This worthy clerk benignely answerde:
"Hooste," quod he, "I am under youre yerde;   yerde: rod (i.e., authority).
Ye han of us as now the governance,
And therfore wol I do yow obeisance,   do yow obeisance: submit to you.
As fer as resoun axeth, hardily.   25   axeth: requires. hardily: certainly.
I wol yow telle a tale which that I
Lerned at Padowe of a worthy clerk,   Padowe: Padua.
As preved by his wordes and his werk.   preved: proved.
He is now deed and nayled in his cheste,   cheste: coffin.
I prey to God so yeve his soule reste!   30
 Frauncyes Petrak, the lauriat poete,   Petrak: Petrarch (who died in 1374).

2294. towne: Sittingbourne? (See Wife of Bath's Prologue, ll. 845–47.)
6. tyme: a season. See Ecclesiastes iii.1.
16. termes: pedantic phrases. colours: rhetorical ornaments. figures: figures of speech.
31. Frauncyes Petrak: Petrarch, Italian poet and humanist, thought that the final story in Boc-
caccio's *Decameron* was so beautiful that it ought to be preserved for all time; he therefore re-
told it in Latin. Chaucer based the Clerk's Tale both on Petrarch's Latin version of the story and
on an anonymous French translation of Petrarch.

Highte this clerk, whos rethorike sweete
Enlumyned al Ytaille of poetrie,   enlumyned: illumined.
As Lynyan dide of philosophie,
Or lawe, or oother art particuler;   35 art: field of study.
But Deeth, that wol nat suffre us dwellen heer,
But as it were a twynklyng of an eye,
Hem bothe hath slayn, and alle shul we dye.
   But forth to tellen of this worthy man
That taughte me this tale, as I bigan,   40
I seye that first with heigh stile he enditeth,   enditeth: writes.
Er he the body of his tale writeth,
A prohemye, in the which discryveth he   prohemye: proem, introduction. dis-
Pemond, and of Saluces the contree,   cryveth: describes. Pemond: Pied-
And speketh of Apennyn, the hilles hye,   45 mont. Saluces: Saluzzo.
That been the boundes of West Lumbardye,
And of Mount Vesulus in special,   Mount Vesulus: Monviso.
Where as the Poo out of a welle smal   welle: spring.
Taketh his firste spryngyng and his sours,
That estward ay encresseth in his cours   50
To Emele-ward, to Ferrare, and Venyse;   to Emele-ward: towards Emilia.
The which a long thyng were to devyse
And trewely, as to my juggement,
Me thynketh it a thyng impertinent,   impertinent: irrelevant.
Save that he wole conveyen his mateere; 55 conveyen: introduce.
But this his tale, which that ye may heere."   this: this is (contracted).

Heere bigynneth the
tale of the Clerk of
Oxenford.

   Ther is, at the west syde of Ytaille,
Doun at the roote of Vesulus the colde,   roote: base, foot.
A lusty playne, habundant of vitaille,   vitaille: produce.
Where many a tour and toun thou mayst
          biholde,   60
That founded were in tyme of fadres olde, fadres: ancestors.
And many another delitable sighte,   delitable: delightful.
And Saluces this noble contree highte.

   A markys whilom lord was of that lond, markys: marquis.
As were his worthy eldres hym bifore;   65 eldres: ancestors.
And obeisant, ay redy to his hond,
Were alle his liges, bothe lasse and moore.

----

34. Giovanni da Legnano was Professor of Canon Law at Bologna.

Thus in delit he lyveth, and hath doon yoore,   yoore: for a long time.
Biloved and drad, thurgh favour of Fortune,   drad: dreaded.
Bothe of his lordes and of his commune. 70 commune: common people.

   Therwith he was, to speke as of lynage,
The gentilleste yborn of Lumbardye,
A fair persone, and strong, and yong of age,   fair: handsome.
And ful of honour and of curteisye;
Discreet ynogh his contree for to gye, 75 gye: guide, govern.
Save in somme thynges that he was to blame;
And Walter was this yonge lordes name.

   I blame hym thus, that he considered noght
In tyme comynge what myghte hym bityde,
But on his lust present was al his thoght, 80
As for to hauke and hunte on every syde.
Wel ny alle othere cures leet he slyde,   cures: cares, responsibilities.
And eek he nolde—and that was worst of alle—
Wedde no wyf, for noght that may bifalle.

   Oonly that point his peple bar so soore 85 bar: bore, endured.
That flokmeele on a day they to hym wente,   flokmeele: in groups or flocks.
And oon of hem, that wisest was of loore—
Or elles that the lord best wolde assente   or elles that: either because.
That he sholde telle hym what his peple mente,
Or elles koude he shewe wel swich matere— 90
He to the markys seyde as ye shal heere:

   "O noble markys, youre humanitee
Assureth us and yeveth us hardinesse,   hardinesse: boldness.
As often as tyme is of necessitee,
That we to yow mowe telle oure hevynesse. 95 hevynesse: grief.
Accepteth, lord, now of youre gentillesse
That we with pitous herte unto yow pleyne,   that: that which.
And lat youre eres nat my voys desdeyne.   eres: ears.

   "Al have I noght to doone in this matere
Moore than another man hath in this place, 100
Yet for as muche as ye, my lord so deere,
Han alwey shewed me favour and grace
I dar the bettre aske of yow a space   a space of: an opportunity for.
Of audience, to shewen oure requeste,
And ye, my lord, to doon right as yow leste. 105

   "For certes, lord, so wel us liketh yow
And al youre werk, and evere han doon, that we
Ne koude nat us self devysen how   devysen: imagine.
We myghte lyven in moore felicitee,
Save o thyng, lord, if it youre wille be, 110

That for to been a wedded man yow leste;
Thanne were youre peple in sovereyn hertes reste.

"Boweth youre nekke under that blisful yok
Of soveraynetee, noght of servyse,
Which that men clepe spousaille or wedlok; 115
And thenketh, lord, among youre thoghtes wyse
How that oure dayes passe in sondry wyse;
For thogh we slepe, or wake, or rome, or ryde,
Ay fleeth the tyme; it nyl no man abyde.   fleeth: flies. nyl: will not.

"And thogh youre grene youthe floure as   floure: may flourish.
      yit,   120
In crepeth age alwey, as stille as stoon,
And deth manaceth every age, and smyt   smyt: (smiteth) smites.
In ech estaat, for ther escapeth noon;
And al so certein as we knowe echon   al so: even as.
That we shul dye, as uncerteyn we alle   125
Been of that day whan deth shal on us falle.

"Accepteth thanne of us the trewe entente,
That nevere yet refuseden youre heste,   heste: command.
And we wol, lord, if that ye wole assente,
Chese yow a wyf, in short tyme at the leeste, 130
Born of the gentilleste and of the meeste   meeste: greatest, highest in rank.
Of al this land, so that it oghte seme
Honour to God and yow, as we kan deeme.

"Delivere us out of al this bisy drede,   bisy drede: deep anxiety.
And taak a wyf, for hye Goddes sake!   135
For if it so bifelle, as God forbede,
That thurgh youre deeth youre lynage sholde
      slake,   slake: come to an end.
And that a straunge successour sholde take
Youre heritage, O, wo were us alyve!
Wherfore we pray you hastily to wyve."   140 hastily: soon. wyve: wed.

Hir meeke prayere and hir pitous cheere
Made the markys herte han pitee.
"Ye wol," quod he, "myn owene peple deere,
To that I nevere erst thoughte streyne me.   that: that which. streyne: constrain.
I me rejoysed of my libertee,   145
That selde tyme is founde in mariage;   selde tyme: infrequent times.
Ther I was free, I moot been in servage.

"But nathelees I se youre trewe entente,
And truste upon youre wit, and have doon ay;   wit: wisdom.
Wherfore of my free wyl I wol assente   150
To wedde me, as soone as evere I may.

But ther as ye han profred me to-day
To chese me a wyf, I yow relesse
That choys, and pray yow of that profre cesse.   profre: offer. cesse: cease, desist.

"For God it woot, that children ofte been   155
Unlyk hir worthy eldres hem bifore;   eldres: ancestors.
Bountee comth al of God, nat of the streen   bountee: goodness. streen: strain,
Of which they been engendred and ybore.   lineage. ybore: born.
I truste in Goddes bountee, and therfore
My mariage and myn estaat and reste   160   reste: peace; quiet life.
I hym bitake; he may doon as hym leste.   hym bitake: entrust to him.

"Lat me allone in chesyng of my wyf,—
That charge upon my bak I wol endure.   charge: load, responsibility.
But I yow pray, and charge upon youre lyf,
What wyf that I take, ye me assure   165
To worshipe hire, whil that hir lyf may dure,   worshipe: honor.
In word and werk, bothe here and everywhere,   werk: deed.
As she an emperoures doghter were.

"And ferthermoore, this shal ye swere, that ye
Agayn my choys shal neither grucche ne   grucche: grumble, complain.
        stryve;   170
For sith I shal forgoon my libertee
At youre requeste, as evere moot I thryve,
Ther as myn herte is set, ther wol I wyve;
And but ye wol assente in swich manere,
I pray yow, speketh namoore of this matere." 175

With hertely wyl they sworen and assenten   hertely: faithful.
To al this thyng, ther seyde no wight nay;
Bisekynge hym of grace, er that they wenten,   bisekynge: beseeching.
That he wolde graunten hem a certein day   graunten: appoint.
Of his spousaille, as soone as evere he may; 180
For yet alwey the peple somwhat dredde,   dredde: dreaded, feared.
Lest that the markys no wyf wolde wedde.

He graunted hem a day, swich as hym leste,
On which he wolde be wedded sikerly,
And seyde he dide al this at hir requeste.   185
And they, with humble entente, buxomly,   buxomly: humbly, meekly.
Knelynge upon hir knees ful reverently,
Hym thanken alle; and thus they han an ende   ende: fulfillment.
Of hire entente, and hom agayn they wende.

And heerupon he to his officers   190
Comaundeth for the feste to purveye,   purveye: provide.
And to his privee knyghtes and squieres   privee: privy, closely attendant.
Swich charge yaf as hym liste on hem leye;   charge: orders.

And they to his comandement obeye,
And ech of hem dooth al his diligence   195
To doon unto the feeste reverence.   doon reverence: show respect.

                    EXPLICIT PRIMA PARS.

                    INCIPIT SECUNDA PARS.

    Noght fer fro thilke paleys honurable,
Wher as this markys shoop his mariage,   shoop: prepared for.
Ther stood a throop, of site delitable,   throop: thorp, hamlet.
In which that povre folk of that village   200
Hadden hir beestes and hir herbergage,   herbergage: lodging.
And of hire labour tooke hir sustenance,
After that the erthe yaf hem habundance.   after that: according as.

    Among thise povre folk ther dwelte a man
Which that was holden povrest of hem alle;   205 holden: held, considered.
But hye God somtyme senden can
His grace into a litel oxes stalle;
Janicula men of that throop hym calle.
A doghter hadde he, fair ynogh to sighte,
And Grisildis this yonge mayden highte.   210

    But for to speke of vertuous beautee,
Thanne was she oon the faireste under sonne;
For povreliche yfostred up was she,   povreliche: in poverty.
No likerous lust was thurgh hire herte yronne.   was yronne: ran.
Wel ofter of the welle than of the tonne   215 ofter: oftener. tonne: cask.
She drank, and for she wolde vertu plese,
She knew wel labour, but noon ydel ese.

    But thogh this mayde tendre were of age,
Yet in the brest of hire virginitee
Ther was enclosed rype and sad corage;   220 sad: firm. corage: temperament.
And in greet reverence and charitee
Hir olde povre fader fostred she.   fostred: tended with care.
A fewe sheep, spynnynge on feeld, she kepte;   spynnynge: while she was spinning.
She wolde noght been ydel til she slepte.

    And whan she homward cam, she wolde
          brynge   225
Wortes or othere herbes tymes ofte,   wortes: cabbages. herbes: edible
The whiche she shredde and seeth for hir lyvynge,   plants. seeth: seethed, boiled.
And made hir bed ful hard and nothyng softe;

----
207. The oxes stalle, with its implications, is one of Chaucer's additions to Petrarch's tale.

And ay she kepte hir fadres lyf on-lofte
With every obeisaunce and diligence   230
That child may doon to fadres reverence.

kepte on-lofte: kept aloft, sustained.

   Upon Grisilde, this povre creature,
Ful ofte sithe this markys sette his eye
As he on huntyng rood paraventure;
And whan it fil that he myghte hire espye,   235
He noght with wantown lookyng of folye
His eyen caste on hire, but in sad wyse
Upon hir cheere he wolde hym ofte avyse,

sithe: times.

fil: befell. espye: see.
folye: lechery.
sad: serious.
hym avyse: take thought, reflect.

   Commendynge in his herte hir wommanhede,
And eek hir vertu, passyng any wight   240
Of so yong age, as wel in cheere as dede.
For thogh the peple have no greet insight
In vertue, he considered ful right
Hir bountee, and disposed that he wolde
Wedde hire oonly, if evere he wedde sholde. 245

passyng: surpassing.

bountee: goodness. disposed: re-
solved.

   The day of weddyng cam, but no wight kan
Telle what womman that it sholde be;
For which merveille wondred many a man,
And seyden, whan they were in privetee,
"Wol nat oure lord yet leve his vanytee?   250
Wol he nat wedde? allas, allas, the while!
Why wol he thus hymself and us bigile?"

vanytee: foolish behavior.

   But nathelees this markys hath doon make
Of gemmes, set in gold and in asure,
Brooches and rynges, for Grisildis sake;   255
And of hir clothyng took he the mesure
Of a mayde lyk to hir stature,
And eek of othere ornamentes alle
That unto swich a weddyng sholde falle.

doon make: caused to be made.
asure: blue enamel made from lapis
lazuli.

ornamentes: adornments; accessories.
falle: be appropriate.

   The time of undren of the same day   260
Approcheth, that this weddyng sholde be;
And al the paleys put was in array,
Bothe halle and chambres, ech in his degree;
Houses of office stuffed with plentee
Ther maystow seen, of deyntevous vitaille   265
That may be founde as fer as last Ytaille.

undren: forenoon.

array: order.
in his degree: according to its use.
houses of office: storage buildings.
deyntevous: delicious.
last: (lasteth) extends.

   This roial markys, richely arrayed,
Lordes and ladyes in his compaignye,
The whiche that to the feeste were yprayed,
And of his retenue the bachelrye,   270
With many a soun of sondry melodye,

yprayed: invited.
bachelrye: the body of knights in at-
tendance upon a superior.

Unto the village of the which I tolde,
In this array the righte wey han holde.   righte: direct. holde: taken.

   Grisilde of this, God woot, ful innocent,
That for hire shapen was al this array,   275 array: magnificence.
To fecchen water at a welle is went,
And cometh hoom as soone as ever she may;
For wel she hadde herd seyd that thilke day
The markys sholde wedde, and if she myghte,
She wolde fayn han seyn som of that sighte.   280

   She thoghte, "I wole with othere maydens
       stonde,
That been my felawes, in oure dore and se
The markysesse, and therfore wol I fonde   markysesse: marchioness. fonde: try.
To doon at hoom, as soone at it may be,
The labour which that longeth unto me;   285
And thanne I may at leyser hir biholde,
If she this wey unto the castel holde."   holde: take.

   And as she wolde over the thresshfold gon,   thresshfold: threshold.
The markys cam, and gan hire for to calle;
And she set doun hir water pot anon,   290
Biside the thresshfold, in an oxes stalle,
And doun upon hir knees she gan to falle,
And with sad contenance kneleth stille,   sad: sober. stille: quietly.
Til she had herd what was the lordes wille.

   This thoghtful markys spak unto this
       mayde   295
Ful sobrely, and seyde in this manere:
"Where is youre fader, O Grisildis?" he sayde.
And she with reverence, in humble cheere,   cheere: spirit.
Answerde, "Lord, he is al redy heere."   redy: at hand.
And in she goth withouten lenger lette,   300 lette: delay.
And to the markys she hir fader fette.   fette: fetched, brought.

   He by the hand than took this olde man,
And seyde thus, whan he hym hadde asyde:
"Janicula, I neither may ne kan

A cassone panel with scenes from *Decameron* X.x: This panel from a Florentine dower chest or cassone and attributed to the school of Francesco Pesellino, of the mid-fifteenth century, depicts three scenes from the crowning story of Boccaccio's *Decameron*. At left the marchese Gualteri of Saluzzo with his entourage is about to leave his home on the way to meet and betroth Griselda. Just right of center he sees her going home from the fountain. In the right background Griselda stands with Gualteri and her father; Gualteri has just had her old garments removed in the presence of all and she is about to be dressed in the new ones provided by him, after which in the *Decameron* Gualteri betroths Griselda; however, their gestures indicate that the artist has the betrothal take place while she is still unclothed. Evidently later scenes from the novella were considered unsuitable for a bridal chest.

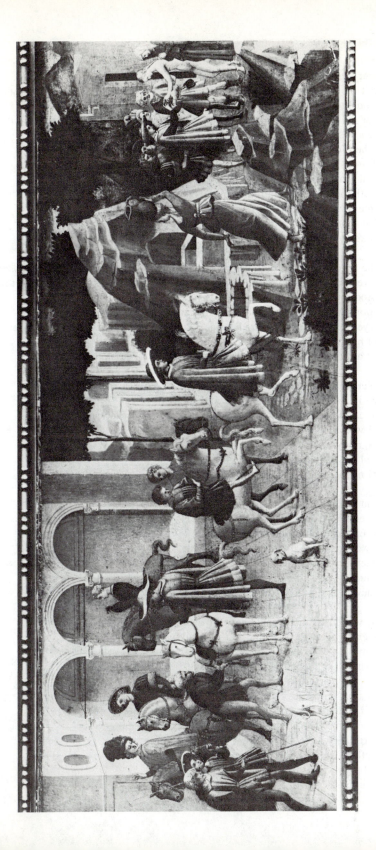

Lenger the plesance of myn herte hyde. 305 plesance: pleasure, desire.
If that thou vouche sauf, what so bityde,   what so bityde: come what may.
Thy doghter wol I take, er that I wende,
As for my wyf, unto my lyves ende.

"Thou lovest me, I woot it wel certeyn,
And art my feithful lige man ybore; 310 ybore: born.
And al that liketh me, I dar wel seyn
It liketh thee, and specially therfore
Tel me that point that I have seyd bifore,
If that thou wolt unto that purpos drawe,   drawe: be inclined.
To take me as for thy sone-in-lawe." 315

The sodeyn cas this man astonyed so   astonyed: astonished, bewildered.
That reed he wax; abayst and al quakyng   wax: became. abayst: startled.
He stood; unnethes seyde he wordes mo,
But oonly thus: "Lord," quod he, "my willyng willyng: desire.
Is as ye wole, ne ayeins youre likynge 320 ayeins: contrary to. likynge: pleasure.
I wol no thyng, ye be my lord so deere;
Right as yow list, governeth this matere."   governeth: arrange.

"Yet wol I," quod this markys softly,
"That in thy chambre I and thou and she
Have a collacioun, and wostow why? 325 collacioun: conference.
For I wol aske if it hir wille be
To be my wyf, and rule hire after me.
And al this shal be doon in thy presence;
I wol noght speke out of thyn audience."   audience: hearing.

And in the chambre, whil they were aboute 330
Hir tretys, which as ye shal after heere,   tretys: discussion of terms.
The peple cam unto the hous withoute,   withoute: outside.
And wondred hem in how honest manere
And tentifly she kepte hir fader deere.   tentifly: attentively.
But outrely Grisildis wondre myghte, 335
For nevere erst ne saw she swich a sighte.

No wonder is thogh that she were astoned astoned: astonished.
To seen so greet a gest come in that place;
She nevere was to swiche gestes woned,   woned: accustomed.
For which she looked with ful pale face. 340
But shortly forth this matere for to chace, chace: pursue.
Thise arn the wordes that the markys sayde
To this benigne, verray, feithful mayde.

"Grisilde," he seyde, "ye shal wel understonde
It liketh to youre fader and to me 345
That I yow wedde, and eek it may so stonde,
As I suppose, ye wol that it so be.

But thise demandes aske I first," quod he,
"That, sith it shal be doon in hastif wyse,
Wol ye assente, or elles yow avyse? 350

   yow avyse: take the matter under advisement.

"I sey this, be ye redy with good herte
To al my lust, and that I frely may,
As me best thynketh, do yow laughe or smerte,
And nevere ye to grucche it, nyght ne day?   *grucche:* murmur at.
And eek whan I sey 'ye,' ne sey nat 'nay,' 355
Neither by word ne frownyng contenance?
Swere this, and here I swere oure alliance."

  Wondrynge upon this word, quakyng for
     drede,
She seyde, "Lord, undigne and unworthy   *undigne:* unworthy.
I am to thilke honour that ye me beede, 360 *beede:* offer.
But as ye wol yourself, right so wol I.
And heere I swere that nevere willyngly,
In werk ne thoght, I nyl yow disobeye,   *werk:* deed. *nyl:* will not.
For to be deed, though me were looth to deye." *for to be deed:* though I die for it.

  "This is ynogh, Grisilde myn," quod he. 365
And forth he goth, with a ful sobre cheere,
Out at the dore, and after that cam she,
And to the peple he seyde in this manere:
"This is my wyf," quod he, "that standeth heere.
Honoureth hire and loveth hire, I preye, 370
Whoso me loveth; ther is namoore to seye."

  And for that no thyng of hir olde geere   *geere:* apparel.
She sholde brynge into his hous, he bad
That wommen sholde dispoillen hir right there; *dispoillen:* strip of clothes, undress.
Of which thise ladyes were nat right glad 375
To handle hir clothes, wherinne she was clad.
But nathelees, this mayde bright of hewe
Fro foot to heed they clothed han al newe.

  Hir heris han they kembd, that lay untressed *untressed:* loose, disheveled.
Ful rudely, and with hir fyngres smale 380
A corone on hir heed they han ydressed,   *corone:* nuptial garland. **ydressed:**
And sette hire ful of nowches grete and smale.   placed. **nowches:** jeweled ornaments.
Of hir array what sholde I make a tale?   ments. **what:** why.
Unnethe the peple hir knew for hire fairnesse,
Whan she translated was in swich richesse. 385 *translated:* transformed.

  This markys hath hire spoused with a ryng *spoused:* wed.
Broght for the same cause, and thanne hire sette *cause:* purpose.
Upon an hors, snow-whit and wel amblyng, *amblyng:* walking at an easy pace.
And to his paleys, er he lenger lette, *lette:* delayed.

With joyful peple that hir ladde and mette,   **390**   ladde: led.
Conveyed hire, and thus the day they spende   conveyed: accompanied, conducted.
In revel, til the sonne gan descende.

    And shortly forth this tale for to chace,
I seye that to this newe markysesse   markysesse: marchioness.
God hath swich favour sent hire of his grace, **395**
That it ne semed nat by liklynesse
That she was born and fed in rudenesse,
As in a cote or in an oxe-stalle,   cote: hut.
But norissed in an emperoures halle.   norissed: nurtured.

    To every wight she woxen is so deere   **400**   woxen: become.
And worshipful that folk ther she was bore,   worshipful: worthy of honor. **bore:**
And from hire birthe knewe hire yeer by yeere,   born.
Unnethe trowed they,—but dorste han swore—   dorste han swore: durst have sworn
That to Janicle, of which I spak bifore,   the contrary.
She doghter were, for, as by conjecture,   **405**   conjecture: surmising.
Hem thoughte she was another creature.

    For though that evere vertuous was she,
She was encressed in swich excellence
Of thewes goode, yset in heigh bountee,   thewes: habits. **heigh bountee:** great
And so discreet and fair of eloquence,   **410**   virtue.
So benigne and so digne of reverence,   digne: deserving.
And koude so the peples herte embrace,
That ech hir lovede that looked on hir face.

    Noght oonly of Saluces in the toun
Publissed was the bountee of hir name,   **415**   publissed: made known, told abroad.
But eek biside in many a regioun,
If oon seide wel, another seyde the same;
So spradde of hire heighe bountee the fame
That men and wommen, as wel yonge as olde,
Goon to Saluce, upon hire to biholde.   **420**

    Thus Walter lowely—nay, but roially—
Wedded with fortunat honestetee,   honestetee: honor.
In Goddes pees lyveth ful esily   esily: comfortably.
At hom, and outward grace ynogh had he;   outward: publicly.
And for he saugh that under low degree   **425**
Was ofte vertu hid, the peple hym helde
A prudent man, and that is seyn ful selde.   seyn: seen.

    Nat oonly this Grisildis thurgh hir wit
Koude al the feet of wyfly hoomlinesse,
But eek, whan that the cas required it,   **430**
The commune profit koude she redresse.   commune profit: public weal. **re-**
    dresse: promote.

———————

429. Knew all the womanly art of managing a home.

Ther nas discord, rancour, ne hevynesse
In al that land, that she ne koude apese   apese: alleviate.
And wisely brynge hem alle in reste and ese.   ese: tranquillity, peace of mind.

   Though that hir housbond absent were,
          anon,   435
If gentil men or othere of hir contree
Were wrothe, she wolde bryngen hem aton;   bryngen aton: reconcile.
So wise and rype wordes hadde she,
And juggementz of so greet equitee,
That she from hevene sent was, as men
          wende,   440
Peple to save and every wrong t'amende.

   Nat longe tyme after that this Grisild
Was wedded, she a doghter hath ybore.
Al had hir levere have born a knave child,   knave: male.
Glad was the markys and the folk therfore; 445
For though a mayde child coome al bifore,
She may unto a knave child atteyne
By liklihede, syn she nys nat bareyne.

       Explicit secunda pars.

       Incipit tercia pars.

   Ther fil, as it bifalleth tymes mo,   fil: befell. mo: other.
Whan that this child had souked but a throwe, 450 souked: sucked. throwe: while.
This markys in his herte longeth so
To tempte his wyf, hir sadnesse for to knowe,   tempte: test. sadnesse: steadfastness.
That he ne myghte out of his herte throwe
This merveillous desir his wyf t'assaye;   assaye: test the character of.
Nedelees, God woot, he thoghte hire for   nedelees: needlessly.
        t'affraye.   455 affraye: disturb deeply; frighten.

   He hadde assayed hire ynogh bifore,
And foond hire evere good; what neded it
Hir for to tempte, and alwey moore and moore,
Though som men preise it for a subtil wit?   wit: piece of wisdom.
But as for me, I seye that yvele it sit   460 yvele it sit: it ill befits.
To assaye a wyf whan that it is no nede,
And putten hire in angwyssh and in drede.

   For which this markys wroghte in this manere:
He cam allone a-nyght, ther as she lay,
With steerne face and with ful trouble cheere, 465
And seyde thus: "Grisilde," quod he, "that day
That I yow took out of youre povre array,   array: condition.

And putte yow in estaat of heigh noblesse,—
Ye have nat that forgeten, as I gesse?

"I seye, Grisilde, this present dignitee,   470
In which that I have put yow, as I trowe,
Maketh yow nat foryetful for to be
That I yow took in povre estaat ful lowe,
For any wele ye mote yourselven knowe.   for: in spite of.
Tak heede of every word that I yow seye;   475
Ther is no wight that hereth it but we tweye.

"Ye woot youreself wel how that ye cam
    heere
Into this hous, it is nat longe ago;
And though to me that ye be lief and deere,   lief: cherished.
Unto my gentils ye be no thyng so.   480 gentils: gentlefolk.
They seyn, to hem it is greet shame and wo
For to be subgetz and been in servage   servage: servitude.
To thee, that born art of a smal village.

"And namely sith thy doghter was ybore   namely: especially.
Thise wordes han they spoken, doutelees.   485
But I desire, as I have doon bifore,
To lyve my lyf with hem in reste and pees.
I may nat in this caas be recchelees;   recchelees: heedless, careless of the
I moot doon with thy doghter for the beste,   consequences. doon: act.
Nat as I wolde, but as my peple leste.   490

"And yet, God woot, this is ful looth to me; looth: repugnant.
But nathelees withoute youre wityng   wityng: knowledge.
I wol nat doon; but this wol I," quod he,   doon: act.
"That ye to me assente as in this thyng.
Shewe now youre pacience in youre werkyng, 495 werkyng: actions, deeds.
That ye me highte and swore in youre village   that: that which. highte: promised.
That day that maked was oure mariage."

Whan she had herd al this, she noght
    ameved   ameved: made a movement, stirred.
Neither in word, or cheere, or contenaunce;
For, as it semed, she was nat agreved.   500
She seyde, "Lord, al lyth in youre plesaunce.
My child and I, with hertely obeisaunce,
Been youres al, and ye mowe save or spille   spille: destroy; kill.
Youre owene thyng; werketh after youre wille.   thyng: property.

"Ther may no thyng, God so my soule save, 505
Liken to yow that may displese me;
Ne I desire no thyng for to have,
Ne drede for to leese, save oonly yee.

This wyl is in myn herte, and ay shal be;
No lengthe of tyme or deeth may this deface, 510
Ne chaunge my corage to another place."

corage: heart, affection.

   Glad was this markys of hir answeryng,
But yet he feyned as he were nat so;
Al drery was his cheere and his lookyng,
Whan that he sholde out of the chambre go. 515
Soone after this, a furlong wey or two,
He prively hath told al his entente
Unto a man, and to his wyf hym sente.

   A maner sergeant was this privee man,
The which that feithful ofte he founden
      hadde   520
In thynges grete, and eek swich folk wel kan
Doon execucioun in thynges badde.
The lord knew wel that he hym loved and dradde;
And whan this sergeant wiste his lordes wille,
Into the chambre he stalked hym ful stille. 525

privee: privy; of his own private com-
panionship.

dradde: feared.

stille: quietly.

   "Madame," he seyde, "ye moote foryeve it me,
Though I do thyng to which I am constreyned.
Ye been so wys that ful wel knowe ye
That lordes heestes mowe nat been yfeyned;
They mowe wel been biwailled or
      compleyned,   530
But men moote nede unto hire lust obeye,
And so wol I; ther is namoore to seye.

heestes: commands. yfeyned: evaded,
shirked.

   "This child I am comanded for to take,"—
And spak namoore, but out the child he hente
Despitously, and gan a cheere make 535
As though he wolde han slayn it er he wente.
Grisildis moot al suffre and al consente;
And as a lamb she sitteth meke and stille,
And leet this cruel sergeant doon his wille.

despitously: cruelly.

leet: let.

   Suspecious was the diffame of this man, 540
Suspect his face, suspect his word also;
Suspect the tyme in which he this bigan.
Allas! hir doghter that she loved so,
She wende he wolde han slawen it right tho.
But nathelees she neither weep ne syked, 545
Conformynge hire to that the markys lyked.

suspecious: suspect. diffame: ill fame.

slawen: slain.
weep: wept. syked: sighed.

   But at the laste speken she bigan,
And mekely she to the sergeant preyde,

---

516. a furlong wey: a brief time (enough to walk a furlong, perhaps two and one-half minutes).

So as he was a worthy gentil man,
That she moste kisse hire child er that it
    deyde.   550   moste: might.
And in hir barm this litel child she leyde   barm: lap.
With ful sad face, and gan the child to blisse,   blisse: bless with the sign of the cross.
And lulled it, and after gan it kisse.

And thus she seyde in hire benigne voys,
"Farewel my child! I shal thee nevere see. 555
But sith I thee have marked with the croys   croys: cross.
Of thilke Fader—blessed moote he be!—
That for us deyde upon a croys of tree,   tree: wood.
Thy soule, litel child, I hym bitake,   bitake: commend.
For this nyght shaltow dyen for my sake." 560

I trowe that to a norice in this cas   norice: nurse.
It had been hard this routhe for to se;   routhe: pitiful sight.
Wel myghte a moder than han cryd "allas!"
But nathelees so sad stedefast was she   sad: quietly.
That she endured al adversitee,   565
And to the sergeant mekely she sayde,
"Have here agayn youre litel yonge mayde.

"Goth now," quod she, "and doth my lordes
    heste;   heste: command.
But o thyng wol I pray yow of youre grace,
That, but my lord forbad yow, atte leeste 570
Burieth this litel body in som place
That beestes ne no briddes it torace."   torace: tear in pieces.
But he no word wol to that purpos seye,
But took the child and wente upon his weye.

This sergeant cam unto his lord agayn, 575
And of Grisildis wordes and hir cheere
He tolde hym point for point, in short and playn,
And hym presenteth with his doghter deere.
Somwhat this lord hath routhe in his manere,
But nathelees his purpos held he stille, 580
As lordes doon, whan they wol han hir wille;

And bad this sergeant that he pryvely
Sholde this child softe wynde and wrappe,
With alle circumstances tendrely,   alle circumstances: the utmost care.
And carie it in a cofre or in a lappe; 585 cofre: basket. lappe: cloth.
But, upon peyne his heed of for to swappe,   of swappe: strike off.
That no man sholde knowe of his entente,
Ne whennes he cam, ne whider that he wente;

But at Boloigne to his suster deere,   Boloigne: Bologna.
That thilke tyme of Panik was countesse, 590 Panik: Panico.

He sholde it take, and shewe hire this matere,
Bisekynge hire to doon hir bisynesse   doon hir bisynesse: devote herself.
This child to fostre in al gentillesse;
And whos child that it was he bad hire hyde
From every wight, for aught that may bityde. 595

The sergeant goth, and hath fulfild this thyng;
But to this markys now retourne we.
For now goth he ful faste ymaginyng   faste: intently. ymaginyng: pondering.
If by his wyves cheere he myghte se,
Or by hire word aperceyve, that she   600
Were chaunged; but he nevere hir koude fynde
But evere in oon ylike sad and kynde.   evere in oon ylike: constantly. sad:
                                         steadfast.

As glad, as humble, as bisy in servyse,
And eek in love, as she was wont to be,
Was she to hym in every maner wise;   605
Ne of hir doghter noght a word spak she.
Noon accident, for noon adversitee,   accident: external sign.
Was seyn in hire, ne nevere hir doghter name   doghter: daughter's.
Ne nempned she, in ernest nor in game.   nempned: named.

Explicit tercia pars.

Sequitur pars quarta.

In this estaat ther passed been foure yeer   610
Er she with childe was, but, as God wolde,
A knave child she bar by this Walter,
Ful gracious and fair for to biholde.
And whan that folk it to his fader tolde,
Nat oonly he, but al his contree merye   615
Was for this child, and God they thanke and
      herye.   herye: praise.

Whan it was two yeer old, and fro the brest
Departed of his norice, on a day   norice: nurse.
This markys caughte yet another lest   lest: desire.
To tempte his wyf yet ofter, if he may.   620 tempte: test. ofter: oftener.
O nedelees was she tempted in assay!   assay: trial.
But wedded men ne knowe no mesure,   mesure: moderation.
Whan that they fynde a pacient creature.

"Wyf," quod this markys, "ye han herd er
      this,

---

618. departed of: removed from, i.e., weaned.

My peple sikly berth oure mariage;   625   sikly berth: dislikes.
And namely sith my sone yborn is,   namely: especially.
Now is it worse than evere in al oure age.   age: lives.
The murmur sleeth myn herte and my corage,   corage: spirit.
For to myne eres comth the voys so smerte   smerte: sharply.
That it wel neigh destroyed hath myn herte.   630

  "Now sey they thus: 'Whan Walter is agon,
Thanne shal the blood of Janicle succede   blood: lineage.
And been oure lord, for oother have we noon.'
Swiche wordes seith my peple, out of drede.   out of drede: without doubt.
Wel oughte I of swich murmur taken heede;   635
For certeinly I drede swich sentence,
Though they nat pleyn speke in myn audience.   pleyn: openly. audience: hearing.

  "I wolde lyve in pees, if that I myghte;
Wherfore I am disposed outrely,
As I his suster servede by nyghte,   640   his: i.e., the son's.
Right so thenke I to serve hym pryvely.
This warne I yow, that ye nat sodeynly
Out of yourself for no wo sholde outreye;   outreye: go to excess.
Beth pacient, and therof I yow praye."

  "I have," quod she, "seyd thus, and evere
        shal: 645
I wol no thyng, ne nyl no thyng, certeyn,   nyl: desire not.
But as yow list. Naught greveth me at al,
Though that my doughter and my sone be
        slayn,—
At youre comandement, this is to sayn.
I have nat had no part of children tweyne   650
But first siknesse, and after, wo and peyne.

  "Ye been oure lord, dooth with youre owene
        thyng
Right as yow list; axeth no reed of me.   reed: advice.
For as I lefte at hom al my clothyng,
Whan I first cam to yow, right so," quod she,   655
"Lefte I my wyl and al my libertee,
And took youre clothyng; wherfore I yow preye,
Dooth youre plesaunce, I wol youre lust obeye.

  "And certes, if I hadde prescience
Youre wyl to knowe, er ye youre lust me
        tolde,   660
I wolde it doon withouten necligence;
But now I woot youre lust, and what ye wolde,

Al youre plesance ferme and stable I holde;
For wiste I that my deeth wolde do yow ese,
Right gladly wolde I dyen, yow to plese.   665

"Deth may noght make no comparisoun
Unto youre love." And whan this markys say   *say: saw.*
The constance of his wyf, he caste adoun   *constance: fortitude under adverse cir-*
His eyen two, and wondreth that she may   *cumstances.*
In pacience suffre al this array;   670 *array: ill-treatment, misery.*
And forth he goth with drery contenance,
But to his herte it was ful gret plesance.

This ugly sergeant, in the same wyse
That he hir doghter caughte, right so he,   *caughte: seized.*
Or worse, if men worse kan devyse,   675
Hath hent hir sone, that ful was of beautee.
And evere in oon so pacient was she   *evere in oon: always.*
That she no cheere made of hevynesse,   *cheere: facial expression.*
But kiste hir sone, and after gan it blesse;   *blesse: i.e., with the sign of the cross.*

Save this, she preyede hym that, if he
    myghte,   680
Hir litel sone he wolde in erthe grave,   *grave: bury.*
His tendre lymes, delicat to sighte,   *lymes: limbs. delicat: delicate, tender.*
Fro foweles and fro beestes for to save.
But she noon answere of hym myghte have.
He wente his wey, as hym no thyng ne roghte; 685 *roghte: concerned, troubled.*
But to Boloigne he tendrely it broghte.

This markys wondreth, ever lenger the moore,
Upon hir pacience, and if that he
Ne hadde soothly knowen therbifoore
That parfitly hir children loved she,   690
He wolde have wend that of som subtiltee,   *wend: thought. subtiltee: treachery.*
And of malice, or of cruel corage,   *corage: heart.*
That she hadde suffred this with sad visage.   *sad: steadfast.*

But wel he knew that next hymself, certayn,
She loved hir children best in every wise.   695
But now of wommen wolde I asken fayn
If thise assayes myghte nat suffise?   *assayes: trials.*
What koude a sturdy housbond moore devyse   *sturdy: cruel.*
To preve hir wyfhod and hir stedefastnesse,   *preve: test.*
And he continuynge evere in sturdinesse?   700 *sturdinesse: cruelty.*

But ther been folk of swich condicion   *condicion: disposition.*
That whan they have a certein purpos take,
They kan nat stynte of hire entencion,

---

663. I hold to all your pleasure unswervingly.

But, right as they were bounden to a stake,
They wol nat of that firste purpos slake.   705   of slake: desist from.
Right so this markys fulliche hath purposed
To tempte his wyf as he was first disposed.   tempte: test.

He waiteth if by word or contenance   waiteth: watches.
That she to hym was changed of corage;
But nevere koude he fynde variance.   710
She was ay oon in herte and in visage;   ay oon: always the same.
And ay the ferther that she was in age,
The moore trewe, if that it were possible,
She was to hym in love, and moore penyble.   penyble: painstaking.

For which it semed thus, that of hem two   715
Ther nas but o wyl; for, as Walter leste,
The same lust was hire plesance also.
And, God be thanked, al fil for the beste.
She shewed wel, for no worldly unreste   for no worldly unreste: on account of
A wyf, as of hirself, nothing ne sholde   720   no earthly discomfort.
Wille in effect, but as hir housbonde wolde.

The sclaundre of Walter ofte and wyde   sclaundre: ill-fame.
        spradde,
That of a cruel herte he wikkedly,
For he a povre womman wedded hadde,
Hath mordred bothe his children prively.   725
Swich murmur was among hem comunly.
No wonder is, for to the peples ere
Ther cam no word, but that they mordred were.

For which, where as his peple therbifore
Hadde loved hym wel, the sclaundre of his
        diffame   730   diffame: bad reputation.
Made hem that they hym hated therfore.   therfore: for it.
To ben a mordrere is an hateful name;
But nathelees, for ernest ne for game,   for ernest ne for game: under no cir-
He of his cruel purpos nolde stente;   cumstances.
To tempte his wyf was set al his entent.   735   tempte: test.

Whan that his doghter twelve yeer was of age,
He to the court of Rome, in subtil wise
Enformed of his wil, sente his message,   message: messengers.
Comaundynge hem swiche bulles to devyse
As to his cruel purpos may suffise,   740
How that the pope, as for his peples reste,   reste: satisfaction.
Bad hym to wedde another, if hym leste.

I seye, he bad they sholde countrefete   countrefete: imitate.
The popes bulles, makyng mencion

That he hath leve his firste wyf to lete,   745   lete: forsake, leave.
As by the popes dispensacion,
To stynte rancour and dissencion
Bitwixe his peple and hym; thus seyde the bulle,
The which they han publissed at the fulle.

  The rude peple, as it no wonder is,   750   rude: ignorant.
Wenden ful wel that it hadde ben right so;
But whan thise tidynges came to Grisildis,
I deeme that hir herte was ful wo.   wo: sad.
But she, ylike sad for everemo,   ylike: unceasingly. sad: steadfast.
Disposed was, this humble creature,   755
The adversitee of Fortune al t'endure,

  Abidynge evere his lust and his plesance,
To whom that she was yeven herte and al,
As to hir verray worldly suffisance.   verray: true. worldly: earthly.
But shortly if this storie telle I shal,   760
This markys writen hath in special   in special: specially; in detail.
A lettre, in which he sheweth his entente,
And secreely he to Boloigne it sente.

  To the Erl of Panyk, which that hadde tho
Wedded his suster, preyde he specially   765
To bryngen hom agayn his children two
In honurable estaat al openly.
But o thyng he hym prayde outrely,   outrely: i.e., emphatically.
That he to no wight, though men wolde enquere,
Sholde nat telle whos children that they were,   770

  But seye, the mayden sholde ywedded be
Unto the Markys of Saluce anon.
And as this erl was preyed, so dide he;
For at day set he on his wey is gon   set: appointed.
Toward Saluce, and lordes many oon   775
In riche array, this mayden for to gyde,
Hir yonge brother ridyng hir bisyde.

  Arrayed was toward hir mariage   toward: for.
This fresshe mayde, ful of gemmes cleere;   cleere: bright.
Hir brother, which that seven yeer was of age,   780
Arrayed eek ful fressh in his manere.   fressh: joyous.
And thus in gret noblesse and with glad cheere,
Toward Saluces shapyng hir journey,
Fro day to day they ryden in hir wey.   ryden: rode.

EXPLICIT QUARTA PARS.

SEQUITUR PARS QUINTA.

Among al this, after his wikke usage,   785
This markys, yet his wyf to tempte moore   tempte: test.
To the outtreste preve of hir corage,   outtreste: utmost. preve: proof.
Fully to han experience and loore   loore: knowledge.
If that she were as stedefast as bifore,
He on a day, in open audience,   790 in open audience: in public.
Ful boistously hath seyd hire this sentence: boistously: rudely, harshly.

"Certes, Grisilde, I hadde ynogh plesance
To han yow to my wyf for youre goodnesse,
As for youre trouthe and for youre obeisance,
Noght for youre lynage, ne for youre richesse; 795
But now knowe I in verray soothfastnesse
That in gret lordshipe, if I wel avyse,   wel avyse: am well advised.
Ther is gret servitute in sondry wyse.

"I may nat do as every plowman may.
My peple me constreyneth for to take   800
Another wyf, and crien day by day;
And eek the pope, rancour for to slake,   slake: make less vehement.
Consenteth it, that dar I undertake;   undertake: assert.
And trewely thus muche I wol yow seye,
My newe wyf is comynge by the weye.   805

"Be strong of herte, and voyde anon hir   voyde: depart from.
      place,
And thilke dowere that ye broghten me.
Taak it agayn; I graunte it of my grace.   agayn: back.
Retourneth to youre fadres hous," quod he;
"No man may alwey han prosperitee.   810
With evene herte I rede yow t'endure   evene: tranquil, steadfast. rede: coun-
The strook of Fortune or of aventure."   sel.

And she agayn answerde in pacience,
"My lord," quod she, "I woot, and wiste alway,
How that bitwixen youre magnificence   815
And my poverte no wight kan ne may
Maken comparison; it is no nay.
I ne heeld me nevere digne in no manere   digne: worthy, deserving.
To be youre wyf, no, ne youre chamberere.   chamberere: chambermaid.

"And in this hous, ther ye me lady made— 820
The heighe God take I for my witnesse,
And also wisly he my soule glade—   also wisly: so surely. glade: may glad-
I never heeld me lady ne maistresse,   den.
But humble servant to youre worthynesse,
And evere shal, whil that my lyf may dure,   825 dure: endure, last.
Aboven every worldly creature.

"That ye so longe of youre benignitee
Han holden me in honour and nobleye,   nobleye: noble estate.
Where as I was noght worthy for to be,
That thonke I God and yow, to whom I preye   830
Foryelde it yow; ther is namoore to seye.   foryelde: repay.
Unto my fader gladly wol I wende,
And with hym dwelle unto my lyves ende.

"Ther I was fostred of a child ful smal,   of: as; from.
Til I be deed my lyf ther wol I lede,   835
A wydwe clene in body, herte, and al.
For sith I yaf to yow my maydenhede,
And am youre trewe wyf, it is no drede,
God shilde swich a lordes wyf to take   shilde: forbid.
Another man to housbond or to make!   840   make: mate.

"And of youre newe wyf God of his grace
So graunte yow wele and prosperitee!   wele: well-being, happiness.
For I wol gladly yelden hire my place,
In which that I was blisful wont to be.   blisful: happy.
For sith it liketh yow, my lord," quod she,   845
"That whilom weren al myn hertes reste,   reste: ease.
That I shal goon, I wol goon whan yow leste.

"But ther as ye me profre swich dowaire   dowaire: dower.
As I first broghte, it is wel in my mynde
It were my wrecched clothes, nothyng faire,   850
The whiche to me were hard now for to fynde.
O goode God! how gentil and how kynde
Ye semed by youre speche and youre visage
The day that maked was oure mariage!

"But sooth is seyd—algate I fynde it trewe,   855   algate: at least.
For in effect it proved is on me—
Love is noght old as whan that it is newe.   old: i.e., when old. as: the same as.
But certes, lord, for noon adversitee,
To dyen in the cas, it shal nat be
That evere in word or werk I shal repente   860   werk: deed.
That I yow yaf myn herte in hool entente.   in hool entente: wholeheartedly.

"My lord, ye woot that in my fadres place
Ye dide me strepe out of my povre weede,   strepe: strip, undress. weede: cloth-
And richely me cladden, of youre grace.   ing.
To yow broghte I noght elles, out of drede,   865   out of drede: without doubt.
But feith, and nakednesse, and maydenhede;
And here agayn your clothyng I restore,
And eek your weddyng ryng, for everemore.

---

859. to dyen in the cas: though I were to die for it.

"The remenant of youre jewels redy be
Inwith youre chambre, dar I saufly sayn. 870 inwith: within.
Naked out of my fadres hous," quod she,
"I cam, and naked moot I turne agayn.   turne agayn: return.
Al youre plesance wol I folwen fayn;
But yet I hope it be nat youre entente
That I smoklees out of youre paleys wente. 875 smoklees: smockless, without under-
          garment.

"Ye koude nat doon so dishonest a thyng,   dishonest: dishonorable.
That thilke wombe in which youre children leye
Sholde biforn the peple, in my walkyng,
Be seyn al bare; wherfore I yow preye,
Lat me nat lyk a worm go by the weye. 880
Remembre yow, myn owene lord so deere,
I was youre wyf, though I unworthy weere.

"Wherfore, in gerdon of my maydenhede,   gerdon: guerdon, recompense.
Which that I broghte, and noght agayn I bere, agayn: back.
As voucheth sauf to yeve me, to my meede, 885 to my meede: for my reward.
But swich a smok as I was wont to were,   were: wear.
That I therwith may wrye the wombe of here wrye: cover, conceal. here: her.
That was youre wyf. And here I take my leeve
Of yow, myn owene lord, lest I yow greve." greve: vex.

"The smok," quod he, "that thou hast on thy
       bak, 890
Lat it be stille, and bere it forth with thee."
But wel unnethes thilke word he spak,
But wente his wey, for routhe and for pitee.
Biforn the folk hirselven strepeth she,   strepeth: undresses.
And in hir smok, with heed and foot al bare, 895
Toward hir fader hous forth is she fare.   fare: gone.

The folk hire folwe, wepynge in hir weye,
And Fortune ay they cursen as they goon;
But she fro wepyng kepte hire eyen dreye,
Ne in this tyme word ne spak she noon. 900
Hir fader, that this tidynge herde anon,
Curseth the day and tyme that Nature
Shoop hym to been a lyves creature.   shoop: created. lyves: living.

For out of doute this olde povre man
Was evere in suspect of hir mariage; 905 in suspect: suspicious.
For evere he demed, sith that it bigan,
That whan the lord fulfild hadde his corage, fulfild . . . corage: had satisfied his
Hym wolde thynke it were a disparage   lust.

---

908. It would seem to him it were a dishonor.

To his estaat so lowe for t'alighte,

alighte: descend.

And voyden hire as soone as ever he myghte. 910

voyden: send away, dismiss.

Agayns his doghter hastiliche goth he,

agayns: to meet.

For he by noyse of folk knew hir comynge,

And with hir olde cote, as it myghte be

as: as well as.

He covered hire, ful sorwefully wepynge.

But on hir body myghte he it nat brynge, 915

brynge: put.

For rude was the clooth, and she moore of age

By dayes fele than at hir mariage.

fele: many.

Thus with hir fader, for a certein space,

Dwelleth this flour of wyfly pacience,

flour: flower.

That neither by hir wordes ne hir face, 920

Biforn the folk, ne eek in hir absence,

hir: their.

Ne shewed she that hir was doon offence;

hir: to her.

Ne of hir heighte estaat no remembrance

Ne hadde she, as by hire contenance.

as by: to judge by, contenance: manner.

No wonder is, for in hir grete estaat 925

Hir goost was evere in pleyn humylitee;

goost: spirit. pleyn: full, perfect.

No tendre mouth, noon herte delicaat,

delicaat: fond of luxury.

No pompe, no semblant of roialtee,

roialtee: splendor.

But ful of pacient benyngnytee,

Discreet and pridelees, ay honurable, 930

And to hir housbonde evere meke and stable.

stable: constant.

Men speke of Job, and moost for his
    humblesse,

moost: chiefly.

As clerkes, whan hem list, kan wel endite,

Namely of men, but as in soothfastnesse,

namely: especially.

Though clerkes preise wommen but a lite, 935

Ther kan no man in humblesse hym acquite

acquite: act, behave.

As wommen kan, ne kan been half so trewe

As wommen been, but it be falle of newe.

be falle: has happened. of newe: recently.

[PART VI.]

Fro Boloigne is this Erl of Panyk come,

Of which the fame up sprang to moore and
    lesse, 940

And to the peples eres, alle and some,

Was kouth eek that a newe markysesse

kouth: known.

He with hym broghte, in swich pompe and
    richesse

That nevere was ther seyn with mannes eye

So noble array in al West Lumbardye. 945

The markys, which that shoop and knew al
    this,

shoop: devised.

Er that this erl was come, sente his message   message: messengers.
For thilke sely povre Grisildis;
And she with humble herte and glad visage,
Nat with no swollen thoght in hir corage,   950 swollen: inflated with pride, puffed up.
Cam at his heste, and on hir knees hir sette,   heste: command.
And reverently and wisely she hym grette.   wisely: attentively. grette: greeted.

    "Grisilde," quod he, "my wille is outrely,   outrely: absolutely.
This mayden, that shal wedded been to me,
Received be to-morwe as roially   955
As it possible is in myn hous to be,
And eek that every wight in his degree   in: according to.
Have his estaat, in sittyng and servyse   have his estaat: be treated according
And heigh plesaunce, as I kan best devyse.   to his rank.

    "I have no wommen suffisaunt, certayn,   960
The chambres for t'arraye in ordynaunce   arraye in ordynaunce: put in order.
After my lust, and therfore wolde I fayn
That thyn were all swich manere governaunce.
Thou knowest eek of old al my plesaunce;
Though thyn array be badde and yvel biseye,   965 biseye: looking.
Do thou thy devoir at the leeste weye."   devoir: duty. at the leeste weye: at the
    very least.

    "Nat oonly, lord, that I am glad," quod she,
"To doon youre lust, but I desire also
Yow for to serve and plese in my degree   in my degree: as befits my rank.
Withouten feyntyng, and shal everemo;   970 feyntyng: flagging of energy or will.
Ne nevere, for no wele ne no wo,
Ne shal the goost withinne myn herte stente
To love yow best with al my trewe entente."   with trewe entente: faithfully.

    And with that word she gan the hous to dighte,   dighte: put in order.
And tables for to sette, and beddes make;   975
And peyned hire to doon al that she myghte,   peyned hire: strove.
Preyynge the chambereres, for Goddes sake,   chambereres: chambermaids.
To hasten hem, and faste swepe and shake;   faste: thoroughly.
And she, the mooste servysable of alle,   servysable: diligent in service.
Hath every chambre arrayed and his halle.   980 arrayed: arranged.

    Abouten undren gan this erl alighte,   abouten undren: in the forenoon. gan
That with hym broghte thise noble children   alighte: arrived.
        tweye,
For which the peple ran to seen the sighte
Of hire array, so richely biseye;   biseye: appearing.
And thanne at erst amonges hem they seye   985 at erst: for the first time. seye: say.
That Walter was no fool, thogh that hym leste
To chaunge his wyf, for it was for the beste.

    For she is fairer, as they deemen alle,
Than is Grisilde, and moore tendre of age,

And fairer fruyt bitwene hem sholde falle,   990   fruyt: offspring.
And moore plesant, for hire heigh lynage.
Hir brother eek so fair was of visage
That hem to seen the peple hath caught
      plesaunce,
Commendynge now the markys governaunce.—   governaunce: behavior.

   "O stormy peple! unsad and evere untrewe! 995   unsad: unsteady, inconstant.
Ay undiscreet and chaungynge as a vane!   undiscreet: undiscerning. vane:
Delitynge evere in rumbul that is newe,   weather vane. rumbul: rumor.
For lyk the moone ay wexe ye and wane!
Ay ful of clappyng, deere ynogh a jane!   clappyng: chatter. a: at a.
Youre doom is fals, youre constance yvele   doom: judgment, opinion.
      preveth;   1000
A ful greet fool is he that on yow leveth."   leveth: believes.

   Thus seyden sadde folk in that citee,   sadde: steadfast.
Whan that the peple gazed up and doun;
For they were glad, right for the noveltee,
To han a newe lady of hir toun.   1005
Namoore of this make I now mencioun,
But to Grisilde agayn wol I me dresse,   me dresse: direct my attention.
And telle hir constance and hir bisynesse.—

   Ful bisy was Grisilde in every thyng
That to the feeste was apertinent.   1010
Right noght was she abayst of hir clothyng,   abayst: upset, embarrassed.
Thogh it were rude and somdel eek torent;   torent: rent in pieces.
But with glad cheere to the yate is went   yate: gate.
With oother folk, to greete the markysesse,
And after that dooth forth hir bisynesse.   1015

   With so glad cheere his gestes she receyveth,
And so konnyngly, everich in his degree,   konnyngly: skilfully. in: according to.
That no defaute no man aperceyveth,   defaute: fault.
But ay they wondren what she myghte be
That in so povre array was for to see,   1020
And koude swich honour and reverence,   koude: understood.
And worthily they preisen hir prudence.

   In al this meene while she ne stente
This mayde and eek hir brother to commende
With al hir herte, in ful benygne entente,   1025
So wel that no man koude hir pris amende.   pris: praise. amende: better.
But at the laste, whan that thise lordes wende
To sitten doun to mete, he gan to calle
Grisilde, as she was bisy in his halle.

---

999. jane: a small silver coin of Genoa, worth ½ d.

"Grisilde," quod he, as it were in his pley, 1030
"How liketh thee my wyf and hir beautee?"
"Right wel," quod she, "my lord; for, in good
        fey,
A fairer saugh I nevere noon than she.
I prey to God yeve hire prosperitee;
And so hope I that he wol to yow sende   1035
Plesance ynogh unto youre lyves ende.

"O thyng biseke I yow, and warne also,
That ye ne prikke with no tormentynge   prikke: goad.
This tendre mayden, as ye han don mo;   mo: others.
For she is fostred in hir norissynge   1040 norissynge: bringing up.
Moore tendrely, and, to my supposynge,
She koude nat adversitee endure
As koude a povre fostred creature."

And whan this Walter saw hir pacience,
Hir glade cheere, and no malice at al,   1045
And he so ofte had doon to hire offence,   offence: harm.
And she ay sad and constant as a wal,   sad: firm.
Continuynge evere hir innocence overal,
This sturdy markys gan his herte dresse   sturdy: stern. dresse: prepare.
To rewen upon hir wyfly stedfastnesse.   1050 rewen: have pity.

"This is ynogh, Grisilde myn," quod he;
"Be now namoore agast ne yvele apayed.   agast: afraid. yvele apayed: dis-
I have thy feith and thy benygnytee,   pleased.
As wel as evere womman was, assayed,
In greet estaat, and povreliche arrayed.   1055
Now knowe I, deere wyf, thy stedfastnesse,"—
And hire in armes took and gan hir kesse.

And she for wonder took of it no keep;   keep: heed, notice.
She herde nat what thyng he to hir seyde;
She ferde as she had stert out of a sleep, 1060 stert: awaked suddenly.
Til she out of hir mazednesse abreyde.   mazednesse: bewilderment. out
"Grisilde," quod he, "by God, that for us deyde, abreyde: recovered from.
Thou art my wyf; noon oother I have,
Ne nevere hadde, as God my soule save!

"This is thy doghter, which thou hast
      supposed   1065
To be my wyf; that oother feithfully   feithfully: indeed.
Shal be myn heir, as I have ay disposed;
Thou bare hym in thy body trewely.
At Boloigne have I kept hem prively;
Taak hem agayn, for now maystow nat seye 1070
That thou hast lorn noon of thy children tweye. lorn: lost.

"And folk that ootherweys han seyd of me,
I warne hem wel that I have doon this deede
For no malice, ne for no crueltee,
But for t'assaye in thee thy wommanhede,   1075 assaye: test.
And nat to sleen my children—God forbede!   sleen: slay.
But for to kepe hem pryvely and stille,
Til I thy purpos knewe and al thy wille."

Whan she this herde, aswowne doun she   aswowne: in a swoon.
    falleth
For pitous joye, and after hir swownynge   1080
She bothe hir yonge children to hire calleth,
And in hir armes, pitously wepynge,
Embraceth hem, and tendrely kissynge
Ful lyk a moder, with hire salte teeres
She bathed bothe hir visage and hir heeres.   1085

O which a pitous thyng it was to se
Hir swownyng, and hir humble voys to heere!
"Grauntmercy, lord, God thanke it yow," quod   grauntmercy: great thanks. **thanke:**
    she,   reward. **it:** for it.
"That ye han saved me my children deere!
Now rekke I nevere to been ded right heere;   1090 rekke: care.
Sith I stonde in youre love and in youre grace,
No fors of death, ne whan my spirit pace!   fors: matter. **pace:** may depart.

"O tendre, o deere, o yonge children myne!
Youre woful moder wende stedfastly
That cruel houndes or som foul vermyne   1095
Hadde eten yow; but God, of his mercy,
And youre benygne fader tendrely
Hath doon yow kept,"—and in that same   doon: had.
    stounde   stounde: moment.
Al sodeynly she swapte adoun to grounde.   swapte: sank into a swoon.

And in hire swough so sadly holdeth she   1100 swough: swoon. **sadly:** firmly.
Hir children two, whan she gan hem t'embrace,
That with greet sleighte and greet difficultee   sleighte: dexterity.
The children from hir arm they gonne arace.   gonne arace: extricated.
O many a teer on many a pitous face
Doun ran of hem that stooden hir bisyde;   1105
Unnethe abouten hire myghte they abyde.

Walter hir gladeth, and hir sorwe slaketh;   slaketh: assuages.
She riseth up, abaysed, from hir traunce,   abaysed: perplexed.
And every wight hir joye and feeste maketh   feeste maketh: i.e., makes much of
Til she hath caught agayn hir contenaunce.   1110   her. **contenaunce:** composure.
Walter hire dooth so feithfully plesaunce

That it was deyntee for to seen the cheere   deyntee: delightful. cheere: joy.
Bitwix hem two, now they been met yfeere.   yfeere: together.

    Thise ladyes, whan that they hir tyme say,   say: saw.
Han taken hire and into chambre gon,   1115
And strepen hire out of hir rude array,   strepen: stripped.
And in a clooth of gold that brighte shoon,
With a coroune of many a riche stoon
Upon hir hed, they into halle hir broghte,
And ther she was honured as hir oghte.   1120

    Thus hath this pitous day a blisful ende,
For every man and womman dooth his myght
This day in murthe and revel to dispende   dispende: spend.
Til on the welkne shoon the sterres lyght.   welkne: welkin, sky.
For moore solempne in every mannes syght   1125   solempne: sumptuous.
This feste was, and gretter of costage,   costage: cost.
Than was the revel of hir mariage.

    Ful many a yeer in heigh prosperitee
Lyven thise two in concord and in reste,   reste: tranquillity.
And richely his doghter married he   1130
Unto a lord, oon of the worthieste
Of al Ytaille; and thanne in pees and reste
His wyves fader in his court he kepeth,
Til that the soule out of his body crepeth.

    His sone succedeth in his heritage   1135
In reste and pees, after his fader day,   fader: father's. day: lifetime.
And fortunat was eek in mariage,
Al putte he nat his wyf in gret assay.
This world is nat so strong, it is no nay,
As it hath been in olde tymes yore,   1140   yore: formerly.
And herkneth what this auctour seith therfore.

    This storie is seyd, nat for that wyves sholde
Folwen Grisilde as in humylitee,
For it were inportable, though they wolde;   inportable: intolerable.
But for that every wight, in his degree,   1145
Sholde be constant in adversitee
As was Grisilde; therfore Petrak writeth
This storie, which with heigh stile he enditeth.

    For, sith a womman was so pacient
Unto a mortal man, wel moore us oghte   1150
Receyven al in gree that God us sent;   in gree: in good part, in good spirit.
For greet skile is, he preeve that he wroghte.   sent: (sendeth) sends.

_____

1152. For it is very reasonable that He test that which He created.

But he ne tempteth no man that he boghte,   boghte: redeemed.
As seith Seint Jame, if ye his pistel rede;   pistel: Epistle of St. James i.13.
He preeveth folk al day, it is no drede,   1155   preeveth: tries, tests.

And suffreth us, as for oure excercise,   suffreth: suffers, permits. **excercise:**
With sharpe scourges of adversitee   discipline.
Ful ofte to be bete in sondry wise;   bete: beaten.
Nat for to knowe oure wyl, for certes he,
Er we were born, knew al oure freletee;   1160   freletee: frailty.
And for oure beste is al his governaunce.
Lat us thanne lyve in vertuous suffraunce.   suffraunce: patient endurance.

But o word, lordynges, herkneth er I go:
It were ful hard to fynde now-a-dayes
In al a toun Grisildis thre or two;   1165
For if that they were put to swiche assayes,   assayes: trials.
The gold of hem hath now so badde alayes   alayes: alloys.
With bras, that thogh the coyne be fair at eye,   at eye: to the eye.
It wolde rather breste a-two than plye.   rather: sooner. **breste a-two:** break in
          two. **plye:** bend.

For which heere, for the Wyves love of   the Wyves love: love of the Wife.
    Bathe—   1170
Whos lyf and al hire secte God mayntene   secte: (heretical) sect; kind of person;
In heigh maistrie, and elles were it scathe—   sex. **scathe:** misfortune; a pity.
I wol with lusty herte, fressh and grene,
Seye yow a song to glade yow, I wene;
And lat us stynte of ernestful matere.   1175
Herkneth my song that seith in this manere:

     Lenvoy de Chaucer.

Grisilde is deed, and eek hir pacience,
And bothe atones buryed in Ytaille;   atones: at once, at the same time.
For which I crie in open audience,
No wedded man so hardy be t'assaille   1180   assaille: test.
His wyves pacience in trust to fynde
Grisildis, for in certein he shal faille.

O noble wyves, ful of heigh prudence,
Lat noon humilitee youre tonge naille,
Ne lat no clerk have cause or diligence   1185
To write of yow a storie of swich mervaille   mervaille: marvel.
As of Grisildis pacient and kynde,
Lest Chichevache yow swelwe in hir entraille!   swelwe: swallow.

Folweth Ekko, that holdeth no silence,   folweth: imitate.
But evere answereth at the countretaille.   1190   countretaille: countertally; reply, re-
          tort.

1166–69. Coins of pure gold could be bent without breaking, but counterfeits whose gold was alloyed with brass would break in two.
1188. **Chichevache:** a cow that fed on patient wives and therefore nearly starved.

Beth nat bidaffed for youre innocence,
But sharply taak on yow the governaille.
Emprenteth wel this lessoun in youre mynde,
For commune profit sith it may availle.

    Ye archewyves, stondeth at defense,   1195
Syn ye be strong as is a greet camaille;
Ne suffreth nat that men yow doon offense.
And sklendre wyves, fieble as in bataille,
Beth egre as is a tigre yond in Ynde;
Ay clappeth as a mille, I yow consaille.   1200

    Ne dreed hem nat, doth hem no reverence
For though thyn housbonde armed be in maille,
The arwes of thy crabbed eloquence
Shal perce his brest, and eek his aventaille.
In jalousie I rede eek thou hym bynde,   1205
And thou shalt make hym couche as doth a
    quaille.

    If thou be fair, ther folk been in presence
Shewe thou thy visage and thyn apparaille;
If thou be foul, be fre of thy dispence;
To gete thee freendes ay do thy travaille;   1210
Be ay of chiere as light as leef on lynde,
And lat hym care, and wepe, and wrynge, and
    waille!

> *Heere endeth the tale of the*
> *Clerk of Oxenford.*

> *The prologe of the Marchantes tale.*

    "Wepyng and waylyng, care and oother sorwe
I knowe ynogh, on even and a-morwe,"
Quod the Marchant, "and so doon othere mo   1215
That wedded been. I trowe that it be so,
For wel I woot it fareth so with me.
I have a wyf, the worste that may be;
For thogh the feend to hire ycoupled were,
She wolde hym overmacche, I dar wel swere.   1220

Glosses (right margin):

bidaffed: fooled.
governaille: mastery.

1195 archewyves: dominating wives.
camaille: camel.

sklendre: slender, thin.
egre: fierce.
1200 clappeth: clatter.

maille: mail-armor.

brest: breastplate. aventaille: chain
  mail for the neck. rede: advise.
couche: cower.

in presence: in company.
apparaille: apparel.
dispence: spending.
1210 do travaille: take pains.
chiere: behavior. lynde: linden-tree.

on even: in the evening. a-morwe: on
  the morrow, in the morning.

1220 overmacche: overmatch.

1212. The following stanza, which occurs in certain manuscripts, seems to have been the orig-inal ending of the tale but was apparently discarded by Chaucer in favor of the verbal echoes linking 1213 with 1212. Apparently he later reworked this so-called "Host's Stanza" to form lines 1889–94 of the Monk's Prologue.

    Bihoold the murye words of the Hoost.

    This worthy Clerk, whan ended was his tale,   1212[a]
    Oure Hooste seyde, and swoor, "By Goddes bones,
    Me were levere than a barel ale
    My wyf at hom had herd this legende ones!
    This is a gentil tale for the nones,
    As to my purpos, wiste ye my wille;
    But thyng that wol nat be, lat it be stille."   1212[b]

What sholde I yow reherce in special   **what**: why.
Hir hye malice? She is a shrewe at al.   **at al**: in every way.
Ther is a long and a large difference
Bitwix Grisildis grete pacience
And of my wyf the passyng crueltee.   1225   **passyng**: surpassing, extreme.
Were I unbounden, also moot I thee!   **unbounden**: unbound, separated, di-
I wolde nevere eft comen in the snare.   vorced. **eft**: again.
We wedded men lyven in sorwe and care.
Assaye whoso wole, and he shal fynde   **assaye**: test, try.
That I seye sooth, by Seint Thomas of Ynde, 1230
As for the moore part, I sey nat alle.
God shilde that it sholde so bifalle!   **shilde**: shield, defend; forbid.
    A! goode sire Hoost, I have ywedded bee
Thise monthes two, and moore nat, pardee;
And yet, I trowe, he that al his lyve   1235
Wyflees hath been, though that men wolde him   **wyflees**: wifeless.
    ryve   **ryve**: pierce.
Unto the herte, ne koude in no manere
Tellen so muchel sorwe as I now heere
Koude tellen of my wyves cursednesse!"
    "Now," quod oure Hoost, "Marchaunt, so
       God yow blesse,   1240
Syn ye so muchel knowen of that art,
Ful hertely I pray yow telle us part."
    "Gladly," quod he, "but of myn owene soore,
For sory herte, I telle may namoore."

Heere bigynneth the
Marchantes tale.

Whilom ther was dwellynge in
       Lumbardye   1245
A worthy knyght, that born was of Pavye,   **Pavye**: Pavia.
In which he lyved in greet prosperitee;
And sixty yeer a wiflees man was he,
And folwed ay his bodily delit
On wommen, ther as was his appetit,   1250
As doon thise fooles that been seculer.   **seculer**: in the world: either secular
And whan that he was passed sixty yeer,   clergy, or laity.

---

the Marchantes Tale. This tale was perhaps originally written for the Monk as a rejoinder to the [Shipman's] Tale originally written for the Wife of Bath, probably preceded by the first 450 lines of her Prologue. If so, the Monk clearly takes offence at the Wife's presentation of "daun John," the monk in her tale; we may also note his jaundiced view of secular life, his ironic twisting, for January, of the Wife's discussion and depiction of marriage in her Prologue, and his satirizing of Alice in his cynical portraits of May and Proserpyne. When the Monk was assigned the tragedies which lead up to the Nuns' Priest's Tale, the Merchant may have seemed an obvious figure to make the rejoinder to the Wife; but this extravagantly elaborated fabliau was never adjusted to the new teller and with him lacks the dramatic unity which it offers when read as if recounted by the Monk.

Were it for holynesse or for dotage,
I kan nat seye, but swich a greet corage   corage: desire.
Hadde this knyght to been a wedded man   1255
That day and nyght he dooth al that he kan
T'espien where he myghte wedded be,   espien: investigate; discover.
Preyinge oure Lord to graunten him that he
Mighte ones knowe of thilke blisful lyf
That is bitwixe an housbonde and his wyf,   1260
And for to lyve under that holy bond
With which that first God man and womman
       bond.   bond: bound.
"Noon oother lyf," seyde he, "is worth a bene;
For wedlok is so esy and so clene,   esy: pleasant. clene: righteous, re-
That in this world it is a paradys."   1265   spectable.
Thus seyde this olde knyght, that was so wys.
    And certeinly, as sooth as God is kyng,
To take a wyf it is a glorious thyng,
And namely whan a man is old and hoor;   namely: especially.
Thanne is a wyf the fruyt of his tresor.   1270   fruyt: choice part.
Thanne sholde he take a yong wyf and a feir,
On which he myghte engendren hym an heir,
And lede his lyf in joye and in solas,   solas: pleasure, comfort.
Where as thise bacheleres synge "allas,"
Whan that they fynden any adversitee   1275
In love, which nys but childissh vanytee.   vanytee: foolishness.
And trewely it sit wel to be so,   sit wel: is fitting.
That bacheleres have often peyne and wo;
On brotel ground they buylde, and brotelnesse   brotel: easily destroyed, insecure.
They fynde, whan they wene sikernesse.   1280   wene: expect. sikernesse: security.
They lyve but as a bryd or as a beest,
In libertee, and under noon areest,   areest: moral restraint.
Ther as a wedded man in his estaat
Lyveth a lyf blisful and ordinaat,   ordinaat: orderly.
Under this yok of mariage ybounde.   1285
Wel may his herte in joy and blisse habounde,
For who kan be so buxom as a wyf?   buxom: humble, obedient, gracious.
Who is so trewe, and eek so ententyf   ententyf: eager, desirous.
To kepe hym, syk and hool, as is his make?   hool: well. make: mate.
For wele or wo she wole hym nat forsake;   1290
She nys nat wery hym to love and serve,
Thogh that he lye bedrede, til he sterve.   bedrede: bedridden. sterve: die.
And yet som clerkes seyn it nys nat so,
Of whiche he Theofraste is oon of tho.
What force though Theofraste liste lye?   1295   force: matter. liste: it pleased (to).
"Ne take no wyf," quod he, "for housbondrye,   housbondrye: domestic economy.
As for to spare in houshold thy dispence.   dispence: expenditure.
A trewe servant dooth moore diligence   dooth diligence: makes effort.

1294. See Wife of Bath's Prologue, l. 671 and note.

Thy good to kepe, than thyn owene wyf,   good: goods, property.
For she wol clayme half part al hir lyf.   1300
And if thou be syk, so God me save,
Thy verray freendes, or a trewe knave,   knave: servant.
Wol kepe thee bet than she that waiteth ay
After thy good and hath doon many a day.
And if thou take a wyf   1305
       "

This sentence, and an hundred thynges worse,
Writeth this man, ther God his bones curse!   ther God: i.e., may God.
But take no kep of al swich vanytee;
Deffie Theofraste, and herke me.   1310 deffie: reject.
   A wyf is Goddes yifte verraily;   yifte: gift.
Alle othere manere yiftes hardily,   hardily: certainly.
As londes, rentes, pasture, or commune,   rentes: incomes.
Or moebles, alle been yiftes of Fortune,   moebles: movable property.
That passen as a shadwe upon a wal.   1315
But drede nat, if pleynly speke I shal:
A wyf wol laste, and in thyn hous endure,   endure: stay.
Wel lenger than thee list, paraventure.
   Mariage is a ful greet sacrament.
He which that hath no wyf, I holde hym
          shent;   1320 shent: ruined.
He lyveth helplees and al desolat,—   desolat: lonely.
I speke of folk in seculer estaat.
And herke why, I sey nat this for noght,
That womman is for mannes helpe ywroght.   for: i.e., to be. helpe: helper.
The hye God, whan he hadde Adam maked,   1325
And saugh him al allone, bely-naked,
God of his grete goodnesse seyde than,
"Lat us now make an helpe unto this man
Lyk to hymself"; and thanne he made him Eve.
Here may ye see, and hereby may ye preve,   1330 preve: prove.
That wyf is mannes helpe and his confort,
His paradys terrestre, and his disport.   disport: solace.
So buxom and so vertuous is she,   buxom: humble, obedient, gracious.
They moste nedes lyve in unitee.
O flessh they been, and o flessh, as I gesse,   1335 o: one.
Hath but oon herte, in wele and in distresse.
   A wyf! a, Seinte Marie, benedicite!
How myghte a man han any adversitee
That hath a wyf? Certes, I kan nat seye.
The blisse which that is bitwixe hem tweye   1340
Ther may no tonge telle, or herte thynke.   thynke: imagine.

1305–06. The MSS read **And if thou take a wyf,** but for the remainder of the couplet a few give nothing while the rest offer seven different unrelated readings. Manly comments, "This is one of the most striking instances of the fact that the CT had not received Chaucer's final touches" (III, 474).

1313. **commune:** the right to use land held in common, as for pasture.

If he be povre, she helpeth hym to swynke;   swynke: labor.
She kepeth his good, and wasteth never a del;
Al that hire housbonde lust, hir likketh wel;
She seith nat ones "nay," whan he seith "ye." 1345
"Do this," seith he; "Al redy, sire," seith she.
O blisful ordre of wedlok precious,
Thou art so murye, and eek so vertuous,
And so commended and approved eek
That every man that halt hym worth a leek, 1350   halt: holds.
Upon his bare knees oughte al his lyf
Thanken his God that hym hath sent a wyf,
Or elles preye to God hym for to sende
A wyf, to laste unto his lyves ende.
For thanne his lyf is set in sikernesse;   1355   sikernesse: security.
He may nat be deceyved, as I gesse,
So that he werke after his wyves reed.   reed: counsel.
Thanne may he boldely beren up his heed,
They been so trewe, and therwithal so wyse;
For which, if thou wolt werken as the wyse, 1360
Do alwey so as wommen wol thee rede.   rede: advise.
      Lo, how that Jacob, as thise clerkes rede,   rede: relate, say.
By good conseil of his moder Rebekke,
Boond the kydes skyn aboute his nekke,
For which his fadres benyson he wan.   1365   benyson: blessing. wan: won.
      Lo Judith, as the storie eek telle kan,
By wys conseil she Goddes peple kepte,   kepte: preserved.
And slow hym Olofernus, whil he slepte.   slow: slew.
      Lo Abigayl, by good conseil, how she
Saved hir housbonde Nabal, whan that he   1370
Sholde han be slayn; and looke, Ester also
By good conseil delyvered out of wo
The peple of God, and made hym Mardochee
Of Assuere enhaunced for to be.   of: by. enhaunced: advanced.
      Ther nys no thyng in gree superlatyf,   1375   gree: degree. superlatyf: surpassing.
As seith Senek, above an humble wyf.
      Suffre thy wyves tonge, as Catoun bit;   suffre: submit to: bit: bids.
She shal comande, and thou shalt suffren it,   suffren: permit, endure.
And yet she wole obeye of curteisye.   of: out of.
A wyf is kepere of thyn housbondrye;   1380   housbondrye: household manage-
Wel may the sike man biwaille and wepe,   ment.
Ther as ther nys no wyf the hous to kepe.

1362–74. For these examples see Genesis xxvii; the apocryphal book of Judith, xi-xiii; I Samuel xxv; Esther vii-viii. They appear, in the same order, in Chaucer's Melibee, II. 1098–1101.
1368. Olofernus: Holofernes.
1370. King David planned to slay Nabal.
1373. Mardochee: Mordecai.
1374. Assuere: Ahasuerus.
1377. Catoun: see Miller's Tale, I. 3227, note.

I warne thee, if wisely thou wolt wirche,　　　wirche: act.
Love wel thy wyf, as Crist loved his chirche.
If thou lovest thyself, thou lovest thy wyf;　　1385
No man hateth his flessh, but in his lyf
He fostreth it, and therfore bidde I thee,
Cherisse thy wyf, or thou shalt nevere thee.　　thee: prosper.
Housbonde and wyf, what so men jape or pleye,　what so: no matter what.
Of worldly folk holden the siker weye;　　1390　worldly: secular, in contrast to re-
They been so knyt ther may noon harm bityde,　　ligious. siker: sure.
And namely upon the wyves syde.　　　namely: especially.
For which this Januarie, of whom I tolde,　　for: because of.
Considered hath, inwith his dayes olde,　　inwith: in.
The lusty lyf, the vertuous quyete,　　1395
That is in mariage hony-sweete;
And for his freendes on a day he sente,
To tellen hem th'effect of his entente.　　effect: gist, purport.
　With face sad his tale he hath hem told.　sad: grave.
He seyde, "Freendes, I am hoor and old,　　1400
And almoost, God woot, on my pittes brynke;　pittes: grave's.
Upon my soule somwhat moste I thynke.
I have my body folily despended;　　folily: lasciviously. despended: used.
Blessed be God that it shal been amended!
For I wol be, certeyn, a wedded man,　　1405
And that anon in al the haste I kan.
Unto som mayde fair and tendre of age,
I pray yow, shapeth for my mariage　　shapeth: prepare.
Al sodeynly, for I wol nat abyde;　　sodeynly: without delay. abyde: wait.
And I wol fonde t'espien, on my syde,　　1410　fonde: try. espien: discover.
To whom I may be wedded hastily.　　hastily: soon.
But forasmuche as ye been mo than I,
Ye shullen rather swich a thyng espyen　　rather: sooner.
Than I, and where me best were to allyen.　allyen: get married.
　But o thyng warne I yow, my freendes
　　　deere,　　1415
I wol noon old wyf han in no manere.　　in no manere: by no means.
She shal nat passe sixteen yeer, certayn;
Old fissh and yong flessh wolde I have fayn.　fayn: gladly.
Bet is," quod he, "a pyk than a pykerel,　pykerel: a young pike.
And bet than old boef is the tendre veel.　　1420
I wol no womman thritty yeer of age;
It is but bene-straw and greet forage.　　bene-straw: refuse of bean plants.
And eek thise olde widwes, God it woot,　　greet: coarse. forage: dry fodder.
They konne so muchel craft on Wades boot,　konne: know. craft: trickery.

1417. sixteen: Some manuscripts read twenty, but Manly's Critical Note shows that he believed
that O' read sixteen (see III, 474). The Autre Balade (Contre les mariages disproportionnés)
by Eustaches Deschamps (DCCCLXXX) gives Janvier ".LX. ans" and Avril ".XV. ans."
1424. Wades boot: Wade was a mythical hero of Germanic legend who performed many strange
exploits in his boat called Guingelot.

So muchel broken harm, whan that hem
    leste,   1425   *broken harm: do harm or mischief.*
That with hem sholde I nevere lyve in reste.
For sondry scoles maken subtile clerkis;
Womman of many scoles half a clerk is.
But certeinly, a yong thyng may men gye,   *gye: guide.*
Right as men may warm wex with handes
    plye.   1430   *plye: bend, mold.*
Wherfore I sey yow pleynly, in a clause,
I wol noon old wyf han right for this cause.
For if so were I hadde swich myschaunce,
That I in hire ne koude han no pleasaunce,
Thanne sholde I lede my lyf in avoutrye,   1435   *avoutrye: adultery.*
And go streight to the devel, when I dye.
Ne children sholde I none upon hire geten;
Yet were me levere houndes had me eten,   *were me levere: I had rather.*
Than that myn heritage sholde falle
In straunge hand, and this I telle yow alle.   1440
I dote nat, I woot the cause why   *dote: behave foolishly.*
Men sholde wedde, and forthermoore woot I,
Ther speketh many a man of mariage
That woot namoore of it than woot my page,
For whiche causes man sholde take a wyf.   1445
If he ne may nat lyven chaast his lyf,
Take hym a wyf with greet devocioun,
By cause of leveful procreacioun   *leveful: lawful.*
Of children, to th'onour of God above,
And nat oonly for paramour or love;   1450   *paramour: sexual love.*
And for they sholde lecherye eschue,
And yelde hir dette whan that it is due;   *yelde: pay.*
Or for that ech of hem sholde helpen oother
In meschief, as a suster shal the brother;   *meschief: misfortune, distress.*
And lyve in chastitee ful holily.   1455
But sires, by youre leve, that am nat I.
For, God be thanked! I dar make avaunt,   *make avaunt: boast.*
I feele my lymes stark and suffisaunt   *stark: strong.*
To do al that a man bilongeth to;   *a man bilongeth to: is a man's duty.*
I woot myselven best what I may do.   1460
Though I be hoor, I fare as dooth a tree
That blosmeth er that fruyt ywoxen be;   *ywoxen: grown.*
And blosmy trees nys neither drye ne deed.
I feele me nowhere hoor but on myn heed;
Myn herte and alle my lymes been as grene   1465
As laurer thurgh the yeer is for to sene.   *laurer: laurel. is for to sene: is*
And syn that ye han herd al myn entente,   *[green] to see.*

1452. See I Corinthians vii.3.
1458. **lymes:** A limb was any organ, part, or member of the body.

I pray yow to my wil ye wol assente."
   Diverse men diversely hym tolde
Of mariage manye ensamples olde.   1470
Somme blamed it, somme preised it, certeyn;
But at the laste, shortly for to seyn,
As al day falleth altercacioun   al day: all the time.
Bitwixe freendes in disputisoun,
Ther fil a stryf bitwix his bretheren two,   1475
Of which that oon was cleped Placebo,
Justinus soothly called was that oother.
   Placebo seyde, "O Januarie, brother,
Ful litel nede hadde ye, my lord so deere,
Conseil to axe of any that is heere,   1480
But that ye been so ful of sapience   sapience: wisdom.
That yow ne liketh, for youre heigh prudence,
To weyven fro the word of Salomon.   weyven: turn aside.
This word seyde he unto us everychon:
'Wirk alle thyng by conseil,' thus seyde he, 1485
'And thanne shaltow nat repente thee.'
But though that Salomon spak swich a word,
Myn owene deere brother and my lord,
So wisly God my soule brynge at reste,   wisly: surely.
I holde your owene conseil is the beste.   1490
For, brother myn, of me tak this motyf,   motyf: proposition.
I have now been a court-man al my lyf,
And God it woot, though I unworthy be,
I have stonden in ful greet degree   stonden: stood. degree: place.
Abouten lordes of ful heigh estat;   1495
Yet hadde I nevere with noon of hem debat. debat: disagreement.
I nevere hem contraried, trewely;   contraried: contradicted.
I woot wel that my lord kan moore than I. kan: knows.
With that he seith, I holde it ferme and stable; with that: as to what.
I seye the same, or elles thyng semblable. 1500 semblable: similar.
A ful greet fool is any conseillour
That serveth any lord of heigh honour,
That dar presume, or elles thenken it,
That his conseil sholde passe his lordes wit. passe: surpass.
Nay, lordes been no fooles, by my fay!   1505
Ye han youreselven shewed heer to-day
So heigh sentence, so holily and weel,   sentence: opinion.
That I consente and conferme everydeel   conferme: support. everydeel: fully.
Youre wordes alle and youre opinioun.
By God, ther nys no man in al this toun, 1510
Ne in Ytaille, koude bet han sayd!
Crist halt hym of this conseil ful wel apayd. halt: holds. conseil: decision. apayd:
And trewely, it is an heigh corage   satisfied. corage: courage (but see
                                        line 1808).

1476: **Placebo:** This name has reference to his complaisant disposition; see Summoner's Tale, l. 2075, note.

Of any man that stapen is in age   stapen: advanced.
To take a yong wyf; by my fader kyn,   1515 fader kyn: father's ancestry.
Youre herte hangeth on a joly pyn!   hangeth . . . pyn: i.e., is amorous.
Dooth now in this matere right as yow leste,
For finally I holde it for the beste."
   Justinus, that ay stille sat and herde,
Right in this wise he to Placebo answerde: 1520
"Now, brother myn, be pacient, I preye,
Syn ye han seyd, and herkneth what I seye.
Senek, amonges othere wordes wise,
Seith that a man oghte hym right wel avyse   hym avyse: take thought.
To whom he yeveth his lond or his catel.   1525 catel: goods.
And syn I oghte avyse me right wel
To whom I yeve my good awey fro me,   good: property.
Wel muchel moore I oghte avysed be   avysed be: to consider.
To whom I yeve my body for alwey.
I warne yow wel, it is no childes pley   1530
To take a wyf withouten avysement.   avysement: consideration.
Men moste enquere, this is myn assent,   assent: opinion.
Wher she be wys, or sobre, or dronkelewe,   dronkelewe: addicted to drink.
Or proud, or elles ootherweys a shrewe,
A chidestere, or wastour of thy good,   1535 chidestere: a scold.
Or riche, or poore, or elles mannyssh wood.   mannyssh wood: inclined to rage like
Al be it so that no man fynden shal   a man; or mad for men.
Noon in this world that trotteth hool in al,   hool: perfectly sound.
Ne man, ne beest, swich as men koude devyse;   devyse: imagine.
But nathelees it oghte ynough suffise   1540
With any wyf, if so were that she hadde
Mo goode thewes than hir vices badde;   thewes: traits.
And al this axeth leyser for t'enquere.
For, God it woot, I have wept many a teere
Ful pryvely, syn that I had a wyf.   1545
Preyse whoso wole a wedded mannes lyf,
Certein I fynde in it but cost and care
And observances, of all blisses bare.   observances: set duties.
And yet, God woot, my neighebores aboute,   aboute: nearby.
And namely of wommen many a route,   1550
Seyn that I have the mooste stedefast wyf,
And eek the mekeste oon that bereth lyf;
But I woot best where wryngeth me my sho.
Ye mowe, for me, right as yow liketh do;
Avyseth yow—ye been a man of age—   1555 avyseth yow: take thought.
How that ye entren into mariage,
And namely with a yong wyf and a fair.
By hym that made water, erthe, and air,
The yongeste man that is in al this route
Is bisy ynough to bryngen it aboute   1560
To han his wyf allone. Trusteth me,   allone: without competitors.
Ye shul nat plesen hire fully yeres thre,—

This is to seyn, to doon hire ful plesaunce.
A wyf axeth ful many an observaunce.
I pray yow that ye be nat yvele apayd."   1565   yvele apayd: displeased.
    "Wel," quod this Januarie, "and hastow ysayd?
Straw for thy Senek, and for thy proverbes!
I counte nat a panyer full of herbes   counte: care. panyer: basket.
Of scole-termes. Wiser men than thow,   of: for. scole-termes: scholastic ex-
As thou hast herd, assenteden right now   1570   pressions; hence, abstract theoriz-
To my purpos. Placebo, what sey ye?"   ing.
    "I seye it is a cursed man," quod he,
"That letteth matrimoigne, sikerly."   letteth: hinders.
And with that word they risen sodeynly,   risen: rose.
And been assented fully that he sholde   1575
Be wedded whan hym liste, and where he wolde.
    Heigh fantasye and curious busynesse   fantasye: imagination. curious:
Fro day to day gan in the soule impresse   eager. busynesse: preoccupation.
Of Januarie aboute his mariage.   gan impresse: became fixed.
Many fair shap and many a fair visage   1580
Ther passeth thurgh his herte nyght by nyght,
As whoso tooke a mirour, polisshed bright,
And sette it in a commune market-place,
Thanne sholde he se ful many a figure pace
By his mirour; and in the same wise   1585   by: across.
Gan Januarie inwith his thoght devyse   inwith: in. devyse of: think about.
Of maydens whiche that dwelten hym bisyde.   hym bisyde: near him.
He wiste nat wher that he myghte abyde.   wher: whether. abyde: adhere to a
For if that oon have beautee in hir face,   decision.
Another stant so in the peples grace   1590   stant: stands.
For hir sadnesse and hir benyngnytee   sadnesse: steadfastness.
That of the peple grettest voys hath she;
And somme were riche, and hadden badde name.
But nathelees, bitwix ernest and game,
He atte laste apoynted hym on oon,   1595   apoynted hym: decided.
And leet alle othere from his herte goon,
And chees hire of his owene auctoritee;   of his owene auctoritee: indepen-
For love is blynd alday, and may nat see.   dently. alday: all the time.
And whan that he was in his bed ybroght,
He purtreyed in his herte and in his thoght   1600   purtreyed: imagined.
Hir fresshe beautee and hir age tendre,
Hir myddel smal, hire armes longe and sklendre,
Hir wise governaunce, hir gentillesse,   governaunce: behavior.
Hir wommanly beryng, and hir sadnesse.
And whan that he on hire was   was condescended: had set his mind.
          condescended,   1605
Hym thoughte his choys myghte nat ben
          amended.   amended: improved.
For whan that he hymself concluded hadde,
Hym thoughte ech oother mannes wit so badde
That inpossible it were to replye

Agayn his choys, this was his fantasye.   **1610**
His freendes sente he to, at his instaunce,   instaunce: urgent entreaty.
And preyed hem to doon hym that plesaunce,
That hastily they wolden to hym come;
He wolde abregge hir labour, alle and some.   abregge: shorten.
Nedeth namoore for hym to go ne ryde;   **1615**   go: walk.
He was apoynted ther he wolde abyde.   apoynted: decided.

    Placebo cam, and eek his freendes soone,
And alderfirst he bad hem alle a boone,   alderfirst: first of all. **bad a boone:**
That noon of hem none argumentes make   made a request.
Agayn the purpos which that he hath take,   **1620**
Which purpos was plesant to God, seyde he,
And verray ground of his prosperitee.

    He seyde ther was a mayden in the toun,
Which that of beautee hadde greet renoun,   of: for.
Al were it so she were of smal degree;   **1625**   smal degree: low rank.
Suffiseth hym hir youthe and hir beautee.
Which mayde, he seyde, he wolde han to his
        wyf,
To lede in ese and holynesse his lyf;   ese: delight.
And thanked God that he myghte han hire al,   al: entirely.
That no wight his blisse parten shal.   **1630**   parten: share.
And preyde hem to laboure in this nede,
And shapen that he faille nat to spede;   shapen: contrive. spede: prosper.
For thanne, he seyde, his spirit was at ese.
"Thanne is," quod he, "no thyng may me
        displese,
Save o thyng priketh in my conscience,   **1635**   priketh: stings with remorse.
The which I wol reherce in youre presence.

    I have," quod he, "herd seyd, ful yoore ago,   yoore ago: long ago.
Ther may no man han parfite blisses two,—
This is to seye, in erthe and eek in hevene.
For though he kepe hym fro the synnes
        sevene,   **1640**
And eek from every branche of thilke tree,
Yet is ther so parfit felicitee
And so greet ese and lust in mariage,   ese: delight. lust: joy.
That evere I am agast now in myn age
That I shal lede now so myrie a lyf,   **1645**
So delicat, withouten wo and stryf,   delicat: luxurious, splendid.
That I shall have myn hevene in erthe heere.
For sith that verray hevene is boght so deere
With tribulacion and greet penaunce,
How sholde I thanne, that lyve in swich
        plesaunce   **1650**
As alle wedded men doon with hire wyvys,
Come to the blisse ther Crist eterne on lyve is?   on lyve: alive.
This is my drede, and ye, my bretheren tweye,
Assoilleth me this question, I preye."   assoilleth: resolve.

Justinus, which that hated his folye,   **1655**   folye: foolishness; lecherousness.
Answerde anon right in his japerye;   japerye: mockery.
And for he wolde his longe tale abregge,   abregge: abridge.
He wolde noon auctoritee allegge,   allegge: cite, quote.
But seide, "Sire, so ther be noon obstacle
Oother than this, God of his hygh myracle   **1660**
And of his mercy may so for yow wirche   wirche: work.
That, er ye have your right of holy chirche,   right: last sacrament.
Ye may repente of wedded mannes lyf,
In which ye seyn ther is no wo ne stryf.
And elles, God forbede but he sente   **1665**
A wedded man hym grace to repente
Wel ofte rather than a sengle man!   rather: sooner.
And therfore, sire—the beste reed I kan—   reed: counsel.
Dispeire yow noght, but have in youre memorie,
Paraunter she may be youre purgatorie!   **1670**   paraunter: perhaps.
She may be Goddes meene and Goddes whippe; meene: means, instrument.
Thanne shal youre soule up to hevene skippe
Swifter than dooth an arwe out of a bowe.
I hope to God, herafter shul ye knowe
That ther nys no so greet felicitee   **1675**
In mariage, ne nevere mo shal be,
That yow shal lette of youre salvacioun,   lette: deprive.
So that ye use, as skile is and reson,   skile: the right thing.
The lustes of youre wyf attemprely,   attemprely: temperately.
And that ye plese hire nat to amorously,   **1680**
And that ye kepe yow eek from oother synne.
My tale is doon, for my wit is thynne.
Beth nat agast herof, my brother deere,
But lat us waden out of this matere.
The Wyf of Bathe, if ye han understonde,   **1685**
Of mariage, which we have on honde,
Declared hath ful wel in litel space.
Fareth now wel, God have yow in his grace."
    And with that word this Justyn and his brother
Han take hir leve, and ech of hem of oother. **1690**
For whan they sawe that it moste nedes be,
They wroghten so, by sly and wys tretee,   tretee: negotiation.
That she, this mayden, which that Mayus highte,
As hastily as ever that she myghte,   hastily: soon.
Shal wedded be unto this Januarie.   **1695**
I trowe it were to longe yow to tarie,   tarie: delay.
If I yow tolde of every scrit and bond   scrit: piece of writing.
By which that she was feffed in his lond,   feffed in: put in possession of, en-
Or for to herknen of hir riche array.   dowed with.
But finally ycomen is the day   **1700**

1660–61. of: some of (partitive); thus myracle and mercy are objects of wirche.
1665–67. but he sente wel ofte: that he should not very often send.

That to the chirche bothe be they went   went: gone.
For to receyve the holy sacrament.
Forth comth the preest, with stole aboute his
      nekke,
And bad hire be lyk Sarra and Rebekke
In wisdom and in trouthe of mariage;   1705
And seyde his orisons, as is usage,
And croucheth hem, and bad God sholde hem   croucheth: makes the sign of the
      blesse,   Cross upon.
And made al siker ynogh with holynesse.
   Thus been they wedded with solempnitee,
And at the feeste sitteth he and she   1710
With othere worthy folk upon the deys.   deys: dais.
Al ful of joye and blisse is the paleys,
And ful of instrumentz and of vitaille,
The mooste deyntevous of all Ytaille.   deyntevous: delightful.
Biforn hem stoode instrumentz of swich soun 1715
That Orpheus, ne of Thebes Amphioun,
Ne maden nevere swich a melodye.
At every cours thanne cam loud mynstralcye,
That nevere tromped Joab for to heere,
Nor he Theodomas, yet half so cleere,   1720
At Thebes, whan the citee was in doute.   doute: peril.
Bacus the wyn hem shenketh al aboute,   shenketh: pours out, serves.
And Venus laugheth upon every wight,
For Januarie was bicome hir knyght,
And wolde bothe assayen his corage   1725 assayen: test. corage: lust.
In libertee, and eek in mariage;
And with hir firbrond in hir hand aboute
Daunceth bifore the bryde and al the route.   route: company.
And certeinly, I dar right wel seyn this,
Ymeneus, that god of weddyng is,   1730 Ymeneus: Hymen.
Saugh nevere his lyf so myrie a wedded man.   his lyf: in his life.
Hoold thou thy pees, thou poete Marcian,
That writest us that ilke weddyng murie
Of hire Philologie and hym Mercurie,
And of the songes that the Muses songe!   1735 songe: sang.
To smal is bothe thy penne, and eek thy tonge,
For to descryven of this mariage.   descryven: describe.
Whan tendre youthe hath wedded stoupyng age,
Ther is swich myrthe that it may nat be writen.
Assayeth it yourself, than may ye witen   1740
If that I lye or noon in this matere.
   Mayus, that sit with so benygne a cheere,   sit: sits.
Hir to biholde it semed fayerye.   fayerye: supernatural enchantment.

1716–21. Orpheus, Amphion, Joab, and Thiodamas, are stock examples of famous musicians.
1732. **Marcian:** Marcianus Capella (5th century), author of *De nuptiis Philologiae et Mercurii,* an allegorical encyclopedia of the seven liberal arts.

Queene Ester looked nevere with swich an eye
On Assuer, so meke a look hath she.   1745
I may yow nat devyse al hir beautee.
But thus muche of hire beautee telle I may,
That she was lyk the brighte morwe of May,   morwe: morning.
Fulfild of alle beautee and plesaunce.
   This Januarie is ravysshed in a traunce   1750
At every tyme he looked on hir face;
But in his herte he gan hir to manace   manace: threaten.
That he that nyght in armes wolde hire streyne
Harder than evere Parys dide Eleyne.
But nathelees yet hadde he gret pitee   1755
That thilke nyght offenden hire moste he,
And thoughte, "Allas! O tendre creature,
Now wolde God ye myghte wel endure
Al my corage, it is so sharp and keene!
I am agast ye shul it nat sustene.   1760
But God forbede that I dide al my myght!
Now wolde God that it were woxen nyght,   woxen: become.
And that the nyght wolde lasten everemo.
I wolde that al this peple were ago."   ago: gone.
And finally he dooth all his labour,   1765
As he best myghte, savyng his honour,
To haste hem fro the mete in subtil wise.   mete: feast.
   The tyme cam that reson was to rise;   reson: good sense.
And after that men daunce and drynken faste,   faste: deeply.
And spices al aboute the hous they caste,   1770
And ful of joye and blisse is every man,—
Al but a squyer, highte Damyan,
Which carf biforn the knyght ful many a day.   carf: carved.
He was so ravysshed on his lady May
That for the verray peyne he was ny wood.   1775 ny: nigh, nearly.
Almoost he swelte and swowned as he stood,   swelte: fainted.
So sore hath Venus hurt hym with hir brond,   brond: torch.
As that she bar it dauncyng in hir hond;
And to his bed he wente hym hastily.
Namoore of hym at this tyme speke I,   1780
But there I lete hym wepe ynogh and pleyne,
Til fresshe May wol rewen on his peyne.   rewen: have pity.
   O perilous fyr, that in the bedstraw bredeth!   bredeth: breeds (i.e., starts).
O famulier foo, that his service bedeth!   bedeth: offers.
O servant traytour, false homly hewe,   1785 hewe: servant.
Lyk to the naddre in bosom sly untrewe,   naddre: adder.
God shilde us alle from youre aqueyntaunce!
O Januarie, dronken in plesaunce
In mariage, se how thy Damyan,

1744–45. See the Book of Esther, especially ii and v.
1784–85. famulier; homly: belonging to one's household.

Thyn owene squier and thy born man,   1790   **thy born man:** your servant from birth.
Entendeth for to do thee vileynye.
God grante thee thyn homly fo t'espye!
For in this world nys worse pestilence
Than homly fo al day in thy presence.
    Parfourned hath the sonne his ark diurne; 1795   **ark diurne:** daily path.
No lenger may the body of hym sojourne
On th'orisonte, as in that latitude.
Night with his mantel, that is derk and rude,   **rude:** rough.
Gan oversprede the hemysperie aboute;
For which departed is this lusty route   1800
Fro Januarie, with thank on every syde.
Hom to hir houses lustily they ryde,
Where as they doon hir thynges as hem leste,
And whan they sye hir tyme, go to reste.   **sye:** saw.
Soone after that, this hastif Januarie   1805   **hastif:** eager, impetuous.
Wol go to bedde, he wol no lenger tarye.
He drynketh ypocras, clarree, and vernage,
Of spices hoote, t'encreessen his corage;   **corage:** sexual desire.
And many a letuarie hadde he ful fyn,
Swich as the cursed monk, daun Constantyn, 1810
Hath writen in his book *De Coitu;*
To eten hem alle he nas no thyng eschu.   **eschu:** averse.
And to his privee freendes thus seyde he:
"For Goddes love, as soone as it may be,
Lat voyden al this hous in curteys wise."   1815   **lat voyden:** empty, clear.
And they han doon right as he wol devyse.
Men drynken, and the travers drawe anon.   **travers:** a curtain across a room.
The bryde was broght abedde as stille as stoon;   **drawe:** drawn.
And whan the bed was with the preest yblessed,   **with:** by.
Out of the chambre hath every wight hym   **hym dressed:** proceeded, gone.
        dressed;   1820
And Januarie hath faste in armes take
His fresshe May, his paradys, his make.   **make:** mate.
He lulleth hire, he kisseth hire ful ofte;
With thikke bristles of his berd unsofte,
Lyk to the skyn of houndfyssh, sharp as   **houndfyssh:** spiny dogfish.
        brere—   1825   **brere:** brier.
For he was shave al newe in his manere—
He rubbeth hire aboute hir tendre face,
And seyde thus, "Allas! I moot trespace
To yow, my spouse, and yow gretly offende,

1807. **ypocras:** a cordial made of wine flavored with spices. **clarree:** a drink made of wine spiced, sweetened with honey, and clarified by straining. **vernage:** a kind of white Italian wine.
1808. **of spices hoote:** biting or peppery with spices.
1809. **letuarie:** a medicine consisting of a powder mixed with syrup.
1810. **daun Constantyn:** Constantinus Africanus, a monk of Carthage, brought Arabic medical learning to Salerno and Monte Cassino in the eleventh century; his little pamphlet on coition consists chiefly of dietary recommendations and recipes for potions.

Er tyme come that I wil doun descende.　1830　doun descende: get down or off.
But nathelees, considereth this," quod he,
"Ther nys no werkman, whatsoevere he be,
That may bothe werke wel and hastily;
This wol be doon at leyser parfitly.
It is no fors how longe that we pleye;　1835
In trewe wedlok coupled be we tweye;
And blessed be the yok that we been inne,
For in our actes we mowe do no synne.
A man may do no synne with his wyf,
Ne hurte hymselven with his owene knyf;　1840
For we han leve to pleye us, by the lawe."
Thus laboureth he til that the day gan dawe;
And thanne he taketh a sop in fyn clarree,
And upright in his bed thanne sitteth he,
And after that he sang ful loude and cleere,　1845
And kiste his wyf, and made wantown cheere.
He was al coltissh, ful of ragerye,　　　　ragerye: wantonness.
And ful of jargon as a flekked pye.　　　jargon: chatter. pye: magpie.
The slakke skyn aboute his nekke shaketh,
Whil that he sang, so chaunteth he and
　　　　craketh.　1850　craketh: trills, quavers.
But God woot what that May thoughte in hir
　　　　herte,
Whan she hym saw up sittyng in his sherte,
In his nyght-cappe, and with his nekke lene;
She preiseth nat his pleyyng worth a bene.　　preiseth: praises.
Thanne seide he thus, "My reste wol I take;　1855
Now day is come, I may no lenger wake."
And doun he leyde his heed, and sleep til pryme.　sleep: slept. pryme: 9 A.M.
And afterward, whan that he saw his tyme,
Up riseth Januarie; but fresshe May
Heeld hire chambre unto the fourthe day,　1860
As usage is of wyves for the beste.
For every labour somtyme moot han reste,　　labour: laborer.
Or elles longe may he nat endure;
This is to seyn, no lyves creature,　　　　lyves: living.
Be it of fissh, or bryd, or beest, or man.　1865　bryd: bird.
　　Now wol I speke of woful Damyan,
That langwissheth for love, as ye shul heere;
Therfore I speke to hym in this manere:
I seye, "O sely Damyan, allas!　　　　　sely: wretched.
Answere to my demaunde, as in this cas.　1870
How shaltow to thy lady, fresshe May,
Telle thy wo? She wol alwey seye nay.
Eek if thou speke, she wol thy wo biwreye.　　biwreye: divulge.

1838–40. Cf. Parson's Tale, l. 859.
1843. sop: a piece of bread dipped in wine.　clarree: see note 1807.

God be thyn help! I kan no bettre seye."
This sike Damyan in Venus fyr   1875
So brenneth that he dyeth for desyr,
For which he putte his lyf in aventure.   aventure: jeopardy.
No lenger myghte he in this wise endure,
But prively a penner gan he borwe,   penner: pen-case.
And in a lettre wroot he al his sorwe,   1880
In manere of a compleynt or a lay,
Unto his faire, fresshe lady May;
And in a purs of sylk, heng on his sherte,   heng: which hung.
He hath it put, and leyde it at his herte.
The moone, that at noon was thilke day   1885
That Januarie hath wedded fresshe May
In two of Tawr, was into Cancre gliden;
So longe hath Mayus in hir chambre abyden,
As custume is unto thise nobles alle.
A bryde shal nat eten in the halle   1890
Til dayes foure, or thre dayes atte leeste,
Ypassed been; thanne lat hir go to feeste.
The fourthe day compleet fro noon to noon,
Whan that the heighe masse was ydoon,
In halle sit this Januarie and May,   1895
As fressh as is the brighte someres day.
And so bifel how that this goode man
Remembred hym upon this Damyan,
And seyde, "Seynte Marie! how may this be,
That Damyan entendeth nat to me?   1900   entendeth to: waits upon, attends.
Is he ay syk, or how may this bityde?"
His squieres, whiche that stooden ther bisyde,
Excused hym by cause of his siknesse,
Which letted hym to doon his bisynesse;   letted hym to doon: prevented him
Noon oother cause myghte make hym tarye. 1905   from doing. bisynesse: duties.
"That me forthynketh," quod this Januarie,   forthynketh: grieves
"He is a gentil squier, by my trouthe!
If that he deyde, it were harm and routhe.
He is as wys, discreet, and as secree
As any man I woot of his degree,   1910
And therto manly, and eek servysable,   servysable: ready to serve.
And for to be a thrifty man right able.   thrifty: thriving.
But after mete, as soone as evere I may,
I wol myself visite hym, and eek May,
To do hym al the confort that I kan."   1915
And for that word hym blessed every man,
That of his bountee and his gentillesse   that: because.
He wolde so conforten in siknesse
His squier, for it was a gentil dede.

1887. In the four days the moon passed from the second degree of Taurus, through Gemini, into Cancer.

"Dame," quod this Januarie, "tak good hede, 1920   hede: heed.
At after-mete ye with youre wommen alle,   at after-mete: after the noon meal.
Whan ye han been in chambre out of this halle,
That alle ye go to see this Damyan.
Dooth hym disport—he is a gentil man;   dooth disport: divert, amuse.
And telleth hym that I wol hym visite,   1925
Have I no thyng but rested me a lite;
And spede yow faste, for I wol abide
Til that ye slepe faste by my syde."
And with that word he gan to hym to calle
A squier, that was marchal of his halle,   1930
And tolde hym certein thynges, what he wolde.
   This fresshe May hath streight hir wey yholde,
With alle hir wommen, unto Damyan.
Doun by his beddes syde sit she than,
Confortyng hym as goodly as she may.   1935
This Damyan, whan that his tyme he say,   say: saw.
In secree wise his purs and eek his bille,   bille: letter, note.
In which that he ywriten hadde his wille,   wille: desire.
Hath put into hir hand, withouten moore,
Save that he siketh wonder depe and soore, 1940   siketh: sighs.
And softely to hire right thus seyde he:
"Mercy! and that ye nat discovere me,   discovere: betray.
For I am deed if that this thyng be kyd."   kyd: known.
This purs hath she inwith hir bosom hyd,   inwith: within.
And wente hir wey; ye gete namoore of me. 1945   of: from.
But unto Januarie ycomen is she,
That on his beddes syde sit ful softe.
He taketh hire, and kisseth hire ful ofte,
And leyde hym doun to slepe, and that anon.
She feyned hire as that she moste gon   1950
Ther as ye woot that every wight moot neede;
And whan she of this bille hath taken heede,
She rente it all to cloutes at the laste,   cloutes: pieces, fragments.
And in the pryvee softely it caste.
   Who studieth now but faire fresshe May? 1955   studieth: thinks intently.
Adoun by olde Januarie she lay,
That sleep til that the coughe hath hym awaked.   sleep: slept.
Anon he preyde hire strepen hire al naked;   strepen: strip.
He wolde of hire, he seyde, han som plesaunce;
He seyde hir clothes dide hym encom-
      braunce,   1960
And she obeyeth, be hir lief or looth.   lief or looth: willing or unwilling.
But lest that precious folk be with me wrooth,   precious: fastidious.
How that he wroghte, I dar nat to yow telle;
Or wheither hire thoughte it paradys or helle.
But heere I lete hem werken in hir wise   1965
Til evensong rong, and that they moste arise.
   Were it by destynee or by aventure,

Were it by influence or by nature,
Or constellacion, that in swich estat
The hevene stood, that tyme fortunat   1970
Was for to putte a bille of Venus werkes—   putte a bille: submit a petition.
For alle thyng hath tyme, as seyn thise clerkes—
To any womman, for to get hir love,
I kan nat seye; but grete God above,
That knoweth that noon act is causelees,   1975
He deme of al, for I wol holde my pees.   He deme: may He judge.
But sooth is this, how that this fresshe May
Hath take swich impression that day
Of pitee of this sike Damyan,
That from hir herte she ne dryve kan   1980
The remembrance for to doon hym ese.
"Certeyn," thoghte she, "whom that this thyng
        displese,
I rekke nat, for here I hym assure   assure: promise.
To love hym best of any creature,
Though he namoore hadde than his sherte."   1985 sherte: undershirt.
Lo, pitee renneth soone in gentil herte!
   Heere may ye se how excellent franchise   franchise: nobility; liberality.
In wommen is, whan they hem narwe avyse.   hem narwe avyse: reflect carefully.
Som tyrant is, as ther be many oon,
That hath an herte as hard as any stoon,   1990
Which wolde han lat hym sterven in the place   sterven: die.
Wel rather than han graunted hym hir grace;
And hem rejoysen in hir cruel pryde,
And rekke nat to been an homycide.
   This gentil May, fulfilled of pitee,   1995
Right of hire hand a lettre maked she,
In which she graunteth hym hir verray grace.
Ther lakketh noght, but oonly day and place,
Wher that she myghte unto his lust suffise;   unto suffise: satisfy.
For it shal be right as he wol devyse.   2000
And whan she saw hir tyme, upon a day,
To visite this Damyan goth May,
And subtilly this lettre doun she threste   subtilly: craftily.
Under his pilwe, rede it if hym leste.
She taketh hym by the hand, and harde hym
        twiste   2005 twiste: twisted.
So secrely that no wight of it wiste,
And bad hym be al hool, and forth she wente
To Januarie, whan that he for hir sente.
   Up riseth Damyan the nexte morwe;
Al passed was his siknesse and his sorwe.   2010
He kembeth hym, he preyneth hym and pyketh,   kembeth: combs. preyneth: prinks.
He dooth al that his lady lust and lyketh;   pyketh: adorns. lust: desires.

1972. See Ecclesiastes iii.1, traditionally ascribed to Solomon.

And eek to Januarie he goth as lowe
As evere dide a dogge for the bowe.
He is so plesant unto every man   2015
(For craft is al, whoso that do it kan)
That every wight is fayn to speke hym good;
And fully in his lady grace he stood.
Thus lete I Damyan aboute his nede,
And in my tale forth I wol procede.   2020
   Somme clerkes holden that felicitee
Stant in delit, and therfore certeyn he,
This noble Januarie, with al his myght,
In honest wise, as longeth to a knyght,
Shoop hym to lyve ful deliciously.   2025
His housyng, his array, as honestly
To his degree was maked as a kynges.
Amonges othere of his honeste thynges,
He made a gardyn, walled al with stoon;
So fair a gardyn woot I nowher noon.   2030
For, out of doute, I verraily suppose
That he that wroot the Romance of the Rose
Ne koude of it the beautee wel devyse;
Ne Priapus ne myghte nat suffise,
Though he be god of gardyns, for to telle   2035
The beautee of the gardyn and the welle,
That stood under a laurer alwey grene.
Ful ofte tyme he Pluto and his queene,
Proserpina, and al hire fayerye,
Disporten hem and maken melodye   2040
Aboute that welle, and daunced, as men tolde.
   This noble knyght, this Januarie the olde,
Swich deyntee hath in it to walke and pleye,
That he wol no wight suffren bere the keye
Save he hymself; for of the smale wyket   2045
He baar alwey of silver a clyket,
With which, whan that hym leste, he it unshette.
And whan he wolde paye his wyf hir dette
In somer seson, thider wolde he go,
And May his wyf, and no wight but they
       two;   2050
And thynges whiche that were nat doon abedde,
He in the gardyn parfourned hem and spedde.
And in this wise, many a murye day,

Glosses (right column):

lowe: tractably, docilely.

hym: of him.
lady: lady's.
lete: leave. aboute: attending to.

stant: stands, consists.

honest: honorable.

shoop hym: prepared himself.
deliciously: luxuriously. honestly: creditably. to: according to.

devyse: describe.
suffise: be able.

laurer: laurel.

fayerye: supernatural creatures.

deyntee: delight.

wyket: wicket, gate.
clyket: latch key.
unshette: unlocked.

spedde: fulfilled.

2014. for the bowe: tracking game wounded by the bowmen.
2032. Guillaume de Lorris opened his allegorical *Roman de la Rose* (c. 1237) with an elaborate description of the garden of Love and its well.
2034. Priapus: the god of procreation and hence of gardens and vineyards.
2038–39. Pluto and Proserpina in this poem are more the king and queen of the fairies than of the classical underworld, and were modeled on their counterparts in the Middle English poem *Sir Orfeo.*

Lyved this Januarie and fresshe May.
But worldly joye may nat alwey dure   2055
To Januarie, ne to no creature.
  O sodeyn hap! o thou Fortune unstable!
Lyk to the scorpion so deceyvable,   deceyvable: deceitful, treacherous.
That flaterest with thyn heed whan thou wolt
          stynge;
Thy tayl is deeth, thurgh thyn envenymynge. 2060
O brotil joye! o sweete venym queynte!   brotil: brittle; precarious. **queynte:**
O monstre, that so subtilly kanst peynte   strange.
Thy yiftes under hewe of stedefastnesse,   yiftes: gifts.
That thou deceyvest bothe moore and lesse!   moore: greater.
Why hastow Januarie thus deceyved,   2065
That haddest hym for thy ful freend receyved?
And now thou hast biraft hym bothe his eyen, biraft: robbed.
For sorwe of which desireth he to dyen.
  Allas! this noble Januarie free,   free: gracious.
Amydde his lust and his prosperitee,   2070
Is woxen blynd, and that al sodeynly.   woxen: become.
He wepeth and he wayleth pitously;
And therwithal the fyr of jalousye,
Lest that his wyf sholde falle in som folye, folye: lechery; adultery.
So brente his herte that he wolde fayn   2075 brente: burned.
That som man bothe hire and hym had slayn.
For neither after his deeth, nor in his lyf,
Ne wolde he that she were love ne wyf,   love ne wyf: i.e., of another.
But evere lyve as wydwe in clothes blake,
Soul as the turtle that lost hath hire make. 2080 soul: sole, single. turtle: turtle-dove.
But atte laste, after a month or tweye,   make: mate.
His sorwe gan aswage, sooth to seye;   gan aswage: became lessened,
For whan he wiste it may noon oother be,   moderated.
He paciently took his adversitee,
Save, out of doute, he may nat forgoon   2085 forgoon: avoid.
That he nas jalous everemoore in oon;   everemoore in oon: all the time.
Which jalousye it was so outrageous,
That neither in halle, ne in noon oother hous,
Ne in noon oother place, neverthemo,
He nolde suffre hire for to ryde or go,   2090 go: walk.
But if that he had hond on hire alway;
For which ful ofte wepeth fresshe May,
That loveth Damyan so benygnely   benygnely: affectionately.
That she moot outher dyen sodeynly,   outher: either.
Or elles she moot han hym as hir leste.   2095
She wayteth whan hir herte wolde breste.   wayteth: expects (the time).
  Upon that oother syde Damyan
Bicomen is the sorwefulleste man
That evere was; for neither nyght ne day
Ne myghte he speke a word to fresshe May, 2100

As to his purpos, of no swich matere,
But if that Januarie moste it heere,
That hadde an hand upon hire everemo.
But nathelees, by writyng to and fro,
And privee signes, wiste he what she mente, 2105
And she knew eek the fyn of his entente.   fyn: end in view, aim.
    O Januarie, what myghte it thee availle,
Thogh thou myghtest se as fer as shippes saille?
For as good is blynd deceyved be   blynd deceyved be: for a blind man to
As to be deceyved whan a man may se.   2110   be deceived.
    Lo, Argus, which that hadde an hondred
        eyen,
For al that evere he koude poure or pryen,   poure: look intently. pryen: spy.
Yet was he blent, and, God woot, so been mo,   blent: blinded, deceived.
That wenen wisly that it be nat so.   wisly: certainly.
Passe over is an ese, I sey namoore.   2115   passe over: i.e., to ignore it. ese:
    This fresshe May, that I spak of so yoore,   relief. yoore: long ago.
In warm wex hath emprented the clyket
That Januarie bar of the smale wyket,
By which into his gardyn ofte he wente;
And Damyan, that knew al hir entente,   2120
The cliket countrefeted pryvely.
Ther nys namoore to seye, but hastily   hastily: soon.
Som wonder by this clyket shal bityde,   bityde: happen.
Which ye shul heeren, if ye wol abyde.
    O noble Ovyde, sooth seystou, God woot, 2125   seystou: sayest thou.
What sleighte is it, thogh it be long and hoot,   sleighte: trick. hoot: hot; dangerous.
That love nyl fynde it out in som manere?   nyl: will not.
By Piramus and Thesbe may men lere;   lere: learn.
Thogh they were kept ful longe streite overal,   kept: guarded. streite: strictly.
They been accorded, rownyng thurgh a wal, 2130   been accorded: came to an under-
Ther no wight koude han founde out swich a   standing. rownyng: whispering.
        sleighte.
    But now to purpos: er that dayes eighte
Were passed [of] the monthe of [Juyn], bifil   of . . . Juyn: see note.
That Januarie hath caught so greet a wil,
Thurgh eggyng of his wyf, hym for to pleye   2135
In his gardyn, and no wight but they tweye,

2111. **Argus:** see Wife of Bath's Prologue, l. 358 and note.

2127. See *Metamorphoses* iv.68.

2133. The latest common original of the extant manuscripts (O') reads **er the monthe of Juyl,** which makes no sense. The editors of the Globe edition (G) emended **Juyl** to **Juyn.** Manly comments: " 'Juyl', the reading of all the MSS, is certainly an error in O'. We learn from 2220 that the sun was in Gemini, which in Chaucer's time would have covered May 11 to June 11. G was therefore justified in emending 'Juyl' to 'Juin'." In further emending **er** to **of,** I have been anticipated by two scribes (and their followers), neither authoritative nor earlier than 1440; but the emendation **of the monthe of Juyn** makes complete sense. (See Manly and Rickert, III, 406 and 477; VI, 474.) I imagine that the scribe of O' picked up **er** from line 2132. A carelessly slanting suprascript mark indicating n could easily have made Ju͞y look like Juyl.

That in a morwe unto his May seith he:
"Rys up, my wyf, my love, my lady free!   free: gracious.
The turtles voys is herd, my dowve sweete;   turtles: turtle-dove's.
The wynter is goon with his reynes wete.   2140
Com forth now, with thyne eyen columbyn!   columbyn: dove-like; innocent; de-
How fairer been thy brestes than is wyn!   mure.
The gardyn is enclosed al aboute;
Com forth, my white spouse! out of doute
Thou hast me wounded in myn herte, O wyf!   2145
No spot of thee ne knew I al my lyf.   spot: fault.
Com forth, and lat us taken oure disport;
I chees thee for my wyf and my confort."
    Swiche olde lewed wordes used he.   lewed: lascivious.
On Damyan a signe made she,   2150
That he sholde go biforn with his cliket.
This Damyan thanne hath opened the wyket,
And in he stirte, and that in swich manere   stirte: hastened.
That no wight myghte it se neither yheere,   yheere: hear.
And stille he sit under a bussh anon.   2155
    This Januarie, as blynd as is a stoon,
With Mayus in his hand, and no wight mo,
Into his fresshe gardyn is ago,   ago: gone.
And clapte to the wyket sodeynly.
    "Now wyf," quod he, "here nys but thou
        and I,   2160
That art the creature that I best love.
For by that Lord that sit in hevene above,
Levere ich hadde to dyen on a knyf,   levere ich hadde: I had rather.
Than thee offende, trewe deere wyf!

2138–48. January's invitation is composed almost entirely of passages from the Song of Songs of Solomon (who is mentioned in ll. 2242, 2277, 2292).

2149. In view of the origin of January's words, such meanings of *lewed* as "lay, not clerical" and "unlearned" add to the irony of this line.

2155. Compare ll. 878–80 of the Wife of Bath's Prologue.

The *hortus conclusus* in the *Speculum Humanæ Salvationis:* The scenes of the last four hundred lines of the Merchant's Tale are concerned with and then laid in January's paradisical "gardyn, walled al with stoon" (2029), with its "welle . . . under a laurer" (2036–37), its "bussh" (2155), and its pear tree (2210, 2217, etc.). As January takes May there he says, "The gardyn is enclosed al aboute" (2143); these and other words in his invitation to May parody phrases in the Song of Songs—the *Canticum Canticorum*—an erotic love song attributed to Solomon in which the singer calls his bride "Hortus conclusus, fons signatus" (iv.12). Whereas in the love song the "enclosed garden" and "sealed fountain" represent the chaste bride of Solomon, they were interpreted by medieval commentators as the Holy Church, bride of Christ; as the individual soul in its relationship to God; and sometimes as the Blessed Virgin Mary: thus in the *Speculum Humanae Salvationis*, of the fourteenth century, above the sketch we read, "Ortus conclusus, Fons signatus, significant Mariam." Hence the central ironies of the tale involve both the erotic and the religious implications of the *Canticum*—the savage parallels and contrasts between the relationships, on the one hand, of Solomon and his bride, of Christ and his Church, and of God and the individual soul, and on the other, of January and May, and of Damian and May with their counterfeited key to the "wiket"; and the Virgin Mary must come to mind too, even before the final line of the poem. The sketch (from an English manuscript of 1390) shows the walled garden, its trees, its "wiket" (with a hole for the "cliket"), and the sealed fountain.

Ortus conclusus
ffons signatus.

significant maria.

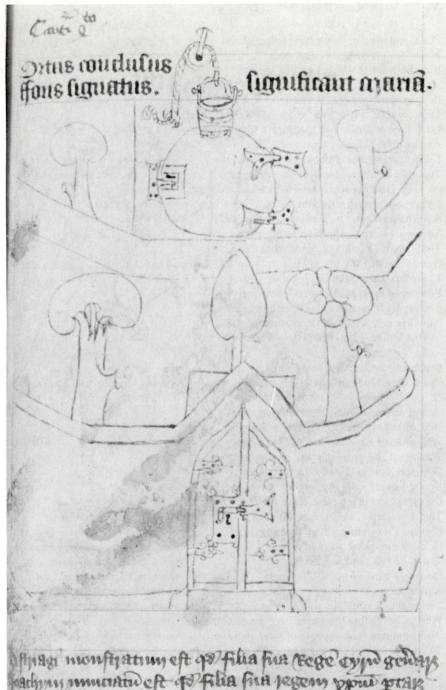

Astragi monstratum est q̄ filia sua rege cyrp geidays
ioachym nunciatu est q̄ filia sua regem ypin ptar
omne Rex libauit iudeos de captiuitate babilonica
et Rex ypt libauit nos de captiuitate dyabolica
ffilia icu Noois altuarie homanu cranan

For Goddes sake, thenk how I thee chees,   2165
Noght for no coveitise, doutelees,
But oonly for the love I had to thee.
And though that I be old, and may nat see,
Beth to me trewe, and I wol telle yow why.
Thre thynges, certes, shal ye wynne therby: 2170
First, love of Crist, and to yourself honour,
And al myn heritage, toun and tour;
I yeve it yow, maketh chartres as yow leste;   maketh chartres: draw up deeds.
This shal be doon to-morwe er sonne reste,   sonne reste: sun's rest, sunset.
So wisly God my soule brynge in blisse.   2175 wisly: surely.
I pray yow first, in covenant ye me kisse;   covenant: compact.
And though that I be jalous, wyte me noght.   wyte: blame.
Ye been so depe enprented in my thoght
That, whan I considere youre beautee,
And therwithal the unlikly elde of me,   2180 unlikly: dissimilar; unsuitable. elde:
I may nat, certes, though I sholde dye,   old age.
Forbere to been out of youre compaignye
For verray love; this is withouten doute.
Now kys me, wyf, and lat us rome aboute."
   This fresshe May, whan she thise wordes
       herde,   2185
Benygnely to Januarie answerde,
But first and forward she bigan to wepe.   first and forward: first and foremost,
"I have," quod she, "a soule for to kepe   first of all.
As wel as ye, and also myn honour,
And of my wyfhod thilke tendre flour,   2190
Which that I have assured in youre hond,   assured: entrusted.
Whan that the preest to yow my body bond;
Wherfore I wole answere in this manere,
By the leve of yow, my lord so deere:
I prey to God that nevere dawe the day   2195
That I ne sterve, as foule as womman may,   sterve: die. foule: shamefully.
If evere I do unto my kyn that shame,
Or elles I empeyre so my name,   elles: otherwise. empeyre: impair, in-
That I be fals; and if I do that lak,   jure. lak: offence, misdeed.
Do strepe me and put me in a sak,   2200 do strepe me: have me stripped.
And in the nexte ryver do me drenche.   do me drenche: have me drowned.
I am a gentil womman and no wenche.   wenche: low or wanton woman.
Why speke ye thus? but men been evere untrewe,
And wommen have repreve of yow ay newe.   repreve: reproach. newe: afresh.
Ye han noon oother contenance, I leeve,   2205 leeve: believe.
But speke to us of untrust and repreeve."
   And with that word she saw wher Damyan
Sat in the bussh, and coughen she bigan,
And with hir fynger signes made she

2205. contenance: pose; i.e., way of covering your own fault.
2206. Except to speak to us of distrust and reproach.

That Damyan sholde clymbe upon a tree,   2210
That charged was with fruyt, and up he wente.   charged: laden.
For verraily he knew al hir entente,
And every signe that she koude make,
Wel bet than Januarie, hir owene make;   make: mate.
For in a lettre she hadde told hym al   2215
Of this matere, how he werken shal.
And thus I lete hym sitte upon the pyrie,   pyrie: pear tree.
And Januarie and May romynge myrie.
   Bright was the day, and blew the firmament;   blew: blue.
Phebus hath of gold his stremes doun ysent,   2220
To gladen every flour with his warmnesse.
He was that tyme in Geminis, as I gesse,
But litel fro his declynacion
Of Cancer, Jovis exaltacion.
And so bifel, that brighte morwe-tyde,   2225
That in that gardyn, in the ferther syde,
Pluto, that is kyng of Fayerye,   Fayerye: the land of supernatural crea-
And many a lady in his compaignye,   tures.
Folwynge his wyf, the queene Proserpyna,
Which that he ravysshed out of Ethna   2230 ravysshed: seized.
Whil that she gadered floures in the mede—
In Claudyan ye may the storie rede,
How in his grisely carte he hire fette—   grisely: causing terror. fette: fetched.
This kyng of Fairye thanne adoun hym sette
Upon a bench of turves, fressh and grene,   2235
And right anon thus seyde he to his queene:
   "My wyf," quod he, "ther may no wight sey
         nay;
Th'experience so preveth every day
The treson whiche that womman dooth to man.
Ten hundred thousand [tales] telle I kan   2240
Notable of youre untrouthe and brotilnesse.
O Salomon, wys, and richest of richesse,   richesse: riches.
Fulfild of sapience and of worldly glorie,   sapience: wisdom.
Ful worthy been thy wordes to memorie
To every wight that wit and reson kan.   2245
Thus preiseth he yet the bountee of man:

2222–24. The time is early June.

2223. declynacion of Cancer: the sun's greatest distance north of the equinoctial; the summer solstice.

2224. exaltacion: the sign of the zodiac in which a planet is supposed to exert its greatest power.

2230. The valley from which Pluto carried off Proserpina was known in the Middle Ages both as Henna and Ethna. (Most MSS erroneously read "Proserpyna," but three suggest that "Ethna" was probably Chaucer's intention.)

2232. The De raptu Proserpinae of Claudius Claudianus was apparently known to Chaucer as part of the medieval school-book Liber Catonianus.

2240. O' reads Ten hundred thousand telle I kan, presumably omitting such a word as tales or stories.

2241. untrouthe: deceit; faithlessness. brotilnesse: moral weakness, fickleness, faithlessness.

'Amonges a thousand men yet foond I oon,
But of wommen alle foond I noon.'
    Thus seith the kyng that knoweth youre
        wikkednesse.
And Jhesus, *filius Syrak,* as I gesse,   2250
Ne speketh of yow but selde reverence.   selde: seldom.
A wilde fyr and corrupt pestilence   corrupt: infectious.
So falle upon youre bodyes yet to-nyght!
Ne se ye nat this honurable knyght,
By cause, allas! that he is blynd and old,   2255
His owene man shal make hym cokewold.
Lo, where he sit, the lechour, in the tree!   sit: sits.
Now wol I graunten, of my magestee,
Unto this olde, blynde, worthy knyght
That he shal have ayein his eyen syght,   2260
Whan that his wyf wold doon hym vileynye.
Thanne shal he knowen al hir harlotrye,
Bothe in repreve of hire and othere mo."   repreve: reproof.
    "Ye shal?" quod Proserpyne, "wol ye so?
Now by my modres sires soule I swere   2265
That I shal yeven hire suffisant answere,
And alle wommen after, for hir sake;
That, though they be in any gilt ytake,   ytake: taken, caught.
With face bold they shul hemself excuse,   bold: brazen.
And bere hem doun that wolde hem accuse.   2270
For lak of answere noon of hem shal dyen.
Al hadde man seyn a thyng with bothe his eyen,   seyn: seen.
Yit shal we wommen visage it hardily,   visage: face, confront. **hardily**: boldly.
And wepe, and swere, and chide subtilly,   subtilly: craftily.
So that ye men shul been as lewed as gees.   2275   lewed: foolish.
    What rekketh me of youre auctoritees?
I woot wel that this Jew, this Salomon,
Foond of us wommen fooles many oon.
But though that he ne foond no good womman,
Yet hath ther founde many another man   2280
Wommen ful trewe, ful goode, and vertuous.
Witnesse on hem that dwelle in Cristes hous;
With martirdom they preved hire constance.
The Romayn geestes eek make remembrance   Romayn geestes: Roman history.
Of many a verray, trewe wyf also.   2285
But, sire, ne be nat wrooth, al be it so,
Though that he seyde he foond no good
        womman,

2250. Jhesus, *filius Syrak:* the supposed author of Ecclesiasticus.
2252. a wilde fyr: such a disease of the skin and flesh as erysipelas or gangrene.
2257. lechour: lecher, grossly unchaste man (there may be a play on the word "lecher" meaning "healer"; it has further been pointed out that St. Damian was the patron saint of physicians).
2265. Proserpina's maternal grandfather was Saturn, who castrated and overthrew his father Uranus and thus brought the Golden Age.

I pray yow take the sentence of the man; sentence: meaning.
He mente thus, that in sovereyn bontee sovereyn bontee: perfect goodness.
Nis noon but God, but neither he ne she. 2290 he ne she: man nor woman.
  Ey! for verray God, that nys but oon,
What make ye so muche of Salomon?
What though he made a temple, Goddes hous?
What though he were riche and glorious?
So made he eek a temple of false goddis. 2295
How myghte he do a thyng that moore forbode forbode: forbidden.
    is?
Pardee, as faire as ye his name emplastre,
He was a lechour and an ydolastre, ydolastre: idolater.
And in his elde he verray God forsook; elde: old age.
And if God ne hadde, as seith the book, 2300
Yspared him for his fadres sake, he sholde
Have lost his regne rather than he wolde. regne: kingdom. rather: sooner.
I sette right noght, of al the vileynye
That ye of wommen write, a boterflye!
I am a womman, nedes moot I speke, 2305
Or elles swelle til myn herte breke.
For sithen he seyde that we been jangleresses, jangleresses: nagging chatterers.
As evere hool I mote brouke my tresses,
I shal nat spare, for no curteisye,
To speke hym harm that wolde us vileynye." 2310 hym harm: ill of him.
  "Dame," quod this Pluto, "be no lenger
    wrooth;
I yeve it up! but sith I swoor myn ooth
That I wolde graunten hym his sighte ageyn,
My word shal stonde, I warne yow certeyn.
I am a kyng, it sit me noght to lye." 2315 sit: befits.
  "And I," quod she, "a queene of Fayerye!
Hir answere shal she have, I undertake.
Lat us namoore wordes heerof make;
For sothe, I wol no lenger yow contrarie." contrarie: contradict.
  Now lat us turne agayn to Januarie, 2320
That in the gardyn with his faire May
Syngeth ful murier than the papejay, papejay: popinjay, parrot.
"Yow love I best, and shal, and oother noon."
So longe aboute the aleyes is he goon, aleyes: paths.
Til he was come agayns thilke pyrie 2325 agayns: in front of. pyrie: pear tree.
Where as this Damyan sitteth ful myrie
An heigh among the fresshe leves grene. an: on.
  This fresshe May, that is so bright and sheene, sheene: fair.
Gan for to syke, and seyde, "Allas, my syde! syke: sigh. syde: womb.
Now sire," quod she, "for aught that may
    bityde, 2330

2297. emplastre: apply a medicinal plaster to; whitewash, gloss over.
2300. the book: the Bible (see I Kings xi.12).
2308. As surely as I may keep (or enjoy) all my hair.

I moste han of the peres that I see,
Or I moot dye, so sore longeth me
To eten of the smale peres grene.
Help, for hir love that is of hevene queene!
I telle yow wel, a womman in my plit   2335   plit: plight, condition.
May han to fruyt so gret an appetit   to: for.
That she may dyen, but she of it have."
    "Allas!" quod he, "that I ne had here a knave
That koude clymbe! Allas, allas," quod he,
"For I am blynd!" "Ye, sire, no fors," quod
        she;   2340
"But wolde ye vouche sauf, for Goddes sake,
The pyrie inwith youre armes for to take,   inwith: within.
For wel I woot that ye mystruste me,
Thanne sholde I clymbe wel ynogh," quod she,
"So I my foot myghte sette upon youre
        bak."   2345
    "Certes," quod he, "theron shal be no lak,
Mighte I yow helpen with myn herte blood."
He stoupeth doun, and on his bak she stood,
And caughte hir by a twiste, and up she goth—   twiste: branch.
Ladyes, I prey yow that ye be nat wroth;   2350
I kan nat glose, I am a rude man—   glose: gloze, veil with specious com-
And sodeynly anon this Damyan   ments.
Gan pullen up the smok, and in he throng.   smok: undergarment. throng: thrust.
    And whan that Pluto saugh this grete wrong,
To Januarie he gaf agayn his sighte,   2355
And made hym see as wel as evere he myghte.
And whan that he hadde caught his sighte agayn,
Ne was ther nevere man of thyng so fayn,
But on his wyf his thoght was everemo.
Up to the tree he caste his eyen two,   2360
And saugh that Damyan his wyf had dressed   dressed: set in a position; treated.
In swich manere it may nat be expressed,
But if I wolde speke uncurteisly;   uncurteisly: rudely.
And up he yaf a roryng and a cry,
As dooth the moder whan the child shal dye: 2365
"Out! help! allas! harrow!" he gan to crye,
"O stronge lady stoore, what dostow?"   stronge: flagrantly guilty. stoore: crude.
    And she answerde, "Sire, what eyleth yow?
Have pacience and reson in youre mynde!
I have yow holpe on bothe youre eyen   holpe: healed, cured.
        blynde.   2370
Up peril of my soule, I shall nat lyen,
As me was taught, to heele with youre eyen,   to heele with youre eyen: to heal your
Was no thyng bet, to make yow to see,   eyes with.
Than strugle with a man upon a tree.
God woot, I dide it in ful good entente."   2375
    "Strugle!" quod he, "ye algate in it wente!   algate: altogether; or nevertheless.

God yeve yow bothe on shames deth to dyen!
He swyved thee, I saw it with myne eyen,
And elles be I hanged by the hals!"

on shames deth: a shameful death.
swyved: copulated with.
hals: neck.

"Thanne is," quod she, "my medicyne fals; 2380
For certeinly, if that ye myghte se,
Ye wolde nat seyn thise wordes unto me.
Ye han som glymsyng, and no parfit sighte."

fals: wrong.
seyn: say.
glymsyng: glimpsing.

"I se," quod he, "as wel as evere I myghte,
Thonked be God! with bothe myne eyen two, 2385
And by my trouthe, me thoughte he dide thee
     so."

"Ye maze, maze, goode sire," quod she;
"This thank have I for I have maad yow see.
Allas," quod she, "that evere I was so kynde!"

maze: are bewildered, stupefied.

"Now, dame," quod he, "lat al passe out of
     mynde.   2390
Com doun, my lief, and if I have myssayd,
God help me so, as I am yvele apayd.
But, by my fader soule, I wende have seyn
How that this Damyan hadde by thee leyn,
And that thy smok hadde leyn upon his
     brest."   2395

lief: dear.
yvele apayd: resentful.
wende have seyn: thought to have
  seen.

"Ye, sire," quod she, "ye may wene as yow
     lest.
But, sire, a man that waketh out of his sleep,
He may nat sodeynly wel taken keep
Upon a thyng, ne seen it parfitly,
Til that he be adawed verraily.   2400
Right so a man that longe hath blynd ybe,
Ne may nat sodeynly so wel yse,
First whan his sighte is newe come ageyn,
As he that hath a day or two yseyn.
Til that youre sighte ysatled be a while,   2405
Ther may ful many a sighte yow bigile.
Beth war, I prey yow; for, by hevene kyng,
Ful many a man weneth to se a thyng,
And it is al another than it semeth.
He that mysconceyveth, he mysdemeth."   2410
And with that word she leep doun fro the tree.

adawed: aroused, awakened.
ybe: been.
yse: see.
newe: newly.
yseyn: seen.
ysatled: settled.
leep: leaped.

This Januarie, who is glad but he?
He kisseth hire, and clippeth hire ful ofte,
And on hir wombe he stroketh hire ful softe,
And to his palays hom he hath hire lad.   2415
Now, goode men, I pray yow to be glad.
Thus endeth here my tale of Januarie;
God blesse us, and his moder Seinte Marie!

clippeth: embraces.

Heere is ended the Marchantes
tale of Januarie.

The prologe of the Squieres tale.

"Ey! Goddes mercy!" seyde oure Hooste tho,
"Now swich a wyf I pray God kepe me fro!   2420
Lo, whiche sleightes and subtilitees   whiche: what. **sleightes**: tricks.
In wommen been! for ay as bisy as bees
Been they, us sely men for to deceyve,   sely: innocent; simple; foolish;
And from a sooth evere wol they weyve;   wretched. weyve: turn aside.
By this Marchauntes tale it preveth weel.   2425 preveth: i.e., is proved.
But doutelees, as trewe as any steel
I have a wyf, though that she povre be,
But of hir tonge a labbyng shrewe is she,   labbyng: blabbing, babbling.
And yet she hath an heep of vices mo;
Therof no fors! lat alle swiche thynges go.   2430
But wyte ye what? In conseil be it seyd.   in conseil: in confidence.
Me reweth soore I am unto hire teyd.   me reweth: I am sorry.
For, and I sholde rekenen every vice   and: if.
Which that she hath, ywis I were to nyce;   nyce: foolish; scrupulous.
And cause why, it sholde reported be   2435
And toold to hire of somme of this meynee,—   of: by. meynee: company.
Of whom, it nedeth nat for to declare,
Syn wommen konnen outen swich chaffare;   konnen: know how to. outen: set
And eek my wit suffiseth nat therto,   forth; offer; utter. chaffare: wares;
To tellen al, wherfore my tale is do.   2440 matter.
Squier, com neer, if it youre wille be,
And sey somwhat of love; for certes ye
Konnen theron as muche as any man."   konnen: know.
    "Nay, sire," quod he, "but I wol seye as I kan
With hertly wyl; for I wol nat rebelle   5
Agayn youre lust; a tale wol I telle.
Have me excused if I speke amys;
My wyl is good, and lo, my tale is this."

Heere bigynneth the
Squieres tale.

    At Sarray, in the land of Tartarye,
Ther dwelte a kyng that werreyed Russye,   10 werreyed: warred against.
Thurgh which ther deyde many a doughty man.

---

the Squieres tale. In this unfinished tale, laid on the bank of the Volga, certain phrases, terms, and names suggest that Chaucer was attempting a sort of science fiction at a time when no sharp boundary separated experimental science and magic. He had been reading of marvelous travels in the East and very likely a French redaction of an oriental romance involving the gift of a flying horse of ebony, and he seems to have learned a few facts concerning the Mongols of Sarai—perhaps from shipmen who frequented the Wool Quay on the Thames when he served as Controller in the Port of London.

9. Sarray: Sarai, on the lower Volga, capital of the Khanate of the Kipchak Mongols of the Golden Horde.

This noble kyng was cleped Cambyuskan,
Which in his tyme was of so greet renoun
That ther was nowher in no regioun
So excellent a lord in alle thyng: 15
Hym lakked noght that longed to a kyng.   longed: was appropriate to.
As of the secte of which that he was born
He kepte his lay, to which that he was sworn;   lay: faith; creed; religious law.
And therto he was hardy, wys, and riche,   therto: besides.
And pitous and just, alwey yliche;   20 alwey yliche: unceasingly, constantly.
Sooth of his word, benigne, and honurable;
Of his corage as any centre stable;   corage: disposition, temperament.
Yong, fressh, and strong; in armes desirous   desirous: eager, keen.
As any bacheler of al his hous.   bacheler: knight.
A fair persone he was and fortunat,   25
And kepte alwey so wel roial estat   estat: ceremonial splendor.
That ther was nowher swich another man.
    This noble kyng, this Tartre Cambyuskan,
Hadde two sones on Elpheta his wyf,
Of whiche the eldeste highte Algarsyf,   30
That oother sone was cleped Cambalo.
A doghter hadde this worthy kyng also,
That yongest was, and highte Canacee.
But for to telle yow al hir beautee,
It lyth nat in my tonge, n'yn my konnyng;   35 konnyng: knowledge.
I dar nat undertake so heigh a thyng.
Myn Englissh eek is insufficient.
It moste been a rethor excellent,   rethor: rhetorician.
That koude his colours longynge for that art,   koude: knew. longynge for: belonging
If he sholde hire discryven every part.   40   to. discryven: describe.
I am noon swich, I moot speke as I kan.
    And so bifel that whan this Cambyuskan
Hath twenty wynter born his diademe,
As he was wont fro yeer to yeer, I deme,
He leet the feeste of his nativitee   45 leet doon cryen: caused to be pro-
Doon cryen thurghout Sarray his citee,   claimed.
The laste Idus of March, after the yeer.
Phebus the sonne ful joly was and cleer;   joly: gay; brilliant.
For he was ny his exaltacioun
In Martes face, and in his mansioun   50

---

12. Cambyuskan: presumably the same name as Genghis Khan (Latin, Camius Khan). Genghis Khan (1162–1227), who founded the Mongol Empire, remained in the East; however, his grandson Batu Khan and later descendants held court at **Sarray**, and **werreyed Russye.**

17. secte: The Kipchak Mongols of the Golden Horde were converted to Islam after 1340.

22. centre: the fixed center about which circles or spheres revolve.

39. colours: stylistic figures or embellishments.

47. the laste Idus of March: March 15, when the sun was in the fourth degree of Aries. The zodiacal sign Aries was the exaltation (l. 49; position of greatest influence) of the Sun. Aries was also the mansion (l. 50) of Mars, the first face (degrees 1 to 10) being known as the face of Mars. after the yeer: according to the year's course.

In Aries, the colerik hote signe.
Ful lusty was the weder and benigne,
For which the foweles, agayn the sonne sheene,   **agayn:** in. **sheene:** bright.
What for the sesoun and the yonge grene,
Ful loude songen hire affeccions.   55
Hem semed han geten hem proteccions
Agayn the swerd of wynter, keene and cold.   **swerd:** sword.
   This Cambyuskan, of which I have yow told,
In roial vestiment sit on his deys,   **sit:** (sitteth) sits. **deys:** dais.
With diademe, ful hye in his paleys,   60
And halt his feeste so solempne and so riche   **halt:** holds.
That in this world ne was ther noon it liche;   **it liche:** like it.
Of which if I shal tellen al th'array,   **array:** festivities.
Thanne wolde it occupie a someres day;
And eek it nedeth nat for to devyse   65
At every cours the ordre of hire servyse.
I wol nat tellen of hir strange sewes,   **sewes:** broths; seasoned dishes.
Ne of hir swannes, ne of hire heronsewes.   **heronsewes:** hernshaws, young
Eek in that land, as tellen knyghtes olde,   herons.
Ther is som mete that is ful deyntee holde,   70 **holde:** held, considered.
That in this land men recche of it but smal;   **recche:** care. **smal:** slightly.
Ther nys no man that may reporten al.
I wol nat taryen yow, for it is pryme,   **taryen:** delay.
And for it is no fruyt, but los of tyme;   **fruyt:** profit.
Unto my firste I wol have my recours.   75 **my firste:** my original matter. **wol have**
   And so bifel that after the thridde cours,   **my recours:** will return.
Whil that this kyng sit thus in his nobleye,   **nobleye:** nobility, splendor.
Herknynge his mynstrals hir thynges pleye
Biforn hym at the bord deliciously,   **bord:** table. **deliciously:** delightfully.
In at the halle dore al sodeynly   80
Ther cam a knyght upon a steede of bras,
And in his hand a brood mirour of glas.   **brood:** broad.
Upon his thombe he hadde of gold a ryng.
And by his syde a naked swerd hangyng;
And up he rideth to the heighe bord.   85
In al the halle ne was ther spoke a word
For merveille of this knyght; hym to biholde
Ful bisily they wayten, yonge and olde.   **wayten:** watch.
   This strange knyght, that cam thus sodeynly,
Al armed, save his heed, ful richely,   90
Salueth kyng and queene and lordes alle,   **salueth:** greets.
By ordre, as they seten in the halle,   **seten:** sat.
With so heigh reverence and obeisaunce,
As wel in speche as in contenaunce,
That Gawayn, with his olde curteisye,   95
Though he were come agayn out of Fairye,

---

51. **colerik:** favorable to the humor choler in living beings, causing irascibility; rousing to passion.
96. **Fairye:** the land of supernatural or legendary creatures.

Ne koude hym nat amende with a word.
And after this, biforn the hye bord,
He with a manly voys seide his message,
After the forme used in his langage, 100
Withouten vice of silable or of lettre;
And, for his tale sholde seme the bettre,
Accordant to his wordes was his cheere,
As techeth art of speche hem that it leere.
Al be that I kan nat sowne his style, 105
Ne kan nat clymben over so heigh a style,
Yet seye I this, as to commune entente,
Thus muche amounteth al that evere he mente,
If it so be that I have it in mynde.
He seyde, "The kyng of Arabe and of Inde, 110
My lige lord, on this solempne day
Salueth yow, as he best kan and may,
And sendeth yow, in honour of youre feeste,
By me, that am al redy at youre heeste,
This steede of bras, that esily and weel 115
Kan in the space of o day naturel —
This is to seyn, in foure and twenty houres—
Wher-so yow list, in droghte or elles shoures,
Beren youre body into every place
To which youre herte wilneth for to pace; 120
Withouten wem of yow, thurgh foul or fair;
Or, if yow list to fleen as hye in the air
As dooth an egle whan hym list to soore,
This same steede shal bere yow everemoore,
Withouten harm, til ye be ther yow leste, 125
Though that ye slepen on his bak or reste,
And turne agayn with writhyng of a pyn.
He that it wroghte koude many a gyn.
He wayted many a constellacion
Er he had doon this operacion, 130
And knew ful many a seel and many a bond.
This mirour eek, that I have in myn hond,
Hath swich a myght that men may in it see
Whan ther shal fallen any adversitee
Unto youre regne or to yourself also, 135
And openly who is youre freend or fo.
And over al this, if any lady bright

amende: improve upon.

forme: established procedure.
vice: fault, imperfection.
for: in order that.
accordant: conforming.
leere: learn.
sowne: imitate in sound.
style: stile.
commune entente: general purport.

solempne: important.
salueth: salutes, greets.

heeste: command.

beren: carry.

wem: hurt, injury.
fleen: fly.
soore: soar.
everemoore: each time, always.

turne: return. writhyng: twisting.
koude: knew. gyn: artifice.
wayted: watched. constellacion: configuration of planets.
seel: (magic) seal; artifice. bond: controlling force.

fallen: happen.
regne: kingdom.

110. In the Middle Ages there were at least three Indias: India Major, India Minor, and India Tertia. India Minor (or Middle India) consisted chiefly of southern Arabia. From 1252 to 1382 Arabia was under the Bahri Mamlūks at Cairo. The diplomatic relations between the Kipchak Mongols of the Golden Horde and the Bahri Mamlūks were steady, and flourished with the conversion of the former to Islam after 1340. We have records of the sending on various occasions of gifts as gold dinars, armor, horses, swords, precious stones, golden lamps, and two magical gifts. Thus the Squire's Tale is laid against a vivid, realistic historical background.
116. o day naturel: twenty-four hours (the artificial day is from sunrise to sunset; see Introduction to the Man of Law's Tale, line 2).

Hath set hir herte on any maner wight,
If he be fals, she shal his tresoun see,
His newe love, and al his subtiltee, 140
So openly that ther shal no thyng hyde.
Wherfore, agayn this lusty someres tyde,   agayn: in anticipation of. tyde: season.
This mirour and this ryng, that ye may see,
He hath sent to my lady Canacee,
Youre excellente doghter that is heere. 145
   The vertu of the ryng, if ye wol heere,
Is this, that if hir list it for to were   were: wear.
Upon hir thombe, or in hir purs it bere,
Ther is no fowel that fleeth under the hevene   fowel: bird. fleeth: flies.
That she ne shal wel understonde his stevene, 150   stevene: language.
And knowe his menyng openly and pleyn,   pleyn: fully.
And answere hym in his langage ageyn;
And every gras that groweth upon roote   gras: herb.
She shal eek knowe, and whom it wol do boote,   do boote: cure.
Al be his woundes never so depe and wyde. 155
   This naked swerd, that hangeth by my syde,
Swich vertu hath that, what man so ye smyte,   what man so: whomsoever.
Thurgh out his armure it wole kerve and byte,
Were it as thikke as is a branched ook;
And what man that is wounded with the   what man that: whomsoever.
       strook 160
Shal never be hool til that yow list, of grace,   hool: whole, well.
To stroke hym with the plat in thilke place   plat: flat surface.
Ther he is hurt; this is as muche to seyn,
Ye moote with the platte swerd ageyn   platte: flat (side of the).
Stroke hym in the wounde, and it wol close. 165
This is a verray sooth, withouten glose;   glose: deceit.
It failleth nat whiles it is in youre hold."
   And whan this knyght hath thus his tale toold,
He rideth out of halle, and doun he lighte.   lighte: alighted.
His steede, which that shoon as sonne brighte, 170
Stant in the court stille as any stoon.   stant: stands. court: courtyard.
This knyght is to his chambre lad anoon,   lad: led.
And is unarmed, and to mete yset.   mete: dinner.
   The presentes been ful roially yfet,—   yfet: fetched, brought.
This is to seyn, the swerd and the mirour, 175
And born anon into the heighe tour
With certein officers ordeyned therfore;   ordeyned: appointed.
And unto Canacee the ryng is bore   bore: carried.
Solempnely, ther she sit at the table.   sit: (sitteth) sits.
But sikerly, withouten any fable, 180
The hors of bras, that may nat be remewed,   remewed: removed.
It stant as it were to the ground yglewed.   yglewed: glued.
Ther may no man out of the place it dryve
For noon engyn of wyndas or polyve;   for: by means of.

184. wyndas: windlass. polyve: pulley.

And cause why? for they kan nat the craft.   185
And therfore in the place they han it laft,
Til that the knyght hath taught hem the manere
To voyden hym, as ye shal after heere.
    Greet was the prees that swarmeth to and fro
To gauren on this hors that stondeth so;   190
For it so heigh was, and so brood and long,
So wel proporcioned for to been strong,
Right as it were a steede of Lumbardye;
Therwith so horsly, and so quyk of eye,
As it a gentil Poilleys courser were.   195
For certes, fro his tayl unto his ere,
Nature ne art ne koude hym nat amende
In no degree, as al the peple wende.
But everemoore hir mooste wonder was
How that it koude go, and was of bras;   200
It was a fairye, as the peple semed.
Diverse folk diversely han demed;
As many heddes, as many wittes ther been.
They murmured as dooth a swarm of been,
And maden skiles after hir fantasies,   205
Rehersynge of thise olde poetries,
And seyden it was lyk the Pegasee,
The hors that hadde wynges for to flee;
Or elles it was the Grekes hors Synon,
That broghte Troye to destruccion,   210
As men in thise olde geestes rede.
"Myn herte," quod oon, "is everemoore in drede;
I trowe som men of armes been therinne,
That shapen hem this citee for to wynne.
It were right good that al swich thyng were
            knowe."   215
Another rowned to his felawe lowe,
And seyde, "He lyeth, for it is rather lyk
An apparence ymaad by som magyk,
As jogelours pleyen at thise feestes grete."
Of sondry doutes thus they jangle and trete,   220
As lewed peple demeth comunly
Of thynges that been maad moore subtilly
Than they kan in hir lewednesse comprehende;
They demen gladly to the badder ende.
    And somme of hem wondred on the mirour, 225

Glosses:

185 for: because. kan: know. craft: device, trick.

188 voyden: remove.

189 prees: press, crowd.

190 gauren on: stare at.

197 amende: improve upon.

198 in no degree: in no way.

201 a fairye: a supernatural contrivance.

203 wittes: opinions.

204 been: bees.

205 skiles: arguments.

208 flee: fly.

211 geestes: histories.

214 shapen hem: prepare themselves, plot.

216 rowned: whispered.

218 apparence: apparition or phantom.

219 jogelours: magicians.

220 jangle: chatter. trete: discuss.

221 lewed: ignorant. demeth: argue.

224 gladly: habitually.

---

195. **Poilleys:** Apulian. Lombardy and Apulia were celebrated for their horses.
201. **the peple semed:** it seemed to the people.
207. **the Pegasee:** Pegasus, a winged horse sprung from the blood of Medusa when Perseus cut off her head.
209. **the Grekes hors Synon:** the horse of Sinon the Greek; the Trojan horse.
224. **to the badder ende:** with the worse result, the wrong way.

That born was up unto the maister-tour.
How men myghte in it swiche thynges se.
    Another answerde, and seyde it myghte wel
        be
Naturelly, by composiciouns   composiciouns: combinations.
Of anglis and of slye reflexiouns,   230   slye: artfully contrived.
And seyde that in Rome was swich oon.
They speke of Alocen, and Vitulon,   speke: spoke.
And Aristotle, that writen in hir lyves   writen: wrote. in: during.
Of queynte mirours and of perspectives,   queynte: curious. perspectives: re-
As knowen they that han hir bookes herd.   235   fracting lenses.
    And oother folk han wondred on the swerd
That wolde percen thurghout every thyng,
And fille in speche of Thelophus the kyng,
And of Achilles for his queynte spere,   for: because of.
For he koude with it bothe heele and dere.   240   heele: heal. dere: injure.
Right in swich wise as men may with the swerd
Of which right now ye han yourselven herd.
They speke of sondry hardyng of metal,
And speke of medicynes therwithal,   medicynes: drugs. therwithal: (used)
And how and whanne it sholde yharded be,   245   besides.
Which is unknowe algates unto me.   algates: altogether.
    Tho speke they of Canacees ryng,
And seyden alle that swich a wonder thyng
Of craft of rynges herde they nevere non,
Save that he Moyses and kyng Salomon   250
Hadde a name of konnyng in swich art.   konnyng: cunning, skill.
Thus seyn the peple, and drawen hem apart.
But nathelees somme seiden that it was
Wonder to maken of fern-asshen glas,   fern-asshen: ashes of ferns.
And yet is glas nat lyk asshen of fern;   255
But, for they han knowen it so fern,   so fern: for so long a time.
Therfore cesseth hir janglyng and hir wonder.
As soore wondren somme on cause of thonder,   soore: sorely.
On ebbe, on flood, on gossomer, and on myst,
And alle thyng, til that the cause is wyst.   260

---

231. The Emperor Nero was reputed to have owned a marvelous mirror of emerald.

232. Alhazen (Alocen), the greatest of Arabic scientists, wrote a treatise on optics which was translated into Latin by the Polish physicist Witelo (Vitulon).

235. A clear reference to the medieval custom of having a book read aloud to a group.

238–39. Telephus, King of Mysia, was wounded by Achilles and then healed by rust from his spear.

243. sondry hardyng: sundry methods of hardening, tempering.

250. Moses was said to have made a Ring of Memory and a Ring of Oblivion. "Solomon's ring" has long been famous as enabling its wearer to understand the speech of birds. Further, Solomon is supposed to have imprisoned demons beneath the gems in rings.

259. on ebbe, on flood: on the ebb and flow of the sea. gossomer: gossamer; cobwebs floating in the air in calm clear weather.

Thus jangle they, and demen, and devyse,   **demen:** argue. **devyse:** discuss.
Til that the kyng gan fro the bord aryse.   **bord:** dinner table.
   Phebus hath laft the angle meridional,   I.e., it was past noon.
And yet ascendynge was the beest roial,
The gentil Leon, with his Aldiran,   265
Whan that this Tartre kyng, Cambyuskan,
Roos fro his bord, ther as he sat ful hye.
Biforn hym gooth the loude mynstralcye,
Til he cam to his chambre of parementz,   **chambre of parementz:** the Presence
There as ther sownen diverse instrumentz,   270   Chamber.
That it is lyk an hevene for to heere.
Now dauncen lusty Venus children deere,   **Venus children:** see page 270.
For in the Fissh hir lady sat ful hye,
And looketh on hem with a freendly eye.
   This noble kyng is set upon his trone.   275
This strange knyght is fet to hym ful soone,
And on the daunce he gooth with Canacee.   **fet:** brought.
Here is the revel and the jolitee
That is nat able a dul man to devyse.   **devyse:** describe.
He moste han knowen love and his servyse,   280 **his:** its. **servyse:** ritual.
And been a feestlych man as fressh as May,   **feestlych:** fond of festivity.
That sholde yow devysen swich array.
   Who koude telle yow the forme of daunces
So unkouthe, and swiche fresshe contenaunces,   **unkouthe:** strange.
Swich subtil lookyng and dissimulynges   285
For drede of jalous mennes aperceyvynges?
No man but Launcelot, and he is deed.
Therfore I passe of al this lustiheed;   **of:** from. **lustiheed:** merriment.
I sey namoore, but in this jolynesse
I lete hem, til men to the soper dresse.   290 **lete:** leave. **dresse:** turn their atten-
   The styward bit spices for to hye,   tion. **bit:** bids. **to hye:** to be brought
And eek the wyn, in al this melodye.   hastily.
The usshers and the squiers been ygon,
The spices and the wyn is come anon.
They ete and drynke; and whan this hadde an
       ende,   295
Unto the temple, as reson was, they wende.   **reson:** i.e., right, proper.
The service doon, they soupen al by day.   **al by day:** still by daylight.
What nedeth yow rehercen hire array?   **array:** festivities.
Ech man woot wel that a kynges feeste
Hath plentee to the meeste and to the leeste,   300 **to:** for.
And deyntees mo than been in my knowyng.
At after-soper gooth this noble kyng
To seen this hors of bras, with al a route   **route:** company.
Of lordes and of ladyes hym aboute.

---

265. **Leon:** the constellation Leo, in which was the star Aldiran.
273. **the Fissh:** Pisces, the sign of the zodiac in which the influence of Venus is greatest.

Swich wondryng was ther on this hors of
    bras   305
That syn the grete sege of Troye was,
Theras men wondreden on an hors also,
Ne was ther swich a wondryng as was tho.
But fynally the kyng axeth this knyght
The vertu of this courser and the myght,   310
And preyed hym to telle his governaunce.   his: its.
   This hors anon bigan to trippe and daunce,
Whan that this knyght leyde hand upon his
    reyne,
And seyde, "Sire, ther is namoore to seyne,
But, whan yow list to ryden anywhere,   315
Ye mooten trille a pyn, stant in his ere,   trille: turn. stant: (which) stands.
Which I shal yow telle bitwix us two.
Ye moote nempne hym to what place also,   nempne: tell.
Or to what contree, that yow list to ryde.
And whan ye come ther as yow list abyde,   320
Bid hym descende, and trille another pyn,
For therin lith th'effect of al the gyn,   effect: essential manner of working.
                                  gyn: contrivance.
And he wol doun descende and doon youre
    wille,
And in that place he wol abiden stille.
Though al the world the contrarie hadde
    yswore,   325 yswore: sworn.
He shal nat thennes be ydrawe nor ybore.   ydrawe: drawn. ybore: carried.
Or, if yow liste bidde hym thennes gon,
Trille this pyn, and he wol vanysshe anon
Out of the sighte of every maner wight,
And come agayn, be it day or nyght,   330
Whan that yow list to clepen hym ageyn
In swich a gyse as I shal to yow seyn   gyse: manner.
Bitwixe yow and me, and that ful soone.
Ride whan yow list, ther is namoore to doone."
   Enformed whan the kyng was of that   of: by.
    knyght   335
And hath conceyved in his wit aright
The manere and the forme of al this thyng,
Ful glad and blithe, this noble doughty kyng
Repeireth to his revel as biforn.
The brydel is unto the tour yborn   340
And kept among his jueles leeve and deere,   leeve: cherished.
The hors vanysshed, I noot in what manere,
Out of hir sighte; ye gete namoore of me.

The magic horse in *Méliacin: Méliacin* or *Le Cheval de Fust* (c. 2190) by Girart d'Amiens, is a
close analogue of the first part of the Squire's Tale. In it the third birthday gift for the king of
Great Armenia is a wooden horse—*cheval de fust*—a magic steed made of ebony. It is not
ridden into the banquet hall; instead the feasters go outside the palace to see it. Making a
demonstration, the donor climbs into the saddle, turns a peg, and rides into the air.

But thus I lete in lust and jolitee
This Cambyuskan his lordes festeyynge, 345
Til wel ny the day bigan to sprynge.

EXPLICIT PRIMA PARS.

lete: leave.

SEQUITUR PARS SECUNDA.

The norice of digestion, the sleep,
Gan on hem wynke and bad hem take keep
That muche drynk and labour wol have reste;
And with a galpyng mouth hem alle he keste, 350
And seyde that it was tyme to lye adoun,
For blood was in his domynacioun.
"Cherisseth blood, natures freend," quod he.
They thanken hym galpynge, by two, by three,
And every wight gan drawe hym to his reste, 355
As sleep hem bad; they tooke it for the beste.
    Hire dremes shul nat now been told for me;
Ful were hire hedes of fumositee,
That causeth dreem of which ther is no charge.
They slepen til that it was pryme large, 360
The mooste part, but it were Canacee.
She was ful mesurable, as wommen be;
For of hir fader hadde she take leve
To goon to reste soone after it was eve.
Hir liste nat appalled for to be, 365
Nor on the morwe unfeestlich for to se,
And slepte hir firste sleep, and thanne awook.
For swich a joye she in hir herte took
Bothe of hir queynte ryng and hir mirour,
That twenty tyme she changed hir colour; 370
And in hir sleep, right for impressioun
Of hir mirour, she hadde a visioun.
Wherfore, er that the sonne gan up glyde,
She cleped upon hir maistresse hir bisyde,
And seyde that hir liste for to ryse. 375
    Thise olde wommen that been gladly wyse,
As is hir maistresse, answerde hir anon,
And seyde, "Madame, whider wil ye gon

norice: nurse.

galpyng: yawning.

in his domynacioun: dominant.

for me: so far as I am concerned.

ther is no charge: it doesn't matter.
slepen: slept. pryme large: 9 A.M.
but: except.
mesurable: temperate.

appalled: faint, tired.
unfeestlich: unfestive, jaded. se: look.

maistresse: governess.

been gladly: would like to be thought.

---

352. On the humor blood, see note on General Prologue, l. 333. Blood was supposed to have domination over the body from midnight to 6 A.M.

358–59. On the fumes that arise from wine-drinking, see the Pardoner's Tale, l. 567; on the theory that dreams caused by fumes are of no significance, see the Nuns' Priest's Tale, ll. 2921–25.

371–72. for impressioun of: because of the effect produced by.

376–77. The intention of this confused construction is "Her governess, who would like to be thought wise, as old women usually do, answered at once. . . ."

Thus erly, for the folk been alle on reste?"   on: at.
  "I wol," quod she, "arise, for me leste   380
Ne lenger for to slepe, and walke aboute."
  Hir maistresse clepeth wommen a gret route,   route: company.
And up they rysen, wel a ten or twelve;
Up riseth fresshe Canacee hirselve,
As rody and bright as dooth the yonge sonne, 385
That in the Ram is foure degrees up ronne—
Noon hyer was he whan she redy was—
And forth she walketh esily a pas,   esily a pas: at an easy pace.
Arrayed after the lusty seson soote   after: appropriately to. soote: sweet.
Lightly, for to pleye and walke on foote,   390 lightly: gaily.
Nat but with fyve or sixe of hir meynee;   meynee: retinue.
And in a trench forth in the park goth she.   trench: an alley through the trees.
  The vapour which that fro the erthe glood   glood: glided.
Made the sonne to seme rody and brood;
But nathelees it was so fair a sighte   395
That it made al hire hertes for to lighte,
What for the seson and the morwenynge,
And for the foweles that she herde synge.
For right anon she wiste what they mente,
Right by hir song, and knew al hire entente. 400
  The knotte why that every tale is told,   knotte: point.
If it be taried til that lust be cold   taried: delayed. lust: interest (in the
Of hem that han it after herkned yoore,   story).
The savour passeth ever lenger the moore,
For fulsomnesse of his prolixitee;   405 his: its.
And by this same reson, thynketh me,
I sholde to the knotte condescende,   condescende: proceed.
And maken of hir walkyng soone an ende.
  Amydde a tree, for drye as whit as chalk,   for drye: on account of dryness.
As Canacee was pleyyng in hir walk,   410
Ther sat a faucon over hir heed ful hye,   faucon: falcon.
That with a pitous voys so gan to crye
That all the wode resouned of hir cry.
Ybeten hadde she hirself so pitously
With bothe hir wynges, til the rede blood   415
Ran endelong the tree ther-as she stood.   endelong: along the side of.
And evere in oon she cryde alwey and shrighte,   evere in oon: continually. shrighte:
And with hir beek hirselven so she prighte,   shrieked. prighte: pricked.
That ther nys tygre, ne noon so cruel beest,
That dwelleth outher in wode or in forest,   420
That nolde han wept, if that he wepe koude,
For sorwe of hire, she shrighte alwey so loude.

---

385. yonge: because its annual course had recently started with the vernal equinox in the zodiacal
sign of Aries, the Ram, about March 12; see footnote for line 7 of the General Prologue.
386. It was about a quarter past six.
403. it after herkned: listened in order to hear it. yoore: for a long time.

For ther nas nevere yet no man on lyve,   on lyve: alive.
If that I koude a faucon wel discryve,   discryve: describe.
That herde of swich another of fairnesse,   425
As wel of plumage as of gentillesse   gentillesse: beauty.
Of shap, of al that myghte yrekened be.   yrekened: taken into account.
A faucon peregryn thanne semed she
Of fremde land; and everemoore, as she stood,   fremde: foreign, remote.
She swowned now and now for lak of blood,   430 now and now: now and again.
Til wel neigh is she fallen fro the tree.
   This faire kynges doghter, Canacee,
That on hir fynger baar the queynte ryng,   queynte: ingeniously contrived.
Thurgh which she understood wel every thyng   wel: indeed.
That any fowel may in his ledene sayn,   435 ledene: language.
And koude answere hym in his ledene agayn,
Hath understonde what this faucon seyde,
And wel neigh for the routhe almoost she deyde.
And to the tree she gooth ful hastily,
And on this faukon looketh pitously,   440
And heeld hir lappe abrood, for wel she wiste   abrood: wide, open.
The faukon moste fallen fro the twiste,   twiste: branch.
Whan that it swowned next, for lak of blood.
A longe while to wayten hir she stood,   wayten: watch.
Til at the laste she spak in this manere   445
Unto the hauk, as ye shal after heere:
   "What is the cause, if it be for to telle,
That ye be in this furial pyne of helle?"   furial: furious, fierce. pyne: torment.
Quod Canacee unto this hauk above.
"Is this for sorwe of deeth or los of love?   450
For, as I trowe, thise been causes two
That causen moost a gentil herte wo;
Of oother harm it nedeth nat to speke.
For ye yourself upon yourself yow wreke,   wreke: avenge.
Which proveth wel that outher ire or drede 455
Moot been encheson of youre cruel dede,   encheson: cause.
Syn that I see noon oother wight yow chace.   chace: pursue.
For love of God, as dooth youreselven grace,   as dooth: do (imperative). grace:
Or what may been youre help? for west nor est   favor.
Ne saw I nevere er now no bryd ne beest   460 bryd: bird.
That ferde with hymself so pitously.   ferde with hymself: behaved, acted.
Ye sle me with youre sorwe verraily,
I have of yow so greet compassioun.
For Goddes love, com fro the tree adoun;
And as I am a kynges doghter trewe,   465
If that I verraily the cause knewe
Of youre disese, if it lay in my myght,   disese: distress.
I wolde amende it er that it were nyght,   amende: relieve.

---

428. faucon peregryn: a species of falcon esteemed for hawking.
432. faire kynges doghter: king's fair daughter.

As wisly helpe me grete God of kynde!   wisly: surely. kynde: nature.
And herbes shal I right ynowe fynde   470
To heele with youre hurtes hastily."
    Tho shrighte this faucon yet moore pitously
Than ever she dide, and fil to ground anon,
And lith aswowne, deed and lik a ston,   lith: (lieth) lies. aswowne: in a swoon.
Til Canacee hath in hir lappe hir take   475
Unto the tyme she gan of swough awake.   of swough: from swoon.
And after that she of swough gan abreyde,   after that: after. gan abreyde: awoke.
Right in hir haukes ledene thus she seyde: ledene: language.
"That pitee renneth soone in gentil herte,
Feelynge his similitude in peynes smerte,   480 his similitude: its counterpart.
Is preved al day, as men may it see,   al day: all the time.
As wel by werk as by auctoritee;   werk: action.
For gentil herte kitheth gentillesse.   kitheth: shows.
I se wel that ye han of my distresse
Compassion, my faire Canacee,   485
Of verray wommanly benignytee   of: because of; from.
That Nature in youre principles hath set.   principles: innate disposition.
But for noon hope for to fare the bet,
But for to obeye unto youre herte free,   free: kind, noble.
And for to maken othere be war by me,   490
As by the whelp chasted is the leon,
Right for that cause and that conclusion,
Whil that I have a leyser and a space,   a leyser: leisure.
Myn harm I wol confessen er I pace."   harm: suffering. confessen: reveal.
    And evere, whil that oon hir sorwe tolde,   495
That oother weep as she to water wolde,
Til that the faucon bad hire to be stille,
And, with a syk, right thus she seyde hir wille: syk: sigh.
    "Ther I was bred—allas, that ilke day!—
And fostred in a roche of marbul gray   500 roche: rock.
So tendrely that no thyng eyled me,   eyled: troubled.
I nyste nat what was adversitee,
Til I koude flee ful hye under the sky.   flee: fly.
Tho dwelte a tercelet me faste by,   tercelet: male peregrine falcon.
That semed welle of alle gentillesse;   505 welle: source.
Al were he ful of treson and falsnesse,
It was so wrapped under humble cheere,
And under hewe of trouthe in swich manere,
Under plesance, and under bisy peyne,   bisy: solicitous. peyne: endeavor.
That no wight koude han wend he koude
      feyne,   510 feyne: feign.
So depe in greyn he dyed his coloures.   in greyn: in a fast color.

---

471. To heal your wounds with promptly.
491. chasted: disciplined (i.e., when the dog is beaten instead of the lion).
496. That other wept as if she would turn to water.
500. roche of marbul gray perhaps signifies a palace.

Right as a serpent hit hym under floures   hit: (hideth) hides.
Til he may se his tyme for to byte,
Right so this god of loves ypocrite
Dooth so his cerymonyes and obeisaunces,   515   obeisaunces: acts of deference.
And kepeth in semblaunt alle his observaunces   semblaunt: semblance.
That sownen into gentillesse of love.   sownen into: are consonant with.
As in a toumbe is al the faire above,   faire: beauty.
And under is the corps, swich as ye woot,
Swich was this ypocrite, bothe coold and hoot. 520
And in this wise he served his entente,   entente: design.
That, save the feend, noon wiste what he mente,
Til he so longe hadde wopen and compleyned,   wopen: wept.
And many a yeer his service to me feyned,
Til that myn herte, to pitous and to nyce,   525   to: too. nyce: foolish.
Al innocent of his crowned malice,   crowned: sovereign, consummate.
Forfered of his deeth, as thoughte me,   forfered: very much afraid.
Upon his othes and his seuretee,
Graunted hym love, upon this condicioun,
That everemoore myn honour and renoun   530
Were saved, bothe privee and apert;   privee: secretly. apert: openly.
This is to seyn, that after his desert,
I yaf hym al myn herte and my thoght—
God woot and he, that ootherwise noght—   ootherwise noght: not on other terms.
And took his herte in chaunge of myn for ay.   535   chaunge: exchange.
But sooth is seyd, goon sithen many a day,   goon . . . . day: many days ago.
'A trewe wight and a theef thenken nat oon.'
And whan he saw the thyng so fer ygon
That I hadde graunted hym fully my love,
In swich a gyse as I have seyd above,   540   gyse: manner.
And yeven hym my trewe herte as free   free: liberally.
As he swoor he yaf his herte to me;
Anon this tigre, ful of doublenesse,   doublenesse: deceitfulness.
Fil on his knees with so devout humblesse,
With so heigh reverence, and, as by his cheere, 545
So lyk a gentil lovere of manere,   of: in.
So ravysshed, as it semed, for the joye,
That nevere Jason ne Parys of Troye—
Jason? certes, ne noon oother man
Syn Lameth was, that alderfirst bigan   550   alderfirst: first of all.
To loven two, as writen folk biforn—   writen: wrote.
Ne nevere, syn the firste man was born,
Ne koude man, by twenty thousand part,   man: one.
Countrefete the sophymes of his art,   sophymes: tricks of logic; deceits.
Ne were worthy unbokele his galoche,   555   galoche: shoe.

---

514. Right so this hypocrite of the god of love.
527. Fearful lest he should die, as it seemed to me.
537. An honest man and a thief do not think one and the same thing.
550. Lameth: Lamek; see Genesis iv.19–23.

Ther doublenesse or feynyng sholde approche, approche: be involved.
Ne so koude thanke a wight as he did me!
His manere was an hevene for to see
Til any womman, were she never so wys, til: to.
So peynted he and kembde at point-devys 560 kembde: combed. at point-devys: to
As wel his wordes as his contenaunce. perfection.
And I so loved hym for his obeisaunce,
And for the trouthe I demed in his herte,
That if so were that any thyng hym smerte, smerte: grieved.
Al were it never so lite, and I it wiste, 565
Me thoughte I felte deeth myn herte twiste. twiste: torment.
And shortly, so ferforth this thyng is went, so ferforth: so far.
That my wyl was his willes instrument;
This is to seyn, my wyl obeyed his wyl
In alle thyng, as fer as reson fil, 570 fil: was concerned.
Kepynge the boundes of my worship evere. worship: honor.
Ne nevere hadde I thyng so lief, ne levere, lief, ne levere: dear, nor dearer.
As hym, God woot! ne nevere shal namo.

 This laste lenger than a yeer or two, laste: lasted.
That I supposed of hym noght but good. 575
But finally, thus at the laste it stood,
That Fortune wolde that he moste twynne twynne: depart.
Out of that place which that I was inne.
Wher me was wo, that is no questioun; wher: whether.
I kan nat make of it discripcioun; 580
For o thyng dar I tellen boldely, boldely: with assurance.
I knowe what is the peyne of deeth therby;
Swich harm I felte for he ne myghte bileve. harm: grief, pain. for: because.
So on a day of me he took his leve, bileve: remain.
So sorwefully eek that I wende verraily 585
That he had felt as muche harm as I,
Whan that I herde hym speke, and saw his hewe.
But nathelees, I thoughte he was so trewe,
And eek that he repaire sholde agayn repaire: return.
Withinne a litel while, sooth to sayn; 590
And reson wolde eek that he moste go
For his honour, as ofte happeth so,
That I made vertu of necessitee,
And took it wel, syn that it moste be.
As I best myghte, I hidde from hym my sorwe, 595
And took hym by the hand, Seint John to borwe, Seint John to borwe: Saint John be
And seyde thus: 'Lo, I am youres al; protector.
Beth swich as I to yow have been and shal.'
What he answerde, it nedeth noght reherse;
Who kan sey bet than he, who kan do werse? 600
Whan he hath al wel seyd, thanne hath he doon.
'Therfore bihoveth hire a ful long spoon
That shal ete with a feend,' thus herde I seye.
So at the laste he moste forth his weye,

And forth he fleeth til he cam ther hym leste. 605   fleeth: flies.
Whan it cam hym to purpos for to reste,
I trowe he hadde thilke text in mynde,
That 'alle thyng, repeiryng to his kynde,   repeiryng: returning. **kynde**: nature.
Gladeth hymself'; thus seyn men, as I gesse.
Men loven of propre kynde newefangelnesse, 610
As briddes doon that men in cages fede.
For though thou nyght and day take of hem
      hede,   hede: care.
And strawe hir cage faire and softe as silk,   strawe: strew, cover the floor of.
And yeve hem sugre, hony, breed and milk,
Yet right anon as that his dore is uppe,   615   anon as that: as soon as.
He with his feet wol spurne doun his cuppe,
And to the wode he wole, and wormes ete;
So newefangel been they of hire mete,   mete: food.
And loven novelries of propre kynde;
No gentillesse of blood ne may hem bynde.   620   bynde: dominate.
   So ferde this tercelet, allas the day!   ferde: behaved.
Though he were gentil born, and fressh and gay,
And goodlich for to seen, and humble and free,
He saw upon a tyme a kyte flee,   kyte: kite, a small bird of prey of the
And sodeynly he loved this kyte so   625   hawk family. flee: fly.
That al his love is clene fro me ago;   ago: gone.
And hath his trouthe falsed in this wise.   trouthe: promise.
Thus hath the kyte my love in hir servyse,
And I am lorn withouten remedye!"   lorn: lost.
And with that word this faucon gan to crye, 630
And swowned eft in Canacees barm.   eft: again. **barm**: lap.
   Greet was the sorwe for the haukes harm   harm: suffering.
That Canacee and alle hir wommen made;
They nyste how they myghte the faucon glade.
But Canacee hom bereth hire in hir lappe,   635
And softely in plastres gan hire wrappe,
Ther as she with hire beek hadde hurt hirselve.
Now kan nat Canacee but herbes delve
Out of the ground, and make salves newe
Of herbes preciouse and fyne of hewe,   640
To heelen with this hauk. Fro day to nyght   to . . . hauk: to heal this hawk with.
She dooth hire bisynesse and al hire myght,
And by hire beddes heed she made a mewe,   mewe: cage.
And covered it with veluettes blewe,   veluettes: velvets.
In signe of trouthe that is in wommen sene.   645   trouthe: loyalty.
And al withoute, the mewe is peynted grene,
In which were peynted alle thise false fowles,
As ben thise tidyves, tercelettes, and owles;   tidyves: some kind of bird, reputed to
Right for despit were peynted hem bisyde,   be inconstant.

---

610. **of propre kynde**: by their own natural inclination, by their very nature.
638. Now Canacee can only dig herbs.

Pyes, on hem for to crye and chyde. 650   pyes: magpies.
    Thus lete I Canacee hir hauk kepyng;   lete: leave. kepyng: taking care of.
I wol namoore as now speke of hir ryng,
Til it come eft to purpos for to seyn   eft: again.
How that this faucon gat hire love ageyn
Repentant, as the storie telleth us, 655
By mediacion of Cambalus,
The kynges sone, of which I yow tolde.
But hennesforth I wol my proces holde   proces: story.
To speke of aventures and of batailles,
That nevere yet was herd so grete mervailles. 660
    First wol I telle yow of Cambyuskan,
That in his tyme many a citee wan;
And after wol I speke of Algarsif,
How that he wan Theodora to his wif,
For whom ful ofte in greet peril he was, 665
Ne hadde he been holpen by the steede of bras;   holpen: helped.
And after wol I speke of Cambalo,
That faught in lystes with the bretheren two
For Canacee er that he myghte hire wynne.
And ther I left I wol ayeyn bigynne. 670

        EXPLICIT SECUNDA PARS.

        INCIPIT PARS TERCIA.

Appollo whirleth up his chaar so hye,
Till that the god Mercurius hous, the slye—

*Heere folwen the wordes
of the Frankeleyn to the
Squier, and the wordes
of the Hoost to the
Frankeleyn.*

  "In feith, Squier, thow hast thee wel yquit   yquit: acquitted.
And gentilly. I preise wel thy wit,"   gentilly: honorably; nobly. wit: judg-
Quod the Frankeleyn, "considerynge thy   ment.
    yowthe 675
So feelyngly thou spekest, sire, I allow the!   allow: laud, commend.
As to my doom, ther is noon that is heere   doom: judgment.
Of eloquence that shal be thy peere,

661–70. Chaucer seems to have had a plan for this unfinished tale.
671–72. It is about the middle of May.

If that thou lyve; God yeve thee good chaunce,   chaunce: luck.
And in vertu sende thee continuance!   680
For of thy speche I have greet deyntee.
I have a sone, and by the Trinitee,
I hadde levere than twenty pound worth lond,
Though it right now were fallen in myn hond,
He were a man of swich discrecioun   685
As that ye been! Fy on possessioun,
But if a man be vertuous withal!
I have my sone snybbed, and yet shal,   snybbed: chided, rebuked.
For he to vertu listeth nat entende;   entende: pay attention, give heed.
But for to pleye at dees, and to despende   690 dees: dice. despende: waste.
And lese al that he hath, is his usage.
And he hath levere talken with a page
Than to comune with any gentil wight
Where he myghte lerne gentillesse aright."   gentillesse: See Basic Glossary.
    "Straw for youre gentillesse!" quod oure
        Hoost.   695
"What, Frankeleyn! pardee, sire, wel thou woost
That ech of yow moot tellen atte leste
A tale or two, or breken his biheste."   biheste: promise.
    "That knowe I wel, sire," quod the Frankeleyn.
"I prey yow, haveth me nat in desdeyn,   700
Though to this man I speke a word or two."
    "Telle on thy tale withouten wordes mo."
    "Gladly, sire Hoost," quod he, "I wole obeye
Unto your wyl; now herkneth what I seye.
I wol yow nat contrarien in no wyse   705 contrarien: antagonize.
As fer as that my wittes wol suffyse.
I prey to God that it may plesen yow;
Thanne woot I wel that it is good ynow."

        Explicit.

        The prologe of the
        Frankeleyns tale.

    Thise olde gentil Britouns in hir dayes   Britouns: Bretons.
Of diverse aventures maden layes,   710 layes: short romances, intended to be
Rymeyed in hir firste Briton tonge;   sung. rymeyed: rimed. firste: orig-
Whiche layes with hir instrumentz they songe,   inal.
Or elles redden hem for hir plesaunce,
And oon of hem have I in remembraunce,
Which I shal seyn with good wyl as I kan.   715
    But, sires, by cause I am a burel man,   burel: coarse, lay, unlearned.

---

681. I take great pleasure in, have great admiration for, your speech.
683. twenty pound worth lond: land yielding income of twenty pounds a year.

At my bigynnyng first I yow biseche,
Have me excused of my rude speche.
I lerned nevere rethorik, certeyn;
Thyng that I speke, it moot be bare and pleyn. 720
I sleep nevere on the Mount of Parnaso,

sleep: slept. on . . . Parnaso: i.e., with the Muses. Scithero: Cicero.

Ne lerned Marcus Tullius Scithero.
Colours ne knowe I none, withouten drede,

colours: (of rhetoric); rhetorical orna-

But swiche colours as growen in the mede,

ments.

Or elles swiche as men dye or peynte. 725
Colours of rhethoryke been to queynte;

to: too. queynte: strange.

My spirit feeleth nat of swich matere.
But if yow list, my tale shul ye heere.

Heere bigynneth the Frankeleyns tale.

In Armorik, that called is Britayne,

Armorik: Armorica; Brittany.

Ther was a knyght that loved and dide his
payne   730

dide his payne: took pains, did his utmost.

To serve a lady in his beste wise;
And many a labour, many a gret emprise

emprise: chivalric enterprise; exploit.

He for his lady wroghte, er she were wonne.
For she was oon the faireste under sonne,
And eek ther to come of so heigh kynrede 735

kynrede: kindred, family.

That wel unnethes dorste this knyght, for drede,

unnethes: scarcely, hardly.

Telle hire his wo, his peyne, and his distresse.
But atte laste she, for his worthynesse,
And namely for his meke obeysaunce,

obeysaunce: deference, attentiveness.

Hath swich a pitee caught of his penaunce 740

penaunce: suffering.

That pryvely she fel of his accord

fel of his accord: came to agreement with him; consented.

To take hym for hir housbonde and hir lord,
Of swich lordshipe as men han over hir wyves.
And for to lede the moore in blisse hir lyves,
Of his fre wyl he swoor hire as a knyght   745
That nevere in al his lyf he, day ne nyght,
Ne sholde upon hym take no maistrye
Agayn hir wyl, ne kithe hire jalousye,

kithe: show, display.

But hire obeye, and folwe hir wyl in al,
As any lovere to his lady shal,   750
Save that the name of soveraynetee,
That wolde he have for shame of his degree.
    She thanked hym, and with ful gret humblesse

---

the Frankeleyns tale. The Franklin's Tale owes its bare plot to a story narrated in the course of Boccaccio's prose romance *Il Filocolo*, where the task is to provide in January a garden as blooming and fruitful as in May.

734. oon the faireste: one of the fairest.

752. for shame of his degree: out of regard for his rank, position.

She seyde, "Sire, sith of youre gentilesse
Ye profre me to have so large a reyne,   755
Ne wolde nevere God bitwix us tweyne,   ne wolde God: God forbid.
As in my gilt, were outher werre or stryf.   as in my gilt: because of my guilt.
Sire, I wol be youre humble trewe wyf;   outher: either.
Have heer my trouthe, til that myn herte breste."   trouthe: troth, pledge.
Thus been they bothe in quiete and in reste.   760
    For o thyng, sires, saufly dar I seye,   saufly: safely.
That freendes everich oother moot obeye,
If they wol longe holden compaignye.
Love wol nat been constreyned by maistrye.
Whan maistrie comth, the God of Love anon 765
Beteth his wynges, and farewel, he is gon!
Love is a thyng as any spirit free.
Wommen, of kynde, desiren libertee,   of kynde: by nature.
And nat to been constreyned as a thral;
And so doon men, if I sooth seyen shal.   770
Looke who that is moost pacient in love,   looke who that: whoever.
He is at his avantage al above.   at his avantage: in a favorable posi-
Pacience is an heigh vertu, certeyn,   tion. al above: over all others.
For it venquysseth, as thise clerkes seyn,
Thynges that rigour sholde nevere atteyne.   775
For every word men may nat chide or pleyne.   pleyne: complain.
Lerneth to suffre, or elles, so moot I gon,   so moot I gon: as I may (still retain
Ye shul it lerne, wher so ye wole or non;   the power to) walk. non: not.
For in this world, certeyn, ther no wight is
That he ne dooth or seith som tyme amys.   780
Ire, siknesse, or constellacioun,
Wyn, wo, or chaungyng of complexioun   wyn: joy.
Causeth ful ofte to doon amys or speken.
On every wrong a man may nat be wreken.   wreken: revenged.
After the tyme moste be temperaunce   785 after: according to.
To every wight that kan on governaunce.   kan on: knows about. governaunce:
And therfore hath this wise, worthy knyght,   self-discipline.
To lyve in ese, suffraunce hire bihight,   suffraunce: forbearance. bihight:
And she to hym ful wisly gan to swere   promised. wisly: seriously; surely.
That nevere sholde ther be defaute in here.   790 defaute: unfaithfulness.
    Here may men seen an humble, wys accord;   accord: agreement.
Thus hath she take hir servant and hir lord,—
Servant in love, and lord in mariage.
Thanne was he bothe in lordshipe and servage.   servage: service, servitude.
Servage? nay, but in lordshipe above,   795

---

755. so large a reyne: so extensive a sovereignty; or so free a rein.
762. That intimates must submit to each other.
781. constellacioun: configuration of planets; horoscope.
782. complexioun: temperament; combination of humors in the body (see General Prologue, note for l. 333).

Sith he hath bothe his lady and his love;
His lady, certes, and his wyf also,
The which that lawe of love acordeth to.   which: who. acordeth: consents.
And whan he was in this prosperitee,
Hom with his wyf he gooth to his contree,   800
Nat fer fro Pedmark, ther his dwellyng was,
Where as he lyveth in blisse and in solas.   solas: delight.

    Who koude telle, but he hadde wedded be,   but: unless.
The joye, the ese, and the prosperitee
That is bitwixe an housbonde and his wyf?   805
A yeer and moore lasted this blisful lyf,
Til that the knyght of which I speke of thus,
That of Kayrrud was cleped Arveragus,
Shoop hym to goon and dwelle a yeer or tweyne   shoop: prepared.
In Engelond, that cleped was eek Briteyne,   810
To seke in armes worshipe and honour;
For al his lust he sette in swich labour;
And dwelled there two yeer, the book seith thus.

    Now wol I stynten of this Arveragus,
And speken I wole of Dorigen his wyf,   815
That loveth hir housbonde as hir hertes lyf.
For his absence wepeth she and siketh,   siketh: sighs.
As doon thise noble wyves whan hem liketh.
She moorneth, waketh, wayleth, fasteth,
    pleyneth;
Desir of his presence hir so destreyneth   820 destreyneth: distresses, torments.
That al this wyde world she set at noght.
Hir freendes, whiche that knewe hir hevy
    thoght,
Conforten hire in al that ever they may.
They prechen hire, they telle hire nyght and day
That causelees she sleeth hirself, allas!   825 causelees: groundlessly.
And every confort possible in this cas
They doon to hire with al hir bisynesse,   hir: their. bisynesse: solicitude.
Al for to make hire leve hir hevynesse.   leve: leave. hir: her.

    By proces, as ye knowen everichoon,   proces: process of time.
Men may so longe graven in a stoon   830 graven in: engrave, carve.
Til som figure therinne emprented be.
So longe han they conforted hire, til she
Receyved hath, by hope and by resoun,
The emprentyng of hire consolacioun,
Thurgh which hir grete sorwe gan aswage;   835 gan aswage: was alleviated.
She may nat alwey duren in swich rage.   duren: continue. rage: violent grief.

    And eek Arveragus, in al this care,
Hath sent hire lettres hom of his welfare,

---

801. **Pedmark:** probably the Breton seaport Penmarch.
808. **Kayrrud:** the name of Arveragus' manor, meaning "Red House."

And that he wol come hastily agayn;
Or elles hadde this sorwe hir herte slayn.   840
    Hire freendes sawe hir sorwe gan to slake,
And preyde hire on knees, for Goddes sake,
To come and romen hire in compaignye,
Awey to dryve hir derke fantasye.
And finally she graunted that requeste,   845
For wel she saugh that it was for the beste.
    Now stood hir castel faste by the see,
And often with hire freendes walketh she,
Hir to disporte, upon the bank an heigh,
Where as she many a ship and barge seigh   850
Seillynge hir cours, where as hem liste go.
But thanne was that a parcel of hir wo,
For to hirself ful ofte, "Allas!" seith she,
"Is ther no ship, of so manye as I se,
Wol bryngen hom my lord? Thanne were myn
          herte   855
Al warisshed of his bittre peynes smerte."
    Another tyme there wolde she sitte and thynke,
And caste hir eyen dounward fro the brynke.
But whan she saugh the grisly rokkes blake,
For verray feere so wolde hir herte quake   860
That on hir feet she myghte hir noght sustene.
Thanne wolde she sitte adoun upon the grene,
And pitously into the see biholde,
And seyn right thus, with sorweful sikes colde:
    "Eterne God, that thurgh thy purveiaunce   865
Ledest the world by certein governaunce,
In ydel, as men seyn, ye no thyng make.
But, Lord, thise grisly feendly rokkes blake,
That semen rather a foul confusion
Of werk than any fair creacion   870
Of swich a parfit wys God and a stable,
Why han ye wroght this werk unresonable?
For by this werk, south, north, ne west, ne eest,
Ther nys yfostred man, ne bryd, ne beest;
It dooth no good, to my wit, but anoyeth.   875
Se ye nat, Lord, how mankynde it destroyeth?
An hundred thousand bodies of mankynde
Han rokkes slayn, al be they nat in mynde,
Which mankynde is so fair part of thy werk
That thou it madest lyk to thyn owene merk.   880
Thanne semed it ye hadde a greet chiertee
Toward mankynde; but how thanne may it be
That ye swiche meenes make, it to destroyen,
Whiche meenes do no good, but evere anoyen?
I woot wel clerkes wol seyn as hem leste,   885

---

agayn: back.

slake: diminish.

romen hire: roam about.

an heigh: on high.
barge: sailing vessel. seigh: saw.

parcel: part.

warisshed: cured. his: its.

sikes: sighs. colde: anguished.
purveiaunce: providence.

in ydel: without purpose.
feendly: fiendish.

stable: steadfast.

anoyeth: is harmful.

mynde: remembrance.

merk: image.
chiertee: love.

make: create.

By argumentz, that al is for the beste,
Though I ne kan the causes nat yknowe.
But thilke God that made wynd to blowe
As kepe my lord! this my conclusion.   as kepe: protect. this: this is.
To clerkes lete I al disputison.   890
But wolde God that alle thise rokkes blake
Were sonken into helle for his sake!
Thise rokkes sleen myn herte for the feere."
Thus wolde she seyn, with many a pitous teere.
    Hire freendes sawe that it was no disport   895   disport: diversion.
To romen by the see, but disconfort,
And shopen for to pleyen somwher elles.   shopen: arranged.
They leden hire by ryveres and by welles,   welles: springs.
And eek in othere places delitables;   delitables: delightful.
They dauncen, and they pleyen at ches and
        tables.   900   tables: backgammon.
    So on a day, right in the morwe-tyde,   morwe-tyde: morning.
Unto a gardyn that was ther bisyde,
In which that they hadde maad hir ordinaunce   ordinaunce: preparation.
Of vitaille and of oother purveiaunce,   vitaille: victuals. purveiaunce: provi-
They goon and pleye hem al the longe day.   905   sion.
And this was on the sixte morwe of May,
Which May hadde peynted with his softe shoures
This gardyn ful of leves and of floures;
And craft of mannes hand so curiously   curiously: exquisitely.
Arrayed hadde this gardyn, trewely,   910
That nevere was ther gardyn of swich prys,   prys: excellence.
But if it were the verray paradys.
The odour of floures and the fresshe sighte
Wolde han maked any herte lighte
That evere was born, but if to greet siknesse, 915   to: too.
Or to greet sorwe helde it in distresse;
So ful it was of beautee with plesaunce.
At after-dyner gonne they to daunce,
And synge also, save Dorigen allone,
Which made alwey hir compleint and hir
        mone,   920   mone: moan.
For she ne saugh hym on the daunce go
That was hir housbonde and hir love also.
But nathelees she moste a tyme abyde,
And with good hope lete hir sorwe slyde.   slyde: pass, go away.
    Upon this daunce, amonges othere men,   925
Daunced a squier bifore Dorigen,
That fressher was and jolyer of array,
As to my doom, than is the monthe of May.   doom: judgment.
He syngeth, daunceth, passyng any man   passyng: surpassing.
That is, or was, sith that the world bigan.   930
Therwith he was, if men sholde hym discryve,   discryve: describe.

Oon of the beste farynge man on lyve;
Yong, strong, right vertuous, and riche, and wys,
And wel biloved, and holden in gret prys.   prys: esteem.
And shortly, if the sothe I tellen shal,   935
Unwityng of this Dorigen at al,
This lusty squier, servant to Venus,
Which that ycleped was Aurelius,
Hadde loved hire best of any creature
Two yeer and moore, as was his aventure, 940 aventure: fortune.
But nevere dorste he tellen hire his grevance.
Withouten coppe he drank al his penance.   penance: suffering.
He was despeyred; no thyng dorste he seye,   despeyred: in despair.
Save in his songes somwhat wolde he wreye   wreye: betray, reveal.
His wo, as in a general compleynyng; 945
He seyde he lovede, and was biloved no thyng. no thyng: not at all.
Of swich matere made he many layes,
Songes, compleintes, roundels, virelayes,
How that he dorste nat his sorwe telle,
But langwissheth as a furye dooth in helle; 950
And dye he moste, he seyde, as dide Ekko
For Narcisus, that dorste nat telle hir wo.
In oother manere than ye heere me seye,
Ne dorste he nat to hire his wo biwreye,   biwreye: reveal.
Save that, paraventure, somtyme at daunces, 955
Ther yonge folk kepen hir observaunces,   kepen hir observaunces: maintain
It may wel be he looked on hir face   their courteous attentions.
In swich a wise as man that asketh grace; grace: mercy.
But nothyng wiste she of his entente.
Nathelees it happed, er they thennes wente, 960
By cause that he was hir neighebour,
And was a man of worship and honour,
And hadde yknowen hym of tyme yoore, hadde: (she) had. of tyme yoore: of
They fille in speche; and forth, moore and old.
     moore,
Unto his purpos drough Aurelius, 965 drough: drew.
And whan he saugh his tyme, he seyde thus:
  "Madame," quod he, "by God that this world
     made,
So that I wiste it myghte youre herte glade,
I wolde that day that youre Arveragus
Wente over the see, that I, Aurelius, 970
Hadde went ther nevere I sholde have come ther: there whence.
     agayn.
For wel I woot my servyce is in vayn;

---

932. oon . . . man: i.e., one man of the most handsome.
936. Altogether unbeknown to this Dorigen.
942. withouten coppe: with trouble; taking a beating; the hard way.
948. roundels, virelayes: kinds of short poems or songs with special rhyme schemes.

My gerdon is but brestyng of myn herte.   gerdon: reward.
Madame, reweth upon my peynes smerte;   reweth: have pity.
For with a word ye may me sleen or save.   975
Here at youre feet God wolde that I were grave!   grave: buried.
I ne have as now no leyser moore to seye;
Have mercy, sweete, or ye wol do me deye!"   do me: cause me to.
  She gan to looke upon Aurelius:
"Is this youre wyl," quod she, "and sey ye
      thus?   980
Nevere erst," quod she, "ne wiste I what ye   erst: before.
      mente.
But now, Aurelie, I knowe youre entente,
By thilke God that yaf me soule and lyf,
Ne shal I nevere been untrewe wyf
In word ne werk, as fer as I have wit;   985   wit: understanding.
I wol been his to whom that I am knyt.
Taak this for fynal answere as of me."
But after that in pley thus seyde she:
  "Aurelie," quod she, "by heighe God above,
Yet wolde I graunte yow to been youre love,   990   graunte: promise.
Syn I yow se so pitously complayne.
Looke what day that endelong Britayne   looke what: whatever. endelong:
Ye remoeve alle the rokkes, stoon by stoon,   lengthwise along.
That they ne lette ship ne boot to goon,—   lette: hinder.
I seye, whan ye han maad the coost so clene   995
Of rokkes that ther nys no stoon ysene,
Thanne wol I love yow best of any man,
Have heer my trouthe, in al that evere I kan.   998   trouthe: troth, pledge.
For wel I woot that it shal never bityde.   1001
Lat swiche folies out of youre herte slyde.
What deyntee sholde a man han in his lyf   deyntee: delight.
For to go love another mannes wyf,
That hath hir body whan so that hym liketh?"
  Aurelius ful ofte soore siketh;   1006   siketh: sighs.
"Is ther noon oother grace in yow?" quod
      he.   999
"No, by that Lord," quod she, "that maked
      me!"   1000
Wo was Aurelie whan that he this herde,   1007
And with a sorweful herte he thus answerde:
  "Madame," quod he, "this were an inpossible!
Thanne moot I dye of sodeyn deth horrible."   1010
And with that word he turned hym anon.   turned hym: turned away.
Tho coome hir othere freendes many oon,   coome: came.

1001–06. These lines are conventionally printed as indicated by the numbering and as written
in the majority of the MSS; but a few MSS give the more satisfactory order presented here. Evi-
dently the lines were placed in the margin of O' and inserted incorrectly by most scribes (see
Manly IV, 485–86, and lines 1541–44 below).

And in the aleyes romeden up and doun,   aleyes: paths.
And nothyng wiste of this conclusioun,
But sodeynly bigonne revel newe   1015
Til that the brighte sonne loste his hewe;
For th'orisonte hath reft the sonne his lyght,—
This is as muche to seye as it was nyght!—
And hoom they goon in joye and in solas,   solas: delight.
Save oonly wrecche Aurelius, allas!   1020 wrecche: wretched.
He to his hous is goon with sorweful herte.
He seeth he may nat from his deeth asterte;   asterte: escape.
Hym semed that he felte his herte colde.   colde: grow cold.
Up to the hevene his handes he gan holde,
And on his knowes bare he sette hym doun, 1025 knowes: knees.
And in his ravyng seyde his orisoun.   orisoun: prayer.
For verray wo out of his wit he breyde.   breyde: started.
He nyste what he spak, but thus he seyde;
With pitous herte his pleynt hath he bigonne
Unto the goddes, and first unto the sonne: 1030

   He seyde, "Appollo, god and governour
Of every plaunte, herbe, tree, and flour,
That yevest, after thy declinacion,
To ech of hem his tyme and his seson,
As thyn herberwe chaungeth lowe or heighe, 1035 herberwe: "house," position in the
Lord Phebus, cast thy merciable eighe   zodiac. eighe: eye.
On wrecche Aurelie, which that am but lorn. lorn: lost.
Lo, lord! my lady hath my deeth ysworn
Withoute gilt, but thy benignytee   withoute gilt: unjustly.
Upon my dedly herte have som pitee.   1040 dedly: dying.
For wel I woot, lord Phebus, if yow lest,
Ye may me helpen, save my lady, best.   save: except for.
Now voucheth sauf that I may yow devyse
How that I may been holpen and in what wyse. holpen: helped.

   Youre blisful suster, Lucina the sheene, 1045 sheene: beautiful, shining.
That of the see is chief goddesse and queene
(Though Neptunus have deitee in the see,   deitee: power of a god.
Yet emperesse aboven hym is she),
Ye knowen wel, lord, that right as hir desir
Is to be quyked and lighted of youre fyr, 1050 quyked: kindled. of: by.
For which she folweth yow ful bisily,
Right so the see desireth naturelly
To folwen hire, as she that is goddesse
Bothe in the see and ryvers moore and lesse. moore and lesse: great and small.
Wherfore, lord Phebus, this is my requeste— 1055

1017. For the horizon had taken away the sun's light. (Here Chaucer appears to feel that the earth turns.)
1027. For true woe he raved.
1033. **after thy declinacion:** according to your angular distance from the equinoctial.
1045. **Lucina:** a title of Diana, here signifying the moon.

Do this miracle, or do myn herte breste—
That now next at this opposicion
Which in the signe shal be of the Leon,
As preyeth hire so greet a flood to brynge   flood: flood tide.
That fyve fadme at the leeste it oversprynge 1060 fadme: fathom (six feet).
The hyeste rokke in Armorik Britayne;
And lat this flood endure yeres twayne.
Thanne certes to my lady may I seye,
'Holdeth youre heste, the rokkes been aweye.'   heste: promise.
    Lord Phebus, dooth this miracle for me.   1065
Prey hire she go no faster cours than ye;
I seye thus, preyeth your suster that she go
No faster cours than ye thise yeres two.
Thanne shal she been evene at the fulle alway,
And spryng flood laste bothe nyght and day. 1070
And but she vouche sauf in swich manere
To graunte me my sovereyn lady deere,
Prey hire to synken every rok adoun
Into hir owene dirke regioun
Under the ground, ther Pluto dwelleth inne, 1075 inne: within.
Or nevere mo shal I my lady wynne.
Thy temple in Delphos wol I barefoot seke.
Lord Phebus, se the teeris on my cheke,
And of my peyne have som compassioun."
And with that word in swowne he fil adoun, 1080
And longe tyme he lay forth in a traunce.
    His brother, which that knew of his penaunce, penaunce: suffering.
Up caughte hym, and to bedde he hath hym
            broght.
Dispeyred in this torment and this thoght   dispeyred: discouraged. thoght: anx-
Lete I this woful creature lye;   1085   iety, grief.
Chese he, for me, wher he wol lyve or dye.   for me: for all I care. wher: whether.
    Arveragus, with heele and greet honour,   heele: health, well-being.
As he that was of chivalrie the flour,   flour: flower.
Is comen hom, and othere worthy men.
O blisful artow now, thou Dorigen,   1090
That hast thy lusty housbonde in thyne armes,
The fresshe knyght, the worthy man of armes,   fresshe: vigorous.
That loveth thee as his owene hertes lyf.
No thyng list hym to been ymaginatyf,
If any wight hadde spoke, whil he was oute, 1095
To hire of love; he hadde of it no doute.   doute: apprehension, fear.
He noght entendeth to no swich matere,   entendeth: devotes himself.

1057. opposicion: i.e., the sun and the moon being opposite to each other as seen from the earth.
1070. spryng flood: the maximum high tide, which occurs shortly after the new and full moon.
1074–75. Diana was a triform goddess, being Luna, the Moon, in heaven, and Proserpina, queen of Pluto, in the lower world.
1094. He had no desire to be suspicious.

But daunceth, justeth, maketh hir good cheere;   **maketh hir good cheere**: treats her
And thus in joye and blisse I lete hem dwelle,   affectionately.
And of the sike Aurelius wol I telle.   1100 **sike**: sick.
    In langour and in torment furyus   **langour**: sickness.
Two yeer and moore lay wrecche Aurelius,   **wrecche**: wretched.
Er any foot he myghte on erthe gon;   **gon**: walk.
Ne confort in this tyme hadde he noon,
Save of his brother, which that was a clerk.   1105
He knew of al this wo and al this werk;   **werk**: trouble, affliction.
For to noon oother creature, certeyn,
Of this matere he dorste no word seyn.
Under his brest he baar it moore secree   **baar**: carried. **secree**: secretly.
Than evere dide Pamphilus for Galathee.   1110
His brest was hool, withoute for to sene,   **withoute**: outwardly.
But in his herte ay was the arwe kene.
And wel ye knowe that of a sursanure   **sursanure**: a wound healed only on the
In surgerye is perilous the cure,   surface. **cure**: treatment.
But men myghte touche the arwe, or come   **but**: unless.
    therby.   1115 **therby**: into possession of it.
His brother weep and wayled pryvely,   **weep**: wept.
Til at the laste hym fil in remembraunce,   **hym**: to him.
That whiles he was at Orliens in Fraunce,
As yonge clerkes, that been lykerous   **lykerous**: eager.
To reden artes that been curious,   1120 **reden**: study. **curious**: occult.
Seken in every halke and every herne   **halke**: nook. **herne**: corner.
Particuler sciences for to lerne—   **particuler**: special.
He hym remembred that, upon a day,
At Orliens in studie a book he say   **studie**: a study. **say**: saw.
Of magyk naturel, which his felawe,   1125 **felawe**: companion.
That was that tyme a bacheler of lawe,
Al were he ther to lerne another craft,
Hadde prively upon his desk ylaft;   **ylaft**: left.
Which book spak muchel of the operaciouns
Touchynge the eighte and twenty mansiouns 1130
That longen to the moone, and swich folye
As in oure dayes is nat worth a flye,—
For holy chirches feith in oure bileve   **bileve**: doctrine.
Ne suffreth noon illusioun us to greve.
And whan this book was in his
    remembraunce,   1135
Anon for joye his herte gan to daunce,
And to hymself he seyde pryvely:
"My brother shal be warisshed hastily;   **warisshed**: cured.

1110. *Pamphilus de Amore* is a twelfth-century amatory poem or comedy whose hero seduces Galatea. The figure of the weapon and wound (ll. 1111–13) comes from its opening lines.

1125. Natural magic, which was regarded as a legitimate science, consisted of practices based on astrology.

1130. The twenty-eight mansions, or stations, of the moon correspond to the twenty-eight days of a lunation.

For I am siker that ther be sciences
By whiche men make diverse apparences,   1140 apparences: apparitions.
Swiche as thise subtile tregetoures pleye.   tregetoures: magicians; mechanical
For ofte at feestes have I wel herd seye   artisans. pleye: practice, perform.
That tregetours, withinne an halle large,
Have maad come in a water and a barge,
And in the halle rowen up and doun.   1145
Somtyme hath semed come a grym leoun;
And somtyme floures sprynge as in a mede;   mede: meadow.
Somtyme a vyne, and grapes white and rede;
Somtyme a castel, al of lym and stoon;
And whan hem lyked, voyded it anon.   1150 voyded: removed.
Thus semed it to every mannes sighte.
    Now thanne conclude I thus, that if I myghte
At Orliens som old felawe yfynde
That hadde thise moones mansions in mynde,
Or oother magyk naturel above,   1155 above: in addition.
He sholde wel make my brother han his love.
For with an apparence a clerk may make,
To mannes sighte, that alle the rokkes blake
Of Britaigne weren yvoyded everichon,   yvoyded: removed.
And shippes by the brynke comen and gon,   1160
And in swich forme enduren a wyke or two.   wyke: week.
Thanne were my brother warisshed of his wo;
Thanne moste she nedes holden hir biheste,   biheste: promise.
Or elles he shal shame hire at the leeste."
    What sholde I make a lenger tale of this? 1165 what: why.
Unto his brotheres bed he comen is,
And swich confort he yaf hym for to gon   confort: encouragement.
To Orliens that he up stirte anon,   stirte: started.
And on his wey forthward thanne is he fare   fare: gone.
In hope for to been lissed of his care.   1170 lissed: relieved.
    Whan they were come almoost to that citee,
But if it were a two furlong or thre,   furlong: an eighth of a mile.
A yong clerk romyng by hymself they mette,
Which that in Latyn thriftily hem grette,   thriftily: suitably. grette: greeted.
And after that he seyde a wonder thyng: 1175
"I knowe," quod he, "the cause of youre
          comyng."
And er they ferther any foote wente,
He tolde hem al that was in hire entente.   entente: mind.
    This Briton clerk hym asked of felawes
The whiche that he had knowe in olde dawes, 1180 dawes: days.
And he answerde hym that they dede were,
For which he weep ful ofte many a teere.   weep: wept.
    Doun of his hors Aurelius lighte anon,   of: off. lighte: alighted.

1142–51. Laura Loomis pointed out that the appearance and disappearance of water, barge, and castle match the great dramatic entertainment staged for King Charles V at a feast in Paris in 1378.

And with this magicien forth is he gon
Hom to his hous, and maden hem wel at ese. 1185
Hem lakked no vitaille that myghte hem plese.   vitaille: provisions.
So wel arrayed hous as ther was oon
Aurelius in his lyf saw nevere noon.
   He shewed hym, er he wente to sopeer,   sopeer: supper.
Forestes, parkes ful of wilde deer;   1190
Ther saw he hertes with hir hornes hye,
The gretteste that evere were seyn with eye.
He saw of hem an hundred slayn with houndes,
And somme with arwes blede of bittre woundes.
He saw, whan voyded were thise wilde deer, 1195   voyded: removed.
Thise fauconers upon a fair ryver,   ryver: hawking ground.
That with hir haukes han the heron slayn.
   Tho saugh he knyghtes justyng in a playn;   tho: then.
And after this he dide hym swich plesaunce
That he hym shewed his lady on a daunce,   1200
On which hymself he daunced, as hym
      thoughte.
And whan this maister that this magyk wroughte
Saugh it was tyme, he clapte his handes two,
And farewel! al oure revel was ago.   revel: sport. ago: gone.
And yet remoeved they nevere out of the   remoeved: moved.
      hous,   1205
Whil they saugh al this sighte merveillous,
But in his studie, ther as his bookes be,
They seten stille, and no wight but they thre.   seten: sat.
   To hym this maister called his squier,
And seyde hym thus: "Is redy oure soper?   1210
Almoost an houre it is, I undertake,
Sith I yow bad oure soper for to make,
Whan that thise worthy men wenten with me
Into my studie, ther as my bookes be."
   "Sire," quod this squier, "whan it liketh
      yow,   1215
It is al redy, though ye wol right now."
"Go we thanne soupe," quod he, "as for the beste.   soupe: sup.
This amorous folk somtyme moote han hir
      reste."
   At after-soper fille they in tretee   tretee: discussion; negotiation.
What somme sholde this maistres gerdon be, 1220   gerdon: recompense.
To remoeven alle the rokkes of Britayne,
And eek from Gerounde to the mouth of Sayne.
   He made it straunge, and swoor, so God hym   straunge: difficult.
      save,
Lasse than a thousand pound he wolde nat have,
Ne gladly for that somme he wolde nat gon. 1225
   Aurelius, with blisful herte anon,
Answerde thus: "Fy on a thousand pound!

This wyde world, which that men seye is round,
I wolde it yeve, if I were lord of it.
This bargayn is ful dryve, for we been knyt. 1230   dryve: concluded. knyt: agreed.
Ye shal be payed trewely, by my trouthe!   trouthe: promise.
But looketh now, for no necligence or slouthe   looketh: make sure.
Ye tarie us heere no lenger than to-morwe."   ye tarie: that you delay.
   "Nay," quod this clerk, "have heer my feith
      to borwe."   to borwe: as pledge.
   To bedde is goon Aurelius whan hym
      leste,   1235
And wel ny al that nyght he hadde his reste.
What for his labour and his hope of blisse,
His woful herte of penaunce hadde a lisse.   penaunce: suffering. lisse: alleviation.
   Upon the morwe, whan that it was day,
To Britaigne tooke they the righte way,   1240   righte: straight.
Aurelius and this magicien bisyde,   bisyde: at his side.
And been descended ther they wolde abyde.   descended: dismounted.
And this was, as thise bookes me remembre,   remembre: remind.
The colde, frosty seson of Decembre.
   Phebus wax old, and hewed lyk latoun,   1245   wax: waxed. latoun: brass.
That in his hote declynacioun
Shoon as the burned gold with stremes brighte;   burned: burnished. stremes: beams.
But now in Capricorn adoun he lighte,   lighte: descended.
Where as he shoon ful pale, I dar wel seyn.
The bittre frostes, with the sleet and reyn,   1250
Destroyed hath the grene in every yerd.   yerd: yard, garden.
Janus sit by the fyr, with double berd,   sit: (sitteth) sits.
And drynketh of his bugle horn the wyn;
Biforn hym stant brawen of the tusked swyn,   stant: stands. brawen: meat. swyn:
And "Nowel" crieth every lusty man.   1255   boar.
   Aurelius, in al that evere he kan,
Dooth to this maister cheere and reverence,
And preyeth hym to doon his diligence   diligence: utmost.
To bryngen hym out of his peynes smerte,
Or with a swerd that he wolde slitte his herte. 1260
   This subtil clerk swich routhe had of this man
That nyght and day he spedde hym that he kan   that: as well as.
To wayten a tyme of his conclusioun;   wayten: watch for. of: for.
This is to seye, to make illusioun,
By swich an apparence or jogelrye—   1265   apparence: apparition. jogelrye: con-
I ne kan no termes of astrologye—   juring. kan: know.
That she and every wight sholde wene and seye

1246. hote declynacioun: the sun's greatest distance north of the equinoctial; the summer solstice.
1248. in Capricorn adoun: far south of the equinoctial; close to the winter solstice.
1252. The clerk waits from December until January for his performance. Janus, as the Roman guardian deity of gates, has long been depicted with two heads or faces. Chaucer describes a scene typically found in medieval Calendars and Books of Hours for the month of January.
1253. bugle horn: drinking horn from a wild ox (bugle).

That of Britaigne the rokkes were aweye,
Or ellis they were sonken under grounde.
So at the laste he hath his tyme yfounde   1270
To maken his japes and his wrecchednesse   japes: tricks. wrecchednesse: mean
Of swich a supersticious cursednesse.   act.
His tables Tolletanes forth he brought,
Ful wel corrected, ne ther lakked nought,
Neither his collect ne his expans yeeris,   1275
Ne his rootes, ne his othere geeris,   geeris: appliances, contrivances.
As been his centris and his argumentz
And his proporcionels convenientz
For his equacions in every thyng.
And by his eighte speere in his wirkyng   1280 eighte speere: eighth sphere.
He knew ful wel how fer Alnath was shove   shove: pushed forward, advanced.
Fro the heed of thilke fixe Aries above,   fixe: fixed.
That in the ninthe speere considered is;
Ful subtilly he kalkuled al this.   kalkuled: calculated.
    Whan he hadde founde his firste mansioun, 1285
He knew the remenaunt by proporcioun,   remenaunt: remainder.
And knew the arisyng of his moone wel,
And in whos face, and terme, and everydel;   everydel: everything.
And knew ful wel the moones mansioun
Acordaunt to his operacioun,   1290 acordaunt to: suitable for, favorable to.
And knew also his othere observaunces   observaunces: practices.
For swiche illusiouns and swiche meschaunces   meschaunces: evil doings.
As hethen folk useden in thilke dayes.
For which no lenger maked he delayes,
But thurgh his magik, for a wyke or tweye,   1295 wyke: week.
It semed that alle the rokkes were aweye.
    Aurelius, which that yet despeired is
Wher he shal han his love or fare amys,   wher: whether. amys: badly.
Awaiteth nyght and day on this myracle;   on: for.

1273. tables Tolletanes: famous astrological tables prepared in the eleventh century by al-Zarqālī and originally calculated for the latitude of Toledo. (They were superseded by the Alphonsine tables, prepared under the direction of Alphonso X the Wise in Toledo, c. 1272.) Corrected (l. 1274) means that the tables Tolletanes were adapted to a given locality. A roote (l. 1276) was the position of a planet at the birth of Christ. A table for collect yeeris (l. 1275) showed the number of degrees to be added to the root for the motion of a planet in multiples of a hundred years; the table for expans yeeris was for shorter periods. A table of centris (l. 1277) shows the distances from the center of an equatory to the centers of planetary orbits, etc.; argumentz are angles or arcs used in calculating the position or motion of a planet; proporcionels convenientz (l. 1278) are tables of proportional parts; an equacion (l. 1279) is the equal partition of the sphere into "houses" for astrological purposes.
1280–83. The true equinoctial point, the head of the fixed Aries, was considered to be in the ninth sphere, the Primum Mobile. The amount of the precession of the equinoxes was ascertained by observing the distance between the true equinoctial point and the star Alnath in the head of Aries in the eighth sphere.
1285. his firste mansioun: the first mansion of the moon, named Alnath (from the star).
1288. face: one of the three parts (of 10° each) into which each sign of the zodiac is divided. terme: one of five unequal parts into which each sign of the zodiac is divided. Each face has its planetary lord.

And whan he knew that ther was noon
      obstacle,   1300
That voyded were thise rokkes everychon,   voyded: removed.
Doun to his maistres feet he fil anon,
And seyde, "I woful wrecche, Aurelius,
Thanke yow, lord, and lady myn Venus,
That me han holpen fro my cares colde."   1305 holpen: delivered. colde: dismal.
And to the temple his wey forth hath he holde, holde: held, gone.
Where as he knew he sholde his lady see.
And whan he saugh his tyme, anon-right he, anon-right: immediately.
With dredful herte and with ful humble cheere, dredful: ful of dread.
Salued hath his sovereyn lady deere: 1310 salued: greeted.
   "My righte lady," quod this woful man,   righte: own.
"Whom I moost drede and love as I best kan,
And lothest were of al this world displese,
Nere it that I for yow have swich disese   disese: misery.
That I moste dyen heere at youre foot anon, 1315
Noght wolde I telle how me is wo bigon.
But certes outher moste I dye or pleyne;   outher: either.
Ye sle me giltlees for verray peyne.
But of my deeth thogh that ye have no routhe, routhe: pity.
Avyseth yow er that ye breke youre trouthe. 1320 avyseth yow: take thought. trouthe:
Repenteth yow, for thilke God above,   pledge.
Er ye me sleen by cause that I yow love. by cause: because.
For, madame, wel ye woot what ye han hight— hight: promised.
Nat that I chalange any thyng of right   chalange: claim.
Of yow, my sovereyn lady, but youre grace— 1325 grace: mercy, favor.
But in a gardyn yond, at swich a place,   yond: yonder.
Ye woot right wel what ye bihighten me; bihighten: promised.
And in myn hand youre trouthe plighten ye trouthe: oath. plighten: pledged.
To love me best—God woot, ye seyde so,
Al be that I unworthy am therto.   1330 therto: of that.
Madame, I speke it for the honour of yow
Moore than to save myn hertes lyf right now,—
I have do so as ye comanded me;   do: done.
And if ye vouche sauf, ye may go see.
Dooth as yow list; have youre biheste in biheste: promise.
      mynde,   1335
For, quyk or deed, right there ye shal me fynde. quyk: alive.
In yow lith al to do me lyve or deye,— do me: cause me to.
But wel I woot the rokkes been aweye."
   He taketh his leve, and she astoned stood; astoned: bewildered.
In al hir face nas a drope of blood.   1340
She wende nevere have come in swich a trappe. wende: expected.
"Allas," quod she, "that evere this sholde happe!
For wende I nevere by possibilitee
That swich a monstre or merveille myghte be! monstre: wonder.
It is agayns the proces of nature."   1345

And hom she goth a sorweful creature;
For verray feere unnethe may she go.   go: walk.
She wepeth, wailleth, al a day or two,
And swowneth, that it routhe was to see.
But why it was to no wight tolde she,   1350
For out of towne was goon Arveragus.
But to hirself she spak, and seyde thus,
With face pale and with ful sorweful cheere,
In hire compleinte, as ye shal after heere:
   "Allas," quod she, "on thee, Fortune, I
       pleyne,   1355
That unwar wrapped hast me in thy cheyne,   unwar: unexpectedly.
Fro which t'escape woot I no socour,   socour: succor, help.
Save oonly deeth or dishonour;
Oon of thise two bihoveth me to chese.
But nathelees, yet have I levere to lese   1360 have I levere: I had rather.
My lif than of my body to have a shame,
Or knowe myselven fals, or lese my name;
And with my deth I may be quyt, ywis.   quyt: freed.
Hath ther nat many a noble wyf er this,
And many a mayde, yslayn hirself, allas!   1365
Rather than with hir body doon trespas?   trespas: wrong.
   Yis, certes, lo, thise stories beren witnesse:
Whan thritty tirauntz, ful of cursednesse,
Hadde slayn Phidon in Atthenes atte feste,
They comanded his doghtres for t'areste,   1370 comanded: i.e., commanded men.
And bryngen hem biforn hem in despit,   despit: malice.
Al naked, to fulfille hir foul delit,
And in hir fadres blood they made hem daunce
Upon the pavement, God yeve hem meschaunce!
For which thise woful maydens, ful of
       drede,   1375
Rather than they wolde lese hir maydenhede,   maydenhede: maidenhood, virginity.
They prively been stirt into a welle,   been stirt: i.e., have leapt.
And dreynte hemselven, as the bookes telle.   dreynte: drowned.
   They of Mecene leete enquere and seke   leete enquere and seke: caused to be
Of Lacedomye fifty maydens eke,   1380   sought.
On whiche they wolden doon hir lecherye.
But was ther noon of al that compaignye
That she nas slayn, and with a good entente   entente: will.
Chees rather for to dye than assente
To been oppressed of hir maydenhede.   1385 oppressed: ravished.
Why sholde I thanne to dye been in drede?
Lo, eek, the tiraunt Aristoclides,
That loved a mayden, heet Stymphalides,   heet: called.

1367. **thise stories**: from St. Jerome's tract *Against Jovinian* Dorigen offers the following examples (ll. 1368–1456) of ancient maidens and women who preferred to die rather than suffer dishonor or who in other ways displayed virtuous conduct.

Whan that hir fader slayn was on a nyght,
Unto Dianes temple goth she right,   1390   right: straightway.
And hente the ymage in hir handes two,
Fro which ymage wolde she nevere go.
No wight ne myghte hir handes of it arace   of: from. arace: pull away.
Til she was slayn, right in the selve place.   selve: same.
   Now sith that maydens hadden swich
       despit   1395   despit: defiance, disdain.
To been defouled with mannes foul delit,
Wel oghte a wyf rather hirselven slee
Than be defouled, as it thynketh me.
What shal I seyn of Hasdrubales wyf,
That at Cartage birafte hirself hir lyf?   1400   birafte: took.
For whan she saw that Romayns wan the toun,
She took hir children alle, and skipte adoun   skipte: leapt.
Into the fyr, and chees rather to dye
Than any Romayn dide hire vileynye.
Hath nat Lucresse yslayn hirself, allas!   1405
At Rome, whan that she oppressed was   oppressed: ravished.
Of Tarquyn, for hir thoughte it was a shame   of: by.
To lyven whan she hadde lost her name?
The sevene maydens of Milesie also
Han slayn hemself, for verray drede and wo,   1410
Rather than folk of Gawle hem sholde oppresse.   folk of Gawle: Galatians.
Mo than a thousand stories, as I gesse,
Koude I now telle as touchyng this matere.
Whan Habradate was slayn, his wyf so deere
Hirselven slow, and leet hir blood to glyde   1415   slow: slew.
In Habradates woundes depe and wyde,
And seyde, 'My body, at the leeste way,
Ther shal no wight defoulen, if I may.'   may: have power (to prevent it).
   What sholde I mo ensamples heerof sayn,
Sith that so many han hemselven slayn   1420
Wel rather than they wolde defouled be?
I wol conclude that it is bet for me
To sleen myself than been defouled thus.
I wol be trewe unto Arveragus,
Or rather sle myself in som manere,   1425
As dide Demociones doghter deere
By cause that she wolde nat defouled be.
O Cedasus, it is ful greet pitee
To reden how thy doghtren deyde, allas!
That slowe hemself for swich maner cas.   1430   cas: reason.
As greet a pitee was it, or wel moore,
The Theban mayden that for Nichanore
Hirselven slow, right for swich manere wo.   slow: slew.
Another Theban mayden dide right so;
For oon of Macedonye hadde hire oppressed, 1435
She with hire deeth hir maydenhed redressed.   maydenhed: maidenhood. redressed:
          vindicated.

What shal I seye of Nicerates wyf,
That for swich cas birafte hirself hir lyf?   birafte: took.
How trewe eek was to Alcibiades
His love, that rather for to dyen chees   1440
Than for to suffre his body unburyed be.
Lo, which a wyf was Alceste," quod she.   which: what.
"What seith Omer of goode Penalopee?
Al Grece knoweth of hir chastitee.
Pardee, of Laodomya is writen thus,   1445
That whan at Troye was slayn Protheselaus,
Ne lenger wolde she lyve after his day.   day: lifetime.
The same of noble Porcia telle I may;
Withoute Brutus koude she nat lyve,
To whom she hadde al hool hir herte yive.   1450 al hool: entirely.
The parfit wyfhod of Arthemesie
Honured is thurgh al the Barbarie.   the Barbarie: the Saracen world.
O Teuta, queene! thy wifly chastitee
To alle wyves may a mirour bee.
The same thyng I seye of Bilyea,   1455
Of Rodogone, and eek Valeria."
   Thus pleyned Dorigen a day or tweye,
Purposynge evere that she wolde deye.
But nathelees, upon the thridde nyght,
Hoom cam Arveragus, this worthy knyght,   1460
And asked hire why that she weep so soore;   weep: wept.
And she gan wepen ever lenger the moore.
"Allas," quod she, "that evere was I born!
Thus have I seyd," quod she, "thus have I
        sworn"—
And tolde hym al as ye han herd bifore;   1465
It nedeth nat reherce it yow namoore.
This housbonde, with glad cheere, in freendly
        wise
Answerde and seyde as I shal yow devyse:
"Is ther oght elles, Dorigen, but this?"   oght: aught, anything.
   "Nay, nay," quod she, "God help me so as
        wys!   1470
This is to muche, and it were Goddes wille."   and: even if.
   "Ye, wyf," quod he, "lat slepen that is stille.   that: that which.
It may be wel, paraventure, yet to day.
Ye shul youre trouthe holden, by my fay!   trouthe: troth, pledge.
For God so wisly have mercy upon me,   1475 wisly: surely.
I hadde wel levere ystiked for to be   ystiked: stabbed to death.
For verray love which that I to yow have,
But if ye sholde youre trouthe kepe and save.   but if: than . . . not. trouthe: vow.
Trouthe is the hyeste thyng that man may
        kepe"—

1470. God help me so as wys!: So surely may God help me!

But with that word he brast anon to wepe,   1480   brast to wepe: burst into weeping.
And seyde, "I yow forbede, up peyne of deeth,   up: upon.
That nevere, whil thee lasteth lyf ne breeth,
To no wight tel thou of this aventure,—   aventure: misfortune.
As I may best, I wol my wo endure,—
Ne make no contenance of hevynesse,   1485   contenance: appearance.
That folk of yow may demen harm or gesse."   gesse: suppose.
    And forth he cleped a squier and a mayde:
"Gooth forth anon with Dorigen," he sayde,
"And bryngeth hire to swich a place anon."
They take hir leve, and on hir wey they gon,   1490
But they ne wiste why she thider wente.
He nolde no wight tellen his entente.
    Paraventure an heep of yow, ywis,
Wol holden hym a lewed man in this   lewed: wicked; foolish.
That he wol putte his wyf in jupartie.   1495   jupartie: jeopardy.
Herkneth the tale er ye upon hire crie.
She may have bettre fortune than yow semeth;   yow: to you.
And whan that ye han herd the tale, demeth.   demeth: judge (imperative).
    This squier, which that highte Aurelius,
On Dorigen that was so amorus,   1500
Of aventure happed hir to meete
Amydde the toun, right in the quykkest strete,   quykkest: liveliest, busiest.
As she was boun to goon the wey forth right   boun: ready; about. forth right:
Toward the gardyn ther as she had hight.   straight forward. hight: promised.
And he was to the gardyn-ward also;   1505   to the gardyn-ward: towards the gar-
For wel he spyed whan she wolde go   den.
Out of hir hous to any maner place.
But thus they mette, of aventure or grace,
And he salueth hire with glad entente,   salueth: greets. with glad entente:
And asked of hire whiderward she wente;   1510   cheerfully.
And she answerde, half as she were mad,
"Unto the gardyn, as myn housbond bad,
My trouthe for to holde, allas! allas!"   trouthe: pledge. holde: keep.
    Aurelius gan wondren on this cas,   cas: situation.
And in his herte hadde greet compassioun   1515
Of hire and of hir lamentacioun,
And of Arveragus, the worthy knyght,
That bad hire holden al that she had hight,   hight: promised.
So looth hym was his wyf sholde breke hir
        trouthe;
And in his herte he caughte of this greet
        routhe,   1520
Considerynge the beste on every syde,
That fro his lust yet were hym levere abyde   abyde: abstain.
Than doon so heigh a cherlyssh wrecchednesse   heigh: extreme.
Agayns franchise and alle gentillesse;   franchise: nobility, generosity.
For which in fewe wordes seyde he thus: 1525
    "Madame, seyth to youre lord Arveragus,

That sith I se his grete gentillesse
To yow, and eek I se wel youre distresse,
That him were levere han shame (and that were
      routhe)
Than ye to me sholde breke thus youre
      trouthe,   1530
I have wel levere evere to suffre wo
Than I departe the love bitwix yow two.   departe: break up.
I yow relesse, madame, into youre hond   yow: to you.
Quyt every serement and every bond   serement: assurance, pledge.
That ye han maad to me as heerbiforn,   1535
Sith thilke tyme which that ye were born.
My trouthe I plighte, I shal yow never repreve   repreve: reproach.
Of no biheste, and here I take my leve,   biheste: promise.
As of the treweste and the beste wyf
That evere yet I knew in al my lyf."   1540
    She thonketh hym upon hir knees al bare,   1545
And hom unto hir housbond is she fare,   fare: gone.
And tolde hym al, as ye han herd me sayd;
And be ye siker, he was so wel apayd   apayd: pleased.
That it were inpossible me to write.   me: for me.
What sholde I lenger of this cas endite?   1550
    But every wyf be war of hire biheste!   1541
On Dorigen remembreth, atte leeste.
Thus kan a squier doon a gentil dede   gentil: noble.
As wel as kan a knyght, withouten drede.   1544   drede: doubt.
    Arveragus and Dorigen his wyf   1551
In sovereyn blisse leden forth hir lyf.
Nevere eft ne was ther angre hem bitwene.   eft: again. angre: resentment.
He cherisseth hire as though she were a queene,
And she was to hym trewe for everemoore.   1555
Of thise two folk ye gete of me namoore.   of: from.
    Aurelius, that his cost hath al forlorn,   cost: outlay. forlorn: lost.
Curseth the tyme that evere he was born:
"Allas," quod he, "allas, that I bihighte   bihighte: promised.
Of pured gold a thousand pound of wighte   1560 of wighte: by weight.
Unto this philosophre! How shal I do?   philosophre: adept in occult science.
I se namoore but that I am fordo.   fordo: ruined.
Myn heritage moot I nedes selle,
And been a beggere; here may I nat dwelle,
And shamen al my kynrede in this place,   1565
But I of hym may gete bettre grace.
But nathelees, I wol of hym assaye,   assaye: endeavor.
At certeyn dayes, yeer by yeer, to paye,
And thanke hym of his grete curteisye.   of: for.

1541–44. These lines clearly belong to the Franklin rather than to Aurelius and were evidently
written in the margin of O′ and inserted incorrectly by most scribes (see Manly IV, 488).
1547. sayd: i.e., say (past participle for infinitive).

My trouthe wol I kepe, I wol nat lye."   1570
  With herte soor he gooth unto his cofre,
And broghte gold unto this philosophre,
The value of fyve hundred pound, I gesse,
And hym bisecheth, of his gentillesse,
To graunte hym dayes of the remenaunt;   1575   dayes of: i.e., days of respite in which
And seyde, "Maister, I dar wel make avaunt,   to pay. avaunt: boast.
I failled nevere of my trouthe as yit.
For sikerly my dette shal be quyt
Towardes yow, howevere that I fare   fare: may fare.
To goon a-begged in my kirtle bare.   1580   goon a-begged: go begging. bare:
But wolde ye vouche sauf, upon seuretee,   scantily clad.
Two yeer or thre for to respiten me,   respiten: grant delay to.
Thanne were I wel; for elles moot I selle   wel: well off.
Myn heritage; ther is namoore to telle."
  This philosophre sobrely answerde,   1585   sobrely: gravely.
And seyde thus, whan he thise wordes herde:
"Have I nat holden covenant unto thee?"
  "Yes, certes, wel and trewely," quod he.
  "Hastow nat had thy lady as thee liketh?"
  "No, no," quod he, and sorwefully he
      siketh.   1590   siketh: sighs.
  "What was the cause? tel me if thou kan."
  Aurelius his tale anon bigan,
And tolde hym al, as ye han herd bifoore;
It nedeth nat to yow reherce it moore.
  He seide, "Arveragus, of gentillesse,   1595
Hadde levere dye in sorwe and in distresse
Than that his wyf were of hir trouthe fals."
The sorwe of Dorigen he tolde hym als;   als: also.
How looth hire was to been a wikked wyf,
And that she levere had lost that day hir lyf,   1600
And that hir trouthe she swoor thurgh innocence,
She nevere erst hadde herd speke of apparence.   erst: before. apparence: apparition.
"That made me han of hire so greet pitee;
And right as frely as he sente hir me,   frely: generously.
As frely sente I hire to hym agayn.   1605
This al and som; ther is namoore to sayn."   this: this is. al and som: the sum
  This philosophre answerde, "Leeve brother,   total.
Everich of yow dide gentilly til oother.
Thou art a squier, and he is a knyght;
But God forbede, for his blisful myght,   1610
But if a clerk koude doon a gentil dede   gentil: noble.
As wel as any of yow, it is no drede!
  Sire, I releesse thee thy thousand pound,
As thou right now were cropen out of the ground,   were cropen: had crawled.
Ne nevere er now ne haddest knowen me.   1615
For, sire, I wol nat taken a peny of thee
For al my craft, ne noght for my travaille.   craft: science; skill. travaille: labor.

Thou hast ypayed wel for my vitaille.
It is ynogh, and fare wel, have good day!"
And took his hors, and forth he goth his way. 1620
    Lordynges, this question than wol I aske now:
Which was the mooste fre, as thynketh yow?   fre: generous, noble.
Now telleth me, er that ye ferther wende;
I kan namoore; my tale is at an ende.   kan: know.

Heere is ended the Frankeleyns tale.

Heere folweth the
Phisiciens tale.

    Ther was, as telleth Titus Livius,
A knyght that called was Virginius,
Fulfild of honour and of worthynesse,
And strong of freendes, and of greet richesse.
    This knyght a doghter hadde by his wyf; 5
No children hadde he mo in al his lyf.
Fair was this mayde in excellent beautee   excellent: excelling.
Aboven every wight that man may see;   wight: creature.
For Nature hath with sovereyn diligence
Yformed hire in so greet excellence, 10
As though she wolde seyn, "Lo! I, Nature,
Thus kan I forme and peynte a creature,
Whan that me list; who kan me countrefete?   countrefete: imitate, emulate.
Pigmalion noght, though he ay forge and bete,   bete: hammer.
Or grave, or peynte; for I dar wel seyn, 15 grave: carve.
Apelles, Zanzis, sholde werche in veyn
Outher to grave, or peynte, or forge, or bete,   outher: either.
If they presumed me to countrefete.
For He that is the formere principal   formere: Creator.
Hath maked me his vicaire general, 20 vicaire: deputy.
To forme and peynten erthely creaturis
Right as me list, and ech thyng in my cure is   cure: care, charge.
Under the moone, that may wane and waxe;
And for my werk right no thyng wol I axe;
My lord and I been ful of oon accord. 25 ful: fully.
I made hire to the worship of my lord;   to the worship of: in honor of.
So do I alle myne othere creatures,
What colour that they han, or what figures."   what: whatever. figures: forms, ap-
Thus semeth me that Nature wolde seye.   pearances.

---

the Phisiciens tale. Although the Physician's Tale derives ultimately from Livy's historical account of the conflict between Apius and Virginius, Chaucer follows Jean de Meun's abridged and modified version of the events, which stresses the wickedness of judges; Chaucer adds emphasis on the beauty and maidenly virtues of Virginia and on the pathos of her death.
14, 16. Pygmalion, Apelles, and Zeuxis are stock examples of famous artists of antiquity.

This mayde of age twelve yeer was and
           tweye,

30 **tweye:** two.

In which that Nature hadde swich delit.
For right as she kan peynte a lilye whit,
And reed a rose, right with swich peynture

reed: red. **right:** just.

She peynted hath this noble creature,
Er she were born, upon hir lymes fre,

35 **fre:** gracious.

Where as by right swiche colours sholde be;
And Phebus dyed hath hir tresses grete

grete: abundant, splendid.

Lyk to the stremes of his burned heete.

stremes: beams, rays. **burned:** burnished, shining.

And if that excellent was hir beautee,
A thousand fold moore vertuous was she.

40

In hir ne lakked no condicioun

condicioun: trait of character.

That is to preyse, as by discrecioun.
As wel in goost as body chast was she;

goost: spirit.

For which she floured in virginitee

floured: flowered, flourished.

With alle humilitee and abstinence,

45

With alle attemperaunce and pacience,
With mesure eek of beryng and array.

mesure: moderation. **array:** dress.

Discreet she was in answeryng alway;
Though she were wis as Pallas, dar I seyn,
Hir facound eek ful wommanly and pleyn,

50 **facound:** eloquence; manner of speaking. **countrefeted:** affected; artificial. **after hir degree:** according to her station.

No countrefeted termes hadde she
To seme wys; but after hir degree
She spak, and alle hir wordes, moore and lesse,
Sownynge in vertu and in gentillesse.

sownynge in: tending towards. **gentillesse:** nobility of character.

Shamefast she was in maydens shamefastnesse,

55

Constant in herte, and evere in bisynesse

shamefast: modest. **in bisynesse:** busy; diligent. **slogardye:** slothfulness, laziness.

To dryve hire out of ydel slogardye.
Bacus hadde of hir mouth right no maistrye;
For wyn and youthe dooth Venus encresse,
As men in fyr wol casten oille or greesse.

60 **men:** (indefinite singular) one.

And of hir owene vertu, unconstreyned,
She hath ful ofte tyme syk hir feyned,

syk: ill.

For that she wolde fleen the compaignye

fleen: avoid, escape from.

Where likly was to treten of folye,
As is at feestes, revels, and at daunces,

65

That been occasions of daliaunces.

daliaunces: amorous or wanton play.

Swich thynges maken children for to be
To soone rype and boold, as men may se,

boold: brazen, shameless.

Which is ful perilous, and hath been yoore.

yoore: for a long time.

For al to soone may she lerne loore

70

Of boldnesse whan she woxen is a wyf.
    And ye maistresses, in youre olde lyf,
That lordes doghtres han in governaunce,

woxen is a wyf: has grown to be a woman. **maistresses:** governesses. **olde lyf:** old age.

---

42. That is to be praised by discerning people.
49. **Pallas:** Pallas Athene was the Greek goddess of Wisdom.
64. Where sinfulness or lechery was likely to be involved.

Ne taketh of my wordes no displesaunce.
Thenketh that ye been set in governynges   75
Of lordes doghtres, oonly for two thynges:
Outher for ye han kept youre honestee,   *outher: either. for: because. hon-*
Or elles ye han falle in freletee,   *estee: virtue. freletee: sinfulness.*
And knowen wel ynough the olde daunce,   *olde daunce: i.e., arts of love.*
And han forsaken fully swich meschaunce   80   *meschaunce: unfortunate conduct.*
For everemo; therfore, for Cristes sake,
To teche hem vertu looke that ye ne slake.   *looke: make sure. slake: become*
    A theef of venysoun, that hath forlaft   *slack. theef: i.e., poacher. forlaft:*
His likerousnesse and al his olde craft,   *given up. likerousnesse: appetite.*
Kan kepe a forest best of any man.   85   *craft: trickery. kepe: guard.*
Now kepeth wel, for if ye wole, ye kan.
Looke wel that ye unto no vice assente,
Lest ye be dampned for youre wikke entente;   *dampned: condemned. wikke: wicked.*
For whoso dooth, a traitour is, certeyn.   *entente: intention.*
And taketh kepe of that that I shal seyn: 90   *taketh kepe: take heed.*
Of alle tresoun sovereyn pestilence   *sovereyn: the greatest. pestilence:*
Is whan a wight bitrayseth innocence.   *destructiveness, wickedness. bitray-*
    Ye fadres and ye modres eek also,   *seth: deceives.*
Though ye han children, be it oon or mo,   *though: if.*
Youre is the charge of al hir surveiaunce,   95   *surveiaunce: surveillance.*
Whil that they been under youre governaunce.
Beth war, if by ensample of youre lyvynge,   *beth war: beware.*
Or by youre necligence in chastisynge,
That they perisse; for I dar wel seye,   *perisse: (perish) incur spiritual death.*
If that they doon, ye shul it deere abeye.   100   *abeye: pay the penalty for.*
Under a shepherde softe and necligent
The wolf hath many a sheep and lamb torent.   *torent: rent in pieces.*
Suffiseth oon ensample now as heere,
For I moot turne agayn to my matere.   *moot: must.*
    This mayde, of which I wol this tale
            expresse,   105   *expresse: tell.*
So kepte hirself hir neded no maistresse;
For in hir lyvyng maydens myghten rede,   *lyvyng: manner of life.*
As in a book, every good word or dede
That longeth to a mayden vertuous,   *longeth: belongs.*
She was so prudent and so bountevous.   110   *bountevous: good, virtuous.*
For which the fame out sprong on every syde,
Bothe of hir beautee and hir bountee wyde,   *bountee: goodness, excellence.*
That thurgh that land they preised hire echone
That loved vertu, save Envye allone,
That sory is of oother mennes wele,   115
And glad is of his sorwe and his unheele.   *unheele: misfortune.*
(The doctour maketh this descripcioun).

---

117. **doctour:** St. Augustine, one of the "Doctors of the Church"; see his *Enarrationes in Psalmos* cv.25; see Parson's Tale, 484.

This mayde upon a day wente in the toun
Toward a temple, with hire moder deere,
As is of yonge maydens the manere.   120   manere: custom.
Now was ther thanne a justice in that toun,
That governour was of that regioun.
And so bifel this juge his eyen caste
Upon this mayde, avysynge hym ful faste,   avysynge hym: taking thought. **faste:**
As she cam forby ther as this juge stood.   125   intently. forby ther as: past where.
Anon his herte chaunged and his mood,
So was he caught with beautee of this mayde,
And to hymself ful pryvely he sayde,
"This mayde shal be myn, for any man!"   for: in spite of.
     Anon the feend into his herte ran,   130
And taughte hym sodeynly that he by slyghte   slyghte: trickery.
The mayden to his purpos wynne myghte.
For certes, by no force ne by no meede,   meede: bribery.
Hym thoughte, he was nat able for to speede;   speede: succeed.
For she was strong of freendes, and eek she   135
Confermed was in swich sovereyn bountee,   confermed: securely established.
That wel he wiste he myghte hire nevere wynne
As for to make hire with hir body synne.
For which, by greet deliberacioun,
He sente after a cherl, was in the toun,   140   cherl: fellow; churl, villain. **was:** i.e.,
Which that he knew for subtil and for bold.   who was. for: to be. subtil: treach-
This juge unto this cherl his tale hath told   erously cunning.
In secree wise, and made hym to ensure   ensure: promise on oath.
He sholde telle it to no creature,
And if he dide, he sholde lese his heed.   145   lese: lose. **heed:** head.
Whan that assented was this cursed reed,   reed: plan.
Glad was this juge, and maked him gret cheere,   maked cheere: treated kindly.
And yaf hym yiftes preciouse and deere.
     Whan shapen was al hire conspiracie   shapen: planned.
Fro point to point, how that his lecherie   150
Parfourned sholde been ful subtilly,
As ye shul heere it after openly,
Hoom gooth the cherl, that highte Claudius.
This false juge, that highte Apius,
(So was his name, for this is no fable,   155
But knowen for historial thyng notable;   historial: historical.
The sentence of it sooth is, out of doute),   sentence: substance.
This false juge gooth now faste aboute
To hasten his delit al that he may.   delit: delightful sport.
And so bifel soone after, on a day,   160
This false juge, as telleth us the storie,
As he was wont, sat in his consistorie,   consistorie: court of justice.
And yaf his doomes upon sondry cas.   doomes: judgments. **cas:** cases.
This false cherl cam forth a ful gret pas,   pas: speed.
And seyde, "Lord, if that it be youre wille,   165

As dooth me right upon this pitous bille,
In which I pleyne upon Virginius;
And if that he wol seyn it is nat thus,
I wol it preve, and fynde good witnesse,
That sooth is that my bille wol expresse." 170
    The juge answerde, "Of this, in his absence,
I may nat yeve diffynytyf sentence.
Lat do hym calle, and I wol gladly heere;
Thou shalt have al right, and no wrong heere."
    Virginius cam to wite the juges wille, 175
And right anon was rad this cursed bille;
The sentence of it was as ye shul heere:
"To yow, my lord, sire Apius so deere,
Sheweth youre povre servant Claudius
How that a knyght, called Virginius, 180
Agayns the lawe, agayn al equitee,
Holdeth, expres agayn the wyl of me,
My servant, which that is my thral by right,
Which fro myn hous was stole upon a nyght,
Whil that she was ful yong; this wol I preve 185
By witnesse, lord, so that it nat yow greeve.
She nys his doghter nat, what so he seye.
Wherfore to yow, my lord the juge, I preye,
Yeld me my thral, if that it be youre wille."
Lo, this was al the sentence of his bille. 190
    Virginius gan upon the cherl biholde,
But hastily, er he his tale tolde,
And wolde have preved it as sholde a knyght,
And eek by witnessyng of many a wight,
That al was fals that seyde his adversarie, 195
This cursed juge wolde no thyng tarie,
Ne heere a word moore of Virginius,
But yaf his juggement, and seyde thus:
    "I deeme anon this cherl his servant have;
Thou shalt no lenger in thyn hous hir save. 200
Go bryng hire forth, and put hire in oure
        warde.
The cherl shal have his thral, this I awarde."
    And whan this worthy knyght Virginius,
Thurgh sentence of this justice Apius,
Moste by force his deere doghter yiven 205
Unto the juge, in lecherie to lyven,
He gooth hym hoom, and sette him in his halle,
And leet anon his deere doghter calle,
And with a face deed as asshen colde
Upon hir humble face he gan biholde, 210
With fadres pitee stikynge thurgh his herte,
Al wolde he from his purpos nat converte.

as dooth: (please) do. bille: i.e., of complaint. pleyne: complain.

preve: prove. witnesse: testimony, evidence. sooth is that: truth is what.

lat do hym calle: have him summoned.

to wite: in order to learn.
rad: read.
sentence: substance.

expres agayn: directly opposed to.
thral: thrall, slave.

so that: provided.

biholde: gaze.

deeme: decree, rule.
save: keep.

warde: custody.

moste: was obliged. yiven: to give.

sette him: sat down.
leet calle: i.e., sent for.
deed: deathlike. asshen: ashes.

stikynge: piercing.
al: although. converte: turn away.

"Doghter," quod he, "Virginia, by thy name,
Ther been two weyes, outher deeth or shame,
That thou most suffre; allas, that I was bore! 215   most: must. bore: born.
For nevere thou deservedest wherfore   wherfore: for any cause
To dyen with a swerd or with a knyf.
O deere doghter, endere of my lyf,
Which I have fostred up with swich plesaunce
That thou were nevere out of my
      remembraunce!   220
O doghter, which that art my laste wo,
And in my lyf my laste joye also,
O gemme of chastitee, in pacience
Take thou thy deeth, for this is my sentence.   sentence: decision.
For love, and nat for hate, thou most be deed; 225
My pitous hand moot smyten of thyn heed.   moot: must. of: off.
Allas, that evere Apius thee say!   say: saw.
Thus hath he falsly juged thee to-day"—
And tolde hire al the cas, as ye bifore
Han herd; nat nedeth for to telle it moore.   230   moore: again.
   "O mercy, deere fader!" quod this mayde,
And with that word she bothe hir armes layde
Aboute his nekke, as she was wont to do.
The teeris bruste out of hir eyen two,   bruste: burst.
And seyde, "Goode fader, shal I dye?   235
Is ther no grace, is ther no remedye?"   grace: mercy.
   "No, certes, deere doghter myn," quod he.
   "Thanne yif me leyser, fader myn," quod she,   leyser: an allowance of time; a res-
"My deeth for to compleyne a litel space;   pite.
For, pardee, Jepte yaf his doghter grace   240   grace: the favor of a delay, respite.
For to compleyne, er he hir slow, allas!   slow: slew.
And, God it woot, no thyng was hir trespas,
But for she ran hir fader first to see,   for: because.
To welcome hym with greet solempnitee."
And with that word she fil aswowne anon,   245   aswowne: in a swoon.
And after, whan hir swownyng is agon,   swownyng: swooning. agon: gone.
She riseth up, and to hir fader sayde,
"Blissed be God, that I shal dye a mayde!
Yif me my deeth, er that I have a shame;   shame: violation of honor, loss of
Dooth with youre child youre wyl, a Goddes   chastity. dooth: do. a: in.
      name!"   250
   And with that word she preyed hym ful ofte
That with his swerd he wolde smyte softe;
And with that word aswowne doun she fil.   fil: fell.
Hir fader, with ful sorweful herte and wil,   wil: intention, determination.

---

240. Jepthah vowed to the Lord that in return for victory over the sons of Ammon, he would sacrifice whoever first came out of his house to meet him on his return; he permitted the victim, his daughter, to bewail her virginity for two months (Judges xi.30–39).

Hir heed of smoot, and by the top it hente,   255   of smoot: smote off. top: hair.
And to the juge he gan it to presente,
As he sat yet in doom in consistorie.   doom: judgment. consistorie: court.
And whan the juge it saugh, as seith the storie,
He bad to take hym and anhange hym faste;   anhange: hang. faste: immediately.
But right anon a thousand peple in thraste, 260   in thraste: pushed their way in,
To save the knyght, for routhe and for pitee,   crowded in.
For knowen was the false iniquitee.
The peple anon had suspect in this thyng,   suspect: suspicion.
By manere of the cherles chalangyng,   manere: reason.
That it was by the assent of Apius;   265
They wisten wel that he was lecherus.
For which unto this Apius they gon,
And caste hym in a prisoun right anon,
Ther as he slow hymself; and Claudius,   slow: slew.
That servant was unto this Apius,   270
Was demed for to hange upon a tree,   demed: sentenced.
But that Virginius, of his pitee,   of: because of.
So preyde for hym that he was exiled;
And elles, certes, he had been bigyled.   bigyled: defrauded (i.e., of his life).
The remenant were anhanged, moore and   moore and lesse: great and small.
     lesse,   275
That were consentant of this cursednesse.
   Heere may men seen how synne hath his
        merite.   merite: due reward.
Beth war, for no man woot whom God wol   beth war: beware.
     smyte
In no degree, ne in which manere wise
The worm of conscience may agrise   280   worm of conscience: i.e., remorse.
Of wikked lyf, though it so pryvee be   agrise of: feel horror toward, shud-
That no man woot therof but God and he.   der at.
For be he lewed man, or ellis lered,   lewed: ignorant. lered: learned.
He noot how soone that he shal been afered.   noot: (ne woot) knows not. afered: ter-
Therfore I rede yow this conseil take: 285   rified (i.e., by death). rede: advise.
Forsaketh synne, er synne yow forsake.   forsaketh: abandon. yow forsake:
                                                      leaves you helpless.

Heere endeth the Phisiciens tale.

The decapitation of Virginia: This scene is from a manuscript of *Les livres des estoires dou commencement dou monde*. Most narrators of the event, including Livy, Boccaccio, and Gower, say that Virginius stabbed his daughter, but Chaucer, following Jean de Meun, wrote that he cut off her head. The artist read in his text simply that Virginius killed her in the center of the city before the people, and assumed that the method was decapitation. Only Chaucer places the scene at home. The manuscript, evidently written in Naples between 1340 and 1350, belonged eventually to Charles V (d. 1380) and later to his brother John, Duke of Berry (d. 1416).

nie esploica si alua a sez
conpaignons que cele po
este leur su coine si uos di
rai comment abnez mozse
uos les nolez enterore.

contre les .x. seingnu[r]
qui la poeste graut ditte
cion furent tel mene. li
senator quil conuint les.
.x. homes hoster de leur po

The wordes of the Hoost
to the Phisicien
and the Pardoner.

Oure Hooste gan to swere as he were wood;
"Harrow!" quod he, "by nayles and by blood!
This was a fals cherl and a fals justise.
As shameful deeth as herte kan devyse   290
Come to thise juges and hire advocatz!
Algate this sely mayde is slayn, allas!   *algate:* at any rate.
Allas, to deere boughte she beautee!   *to deere:* too dearly. *boughte:* paid
Wherfore I seye al day that men may see   for. *al day:* all the time.
That yiftes of Fortune and of Nature   *yiftes:* gifts.
Been cause of deeth to many a creature.   296
Of bothe yiftes that I speke of now   299
Men han ful ofte moore for harm than prow.   *for:* i.e., which does. *prow:* benefit.
    But trewely, myn owene maister deere,
This is a pitous tale for to heere.
But nathelees, passe over, is no fors.   *no fors:* no matter.
I pray to God so save thy gentil cors,   *cors:* person.
And eek thyne urynals and thy jurdones,   305
Thyn ypocras, and eek thy galiones,
And every boyste ful of thy letuarie;   *boyste:* box. *letuarie:* electuary, rem-
God blesse hem, and oure lady Seinte Marie!   edy.
So moot I theen, thou art a propre man,   *propre:* handsome, perfect.
And lyk a prelat, by Seint Ronyan!   310
Seyde I nat wel? I kan nat speke in terme;   *in terme:* with formal accuracy.
But wel I woot thou doost myn herte to erme,   *doost:* causest. *erme:* grieve.
That I almoost have caught a cardynacle.
By corpus bones! but I have triacle,   *triacle:* a remedy, medicine.
Or elles a draughte of moyste and corny ale, 315   *moyste:* new. *corny:* tasting strong of
                                                             the malt.

287–96, 299–300. Chaucer wrote a 12-line "endlink" for The Physician's Tale and later revised it; I print the later version. Some editors gratuitously insert into this revision (as lines 297–98) a couplet from the earlier version:

> Hire beautee was hire deth, I dar wel sayn.
> Allas, so pitously as she was slayn!

This insertion has no manuscript authority and cannot represent the intention of the poet; in fact he presented a corresponding thought in lines 292–93 of the revision. (See Manly and Rickert, IV, 79–80, 490–91.)

288. harrow!: help!, a cry of distress. by nayles and by blood: a familiar oath, by the nails of the Cross and the blood of Christ.

305. urynals, jurdones: glass vessels used in diagnosing diseases by uroscopy.

306. ypocras: an aphrodisiac drink named after Hippocrates (see Merchant's Tale, 1807–8 and note). galiones: Only Herry Bailey knows what he meant by this; perhaps a similar drink named after Galen.

310. Chaucer's audience was presumably less interested in identifying Seint Ronyan (line 320, Ronyon) with St. Ronan (of the Well) or St. Ninian than in noting the pun on "runnion" meaning "reins," "kidneys"; hence perhaps for line 320, "loins," the seat of generative power.

313. cardynacle: Herry Bailey's valiant word for cardiacle, palpitation caused by excessive emotion.

314. corpus bones: a meaningless blunder of an oath.

Or but I heere anon a myrie tale,
Myn herte is lost for pitee of this mayde.
Thou beel amy, thou Pardoner," he sayde,
"Telle us som myrthe or japes right anon."   japes: jokes.
   "It shal be doon," quod he, "by Seint
      Ronyon!   320
But first," quod he, "heere at this ale-stake
I wol bothe drynke, and eten of a cake."   cake: loaf of bread.
   But right anon thise gentils gonne to crye,
"Nay, lat hym telle us of no ribaudye!   ribaudye: ribaldry.
Telle us som moral thyng, that we may leere 325 leere: learn.
Som wit, and thanne wol we gladly heere."   wit: wisdom.
   "I graunte, ywis," quod he, "but I moot
      thynke
Upon som honeste thyng while that I drynke."   honeste: fitting, virtuous.

*Heere folweth the
prologe of the
Pardoners tale.*

*Radix malorum est cupiditas,
ad Thimotheum, 6°.*

"Lordynges," quod he, "in chirches whan I
    preche,
I peyne me to han an hauteyn speche, 330 peyne me: take pains. hauteyn: lofty,
And rynge it out as round as gooth a belle,   elevated.
For I kan al by rote that I telle.   kan: know.
My theme is alwey oon, and evere was—   theme: text. oon: the same.
Radix malorum est Cupiditas.
   First I pronounce whennes that I come, 335 whennes: whence.
And thanne my bulles shewe I, alle and some.
Oure lige lordes seel on my patente,
That shewe I first, my body to warente,   my body: myself. warente: protect.
That no man be so boold, ne preest ne clerk,
Me to destourbe of Cristes hooly werk. 340 destourbe of: prevent from doing.
And after that thanne telle I forth my tales;
Bulles of popes and of cardynales,
Of patriarkes and bishopes I shewe,
And in Latyn I speke a wordes fewe,

---

318. beel amy: fair friend (here an expression of contempt).
321–22. See General Prologue, ll. 666–670.
331. round: roundly; with full tone.
334. The root of evils is avarice (I Timothy vi.10).
336. bulles: papal bulls, presumably concerning indulgences.
337. The certificate, permitting the Pardoner to preach and to sell papal indulgences, had a bishop's seal.

To saffron with my predicacioun,   345
And for to stire hem to devocioun.
Thanne shewe I forth my longe cristal stones,
Ycrammed ful of cloutes and of bones,—   cloutes: rags.
Relikes been they, as wenen they echoon.
Thanne have I in latoun a sholder-boon   350 latoun: latten, an alloy resembling
Which that was of an hooly Jewes sheep.   brass.
'Goode men,' I seye, 'taak of my wordes keep; keep: heed.
If that this boon be wasshe in any welle,
If cow, or calf, or sheep, or oxe swelle
That any worm hath ete, or worm ystonge, 355 worm: snake.
Taak water of that welle and wassh his tonge,
And it is hool anon; and forthermoore,   hool: healed, cured.
Of pokkes and of scabbe, and every soore   pokkes: pocks.
Shal every sheep be hool that of this welle
Drynketh a draughte. Taak kep eek what I   kep: heed.
     telle: 360
If that the good-man that the beestes oweth   oweth: owns.
Wol every wyke, er that the cok hym croweth, wyke: week.
Fastynge, drynken of this welle a draughte,
As thilke hooly Jew oure eldres taughte,   eldres: ancestors.
His beestes and his stoor shal multiplie. 365 stoor: livestock.
  And, sires, also it heeleth jalousie;
For though a man be falle in jalous rage,
Lat maken with this water his potage,   potage: soup.
And nevere shal he moore his wyf mystriste,
Though he the soothe of hir defaute wiste, 370 soothe: truth. defaute: guilt.
Al had she taken prestes two or thre.
  Heere is a miteyn eek, that ye may se.   miteyn: mitten.
He that his hand wol putte in this mitayn,
He shal have multipliyng of his grayn,
Whan he hath sowen, be it whete or otes, 375
So that he offre pens, or elles grotes.   pens: pence.
  Goode men and wommen, o thyng warne I
     yow:
If any wight be in this chirche now
That hath doon synne horrible, that he
Dar nat, for shame, of it yshryven be,   380 yshryven: shrived.
Or any womman, be she yong or old,
That hath ymaked hir housbonde cokewold,   cokewold: cuckold.
Swich folk shal have no power ne no grace
To offren to my relikes in this place.
And whoso fyndeth hym out of swich blame, 385
They wol come up and offre a Goddes name,   a: in.
And I assoille hem by the auctoritee   assoille: absolve.

---

345. To spice and color my preaching with.
347. cristal stones: jars made of crystal. (For Chaucer's statement see General Prologue, l. 700.)
355. The word **worm** is first the object of **hath ete** and then the subject of **hath ystonge**.

Which that by bulle ygraunted was to me.'
   By this gaude have I wonne, yeer by yeer,   gaude: trick.
An hundred mark sith I was pardoner.   390
I stonde lyk a clerk in my pulpet,
And whan the lewed peple is doun yset,   lewed: ignorant.
I preche so as ye han herd bifore,
And telle an hundred false japes more.
Thanne peyne I me to strecche forth the   peyne I me: I strive.
       nekke,   395
And est and west upon the peple I bekke,   bekke: nod.
As dooth a dowve sittynge on a berne.   berne: barn.
Myne handes and my tonge goon so yerne   yerne: eagerly, quickly.
That it is joye to se my bisynesse.
Of avarice and of swich cursednesse   400   cursednesse: sinfulness.
Is al my prechyng, for to make hem free   free: generous.
To yeven hir pens, and namely unto me.   namely: especially.
For myn entente is nat but for to wynne,
And nothyng for correccioun of synne.
I rekke nevere, whan that they been beryed, 405   beryed: buried.
Though that hir soules goon a-blakeberyed!   goon a-blakeberyed: go to perdition.
For certes, many a predicacioun   predicacioun: sermon.
Comth ofte tyme of yvel entencioun;
Som for plesance of folk and flaterye,   plesance: the pleasing.
To been avaunced by ypocrisye,   410
And som for veyne glorie, and som for hate.
For whan I dar noon oother weyes debate,   debate: quarrel.
Thanne wol I stynge hym with my tonge smerte
In prechyng, so that he shal nat asterte   asterte: escape.
To been defamed falsly, if that he   415
Hath trespased to my bretheren or to me.   trespased: done wrong.
For though I telle noght his propre name,
Men shal wel knowe that it is the same,
By signes, and by othere circumstances.
Thus quyte I folk that doon us displesances; 420
Thus spitte I out my venym under hewe
Of holynesse, to seme holy and trewe.
   But shortly myn entente I wol devyse:
I preche of no thyng but for coveityse.
Therfore my theme is yet, and evere was,   425
Radix malorum est Cupiditas.
Thus kan I preche agayn that same vice   agayn: against.
Which that I use, and that is avarice.
But though myself be gilty in that synne,
Yet kan I maken oother folk to twynne   430   twynne from: forsake, renounce.
From avarice, and soore to repente.
But that is nat my principal entente;
I preche nothyng but for coveitise.

---

390. A mark would be worth today between $25.00 and $30.00.

Of this mateere it oghte ynogh suffise.
    Thanne telle I hem ensamples many oon   435   **ensamples:** illustrative tales.
Of olde stories longe tyme agoon.
For lewed peple loven tales olde;   **lewed:** ignorant.
Swiche thynges kan they wel reporte and holde.
What, trowe ye, that whiles I may preche,
And wynne gold and silver for I teche,   440   **for:** because.
That I wol lyve in poverte wilfully?
Nay, nay, I thoghte it nevere, trewely!
For I wol preche and begge in sondry landes;
I wol nat do no labour with myne handes,
Ne make baskettes, and lyve therby,   445
By cause I wol nat beggen ydelly.   **ydelly:** uselessly; i.e., without profit.
I wol noon of the apostles countrefete;   **countrefete:** imitate.
I wol have moneie, wolle, chese, and whete,
Al were it yeven of the povereste page,   **page:** servant.
Or of the povereste wydwe in a village,   450
Al sholde hir children sterve for famyne.   **sterve:** die.
Nay, I wol drynke licour of the vyne,
And have a joly wenche in every toun.
    But herkneth, lordynges, in conclusioun:
Youre likyng is that I shal telle a tale.   455
Now have I dronke a draughte of corny ale,   **corny:** tasting strong of the malt.
By God, I hope I shal yow telle a thyng
That shal by reson been at youre likyng.   **by reson:** naturally; of course.
For though myself be a ful vicious man,
A moral tale yet I yow telle kan,   460
Which I am wont to preche for to wynne.
Now hoold youre pees! my tale I wol bigynne."

Heere bigynneth the
Pardoners tale.

    In Flaundres whilom was a compaignye
Of yonge folk that haunteden folye,   **haunteden:** habitually practiced.
As riot, hasard, stywes, and tavernes,   465   **folye:** sinfulness.
Where as with harpes, lutes, and gyternes,   **gyternes:** guitars.
They daunce and pleyen at dees bothe day and   **dees:** dice.
      nyght,
And eten also and drynken over hir myght,   **over hir myght:** to excess.
Thurgh which they doon the devel sacrifise
Withinne that develes temple, in cursed wise, 470
By superfluytee abhomynable.   **superfluytee:** overindulgence.

---

441. Voluntary poverty was enjoined by the religious orders.
445. St. Jerome enjoined Rusticus to imitate the apostles by working with his hands and sug-
gested that he weave baskets; see *Epistola CXXV: Ad Rusticum Monachum*, § 11.
465. **riot:** debauchery. **hasard:** medieval craps. **stywes:** brothels.

Hir othes been so grete and so dampnable   othes: oaths.
That it is grisly for to heere hem swere.   grisly: horrible.
Oure blissed Lordes body they totere,—
Hem thoughte that Jewes rente hym noght   hem thoughte: it seemed to them.
       ynough;   475
And ech of hem at otheres synne lough.   lough: laughed.
And right anon thanne comen tombesteres
Fetys and smale, and yonge frutesteres,   fetys: shapely. smale: slender.
Syngeres with harpes, baudes, wafereres,   baudes: bawds.
Whiche been the verray develes officeres   480
To kyndle and blowe the fyr of lecherye,
That is annexed unto glotonye.   annexed: connected.
The hooly writ take I to my witnesse
That luxurie is in wyn and dronkenesse.   luxurie: lust, licentiousness.
   Lo, how that dronken Loth, unkyndely,   485   unkyndely: unnaturally.
Lay by his doghtres two, unwityngly;
So dronke he was, he nyste what he wroghte.
   Herodes, whoso wel the stories soghte,
Whan he of wyn was repleet at his feeste,
Right at his owene table he yaf his heeste   490   heeste: command.
To sleen the Baptist John, ful giltelees.   sleen: slay.
   Senec seith a good word doutelees;
He seith he kan no difference fynde
Bitwix a man that is out of his mynde
And a man which that is dronkelewe,   495   dronkelewe: addicted to drink.
But that woodnesse, yfallen in a shrewe,
Persevereth lenger than dooth dronkenesse.
O glotonye, ful of cursednesse!
O cause first of oure confusioun!   confusioun: ruin.
O original of oure dampnacioun,   500   original: origin.
Til Crist hadde boght us with his blood agayn!   boght agayn: redeemed.
Lo, how deere, shortly for to sayn,   deere: dearly.
Aboght was thilke cursed vileynye!   aboght: paid for.
Corrupt was al this world for glotonye.   for: because of.
   Adam oure fader, and his wyf also,   505
Fro Paradys to labour and to wo
Were dryven for that vice, it is no drede.   drede: doubt.
For whil that Adam fasted, as I rede,
He was in Paradys; and whan that he
Eet of the fruyt deffended on the tree,   510   eet: ate. deffended: forbidden.
Anon he was out cast to wo and peyne.

---

474. **totere:** tear in pieces (through oaths by the parts of the body of Christ).
477–79. **tombesteres; frutesteres; wafereres:** female tumblers or dancers; fruit girls; girls selling wafers (thin, crisp, hot cakes; cf. Miller's Tale, l. 3379) and other confections.
484. See Ephesians v.18.
485. **Loth:** Lot; see Genesis xix.30–38.
488. **whoso . . . soghte:** (as anyone would learn) who searched the stories carefully.
496. **woodnesse, yfallen in a shrewe:** madness, when it possesses a person of evil disposition.

O glotonye, on thee wel oghte us pleyne!   pleyne: complain.
O, wiste a man how manye maladyes   wiste a man: if a man knew.
Folwen of excesse and of glotonyes,   of: from.
He wolde been the moore mesurable   515   mesurable: moderate.
Of his diete, sittynge at his table.
Allas! the shorte throte, the tendre mouth,
Maketh that est and west and north and south,
In erthe, in eir, in water, men to swynke   swynke: labor.
To gete a glotoun deyntee mete and drynke!   520
Of this matiere, o Paul, wel kanstow trete: kanstow: canst thou.
"Mete unto wombe, and wombe eek unto mete,   wombe: belly.
Shal God destroyen bothe," as Paulus seith.
Allas! a foul thyng is it, by my feith,
To seye this word, and fouler is the dede,   525
Whan man so drynketh of the white and rede
That of his throte he maketh his pryvee,
Thurgh thilke cursed superfluitee.
    The apostel wepyng seith ful pitously,
"Ther walken manye of whiche yow toold
        have I—   530
I seye it now wepyng, with pitous voys—
They been enemys of Cristes croys,   croys: cross.
Of whiche the ende is deeth, wombe is hir god!"
O wombe! O bely! O stynkyng cod,   cod: bag (here for stomach).
Fulfilled of dong and of corrupcioun!   535   fulfilled: filled full.
At either ende of thee foul is the soun.   soun: sound.
How greet labour and cost is thee to fynde!   fynde: provide for.
Thise cookes, how they stampe, and streyne,   stampe: pulverize.
        and grynde,
And turnen substaunce into accident,
To fulfillen al thy likerous talent!   540   likerous talent: dainty appetite.
Out of the harde bones knokke they
The mary, for they caste noght awey   mary: marrow.
That may go thurgh the golet softe and swoote.   golet: gullet, throat. swoote: sweetly.
Of spicerie of leef, and bark, and roote
Shal been his sauce ymaked by delit,   545
To make hym yet a newer appetit.
But, certes, he that haunteth swiche delices   haunteth: resorts to. delices: delica-
Is deed, whil that he lyveth in tho vices.   cies.
    A lecherous thyng is wyn, and dronkenesse
Is ful of stryvyng and of wrecchednesse.   550
O dronke man, disfigured is thy face,

---

517. The brief pleasures of swallowing, of tasting.
522. See I Corinthians vi.13.
530. See Philippians iii.18–19.
535. corrupcioun: decomposed matter.
539. substaunce: immaterial essence.   accident: physical property (such as form, color, taste).

Sour is thy breeth, foul artow to embrace,
And thurgh thy dronke nose semeth the soun   semeth: seems.
As though thou seydest ay "Sampsoun,
       Sampsoun!"
And yet, God woot, Sampsoun drank nevere no
       wyn.   555
Thou fallest as it were a styked swyn;
Thy tonge is lost, and al thyn honeste cure;
For dronkenesse is verray sepulture   sepulture: burial.
Of mannes wit and his discrecioun.
In whom that drynke hath dominacioun   560
He kan no conseil kepe, it is no drede.   conseil: secret.
Now kepe yow fro the white and fro the rede,
And namely fro the white wyn of Lepe,   namely: especially.
That is to selle in Fysshstrete or in Chepe.
This wyn of Spaigne crepeth subtilly   565
In othere wynes, growynge faste by,
Of which ther ryseth swich fumositee   fumositee: fumes arising from drunk-
That whan a man hath dronken draughtes   enness.
       thre,
And weneth that he be at hoom in Chepe,
He is in Spaigne, right at the toune of Lepe,— 570
Nat at the Rochele, ne at Burdeux toun;
And thanne wol he seye "Sampsoun, Sampsoun!"
   But herkneth, lordynges, o word, I yow preye,
That alle the sovereyn actes, dar I seye,   sovereyn: supreme.
Of victories in the Olde Testament,   575
Thurgh verray God, that is omnipotent,
Were doon in abstinence and in prayere.
Looketh the Bible, and ther ye may it leere.   leere: learn.
   Looke, Attilla, the grete conquerour,
Deyde in his sleep, with shame and
       dishonour,   580
Bledynge at his nose in dronkenesse.
A capitayn sholde lyve in sobrenesse.
And over al this, avyseth yow right wel
What was comaunded unto Lamuel—
Nat Samuel, but Lamuel, seye I—   585
Redeth the Bible, and fynde it expresly
Of wyn-yevying to hem than han justise.   han: have charge of.
Namoore of this, for it may wel suffise.

---

556. You fall like a stuck pig.
557. **honeste cure:** care for honorable things, sense of decency.
563. **Lepe:** a town on the southwest coast of Spain, known for its strong wines.
564. **Fysshstrete . . . Chepe:** London streets known for wine merchants and taverns.
565. The cheaper Spanish wine would mysteriously contaminate the French wines (see l. 571) produced near by.
585. **Lamuel:** Lemuel; see Proverbs xxxi.4–5.

And now that I have spoken of glotonye,
Now wol I yow deffenden hasardrye.   590   deffenden: forbid. hasardrye: dicing.
Hasard is verray moder of lesynges,   lesynges: lies.
And of deceite, and cursed forswerynges,   forswerynges: false oaths.
Blaspheme of Crist, manslaughtre, and wast also   blaspheme: blaspheming.
Of catel and of tyme; and forthermo,   catel: goods.
It is repreeve and contrarie of honour   595   repreeve: shame. contrarie: opposite.
For to ben holde a commune hasardour.   hasardour: gambler.
And ever the hyer he is of estaat,
The moore is he holden desolaat.   holden: considered. desolaat: aban-
If that a prynce useth hasardrye,   doned; dissolute.
In alle governaunce and policye   600
He is, as by commune opinioun,
Yholde the lasse in reputacioun.

  Stilboun, that was a wys embassadour,
Was sent to Corynthe, in ful greet honour,
Fro Lacidomye, to make hire alliaunce.   605
And whan he cam, hym happede, par chaunce,
That alle the gretteste that were of that lond,
Pleyynge atte hasard he hem fond.
For which, as soone as it myghte be,
He stal hym hoom agayn to his contree,   610   stal hym: stole away.
And seyde, "Ther wol I nat lese my name,
N'I wol nat take on me so greet defame,   defame: dishonor.
Yow for to allie unto none hasardours.
Sendeth othere wise embassadours;
For, by my trouthe, me were levere dye   615
Than I yow sholde to hasardours allye.
For ye, that been so glorious in honours,
Shul nat allyen yow with hasardours
As by my wyl, ne as by my tretee."
This wise philosophre, thus seyde he.   620

  Looke eek that to the kyng Demetrius   looke: consider.
The kyng of Parthes, as the book seith us,   Parthes: Parthians.
Sente him a paire of dees of gold in scorn,   dees: dice.
For he hadde used hasard ther-biforn;
For which he heeld his glorie or his renoun   625
At no value or reputacioun.
Lordes may fynden oother maner pley
Honest ynough to dryve the day awey.

  Now wol I speke of othes false and grete   othes: oaths.
A word or two, as olde bookes trete.   630
Gret sweryng is a thyng abhominable,
And fals sweryng is yet moore reprevable.   reprevable: reprehensible.
The heighe God forbad sweryng at al,
Witnesse on Mathew; but in special
Of sweryng seith the hooly Jeremye,   635

---

622. the book: the *Communiloquium* of John of Wales, who retold this and the preceding story from John of Salisbury's *Policraticus*.

"Thou shalt swere sooth thyne othes, and nat
      lye,
And swere in doom, and eek in rightwisnesse";
But ydel sweryng is a cursednesse.
Bihoold and se that in the firste table
Of heighe Goddes heestes honurable,   640
Hou that the seconde heeste of hym is this:
"Take nat my name in ydel or amys."
Lo, rather he forbedeth swich sweryng
Than homycide or many a cursed thyng;
I seye that, as by ordre, thus it standeth;   645
This knowen, that his heestes understandeth,
How that the seconde heeste of God is that.
And forther over, I wol thee telle al plat,
That vengeance shal nat parten from his hous
That of his othes is to outrageous.   650
"By Goddes precious herte," and "By his nayles,"
And "By the blood of Crist that is in Hayles,
Sevene is my chaunce, and thyn is cynk and
      treye!"
"By Goddes armes, if thou falsly pleye,
This daggere shal thurghout thyn herte go!"— 655
This fruyt cometh of the bicched bones two,
Forsweryng, ire, falsnesse, homycide.
Now, for the love of Crist, that for us dyde,
Lete youre othes, bothe grete and smale.
But, sires, now wol I telle forth my tale.   660

    Thise riotoures thre of whiche I telle,
Longe erst er prime rong of any belle,
Were set hem in a taverne to drynke,
And as they sat, they herde a belle clynke
Biforn a cors, was caried to his grave.   665
That oon of hem gan callen to his knave:
"Go bet," quod he, "and axe redily
What cors is this that passeth heer forby;
And looke that thou reporte his name weel."
    "Sire," quod this boy, "it nedeth never-a-
      deel;   670
It was me toold er ye cam heer two houres.
He was, pardee, an old felawe of youres;
And sodeynly he was yslayn to-nyght,
Fordronke, as he sat on his bench upright.

Glosses:

sooth: truthfully.

in doom: i.e., in court. rightwisnesse: righteousness.

heestes: commandments.

in ydel: in vain.
rather: sooner.

knowen, that: (they) know, (i.e., he) who.

forther over: furthermore. plat: flatly, plainly. parten: depart.

to: too.

cynk: five.
treye: three.

thurghout: quite through.
bicched: cursed (bitched).
forsweryng: perjury.

lete: let alone, give up.

riotoures: debauchees.
erst er: before.

cors: corpse. was: (which) was.

redily: quickly.
forby: by.

never-a-deel: not at all.

to-nyght: last night.
fordronke: very drunk. upright: lying on his back (asleep).

---

636. See Jeremiah iv.2.
639. firste table: the first five commandments, which teach man's duty to God.
641. seconde: the third in the Protestant Bible.
652. Some of Christ's blood was supposed to be preserved at Hayles in Gloucestershire.
653. chaunce: the number a dicer must throw in order to win.
667. bet: (better) i.e., faster, as quickly as possible.

Ther cam a privee theef, men clepeth Deeth,   675
That in this contree al the peple sleeth,
And with his spere he smoot his herte atwo,   atwo: in two.
And wente his wey withouten wordes mo.
He hath a thousand slayn this pestilence.
And, maister, er ye come in his presence,   680
Me thynketh that it were necessarie
For to be war of swich an adversarie.
Beth redy for to meete hym everemoore;   beth everemoore: always be.
Thus taughte me my dame; I sey namoore."   dame: mother.
"By Seinte Marie!" seyde this taverner,   685
"The child seith sooth, for he hath slayn this
          yeer,
Henne over a mile, withinne a greet village,   henne: hence.
Bothe man and womman, child, and hyne, and   hyne: servant.
          page;
I trowe his habitacioun be there.
To been avysed greet wysdom it were,   690 been avysed: take thought.
Er that he dide a man a dishonour."
    "Ye, Goddes armes!" quod this riotour,
"Is it swich peril with hym for to meete?
I shal hym seke by wey and eek by strete,   wey: road. strete: highway.
I make avow to Goddes digne bones!   695 avow: vow. digne: worthy.
Herkneth, felawes, we thre been al ones;   ones: of one mind.
Lat ech of us holde up his hand til oother,   til: to.
And ech of us bicomen otheres brother,
And we wol sleen this false traytour Deeth.
He shal be slayn, he that so manye sleeth,   700
By Goddes dignitee, er it be nyght!"
    Togidres han thise thre hir trouthes plight   hir trouthes plight: pledged their
To lyve and dyen ech of hem for oother,   promises.
As though he were his owene ybore brother.   ybore: born.
And up they stirte, al dronken in this rage,   705
And forth they goon towardes that village
Of which the taverner hadde spoke biforn.
And many a grisly ooth thanne han they sworn,
And Cristes blessed body they torente—   torente: rent in pieces (by their
Deeth shal be deed, if that they may hym   oaths).
          hente!   710
    Whan they han goon nat fully half a mile,
Right as they wolde han troden over a stile,
An old man and a povre with hem mette.   povre: poor.
This olde man ful mekely hem grette,   grette: greeted.
And seyde thus, "Now, lordes, God yow see!" 715 God yow see!: may God protect you!
    The proudeste of thise riotoures three
Answerde agayn, "What, carl, with sory grace!   carl: fellow. with sory grace: i.e., con-
                                                                 found you!
_____

675. **privee:** stealthy. **theef:** villain; thief.
696–704. See Knight's Tale, l. 1132 and footnote.

Why artow al forwrapped save thy face?   forwrapped: wrapped up.
Why lyvestow so longe in so greet age?"   lyvestow: do you live.
    This olde man gan looke in his visage,   720
And seyde thus, "For I ne kan nat fynde
A man, though that I walked into Inde,
Neither in citee ne in no village,
That wolde chaunge his youthe for myn age;
And therfore moot I han myn age stille,   725
As longe tyme as it is Goddes wille.
Ne Deeth, allas! ne wol nat han my lyf.
Thus walke I, lyk a restelees kaityf,   kaityf: captive; wretch.
And on the ground, which is my modres gate,
I knokke with my staf, bothe erly and late,   730
And seye 'Leeve moder, leet me in!
Lo how I vanysshe, flessh, and blood, and skyn!
Allas! whan shul my bones been at reste?
Moder, with yow wolde I chaunge my cheste   cheste: storage chest (with contents).
That in my chambre longe tyme hath be,   735   be: been.
Ye, for an heyre clowt to wrappe me!'   heyre clowt: a piece of hair cloth.
But yet to me she wol nat do that grace,
For which ful pale and welked is my face.   welked: withered.
    But, sires, to yow it is no curteisye
To speken to an old man vileynye,   740
But he trespasse in word, or elles in dede.   but: unless.
In holy writ ye may yourself wel rede:
'Agayns an old man, hoor upon his heed,   agayns: before, in presence of.
Ye sholde arise'; wherfore I yeve yow reed,   reed: counsel.
Ne dooth unto an old man noon harm now,   745
Namoore than that ye wolde men did to yow
In age, if that ye so longe abyde.
And God be with yow, wher ye go or ryde!   wher: whether. go: walk.
I moot go thider as I have to go."
    "Nay, olde cherl, by God, thou shalt nat
       so,"   750
Seyde this oother hasardour anon;   hasardour: dicer.
"Thou partest nat so lightly, by Seint John!
Thou spak right now of thilke traytour Deeth,
That in this contree alle oure freendes sleeth.
Have heer my trouthe, as thou art his espye,   755   trouthe: promise.
Telle where he is, or thou shalt it abye,   abye: pay for.
By God, and by the holy sacrament!
For soothly thou art oon of his assent   assent: conspiracy.
To sleen us yonge folk, thou false theef!"
    "Now, sires," quod he, "if that yow be so   yow be so leef: you desire so.
       leef   760
To fynde Deeth, turne up this croked wey,

---

743. See Leviticus xix.32.

For in that grove I lafte hym, by my fey,   lafte: left. fey: faith.
Under a tree, and there he wol abyde;
Noght for youre boost he wol him no thyng boost: boasting, loud talk.
   hyde.
Se ye that ook? Right there ye shal hym fynde. 765 ook: oak.
God save yow, that boghte agayn mankynde, boghte agayn: redeemed.
And yow amende!" Thus seyde this olde man; amende: save.
And everich of thise riotoures ran
Til they came to that tree, and ther they founde
Of floryns fyne of gold ycoyned rounde   770
Wel ny an eighte busshels, as hem thoughte.
No lenger thanne after Deeth they soughte,
But ech of hem so glad was of the sighte,
For that the floryns been so faire and brighte,
That doun they sette hem by this precious
   hoord.   775
The worste of hem, he spak the firste word.
 "Bretheren," quod he, "taak kepe what I seye;
My wit is greet, though that I bourde and pleye. bourde: jest.
This tresor hath Fortune unto us yiven,
In myrthe and jolitee oure lyf to lyven,   780
And lightly as it cometh, so wol we spende.
Ey! Goddes precious dignitee! who wende wende: would have thought.
To-day that we sholde han so fair a grace? grace: fortune.
But myghte this gold be caried fro this place
Hoom to myn hous, or elles unto youres— 785
For wel ye woot that al this gold is oures—
Thanne were we in heigh felicitee.
But trewely, by daye it may nat be.
Men wolde seyn that we were theves stronge, stronge: flagrantly guilty.
And for oure owene tresor doon us honge. 790 doon us honge: have us hanged.
This tresor moste ycaried be by nyghte
As wisely and as slyly as it myghte.
Wherfore I rede that cut among us alle   rede: advise. cut: lots.
Be drawe, and lat se wher the cut wol falle;
And he that hath the cut with herte blithe 795
Shal renne to the town, and that ful swithe, swithe: quickly.
And brynge us breed and wyn ful prively.
And two of us shul kepen subtilly   kepen: guard. subtilly: skilfully.
This tresor wel; and if he wol nat tarie,
Whan it is nyght, we wol this tresor carie, 800
By oon assent, where as us thynketh best." by oon assent: in complete agree-
That oon of hem the cut broghte in his fest,   ment.
And bad hem drawe, and looke where it wol
   falle;
And it fil on the yongeste of hem alle,
And forth toward the toun he wente anon. 805

---

779. Henri de Bracton, the thirteenth-century English legal writer, said, "It is believed that treasure is the gift of Fortune": "Thesaurus donum fortunae creditur." He also makes clear that concealment of treasure-trove (treasure which someone finds) such as this, is theft of the King's gold.

And also soone as that he was gon,
That oon of hem spak thus unto that oother:
"Thow knowest wel thou art my sworn brother;
Thy profit wol I telle thee anon.
Thou woost wel that oure felawe is agon,   810
And heere is gold, and that ful greet plentee,
That shal departed been among us thre.   departed: divided.
But nathelees, if I kan shape it so
That it departed were among us two,
Hadde I nat doon a freendes torn to thee?"   815 torn: turn.
    That oother answerde, "I noot hou that may
        be.
He woot that the gold is with us tweye;
What shal we doon? What shal we to hym seye?"
    "Shal it be conseil?" seyde the firste shrewe,   conseil: a secret.
"And I shal tellen in a wordes fewe   820
What we shal doon, and brynge it wel aboute."
    "I graunte," quod that oother, "out of doute,   graunte: promise.
That, by my trouthe, I wol thee nat biwreye."   biwreye: betray.
    "Now," quod the firste, "thou woost wel we
        be tweye,
And two of us shul strenger be than oon.   825
Looke whan that he is set, that right anoon   looke: make sure.
Arys as though thou woldest with hym pleye,   arys: arise.
And I shal ryve hym thurgh the sydes tweye,   ryve: pierce.
Whil that thou strogelest with hym as in game,   game: sport.
And with thy daggere looke thou do the same; 830
And thanne shal al this gold departed be,   departed: divided.
My deere freend, bitwixen me and thee.
Thanne may we bothe oure lustes all fulfille,
And pleye at dees right at oure owene wille."   dees: dice.
And thus acorded been thise shrewes tweye   835
To sleen the thridde, as ye han herd me seye.
    This yongeste, which that wente to the toun,
Ful ofte in herte he rolleth up and doun
The beautee of thise floryns newe and brighte.
"O Lord!" quod he, "if so were that I myghte 840
Have al this tresor to myself allone,
Ther is no man that lyveth under the trone   trone: throne.
Of God that sholde lyve so murye as I!"
And atte laste the feend, oure enemy,
Putte in his thought that he sholde poyson
        beye,   845 beye: buy.
With which he myghte sleen his felawes tweye;
For-why the feend foond hym in swich lyvynge   for-why: because. lyvynge: state of
That he hadde leve him to sorwe brynge.   life.
For this was outrely his fulle entente,
To sleen hem bothe, and nevere to repente.   850

---

848. That he had permission to bring him to sorrow.

And forth he goth, no lenger wolde he tarie,
Into the toun, unto a pothecarie,
And preyde hym that he hym wolde selle
Som poyson, that he myghte his rattes quelle;   quelle: kill.
And eek ther was a polcat in his hawe,   855   hawe: yard.
That, as he seyde, his capouns hadde yslawe,   yslawe: slain, killed.
And fayn he wolde wreke hym, if he myghte,   wreke: avenge.
On vermyn that destroyed hym by nyghte.   destroyed: ruined, harassed.
   The pothecarie answerde, "And thou shalt
      have
A thyng that, also God my soule save,   860
In al this world ther is no creature,
That ete or dronke hath of this confiture   confiture: mixture.
Nat but the montance of a corn of whete,   montance: amount. corn: grain.
That he ne shal his lif anon forlete;   forlete: yield up.
Ye, sterve he shal, and that in lasse while   865   sterve: die.
Than thou wolt goon a paas nat but a mile,   goon a paas: walk at a footpace.
The poysoun is so strong and violent."
   This cursed man hath in his hond yhent   yhent: taken.
This poysoun in a box, and sith he ran   sith: then.
Into the nexte strete unto a man,   870
And borwed hym large botels thre;   hym: i.e., for himself.
And in the two his poyson poured he;
The thridde he kepte clene for his drynke.
For al the nyght he shoop hym for to swynke   shoop: intended. swynke: labor.
In cariynge of the gold out of that place.   875
And whan this riotour, with sory grace,   with sory grace: i.e., confound him!
Hadde filled with wyn his grete botels thre,
To his felawes agayn repaireth he.
   What nedeth it to sermone of it moore?
For right as they hadde cast his deeth bifore, 880   cast: plotted.
Right so they han hym slayn, and that anon.
And whan that this was doon, thus spak that oon:
"Now lat us sitte and drynke, and make us merie,
And afterward we wol his body berie."
And with that word it happed hym, par cas,   885   par cas: perchance.
To take the botel ther the poyson was,
And drank, and yaf his felawe drynke also,
For which anon they storven bothe two.   storven: died.

Part of a chest-front depicting scenes from the Pardoner's Tale: In the catalogue of the exhibition, "Chaucer's London," in the London Museum (1972) Brian Spencer dates this elm chest-front "c. 1400" on the evidence of costume and hairstyle. Indeed the scenes themselves appear to be closer to the Pardoner's Tale than to any of its analogues. The scene at left brings to mind how the youngest "riotour" "borwed hym large botels thre" (871). In the central scene all three "riotoures" are about to succeed in their quest "To fynde Deeth" (761; 880–88). At right the two older "riotoures" are shown with the "breed and wyn" (797) brought from town; one "felawe" is finishing "the botel ther the poyson was" (886); the other appears already to have had his share. The fox in the lower right corner is perhaps intended to bring to mind the "feend" (844–48), who now goes about other business. The missing left-hand portion of the chest-front may have balanced these scenes with the tavern, the old man, and the florins under the oak.

But certes, I suppose that Avycen
Wroot nevere in no canon, ne in no fen,   890   fen: section.
Mo wonder signes of empoisonyng   wonder: strange. signes: symptoms.
Than hadde thise wrecches two, er hir endyng.
Thus ended been thise homicides two,
And eek the false empoysonere also.

  O cursed synne of alle cursednesse!   895
O traytours homicide, O wikkednesse!   traytours: traitorous.
O glotonye, luxurie, and hasardrye!   hasardrye: gambling.
Thou blasphemour of Crist with vileynye   vilyeynye: vile speech.
And othes grete, of usage and of pride!   of usage: from habit.
Allas! mankynde, how may it bitide   900
That to thy creatour, which that thee wroghte,
And with his precious herte-blood thee boghte,   boghte: redeemed.
Thou art so fals and so unkynde, allas?   unkynde: ungrateful.
  Now, goode men, God foryeve yow youre
          trespas,
And ware yow fro the synne of avarice!   905   ware yow fro: beware of, avoid.
Myn hooly pardoun may yow alle warice,   warice: save.
So that ye offre nobles or sterlynges,   so that: provided that.
Or elles silver broches, spoones, rynges.
Boweth youre heed under this holy bulle!
Cometh up, ye wyves, offreth of youre wolle!   910
Youre name I entre here in my rolle anon;
Into the blisse of hevene shul ye gon.
I yow assoille, by myn heigh power,   assoille: absolve.
Yow that wol offre, as clene and eek as cleer   cleer: pure.
As ye were born.—And lo, sires, thus I
          preche.   915
And Jhesu Crist, that is oure soules leche,   leche: physician.
So graunte yow his pardoun to receyve,
For that is best; I wol yow nat deceyve.
  But, sires, o word forgat I in my tale:
I have relikes and pardon in my male,   920   male: bag, wallet.
As faire as any man in Engelond,
Whiche were me yeven by the popes hond.
If any of yow wol, of devocion,
Offren, and han myn absolucion,
Com forth anon, and kneleth here adoun,   925
And mekely receyveth my pardoun;
Or elles taketh pardoun as ye wende,
Al newe and fressh at every miles ende,

---

889. Avycen: Avicenna (see General Prologue, I. 432), who wrote on medicine.
890. canon: rule of procedure.
907. nobles: gold coins, valued at 6s 8d (a third of a pound). **sterlynges:** silver pennies; a penny was worth perhaps between $1.50 and $2.00 in modern money.
928. every miles ende: perhaps refers to the Roman milestones (*miliaria*) which formerly were situated along the London–Canterbury road.

So that ye offren, alwey newe and newe,   newe and newe: continually.
Nobles or pens, whiche that be goode and   pens: pence.
     trewe.   930
It is an honour to everich that is heer
That ye mowe have a suffisant pardoner
T'assoille yow, in contree as ye ryde,
For aventures whiche that may bityde.   aventures: misfortunes.
Paraventure ther may fallen oon or two   935
Doun of his hors, and breke his nekke atwo.   of: off. atwo: in two.
Looke which a seuretee is it to yow alle   seuretee: security.
That I am in youre felaweshipe yfalle,
That may assoille yow, bothe moore and lasse,
Whan that the soule shal fro the body passe.   940
I rede that oure Hoost shal bigynne,   rede: counsel.
For he is moost enveluped in synne.   enveluped: wrapped up.
Com forth, sire Hoost, and offre first anon,
And thou shalt kisse the relikes everychon,
Ye, for a grote! Unbokele anon thy purs."   945
   "Nay, nay!" quod he, "thanne have I Cristes
     curs!
Lat be," quod he, "it shal nat be, so theech!   so theech!: so may I prosper!
Thou woldest make me kisse thyn olde breech,   breech: underpants.
And swere it were a relyk of a seint,
Though it were with thy fundement depeint!   950   fundement: fundament, anus. depeint:
But, by the croys which that Seint Eleyne fond,   painted, stained.
I wolde I hadde thy coillons in myn hond   coillons: testicles.
In stide of relikes or of seintuarie.   seintuarie: a box containing relics.
Lat kutte hem of, I wol thee helpe hem carie;
They shul be shryned in an hogges toord!"   955   shryned: enshrined. toord: turd.
   This Pardoner answerde nat a word;
So wrooth he was, no word ne wolde he seye.
   "Now," quod oure Hoost, "I wol no lenger
     pleye
With thee, ne with noon oother angry man."
But right anon the worthy Knyght bigan,   960
Whan that he saugh that al the peple lough,   lough: laughed.
"Namoore of this, for it is right ynough!
Sire Pardoner, be glad and myrie of cheere;
And ye, sire Hoost, that been to me so deere,
I pray yow that ye kisse the Pardoner.   965
And Pardoner, I prey thee, drawe thee neer,
And, as we diden, lat us laughe and pleye."
Anon they kiste, and ryden forth hir weye.   ryden: rode.

Here is ended the Pardoners tale.

---

945. grote: groat, a silver coin valued at fourpence.
951. Seint Eleyne: St. Helen, the mother of Constantine, is said to have found the true Cross.

The prologe of the
Seconde Nonnes tale.

The ministre and the norice unto vices,   ministre: servant. **norice**: nurse.
Which that men clepe in Englissh ydelnesse,
That porter of the gate is of delices,   delices: sensual pleasures.
To eschue, and by hir contrarie hire oppresse,   oppresse: put down.
That is to seyn, by leveful bisynesse,   5 leveful: permissible.
Wel oghte we to doon al oure entente,   doon al oure entente: take all pains.
Lest that the feend thurgh ydelnesse us hente.

For he that with his thousand cordes slye
Continuelly us waiteth to biclappe,   biclappe: trap suddenly.
Whan he may man in ydelnesse espye,   10
He kan so lightly cacche hym in his trappe,
Til that a man be hent right by the lappe,   lappe: edge of a garment.
He nys nat war the feend hath hym in honde.
Wel oghte us werche, and ydelnesse withstonde.

And though men dradden nevere for to dye, 15
Yet seen men wel by resoun, doutelees,
That ydelnesse is roten slogardye,   slogardye: slothfulness.
Of which ther nevere comth no good n'encrees, encrees: profit.
And syn that slouthe hir holdeth in a lees   hir: i.e., idleness. lees: leash.
Oonly to slepe, and for to ete and drynke,   20
And to devouren al that othere swynke,   othere swynke: others work for.

And for to putte us from swich ydelnesse,
That cause is of so greet confusioun,   confusioun: ruin.
I have here doon my feithful bisynesse,
After the legende, in translacioun   25
Right of thy glorious lif and passioun,   passioun: martyrdom.
Thou with thy gerland wroght of rose and lilie,—
Thee meene I, mayde and martyr, Seint Cecilie.

Invocacio ad Mariam

And thow that flour of virgines art alle,
Of whom that Bernard list so wel to write, 30
To thee at my bigynnyng first I calle;
Thou confort of us wrecches, do me endite   do me endite: help me to relate.
Thy maydens deeth, that wan thurgh hir merite
The eternal lyf, and of the feend victorie,   of: over.
As man may after reden in hir storie.   35

---

8. his thousand cordes slye: i.e., the devil's net.
15. Even if men never feared to die.
27. rose and lilie: i.e., symbols respectively of martyrdom and purity.
30. The devotion of St. Bernard (1090–1153) to the Virgin was such that Dante had him offer the prayer to Mary which opens the final canto of the *Paradiso;* on this prayer are based the next three stanzas.

Thow Mayde and Moder, doghter of thy Sone,
Thow welle of mercy, synful soules cure,   welle: source.
In whom that God for bountee chees to wone,   wone: dwell.
Thow humble, and heigh over every creature,
Thow nobledest so forforth oure nature,   40 so forforth: so much.
That no desdeyn the Makere hadde of kynde   kynde: nature.
His Sone in blood and flessh to clothe and wynde. wynde: wrap.

Withinne the cloistre blisful of thy sydis
Took mannes shap the eternal love and pees,
That of the tryne compas lord and gyde is,   45 tryne compas: three realms. **gyde:**
Whom erthe and see and hevene, out of relees,   ruler. **out of relees:** without cease.
Ay heryen; and thou, Virgine wemmelees,   heryen: praise. wemmelees: spotless.
Baar of thy body—and dweltest mayde pure—   dweltest: remained.
The Creatour of every creature.

Assembled is in thee magnificence   50
With mercy, goodnesse, and with swich pitee
That thou, that art the sonne of excellence   sonne: sun.
Nat oonly helpest hem that prayen thee,   prayen: pray to.
But often tyme, of thy benygnytee,
Ful frely, er that men thyn help biseche,   55
Thou goost biforn, and art hir lyves leche.   leche: physician.

Now help, thow meeke and blisful faire mayde,
Me, flemed wrecche, in this desert of galle;   flemed wrecche: banished exile.
Thynk on the womman Cananee, that sayde   Cananee: of Canaan.
That whelpes eten somme of the crommes alle 60
That from hir lordes table been yfalle;
And though that I, unworthy sone of Eve,
Be synful, yet accepte my bileve.   bileve: devotion.

And, for that feith is deed withouten werkis, deed: dead.
So for to werken yif me wit and space,   65 space: time.
That I be quit fro thennes that most derk is! quit: set free, i.e., saved. **fro**
O thou, that art so fair and ful of grace,   **thennes:** from the place.
Be myn advocat in that heighe place
Theras withouten ende is songe "Osanne,"
Thow Cristes moder, doghter deere of Anne! 70

And of thy light my soule in prison lighte,   lighte: lighten; illuminate.
That troubled is by the contagioun
Of my body, and also by the wighte   wighte: weight.
Of erthely lust and fals affeccioun;
O havene of refut, o salvacioun   75 refut: refuge.

59–61. See Matthew xv.21–28.

62. sone of Eve: descendant of Eve. This phrase, like **flemed wrecche** (l. 58), echoes a line in the antiphon of our Lady, *Salve Regina,* which the Nun sang every day: "To thee we cry, exiled sons of Eve" ("Ad te clamamus exules filii Evae").

Of hem that been in sorwe and in distresse,
Now help, for to my work I wol me dresse.   me dresse: devote myself.

Yet praye I yow that reden that I write,   that: that which.
Foryeve me that I do no diligence   do no diligence: take no pains.
This ilke storie subtilly to endite,   80
For bothe have I the wordes and sentence   sentence: meaning.
Of hym that at the seintes reverence   at the seintes reverence: in reverence
The storie wroot, and folwe hir legende,   for the saint.
And pray yow that ye wol my work amende.   amende: correct.

Interpretacio nominis Cecilie quam ponit
frater Jacobus Januensis in legenda aurea

   First wolde I yow the name of Seinte Cecilie 85
Expowne, as men may in hir storie see.   expowne: expound, give the meaning
It is to seye in Englissh "hevenes lilie,"   of.
For pure chastnesse of virginitee;
Or, for she whitnesse hadde of honestee,   for: because. honestee: chastity.
And grene of conscience, and of good fame   90 conscience: tenderness.
The swote savour, "lilie" was hir name.   swote: sweet.

Or Cecile is to seye "the wey to blynde,"   is to seye: means. wey to blynde: path
For she ensample was by good techynge;   for the blind.
Or elles Cecile, as I writen fynde,
Is joyned, by a manere conjoinynge   95 conjoinynge: joining.
Of "hevene" and "Lia"; and here, in figurynge,   in figurynge: figuratively, symbolically.
The "hevene" is set for thoght of hoolynesse,   thoght of: meditation on.
And "Lia" for hir lastyng bisynesse.   lastyng: constant. bisynesse: dili-
    gence, industry.

Cecile may eek be seyd in this manere,   be seyd: be taken.
"Wantynge of blyndnesse," for hir grete light 100 wantynge: lack.
Of sapience, and for hir thewes cleere;   sapience: wisdom. thewes: virtues.
Or elles, lo, this maydens name bright   cleere: shining.
Of "hevene" and "leos" comth, for which by right of: from. leos: (Greek) people.
Men myghte hire wel "the hevene of peple"
    calle,
Ensample of goode and wise werkes alle.   105

For "leos" "peple" in Englissh is to seye,
And right as men may in the hevene see
The sonne and moone, and sterres every weye,   weye: direction.

Interpretacio . . . . aurea: the interpretation of the name Cecilia which James of Genoa offers in his *Golden Legend.* (Chaucer based the *Interpretacio,* and the Tale through line 357, on the *Legenda Aurea* of Jacobus de Voragine of Genoa (c. 1230–1298); for the remainder of the poem he used a different account. All the etymologies here proposed are wrong.)
95. joyned: i.e., made by joining etymological parts.
96. Lia: Leah, symbol of the active life (Genesis xxix.32–35).

Right so men goostly in this mayden free
Syen of feith the magnanymytee, 110
And eek the cleernesse hool of sapience,
And sondry werkes, brighte of excellence.

And right so as thise philosophres write
That hevene is swift and round and eek
       brennynge,
Right so was faire Cecilie the white 115
Ful swift and bisy evere in good werkynge,
And round and hool in good perseverynge,
And brennyng evere in charite ful brighte.
Now have I yow declared what she highte.

goostly: spiritually. **free**: noble.
syen: saw.
cleernesse: brightness, radiance.
  hool: whole, perfect.

brennynge: burning.

declared: explained, interpreted.

> ### Explicit.

Heere bigynneth the
Seconde Nonnes tale of
the lyf of Seinte Cecile.

  This mayden bright Cecilie, as hir lif seith, 120
Was come of Romayns, and of noble kynde,
And from hir cradel up fostred in the feith
Of Crist, and bar his gospel in hir mynde.
She nevere cessed, as I writen fynde,
Of hir prayere, and God to love and drede, 125
Bisekyng hym to kepe hir maydenhede.

And whan this mayden sholde unto a man
Ywedded be, that was ful yong of age,
Which that ycleped was Valerian,
And day was comen of hir marriage, 130
She, ful devout and humble in hir corage,
Under hir robe of gold, that sat ful faire,
Hadde next hir flessh yclad hire in an haire.

And whil the organs maden melodie,
To God allone in herte thus sang she: 135
"O Lord, my soule and eek my body gye
Unwemmed, lest that I confounded be."
And, for his love that deyde upon a tree,
Every seconde and thridde day she faste,
Ay biddyng in hir orisons ful faste. 140

kynde: birth, descent.
up fostred: brought up; instructed.
bar: bore, kept.
cessed: ceased.

bisekyng: beseeching. **kepe**: guard;
  preserve. **maydenhede**: maiden-
  hood, virginity.

ycleped: called.

corage: heart, spirit.
sat: fitted; suited.
yclad: clothed. **haire**: a shirt of hair-
  cloth.
organs: organ.

gye: preserve.
unwemmed: spotless, immaculate.
  confounded: condemned, cursed. **a
  tree**: the Cross. **faste**: fasted.
biddyng: praying. **faste**: devoutly.

---

119. **what she highte**: what she was called; her name.

The nyght cam, and to bedde moste she gon
With hire housbonde, as ofte is the manere,
And pryvely to hym she seyde anon,
"O sweete and wel biloved spouse deere,
Ther is a conseil, and ye wolde it heere, 145   conseil: secret. and: if.
Which that right fayn I wolde unto yow seye,   fayn: gladly.
So that ye swere ye shul it nat biwreye."   so that: if. biwreye: divulge.

    Valerian gan faste unto hir swere   faste: solemnly.
That for no cas, ne thyng that myghte be,   for no cas: under no circumstances.
He sholde nevere mo biwreyen here; 150   here: her.
And thanne at erst to hym thus seyde she: thanne at erst: then for the first time;
"I have an aungel which that loveth me,   not until then.
That with gret love, wher so I wake or sleepe,   wher so: whether.
Is redy ay my body for to kepe.   kepe: guard, protect.

"And if that he may feelen, out of drede, 155   feelen: perceive. drede: doubt.
That ye me touche, or love in vileynye,   in vileynye: shamefully.
He right anon wol sle yow with the dede,   sle: slay. with the dede: i.e., immedi-
And in youre youthe thus ye shullen dye;   ately.
And if that ye in clene love me gye,   clene: chaste. gye: keep, preserve.
He wol yow love as me, for youre clennesse, 160
And shewen yow his joye and his brightnesse."

    Valerian, corrected as God wolde,   corrected: admonished.
Answerde agayn, "If I shal trusten thee,
Lat me that aungel se, and hym biholde;
And if that it a verray angel be, 165   verray: true.
Thanne wol I doon as thou hast prayed me;
And if thou love another man, for sothe
Right with this swerd than wol I sle yow bothe."

    Cecile answerde anon-right in this wise: anon-right: immediately.
"If that yow list, the angel shal ye see, 170
So that ye trowe on Crist and yow baptise.   so that: provided that. yow baptise:
  receive baptism.

Eight scenes from the life of Saint Cecilia: Of the early fourteenth century, the anonymous altar-piece of the church of Santa Cecilia, Florence, depicts in the center the saint enthroned (here omitted) and on each side four scenes from her life. The church was razed in 1367 to permit enlargement of the Piazza dei Priori and was soon rebuilt near the Piazza Signoria. If the construction was completed before Chaucer came to Florence in 1373, it was a very new edifice in a central location and might have attracted such a visitor. It was demolished in the late eighteenth century and the altarpiece is now in the Uffizi. The sequence of the scenes is from the two upper scenes on the left to those below them, and then to the upper and lower scenes on the right. 1. St. Cecilia at her wedding feast; the painter has forgotten her "robe of gold" (see line 132) which was mentioned in the *Legenda Aurea*. 2. The wedding night (ll. 141–182): "I have an aungel which that loveth me" (152). 3. The angel crowns Valerian (218–224). 4. St. Cecilia preaches to Tiburce (left) while Valerian listens too (319–48). 5. Pope Urban christens Tiburce (349–53). 6. St. Cecilia at the house of Maximus (372–90). 7. Cecilia baits Almachius (321–511). 8. The martyrdom. The artist presents a strange concept of a Roman bath which he sets in an idealized Tuscan landscape (515–18). The "tormentour" is in the act of smiting Cecilia in the neck with the first stroke of his sword (526).

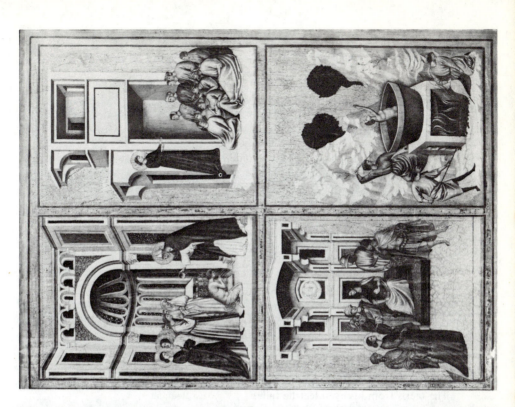

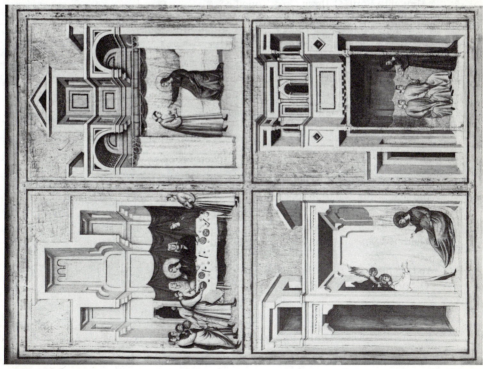

Gooth forth to Via Apia," quod she,
"That fro this toun ne stant but miles three,   stant: (standeth) stands.
And to the povre folkes that ther dwelle,
Sey hem right thus, as that I shal yow telle. 175

"Telle hem that I, Cecile, vow to hem sente,
To shewen yow the goode Urban the olde,   Urban: Pope Urban I.
For secree nedes and for good entente.   secree nedes: secret necessary busi-
And whan that ye Seint Urban han biholde,   ness. biholde: beheld, seen.
Telle hym the wordes whiche that I to yow
        tolde; 180
And whan that he hath purged yow fro synne,   purged: i.e., by baptism.
Thanne shal ye se that angel, er ye twynne."   twynne: depart.

   Valerian is to the place ygon,
And right as hym was taught by his lernynge,   lernynge: direction.
He foond this holy olde Urban anon 185
Among the seintes buryels lotynge.   buryels: graves. lotynge: lurking,
And he anon, withouten tariynge,   lying hid.
Dide his message; and whan that he it tolde,   dide: delivered.
Urban for joye his handes gan up holde.

The teeris from his eyen leet he falle.   190 leet: let.
"Almyghty Lord, O Jhesu Crist," quod he,
"Sower of chaast conseil, hierde of us alle,   chaast: virtuous. hierde: shepherd.
The fruyt of thilke seed of chastitee
That thou hast sowe in Cecile, taak to thee!   sowe: sown.
Lo, lyk a bisy bee, withouten gile, 195
Thee serveth ay thyn owene thral Cecile.   thral: servant.

"For thilke spouse that she took but now
Ful lyk a fiers leoun, she sendeth heere,
As meke as evere was any lamb, to yow!"
And with that word anon ther gan appeere 200
An old man, clad in white clothes cleere,   cleere: shining, radiant.
That hadde a book with lettres of gold in honde,
And gan bifore Valerian to stonde.

Valerian as deed fil doun for drede   deed: dead. fil: fell.
Whan he hym saugh, and he up hente hym   up hente: lifted up.
        tho, 205
And on his book right thus he gan to rede:
"O Lord, o feith, o God, withouten mo,   o: one.

---

172. The Appian Way leads south from Rome past four famous catacombs: cf. **seintes buryels**
(l. 186); the *Legenda Aurea* actually says that Valerian is to go along the Via Appia to the third
milestone.
201. an old man: i.e., an angel in the form of St. Paul.

O cristendom, and Fader of alle also,"   o cristendom: one christening.
Aboven alle and over alle everywhere."
Thise wordes al with gold ywriten were.   210

Whan this was rad, thanne seyde this olde man,   rad: read.
"Leevestow this thyng or no? Sey ye or nay."   leevestow: dost thou believe. sey ye:
"I leeve al this thyng," quod Valerian,   say 'yea'. leeve: believe.
"For sother thyng than this, I dar wel say,   sother: truer.
Under the hevene no wight thynke may."   215   thynke: imagine.
Tho vanysshed this olde man, he nyste where,   nyste: (ne wiste) knew not.
And Pope Urban hym cristned right there.

   Valerian gooth hoom and fynt Cecilie   fynt stonde: finds standing.
Withinne his chambre with an angel stonde.
This angel hadde of roses and of lilie   220
Corones two, the which he bar in honde;   corones: crowns.
And first to Cecile, as I understonde,
He yaf that oon, and after gan he take   gan take: gave.
That oother to Valerian, hir make.   make: mate.

"With body clene and with unwemmed thoght 225   clene: pure, chaste. unwemmed:
Kepeth ay wel thise corones," quod he;   spotless, pure. kepeth ay: always
"Fro paradys to yow have I hem broght,   guard.
Ne nevere mo ne shal they roten bee,   nevere mo: at no future time. roten
Ne lese hir swote savour, trusteth me;   bee: decay. lese: lose. swote:
Ne nevere wight shal seen hem with his eye, 230   sweet.
But he be chaast and hate vileynye.   but: unless. vileynye: wickedness;
     lechery.

"And thow, Valerian, for thow so soone   for: because.
Assentedest to good conseil also,
Sey what thee list, and thou shalt han thy boone."   what thee list: what you would like.
"I have a brother," quod Valerian tho,   235   boone: request.
"That in this world I love no man so.
I pray yow that my brother may han grace
To knowe the trouthe as I do in this place."   in this place: immediately.

   The angel seyde, "God liketh thy requeste,
And bothe, with the palm of martirdom,   240
Ye shullen come unto his blisful feste."   feste: feast.
And with that word Tiburce his brother coom.   coom: came.
And whan that he the savour undernoom,   undernoom: perceived.
Which that the roses and the lilies caste,
Withinne his herte he gan to wondre faste,   245   faste: greatly.

And seyde, "I wondre, this tyme of the yeer,
Whennes that swote savour cometh so
Of rose and lilies that I smelle heere.
For though I hadde hem in myne handes two,   though: even if.

The savour myghte in me no depper go.   250   depper: deeper.
The sweete smel that in myn herte I fynde
Hath chaunged me al in another kynde."   in: into. kynde: nature.

Valerian seyde: "Two corones han we,
Snow white and rose reed, that shynen cleere,   cleere: brightly.
Which that thyne eyen han no myght to see;   255
And as thou smellest hem thurgh my prayere,
So shaltow seen hem, leeve brother deere,   leeve: beloved.
If it so be thou wolt, withouten slouthe,   slouth: slowness, tardiness.
Bileve aright and knowen verray trouthe."   knowen: recognize; acknowledge.

Tiburce answerde, "Seistow this to me   260
In soothnesse, or in dreem I herkne this?"   soothnesse: truth.
"In dremes," quod Valerian, "han we be
Unto this tyme, brother myn, ywis.
But now at erst in trouthe oure dwellyng is."   at erst: for the first time.
"How wostow this?" quod Tiburce, "and in
    what wyse?"   265
Quod Valerian, "That shal I thee devyse.   devyse: tell, explain.

"The aungel of God hath me the trouthe
    ytaught
Which thou shalt seen, if that thou wolt reneye   reneye: renounce.
The ydoles and be clene, and elles naught."   clene: chaste. elles naught: not
And of the myracle of thise corones tweye   270   otherwise.
Seint Ambrose in his preface list to seye;
Solempnely this noble doctour deere
Commendeth it, and seith in this manere:

"The palm of martirdom for to receyve,
Seinte Cecile, fulfild of Goddes yifte,   275   fulfild of: filled with.
The world and eek hir chambre gan she weyve;   chambre: bridal chamber. weyve: put
Witnesse Tyburces and Valerians shrifte,   aside. shrifte: confession of faith.
To whiche God of his bountee wolde shifte   whiche: whom. wolde shifte: willed
Corones two of floures wel smellynge,   to assign.
And made his angel hem the corones brynge.   280

The mayde hath broght thise men to blisse
    above;
The world hath wist what it is worth, certeyn,   wist: come to know.
Devocioun of chastitee to love."   devocioun of chastitee to love: to
Tho shewed hym Cecile al open and pleyn   love devotion to chastity.
That alle ydoles nys but a thyng in veyn,   285   in veyn: in vain, worthless.

---

271. The reference is to the proper preface to the mass for St. Cecilia's Day in the Ambrosian liturgy. (The "preface" is the prelude to the central part of the mass. The Ambrosian rite was the liturgy of Milan, whose bishop from 374 to 397 was St. Ambrose.)
276. hir chambre gan she weyve: she remained a virgin.

For they been dombe, and therto they been
      deve,   *therto:* also.
And charged hym his ydoles for to leve.   *deve:* deaf.

"Whoso that troweth nat this, a beest he is,"
Quod tho Tiburce, "if that I shal nat lye."
And she gan kisse his brest, that herde this, 290
And was ful glad he koude trouthe espye.   *espye:* discern.
"This day I take thee for myn allye,"   *allye:* kinsman.
Seyde this blisful faire mayde deere,
And after that, she seyde as ye may heere:

"Lo, right so as the love of Crist," quod
      she,   295
"Made me thy brotheres wyf, right in that wise
Anon for myn allye heer take I thee,
Syn that thou wolt thyne ydoles despise.   *despise:* renounce.
Go with thy brother now, and thee baptise, *thee baptise:* receive baptism.
And make thee clene, so that thou mowe   *mowe:* may.
      biholde   300
The angeles face of which thy brother tolde."

  Tiburce answerde and seyde, "Brother deere,
First tel me whider I shal, and to what man?" *shal:* i.e., must go.
"To whom?" quod he, "com forth with right
      good cheere,
I wol thee lede unto the Pope Urban."   305
"Til Urban? brother myn Valerian,"   *til:* to.
Quod tho Tiburce, "woltow me thider lede?
Me thynketh that it were a wonder dede.

"Ne menestow nat Urban," quod he tho,   *ne menestow nat:* don't you mean.
"That is so ofte dampned to be deed,   310 *dampned:* condemned. **to be deed:**
And woneth in halkes alwey to and fro,   i.e., to death. *woneth:* dwells.
And dar nat ones putte forth his heed?   *halkes:* corners, hidding places.
Men sholde hym brennen in a fyr so reed   *heed:* head. **brennen:** burn.
If he were founde, or that men myghte hym spye,
And we also, to bere hym compaignye;   315

"And whil we seken thilke divinitee
That is yhid in hevene pryvely,   *yhid:* hidden.
Algate ybrend in this world shul we be!"   *algate:* altogether. **ybrend:** burned.
To whom Cecile answerde boldely,
"Men myghten dreden wel and skilfully   320 *skilfully:* with good reason.
This lyf to lese, myn owene deere brother, *lese:* lose.
If this were lyvyng oonly and noon oother. *lyvyng oonly:* the only state of life.

"But ther is bettre lif in oother place,
That nevere shal be lost, ne drede thee noght,

Which Goddes Sone us tolde thurgh his grace. 325
That Fadres Sone hath alle thynges wroght,
And al that wroght is with a skilful thoght,
The Goost, that fro the Fader gan procede,
Hath souled hem, withouten any drede.

> wroght . . . thoght: is endowed with reason. Goost: Holy Ghost.
> souled: endowed with souls. hem: i.e., all rational creatures.

By word and by myracle heigh Goddes Sone, 330
Whan he was in this world, declared heere
That ther was oother lyf ther men may wone."
To whom answerde Tiburce, "O suster deere,
Ne seydestow right now in this manere,
Ther nys but o God, lord in soothfastnesse? 335
And now of three how maystow bere witnesse?"

> lyf: state of existence. ther: in which. wone: dwell.
> o: one.

"That shal I telle," quod she, "er I go.
Right as a man hath sapiences three,
Memorie, engyn, and intellect also,
So in o beynge of divinitee, 340
Thre persones may ther right wel bee."
Tho gan she hym ful bisily to preche
Of Cristes come, and of his peynes teche,

> sapiences: mental faculties.
> engyn: innate ingenuity. intellect: reason, thought.
> bisily: earnestly.
> Cristes come: Advent; the birth of Christ.

And manye pointes of his passioun;
How Goddes Sone in this world was withholde 345
To doon mankynde pleyn remissioun,
That was ybounde in synne and cares colde;
Al this thyng she unto Tiburce tolde.
And after this, Tiburce in good entente
With Valerian to Pope Urban he wente, 350

> withholde: retained, kept.
> pleyn: full.
> cares colde: anguish.

That thanked God, and with glad herte and light
He cristned hym, and made hym in that place
Parfit in his lernynge, Goddes knyght.
And after this, Tiburce gat swich grace
That every day he saugh, in tyme and space, 355
The aungel of God; and every maner boone
That he God axed, it was sped ful soone.

> that: who.
> lernynge: doctrine.
> space: time, leisure. in tyme and space: when there was opportunity.
> boone: request, favor.

It were ful hard by ordre for to seyn
How manye wondres Jhesus for hem wroghte;
But at the laste, to tellen short and pleyn, 360
The sergeantz of the toun of Rome hem soghte,
And hem biforn Almache, the prefect, broghte
Which hem apposed, and knew al hire entente,
And to the ymage of Juppiter hem sente,

> wondres: miracles.
> apposed: questioned, examined.
> entente: spiritual attitude.

352–53. I.e., he christened and confirmed him.

And seyde, "Whoso wol nat sacrifise,   365

Swape of his heed; this my sentence heer."   swape of: smite off. this: this is.

Anon thise martirs that I yow devyse,

Oon Maximus, that was an officer

Of the prefectes, and his corniculer,

Hem hente, and whan he forth the seintes   hente: seized.

      ladde,   370   ladde: led.

Hymself he weep for pitee that he hadde.   weep: wept.

Whan Maximus had herd the seintes loore,   loore: teaching.

He gat hym of the tormentoures leve,   leve: leave, permission.

And ladde hem to his hous withoute moore,   withoute moore: without more ado.

And with hir prechyng, er that it were eve,   375   with hir: by their.

They gonnen fro the tormentours to reve,   gonnen to reve: took away.

And fro Maxime, and fro his folk echone,

The false feith, to trowe in God allone.   to trowe: with the result that they believed.

   Cecilie cam, whan it was woxen nyght,   was woxen: had become.

With preestes that hem cristned alle yfeere;   380   yfeere: together.

And afterward, whan day was woxen light,

Cecile hem seyde with a ful stedefast cheere,

"Now, Cristes owene knyghtes leeve and deere,

Cast al awey the werkes of derknesse,

And armeth yow in armure of brightnesse.   385

"Ye han for sothe ydoon a greet bataille,   ydoon: i.e., fought.

Youre cours is doon, youre feith han ye   youre cours: i.e., the course of your

      conserved.   life. conserved: kept.

Gooth to the corone of lif that may nat faille;   gooth: go.

The rightful Juge, which that ye han served,

Shal yeve it yow, as ye han it deserved."   390

And whan this thyng was seyd as I devyse,

Men ledde hem forth to doon the sacrifise.

But whan they weren to the place broght

To tellen shortly the conclusioun,

They nolde encense ne sacrifise right noght,   395   nolde: (ne wolde) would not. encense: offer incense.

But on hir knees they setten hem adoun

With humble herte and sad devocioun,   sad: steadfast.

And losten bothe hir hevedes in the place.   hevedes: heads. in the place: then and there; immediately.

Hir soules wenten to the Kyng of grace.

This Maximus, that saugh this thyng bityde,   400   bityde: happen.

With pitous teeris tolde it anonright,   anonright: at once.

368–69. an officer . . . corniculer: an officer and assistant of the prefect's.

373. of the tormentoures: from the executioners.

386–390. See II Timothy iv.7–8.

That he hir soules saugh to hevene glyde
With aungels ful of cleernesse and of light,   cleernesse: brightness; splendor.
And with his word converted many a wight;
For which Almachius dide hym so bete   405 dide hym so bete: caused him to be
With whippe of leed, til he his lif gan lete.   so beaten. til: that. gan lete: gave
    up.

    Cecile hym took and buryed hym anon
By Tiburce and Valerian softely   softely: tenderly.
Withinne hire buryyng place, under the stoon;
And after this, Almachius hastily   410
Bad his ministres fecchen openly   ministres: officers.
Cecile, so that she myghte in his presence
Doon sacrifice, and Juppiter encense.   encense: offer incense to.

But they, converted at hir wise loore,   at: by. loore: teaching.
Wepten ful soore, and yaven ful credence   415 yaven: gave.
Unto hir word, and cryden moore and moore,   moore and moore: again and again.
"Crist, Goddes Sone, withouten difference,
Is verray God—this is al oure sentence—   sentence: opinion.
That hath so good a servant hym to serve.
This with o voys we trowen, thogh we sterve!" 420 with o voys: unanimously. sterve: die.

    Almachius, that herde of this doynge,
Bad feechen Cecile, that he myghte hir see,
And alderfirst, lo! this was his axynge.   alderfirst: first of all. axynge: ques-
"What maner womman artow?" tho quod he.   tion.
"I am a gentil womman born," quod she.   425
"I axe thee," quod he, "though it thee greeve,
Of thy religioun and of thy bileeve."   of: about. bileeve: creed.

    "Ye han bigonne youre questioun folily,"   folily: foolishly.
Quod she, "that wolden two answeres conclude   conclude: include.
In o demande; ye axed lewedly."   430 o demande: one question. axed:
Almache answerde unto that similitude,   asked. lewedly: ignorantly.
"Of whennes comth thyn answeryng so rude?"
"Of whennes?" quod she, whan that she was
    freyned,   freyned: asked.
"Of conscience and of good feith unfeyned."   unfeyned: unfeigning, sincere.

    Almachius seyde, "Ne takestow noon heede 435
Of my power?" And she answerde hym this:
"Youre myght," quod she, "ful litel is to drede,   to drede: to be feared.
For every mortal mannes power nys
But lyk a bladdre ful of wynd, ywys.
For with a nedles poynt, whan it is blowe,   440 blowe: blown up.
May al the boost of it be leyd ful lowe."   boost: pride. leyd: cast down.

---

406. whippe of leed: i.e., a whip furnished with leaden plummets.

"Ful wrongfully bigonne thow," quod he,
"And yet in wrong is thy perseveraunce.
Wostow nat how oure myghty princes free   free: noble.
Han thus comanded and maad ordinaunce,   445
That every Cristen wight shal han penaunce   penaunce: punishment.
But if that he his Cristendom withseye,   but if: unless. withseye: deny.
And goon al quit, if he wol it reneye?"   goon quit: go free. reneye: renounce.

"Yowre princes erren, as youre nobleye dooth,"   nobleye: nobility (i.e., nobles).
Quod tho Cecilie, "and with a wood sentence   450   wood: mad, senseless.
Ye make us gilty, and it is nat sooth.
For ye, that knowen wel oure innocence,
For as muche as we doon a reverence
To Crist, and for we bere a Cristen name,   for . . . name: because we are called
Ye putte on us a cryme, and eek a blame.   455   "Christians". putte on: impute to.
                                           blame: offense.

But we that knowen thilke name so
For vertuous, we may it nat withseye."
Almache answerde, "Chees oon of thise two: chees: choose.
Do sacrifice, or Cristendom reneye,
That thou mowe now escapen by that weye."   460
At which the holy blisful faire mayde
Gan for to laughe, and to the juge sayde:

"O juge, confus in thy nycetee,   confus: disconcerted. nycetee: folly.
Woltow that I reneye innocence,
To make me a wikked wight?" quod she.   465
"Lo, he dissimuleth heere in audience;   dissimuleth: dissembles. in audience:
He stareth, and woodeth in his advertence!"   at a hearing. woodeth: raves. ad-
To whom Almachius, "Unsely wrecche,   vertence: spirit. unsely: unhappy.
Ne wostow nat how fer my myght may strecche?

"Han noght oure myghty princes to me yiven, 470
Ye, bothe power and auctoritee   ye: yea.
To maken folk to dyen or to lyven?
Why spekestow so proudly thanne to me?"
"I speke noght but stedfastly," quod she;   stedfastly: with firm belief.
"Nat proudly, for I seye, as for my syde,   475   syde: part.
We haten dedly thilke vice of pryde.   dedly: mortally; intensely.

"And if thou drede nat a sooth to heere,
Thanne wol I shewe al openly, by right,
That thou hast maad a ful gret lesyng heere.   lesyng: falsehood.
Thou seyst thy princes han thee yeven myght 480
Bothe for to sleen and for to quyken a wight;   sleen: slay. quyken: make live.
Thou, that ne mayst but oonly lyf bireve,   lyf bireve: i.e., put to death.
Thou hast noon oother power ne no leve.

"But thou mayst seyn thy princes han thee maked   seyn: say.
Ministre of deeth; for if thou speke of mo,   485
Thou lyest, for thy power is ful naked."   ful naked: completely lacking.
"Do wey thy boldnesse," seyde Almachius tho,   boldnesse: impudence.
"And sacrifice to oure goddes, er thou go!
I recche nat what wrong that thou me profre,   recche: reck, care.
For I kan suffre it as a philosophre;   490

"But thilke wronges may I nat endure
That thou spekest of oure goddes here," quod he.
Cecilie answerde, "O nyce creature!   nyce: foolish.
Thou seydest no word syn thou spak to me
That I ne knew therwith thy nycetee;   495   therwith: from it. nycetee: foolishness.
And that thou were, in every maner wise,   every maner wise: every way.
A lewed officer and a veyn justise.   lewed: ignorant. veyn: worthless.

"Ther lakketh no thyng to thyne outter eyen
That thou n'art blynd; for thyng that we seen alle
That is a stoon,—that men may wel espyen,—   500
That ilke stoon a god thow wolt it calle.
I rede thee, lat thyn hand upon it falle,   rede: counsel.
And taste it wel, and stoon thou shalt it fynde,   taste: examine by touch; handle.
Syn that thou seest nat with thyne eyen blynde.   syn: since.

"It is a shame that the peple shal   505
So scorne thee, and laughe at thy folye;
For communly men woot it wel overal   overal: above everything, especially.
That myghty God is in his hevenes hye;
And thise ymages, wel thou mayst espye,
To thee ne to hemself mowe noght profite,   510   mowe: may.
For in effect they been nat worth a myte."

Thise wordes and swiche othere seyde she,
And he weex wroth, and bad men sholde hir lede   weex: grew. wroth: angry.
Hom til hir hous, and "In hir hous," quod he,   til: to.
"Brenne hire right in a bath of flambes rede."   515   brenne: burn.
And as he bad, right so was doon the dede;
For in a bath they gonne hire faste shetten,   shetten: shut.
And nyght and day greet fyr they under betten.   under: underneath. betten: fed.

The longe nyght, and eek a day also,
For al the fyr, and eek the bathes heete,   520
She sat al coold, and feelede no wo.   feelede: felt.
It made hir nat a drope for to swete.   swete: sweat.
But in that bath hir lyf she moste lete,   moste lete: must give up.

498–99. ther . . . blynd: i.e., your bodily eyes are deficient so that you are blind (n.b. intensive cumulative negatives).
517. bath: i.e., the *sudatorium* (sweating-room) of the bath.

For he Almachius, with a ful wikke entente,
To sleen hire in the bath his sonde sente. 525   sleen: slay. **sonde**: emissary.

Thre strokes in the nekke he smoot hire tho,
The tormentour, but for no maner chaunce   **for no maner chaunce**: under no cir-
He myghte noght smyte al hir nekke atwo;   cumstances. **atwo**: in two.
And for ther was that tyme an ordinaunce
That no man sholde doon man swich penaunce 530   penaunce: suffering.
The ferthe strook to smyten, softe or soore,   to: as to.
This tormentour ne dorste do namoore,

But half deed, with hir nekke ycorven there,   ycorven: cut.
He lefte hir lye, and on his wey he went.
The Cristen folk, which that aboute hire were, 535
With sheetes han the blood ful faire yhent.   sheetes: cloths. **faire**: gently. **yhent**:
Thre dayes lyved she in this torment,   wiped.
And nevere cessed hem the feith to teche   cessed: ceased.
That she hadde fostred; hem she gan to preche,   that: whom. **fostred**: i.e., converted.

And hem she yaf hir moebles and hir thyng, 540   moebles: movable goods. **thyng**:
And to the Pope Urban bitook hem tho,   property. **bitook**: entrusted.
And seyde, "I axed this of hevene kyng,
To han respit thre dayes and namo,
To recomende to yow, er that I go,   recomende: commend.
Thise soules, lo! and that I myghte do werche 545   do werche: have made.
Here of myn hous perpetuelly a cherche."

   Seint Urban, with his deknes, prively   deknes: deacons.
The body fette, and buryed it by nyghte   fette: fetched.
Among his othere seintes honestly.   honestly: honorably.
Hir hous the chirche of Seinte Cecilie highte; 550
Seint Urban halwed it, as he wel myghte;   halwed: hallowed, consecrated.
In which, into this day, in noble wyse,
Men doon to Crist and to his seinte servyse.

Heere is ended the
Seconde Nonnes Tale.

---

550. The remains of a classical house, with a bath (*calidarium*), may be seen in Rome in the
basilica of St. Cecilia in Trastevere.

The prologe of the
Chanons Yemannes tale.

Whan ended was the lyf of Seinte Cecile,
Er we hadde riden fully fyve mile,   555
At Boghtoun under Blee us gan atake   us gan atake: overtook us.
A man that clothed was in clothes blake,
And under that he hadde a whyt surplys.
His hakeney, that was al pomely grys,   pomely grys: dappled gray.
So swatte that it wonder was to see;   560 swatte: sweated.
It semed he had priked miles three.   priked: spurred.
   The hors eek that his yeman rood upon   yeman: yeoman, servant, assistant.
So swatte that unnethe myghte he gon.
Aboute the peytrel stood the foom ful hye;   peytrel: poitrel; ornamental breast-
He was of foom al flekked as a pye.   565   plate for a horse. he: the horse.
A male tweyfoold on his croper lay.   pye: magpie. croper: hindquarters.
   It semed that he caried lite array.   he: the canon. array: equipment;
Al light for somer rood this worthy man,   clothing.
And in myn herte wondren I bigan
What that he was, til that I understood   570
How that his cloke was sowed to his hood;
For which, whan I longe hadde avysed me,   avysed: me: deliberated.
I demed hym som chanoun for to be.
His hat heeng at his bak doun by a laas,   laas: cord.
For he hadde riden moore than trot or paas; 575 paas: footpace.
He hadde ay priked lik as he were wood.
A clote-leef he hadde under his hood   clote-leef: burdock-leaf.
For swoot, and for to keep his heed from heete.   for swoot: to prevent sweat.
But it was joye for to seen hym swete!
His forheed dropped as a stillatorie,   580 stillatorie: still.
Were ful of plantayne and of paritorie.   were: as if it were.
And whan that he was come, he gan to crye,
"God save," quod he, "this joly compaignye!
Faste have I priked," quod he, "for youre sake,
By cause that I wolde yow atake,   585 atake: overtake.
To riden in this myrie compaignye."
His yemen eek was ful of curteisye,

The prologe of the Chanons Yemannes tale. In the Prologue and the first part of the Tale the Canon's Yeoman tells something of his work in assisting the Canon's alchemical activities, then ("pars secunda") tells a story of three alchemical tricks used by a canon to victimize a London priest, and finally (ll. 1388–481) expresses his personal views on alchemy. See the paragraph on alchemy and the Tale in the Introduction, pp. 00. Edgar Hill Duncan has kindly reviewed for me that paragraph and the glosses, notes, and illustration for the Tale.

556. Boghtoun under Blee: the village of Boughton in the Blean Forest, about five miles beyond Ospringe (probably referred to in l. 589) and about seven from Canterbury.

566. male tweyfoold: a double bag.

571. This bit of evidence shows the company that the newcomer was a Black Canon, a Canon Regular of St. Augustine, who presumably was supposed to serve a cathedral church.

581. paritorie: pellitory, an herb; like plantain, this was used for medicine.

And seyde, "Sires, now in the morwe-tyde
Out of youre hostelrie I saugh yow ryde,
And warned here my lord and my soverayn,   590
Which that to ryden with yow is ful fayn
For his desport; he loveth daliaunce."

   "Freend, for thy warnyng God yeve thee good
      chaunce!"

Thanne seyde oure Hoost, "for certein it wolde
      seme
Thy lord were wys, and so I may wel deme.   595
He is ful jocunde also, dar I leye!
Can he oght telle a myrie tale or tweye,
With which he glade may this compaignye?"

   "Who, sire? my lord? ye, ye, withouten lye,
He kan of murthe and eek of jolitee   600
Nat but ynough; also, sire, trusteth me,
And ye hym knewe as wel as do I,
Ye wolde wondre how wel and craftily
He koude werke, and that in sondry wise.
He hath take on hym many a greet emprise,   605
Which were ful hard for any that is heere
To brynge aboute, but they of hym it leere.
As hoomly as he rit amonges yow,
If ye hym knewe, it wolde be for youre prow.
Ye wolde nat forgoon his aqueyntaunce   610
For muchel good, I dar leye in balaunce
Al that I have in my possessioun.
He is a man of heigh discrecioun;
I warne yow wel, he is a passyng man."

   "Wel," quod oure Hoost, "I pray thee, tel
      me than,   615
Is he a clerk, or noon? telle what he is."

   "Nay, he is gretter than a clerk, ywis,"
Seyde this Yeman, "and in wordes fewe,
Hoost, of his craft somwhat I wol yow shewe.

   I seye, my lord kan swich subtilitee—   620
But al his craft ye may nat wite of me,
And somwhat helpe I yet to his wirkyng—
That al this ground on which we been ridyng,
Til that we come to Caunterbury toun,
He koude al clene turnen up-so-doun,   625
And pave it al of silver and of gold."

   And whan this Yeman hadde thus ytold
Unto oure Hoost, he seyde, "Benedicitee!
This thyng is wonder merveillous to me,
Syn that thy lord is of so heigh prudence,   630
By cause of which men sholde hym reverence,
That of his worshipe rekketh he so lite.

---

desport: diversion. daliaunce: socia-
bility; mirth.
chaunce: luck.

leye: wager.
oght: at all.

kan: knows.
nat but: quite.

emprise: enterprise, undertaking.

leere: learn.
hoomly: unpretentiously. rit: (rideth)
rides. prow: profit, advantage.

good: wealth. leye in balaunce: put
in the balance, wager.

passyng: surpassing, excellent.

subtilitee: abstruse science.
wite: discover. of: from.

worshipe: dignity; respectable ap-
pearance. rekketh: recks, cares.

His overslope nys nat worth a myte,
As in effect, to hym, so moot I go!
It is al baudy and totore also.   635   baudy: dirty. **totore**: torn in pieces.
Why is thy lord so sluttissh, I the preye,   sluttissh: slovenly.
And is of power bettre clooth to beye,   clooth: clothing. **beye**: buy.
If that his dede accorde with thy speche?
Telle me that, and that I thee biseche."
    "Why?" quod this Yeman, "wherto axe ye   wherto: why.
        me?   640
God help me so, for he shal nevere thee!   thee: prosper.
(But I wol nat avowe that I seye,
And therfore keepe it secree, I yow preye.)
He is to wys, in feith, as I bileeve.
That that is overdoon, it wol nat preeve   645   that that: that which. **preeve**: turn out.
Aright, as clerkes seyn; it is a vice.
Wherfore in that I holde hym lewed and nyce.   lewed: ignorant. **nyce**: foolish.
For whan a man hath over-greet a wit,
Ful oft hym happeth to mysusen it.
So dooth my lord, and that me greveth soore; 650
God it amende! I kan sey yow namoore."
    "Ther-of no fors, good Yeman," quod oure   no fors: no matter.
        Hoost;
"Syn of the konnyng of thy lord thow woost,
Telle how he dooth, I pray thee hertely,
Syn that he is so crafty and so sly.   655   crafty: skillful; intelligent. **sly**: skillful;
Where dwelle ye, if it to telle be?"   artful.
    "In the suburbes of a toun," quod he,
"Lurkynge in hernes and in lanes blynde,   hernes: corners.
Whereas thise robbours and thise theves by
        kynde   kynde: nature.
Holden hir pryvee fereful residence,   660
As they that dar nat shewen hir presence;
So faren we, if I shal seye the sothe."
    "Now," quod oure Hoost, "yit lat me talke
        to the.
Why artow so discoloured of thy face?"
    "Peter!" quod he, "God yeve it harde grace, 665   grace: luck.
I am so used in the fyr to blowe
That it hath chaunged my colour, I trowe.
I am nat wont in no mirour to prie,   prie: pry, peer.
But swynke soore and lerne multiplie.   swynke: labor, toil.
We blondren evere and pouren in the fir,   670   pouren: gaze.
And for al that we faille of oure desir,   of: in.

633–34. His upper garment is not worth a mite, really, for a man like him, so may I have the power to walk.

669. **multiplie**: increase the amount of precious metal by transmutation of baser metal.

670. **blondren**: blunder, proceed ignorantly.

For evere we lakken oure conclusioun.
    conclusioun: successful outcome.
To muchel folk we doon illusioun,
And borwe gold, be it a pound or two,
Or ten, or twelve, or manye sommes mo,   675
And make hem wenen, at the leeste weye,   leeste weye: very least.
That of a pound we koude make tweye.
Yet is it fals, and ay we han good hope
It for to doon, and after it we grope.
But that science is so fer us biforn,   680
We mowen nat, although we hadden it sworn,   mowen: may.
It overtake, it slit awey so faste.   slit: (slideth) slides.
It wole us maken beggers atte laste."
   Whil this Yeman was thus in his talkyng,
This Chanoun drough hym neer, and herde al   drough hym neer: drew near.
    thyng   685
Which this Yeman spak, for suspecioun
Of mennes speche evere hadde this Chanoun.
For Catoun seith, "He that gilty is
Demeth alle thyng be spoke of hym, ywis."
That was the cause he gan so ny hym drawe   690
To his Yeman, to herknen al his sawe.   sawe: speech.
And thus he seyde unto his Yeman tho:
"Hoold thou thy pees, and spek no wordes mo,
For if thou do, thou shalt it deere abye.   abye: pay for.
Thou sclaundrest me heere in this compaignye, 695   sclaundrest: slanderest.
And eek discoverest that thou sholdest hyde."   discoverest: revealest. that: that
    which.
   "Ye," quod oure Hoost, "telle on, what so
    bityde.
Of al this thretyng rekke nat a myte!"   thretyng: threatening.
   "In feith," quod he, "namoore I do but lyte."
   And whan this Chanon saugh it wolde nat
    bee,   700
But his Yeman wolde telle his pryvetee,   pryvetee: private affairs.
He fledde awey for verray sorwe and shame.
   "A!" quod the Yeman, "heere shal arise game;
Al that I kan anon now wol I telle.
Syn he is goon, the foule feend hym quelle!   705   quelle: kill.
For nevere heerafter wol I with hym meete
For peny ne for pound, I yow biheete.   biheete: promise.
He that me broghte first unto that game,
Er that he dye, sorwe have he and shame!
For it is ernest to me, by my feith;   710   ernest: serious matter.
That feele I wel, what so any man seith.
And yet, for al my smert and al my grief,   grief: hardship.
For al my sorwe, labour, and meschief,   meschief: misfortune.
I koude nevere leve it in no wise.
Now wolde God my wit myghte suffise   715
To tellen al that longeth to that art!   longeth: belongs.

But nathelees yow wol I tellen part.
Syn that my lord is goon, I wol nat spare;
Swich thyng as I knowe, I wol declare.

*Heere endeth the prologe of the
Chanouns Yemannes tale.*

*Heere bigynneth the
Chanouns Yeman his tale.*

With this Chanoun I dwelt have seven yeer, 720	
And of his science am I never the neer.	of: from. never the neer: no better off
Al that I hadde I have lost therby,	(i.e., no nearer to my purpose).
And, God woot, so hath many mo than I.	
Ther I was wont to be right fressh and gay	ther: whereas.
Of clothyng and of oother good array, 725	
Now may I were an hose upon myn heed;	were: wear. hose: stocking.
And wher my colour was bothe fressh and reed,	
Now is it wan and of a leden hewe—	leden: leaden.
Whoso it useth, soore shal he rewe!—	rewe: rue, repent.
And of my swynk yet blered is myn eye. 730	swynk: labor.
Lo! which avantage is to multiplie!	which: what (an).
That slidynge science hath me maad so bare	slidynge: slippery, unreliable.
That I have no good, wher that evere I fare;	good: goods.
And yet I am endetted so therby,	endetted: in debt.
Of gold that I have borwed, trewely, 735	of: for.
That whil I lyve I shal it quite nevere.	quite: repay.
Lat every man be war by me for evere!	
What maner man that casteth hym therto,	casteth hym therto: devotes himself
If he continue, I holde his thrift ydo.	to it, practises it. thrift: prosperity.
For so helpe me God, therby shal he nat wynne, 740	ydo: done, finished.
But empte his purs, and make his wittes thynne.	empte: empty, drain.
And whan he, thurgh his madnesse and folye,	
Hath lost his owene good thurgh jupartye,	jupartye: jeopardy, risk.
Thanne he exciteth oother folk therto,	exciteth: incites.
To lese hir good, as he hymself hath do. 745	lese: lose. hath do: has done.
For unto shrewes joye it is and ese	shrewes: rascals.
To have hir felawes in peyne and disese.	disese: misfortune.
Thus was I ones lerned of a clerk.	ones: once. lerned of: taught by.
Of that no charge, I wol speke of oure werk.	no charge: no matter.

---

727. reed: red (healthy); (n.b., that red was the conventional color of gold).
729. it useth: practises it (i.e., the science).
730. blered is myn eye: my eye is bleared; I have been hoodwinked (double meaning).
731. multiplie: see line 669, note.
733. wher that evere I fare: wherever I go; whatever I do.

Whan we been there as we shul exercise   750
Oure elvysshe craft, we semen wonder wise,
Oure termes been so clergial and so queynte.
I blowe the fyr til that myn herte feynte.
What sholde I tellen ech proporcion
Of thynges whiche that we werche upon —   755
As on fyve or sixe ounces, may wel be,
Of silver, or som oother quantitee—
And bisye me to telle yow the names
Of orpyment, brent bones, iren squames,
That into poudre grounden been ful smal;   760
And in an erthen pot how put is al,
And salt yput in, and also papeer,
Biforn thise poudres that I speke of heer;
And wel ycovered with a lampe of glas;
And of muche oother thyng which that ther
      was;   765
And of the pot and glasses enlutyng,
That of the eyr myghte passe out nothyng;
And of the esy fyr, and smart also,
Which that was maad, and of the care and wo
That we hadde in oure matires sublymyng,   770
And in amalgamyng and calcenyng
Of quyksilver, yclept mercurie crude?
For alle oure sleightes we kan nat conclude.
Oure orpyment and sublymed mercurie,
Oure grounden litarge eek on the porfurie,   775
Of ech of thise of ounces a certeyn—
Noght helpeth us, oure labour is in veyn.
Ne eek oure spirites ascencioun,
Ne oure materes that lyen al fix adoun,
Mowe in oure werkyng no thyng us availle,   780
For lost is al oure labour and travaille;
And al the cost, a twenty devel waye,
Is lost also, which we upon it laye.
    Ther is also ful many another thyng
That is unto oure craft apertenyng.   785
Though I by ordre hem nat reherce kan,
By cause that I am a lewed man,

elvysshe: mysterious, weird. **semen:** seem. **clergial:** learned. **queynte:** curious, strange.

what: why.

werche upon: work with.

bisye: busy.

brent: burned, calcined. **squames:** scales. **poudre:** powder.

papeer: paper.

lampe: ? lamina, thin plate; (more likely:) alembic, upper part of a distilling vessel.

eyr: air, gas.

esy fyr: slow or moderate fire. **smart:** brisk.

oure matires sublymyng: sublimation of our substances.

sleightes: skills, tricks.

litarge: litharge, protoxide of lead.

a certeyn: a certain number.

materes: substances. **fix:** fixed, not transmutable.

cost: expenditure. **a twenty devel waye:** to the devils. **laye:** lay out.

by: in.

lewed: ignorant.

---

759. orpyment: trisulphide of arsenic; yellow arsenic.
766. And of the sealing with a cement of (the joint between) the **pot** and **glas**.
770. sublymyng: sublimation; conversion of a solid into vapor by means of heat.
771. amalgamyng: amalgamating; the process of alloying another metal with mercury. **calcenyng:** the process of reducing to a powder by fire.
773. conclude: i.e., bring our work to its proper conclusion.
774. sublymed mercurie: mercury sublimate, mercuric chloride.
775. porfurie: a slab of porphyry upon which to grind drugs and chemicals.
778. oure spirites ascencioun: vaporization or distillation of our spirits; see line 820 and note.

Yet wol I telle hem as they come to mynde,
Thogh I ne kan nat sette hem in hir kynde:
As bole armonyak, verdegrees, boras,   790 boras: borax.
And sondry vessels maad of erthe and glas,   erthe: potter's clay.
Oure urynales and oure descensories,   urynales: glass vessels for making
Violes, crosletz, and sublymatories,   solutions. violes: vials, phials.
Cucurbites and alambikes eek,   crosletz: crucibles.
And othere swiche, deere ynough a leek.   795 a leek: i.e., (for) a thing of no value.
Nat nedeth it for to reherce hem alle,—
Watres rubifiyng, and boles galle,   rubifiyng: tingeing a red color.
Arsenyk, sal armonyak, and brymstoon;   sal armonyak: sal ammoniac, am-
And herbes koude I telle eek many oon,   monium chloride. brymstoon: sul-
As egremoyne, valerian, and lunarie,   800 phur. egremoyne: agrimony.
And othere swiche, if that me liste tarie;
Oure lampes brennyng bothe nyght and day,
To brynge aboute oure craft, if that we may;   craft: art.
Oure fourneys eek of calcinacioun,   calcinacioun: reduction of a substance
And of watres albificacioun;   805 to powder by heating it.
Unslekked lym, chalk, and gleyre of an ey,   unslekked lym: unslaked lime. chalk:
Poudres diverse, asshes, donge, pisse, and cley,   calx; slaked lime. poudres: pow-
Cered pokkets, sal peter, vitriole,   ders. sal peter: saltpeter.

---

789. Though I do not know how to classify them.
790. bole armonyak: a red astringent earth brought from Armenia. verdegrees: copper rust or copper acetate.
792. descensories: retorts and furnace for distilling by condensation (descent).
793. sublymatories: vessels for sublimation, subliming pots.
794. A cucurbit is the gourd-shaped lower part of a distilling vessel; an alembic, the upper part of a distilling vessel, consists of a head or cap with a delivery spout. See illustration opposite and note below.
797. boles galle: a bitter fluid secreted by the liver of oxen.
800. lunarie: lunary; probably moonwort (a fern described in Ashmole's *Theatrum Chemicum*).
805. albificacioun: the process of making white, or coloring like silver.
806. gleyre of an ey: white of an egg.
808. cered pokkets: bags impregnated with wax (so as to be waterproof). vitriole: one or other of the various sulphates of metals.

Processes of distillation and sublimation in the laboratory of John Norton, an alchemist of Bristol (c. 1477): In the upper left and lower right are shown distilling processes. A "stillatorie" (see line 580) consists of an alembic, a cucurbit (for both see l. 794 and notes), and a receiver. In the upper left a double alembic is atop a cucurbit mounted on a furnace. To each mouth of the alembic is affixed its own receiver. In the lower right seven single "stillatories" are on a flat-topped furnace. The attendant may be on the point of emptying one of the receivers: see the flat vessel (on the small furnace at his knee) which he has just uncovered. The covered vessel near his right foot is being kept warm on a small furnace. At the lower left, top center, and upper right are sublimating processes. At top center is a sublimatory furnace (sublimatorium; see line 793 and note for line 770); or the sublimatory may be the aludel (the vessel atop the furnace equipped with a close-fitting top or cap [extending down the sides of the aludel] for collecting the sublimate). The active vents in the four corners of the furnace top indicate that this furnace is for producing considerable heat necessary in certain sublimations. The attendant is probably stoking or prodding the fire; but if the instrument is a bellows, he is doing the Canon's Yeoman's work (ll. 753, 923–24). At the lower left and upper right are sublimating processes for substances requiring, apparently, less heat. The vessels are aludels. The grill in the middle of the top of the furnace at lower left appears to be an opening for bringing a vessel in direct contact with the fire. The circle in the middle of the furnace top at the lower right is probably a removable lid for the same purpose.

And diverse fires maad of wode and cole;   cole: charcoal.
Sal tartre, alkaly, and sal preparat,   810   sal tartre: salt of tartar, potassium car-
And combust materes and coagulat;   bonate. combust: burnt, calcined.
Cley maad with hors or mannes heer,   hors: horse's. mannes: man's. heer:
        and oille   hair.
Of tartre, alum glas, berme, wort, and argoille,   alum glas: rock alum. berme: barm,
Resalgar, and oure materes embibyng,   yeast.
And eek of oure materes encorporyng,   815   encorporyng: precipitation; incorporat-
And of oure silver citrinacioun,   ing, amalgamating.
Oure cementyng and fermentacioun,   fermentacioun: chemical change with
Oure ingottes, testes, and many mo.   heat and effervescence. ingottes:
    I wol yow telle, as was me taught also,   molds for casting molten metal.
The foure spirites and the bodies sevene,   820
By ordre, as ofte I herde my lord hem nevene.   nevene: call.
    The firste spirit quyksilver called is,   quyksilver: mercury.
The seconde orpyment, the thridde, ywis,   orpyment: trisulphide of arsenic, yel-
Sal armonyak, and the ferthe brymstoon.   low arsenic.
The bodyes sevene eek, lo! hem heer anoon: 825
Sol gold is, and Luna silver we threpe,   Sol: the sun. Luna: the moon. threpe:
Mars iren, Mercurie quyksilver we clepe,   assert. clepe: call.
Saturnus leed, and Juppiter is tyn,   leed: lead.
And Venus coper, by my fader kyn!   fader: father's.
    This cursed craft whoso wole excercise,   830
He shal no good han that hym may suffise;   good: wealth.
For al the good he spendeth theraboute
He lese shal; therof have I no doute.
Whoso that listeth outen his folie,   outen: disclose, exhibit.
Lat hym come forth and lerne multiplie;   835
And every man that hath oght in his cofre,
Lat hym appere, and wexe a philosophre.   wexe: become.
Ascaunce that craft is so light to lere?   ascaunce: as if. light: easy. lere:
Nay, nay, God woot, al be he monk or frere,   learn.
Preest or chanoun, or any oother wight,   840
Though he sitte at his book bothe day and nyght
In lernyng of this elvyssh nyce loore,   elvyssh: mysterious, weird. nyce:
                                                                    foolish.
_____

810. alkaly: salt alkali, impure sodium carbonate. sal preparat: any prepared (i.e., purified) salt.
811. materes: substances. coagulat: solidified.
812. cley: a mixture of the consistency of clay.
812–13. oille of tartre: a saturated solution of potassium carbonate.
813. wort: infusion of malt. argoille: crude tartar (potassium bitartrate).
814. resalgar: realgar, disulphide of arsenic; also called red arsenic, red orpiment. embibyng:
imbibition, absorption, saturation.
816. silver citrinacioun: imparting a yellow color to silver by fusing into it certain compounds of
sulphur or mercury.
817. cementyng: the process by which one solid is made to penetrate and combine with an-
other at high temperature.
818. testes: vessels for assaying or refining metals; cupels.
820. The spirites and bodies, two main classes of alchemical ingredients, are named in lines
822–29. The four spirites are turned by fire into vapor; the seven bodies are metals.
837. a philosophre: an adept in occult science; an alchemist.

Al is in veyn, and parde! muchel moore.
To lerne a lewed man this subtiltee—
Fy! spek nat therof, for it wol nat be; 845
And konne he letterure, or konne he noon,
As in effect, he shal fynde it al oon.
For bothe two, by my savacioun,
Concluden in multiplicacioun
Ylike wel, whan they han al ydo; 850
This is to seyn, they faillen bothe two.

    Yet forgat I to maken rehersaille
Of watres corosif, and of lymaille,
And of bodies mollificacioun,
And also of hire induracioun; 855
Oilles, ablucioun, and metal fusible,—
To tellen al wolde passen any bible
That owher is; wherfore, as for the beste,
Of alle thise names now wol I me reste.
For, as I trowe, I have yow told ynowe 860
To reyse a feend, al looke he never so rowe.

    A! nay! lat be; the philosophres stoon,
Elixer clept, we sechen faste echoon;
For hadde we hym, thanne were we siker ynow.
But unto God of hevene I make avow, 865
For al oure craft, whan we han al ydo,
And al oure sleighte, he wol nat come us to.
He hath ymaad us spende muchel good,
For sorwe of which almoost we wexen wood,
But that good hope crepeth in oure herte, 870
Supposynge evere, though we sore smerte,
To be releeved by hym afterward.
Swich supposyng and hope is sharp and hard;
I warne yow wel, it is to seken evere.
That futur temps hath maad men to
        dissevere, 875
In trust therof, from al that evere they hadde.
Yet of that art they kan nat wexen sadde,
For unto hem it is a bitter sweete,—
So semeth it,—for nadde they but a sheete,
Which that they myghte wrappe hem in
        a-nyght, 880
And a brat to walken in by daylyght,
They wolde hem selle and spenden on this craft.
They kan nat stynte til no thyng be laft.
And everemoore, where that evere they goon,
Men may hem knowe by smel of brymstoon. 885

Glosses (right column):

lerne: teach. lewed: ignorant. subtil-
tee: abstruse science.
letterure: learning. noon: none.
in effect: in fact. oon: the same.

ylike: equally.

watres corosif: acids. lymaille: metal
  filings.

induracioun: hardening or congealing.
ablucioun: washing, cleansing.
passen: surpass, outdo. bible: book.
owher: anywhere.

reyse: raise. rowe: rough.

faste: eagerly, intently.
were we siker: were we secure, had
  we sure mastery. make avow:
  swear an oath.
sleighte: skill. he: i.e., the elixer.
he: the elixer. good: money.
wexen wood: go mad.

hym: the elixer.

is to seken evere: needs to be sought
  forever. futur temps: time to come.
dissevere from: part with, give up.

wexen sadde: become sated, have
  their fill.
for . . . sheete: for had they only one
  sheet.

brat: a cloak of coarse cloth.

stynte: stop.

---

854. mollificacioun: softening, rendering wax-like.
862–63. philosophres stoon, elixer: the means or the substance by which a lower or baser metal could be transmuted to a higher one.

For al the world they stynken as a goot;

goot: goat.

Hir savour is so rammyssh and so hoot

savour: smell. **rammyssh:** ramlike,

That though a man from hem a mile be,

rank. hoot: pungent.

The savour wol infecte hym, trusteth me.

infecte: pollute with stench.

Lo thus by smellyng and threedbare array, 890

If that men liste, this folk they knowe may.

And if a man wol aske hem pryvely

Why they been clothed so unthriftily,

unthriftily: poorly.

They right anon wol rownen in his ere,

rownen: whisper.

And seyn if that they espied were, 895

espied: discovered, found out.

Men wolde hem slee by cause of hir science.

Lo, thus this folk bitrayen innocence!

    Passe over this; I go my tale unto.

Er that the pot be on the fyr ydo,

ydo: put.

Of metals with a certeyn quantitee, 900

My lord hem trempreth, and no man but he—

trempreth: mixes, blends together.

Now he is goon, I dar seyn boldely—

For, as men seyn, he kan doon craftily.

kan doon craftily: knows how to pro-

Algate I woot wel he hath swich a name,

ceed skillfully. **algate:** at any rate.

And yet ful ofte he renneth in a blame. 905

name: reputation. **renneth in a**

And wite ye how? ful ofte it happeth so,

blame: does wrong, blunders.

The pot tobreketh, and farewel, al is go!

tobreketh: breaks in pieces, bursts

Thise metals been of so greet violence,

asunder. go: gone.

Oure walles mowe nat make hem resistence,

But if they weren wroght of lym and stoon; 910

lym: mortar.

They percen so, and thurgh the wal they goon.

And somme of hem synken into the ground—

Thus han we lost by tymes many a pound—

by tymes: betimes, in a short time.

And somme are scatered al the floor aboute;

Somme lepe into the roof. Withouten doute, 915

Though that the feend noght in oure sighte hym
        shewe,

I trowe he with us be, that ilke shrewe!

In helle, where that he is lord and sire,

Nis ther moore wo, ne moore rancour ne ire.

Whan that oure pot is broke, as I have sayd, 920

Every man chit, and halt hym yvele apayd.

yvele apayd: dissatisfied.

    Somme seyde it was long on the fir makyng;

long on: the fault of. **the fir makyng:**

Somme seyde nay, it was on the blowyng,—

i.e., how the fire was made.

Thanne was I fered, for that was myn office.

fered: afraid.

"Straw!" quod the thridde, "ye been lewed and

lewed: ignorant.

      nyce. 925

nyce: foolish.

It was nat tempred as it oghte be."

"Nay," quod the fourthe, "stynt and herkne me.

By cause oure fyr was nat maad of beech,

That is the cause, and oother noon, so theech!"

so theech: so may I thrive, prosper.

I kan nat telle wheron it was long, 930

wheron it was long: i.e., what caused
    it.

---

921. chit: (chideth) chides. halt: (halteth) holds.

But wel I woot greet strif is us among.
   "What," quod my lord, "ther is namoore to
      doone;
Of thise perils I wol be war eftsoone.   eftsoone: hereafter.
I am right siker that the pot was crased.   crased: cracked.
Be as be may, be ye no thyng amased;   935 amased: stunned, bewildered.
As usage is, lat swepe the floor as swithe;   lat swepe: let . . . be swept. as
Plukke up youre hertes, and beeth glad and   swithe: at once.
      blithe."
   The mullok on an heep ysweped was,   mullok: rubbish, refuse. on: into.
And on the floor ycast a canevas,
And al this mullok in a syve ythrowe,   940 syve: sieve.
And sifted, and ypiked many a throwe.   ypiked: picked over. many a throwe:
   "Pardee," quod oon, "somwhat of oure metal   many a time, often.
Yet is ther heere, though that we han nat al.
And though this thyng myshapped have as now, myshapped: happened unfortunately.
Another tyme it may be well ynow.   945 as now: just now. ynow: enough.
Us moste putte oure good in aventure.   putte in aventure: stake, risk. good:
A marchant, pardee, may nat ay endure,   goods; property, wealth.
Trusteth me wel, in his prosperitee.
Somtyme his good is drowned in the see,
And somtyme comth it sauf unto the londe." 950 sauf: safe.
   "Pees!" quod my lord, "the nexte tyme I wol
      fonde   fonde: endeavor.
To bryngen oure craft al in another plite,   plite: plight, state.
And but I do, sires, lat me han the wite.   wite: blame.
Ther was defaute in somwhat, wel I woot."   defaute: defect, fault. somwhat: some-
   Another seyde the fir was over-hoot,—   955 thing.
But, be it hoot or coold, I dar seye this,
That we concluden everemoore amys.
We faille of that which that we wolden have,
And in oure madnesse everemoore we rave.
And whan we been togidres everichon,   960
Every man semeth a Salomon.
But al thyng which that shineth as the gold
Nis nat gold, as that I have herd told;
Ne every appul that is fair at eye   at eye: to the eye.
Ne is nat good, what so men clappe or crye. 965 clappe: chatter.
Right so, lo, fareth it amonges us:
He that semeth the wisest, by Jhesus!
Is moost fool, whan it cometh to the preef;   preef: proof, test.
And he that semeth trewest is a theef.   theef: scoundrel.
That shul ye knowe, er that I fro yow wende, 970
By that I of my tale have maad an ende.   by that: by the time that.

      EXPLICIT PRIMA PARS.
    ET SEQUITUR PARS SECUNDA.

   Ther is a chanoun of religioun
Amonges us, wolde infecte al a toun,   wolde infecte: (who) would pollute
                               with stench.

Thogh it as greet were as was Nynyvee,
Rome, Alisaundre, Troye, and othere three. 975
His sleightes and his infinite falsnesse   sleightes: deceits.
Ther koude no man writen, as I gesse,
Though that he myghte lyve a thousand yeer.
In al this world of falshede nis his peer;   of: for. nis: there is not.
For in his termes he wol hym so wynde, 980   termes: technical expressions. wynde:
And speke his wordes in so sly a kynde,   entangle. sly: crafty, skillful. kynde:
Whanne he commune shal with any wight,   manner.
That he wol make hym doten anonright,   doten: behave foolishly. anonright:
But it a feend be, as hymselven is.   right off, immediately.
Ful many a man hath he bigiled er this, 985
And wol, if that he lyve may a while;
And yet men ride and goon ful many a mile   goon: walk.
Hym for to seke and have his aqueyntaunce,   seke: visit.
Noght knowynge of his false governaunce.   governaunce: behavior.
And if yow list to yeve me audience, 990
I wol it tellen here in youre presence.
   But worshipful chanons religious,
Ne demeth nat that I sclaundre youre hous,   sclaundre: slander; reproach.
Although my tale of a chanoun bee.
Of every ordre som shrewe is, pardee, 995   of: in.
And God forbede that al a compaignye
Sholde rewe a singuleer mannes folye.   rewe: rue, feel remorse for. singuleer:
To sclaundre yow is no thyng myn entente,   single, individual. no thyng: not at
But to correcten that is mys I mente.   all. that: what. mys: amiss; wrong.
This tale was nat oonly told for yow, 1000
But eek for othere mo; ye woot wel how
That among Cristes apostles twelve
Ther was no traytour but Judas hymselve.
Thanne why sholde al the remenant have a blame
That giltlees were? By yow seye I the same, 1005   by: of.
Save oonly this, if ye wol herkne me:
If any Judas in youre covent be,   covent: body of canons, religious
Remoeveth hym bitymes, I yow rede,   house. bitymes: promptly. rede:
If shame or los may causen any drede.   advise.
And beeth no thyng displesed, I yow preye, 1010   beeth: be.
But in this cas herketh what I shal seye.
   In London was a preest, an annueleer,
That therinne dwelled hadde many a yeer,
Which was so plesaunt and so servysable   which: who.
Unto the wyf, where as he was at table, 1015   wyf: woman. was at table: i.e.,
That she wolde suffre hym no thyng for to paye   boarded.
For bord ne clothyng, wente he never so gaye;
And spendyng silver hadde he right ynow.   silver: money.
Therof no fors; I wol procede as now,   no fors: no matter.

---

979. falshede: falseness, deceitfulness.
1012. annueleer: a priest endowed to celebrate anniversary memorial masses for the dead.

And telle forth my tale of the chanoun   1020
That broghte this preest to confusioun.   confusioun: ruin.
    This false chanon cam upon a day
Unto this preestes chambre, wher he lay,   lay: lodged.
Bisechynge hym to lene hym a certeyn   lene: lend. a certeyn: a certain
Of gold, and he wolde quyte it hym ageyn.   1025   amount. quyte: repay.
"Lene me a marke," quod he, "but dayes three,
And at my day I wol it quyten thee.   day: i.e., day agreed upon.
And if so be that thow me fynde fals,
Another day do hange me by the hals!"   hals: neck.
    This preest hym took a marke, and that as   took: gave. as swithe: at once.
     swithe,   1030
And this chanoun hym thanked ofte sithe,   ofte sithe: oft-times, many times.
And took his leve, and wente forth his weye,
And at the thridde day broghte his moneye,
And to the preest he took his gold agayn,   took: gave. agayn: back.
Wherof this preest was wonder glad and
     fayn.   1035
    "Certes," quod he, "no thyng anoyeth me
To lene a man a noble, or two, or thre,   noble: gold coin worth one-third of a
Or what thyng were in my possessioun,   pound. what: whatever.
Whan he so trewe is of condicioun   condicioun: character, moral nature.
That in no wise he breke wol his day;   1040   breke his day: fail to make his pay-
To swich a man I kan never seye nay."   ment by the agreed day.
    "What!" quod this chanoun, "sholde I be
     untrewe?
Nay, that were thyng yfallen al of newe.   of newe: recently.
Trouthe is a thyng that I wol evere kepe   trouthe: (my) pledge.
Unto that day in which that I shal crepe   1045
Into my grave, and ellis God forbede.
Bileveth this as siker as your Crede.
God thanke I, and in good tyme be it sayd,   in good tyme: in fortunate time, for-
That ther was nevere man yet yvele apayd   tunately. yvele apayd: dissatisfied.
For gold ne silver that he to me lente,   1050
Ne nevere falshede in myn herte I mente.   falshede: falseness, deceitfulness.
And sire," quod he, "now of my pryvetee,
Syn ye so goodlich han been unto me,   goodlich: friendly, kind.
And kithed to me so greet gentillesse,   kithed: shown.
Somwhat to quyte with youre kyndenesse   1055   to quyte . . . kyndenesse: to repay
I wol yow shewe, and if yow list to lere,   your kindness with. lere: learn.
I wol yow teche pleynly the manere
How I kan werken in philosophye.
Taketh good heede, ye shul wel seen at eye   at eye: i.e., with your own eyes;
That I wol doon a maistrie er I go."   1060   clearly. doon a maistrie: make a
    "Ye," quod the preest, "ye, sire, and wol ye so?   magistery, prepare the philosopher's
Marie! therof I pray yow hertely."   stone.

1026. marke: the sum of money of the value of eight ounces of silver; two-thirds of a pound.

"At youre comandement, sire, trewely,"
Quod the chanoun, "and ellis God forbede!"
Lo, how this theef koude his service bede! 1065   theef: scoundrel. bede: offer.
Ful sooth it is that swich profred servyse
Stynketh, as witnessen thise olde wyse,   olde wyse: ancient sages.
And that, ful soone I wol it verifie
In this chanoun, roote of al trecherie,
That everemoore delit hath and gladnesse— 1070
Swiche feendly thoghtes in his herte impresse—   impresse: become fixed.
How Cristes peple he may to meschief brynge.   meschief: misfortune; poverty.
God kepe us from his false dissymulynge!
    Noght wiste this preest with whom that he
        delte,
Ne of his harm comynge he no thyng felte. 1075   harm comynge: approaching ruin.
O sely preest! o sely innocent!   sely: simple, foolish.
With coveitise anon thou shalt be blent!   blent: blinded.
O gracelees, ful blynd is thy conceit,   gracelees: unwary man. conceit:
No thyng artow war of the deceit   mind. no thyng: not at all. war:
Which that this fox yshapen hath to thee! 1080   aware. yshapen to: contrived for.
His wily wrenches thou ne mayst nat flee.   wrenches: tricks.
Wherfore, to go to the conclusion,
That refereth to thy confusion,   refereth: has reference. confusion:
Unhappy man, anon I wol me hye   ruin. hye: hasten.
To tellen thyn unwit and thy folye,   1085   unwit: stupidity.
And eek the falsnesse of that oother wrecche,
As ferforth as my konnyng wol strecche.   ferforth: far.
    This chanon was my lord, ye wolden wene?
Sire hoost, in feith, and by the hevenes queene,
It was another chanoun, and nat he,   1090
That kan an hundred fold moore subtiltee.   subtiltee: cunning, craftiness.
He hath bitrayed folkes many tyme;   bitrayed: deceived, duped.
Of his falsnesse it dulleth me to ryme.   dulleth: depresses.
Evere whan I speke of his falshede,
For shame of hym my chekes wexen rede.   1095
Algates they bigynnen for to glowe,   algates: at any rate.
For reednesse have I noon, right wel I knowe,
In my visage; for fumes diverse
Of metals, which ye han herd me reherce,
Consumed and wasted han my reednesse.   1100
Now tak heede of this chanons cursednesse!
    "Sire," quod he to the preest, "lat youre man   lat gon: cause to go; send.
        gon
For quyksilver, that we it hadde anon;   that: so that. hadde: might have.
And lat hym bryngen ounces two or three;
And whan he comth, as faste shal ye see   1105   as faste: very quickly.
A wonder thyng, which ye saugh nevere er this."
    "Sire," quod the preest, "it shal be doon, ywis."
He bad his servant fecchen hym this thyng,
And he al redy was at his biddyng,

And wente hym forth, and cam anon agayn   1110
With this quyksilver, shortly for to sayn,
And took thise ounces thre to the chanoun;   took: gave.
And he hem leyde faire and wel adoun,   leyde: laid. faire: carefully.
And bad the servant coles for to brynge,   coles: charcoal.
That he anon myghte go to his werkynge.   1115
   The coles right anon weren yfet,   yfet: fetched.
And this chanoun took out a crosselet   crosselet: crucible.
Of his bosom, and shewed it the preest.   of: from.
"This instrument," quod he, "which that thou
        seest,
Taak in thyn hand, and put thyself therinne   1120
Of this quyksilver an ounce, and heer bigynne,
In the name of Crist, to wexe a philosofre.
Ther been ful fewe whiche that I wolde profre
To shewen hem thus muche of my science.
For ye shul seen heer, by experience,   1125
That this quyksilver I wol mortifye   mortifye: alter or destroy the outward
Right in youre sighte anon, withouten lye,   form of (e.g., a metal).
And make it as good silver and as fyn
As ther is any in youre purs or myn
Or elleswhere, and make it malliable;   1130
And elles holdeth me fals and unable   unable: unfit.
Amonges folk for evere to appeere.
I have a poudre heer, that coste me deere,   poudre: powder.
Shal make al good, for it is cause of al
My konnyng, which that I yow shewen shal.   1135
Voyde youre man, and lat hym be theroute,   voyde: send away. theroute: outside.
And shette the dore, whiles we been aboute
Oure pryvetee, that no man us espye,   pryvetee: secret affairs.
Whils that we werke in this philosophye."   philosophye: alchemy.
   Al as he bad fulfilled was in dede.   1140   bad: bade, directed.
This ilke servant anonright out yede   yede: went.
And his maister shette the dore anon,
And to hire labour spedily they gon.
   This preest, at this cursed chanons biddyng,
Upon the fir anon sette this thyng,   1145
And blew the fir, and bisied hym ful faste.   faste: intently.
And this chanoun into the crosselet caste
A poudre, noot I wherof that it was
Ymaad, outher of chalk, outher of glas,   outher: either; or.
Or somwhat elles, was nat worth a flye,   1150
To blynde with this preest; and bad hym hye   to blynde . . . preest: to blind this
The coles for to couchen al above   priest with. hye: hasten. couchen:
The crosselet. "For in tokenyng I thee love,"   set, arrange. in tokenyng: as a
Quod this chanoun, "thyne owene handes two   token that.
Shul werche al thyng which that shal here be   werche: perform. al: every.
        do."   1155

"Graunt mercy," quod the preest, and was ful
    glad,

      graunt mercy: great thanks.

And couched coles as the chanoun bad.
And while he bisy was, this feendly wrecche,
This false chanoun—the foule feend hym
      fecche!—
Out of his bosom took a bechen cole,   1160

      bechen cole: a piece of charcoal made

In which ful subtilly was maad an hole,

      of beechwood. *subtilly:* craftily,

And therinne put was of silver lymaille

      cunningly. *lymaille:* filings.

An ounce, and stopped was, withouten faille,
This hole with wex, to kepe the lemaille in.

      wex: wax.

And understondeth that this false gyn   1165

      gyn: contrivance.

Was nat maad ther, but it was maad bifore;

      ther: on that occasion, then.

And othere thynges I shal tellen moore
Herafterward, which that he with hym broghte.
Er he cam there, hym to bigile he thoghte,

      hym: i.e., the priest. *bigile:* cheat.

And so he dide, er that they wente atwynne; 1170

      wente atwynne: went apart, parted

Til he had terved hym, koude he nat blynne.

      company. *terved:* flayed, skinned.

It dulleth me whan that I of hym speke.

      blynne: cease. *dulleth:* depresses.

On his falshede fayn wolde I me wreke,

      falshede: falseness, deceitfulness.

If I wiste how, but he is here and there;

      wreke: avenge.

He is so variaunt, he abit nowhere.   1175

      variaunt: varying, shifty. *abit:* (abideth)

    But taketh heede now, sires, for Goddes love!

      abides.

He took his cole of which I spak above,
And in his hand he baar it pryvely.
And whiles the preest couched bisily
The coles, as I tolde yow er this,   1180
This chanoun seyde, "Freend, ye doon amys.
This is nat couched as it oghte be;
But soone I shal amenden it," quod he.

      amenden: correct.

"Now lat me medle therwith but a while,

      medle: busy myself.

For of yow have I pitee, by Seint Gile!   1185
Ye been right hoot; I se wel how ye swete.

      hoot: hot. *swete:* sweat.

Have here a clooth, and wipe awey the wete."
And whiles that the preest wiped his face,
This chanoun took his cole—with sory grace!—

      with sory grace: bad luck to him!

And leyde it above upon the myddeward   1190

      myddeward: middle.

Of the crosselet, and blew wel afterward,
Til that the coles gonne faste brenne.
    "Now yeve us drynke," quod the chanoun
      thenne;
"As swithe al shal be wel, I undertake.

      as swithe: soon.

Sitte we doun, and lat us myrie make."   1195
And whan that this chanounes bechen cole
Was brent, al the lemaille out of the hole

      brent: burned. *lemaille:* filings.

Into the crosselet fil anon adoun;
And so it moste nedes, by resoun,

      by resoun: with good reason.

Syn it so evene above couched was.   1200

      evene: exactly. *couched:* set.

But therof wiste the preest nothyng, alas!

He demed alle the coles yliche good;
For of the sleighte he nothyng understood.
And whan this alkamystre saugh his tyme,
"Ris up," quod he, "sire preest, and stondeth by
      me;   1205
And for I woot wel ingot have ye noon,
Gooth, walketh forth, and bryngeth a chalk
      stoon;
For I wol make it of the same shap
That is an ingot, if I may han hap.
And bryngeth eek with yow a bolle or a
      panne   1210
Ful of water, and ye shul se wel thanne
How that oure bisynesse shal thryve and preve.
And yet, for ye shul han no mysbileeve
Ne wrong conceite of me in youre absence,
I wol nat been out of youre presence,   1215
But go with yow, and come with yow ageyn."
The chambre dore, shortly for to seyn,
They opened and shette, and wente hir weye.
And forth with hem they carieden the keye,
And come agayn withouten any delay.   1220
What sholde I tarien al the longe day?
He took the chalk, and shoop it in the wise
Of an ingot, as I shal yow devyse.
   I seye, he took out of his owene sleeve
A teyne of silver—yvele moot he cheve!—   1225
Which that ne was nat but an ounce of weighte.
And taketh heede now of his cursed sleighte!
   He shoop his ingot, in lengthe and in brede
Of this teyne, withouten any drede,
So slyly that the preest it nat espide,   1230
And in his sleve agayn he gan it hide,
And fro the fyr he took up his matere,
And in th'yngot putte it with myrie cheere,
And in the water-vessel he it caste,
Whan that hym lyste, and bad the preest as
      faste,   1235
"Look what ther is, put in thyn hand and grope.
Thow fynde shalt ther silver, as I hope."
What, devel of helle! sholde it elles be?
Shaving of silver silver is, pardee!
He putte his hand in and took up a teyne   1240
Of silver fyn, and glad in every veyne
Was this preest, whan he saugh it was so.
"Goddes blessyng, and his modres also,
And alle halwes, have ye, sire chanoun,"
Seyde the preest; "and I hir malisoun,   1245
But, and ye vouche-sauf to techen me

Glosses

yliche: equally.
sleighte: trick.
alkamystre: alchemist.
stondeth: stand.

ingot: mold for molten metal.
chalk stoon: a piece of soft limestone (chalk).

hap: good fortune; success.

bolle: bowl.

preve: succeed.
mysbileeve: false opinion.
conceite: opinion.

come: came.
what: why.
shoop: shaped. wise: fashion.
ingot: mold.

teyne: small bar. cheve: fare.

sleighte: trick, trickery.

shoop: shaped. brede: breadth.

matere: material.

as faste: very quickly.

halwes: saints.
hir malisoun: their malediction, curse.
but: unless. and: if.

This noble craft and this subtilitee,   subtilitee: abstruse science.
I wol be youre in al that evere I may."   youre: yours.
     Quod the chanoun, "Yet wol I make assay
The seconde tyme, that ye may taken heede   1250
And been expert of this, and in youre neede   expert of: experienced in. in: at.
Another day assaye in myn absence   assaye: practise.
This disciplyne and this crafty science.   crafty: learned, subtle.
Lat take another ounce," quod he tho,
"Of quyksilver, withouten wordes mo,   1255
And do therwith as ye han doon er this
With that oother, which that now silver is."
     This preest hym bisieth in al that he kan
To doon as this chanoun, this cursed man,
Comanded hym, and faste blew the fir,   1260
For to come to th'effect of his desir.   effect: achievement.
And this chanon, right in the meene while,
Al redy was this preest eft to bigile,   eft: again, once more.
And for a contenaunce in his hand he bar   for a contenaunce: for show; for de-
An holwe stikke—taak keep and be war!—   1265   ception. holwe: hollow.
In the ende of which an ounce, and namoore,
Of silver lemaille put was, as bifore
Was in his cole, and stopped with wex weel   wex: wax.
For to kepe in his lemaille every deel.
And whil this preest was in his bisinesse,   1270
This chanoun with his stikke gan hym dresse   gan hym dresse: went.
To hym anon, and his poudre caste in
As he dide er—the devel out of his skyn
Hym terve, I pray to God, for his falshede!   terve: flay.
For he was evere fals in thoght and dede—   1275
And with his stikke, above the crosselet,
That was ordeyned with that false jet   ordeyned: prepared, equipped. jet: de-
He stired the coles til relente gan   vice. relente gan: melted.
The wex agayn the fyr, as every man,   agayn: in.
But it a fool be, woot wel it moot nede,   1280
And al that in the stikke was out yede,   out yede: went out, i.e., poured out.
And in the crosselet hastily it fel.
     Now, good sires, what wol ye bet than wel?   bet: better.
Whan that this preest thus was bigiled ageyn,
Supposynge noght but trouthe, sooth to seyn,   1285   trouthe: honesty, integrity.
He was so glad that I kan nat expresse
In no manere his myrthe and his gladnesse;
And to the chanoun he profred eftsoone   eftsoone: again.
Body and good. "Ye," quod the chanoun soone,
"Though poure I be, crafty thou shalt me   crafty: skillful, learned.
        fynde.   1290
I warne thee, yet is ther moore bihynde.   bihynde: still to come.
Is ther any coper herinne?" seyde he.
     "Ye," quod the preest, "sire, I trowe wel ther
        be."

"Elles go bye us som, and that as swithe;

Now, goode sire, go forth thy wey and hy
   the." 1295

He wente his wey, and with this coper cam,

And this chanon it in his handes nam,

And of that coper weyed out but an ounce.

Al to symple is my tonge to pronounce,

As ministre of my wit, the doublenesse 1300

Of this chanoun, roote of alle cursednesse!

He semed freendly to hem that knewe hym
   noght,

But he was feendly bothe in werk and thoght.

It weerieth me to telle of his falsnesse,

And nathelees yet wol I it expresse, 1305

To th'entente that men may be war therby,

And for noon oother cause, trewely.

He putte this ounce of coper in the crosselet,

And on the fyr as swithe he hath it set,

And caste in poudre, and made the preest to
   blowe, 1310

And in his werkyng for to stoupe lowe,

As he dide er,—and al nas but a jape;

Right as hym liste, the preest he made his ape!

And afterward in the ingot he it caste,

And in the panne putte it at the laste 1315

Of water, and in he putte his owene hand,

And in his sleve (as ye biforen-hand

Herde me telle) he hadde a silver teyne.

He slyly took it out, this cursed heyne,

Unwityng this preest of his false craft, 1320

And in the pannes botme he hath it laft;

And in the water rombled to and fro,

And wonder pryvely took up also

The coper teyne, noght knowyng this preest,

And hidde it, and hym hente by the breest, 1325

And to hym spak, and thus seyde in his game:

"Stoupeth adoun, by God, ye be to blame!

Helpeth me now, as I dide yow whileer;

Putte in youre hand, and looketh what is theer."

This preest took up this silver teyne anon, 1330

And thanne seyde the chanoun, "Lat us gon

With thise thre teynes, whiche that we han
   wroght,

To som goldsmyth, and wite if they been oght.

For, by my feith, I nolde, for myn hood,

---

as swithe: at once.

hy the: hurry.

nam: took.

weyed: weighed.

ministre: servant, agent. **doublenesse:**
 duplicity.

weerieth: wearies.

cause: purpose.

as swithe: at once.

stoupe: stoop.

jape: trick.

ingot: mold.

teyne: small bar.

heyne: mean wretch.

pannes botme: bottom of the pan.

rombled: rambled, fumbled, groped
 about. **wonder:** very. **pryvely:**
 stealthily.

hente: grasped.

in his game: playfully.

stoupeth: stoop. **ye be:** (or) you are.

whileer: a while ago.

oght: aught, worth anything.

1320. **unwityng this preest:** this priest unaware.

1324. **noght knowyng this preest:** the priest knowing nothing (of it).

1334–35. **I nolde . . . were:** i.e., I wager my hood that they be.

But if they were silver fyn and good,   1335
And that as swithe preved shal it bee."

    Unto the goldsmyth with thise teynes three
They wente, and putte thise teynes in assay
To fyr and hamer; myghte no man seye nay,
But that they weren as hem oghte be.   1340
    This sotted preest, who was gladder than he?
Was nevere brid gladder agayn the day,
Ne nyghtyngale, in the sesoun of May,
Was nevere noon that lyste bet to synge;
Ne lady lustier in carolynge,   1345
Or for to speke of love and wommanhede,
Ne knyght in armes to doon an hardy dede,
To stonde in grace of his lady deere,
Than hadde this preest this sory craft to leere.
And to the chanoun thus he spak and seyde: 1350
"For love of God, that for us alle deyde,
And as I may deserve it unto yow,
What shal this receite coste? telleth now!"

    "By oure Lady," quod this chanon, "it is dere,
I warne yow wel; for save I and a frere,   1355
In Engelond ther kan no man it make."

    "No fors," quod he, "now, sire, for Goddes
        sake,
What shal I paye? telleth me, I preye."

    "Ywis," quod he, "it is ful deere, I seye.
Sire, at o word, if that thee list it have,   1360
Ye shul paye fourty pound, so God me save!
And nere the freendshipe that ye dide er this
To me, ye sholde paye moore, ywis."

    This preest the somme of fourty pound anon
Of nobles fette, and took hem everichon   1365
To this chanoun, for this ilke receite.
Al his werkyng nas but fraude and deceite.

    "Sire preest," he seyde, "I kepe han no loos
Of my craft, for I wolde it kept were cloos;
And, as ye love me, kepeth it secree.   1370
For, and men knewen al my soutiltee,
By God, they wolden han so greet envye
To me, by cause of my philosophye,
I sholde be deed; ther were noon oother weye."

    "God it forbede," quod the preest, "what sey
        ye?   1375
Yet hadde I levere spenden al the good
Which that I have, and elles wexe I wood,
Than that ye sholden falle in swich mescheef."

    "For youre good wil, sire, have ye right good
        preef,"

---

as swithe: at once. preved: tested.

assay: trial.

sotted: besotted, stupid.

brid: bird. agayn the day: toward day-
  break.

lyste bet: it better pleased.

lustier: more joyful. carolynge: danc-
  ing a carol (a round dance with
  singing).

leere: learn.

deyde: died.
unto: from.
receite: recipe, formula.

and nere: if it were not (for).

fette: fetched. took: gave.

nas but: was nothing but.
I kepe han no loos: I care to have no
  renown, fame. kept cloos: held in
  confidence.
and: if. soutiltee: skill; craftiness.

philosophye: abstruse science.
deed: dead.

good: money; goods.
elles wexe I wood: otherwise may I
  go mad. mescheef: misfortune.
have ye: may you have.
preef: result, fulfillment.

Quod the chanoun, "and farwel, grant
     mercy!" 1380

grant mercy: great thanks.

He wente his wey, and never the preest hym sy

sy: saw.

After that day; and whan that this preest sholde
Maken assay, at swich tyme as he wolde,
Of this receit, farwel! it wolde nat be.
Lo, thus byjaped and bigiled was he! 1385

byjaped: tricked, deceived.

Thus maketh he his introduccioun,

introduccioun: preliminary action.

To brynge folk to hir destruccioun.
    Considereth, sires, how that, in ech estaat,

estaat: class of society.

Bitwixe men and gold ther is debaat

debaat: conflict.

So ferforth that unnethes is ther noon. 1390
This multiplying blent so many oon

multiplying: see line 669, note. blent:
   (blendeth) blinds.

That in good feith I trowe that it be
The cause grettest of swich scarsetee.
Philosophres speken so mystily

philosophres: alchemists.

In this craft that men kan nat come therby, 1395

come therby: come by it, grasp it.

For any wit that men han now-a-dayes.
They mowe wel chiteren as doon jayes,

chiteren: chatter, jabber.

And in hire termes sette hir lust and peyne,

termes: technical jargon. lust and
   peyne: delight and sorrow.

But to hir purpos shul they nevere atteyne.
A man may lightly lerne, if he have aught, 1400

lightly: easily; quickly.

To multiplie, and brynge his good to naught!

good: goods, wealth.

    Lo! swich a lucre is in this lusty game,

lucre: profit.

A mannes myrthe it wol turne into grame,

grame: grief, sorrow.

And empten also grete and hevye purses,

empten: empty.

And maken folk for to purchasen curses 1405

purchasen: acquire.

Of hem that han hir good therto ylent.

therto: for that purpose.

O! fy, for shame! they that han been brent,
Allas! kan they nat flee the fires heete?
Ye that it use, I rede ye it lete,

use: practise. rede: advise. lete:
   abandon, forsake.

Lest ye lese al; for bet than nevere is late. 1410

to long a date: too long a time.

Nevere to thryve were to long a date.
Though ye prolle ay, ye shul it nevere fynde.

prolle ay: prowl about forever.

Ye been as boold as is Bayard the blynde,

boold: overconfident, rash.

That blondreth forth, and peril casteth noon.

casteth: notices.

He is as boold to renne agayn a stoon 1415

agayn: against.

As for to goon bisides in the weye.

goon bisides: go astray.

So faren ye that multiplie, I seye.
If that youre eyen kan nat seen aright,
Looke that youre mynde lakke noght his sight.

looke: make sure. his: its.

For though ye looke never so brode and
    stare, 1420

brode: wide-eyed.

Ye shul nothyng wynne on that chaffare,

chaffare: traffic, transaction.

But wasten al that ye may rape and renne.

rape and renne: seize and grasp.

1390. To such a degree that there is hardly any (gold) left.
1410. bet than nevere is late: better late than never.
1413. Bayard: a horse who proverbially was ignorant and reckless.

Withdraweth the fyr, lest it to faste brenne;   to faste: too fast, too hard.
Medleth namoore with that art, I mene,   mene: say.
For if ye doon, youre thrift is goon ful clene. 1425   thrift: prosperity.
And right as swithe I wol yow tellen here   as swithe: at once.
What philosophres seyn in this matere.

  Lo, thus seith Arnold of the Newe Toun,
As his Rosarie maketh mencioun;
He seith right thus, withouten any lye: 1430
"Ther may no man mercurie mortifye   mortifye: transmute.
But it be with his brother knowlechyng";
How that he which that first seyde this thyng   how: i.e., he says how.
Of philosophres fader was, Hermes—   of philosophres fader: (the) first of
He seith how that the dragon, doutelees,   1435   alchemists.
Ne dieth nat, but if that he be slayn
With his brother; and that is for to sayn,   with: by.
By the dragon, Mercurie, and noon oother
He understood, and brymstoon by his brother,
That out of Sol and Luna were ydrawe.   1440   ydrawe: drawn, extracted.
"And therfore," seyde he,—tak heede to my
    sawe—   sawe: speech, discourse.
"Lat no man bisy hym this art for to seche,   seche: pursue.
But if that he th'entencioun and speche   entencioun: meaning. speche: (tech-
Of philosophres understonde kan;   nical) language. philosophres: al-
And if he do, he is a lewed man.   1445   chemists. lewed: foolish.
For this science and this konnyng," quod he,   konnyng: skill.
"Is of the secree of the secretes, pardee."   secree of the secretes: secret of se-
  Also ther was a disciple of Plato,   crets, greatest of secrets.
That on a tyme seyde his maister to,   his . . . to: to his master.
As his book Senior wol bere witnesse,   1450
And this was his demande in soothfastnesse:
"Telle me the name of the privee stoon?"   privee: secret. stoon: i.e., the phi-
  And Plato answerde unto hym anoon,   losopher's stone, the elixer.
"Take the stoon that Titanos men name."   titanos: magnesia (see line 1455,
  "Which is that?" quod he. "Magnasia is the   note).
    same,"   1455
Seyde Plato. "Ye, sire, and is it thus?

1428–29. The source of lines 1431–47 is actually *De Lapide Philosophorum* by Arnald of Vill: Nova (c. 1240–1311) rather than his *Rosarium*, although this too offers ideas used in line 1431–40.

1432. Without [mercury] uniting with his brother (a "sulphur").

1434. Hermes: Hermes Trismegistus ("thrice greatest"), the Egyptian god Thoth, regarded a the author of the secrets of alchemy.

1435–40. Mercury (the dragon) may not be transmuted (be mortifed, die) unless he be mortifie (slayn) with a "sulphur" (his brother) extracted (ydrawe) from gold (Sol) and silver (Luna).

1445. do: i.e., attempt to practise it.

1450. book Senior: an alchemical treatise (*Tabula Chemica*) attributed to Zadith ibn Hamue who was known in Latin as "Senior" (Arabic, "Sheikh").

1455. magnasia: magnesia, a mineral thought to be one of the ingredients of the philosopher stone.

This is *ignotum per ignocius.*
What is Magnasia, good sire, I yow preye?"
   "It is a water that is maad, I seye,
Of elementes foure," quod Plato.   1460
   "Telle me the roote, good sire," quod he tho,   the roote: real basis, essential part.
"Of that water, if it be youre wille."
   "Nay, nay," quod Plato, "certein, that I nylle,   nylle: (he wylle) will not.
The philosophres sworn were everychoon
That they sholden discovere it unto noon,   1465   discovere: reveal.
Ne in no book it write in no manere.
For unto Crist it is so lief and deere   lief: precious.
That he wol nat that it discovered be,   discovered: revealed.
But where it liketh to his deitee   liketh to: pleases.
Men for t'enspire, and eek for to defende   1470   men for t'enspire: to enlighten men.
Whom that hym liketh; lo, this is the ende."   defende: restrain. ende: essential
   Thanne conclude I thus, sith that God of   truth about it.
       hevene
Ne wil nat that the philo   ʰres nevene   nevene: tell.
How that a man shal co   .nto this stoon,
I rede, as for the beste, lete it goon.   1475   rede: counsel.
For whoso maketh God his adversarie,
As for to werken any thyng in contrarie
Of his wil, certes, never shal he thryve,
Thogh that he multiplie terme of his lyve.   terme: (for the) length (i.e., rest).
And there a poynt; for ended is my tale.   1480   poynt: full point, full stop, period.
God sende every trewe man boote of his bale!   boote of his bale: deliverance from his
                                                        suffering; redemption.

*Heere is ended the
Chanouns Yemannes tale.*

*Heere folweth the
prologe of the
Maunciples tale.*

   Woot ye nat where ther stant a litel toun
Which that ycleped is Bobbe-up-and-doun,
Under the Blee, in Caunterbury Weye?
Ther gan oure Hooste for to jape and pleye,
And seyde, "Sires, what! Dun is in the myre!   5   Dun: a general name for a horse.
Is ther no man, for preyere ne for hyre,
That wole awake oure felawe al bihynde?
A theef myghte hym ful lightly robbe and bynde. lightly: easily.
See how he nappeth! see how, for cokkes bones,

1457. This is (explaining) the unknown by the more unknown.
1459. a water: i.e., a kind of water (in Senior it is composite and congealed: *"aqua composita, congelata"*).
2. Bobbe-up-and-doun: Harbledown, two miles from Canterbury by the Blean forest.
9. cokkes bones: another of the Host's amazing oaths.

That he wol falle from his hors atones!   10   atones: at once.
Is that a cook of Londoun, with meschaunce?   with meschaunce: ill luck to him.
Do hym come forth, he knoweth his penaunce;   do . . . forth: make him come forth.
For he shal telle a tale, by my fey,
Although it be nat worth a botel hey.   botel hey: small bundle of hay.
Awake, thou Cook," quod he, "God yeve thee
        sorwe!   15
What eyleth thee to slepe by the morwe?   by the morwe: in the morning.
Hastow had fleen al nyght, or artow dronke?   fleen: fleas.
Or hastow with som quene al nyght yswonke,   quene: quean, concubine. yswonke:
So that thow mayst nat holden up thyn heed?"   labored, toiled.
   This Cook, that was ful pale and no thyng
        reed,   20
Seyde to oure Hoost, "So God my soule blesse,
As ther is falle on me swich hevynesse,
Noot I nat why, that me were levere slepe
Than the beste galon wyn in Chepe."
   "Wel," quod the Maunciple, "if it may doon
        ese   25
To thee, sire Cook, and to no wight displese,
Which that heere rideth in this compaignye,
And that oure Hoost wole, of his curteisye,
I wol as now excuse thee of thy tale.   as now: for now.
For, in good feith, thy visage is ful pale,   30
Thyne eyen daswen eek, as that me thynketh,   daswen: grow dim.
And, wel I woot, thy breeth ful soure stynketh:
That sheweth wel thou art nat wel disposed.   wel disposed: in good health.
Of me, certeyn, thou shalt nat been yglosed.   yglosed: flattered.
See how he ganeth, lo! this dronken wight,   35   ganeth: yawns.
As though he wolde swolwe us anonright.   anonright: immediately.
Hoold cloos thy mouth, man, by thy fader kyn!   fader kyn: father's kindred.
The devel of helle sette his foot therin!
Thy cursed breeth infecte wole us alle.
Fy, stynkyng swyn! fy, foule moote thee falle! 40   falle: befall.
A! taketh heede, sires, of this lusty man.

23–24. I had rather sleep than (have) the best gallon of wine in Cheapside.

26. sire Cook: the Cook's name was probably Roger Knyght de Ware (n.b. also line 50).

29. excuse thee of: relieve you of and act as your substitute for.

The Ellesmere Cook and the Oxford Cook: Chaucer presents Roger Knyght de Ware, the London Cook, on three occasions: in the General Prologue (ll. 379–87), in the Cook's Prologue, and in the Manciple's Prologue. The Ellesmere artist, the most faithful of those who illustrated that manuscript (1400–10), seems to understand these passages well. He notes the mormal (General Prologue, l. 386) and even bandages its unspeakable suppuration. From top to toe Roger is disgraceful and filthy. Who would choose to eat food prepared by this repulsive scoundrel? Who would desire to incur his wrath? How long will he manage to stay on the unhappy mare? Did the Ellesmere artist know of the reputation of the real Roger Knyght? Had he by chance ever laid eyes on him? Just as the Ellesmere portrait symbolizes Roger's profession with an apron and a fleshhook, so some forty years later the Oxford manuscript (1440–50) has an apron and a great cleaver. This cook, too, is bareheaded, but he is without hint of mormal, poverty, or low living. Though heavy-eyed and somewhat careless of the knotted rope halter, he has so far preserved a sort of flamboyant dignity.

Now, sweete sire, wol ye justen atte fan?
Therto me thynketh ye been wel yshape!   yshape: prepared.
I trowe that ye dronken han wyn ape,
And that is whan men pleyen with a straw." 45
And with this speche the Cook wax wrooth and   wax: became. **wrooth:** wroth, angry.
     wraw,   wraw: angry, fretful.
And on the Manciple he gan nodde faste
For lakke of speche, and doun the hors hym
     caste,
Where as he lay, til that men hym up took.
This was a fair chyvachee of a cook!   50 chyvachee: feat of horsemanship.
Allas! he nadde holde hym by his ladel!
And er that he agayn were in his sadel,
Ther was greet showvyng bothe to and fro
To lifte hym up, and muchel care and wo,
So unweeldy was this sory palled goost.   55 palled: pale; enfeebled.
And to the Manciple thanne spak oure Hoost:
   "By cause drynke hath dominacioun
Upon this man, by my savacioun,
I trowe he lewedly telle wolde his tale.   lewedly: ignorantly; coarsely; rudely.
For, were it wyn, or old or moisty ale,   60 moisty: new.
That he hath dronke, he speketh in his nose,
And fneseth faste, and eek he hath the pose.   fneseth: snorts. **pose:** head-cold.
   He hath also to do moore than ynough
To kepen hym and his capul out of the slough; capul: horse.
And if he falle from his capul eftsoone,   65 eftsoone: again.
Thanne shal we alle have ynogh to doone,
In liftyng up his hevy dronken cors.   cors: body.
Telle on thy tale; of hym make I no fors.   no fors: no matter.
   But yet, Manciple, in feith thou art to nyce, nyce: foolish.
Thus openly repreve hym of his vice.   70 repreve: reprove.
Another day he wole, peraventure,
Reclayme thee and brynge thee to lure;   reclayme: bring a hawk to the lure;
I meene, he speke wole of smale thynges,   entice into his power.
As for to pynchen at thy rekenynges.   pynchen at: find fault with.
That were nat honest, if it cam to preef." 75 honest: decent; worthy. **preef:** proof,
   "No," quod the Manciple, "that were a greet   test.
     mescheef!   mescheef: misfortune.
So myghte he lightly brynge me in the snare.
Yet hadde I levere payen for the mare
Which he rit on, than he sholde with me stryve. rit: (rideth) rides.
I wol nat wratthen hym, also moot I thryve! 80 wratthen: anger.
That that I spak, I seyde it in my bourde.   that that: that which. **bourde:** jest.

---

42. fan: the fan of a quintain, a pivoted swinging board with a club or bag of sand at the other end, swift to hit a careless jouster.
44. wyn ape: but the Cook is not foolishly playful; the Manciple is teasing him. He is, instead, hog-drunk.
51. Alas that he did not stick to his ladle!
78. payen for: pay for the hire of the mare on the pilgrimage.

And wite ye what? I have heer in a gourde
A draghte of wyn, ye, of a ripe grape,
And right anon ye shul seen a good jape.
This Cook shal drynke therof, if I may.   85
Up peyne of deeth, he wol nat seye me nay."
    And certeynly, to tellen as it was,
Of this vessel the Cook drank faste, allas!
What neded it? he drank ynough biforn.
And whan he hadde pouped in this horn,   90
To the Manciple he took the gourde agayn;
And of that drynke the Cook was wonder fayn,
And thanked hym in swich wise as he koude.
    Thanne gan oure Hoost to laughen wonder
      loude,
And seyde, "I se wel it is necessarie,   95
Where that we goon, good drynke with us carie;
For that wol turne rancour and disese
T'acord and love, and many a wrong apese.
    O Bacus, yblessed be thy name,
That so kanst turnen ernest into game!   100
Worshipe and thank be to thy deitee!
Of that matere ye gete namoore of me.
Telle on thy tale, Manciple, I thee preye."
    "Wel, sire," quod he, "now herkneth what I
      seye."

gourde: flask; bottle.

up: upon.

faste: deep.

took agayn: gave back.
fayn: fond, glad.

disese: vexation.

apese: appease.

ernest: a serious matter.

Heere bigynneth the Maunciples tale of the Crowe.

Whan Phebus dwelled here in this erthe
    adoun,
As olde bookes maken mencioun,
He was the mooste lusty bachiler
In al this world, and eek the beste archer.
He slow Phitoun, the serpent, as he lay
Slepynge agayn the sonne upon a day;
And many another noble worthy dede
He with his bowe wroghte, as men may rede.
    Pleyen he koude on every mynstralcye,
And syngen, that it was a melodye
To heeren of his cleere voys the soun.

105 *adoun: below.*

bachiler: knight.

Phitoun: the Python.
110 *agayn: in.*

every mynstralcye: every musical in-
strument.

115 *cleere: magnificent.*

---

90. pouped: blown (with a play on horn for drinking and horn for blowing).

the Maunciples tale. The Manciple's Tale has its ultimate source in Ovid's story of Apollo and the raven (*Metamorphoses* ii.531–632); Chaucer knew also several of the medieval redactions, including that of John Gower in his *Confessio Amantis* (iii. 768–835).

Certes the kyng of Thebes, Amphioun,
That with his syngyng walled that citee,
Koude nevere syngen half so wel as he.
Therto he was the semelieste man
That is or was, sith that the world bigan.   120
What nedeth it his fetures to discryve?   discryve: describe.
For in this world was noon so faire on lyve.   on lyve: alive.
He was therwith fulfild of gentillesse,   gentillesse: noble kindness.
Of honour, and of parfit worthynesse.

   This Phebus, that was flour of bachelrie,   125 flour: flower. bachelrie: knighthood.
As wel in fredom as in chivalrie,   fredom: nobility; generosity.
For his desport, in signe eek of victorie   desport: pleasure.
Of Phitoun, so as telleth us the storie,   of: over.
Was wont to beren in his hand a bowe.
   Now hadde this Phebus in his hous a
      crowe   130
Which in a cage he fostred many a day,   fostred: cared for.
And taughte it speke, as men teche a jay.
Whit was this crowe as is a snow-whit swan,
And countrefete the speche of every man   countrefete: imitate.
He koude, whan he sholde telle a tale.   135
Therwith in al this world no nyghtyngale
Ne koude, by an hondred thousand deel,   thousand deel: thousandth part.
Syngen so wonder myrily and weel.   wonder: wondrously, very.
   Now hadde this Phebus in his hous a wyf
Which that he lovede moore than his lyf,   140
And nyght and day dide evere his diligence   his diligence: i.e., his utmost.
Hir for to plese, and doon hire reverence,
Save oonly, if the sothe that I shal sayn,   if that: if.
Jalous he was, and wolde have kept hire fayn.   kept: guarded. fayn: gladly.
For hym were looth byjaped for to be,   145 byjaped: deceived.
And so is every wight in swich degree;   degree: state.
But al for naught, for it availleth noght.
A good wyf, that is clene of werk and thoght,
Sholde nat been kept in noon awayt, certayn;   in awayt: under surveillance.
And trewely, the labour is in vayn   150
To kepe a shrewe, for it wol nat be.   kepe: guard. shrewe: wicked person.
This holde I for a verray nycetee,   nycetee: folly.
To spille labour for to kepe wyves: spille: waste.
Thus writen olde clerkes in hir lyves.   writen: wrote. in: during.
   But now to purpos, as I first bigan: 155 purpos: the matter in hand.
This worthy Phebus dooth al that he kan
To plesen hire, wenynge by swich plesaunce,   wenynge: supposing.
And for his manhode and his governaunce,   governaunce: behavior.
That no man sholde han put hym from hir grace.
But God it woot, ther may no man embrace   160 embrace: manage.
As to destreyne a thyng which that nature   as to: so as to. destreyne: restrain.
Hath naturelly set in a creature.

Take any bryd, and put it in a cage,
And do al thyn entente and thy corage   entente: diligence. **corage**: desire.
To fostre it tendrely with mete and drynke   165   mete: food.
Of alle deyntees that thou kanst bithynke,   bithynke: think of.
And keep it al so clenly as thou may,
Although his cage of gold be never so gay,
Yet hath this brid, by twenty thousand fold,   fold: times.
Levere in a forest, that is rude and cold,   170
Goon ete wormes and swich wrecchednesse.   wrecchednesse: miserable fare.
For evere this brid wol doon his bisynesse   doon his bisynesse: exert himself.
To escape out of his cage, if he may.
His libertee this brid desireth ay.
    Lat take a cat, and fostre hym wel with milk 175
And tendre flessh, and make his couche of silk,
And lat hym seen a mous go by the wal,
Anon he weyveth milk and flessh and al,   weyveth: rejects.
And every deyntee that is in that hous,
Swich appetit hath he to ete a mous.   180
Lo, heere hath lust his dominacioun,
And appetit flemeth discrecioun.   flemeth: drives out.
    A she-wolf hath also a vileyns kynde.   vileyns: villainous. **kynde**: nature.
The lewedeste wolf that she may fynde,
Or leest of reputacioun, that wol she take,   185
In tyme whan hir lust to han a make.   hir lust: she desires. **make**: mate.
    Alle thise ensamples speke I by thise men   by: with reference to.
That been untrewe, and no thyng by wommen.   no thyng: not at all.
For men han evere a likerous appetit   likerous: lecherous.
On lower thyng to parformen hire delit   190   parformen: fulfil.
Than on hire wyves, be they never so faire,
Ne never so trewe, ne so debonaire.
Flessh is so newefangel, with meschaunce,   newefangel: fond of novelty.
That we ne konne in no thyng han plesaunce
That sowneth into vertu any while.   195   sowneth into: conduces to, tends to-
    This Phebus, which that thoghte upon no gile,   wards.
Deceyved was, for al his jolitee.   jolitee: splendor.
For under hym another hadde she,   under: in addition to.
A man of litel reputacioun,
Nat worth to Phebus in comparisoun.   200   worth to: equivalent to.
The moore harm is, it happeth ofte so,
Of which ther cometh muchel harm and wo.
    And so bifel, whan Phebus was absent,
His wyf anon hath for hir lemman sent.   lemman: unlawful lover.
Hir lemman? Certes, this is a knavyssh
              speche!   205
Foryeveth it me, and that I yow biseche.
    The wise Plato seith, as ye may rede,

---

164. And take all pains.

The word moot nede accorde with the dede.
If men shal telle proprely a thyng,
The word moot cosyn be to the werkyng. 210 werkyng: deed.
I am a boystous man, right thus seye I,   boystous: rough.
Ther nys no difference, trewely,
Bitwixe a wyf that is of heigh degree,   degree: rank.
If of hir body dishonest she be,   dishonest: unchaste.
And a povre wenche, oother than this— 215
If it so be they werke bothe amys—   werke amys: do wrong.
But that the gentile, in estat above,   gentile: gentlewoman.
She shal be cleped his lady, as in love;
And for that oother is a povre womman,   for: because.
She shal be cleped his wenche or his lemman. 220
And, God it woot, myn owene deere brother,
Men leyn that oon as lowe as lith that oother. leyn: lay. lith: lieth.
    Right so bitwixe a titlelees tiraunt   titlelees: usurping.
And an outlawe, or a theef erraunt,   theef erraunt: roving robber.
The same I seye, ther is no difference. 225
To Alisaundre was told this sentence,
That, for the tiraunt is of gretter myght,
By force of meynee, for to sleen dounright, meynee: his retainers.
And brennen hous and hoom, and make al playn, make al playn: level everything.
Lo, therfore is he cleped a capitayn; 230
And for the outlawe hath but smal meynee, meynee: retinue.
And may nat doon so gret an harm as he,
Ne brynge a contree to so gret meschief,   meschief: misfortune.
Men clepen hym an outlawe or a theef.
But, for I am a man noght textuel, 235 textuel: well read.
I wol noght telle of textes never a del;
I wol go to my tale, as I bigan.
Whan Phebus wyf had sent for hir lemman,
Anon they wroghten al hire lust volage. volage: fickle.
    The white crowe, that heng ay in the cage, 240 heng: hung.
Biheld hire werk, and seyde never a word.
And whan that hoom was come Phebus, the lord,
This crowe sang "Cokkow! cokkow! cokkow!" Cokkow!: a cry implying that Phoebus
    "What, bryd!" quod Phebus, "what song   is a cuckold.
            syngestow?
Ne were thow wont so myrily to synge 245
That to myn herte it was a rejoysynge
To heere thy voys? Allas! what song is this?"
    "By God!" quod he, "I synge nat amys.
Phebus," quod he, "for al thy worthynesse,
For al thy beautee and thy gentilesse, 250
For al thy song and al thy mynstralcye,
For al thy waityng, blered is thyn eye waityng: watching. blered is thyn eye
With oon of litel reputacioun,   with: you are hoodwinked by.

---

226. This anecdote was told as early as Cicero and was popular in medieval preachers' manuals.

Noght worth to thee, as in comparisoun,

The montance of a gnat, so moote I thryve! 255   montance: amount, value.

For on thy bed thy wyf I saugh hym swyve."   swyve: lie with.

    What wol ye moore? The crowe anon hym
        tolde,

By sadde tokenes and by wordes bolde,   sadde tokenes: sure signs. bolde:

How that his wyf had doon hire lecherye,   confident, certain.

Hym to gret shame and to gret vileynye; 260   hym to: to his.

And tolde hym ofte he saugh it with his eyen.

    This Phebus gan aweyward for to wryen;   wryen: turn.

Hym thoughte his sorweful herte brast atwo.   brast: would burst.

His bowe he bente, and sette therinne a flo,   flo: arrow.

And in his ire his wyf thanne hath he slayn. 265

This is th'effect, ther is namoore to sayn;

For sorwe of which he brak his mynstralcie,   brak: broke.

Bothe harpe, and lute, gyterne, and sautrie;   gyterne: guitar. sautrie: small harp.

And eek he brak his arwes and his bowe,

And after that thus spak he to the crowe: 270

    "Traitour," quod he, "with tonge of scorpioun,

Thou hast me broght to my confusioun;   confusioun: destruction.

Allas, that I was wroght! why nere I ded?

O deere wyf! o gemme of lustihed!   lustihed: delight.

That were to me so sad and eek so trewe, 275   sad: constant.

Now listow deed, with face pale of hewe,   listow: you lie.

Ful giltelees, that dorste I swere, ywys!

O rakel hand, to doon so foule amys!   rakel: rash.

O trouble wit, o ire recchelees,   trouble wit: troubled mind.

That unavysed smytest gilteles! 280   unavysed: thoughtless.

O wantrust, ful of fals suspecioun,   wantrust: distrust.

Where was thy wit and thy discrecioun?

O every man, be war of rakelnesse!   rakelnesse: rashness.

Ne trowe no thyng withouten strong witnesse.

Smyt nat to soone, er that ye witen why, 285

And beeth avysed wel and sobrely   beeth avysed: take thought.

Er ye doon any execucioun   doon execucioun upon: give vent to.

Upon youre ire for suspecioun.

Allas! a thousand folk hath rakel ire

Fully fordoon, or broght hem in the mire. 290   fordoon: ruined.

Allas! for sorwe I wol myselven slee!"

    And to the crowe, "O false theef!" seyde he,   theef: scoundrel.

"I wol thee quite anon thy false tale.

Thou songe whilom lyk a nyghtyngale;

Now shaltow, false theef, thy song forgon, 295

And eek thy white fetheres everichon,

Ne nevere in al thy lif ne shaltow speke.

Thus shal men on a traytour been awreke;   awreke: avenged.

Thou and thyn ofspryng evere shul be blake,

Ne nevere sweete noyse shul ye make, 300

But evere cry agayn tempest and rayn,   agayn: shortly before; in anticipation
    of.

In tokenynge that thurgh thee my wyf is slayn."
And to the crowe he stirte, and that anon,
And pulled his white fetheres everychon,   pulled: plucked.
And made hym blak, and refte hym al his
   song, 305 refte: took from.
And eek his speche, and out at dore hym slong
Unto the devel, which I hym bitake; which: to whom. bitake: consign.
And for this caas been alle crowes blake. caas: reason.
 Lordynges, by this ensample I yow preye,
Beth war, and taketh kepe what ye seye: 310
Ne telleth nevere no man in youre lyf
How that another man hath dight his wyf; dight: lain with.
He wol yow haten mortally, certeyn.
Daun Salomon, as wise clerkes seyn, daun: master.
Techeth a man to kepen his tonge wel. 315 kepen: guard.
But, as I seyde, I am nat textuel.
But nathelees, thus taughte me my dame: dame: mother.
"My sone, thenk on the crowe, a Goddes name!
My sone, keep wel thy tonge, and keep thy
   freend.
A wikked tonge is worse than a feend; 320
My sone, from a feend men may hem blesse. blesse: protect.
My sone, God of his endelees goodnesse
Walled a tonge with teeth and lippes eke,
For man sholde hym avyse what he speeke. hym avyse: consider.
My sone, ful ofte, for to muche speche 325 to: too.
Hath many a man been spilt, as clerkes teche; spilt: ruined.
But for litel speche avysely avysely: thoughtfully.
Is no man shent, to speke generally. shent: injured.
My sone, thy tonge sholdestow restreyne
At alle tymes, but whan thou doost thy peyne 330 but: except.
To speke of God, in honour and preyere.
The firste vertu, sone, if thou wolt leere, leere: learn.
Is to restreyne and kepe wel thy tonge;
Thus lerne children whan that they been yonge.
My sone, of muchel spekyng yvele avysed, 335 yvele avysed: thoughtless.
Ther lasse spekyng hadde ynough suffised,
Comth muchel harm; thus was me told and
   taught.
In muchel speche synne wanteth naught. wanteth: is lacking.
Wostow wherof a rakel tonge serveth? wostow: do you know.
Right as a swerd forkutteth and forkerveth 340 forkutteth, forkerveth: cuts off.
An arm a-two, my deere sone, right so
A tonge kutteth frendship al a-two.
A jangler is to God abhomynable. jangler: talebearer.
Reed Salomon, so wys and honurable;

---

326. clerkes: learned authors (e.g., David, Solomon, Seneca, Dionysius Cato, Albertano of Brescia).

Reed David in his psalmes, reed Senekke.   345
My sone, spek nat, but with thyn heed thou
     bekke.   bekke: nod.
Dissimule as thou were deef, if that thou heere
A janglere speke of perilous mateere.
The Flemyng seith, and lerne it if thee leste,
That litel janglyng causeth muchel reste.   350
My sone, if thou no wikked word hast seyd,
Thee thar nat drede for to be biwreyd;   thee thar: you need. biwreyd: be-
But he that hath mysseyd, I dar wel sayn,   trayed.
He may by no wey clepe his word agayn.   clepe agayn: call back.
Thyng that is seyd is seyde, and forth it
     gooth,   355
Though hym repente, or be hym nevere so looth.
He is his thral to whom that he hath sayd   thral: slave.
A tale of which he is now yvele apayd.   yvele apayd: displeased.
My sone, be war, and be noon auctour newe
Of tidynges, wheither they been false or
     trewe.   360
Wherso thou come, amonges hye or lowe,
Kepe wel thy tonge, and thenk upon the crowe."

     Heere is ended the Maunciples
        tale of the Crowe.

      Heere folweth the
       prologe of the
       Persouns tale.

  By that the Maunciple hadde his tale ended,   by that: by the time that.
The sonne fro the south lyne was descended
So lowe that he nas nat, to my sighte,
Degreës nyne and twenty as of highte.
Foure of the clokke it was, so as I gesse,   5
For ellevene foot, or litel moore or lesse,
My shadwe was at thilke tyme, as there,
Of swiche feet as my lengthe parted were
In sixe feet equal of proporcioun.
Therwith the moones exaltacioun,   10
I meene Libra, alwey gan ascende,
As we were entryng at a thropes ende;   thropes: thorp's, of a village.
For which oure Hoost, as he was wont to gye,   gye: guide, govern.

---

2. **south lyne:** meridian. The altitude of the sun was almost 29° at 4 P.M. in mid-April; the length of Chaucer's shadow (ll. 6–9) gives the same altitude.

10. **exaltacioun:** the position of a planet in the zodiac (here Libra, the Balance) where it was thought to exert its greatest influence.

11. **alwey gan ascende:** all the while ascended.

As in this caas, oure joly compaignye,
Seyde in this wise: "Lordynges everichoon,   15
Now lakketh us no tales mo than oon.
Fulfilled is my sentence and my decree;
I trowe that we han herd of ech degree;   of: from.
Almoost fulfild is al myn ordinaunce.
I pray to God, so yeve hym right good
        chaunce,   20   chaunce: luck.
That telleth this tale to us lustily.   lustily: delightfully, pleasurably.
    Sire preest," quod he, "artow a vicary?   vicary: vicar.
Or artow a person? sey sooth, by thy fey!   person: parson.
Be what thou be, ne breke thou nat oure pley;
For every man, save thou, hath toold his tale.   25
Unbokele, and shewe us what is in thy male;   male: bag, wallet.
For, trewely, me thynketh by thy cheere   cheere: appearance, behavior.
Thou sholdest knytte up wel a greet mateere.   knytte: knit, gather together.
Telle us a fable anon, for cokkes bones!"
    This Persoun answerde, al atones,   30   atones: at once.
"Thou getest fable noon ytoold for me;   for: by.
For Paul, that writeth unto Thymothee,
Repreveth hem that weyven soothfastnesse,   weyven: waive, put aside, neglect.
And tellen fables and swich wrecchednesse.
Why sholde I sowen draf out of my fest,   35   draf: draff, chaff. fest: fist.
Whan I may sowen whete, if that me lest?   me lest: it pleases me.
For which I seye, if that yow list to heere
Moralitee and vertuous mateere,
And thanne that ye wol yeve me audience,
I wol ful fayn, at Cristes reverence,   40
Do yow plesaunce leefful, as I kan.   plesaunce leefful: lawful pleasure.
But trusteth wel, I am a Southren man,
I kan nat geeste 'rum, ram, ruf,' by lettre,
Ne, God woot, rym holde I but litel bettre;
And therfore, if yow list—I wol nat glose—   45   glose: talk speciously.
I wol yow telle a myrie tale in prose
To knytte up al this feeste, and make an ende.   feeste: feast (of stories).
And Jhesu, for his grace, wit me sende
To shewe yow the wey, in this viage,
Of thilke parfit glorious pilgrymage   50
That highte Jerusalem celestial.
And if ye vouche sauf, anon I shal
Bigynne upon my tale, for which I preye

---

29. cokkes bones: see Manciple's Prologue, l. 9.

43. geeste: tell a tale, a romance; 'rum, ram, ruf' suggests that the Parson means that he does not know how to tell an *alliterative* romance.

"Jerusalem celestial": The Cloisters Apocalypse, a Norman manuscript of the early fourteenth century, thus illustrates Revelation xxi.9–27. The editor of the facsimile entitles the illumination, "John Led to the New Jerusalem," and comments as follows: "Sun and moon have vanished: the heavenly Jerusalem is resplendent in its own light. John is led by one of the angels of the seven bowls up the mountain, above the tree line and the clouds, to behold the glorious sight." See lines 49–51 and Parson's Tale, l. 80.

Et uenit unus de septem angelis habentibus phi-
alas plenis septem plagis nouissimis:
et loqutus est mecum dicens. Veni ostendā
tibi sponsam uxorem agni. Et sustulit me in spiritu in montem
magnum et altum : et ostendit michi ciuitatem
sanctam iherusalem descendentem de celo a deo haben-
tem claritatem dei. lumen eius sile lapidi preciosissi-
mo tanq̄ lapidi iaspidis sile cristallum. Et habebat mu-
rum magnum et altum : habentem portas duode-
cim: et in portis angulos duodecim : et nomina scripta
que sunt nomina duodecim tribuum filiorum isrl. ab ori-
ente porte tres. Ab aquilone porte tres. Ab austro por-
te tres. Et ab occidente porte tres. Et murus ciuita-
tis habens fundamenta duodecim et in ipsis duode-
cim nomina duodecim aplorum et agni. Et qui loquebatur mecum
habebat arundineam mensuram auream: ut metire-
tur ciuitatem. et portas eius. et murum. et ciuitas i̅
quadro posita est. Longitudo eius tanta est quanta e la-
titudo. Et mensus est ciuitatem de arundine: p̄ sta-
dia duodecim milia. longitudo. et latitudo. et alti-
tudo eius equalia sunt. Et mensus est muros
eius centum quadraginta quattuor cubitos. Mensura
hois q̄ est angeli. Et erat structura muri eius : et lapidis

iaspidis. Ipsa uero ciuitas aurum mundum: simile
uitro mundo. Et fundamenta muri ciuitatis. omni la-
pide precioso ornata. Fundamentum primum aspis
secundus saphirus: tercius calcedonius · quartus
smaragdus. quintus sardonix. sextus sardius ·
septimus crisolitus. octauus berillus. nonus to-
pazius. decimus crisoprassus. undecimus iacin-
ctus · duodecimus ametistus. Et duodecim por-
te. duodecim margarite sunt per singulas.
Et singule porte erant ex singulis margaritis.
Et platea ciuitatis aurum mundum. tanquam uitrum
perlucidum. Et templum non uidi in ea. dn̄s enim de-
omps templum illius est. et agnus. Et ciuitas
non eget sole neq̄ luna ut luceant in ea. nā
claritas dei illuminabit eam. et lucerna eius ē
agnus. Et ambulabunt gentes in lumine
eius. et reges terre afferent gloriam suam
et honorem in illam · Et porte eius non claudē-
tur per diem. nox enim non erit illic · Et af-
ferent gloriam et honorem gentium in illā
nec in illam aliquid coinquinatum et fa-
ciens abhominationem et mendacium.

nisi qui scripta sunt in libro uite agni.

Telle youre avys, I kan no bettre seye.   avys: opinion.
  But nathelees, this meditacioun   55
I putte it ay under correccioun
Of clerkes, for I am nat textuel;   textuel: learned in texts.
I take but the sentence, trusteth wel.   sentence: essential meaning.
Therfore I make protestacioun
That I wol stonde to correccioun."   60
  Upon this word we han assented soone,
For, as it semed, it was for to doone,   for to doone: the thing to do.
To enden in som vertuous sentence,   sentence: theme, opinion.
And for to yeve hym space and audience;   space: time; opportunity.
And bede oure Hoost he sholde to hym seye   65   bede: we bade.
That alle we to telle his tale hym preye.
  Oure Hoost hadde the wordes for us alle:
"Sire preest," quod he, "now faire yow bifalle!
Telleth," quod he, "youre meditacioun.
But hasteth yow, the sonne wole adoun;   70
Beth fructuous, and that in litel space,   fructuous: fruitful.
And to do wel God sende yow his grace!
Sey what yow list, and we wol gladly heere."
And with that word he seyde in this manere.

Explicit prohemium.

Heere bigynneth the Persouns tale.

Jer. 6°. State super vias, et videte, et interrogate de viis antiquis que sit via bona, et ambulate in ea; et inuenietis refrigerium animabus vestris, etc.

Oure sweete Lord God of hevene, that no man wole perisse, but wole that we comen alle to the knoweleche of hym, and to the blisful lif that is perdurable, [75] amonesteth us by the prophete Jeremie, that seith in this wise:/ Stondeth upon the

73–74. In the manuscripts this couplet follows line 68; Manly emends.

the Persouns Tale. The Parson's Tale is not a sermon but a *tretice* (see 957 and 1081, below), a confessional manual for layman or priest. W. A. Pantin describes it as "a good, straightforward, rather conventional example of a treatise on confession and on the seven sins and their remedies." The opening and closing portions on penitence (75–386, 958–1080) derive ultimately (after various intervening tracts) from the *Summa de Paenitentia* of the Spanish Dominican St. Raymond of Pennaforte, written shortly after the Lateran Council of 1215 made annual confession compulsory. The central section on sins and their remedies (387–957) is similarly related to the second half of the *Summa Virtutum ac Vitiorum* of the French Dominican William Peraldus (before 1261). However, the phraseology of Chaucer's treatise again and again suggests that its immediate source was not Latin but French. Judging by the parallels to the Parson's Tale so far discovered in similar manuals, it seems possible that the colorful, humanizing touches—the specific illustrative details which enliven the accounts of sins and sinners—may be the poet's original contributions to this "myrie tale in prose" (46). Biblical and patristic sources have been indicated whenever possible.

Jer. 6°.: Jeremiah vi.16.

75. no man wole perisse: wishes no man to perish (i.e., to incur spiritual death, be lost); see II Peter iii.9. perdurable: thoroughly enduring, everlasting.

76. amonesteth: admonishes.

weyes, and seeth and axeth of olde pathes (that is to seyn, of olde sentences) which is the goode wey,/ and walketh in that wey, and ye shal fynde refresshynge for youre soules, etc./

Manye been the weyes espirituels that leden folk to oure Lord Jhesu Crist, and to the regne of glorie./ Of whiche weyes, ther is a ful noble wey and a ful covenable, which may nat fayle to man ne to womman that thurgh synne hath mysgoon fro the righte wey of Jerusalem celestial; [80] and this wey is cleped Penitence, of which man sholde gladly herknen and enquere with al his herte,/ to wite what is Penitence, and whennes it is cleped Penitence, and in how manye maneres been the acciouns or werkynges of Penitence,/ and how manye speces ther ben of Penitence, and whiche thynges apertenen and bihoven to Penitence, and whiche thynges destourben Penitence./

Seint Ambrose seith that Penitence is the pleynynge of man for the gilt that he hath doon, and namoore to do any thyng for which hym oghte to pleyne./ And som doctour seith, "Penitence is the waymentynge of man that sorweth for his synne, and pyneth hymself for he hath mysdoon." [85] Penitence, with certeyne circumstances, is verray repentance of a man that halt hymself in sorwe and oother peyne for his giltes./ And for he shal be verray penitent, he shal first biwaylen the synnes that he hath doon, and stedefastly purposen in his herte to have shrift of mouthe, and to doon satisfaccioun,/ and nevere to doon thyng for which hym oghte moore to biwayle or to compleyne, and to continue in goode werkes, or elles his repentance may nat availle./ For, as seith Seint Ysidre, "he is a japere and a gabbere, and no verray repentant, that eftsoone dooth thyng for which hym oghte repente."/ Wepynge, and nat for to stynte to do synne, may nat availe. [90] But nathelees, men shal hope that at every tyme that man falleth, be it never so ofte, that he may arise thurgh Penitence, if he have grace; but certeinly it is greet doute./ For, as seith Seint Gregorie, "unnethe ariseth he out of his synne, that is charged with the charge of yvel usage."/ And therfore repentant folk, that stynte for to synne, and forlete synne er that synne forlete hem, holy chirche holdeth hem siker of hire savacioun./

---

77. **seeth:** look. **axeth of:** ask concerning. **sentences:** opinions.

78. **refresshynge:** refreshment.

79. **espirituels:** spiritual. **regne:** kingdom.

80. **covenable:** appropriate. **mysgoon:** gone astray. **right:** direct. **of:** to.

81. **cleped:** called. **penitence:** penance. **herknen:** harken.

82. **wite:** know. **whennes:** from which cause, why.

83. **speces:** kinds. **apertenen:** belong. **bihoven:** are necessary. **destourben:** hinder.

84. **Seint Ambrose:** see *Sermo* xxv.§1. **pleynynge:** lamentation. **gilt:** sins.

85. **doctour:** Church Father. **waymentynge:** lamentation. **pyneth:** torments. **for:** because. **mysdoon:** done evil.

86. **with:** under. **verray:** true. **halt:** (holdeth) holds. **giltes:** sins.

87. **for:** so that. **verray:** truly. **shrift of mouthe:** i.e., auricular confession. **satisfaccioun:** the performance by a penitent of the penance enjoined by his confessor as payment of the temporal punishment due to his sin.

89. **japere:** trickster. **gabbere:** mocker. **verray:** true. **eftsoone:** soon after. **thyng:** a deed.

90. **stynte:** cease. **availe:** help; be of use.

92. **Seint Gregorie:** see *In Septem Psalmos Poenitentiales Expositio,* Psalm xxxvii.8 **unnethe:** not easily; hardly. **charged:** burdened. **charge:** burden. **usage:** habit.

93. **forlete synne:** renounce sin. **forlete hem:** leaves them helpless. **siker:** sure.

And he that synneth and verraily repenteth hym in his laste, holy chirche yet hopeth his savacioun, by the grete mercy of oure Lord Jhesu Crist, for his repentaunce; but taak the siker wey./

And now, sith I have declared yow what thyng is Penitence, now shul ye understonde that ther been three acciouns of Penitence. [95] The firste is that if a man be baptized after that he hath synned,/ Seint Augustyn seith, "But he be penitent for his olde synful lyf, he may nat bigynne the newe clene lif."/ For, certes, if he be baptized withouten penitence of his olde gilt, he receyveth the mark of baptesme, but nat the grace ne the remission of his synnes, til he have repentance verray./ Another defaute is this, that men doon deedly synne after that they han receyved baptesme./ The thridde defaute is that men fallen in venial synnes after hir baptesme, fro day to day. [100] Therof seith Seint Augustyn that penitence of goode and humble folk is the penitence of every day./

The speces of Penitence been three. That oon of hem is solempne, another is commune, and the thridde is privee./ Thilke penance that is solempne is in two maneres; as to be put out of holy chirche in Lente, for slaughtre of children, and swich maner thyng./ Another is, whan a man hath synned openly, of which synne the fame is openly spoken in the contree, and thanne holy chirche by jugement destreyneth hym for to do open penaunce./ Commune penaunce is that preestes enjoynen men communly in certeyn cas, as for to goon peraventure naked in pilgrimage, or barefoot. [105] Pryvee penaunce is thilke that men doon alday for privee synnes, of which we shryve us prively and receyve privee penaunce./

Now shaltow understande what is bihovely and necessarie to verray perfit Penitence. And this stant on three thynges:/ Contricioun of herte, Confessioun of Mouth, and Satisfaccioun./ For which seith Seint John Crisostom: "Penitence destreyneth a man to accepte benygnely every peyne that hym is enjoyned, with contricioun of herte, and shrift of mouth, with satisfaccioun; and in werkynge of alle manere humylitee."/ And this is fruytful penitence agayn three thynges in

---

94. laste: last moments. hopeth: hopes for. for: on account of. taak: take. siker: sure.

95. declared: told. acciouns: functions. penitence: penance.

97. Seint Augustyn: see *Sermo* cccli, c. 2. clene: pure.

98. gilt: sins. verray: true.

99. defaute: need (i.e., for penance). deedly: deadly, mortal.

100. venial: pardonable. fro day to day: continuously.

101. Seint Augustyn: see *Epistola* cclxv.§8.

102. speces: kinds. penitence: penance. solempne: solemn. commune: general, public. privee: private, i.e., auricular.

103. slaughtre: see line 575, below.

104. fame: report. contree: region. destreyneth: constrains.

105. communly: in a common body; together. cas: cases, circumstances. peraventure: perhaps. naked: i.e., in only an undergarment.

106. pryvee: private. alday: again and again. prively: privately.

107. bihovely: suitable. penitence: penance. stant on: consists in.

108. confessioun of mouth: auricular confession. satisfaccioun: see 87 above.

109. for: concerning. destreyneth: constrains. benygnely: patiently. peyne: punishment. enjoyned: imposed on. werkynge: deeds, actions.

110. agayn: against.

which we wrathe oure Lord Jhesu Crist: [110] this is to seyn, by delit in thynkynge, by recchelesnesse in spekynge, and by wikked synful werkynge./ And agayns thise wikkede giltes is Penitence, that may be likned unto a tree./

The roote of this tree is Contricioun, that hideth hym in the herte of hym that is verray repentaunt, right as the roote of a tree hideth hym in the erthe./ Of the roote of Contricioun spryngeth a stalke that bereth braunches and leves of Confessioun, and fruyt of Satisfaccioun./ For which Crist seith in his gospel: "Dooth digne fruyt of Penitence"; for by this fruyt may men knowe this tree, and nat by the roote that is hyd in the herte of man, ne by the braunches, ne by the leves of Confessioun. [115] And therfore oure Lord Jhesu Crist seith thus: "By the fruyt of hem shul ye knowe hem."/ Of this roote eek spryngeth a seed of grace, the which seed is moder of sikernesse, and this seed is egre and hoot./ The grace of this seed spryngeth of God thurgh remembrance of the day of doom and on the peynes of helle./ Of this matere seith Salomon that in the drede of God man forleteth his synne./ The heete of this seed is the love of God, and the desiryng of the joye perdurable. [120] This heete draweth the herte of man to God, and dooth hym hate his synne./ For soothly ther is nothyng that savoureth so wel to a child as the milk of his norice, ne nothyng is to hym moore abhomynable than thilke milk whan it is medled with oother mete./ Right so the synful man that loveth his synne, hym semeth that it is to him moost sweete of anythyng;/ but fro that tyme that he loveth sadly oure Lord Jhesu Crist, and desireth the lif perdurable, ther nys to him no thyng moore abhomynable./ For soothly the lawe of God is the love of God; for which David the prophete seith: "I have loved thy lawe, and hated wikkednesse and hate"; he that loveth God kepeth his lawe and his word. [125] This tree saugh the prophete Daniel in spirit, upon the avysioun of Nabugodonosor, whan he conseiled hym to do penitence./ Penaunce is the tree of lyf to hem that it receyven, and he that holdeth hym in verray penitence is blessed, after the sentence of Salomon./

---

110. wrathe: anger.

111. delit: (sensuous) delight. recchelesnesse: carelessness. (i.e., shamelessness). werkynge: deeds, actions.

112. agayns: over against. giltes: sins.

113. verray: truly.

114. stalke: main stem, trunk.

115. Crist: actually John the Baptist; see Matthew iii.8. dooth: give. digne: worthy.

116. Crist: see Matthew vii.20.

117. sikernesse: security. egre: sharp. hoot: biting.

118. of God: from God. remembrance: recollection, calling to mind. doom: judgment.

119. Salomon: see Proverbs xvi.6. forleteth: renounces.

120. perdurable: everlasting.

121. dooth: makes.

122. savoureth: tastes. norice: nurse. medled: mixed. mete: food.

124. sadly: steadfastly.

125. David: see Psalms cxix.113. hate: hatred.

126. saugh: saw. Daniel: see Daniel iv.10–27. in spirit: in the eye of his spirit, so to speak. upon: following on; right after. avysioun: vision. Nabugodonosor: Nebuchadnezzar.

127. holdeth hym in: remains in (the state of). after: according to. sentence: opinion. Salomon: cf. Proverbs xxviii.13.

In this Penitence or Contricioun man shal understonde foure thynges; that is to seyn, what is Contricioun, and whiche ben the causes that moeven a man to Contricioun, and how he sholde be contrit, and what Contricioun availleth to the soule./ Thanne is it thus: that Contricioun is the verray sorwe that a man receyveth in his herte for his synnes, with sad purpos to shryve hym, and to do penaunce, and neveremoore to do synne./ And this sorwe shal been in this manere, as seith Seint Bernard: "It shal ben hevy and grevous, and ful sharp and poynaunt in herte." [130] First, for man hath agilt his Lord and his Creatour; and moore sharp and poynaunt, for he hath agilt his Fader celestial;/ and yet moore sharp and poynaunt, for he hath wrathed and agilt hym that boghte hym, that with his precious blood hath delivered us fro the bondes of synne, and fro the crueltee of the devel, and fro the peynes of helle./

The causes that oghte moeve a man to Contricioun been sixe. First a man shal remembre hym of his synnes;/ but looke that thilke remembraunce ne be to hym no delit by no wey, but gret shame and sorwe for his gilt. For Job seith, "Synful men doon werkes worthy of confusioun."/ And therfore seith Ezechie, "I wol remembre me alle the yeres of my lyf in bitternesse of myn herte." [135] And God seith in the Apocalipse, "Remembre yow fro whennes that ye ben falle"; for biforn that tyme that ye synned, ye were the children of God, and lymes of the regne of God;/ but for youre synne ye ben woxen thral, and foul, and membres of the feend, hate of aungels, sclaundre of holy chirche, and foode of the false serpent; perpetuel matere of the fir of helle;/ and yet moore foul and abhomynable, for ye trespassen so ofte tyme as dooth the hound that retourneth to eten his spewyng./ And yet be ye fouler for youre longe continuyng in synne and youre synful usage, for which ye be roten in youre synne, as a beest in his dong./ Swiche manere of thoughtes maken a man to have shame of his synne, and no delit, as God seith by the prophete Ezechiel: [140] "Ye shal remembre yow of youre weyes, and they shuln displese yow." Soothly synnes been the weyes that leden folk to helle./

The seconde cause that oghte make a man to have desdeyn of synne is this: that,

---

128. **what availleth**: what is the benefit of.

129. **sad**: firm.

130. **poynaunt**: poignant; painfully sharp.

131. **for**: because. **agilt**: sinned against; offended.

132. **wrathed**: angered. **boghte**: redeemed.

134. **looke**: make sure. **by no wey**: by no means, not at all. **gilt**: sins. **Job**: see Proverbs xii.4. **werkes**: deeds, acts. **confusioun**: damnation.

135. **Ezechie**: Hezekiah; see Isaiah xxxviii.15.

136. **God**: see Revelation ii.5. **lymes**: members. **regne**: kingdom.

137. **ben woxen**: have become. **thral**: enslaved. **foul**: vile. **membres**: limbs; agents. **sclaundre**: disgrace, scandal. **matere of**: material for. **fir**: fire.

138. **for**: because. **hound**: cf. II Peter ii.22. **spewyng**: vomit.

139. **usage**: habits.

140. **Ezechiel**: see Ezekiel xx.43.

141. **shuln**: shall. **leden**: lead.

142. **desdeyn**: loathing.

as seith Seint Peter, "whoso that dooth synne is thral of synne"; and synne put a man in greet thraldom./ And therfore seith the prophete Ezechiel: "I wente sorweful in desdayn of myself." Certes, wel oghte a man have desdayn of synne, and withdrawe hym from that thraldom and vileynye./ And lo, what seith Seneca in this matere? He seith thus: "Though I wiste that neither God ne man ne sholde nevere knowe it, yet wolde I have desdayn for to do synne."/ And the same Seneca also seith: "I am born to gretter thynges than to be thral to my body, or than for to maken of my body a thral." [145] Ne a fouler thral may no man ne womman maken of his body than for to yeve his body to synne./ Al were it the fouleste cherl or the fouleste womman that lyveth, and leest of value, yet is he thanne moore foul and moore in servitute./ Evere fro the hyer degree that man falleth, the moore is he thral, and moore to God and to the world vile and abhomynable./ O goode God, wel oghte man have desdayn of synne, sith that thurgh synne, ther he was free, now is he maked bonde./ And therfore seyth Seint Augustyn: "If thou hast desdayn of thy servant, if he agilte or synne, have thou thanne desdayn that thou thyself sholdest do synne." [150] Take reward of thy value, that thou ne be to foul to thyself./ Allas! wel oghten they thanne have desdayn to ben servauntz and thralles to synne, and soore ben ashamed of hemself,/ that God of his endelees goodnesse hath set hem in heigh estaat, or yeven hem wit, strengthe of body, heele, beautee, prosperitee,/ and boghte hem fro the deeth with his herte-blood, that they so unkyndely, agayns his gentilesse, quiten hym so vileynsly to slaughtre of hir owene soules./ O goode God, ye wommen that been of so greet beautee, remembreth yow of the proverbe of Salomon. He seith: [155] "Likneth a fair womman that is a fool of hire body lyk to a ryng of gold that were in the groyn of a sowe."/ For right as a sowe wroteth in everich ordure, so wroteth she hire beautee in stynkynge ordure of synne./

The thridde cause that oghte moeve a man to Contricioun is drede of the day of doom and of the horrible peynes of helle./ For, as Seint Jerome seith, "At every tyme that me remembreth of the day of doom I quake;/ for whan I ete or drynke, or what so that I do, evere semeth me that the trompe sowneth in myn ere: [160]

---

142. **Seint Peter:** see II Peter ii.19; but even closer is John viii.34. **dooth:** commits. **thral:** slave. **put:** (putteth) puts. **thraldom:** servitude.

143. **vileynye:** bondage.

148. **thral:** enslaved.

149. **ther:** whereas. **bonde:** enslaved.

150. **Seint Augustyn:** see *Sermo* ix.§16. **agilte:** transgress.

151. **reward:** regard, heed. **to foul:** too vile.

153. **wit:** intellect. **heele:** health.

154. **boghte:** redeemed. **unkyndely:** unnaturally. **agayns:** in return for. **gentilesse:** noble goodness. **quiten:** requite. **vileynsly:** evilly. **to slaughtre:** to the destruction.

155. **Salomon:** see Proverbs xi.22.

156. **a fool of hire body:** i.e., unchaste. **groyn:** snout.

157. **wroteth:** roots, digs with the snout, pokes into. **ordure:** filth.

158. **doom:** judgment. **peynes:** torments.

159. **Seint Jerome:** see the pseudo-Jerome *Regula Monachorum*. **quake:** tremble.

160. **trompe:** trumpet. **sowneth:** sounds.

'Riseth ye up, that ben dede, and cometh to the jugement.' "/ O goode God, muchel oghte a man to drede swich a jugement, "ther as we shullen ben alle," as Seint Poul seith, "biforn the seete of oure Lord Jhesu Crist";/|whereas he shal make a general congregacioun, whereas no man may ben absent./ For certes there availeth noon essoyne ne excusacioun./ And nat oonly that oure defautes shullen be juged, but eek that alle oure werkes shullen openly be knowe. [165] And, as seith Seint Bernard, "Ther ne shal no pledynge availle, ne no sleighte; we shullen yeve rekenynge of everich ydel word."/ Ther shul we han a juge that may nat ben deceyved ne corrupt. And why? For, certes, alle oure thoghtes ben discovered as to hym; ne for preyere ne for meede he shal nat ben corrupt./ And therfore seith Salomon, "The wrathe of God ne wol nat spare no wight, for prayere ne for yifte"; and therfore, at the day of doom, ther nys noon hope to escape./ Wherfore, as seith Seint Anselm, "Ful gret angwyssh shul the synful folk have at that tyme;/ ther shal the stierne and wrothe juge sitte above, and under hym the horrible pit of helle open to destroyen hym that moot biknowen his synnes, whiche synnes openly ben shewed biforn God and biforn every creature; [170] and on the left syde mo develes than herte may bithynke, for to harye and drawe the synful soules to the peyne of helle;/ and withinne the hertes of folk shal be the bitynge conscience, and withoute forth shal be the world al brennynge./ Whider shal thanne the wrecched synful man flee to hyde hym? Certes, he may nat hyde hym; he moste come forth and shewe hym."/ For certes, as seith Seint Jerome, "the erthe shal caste hym out of hym, and the see also, and the eyr also, that shal be ful of thonder-clappes and lightnynges."/ Now soothly, whoso wel remembreth hym of thise thynges, I gesse that his synne shal nat turne hym in delit, but to gret sorwe, for drede of the peyne of helle. [175] And therfore seith Job to God: "Suffre, Lord, that I may a while biwaille and wepe, er I go withoute returnyng to the derke lond, covered with the derknesse of deeth;/ to the lond of mysese and of derknesse, whereas is the shadwe of deeth; whereas ther is noon ordre or ordinaunce, but grisly drede that evere shal laste."/

Lo, here may ye seen that Job preyde respit a while, to biwepe and waille his

---

162. **ther as:** where. **Seint Poul:** see Romans xiv.10. **seete:** throne.

163. **whereas:** where. **general congregacioun:** assembly (of all mankind).

164. **essoyne:** excuse for non-appearance in court. **excusacioun:** defence; plea.

165. **defautes:** sins. **knowe:** known.

166. **Seint Bernard:** see *Sermo ad Prelatos in Concilio* §5. **sleighte:** trickery. **ydel:** empty; vain; frivolous.

167. **corrupt:** corrupted. **discovered:** disclosed. **meede:** bribery.

168. **Salomon:** cf. Proverbs i.28.

169. **Seint Anselm:** see *Meditatio Secunda*. **angwyssh:** anxiety.

170. **stierne:** stern. **wrothe:** wrathful. **moot biknowen:** must acknowledge.

171. **bithynke:** imagine. **harye:** drag.

172. **withoute forth:** everywhere outside. **brennynge:** burning.

174. **see:** sea. **eyr:** air.

175. **in:** to.

176. **Job:** see Job x.20–22.

177. **mysese:** misery. **ordinaunce:** orderly arrangement. **grisly:** inspired by fear.

178. **biwepe:** shed tears over. **waille:** bewail.

trespas; for soothly o day of respit is bettre than al the tresor of this world./ And forasmuche as a man may acquiten hymself biforn God by penitence in this world, and nat by tresor, therfore sholde he preye to God to yeve hym respit a while to biwepe and biwaillen his trespas./ For certes, al the sorwe that a man myghte make fro the bigynnyng of the world nys but a litel thyng at regard of the sorwe of helle. [180]

The cause why that Job clepeth helle the lond of derknesse;/ understondeth that he clepeth it "lond" or erthe, for it is stable, and nevere shal faille; "derk," for he that is in helle hath defaute of light material./ For certes, the derke light that shal come out of the fyr that evere shal brenne, shal turne hym al to peyne that is in helle; for it sheweth him to the horrible develes that hym tormenten./ "Covered with the derknesse of deeth," that is to seyn, that he that is in helle shal have defaute of the sighte of God; for certes, the sighte of God is the lyf perdurable./ "The derknesse of deeth" ben the synnes that the wrecched man hath doon, whiche that destourben hym to see the face of God, right as a derk clowde bitwixe us and the sonne. [185] "Lond of misese," by cause that ther ben three maneres of defautes, agayn three thynges that folk of this world han in this present lyf, that is to seyn, honours, delices, and richesses./ Agayns honour, have they in helle shame and confusioun./ For wel ye woot that men clepen honour the reverence that man doth to man; but in helle is noon honour ne reverence. For certes, namoore reverence shal be doon there to a kyng than to a knave./ For which God seith by the prophete Jeremye, "Thilke folk that me despisen shul been in despit."/ Honour is eek cleped greet lord-shipe; ther shal no wight serven other, but of harm and torment. Honour is eek cleped greet dignytee and heighnesse, but in helle shul they ben al fortroden of develes. [190] As God seith, "The horrible develes shulle goon and comen upon the hevedes of dampned folk." And this is for as muche as the hyer that they were in this present lyf, the moore shulle they ben abated and defouled in helle./

Agayns the richesse of this world shul they han mysese of poverte, and this poverte shal be in foure thynges:/ In defaute of tresor, of which that David seith, "The

---

180. at regard of: in comparison with.

182. faille: cease to exist, come to an end. hath defaute of: is deprived of. light material: i.e., physical light.

183. shal turne hym al to peyne: shall turn to pain for him all.

184. have defaute of: lack. perdurable: everlasting.

185. destourben . . . see: prevent him from seeing.

186. misese: misery. defautes: lacks. agayn: over against. delices: pleasures. richesses: riches.

187. agayns: in place of. confusioun: disgrace.

188. clepen: call. a knave: a male servant; one of low condition.

189. Jeremye: not Jeremiah but I Samuel ii.30 (Vulgate, Liber Primus Regum ii.30). in despit: despised.

190. of harm: with harm. fortroden of: trampled upon by.

191. God: see Job xx.25. hevedes: heads. dampned: damned. abated: degraded. defouled: trampled upon.

192. agayns: over against. mysese: misery.

193. defaute: lack. David: see Vulgate, Psalms lxxv.6.

riche folk, that embraceden and oneden al hire herte to tresor of this world, shul slepe in the slepynge of deeth; and nothyng ne shal they fynden in hire handes of al hir tresor."/ And mooreover the myseyse of helle shal ben in defaute of mete and drinke./ For God seith thus by Moyses: "They shul ben wasted with hunger, and the briddes of helle shul devouren hem with bitter deeth, and the galle of the dragon shal ben hire drynke, and the venym of the dragon hire morsels." [195] And forther over, hire myseyse shal ben in defaute of clothyng; for they shulle be naked in body as of clothyng, save the fyr in which they brenne, and othere filthes;/ and naked shul they ben of soule, of alle manere vertues, which that is the clothyng of soule. Where ben thanne the gaye robes, and the softe shetes, and the smale shertes?/ Loo, what seith God of hem by the prophete Ysaye: that "under hem shul ben strawed motthes, and hire covertures shulle ben of wormes of helle."/ And forther over, hir myseyse shal ben in defaute of frendes. For he is nat povre that hath goode frendes; but there is no frend,/ for neither God ne no creature shal ben freend to hem, and everich of hem shal haten oother with deedly hate. [200] "The sones and the doghtren shullen rebellen agayns fader and moder, and kynrede agayns kynrede, and chiden and despisen everich of hem oother bothe day and nyght," as God seith by the prophete Michias./ And the lovynge children, that whilom loveden so flesshly everich oother, wolden everich of hem eten oother if they myghte./ For how sholden they love hem togidre in the peyne of helle, whan they hated everich of hem oother in the prosperitee of this lyf?/ For truste wel, hire flesshly love was deedly hate, as seith the prophete David: "Whoso that loveth wikkednesse, he hateth his soule."/ And whoso hateth his owene soule, certes, he may love noon oother wight in no manere. [205] And therfore, in helle is no solas ne no frendshipe, but evere the moore flesshly kynredes that ben in helle, the moore cursynges, the more chidynges, and the moore deedly hate ther is among hem./

And forther over, they shul have defaute of alle manere delices. For certes, delices ben after the appetites of the fyve wittes, as sighte, herynge, smellynge, savorynge, and touchynge./ But in helle hir sighte shal be ful of derknesse and of smoke, and therfore ful of teeres; and hire herynge ful of waymentynge and of gryntynge of teeth, as seith Jhesu Crist./ Hire nosethirles shullen be ful of stynk-

---

193. oneden: united.

194. myseyse: misery. mete: food.

195. Moyses: see Deuteronomy xxxii.24, 33. galle: poison. morsels: mouthfuls.

196. forther over: furthermore. defaute: lack. filthes: foul treatment.

197. shetes: sheets. smale shertes: fine undergarments.

198. Ysaye: see Isaiah xiv.11. strawed: strewn. covertures: coverlets.

199. there: i.e., in hell.

200. deedly: mortal.

201. kynrede: kindred. everich of hem oother: each other. Michias: see Micah vii.6.

202. whilom: formerly. flesshly: carnally. everich oother: each other.

203. hem togidre: i.e., each other.

204. deedly: mortal. David: see Psalms xi.5 (Vulgate, x.6).

206. solas: solace. flesshly: carnal. kynredes: kinships. deedly: mortal.

207. forther over: furthermore. defaute: lack. delices: pleasures. after: according to. wittes: senses. savorynge: tasting.

208. waymentynge: lamentation. gryntynge: gnashing. Crist: see Matthew xiii.42; xxv.30.

209. nosethirles: nostrils.

ynge stynk; and, as seith Ysaye the prophete, "hire savoryng shal be ful of bitter galle";/ and touchynge of al hir body ycovered with "fyr that nevere shal quenche, and with wormes that nevere shul dyen," as God seith by the mouth of Ysaye. [210]

And for as muche as they shul nat wene that they may dyen for peyne, and by hire deeth flee fro peyne, that may they understonde in the word of Job, that seith, "ther as is the shadwe of deth."/ Certes, a shadwe hath the liknesse of the thyng of which it is shadwe, but shadwe is nat the same thyng of which it is shadwe./ Right so fareth the peyne of helle; it is lyk deeth for the horrible angwissh, and why? For it peyneth hem evere, as though men sholde dye anon; but certes, they shal nat dye./For, as seith Seint Gregorie, "To wrecche caytyves shal be deeth withoute deeth, and ende withouten ende, and defaute withoute failynge./ For hire deeth shal alwey lyven, and hir ende shal everemo bigynne, and hir defaute shal nat faille." [215] And therfore seith Seint John the Evaungelist: "They shullen folwe deeth, and they shul nat fynde hym; and they shul desiren to dye, and deeth shal flee fro hem."/

And eek Job seith that in helle is noon ordre of rule./ And al be it so that God hath creat alle thynges in right ordre, and no thyng withouten ordre, but alle thynges ben ordeyned and nombred; yet, nathelees, they that ben dampned ben nothyng in ordre, ne holden noon ordre./ For the erthe ne shal bere hem no fruyt./ For, as the prophete David seith, "God shal destroye the fruyt of the erthe as fro hem; ne water shal yeve hem no moisture, ne the eyr no refresshyng, ne fyr no light." [220] For, as seith Seint Basilie, "The brennynge of the fyr of this world shal God yeven in helle to hem that been dampned,/ but the light and the cleernesse shal be yeven in hevene to his children"; right as the goode man yeveth flessh to his children and bones to his houndes./ And for they shullen have noon hope to escape, seith Seint Job atte laste that "ther shal horrour and grisly drede dwelle withouten ende."/

Horrour is alwey drede of harm that is to come, and this drede shal evere dwelle in the hertes of hem that been dampned. And therfore han they lorn al hire hope, for sevene causes./ First, for God, that is hir juge, shal be withouten mercy to hem; ne they may nat plese hym ne noon of his halwes; ne they ne may yeve no

---

209. **Ysaye:** see Isaiah xxiv.9.

210. **touchynge:** (sense of) touch. **quenche:** be quenched. **Ysaye:** see Isaiah lxvi.24.

211. **wene:** imagine. **for peyne:** from torment. **Job:** see Job x.22.

213. **for:** because of. **evere:** constantly.

214. **Seint Gregorie:** see *Moralium,* lib. vi. c. 66. **wrecche:** wretched. **caytyves:** miserable persons. **defaute:** lack, want. **failynge:** end.

215. **faille:** end.

216. **Seint John:** see Revelation ix.6. **folwe:** seek after.

217. **Job:** see Job x.22.

218. **creat:** created. **ordeyned:** ordered. **nothyng:** not at all. **holden:** maintain.

220. **David:** see Psalms cvii.33–34 (Vulgate, cvi.33–34). **as fro hem:** i.e., depriving them. **eyr:** air. **refresshyng:** refreshment.

221. **Seint Basilie:** see St. Basil, *Homilies on the Psalms,* Psalm xxviii.7, §6.

222. **cleernesse:** brightness. **flessh:** meat.

223. **for:** because. **Seint Job:** see Job x.22. **ther:** i.e., in hell. **grisly:** full of fear.

224. **lorn:** lost. **causes:** reasons.

225. **for:** because. **halwes:** saints.

thyng for hir raunsoun; [225] ne they have no voys to speke to hym; ne they may nat fle fro peyne; ne they have no goodnesse in hem, that they may shewe to delivere hem fro peyne./ And therfore seith Salomon: "The wikked man dieth, and whan he is deed, he shal have noon hope to escape fro peyne."/ Whoso thanne wolde wel understande thise peynes, and bithynke hym wel that he hath deserved thilke peynes for his synnes, certes, he sholde have moore talent to siken and to wepe, than for to syngen and to pleye./ For, as that seith Salomon, "Whoso that hadde the science to knowe the peynes that ben establised and ordeyned for synne, he wolde make sorwe."/ "Thilke science," as seith Seint Augustyn, "maketh a man to waymente in his herte." [230]

The fourthe point that oghte make a man have contricion is the sorweful remembraunce of the good that he hath left to doon here in erthe, and eek the good that he hath lorn./ Soothly, the goode werkes that he hath lost, either they ben the goode werkes that he wroghte er he fel into deedly synne, or elles the goode werkes that he wroghte while he lay in synne./ Soothly, the goode werkes that he dide biforn that he fil in synne ben al mortefied and astoned and dulled by the ofte synnyng./ The othere goode werkes, that he wroghte whil he lay in deedly synne, they been outrely dede, as to the lyf perdurable in hevene./

Thanne thilke goode werkes that ben mortefied by ofte synnyng, whiche goode werkes he dide while he was in charitee, ne mowe nevere quyken agayn withouten verray penitence. [235] And therof seith God by the mouth of Ezechiel, that "if the rightful man returne agayn from his rightwisnesse and werke wikkednesse, shal he lyve?"/ Nay, for alle the goode werkes that he hath wroght ne shul nevere ben in remembraunce, for he shal dyen in his synne./ And upon thilke chapitre seith Seint Gregorie thus: that "we shulle understonde this principally;/ that whan we doon deedly synne, it is for noght thanne to reherce or drawen into memorie the goode werkes that we han wroght biforn."/ For certes, in the werkynge of the dedly synne, ther is no trust to no good werk that we han doon biforn; that is to seyn, as for to have therby the lyf perdurable in hevene. [240] But nathelees, the goode werkes quyken agayn, and comen agayn, and helpen, and availlen to have the lyf perdurable in hevene, whan we han contricioun./ But soothly, the goode werkes that men doon whil they been in dedly synne, for as muche as they were doon in

---

225. **hir raunsoun**: their ransom.

227. **Salomon**: see Proverbs xi.7.

228. **bithynke hym wel**: consider carefully.   **talent**: inclination.   **siken**: sigh.

229. **science**: knowledge.   **make sorwe**: lament.

230. **waymente**: lament.

231. **left**: omitted.   **lorn**: lost.

232. **deedly**: mortal.

233. **mortefied**: killed; rendered ineffective.   **astoned**: deadened.   **dulled**: nullified.   **ofte**: frequent.

234. **outrely**: utterly.   **dede**: dead.   **as to**: as regards.   **perdurable**: everlasting.

235. **was in charitee**: had the supreme virtue of charity; was in favor with God.   **quyken**: recover life.

236. **Ezechiel**: see Ezekiel xviii.24.   **returne**: revert.   **rightwisnesse**: righteousness.   **werke**: do.

238. **chapitre**: subject.

239. **doon**: commit.   **deedly**: deadly.

240. **werkynge**: effect.   **werk**: deed.

241. **quyken**: recover life.   **availlen to have**: assist in obtaining.

dedly synne, they may nevere quyken agayn./· For certes, thyng that nevere hadde lyf may nevere quykene; and nathelees, al be it that they ne availle noght to han the lyf perdurable, yet availlen they to abregge of the peyne of helle, or elles to gete temporal richesse,/ or elles that God wole the rather enlumyne and lightne the herte of the synful man to have repentaunce;/ and eek they availlen for to usen a man to doon goode werkes, that the feend have the lasse power of his soule. [245] And thus the curteys Lord Jhesu Crist ne wole that no good werk be lost; for in somwhat it shal availle./ But, for as muche as the goode werkes that men doon whil they ben in good lyf ben al mortefied by synne folwynge, and eek sith that alle the goode werkes that men doon whil they ben in dedly synne ben outrely dede as for to have the lyf perdurable;/ wel may that man that no good werk ne dooth synge thilke newe Frenshe song, *"Jay tout perdu mon temps et mon labour."*/

For certes, synne bireveth a man bothe goodnesse of nature and eek the goodnesse of grace./ For soothly, the grace of the Holy Goost fareth lyk fyr, that may nat been ydel; for fyr fayleth anon as it forleteth his werkynge, and right so grace faileth anon as it forleteth his werkynge. [250] Then leseth the synful man the goodnesse of glorie, that oonly is bihight to goode men that labouren and werken./ Wel may he be sory thanne, that oweth al his lif to God as longe as he hath lyved, and eek as longe as he shal lyve, that no goodnesse ne hath to paye with his dette to God to whom he oweth al his lyf./ For trust wel, "he shal yeve acountes," as seith Seint Bernard, "of alle the goodes that han be yeven hym in this present lyf, and how he hath hem despended;/ nat so muche that ther shal nat perisse an heer of his heed, ne a moment of an houre ne shal nat perisse of his tyme, that he ne shal yeve of it a rekenyng."/

The fifthe thyng that oghte moeve a man to contricioun is remembrance of the passioun that oure Lord Jhesu Crist suffred for oure synnes. [255] For, as seith Seint Bernard, "Whil that I lyve I shal have remembrance of the travailles that oure Lord Jhesu Crist suffred in prechyng;/ his werynesse in travaillyng, his temptaciouns whan he fasted, his longe wakynges whan he preyde, hise teeres whan that he weep for pitee of good peple;/ the wo and the shame and the filthe that men seyden to hym; of the foule spittyng that men spitte in his face, of the buffettes that men yave hym, of the foule mowes, and of the repreves that men to hym seyden;/ of the nayles with whiche he was nayled to the croys, and of al the

---

243. **abregge:** reduce the severity. **richesse:** riches.
244. **rather:** sooner. **enlumyne:** enlighten. **lightne:** kindle.
245. **usen:** accustom. **lasse:** less. **of:** over.
246. **curteys:** merciful. **in somwhat:** to some extent. **availle:** be of use.
247. **folwynge:** occurring later. **as . . . have:** as regards having.
248. **werk:** deed. *Jay . . . labour:* "I have lost my time and my labor."
249. **bireveth a man:** deprives a man of.
250. **fareth:** acts. **ydel:** idle, inactive. **fayleth:** ceases to exist. **anon as:** as soon as. **forleteth:** ceases. **werkynge:** function.
251. **leseth:** loses. **bihight:** promised.
252. **to . . . dette:** to pay his debt with.
253. **despended:** spent.
254. **perisse:** perish. **heer:** hair. **heed:** head. **perisse:** be wasted.
256. **travailles:** hardships.
257. **travaillyng:** toiling. **wakynges:** vigils. **weep:** wept.
258. **spittyng:** spittle. **spitte:** spat. **yave:** gave. **mowes:** grimaces. **repreves:** insults.

remenant of his passioun that he suffred for my synnes, and no thyng for his gilt."/

And ye shul understonde that in mannes synne is every manere of ordre or ordinaunce turned up-so-doun. [260] For it is sooth that God, and reson, and sensualitee, and the body of man ben so ordeyned that everich of thise foure thynges sholde have lordshipe over that oother;/ as thus: God sholde have lordshipe over resoun, and resoun over sensualitee, and sensualitee over the body of man./ But soothly, whan man synneth, al this ordre or ordinaunce is turned up-so-doun./ And therfore, thanne, for as muche as the reson of man ne wol nat be subget ne obeisant to God, that is his lord by right, therfore leseth it the lordshipe that it sholde have over sensualitee, and eek over the body of man./ And why? For sensualitee rebelleth thanne agayns resoun, and by that way leseth resoun the lordshipe over sensualitee and over the body. [265] For right as resoun is rebel to God, right so is bothe sensualitee rebel to reson and the body also./

And certes this disordinaunce and this rebellioun oure Lord Jhesu Crist aboghte upon his precious body ful deere, and herkneth in which wise./ For as muche thanne as reson is rebel to God, therfore is man worthy to have sorwe and to be deed./ This suffred oure Lord Jhesu Crist for man, after that he hadde be bitraysed of his disciple, and distreyned and bounde, so that his blood brast out at every nayl of his handes, as seith Seint Augustyn./ And forther over, for as muchel as reson of man ne wol nat daunte sensualitee whan it may, therfore is man worthy to have shame; and this suffred oure Lord Jhesu Crist for man, whan they spette in his visage. [270] And forther over, for as muche thanne as the caytyf body of man is rebel bothe to resoun and to sensualitee, therfore is it worthy the deeth./ And this suffred oure Lord Jhesu Crist for man upon the croys, where as ther was no part of his body free withoute gret peyne and bitter passioun./ And al this suffred Jhesu Crist, that nevere forfeted: "To muchel am I peyned for the thynges that I nevere deserved, and to muche defouled for shendshipe that man is worthy to have."/ And therfore may the synful man wel seye, as seith Seint Bernard, "Acursed be the bitternesse of my synne, for which ther moste be suffred so muche bitternesse."/ For certes, after the diverse disordinaunces of oure wikkednesses was the passioun of Jhesu Crist ordeyned in diverse thynges, [275] as thus. Certes, synful mannes

---

259. remenant: rest. no thyng: not at all.

260. ordinaunce: orderly arrangement. up-so-doun: upside-down.

261. sensualitee: the bodily nature; perceptive sense. ordeyned: ordered, arranged.

264. subget: subject. obeisant: obedient. leseth: loses.

265. for: because.

266. right: just.

267. disordinaunce: disorder. aboghte upon: redeemed with. deere: dearly. which wise: what manner.

268. deed: dead.

269. hadde be bitraysed of: had been betrayed by. distreyned: arrested. brast: burst.

270. forther over: furthermore. daunte: subdue. spette: spat.

271. catyf: wretched.

272. croys: cross. free withoute: free from.

273. forfeted: sinned. to muchel . . . to have: probably a reference to Psalms lxix, which was commonly applied to the sufferings of Christ; see verses 7, 9, 18–21. to muchel: too much. peyned: punished; tormented. that I nevere deserved: i.e., for which I never deserved punishment. defouled: tormented. shendshipe: disgrace. is worthy: deserves.

275. after: in accordance with. disordinaunces: disorders. in: in accordance with.

soule is bitraysed of the devel by coveitise of temporel prosperitee, and scorned by deceite whan he cheseth flesshly delices; and yet is it tormented by inpacience of adversitee, and bispet by servage and subjeccioun of synne; and atte laste it is slayn fynally./ For this disordinaunce of synful man was Jhesu Crist first bitraysed, and after that was he bounde, that cam for to unbynde us of synne and of peyne./ Thanne was he biscorned, that oonly sholde ben honoured in alle thynges and of alle thynges./ Thanne was his visage, that oghte be desired to be seyn of al man-kynde, in which visage angels desiren to looke, vileynsly bispet./ Thanne was he scourged, that no thyng hadde agilt; and finally, thanne was he crucified and slayn. [280] Thanne was acompliced the word of Ysaye, "He was wounded for oure mys-dedes and defouled by oure felonies."/ Now sith that Jhesu Crist took upon hym-self the peyne of alle oure wikkednesses, muche oghte synful man wepen and bi-wayle, that for his synnes Goddes sone of hevene sholde al this peyne endure./

The sixte thyng that oghte moeve a man to contricioun is the hope of three thynges; that is to seyn, foryifnesse of synne, and the yifte of grace wel for to do, and the glorie of hevene, with which God shal gerdone man for his goode dedes./ And for as muche as Jhesu Crist yeveth us thise yiftes of his largesse and of his sovereyn bountee, therfore is he cleped *Jhesus Nazarenus rex Judeorum./ Jhesus* is to seyn "saveour" or "salvacioun," on whom men shul hope to have foryifnesse of synnes, which that is proprely salvacioun of synnes. [285] And therfore seyde the aungel to Joseph, "Thou shalt clepen his name Jhesus, that shal save his peple of hire synnes."/ And heerof seith Seint Peter: "Ther is noon oother name under hevene that is yeve to any man, by which a man may be saved, but oonly Jhesus."/ *Nazarenus* is as muche for to seye as "florisshynge," in which a man shal hope that he that yeveth hym remissioun of synnes shal yeve hym eek grace wel to do. For in the flour is hope of fruyt in tyme comynge, and in foryifnesse of synnes hope of grace wel to do./ "I was atte dore of thyn herte," seith Jhesus, "and cleped for to entre. He that openeth to me shal have foryifnesse of synne./ I wol entre into hym by my grace, and soupe with hym," by the goode werkes that he shal doon, whiche werkes been the foode of God; "and he shal soupe with me," by the grete joye that I shal yeve hym. [290] Thus shal man hope, that for his werkes of pen-aunce, God shal yeve hym his regne, as he byheteth hym in the gospel./

---

276. bitraysed of: deceived by.   coveitise: covetousness.   cheseth: chooses.   delices: pleas-ures.   bispet: spat upon.   servage: servitude.   of synne: to sin.
277. disordinaunce: disorder.   bitraysed: betrayed.   peyne: punishment.
278. biscorned: scoffed at.
279. seyn of: seen by.   vileynsly: evilly.   bispet: spat upon.
280. no thyng: not at all.   agilt: sinned.
281. Ysaye: see Isaiah liii.5.   defouled: tormented.
282. Goddes sone of hevene: the Son of God in heaven.
283. gerdone: reward.
284. largesse: generosity.   bountee: noble goodness.   cleped: called.   *Jhesus Nazarenus rex Judeorum:* see John xix.19.
285. on: through.
286. the aungel: see Matthew i.20–21.   of: from.
287. Seint Peter: see Acts iv.12.
288. flour: flower.
289. Jhesus: see Revelation iii.20.   cleped: called.   entre: enter.
290. soupe: sup.
291. for: on account of.   regne: kingdom.   byheteth: promises.

Now shal man understonde in which manere shal ben his contricioun. I seye that it shal ben universal and total. This is to seyn, a man shal be verray repentaunt for alle his synnes that he hath doon in delit of his thoght; for delit is ful perilous./ For ther ben two manere of consentynges: that oon of hem is cleped consentynge of affeccioun, whan a man is moeved to do synne, and deliteth hym longe for to thynke on that synne;/ and his reson aperceyveth wel that it is synne agayns the lawe of God, and yet his reson refreyneth nat his foul delit or talent, though he se wel apertly that it is agayns the reverence of God. Although his reson ne consente nat to doon that synne in dede,/ yet seyn somme doctours that swich delit that dwelleth longe, it is ful perilous, al be it never so lite. [295] And also a man sholde sorwe namely for al that evere he hath desired agayn the lawe of God with parfit consentynge of his resoun; for therof is no doute, that it is dedly synne in consentynge./ For certes, ther is no dedly synne, that it nas first in mannes thought, and after that in his delit, and so forth into consentynge and into dede./ Wherfore I seye that many men ne repenten hem nevere of swiche thoghtes and delites, ne nevere shryven hem of it, but oonly of the dede of grete synnes outward./ Wherfore I seye that swiche wikked delites and wikked thoghtes been subtile bigileres of hem that shullen be dampned./

Mooreover man oghte to sorwe for his wikked wordes as wel as for his wikked dedes. For certes, the repentaunce of a singuler synne, and nat repente of alle his othere synnes, or elles repente hym of alle his othere synnes, and nat of a synguler synne, may nat availe. [300] For certes, God almyghty is al good; and therfore he foryeveth al, or elles right noght./ And heerof seith Seint Augustyn:/ "I wot certeynly that God is enemy to everich synnere"; and how thanne, he that observeth o synne, shal he have foryifnesse of the remenant of his othere synnes? Nay./

And forther over, contricioun sholde be wonder sorweful and anguissous; and therfore yeveth hym God pleynly his mercy; and therfore, whan my soule was anguissous withinne me, I hadde remembrance of God that my prayere myghte come to hym./

Forther over, contricioun moste be continuel, and that man have stedefast purpos to shrive hym, and for to amende hym of his lyf. [305] For soothly, whil contricioun lasteth, man may evere have hope of foryifnesse; and of this cometh hate of synne, that destroyeth synne, bothe in himself, and eek in oother folk, at his power./ For which seith David: "Ye that loven God, hateth wikkednesse." For trusteth wel, to love God is for to love that he loveth, and hate that he hateth./

---

292. verray: truly. doon: committed. in delit of his thoght: in the pleasure of contemplation.
293. consentynges: acquiescence. affeccioun: feeling.
294. aperceyveth: apprehends. refreyneth: restrains. foul delit: sinful pleasure. talent: appetite. wel apertly: very clearly. the reverence of God: the reverence due to God.
295. doctours: authorities. lite: little.
296. namely: especially. parfit: complete.
298. shryven: confess. dede: commission. outward: outwardly.
300. singuler: single. nat repente: not to repent.
301. al: wholly. right noght: nothing at all.
302. Seint Augustyn: see [Pseudo-Augustine] De Vera et Falsa Poenitentia I.9, §24.
303. observeth: gives heed to. remenant: rest.
304. forther over: furthermore. wonder: exceedingly. anguissous: anxious. pleynly: fully.
306. hate: hatred. at his power: to the utmost of his power.
307. David: see Psalms xcvii.10 (Vulgate, xcvi.10). that he loveth: what he loves.

The laste thyng that men shal understonde in contricioun is this: wherof availeth contricioun. I seye that somtyme contricioun delivereth man fro synne;/ of which that David seith, "I seye," quod David (that is to seyn, I purposed fermely) "to shryve me, and thow, Lord, relessedest my synne."/ And right so as contricion availeth nat withouten sad purpos of shrifte, if man have oportunitee, right so litel worth is shrifte or satisfaccioun withouten contricioun. [310] And mooreover contricion destroyeth the prisoun of helle, and maketh wayk and fieble alle the strengthes of the develes, and restoreth the yiftes of the Holy Goost and of alle goode vertues;/ and it clenseth the soule of synne, and delivereth the soule fro the peyne of helle, and fro the compaignye of the devel, and fro the servage of synne, and restoreth it to alle goodes espirituels, and to the compaignye and communyoun of holy chirche./ And forther over, it maketh hym that whilom was sone of ire to be sone of grace; and alle thise thynges ben preved by holy writ./ And therfore, he that wolde sette his entente to thise thynges, he were ful wys; for soothly he ne sholde nat thanne in al his lyf have corage to synne, but yeve his body and al his herte to the service of Jhesu Crist, and therof doon hym hommage./ For certes oure sweete Lord Jhesu Crist hath spared us so debonairly in oure folies, that if he ne hadde pitee of mannes soule, a sory song we myghten alle synge. [315]

Explicit prima pars Penitentie; Et sequitur secunda pars eiusdem.

The seconde partie of Penitence is Confessioun, that is signe of contricioun./ Now shul ye understonde what is Confessioun, and wheither it oghte nedes be doon or noon, and whiche thynges been covenable to verray Confessioun./

First shaltow understonde that Confessioun is verray shewynge of synnes to the preest./ This is to seyn "verray," for he moste confessen hym of alle the condiciouns that bilongen to his synne, as ferforth as he kan./ Al moot be seyd, and no thyng excused ne hid ne forwrapped, and nat avaunte hym of hise goode werkes. [320]

And forther over, it is necessarie to understonde whennes that synnes spryngen, and how they encreessen and whiche they ben./

Of the spryngynge of synnes seith Seint Paul in this wise: that "right as by a man synne entred first into this world, and thurgh that synne deth, right so thilke deth entred into alle men that synneden."/ And this man was Adam, by whom synne entred into this world, whan he brak the comaundementz of God./ And therfore,

---

308. **wherof:** in what respect.   **availeth:** is of use.

309. **David:** see Psalms xxxii.5 (Vulgate, xxxi.5).   **purposed:** resolved.   **fermely:** firmly, faithfully. **relessedest:** remitted.

310. **sad:** firm, steadfast.

311. **wayk:** weak.

312. **servage:** servitude.   **goodes espirituels:** spiritual blessings.   **communyoun:** fellowship.

313. **whilom:** formerly.   **sone:** son.   **holy writ:** cf. Ephesians ii.3–8.

314. **sette his entente:** pay attention.   **corage:** desire.   **therof:** thereby.

315. **debonairly:** mercifully.   **folies:** sins.

316. **partie:** part.

317. **covenable:** appropriate.

318. **verray:** true.

319. **condiciouns:** circumstances.   **as ferforth as:** insofar as.

320. **moot:** must.   **forwrapped:** covered up.   **avaunte hym:** boast.

321. **whennes:** whence.   **spryngen:** originate.   **encreessen:** increase.   **whiche:** what.

322. **spryngynge:** origin.   **Seint Paul:** see Romans v.12.   **right:** just.

323. **brak:** broke.

he that first was so myghty that he sholde nat have dyed, bicam swich oon that he moste nedes dye, wheither he wolde or noon, and al his progenye in this world, that in thilke man synneden./ Looke that in th'estat of innocence, whan Adam and Eve naked weren in Paradys, and nothyng ne hadden shame of hir nakednesse, [325] how that the serpent, that was moost wily of alle othere beestes that God hadde maked, seyde to the womman: "Why comaunded God to yow ye sholde nat eten of every tree in Paradys?"/ The womman answerde: "Of the fruyt," quod she, "of the trees in Paradys we feden us, but soothly, of the fruyt of the tree that is in the myddel of Paradys, God forbad us for to ete, ne nat touchen it, lest per aventure we sholde dyen."/ The serpent seyde to the womman: "Nay, nay, ye shul nat dyen of deth; for sothe, God woot that what day that ye eten therof, youre eyen shul opene, and ye shul ben as goddes, knowynge good and harm."/ The womman thanne saugh that the tree was good to feedyng, and fair to the eyen, and delitable to sighte. She took of the fruyt of the tree, and eet it, and yaf to hire housbonde, and he eet, and anon the eyen of hem bothe openeden./ And whan that they knewe that they were naked, they sowed of figge leves a maner of breches to hiden hire membres. [330] There may ye seen that dedly synne hath, first, suggestion of the feend, as sheweth heere by the naddre; and afterward, the delit of the flessh, as sheweth heere by Eve; and after that, the consentynge of reson, as sheweth heere by Adam./ For trust wel, though so were that the feend tempted Eve, that is to seyn, the flessh, and the flessh hadde delit in the beautee of the fruyt defended, yet certes, til that reson, that is to seyn, Adam, consented to the etynge of the fruyt, yet stood he in th' estaat of innocence./ Of thilke Adam tooke we thilke synne original; for of hym flesshly descended be we alle, and engendred of vile and corrupt matere./ And whan the soule is put in oure body, right anon is contract original synne; and that that was erst but oonly peyne of concupiscence, is afterward bothe peyne and synne./ And therfore be we alle born sones of wratthe and of dampnacioun perdurable, if it nere baptesme that we receyven, which bynymeth us the culpe. But for sothe, the peyne dwelleth with us, as to temptacioun, which peyne highte concupiscence. [335] And this concupiscence, whan it is wrongfully disposed or ordeyned in man, it maketh hym coveite, by coveitise of flessh, flesshly synne, by sighte of his eyen as to erthely thynges, and eek coveitise of hynesse by pride of herte./

Now, as to speken of the firste coveitise, that is concupiscence, after the lawe of oure membres, that weren lawefulliche ymaked and by rightful jugement of God;/

---

324. swich oon: such a one. noon: no.
325. looke: consider. Adam and Eve: see Genesis iii.1–7. nothyng: not at all.
326. eten: eat.
327. feden us: eat.
328. harm: evil.
329. to feedyng: for eating. delitable: delightful, pleasing. eet: ate.
330. sowed: sewed. maner: kind. membres: sexual organs.
331. sheweth: is manifest. naddre: serpent.
332. defended: forbidden. yet stood he: he still remained.
333. flesshly: physically.
334. contract: incurred. erst: first. peyne: affliction.
335. bynymeth: takes away from. culpe: guilt.
336. ordeyned: ordered, disposed. coveitise: covetousness; immoderate desire. hynesse: high rank or position.
337. after: according to. lawe of oure membres: the law of God concerning our sexual organs.

I seye, forasmuche as man is nat obeisaunt to God, that is his lord, therfore is the flessh to hym disobeisaunt thurgh concupiscence, which yet is cleped norissynge of synne and occasioun of synne./ Therfore, al the while that a man hath in hym the peyne of concupiscence, it is impossible but he be tempted somtime and moeved in his flessh to synne./ And this thyng may nat faille as longe as he lyveth; it may wel wexe fieble and faile by vertu of baptesme, and by the grace of God thurgh peni- tence; [340] but fully ne shal it nevere quenche, that he ne shal som tyme be moeved in hymself, but if he were al refreyded by siknesse, or by malefice of sorcerye, or colde drynkes./ For lo, what seith Seint Paul: "The flessh coveiteth agayn the spirit, and the spirit agayn the flessh; they been so contrarie and so stryven that a man may nat alway doon as he wolde."/ The same Seint Paul, after his grete penaunce in water and in lond,—in water by nyght and by day in gret peril and in gret peyne; in lond, in famyne and thurst, in coold and clothlees, and ones stoned almoost to the deth,/—yet seyde he, "Allas, I catyf man! who shal delivere me fro the prison of my caytyf body?"/ And Seint Jerome, whan he longe tyme hadde woned in desert, where as he hadde no compaignye but of wilde beestes, where as he hadde no mete but herbes, and water to his drynke, ne no bed but the naked erthe, for which his flessh was blak as an Ethiopen for heete, and ny destroyed for cold, [345] yet seyde he that "the brennynge of lecherye boyled in al his body."/ Wherfore I woot wel sikerly that they ben deceyved that seyn that they ne be nat tempted in hir body./ Witnesse on Seint Jame the Apostel, that seith that "every wight is tempted in his owene concupiscence"; that is to seyn, that everich of us hath matere and occasioun to be tempted of the norissynge of synne that is in his body./ And therfore seith Seint John the Evaungelist: "If that we seyn that we be withoute synne, we deceyve us selve, and trouthe is nat in us."/

Now shal ye understonde in what manere that synne wexeth and encreesseth in man. The firste thyng is thilke norissynge of synne of which I spak biforn, thilke flesshly concupiscence. [350] And after that comth the subjeccioun of the devel, this is to seyn, the develes bely, with which he bloweth in man the fyr of flesshly concupiscence./ And after that, a man bithynketh hym wheither he wol doon, or no, thilke thing to which he is tempted./ And thanne, if that a man withstonde and weyve the firste entisynge of his flessh and of the feend, thanne is it no synne; and if so be that he do nat so, thanne feeleth he anoon a flambe of delit./ And thanne

---

338. **obeisaunt:** obedient. **norissynge:** nourishment. **occasioun:** cause.

340. **wexe:** wax, grow, become.

341. **quenche:** be quenched. **moeved:** moved, stirred. **refreyded:** cooled. **malefice:** wicked enchantments.

342. **Seint Paul:** see Galatians v.17. **coveiteth agayn:** strives eagerly against.

343. **Seint Paul:** see II Corinthians xi.25–27; Romans vii.24. **clothlees:** without clothes; without adequate clothing. **ones:** once.

344. **caytyf:** wretched.

345. **Seint Jerome:** see *Epistola xxii: Ad Eustochium, De Virginitate*, §7. **woned:** lived. **where as:** where. **mete:** food. **for heete:** because of heat.

348. **Seint Jame:** see James i.14. **matere:** reason. **occasioun:** cause. **of the norissynge:** by the nourishment.

349. **Seint John:** see I John i.8.

350. **wexeth:** waxes, grows. **norissynge:** nourishment.

351. **subjeccioun:** suggestioun, i.e., temptation. **bely:** bellows.

352. **bithynketh hym:** considers.

353. **weyve:** put aside. **flambe:** flame.

is it good to be war, and kepe hym wel, or elles he wol falle anon into consentynge of synne; and thanne wol he do it, if he may have tyme and place./ And of this matere seith Moyses by the devel in this manere: "The feend seith, 'I wole chace and pursue the man by wikked suggestioun, and I wole hente hym by moevynge or stirynge of synne. And I wol departe my prise or my praye by deliberacioun, and my lust shal ben acompliced in delit. I wol drawe my swerd in consentynge'—[355] for certes, right as a swerd departeth a thyng in two peces, right so consentynge departeth God fro man—'and thanne wol I sleen hym with myn hand in dede of synne'; thus seith the feend."/ For certes, thanne is a man al deed in soule. And thus is synne acompliced by temptacioun, by delit, and by consentynge; and thanne is the synne cleped actuel./

For sothe, synne is in two maneres; outher it is venial, or dedly synne. Soothly, whan man loveth any creature moore than Jhesu Crist oure Creatour, thanne is it dedly synne. And venial synne is it, if man love Jhesu Crist lasse than hym oghte./ For sothe, the dede of this venial synne is ful perilous; for it amenuseth the love that men sholde han to God moore and moore./ And therfore, if a man charge hymself with manye swiche venial synnes, certes, but if so be that he somtyme descharge hym of hem by shrifte, they mowe ful lightly amenuse in hym al the love that he hath to Jhesu Crist; [360] and in this wise skippeth venial into dedly synne. For certes, the moore that a man chargeth his soule with venial synnes, the moore is he enclyned to falle in dedly synne./ And therfore lat us nat be necligent to deschargen us of venial synnes. For the proverbe seith that "manye smale maken a greet."/ And herkne this ensample. A greet wawe of the see comth som tyme with so greet a violence that it drencheth the ship. And the same harm doon som tyme the smale dropes of water, that entren thurgh a litel crevace into the thurrok, and in the botme of the ship, if men be so necligent that they ne descharge hem nat by tyme./ And therfore, although ther be a difference bitwixe thise two causes of drenchynge, algates the ship is dreynt./ Right so fareth it somtyme of dedly synne, and of anoyouse veniale synnes, whan they multiplie in a man so gretly that thilke worldly thynges that he loveth, thurgh which he synneth venially, is as gret in his herte as the love of God, or moore. [365] And therfore, the love of every thyng that is nat biset in God, ne doon principally for Goddes sake, although that a man love it lasse than God, yet is it venial synne;/ and dedly synne whan the love of any thyng weyeth in the herte of man as muche as the love of God, or moore./ "Dedly

354. kepe hym: be on his guard.   consentynge of: yielding to.
355. Moyses: see Exodus xv.9.   by: concerning.   hente: ensnare.   departe: separate or single (as from the hunted herd).   prise: prey.   praye: prey, quarry.   by deliberacioun: deliberately. lust: desire.   in consentynge: i.e., in his consenting to sin.
356. right: just.   departeth: separates, divides.   sleen: slay.   in dede: in (his) deed, act.
357. al: utterly.   deed: dead.
358. venial: pardonable.   dedly: mortal.
359. dede: commission.   amenuseth: diminishes.
360. charge: burden.   discharge: unburden.   lightly: easily.
361. skippeth: passes directly.
363. herkne: take heed of.   wawe: wave.   drencheth: sinks.   crevace: crack.   thurrok: bilge. descharge: bail.   by tyme: in time, promptly.
364. algates: in any case.   dreynt: sunk.
365. anoyouse: harmful.
366. biset: set.
367. weyeth: weighs.

synne," as seith Seint Augustyn, "is whan a man turneth his herte fro God, which that is verray sovereyn bountee, that may nat chaunge, and yeveth his herte to thyng that may chaunge and flitte."/ And certes, that is every thyng save God of hevene. For sooth is that if a man yeve his love, the which that he oweth al to God with al his herte, unto a creature, certes, as muche of his love as he yeveth to thilke creature, so muche he bireveth fro God;/ and therfore dooth he synne. For he that is dettour to God ne yeldeth nat to God al his dette, that is to seyn, al the love of his herte. [370]

Now sith man understondeth generally which is venial synne, thanne is it covenable to tellen specially of synnes whiche that many a man peraventure ne demeth hem nat synnes, and ne shryveth him nat of the same thynges, and yet natheless they been synnes/ soothly, as thise clerkes writen; this is to seyn, that at every tyme that man eteth or drynketh moore than suffiseth to the sustenaunce of his body, in certein he dooth synne./ And eek whan he speketh moore than it nedeth, it is synne. Eek whan he herkneth nat benignely the compleint of the povre;/ eek whan he is in heele of body, and wol nat faste whan other folk faste, withouten cause resonable; eek whan he slepeth moore than nedeth, or whan he comth by thilke enchesoun to late to chirche, or to othere werkes of charitee;/ eek whan he useth his wyf, withoute sovereyn desir of engendrure to the honour of God, or for the entente to yelde to his wyf the dette of his body; [375] eek whan he wol nat visite the sike and the prisoner, if he may; eek if he love wyf or child, or oother worldly thyng, moore than reson requireth; eek if he flatere or blandise moore than hym oghte for any necessitee;/ eke if he amenuse or withdrawe the almesse of the povre; eke if he apparaileth his mete moore deliciously than nede is, or ete it to hastily by likerousnesse;/ eek if he tale vanytees at chirche or at Goddes service, or that he be a talker of ydel wordes of folye or of vileynye, for he shal yelde acountes of it at the day of doom;/ eek whan he biheteth or assureth to do thynges that he may nat perfourne; eek whan that he by lightnesse or folye mysseyeth or scorneth his neighebor;/ eek whan he hath any wikked suspecioun of thyng ther he ne woot of it no soothfastnesse: [380] thise thynges, and mo withoute nombre, ben synnes, as seith Seint Augustyn./

Now shal men understonde that, al be it so that noon erthely man may eschue alle venial synnes, yet may he refreyne hym by the brennynge love that he hath to

---

368. **bountee:** goodness. **flitte:** vary.

369. **bireveth:** takes away.

370. **yeldeth:** pays.

371. **covenable:** appropriate. **demeth:** considers.

372. **in certein:** certainly.

373. **benignely:** graciously.

374. **heele:** health, sound physical condition. **by thilke enchesoun:** for that reason. **to late:** too late. **werkes:** acts.

375. **yelde:** pay.

376. **visite:** see Matthew xxv.43. **blandise:** blandish.

377. **amenuse:** reduce. **withdrawe:** withhold. **the almesse of:** (his) alms for. **apparaileth:** prepares. **mete:** food. **deliciously:** sumptuously. **ete:** eat. **to hastily:** too hastily. **by likerousnesse:** because of fondness for delicious food.

378. **tale vanytees:** tell idle tales. **vileynye:** wickedness. **yelde:** render. **doom:** judgment.

379. **biheteth:** promises. **assureth:** gives a pledge. **lightnesse:** thoughtlessness. **mysseyeth:** slanders. **scorneth:** mocks, derides.

382. **al be it so that:** although. **eschue:** avoid. **refreyne hym:** curb himself. **brennynge:** burning.

oure Lord Jhesu Crist, and by preyeres and confessioun and othere goode werkes, so that it shal but litel greve./ For, as seith Seint Augustyn, "If a man love God in swich manere that al that evere he dooth is in the love of God, or for the love of God, verraily, for he brenneth in the love of God,/ looke how muche that a drope of water that falleth in a fourneys ful of fyr anoyeth or greveth, so muche anoyeth a venial synne unto a man that is perfit in the love of Jhesu Crist."/ Men may also refreyne venial synne by receyvynge worthily of the precious body of Jhesu Crist; [385] by receyvynge eek of holy water; by almesdede; by general confessioun of *Confiteor* at masse and at complyn; and by blessynge of bisshopes and of preestes, and by othere goode werkes.

Explicit secunda pars penitentie.

*Sequitur de septem peccatis mortalibus
et eorum dependenciis, circumstanciis, et speciebus.*

Now is it bihovely thyng to telle which ben deedly synnes, this is to seyn, chief-taynes of synnes. Alle they renne in o lees, but in diverse manneres. Now ben they cleped chieftaynes, for as muche as they been chief and spryng of alle othere synnes./ Of the roote of thise sevene synnes, thanne, is Pride the general roote of alle harmes. For of this roote spryngen certein braunches, as Ire, Envye, Accidie or Slewthe, Avarice or Coveitise (to commune understondynge), Glotonye, and Lecherye./ And everich of thise chief synnes hath his braunches and his twigges, as shal be declared in hire chapitres folwynge./

De Superbia.

And thogh so be that no man kan outrely telle the nombre of the twigges and of the harmes that comen of Pride, yet wol I shewe a partie of hem, as ye shul under-stonde. [390] Ther is Inobedience, Avauntynge, Ypocrisie, Despit, Arrogance, In-pudence, Swellynge of Herte, Insolence, Elacioun, Inpacience, Strif, Contumacie, Presumpcioun, Irreverence, Pertinacie, Veyne Glorie, and many another twig that I kan nat declare./ Inobedient is he that disobeyeth for despit to the comandementz of God, and to his sovereyns, and to his goostly fader./ Avauntour is he that bosteth of the harm or of the bountee that he hath doon./ Ypocrite is he that hideth

---

382. but litel greve: disturb but little.
383. for he brenneth: because he burns.
384. looke how: however.
385. refreyne: curb. worthily: devoutly.
386. almesdede: almsgiving. of bisshopes: by bishops.
387. bihovely: necessary. alle they renne: they all run. in o lees: on one leash. spryng: source.
388. Pride: see Ecclesiasticus x.15. harmes: sins. ire: wrath. slewthe: sloth. coveitise: covetousness.
389. declared: told. chapitres: sections.
390. outrely: fully. telle: count. partie: part.
391. inobedience: disobedience. avauntynge: boasting. despit: disdain. pertinacie: perverse obstinacy. declare: set down.
392. goostly: spiritual.
393. avauntour: boaster. harm: evil. bountee: good.
394. hideth to shewe hym: withholds showing himself.

to shewe hym swich as he is, and sheweth hym swich as he noght is./ Despitous is he that hath desdeyn of his neighebor, that is to seyn, of his evene-Cristene, or hath despit to doon that hym oghte to do. [395] Arrogant is he that thynketh that he hath thilke bountees in hym that he hath nat, or weneth that he sholde have hem by his desertes, or elles he demeth that he be that he nys nat./ Inpudent is he that for his pride hath no shame of his synnes./ Swellynge of herte is whan a man rejoyseth hym of harm that he hath doon./ Insolent is he that despiseth in his juggement alle othere folk, as to regard of his value, and of his konnyng, and of his spekyng, and of his beryng./ Elacioun is whan he ne may neither suffre to have maister ne felawe. [400] Inpacient is he that wol nat been ytaught ne undernome of his vice, and by strif werreieth trouthe wityngly, and deffendeth his folye./ *Contumax* is he that thurgh his indignacioun is agayns everich auctoritee or power of hem that ben his sovereyns./ Presumpcioun is whan a man undertaketh an emprise that hym oghte nat do, or elles that he may nat do; and this is called Surquidrie. Irreverence is whan men do nat honour there as hem oghte to doon, and waiten to be reverenced./ Pertinacie is whan a man deffendeth his folye, and trusteth to muche to his owene wit./ Veyneglorie is for to have pompe and delit in temporel hynesse, and glorifie hym in worldly estat. [405] Janglynge is whan a man speketh to muche biforn folk, and clappeth as a mille, and taketh no keep what he seith./

And yet is ther a privee spece of Pride, that waiteth first to be salewed er he wole salewe, al be he lasse worthy than that oother is, peraventure; and eek he waiteth or desireth to sitte, or elles to goon above hym in the wey, or kisse pax, or been encensed, or goon to offryng biforn his neighebor,/ and swiche semblable thynges, agayns his duetee, peraventure, but that he hath his herte and his entente in swich a proud desir to be magnified and honoured biforn the peple./

Now ben ther two maneres of Pride: that oon of hem is withinne the herte of man, and that oother is withoute./ Of whiche, soothly, thise forseyde thynges, and mo than I have seyd, apertenen to Pride that is in the herte of man; and that othere speces of Pride ben withoute. [410] But natheles that oon of thise speces of Pride is signe of that oother, right as the gaye leefsel atte taverne is signe of the wyn that is in the celer./ And this is in manye thynges: as in speche and contenaunce, and

---

395. despitous: disdainful.　evene-Cristene: fellow Christian.　despit: disdain.　that: that which, what.

399. as . . . value: in comparison with his own worth.

400. felawe: equal.

401. undernome: reproved.　werreieth: makes war upon.

402. sovereyns: rulers.

403. emprise: enterprise.　waiten: wait with expectant desire.

404. pertinacie: perverse obstinacy.　wit: intellect.

405. hynesse: rank.

406. to muche: too much.　clappeth: clatters.

407. privee: private.　spece: sort.　waiteth: expects.　salewed: saluted, greeted.　al: although. to sitte . . . wey: to sit in a higher place than he (at the table) or to precede him in the street. kisse pax: (i.e., after Mass).　encensed: censed (with the smoke of incense).

408. agayns his duetee: contrary to propriety.

409. that oon: the one.

410. apertenen: belong.　speces: kinds.

411. speces: kinds.　leefsel: leafy arbor.

412. contenaunce: bearing.

in outrageous array of clothyng./ For certes, if ther ne hadde be no synne in cloth-yng, Crist wolde nat so soone have noted and spoken of the clothyng of thilke riche man in the gospel./ And, as seith Seint Gregorie, that "precious clothyng is cow-pable for the derthe of it, and for his softenesse, and for his strangenesse and degisynesse, and for the superfluitee, or for the inordinat scantnesse of it."/ Allas! may man nat seen, as in oure dayes, the synful costlewe array of clothynge, and namely in to muche superfluitee, or elles in to desordinat scantnesse? [415]

As to the first synne, that is in superfluitee of clothynge, which that maketh it so deere, to harm of the peple;/ nat oonly the cost of embrowdynge, the degise en-dentynge or barrynge, owndynge, palynge, wyndynge or bendynge, and semblable wast of clooth in vanitee;/ but ther is also costlewe furrynge in hire gownes, so muche pownsonynge of chisels to maken holes, so muche daggynge of sheres;/ forthwith the superfluitee in lengthe of the forseide gownes, trailynge in the dong and in the mire, on horse and eek on foote, as wel of man as of womman, that al thilke trailyng is verraily as in effect wasted, consumed, thredbare, and roten with donge, rather than it is yeven to the povre, to gret damage of the forseyde povre folk./ And that in sondry wise; this is to seyn that the moore that clooth is wasted, the moore moot it coste to the peple for the scarsnesse. [420] And forther over, if so be that they wolde yeven swich pownsoned and dagged clothyng to the povre folk, it is nat convenient to were for hire estaat, ne suffisant to beete hire necessitee, to kepe hem fro the distemperance of the firmament./

Upon that oother side, to speken of the horrible disordinat scantnesse of cloth-yng, as ben thise kutted sloppes, or haynselyns, that thurgh hire shortnesse ne covere nat the shameful membres of man, to wikked entente./ Allas! somme of hem shewen the shap and the boce of the horrible swollen membres, that semeth lik the maladie of hirnia, in the wrappynge of hire hoses;/ and eek the buttokes of hem that faren as it were the hyndre part of a she-ape in the fulle of the moone./ And mooreover, the wrecched swollen membres that they shewe thurgh disgisynge, in departynge of hire hoses in whit and reed,—semeth that half hir shameful privee membres weren flayne. [425] And if so be that they departen hire hoses in othere colours, as is whit and blew, or whit and blak, or blak and reed, and so forth,/ thanne semeth it, as by variaunce of colour, that half the partie of hire privee

---

413. gospel: see Luke xvi.19.

414. Seint Gregorie: see St. Gregory, *Homiliarum in Evangelia* ii.40.§3. cowpable: blameworthy, sinful. for: because of. derthe: scarcity; costliness. degisynesse: newfangledness, elaborate-ness.

415. costlewe: costly. to muche: too much. desordinat: inordinate, immoderate.

417. embrowdynge: embroidering. degise: newfangled, ostentatious. endentynge: notching. barrynge: ornamenting with bars or stripes. owndynge: undulating. palynge: vertical stripes. wyndynge: coiling. bendynge: decorative borders.

418. pownsonynge: punching. chisels: blades. daggynge: slitting. sheres: shears.

419. al thilke trailyng: all that (cloth which is) trailing.

420. moot: must.

421. pownsoned: punched. dagged: slitted. convenient: suitable. were: wear. for: because of. beete: relieve. necessitee: need. distemperance: inclemency.

422. kutted: short-cut. sloppes: coats. haynselyns: short jackets. entente: intention.

423. shap: sexual organ. boce: protuberance or swelling.

424. faren: seem. in the fulle of the moone: i.e., in heat.

425. disgisynge: newfangled clothing. departynge of hire hoses in: dividing of their hose into. semeth: it seems. flayne: flayed.

427. partie: part.

membres beh corrupt by the fyr of Seint Antony, or by cancre, or oother swich meschaunce./ Of the hyndre part of hire buttokes, it is ful horrible for to see. For certes, in that partie of hire body ther as they purgen hir stynkynge ordure,/ that foule partie shewe they to the peple proudly in despit of honestitee, which honestitee that Jhesu Crist and his frendes observede to shewen in hir lyve./ Now, as of the outrageous array of wommen, God woot that though the visages of somme of hem seme ful chaast and debonaire, yet notifie they in hire array of atyr likerousnesse and pride. [430] I sey nat that honestitee in clothynge of man or womman is uncovenable, but certes the superfluitee or disordinat scantitee of clothynge is reprevable./

Also the synne of aornement or of apparaille is in thynges that apertenen to ridynge, as in to manye delicat horses that ben holden for delit, that ben so faire, fatte, and costlewe;/ and also many a vicious knave that is sustened by cause of hem; in to curious harneys, as in sadeles, in crouperes, peytrels, and bridles covered with precious clothyng, and riche barres and plates of gold and of silver./ For which God seith by Zakarie the prophete, "I wol confounde the rideres of swiche horses."/ Thise folk taken litel reward of the ridynge of Goddes sone of hevene, and of his harneys whan he rood upon the asse, and ne hadde noon oother harneys but the povre clothes of his disciples; ne we ne rede nat that evere he rood on oother beest. [435] I speke this for the synne of superfluitee, and nat for resonable honestitee, whan reson it requireth./ And further over, certes, pride is gretly notified in holdynge of gret meynee, whan they be of litel profit or of right no profit;/ and namely whan that meynee is felonous and damageous to the peple by hardynesse of heigh lordshipe or by wey of offices./ For certes, swiche lordes sellen thanne hir lordship to the devel of helle, whan they sustenen the wikkednesse of hire meynee./ Or elles, whan thise folk of lowe degree, as thilke that holden hostelries, sustenen the thefte of hire hostilers, and that is in many manere of deceites. [440] Thilke manere of folk ben the flyes that folwen the hony, or elles the houndes that folwen the careyne. Swich forseyde folk stranglen spiritually hire lordshipes;/ for which thus seith David the prophete: "Wikked deth mote come upon thilke lordshipes, and God yeve that they mote descenden into helle al doun;

---

427. **corrupt:** corrupted. **fyr of Seint Antony:** erysipelas. **cancre:** cancer.

429. **honestitee:** decency. **observede:** took care. **in hir lyve:** during their lives.

430. **debonaire:** gracious. **notifie:** indicate. **array of atyr:** arrangement of apparel. **likerousnesse:** lechery.

431. **uncovenable:** inappropriate. **disordinat:** inordinate, excessive. **reprevable:** blameworthy, reprehensible.

432. **aornement:** adornment, embellishment. **apparaille:** ornaments, trappings. **apertenen:** pertain. **to manye:** too many. **delicat:** dainty. **holden:** kept. **costlewe:** costly.

433. **knave:** servant; base rogue. **sustened:** kept. **to curious:** too sumptuous. **harneys:** harness or fittings for a horse. **crouperes:** cruppers, often richly ornamented. **peytrels:** poitrels (a poitrel is an ornamental breastplate for a horse). **clothyng:** cloth.

434. **Zakarie:** see Zachariah x.5.

435. **reward:** regard. **Goddes sone:** see Matthew xxi.7. **harneys:** trappings.

436. **for:** with regard to.

437. **notified:** indicated. **holdynge:** maintaining. **meynee:** retinue, household.

438. **felonous:** cruel. **hardynesse:** insolence. **offices:** official positions.

439. **sustenen:** support.

440. **holden:** keep. **hostilers:** hostlers or other servants (at an inn).

441. **flyes:** flying insects. **folwen:** seek. **careyne:** carrion. **lordshipes:** dominion, authority.

442. **David:** see Psalms lv.15 (Vulgate, liv.16). **wikked deth mote:** may an evil death. **yeve:** grant. **al doun:** deep down.

for in hire houses been iniquitees and shrewednesses, and nat God of hevene."/ And certes, but if they doon amendement, right as God yaf his benysoun to [Laban] by the service of Jacob, and to [Pharao] by the service of Joseph, right so God wol yeve his malisoun to swiche lordshipes as sustenen the wikkednesse of hire servauntz, but they come to amendement./

Pride of the table appeereth eek ful ofte; for certes, riche men ben cleped to festes, and povre folk ben put awey and rebuked./ Also in excesse of diverse metes and drynkes, and namely swich manere bake-metes and dissh-metes, brennynge of wilde fyr and peynted and castelled with papir, and semblable wast, so that it is abusioun for to thynke. [445] And eek in to gret preciousnesse of vessel and curiositee of mynstralcye, by whiche a man is stired the moore to delices of luxurie,/ if so be that he sette his herte the lasse upon oure Lord Jhesu Crist, certeyn it is a synne; and certeinly the delices myghte ben so grete in this cas that man myghte lightly falle by hem into dedly synne./ The especes that sourden of Pride, soothly whan they sourden of malice ymagined, avised, and forncast, or elles of usage, been dedly synnes, it is no doute./ And whan they sourden by freletee unavysed, and sodeynly withdrawe ayeyn, al be they grevouse synnes, I gesse that they ne be nat deedly./

Now myghte men axe wherof that Pride sourdeth and spryngeth, and I seye, somtyme it spryngeth of the goodes of nature, and somtyme of the goodes of fortune, and somtyme of the goodes of grace. [450] Certes, the goodes of nature stonden outher in goodes of body or goodes of soule./ Certes, goodes of body been heele of body, strengthe, delivernesse, beautee, gentrice, franchise./ Goodes of nature of the soule ben good wit, sharp understondynge, subtil engyn, vertu naturel, good memorie./ Goodes of fortune been richesses, hyghe degrees of lordshipes, preisynges of the peple./ Goodes of grace been science, power to suffre spiritual travaille, benignitee, vertuous contemplacioun, withstondynge of temptacioun, and semblable thynges. [455] Of whiche forseyde goodes, certes it is a ful gret folye a man to priden hym in any of hem alle./ Now as for to speken of goodes of nature,

---

442. **shrewednesses:** wickedness.

443. **doon amendement:** make amends. **God:** see Genesis xxxi, xlvii.7. **benysoun:** blessing. **malisoun:** curse.

444. **cleped:** invited. **put awey:** turned away. **rebuked:** repulsed.

445. **metes:** foods. **bake-metes:** food baked in shells of pastry. **dissh-metes:** food cooked in dishes. **brennynge of wilde fyr:** with flames of burning spirits. **castelled:** castellated. **abusioun:** outrage. **thynke:** imagine.

446. **vessel:** vessels or utensils for the table, especially those made of gold and silver. **curiositee:** elaborateness. **stired:** stirred, moved. **delices:** pleasures.

447. **lightly:** easily.

448. **especes:** kinds. **sourden of:** arise from. **soothly:** as a matter of fact. **ymagined:** conceived, meditated. **avised:** considered beforehand. **forncast:** premeditated, aforethought. **of usage:** from habit.

449. **sourden by:** arise from. **freletee:** moral weakness. **unavysed:** without reflection. **withdrawe:** disappear. **al be they:** although they be. **grevouse:** grave.

450. **sourdeth:** arises. **goodes:** good things, benefits, blessings. **of nature:** bestowed by nature. **of fortune:** bestowed by fortune. **of grace:** bestowed by God's grace.

451. **stonden in:** consist in. **outher:** either.

452. **heele:** health. **delivernesse:** agility. **gentrice:** nobility of birth. **franchise:** freedom.

453. **wit:** intellect. **sharp:** acute. **engyn:** ingenuity; talent. **vertu naturel:** native ability.

454. **preisynges:** praises.

455. **science:** knowledge as a personal attribute. **suffre:** endure. **travaille:** suffering.

456. **a man:** for a man.

God woot that somtyme we han hem in nature as muche to oure damage as to oure profit./ As for to speke of heele of body, certes it passeth ful lightly, and eek it is ful ofte enchesoun of the siknesse of oure soule. For, God woot, the flessh is a ful greet enemy to the soule; and therfore, the moore that the body is hool, the moore be we in peril to falle./ Eke for to pride hym in his strengthe of body, it is an heigh folye. For certes, the flessh coveiteth agayn the spirit; and ay the moore strong that the flessh is, the sorier may the soule be./ And over al this, strengthe of body and worldly hardynesse causeth ful ofte many a man to peril and meschaunce. [460] Eek for to pride hym of his gentrie is ful gret folie; for ofte tyme the gentrie of the body binymeth the gentrie of the soule; and eek we ben alle of o fader and of o moder; and alle we ben of o nature, roten and corrupt, bothe riche and povre./ For sothe, o manere gentrye is for to preise, that apparailleth mannes corage with vertues and moralitees, and maketh hym Cristes child./ For truste wel that over what man that synne hath maistrie, he is a verray cherl to synne./

Now ben ther generale signes of gentillesse, as eschewynge of vice and ribaudye and servage of synne, in word, in werk, and contenaunce;/ and usynge vertu, curteisye, and clennesse, and to be liberal, that is to seyn, large by mesure; for thilke that passeth mesure is folye and synne. [465] Another is to remembre hym of bountee, that he of oother folk hath receyved./ Another is to be benigne to his goode subgetz; wherfore seith Senek, "Ther is no thing moore covenable to a man of heigh estaat than debonairetee and pitee./ And therfore thise flyes that men clepen bees, whan they maken hire kyng, they chesen oon that hath no prikke wherwith he may stynge."/ Another is, a man to have a noble herte and a diligent, to attayne to heighe vertuouse thynges./

Now certes, a man to pride hym in the goodes of grace is eek an outrageous folye; for thilke yiftes of grace that sholde have turned hym to goodnesse and to medicine, turneth hym to venym and to confusioun, as seith Seint Gregorie. [470] Certes also, whoso prideth hym in the goodes of fortune, he is a ful gret fool; for somtyme is a man a gret lord by the morwe, that is a caytyf and a wrecche er it be nyght;/ and somtyme the richesse of a man is cause of his deth; somtyme the delices of a man is cause of the grevous maladye thurgh which he dyeth./ Certes,

---

457. in: by. damage: harm.

458. heele: health. passeth: departs. lightly: easily; quickly. enchesoun: cause. hool: healthy.

459. For certes . . . the spirit: see Galatians v.17. coveiteth agayn: strives eagerly against.

460. hardynesse: rashness. causeth: drives.

461. hym: himself. gentrie: nobility. binymeth: destroys. o: one.

462. apparailleth: adorns. corage: spirit. moralitees: moral qualities. Cristes child: i.e., a good Christian.

463. cherl: slave.

464. ribaudye: debauchery. servage of: servitude to. werk: deed. contenaunce: manner.

465. usynge: the practising of. clennesse: purity. large: generous. by mesure: in moderation. passeth: exceeds.

466. bountee: kindness.

467. subgetz: subordinates. Senek: see Seneca, *De Clementia* i.3.3, and i.19.2. covenable: appropriate. debonairetee: graciousness.

468. flyes: flying insects.

469. a man: for a man. thynges: deeds.

470. turned: directed. medicine: a remedy. venym: poison. confusioun: ruin.

471. by the morwe: in the morning. caytyf: miserable person.

472. delices: sensual pleasures.

the commendacioun of the peple is somtyme ful fals and ful brotel for to triste;/ this day they preyse, tomorwe they blame./ God woot, desir to have commendacioun eek of the peple hath caused deth to many a bisy man./

Remedium contra peccatum Superbie.

Now sith that so is that ye han understonde what is Pride, and whiche ben the speces of it, and whennes Pride sourdeth and spryngeth, [475] now shul ye understonde which is the remedie agayns Pride; and that is humylitee, or mekenesse./ That is a vertu thurgh which a man hath verray knoweleche of hymself, and holdeth of hymself no pris ne deyntee, as in regard of his desertes, considerynge evere his freletee./ Now ben ther three maneres of humylitee: as humylitee in herte; another humylitee in his mouth; the thridde in his werkes./ The humilitee in herte is in foure maneres. That oon is whan a man holdeth hymself as noght worth biforn God of hevene. Another is whan he ne despiseth noon oother man./ The thridde is whan he rekketh nat, though men holde hym noght worth. The ferthe is whan he nys nat sory of his humiliacioun. [480] Also the humilitee of mouth is in foure thynges: in attempree speche, and in humblesse of speche, and whan he biknoweth with his owene mouth that he is swich as hym thynketh that he is in his herte. Another is whan he preiseth the bountee of another man, and nothyng therof amenuseth./ Humilitee eek in werkes is in foure maneres. The firste is whan he putteth othere men biforn hym. The seconde is to chese the loweste place over al. The thridde is gladly to assente to good conseil./ The ferthe is to stonde gladly to the award of his sovereyns, or of hym that is in hyer degree. Certein, this is a gret werk of humylitee./

Sequitur de Invidia.

After Pride wol I speken of the foule synne of Envye, which that is, as by the word of the philosophre, "sorwe of othere mennes prosperitee"; and after the word of Seint Augustyn, it is "sorwe of othere mennes wele, and joye of othere mennes harm."/ This foule synne is platly agayns the Holy Goost. Al be it so that every synne is agayns the Holy Goost, yet nathelees, for as muche as bountee aperteneth proprely to the Holy Goost, and Envye cometh proprely of malice, therfore it is proprely agayns the bountee of the Holy Goost. [485] Now hath malice two speces; that is to seyn, hardnesse of herte in wikkednesse, or elles the flessh of man is so

---

473. **brotel:** brittle; fickle. **triste:** trust.

475. **sourdeth:** arises.

477. **holdeth . . . deyntee:** i.e., has no esteem nor respect for himself. **considerynge:** being aware of. **freletee:** moral weakness.

478. **werkes:** deeds.

479. **noght:** nothing. **noon:** no.

480. **rekketh:** cares.

481. **attempree:** moderate. **biknoweth:** confesses. **bountee:** goodness. **nothyng:** not at all. **amenuseth:** belittles.

482. **chese:** choose. **over al:** in every way.

483. **stonde to the award:** accept the decision. **werk:** act.

484. **sorwe of:** sorrow for. **Seint Augustyn:** see his *Enarrationes in Psalmos* cv.25. **harm:** bad fortune; suffering.

485. **platly:** directly. **al be it so that:** although. **bountee:** goodness. **aperteneth proprely:** belongs naturally to.

blynd that he considereth nat that he is in synne, or rekketh nat that he is in synne, which is the hardnesse of the devel./ That oother spece of malice is whan that a man werreyeth trouthe, whan that he woot that it is trouthe; and eek whan he werreyeth the grace that God hath yeve to his neighebor; and al this is by Envye./ Certes, thanne is Envye the worste synne that is. For soothly, alle othere synnes ben somtyme oonly agayns o special vertu;/ but certes, Envye is agayns alle vertues and agayns alle goodnesses. For it is sory of alle the bountees of his neighebor, and in this manere it is divers from alle othere synnes./ For wel unnethe is ther any synne that it ne hath som delit in itself, save oonly Envye, that evere hath in itself angwissh and sorwe. [490]

The speces of Envye ben thise. Ther is first, sorwe of othere mennes goodnesse and of hir prosperitee; and prosperitee is kyndely matere of joye; thanne is Envye a synne agayns kynde./ The seconde spece of Envye is joye of oother mannes harm; and that is proprely lyk to the devel, that evere rejoyseth hym of mannes harm.

Of thise two speces comth bakbityng; and this synne of bakbityng or detraccion hath certeine speces, as thus. Som man preiseth his neighebor by a wikked entente;/ for he maketh alwey a wikked knotte atte laste ende. Alwey he maketh a "but" at the laste ende, that is digne of moore blame, than worth is al the preisynge./ The seconde spece is that if a man be good, and dooth or seith a thing to good entente, the bakbitere wol turne al thilke goodnesse up-so-doun to his shrewed entente. [495] The thridde is to amenuse the bountee of his neighebor./ The fourthe spece of bakbityng is this, that if men speke goodnesse of a man, thanne wol the bakbitere seyn, "parfey, swich a man is yet bet than he"; in dispreisynge of hym that men preise./ The fifte spece is this, for to consente gladly and herkne gladly to the harm that men speke of oother folk. This synne is ful greet, and ay encreesseth after the wikked entente of the bakbitere./

After bakbityng cometh gruchchyng or murmuracioun; and somtyme it spryngeth of inpacience agayns God, and somtyme agayns man./ Agayns God it is, whan a man gruccheth agayn the peyne of helle, or agayns poverte, or los of catel, or agayn reyn or tempest; or elles gruccheth that shrewes han prosperitee, or elles for that goode men han adversitee. [500] And alle thise thynges sholde men suffre paciently, for they comen by the rightful juggement and ordinaunce of God./ Somtyme cometh grucching of avarice; as Judas grucched agayns the Magdaleyne, whan she enoynted

---

486. considereth: is aware.
487. werreyeth: wars against. by: concerning.
488. agayns: opposed to.
489. divers: different.
490. unnethe: scarcely.
491. kyndely: naturally. kynde: nature.
492. harm: misfortune; suffering.
494. digne of: deserving of.
495. shrewed: wicked.
496. amenuse: belittle.
498. harm: evil; defamation. greet: great. ay: constantly. after: in proportion to.
499. gruchchyng: grumbling. murmuracioun: complaining.
500. agayn: against. catel: property, goods, money. or elles . . . prosperitee: see Psalms xxxvii.7 (Vulgate, xxxvi.7). shrewes: scoundrels.
502. the Magdaleyne: actually Mary, the sister of Martha; see John xii.4–6. enoynted: anointed.

the heved of oure Lord Jhesu Crist with hir precious oynement./ This manere murmure is swich as whan man gruccheth of goodnesse that hymself dooth, or that oother folk doon of hire owene catel./ Somtyme comth murmure of Pride; as whan Simon the Pharisee grucched agayn the Magdaleyne, whan she approched to Jhesu Crist, and weep at his feet for hire synnes./ And somtyme it sourdeth of Envye; whan men discovereth a mannes harm that was pryvee, or bereth hym on hond thyng that is fals. [505] Murmure eek is ofte amonges servauntz that grucchen whan hire sovereyns bidden hem to doon leveful thynges;/ and forasmuche as they dar nat openly withseye the comaundementz of hire sovereyns, yet wol they seyn harm, and grucche, and murmure prively for verray despit;/ whiche wordes men clepen the develes *Pater noster,* though so be that the devel ne hadde nevere *Pater noster,* but that lewed folk yeven it swich a name./ Somtyme it comth of Ire or privee hate, that norisseth rancour in herte, as afterward I shal declare./ Thanne cometh eek bitternesse of herte, thurgh which bitternesse every good dede of his neighebor semeth to hym bitter and unsavory. [510] Thanne cometh discord, that unbyndeth alle manere of frendshipe. Thanne comth scornynge of his neighebor, al do he never so wel./ Thanne comth accusynge, as whan man seketh occasioun to anoyen his neighebor, which that is lyk the craft of the devel, that waiteth bothe nyght and day to accusen us alle./ Thanne comth malignitee, thurgh which a man anoyeth his neighebor prively, if he may;/ and if he nat may, algate his wikked wil ne shal nat wante, as for to brennen his hous pryvely, or empoysone or sleen his beestes, and semblable thynges./

Remedium contra peccatum Invidie.

Now wol I speke of the remedye agayns this foule synne of Envye. First is the love of God principal, and lovyng of his neighebor as himself; for soothly, that oon ne may nat ben withoute that oother. [515] And truste wel that in the name of thy neighebor thou shalt understonde the name of thy brother; for certes alle we have o fader flesshly, and o moder, that is to seyn, Adam and Eve; and eek o fader spirituel that is God of hevene./ Thy neighebor artow holden for to love, and wilne hym alle goodnesse; and therfore seith God, "Love thy neighebor as thyself," that is to seyn, to salvacioun bothe of lyf and of soule./ And mooreover thou shalt love hym in word, and in benigne amonestynge and chastisynge, and conforte hym in his

---

502. heved: head.
503. murmure: muttered complaint. doon of: do with.
504. Simon: see Luke vii.39. weep: wept.
505. sourdeth: arises from. men: one (unemphatic indefinite pronoun). discovereth: discloses, reveals. harm: misfortune. bereth hym on hond: accuses him of.
506. leveful: lawful.
507. withseye: refuse to obey. seyn harm: speak ill. verray: sheer. despit: spite.
508. lewed: ignorant.
509. norisseth: nourishes.
510. unsavory: displeasing.
511. al do he: although he do.
512. occasioun: pretext.
514. algate: nevertheless. wante: fail. brennen: burn. empoysone: poison. sleen: slay.
515. principal: foremost. ben: exist.
516. o fader flesshly: one physical father.
517. artow holden: you are under an obligation. wilne: desire.
518. benigne: kindly. amonestynge: admonishing.

anoyes, and preye for hym with al thyn herte./ And in dede thou shalt love hym in swich wise that thou shalt doon to hym in charitee as thou woldest that it were doon to thyn owene persone./ And therfor thou ne shalt doon hym no damage in wikked word, ne harm in his body, ne in his catel, ne in his soule, by entisynge of wikked ensample. [520] Thou shalt nat desiren his wyf, ne none of his thynges. Understoond eek that in the name of neighebor is comprehended his enemy./ Certes, man shal love his enemy, by the comandement of God; and soothly thy freend shaltow love in God./ I seye, thyn enemy shaltow love for Goddes sake, by his comandement. For if it were reson that man sholde haten his enemy, for sothe God nolde nat receyven us to his love that ben his enemys./

Agayns three manere of wronges that his enemy dooth to hym, he shal doon three thynges, as thus./ Agayns hate and rancour of herte, he shal love hym in herte. Agayns chidyng and wikked wordes, he shal preye for his enemy. Agayns the wikked dede of his enemy, he shal doon hym bountee. [525] For Crist seith: "Loveth youre enemys, and preyeth for hem that speke yow harm, and eek for hem that yow chacen and pursuen, and dooth bountee to hem that yow haten." Loo, thus comaundeth us oure Lord Jhesu Crist to do to oure enemys./ For soothly, nature dryveth us to loven oure frendes, and parfey, oure enemys han moore nede to love than oure frendes; and they that moore nede have, certes to hem shal men doon goodnesse;/ and certes, in thilke dede have we remembraunce of the love of Jhesu Crist that deyde for his enemys./ And in as muche as thilke love is the moore grevous to perfourne, so muche is the moore gret the merite; and therfore the lovynge of oure enemy hath confounded the venym of the devel./ For right as the devel is disconfited by humylitee, right so is he wounded to the deeth by love of oure enemy. [530] Certes, thanne is love the medicine that casteth out the venym of Envye fro mannes herte./ The speces of this paas shullen be moore largely declared in hire chapitres folwynge./

Sequitur de Ira.

After Envye wol I discryven the synne of Ire. For soothly, whoso hath envye upon his neighebor, anon he wole comunly fynde hym a matere of wratthe, in word or in dede, agayns hym to whom he hath envye./ And as wel comth Ire of Pride, as of Envye; for soothly, he that is proud or envyous is lightly wrooth./

This synne of Ire, after the discryvyng of Seint Augustyn, is wikked wil to ben

---

518. **anoyes:** afflictions.
519. **in dede:** in deeds.
520. **catel:** goods, property.   **entisynge:** the enticement.
521. **his:** i.e., a man's.
523. **reson:** agreeable to reason.
524. **agayns:** in return for.
525. **bountee:** a good deed.
526. **Crist:** see Matthew v.44.   **speke harm:** speak ill of.   **chacen:** harass.   **pursuen:** persecute. **yow haten:** hate you.
527. **nede to:** need of.
529. **grevous:** difficult.   **perfourne:** achieve, carry into action.
530. **by love:** i.e., by our love.
532. **speces:** kinds (of love).   **paas:** section.   **declared:** explained.   **chapitres:** sections.
533. **hym:** himself.   **matere:** ground.   **of wratthe:** for wrath.
534. **lightly:** easily; quickly; commonly.
535. **discryvyng:** description.   **wil:** desire.

avenged by word or by dede. [535] Ire, after the philosophre, is the fervent blood of man yquyked in his herte, thurgh which he wole harm to hym that he hateth./ For certes, the herte of man, by eschawfynge and moevynge of his blood, wexeth so trouble that he is out of all jugement of resoun./

But ye shal understonde that Ire is in two maneres; that oon of hem is good, and that oother is wikked./ The goode Ire is by jalousie of goodnesse, thurgh which a man is wrooth with wikkednesse and agayns wikkednesse; and therfore seith a wys man that Ire is bet than pley./ This Ire is with debonairetee, and it is wrooth withoute bitternesse; nat wrooth agayns the man, but wrooth with the mysdede of the man, as seith the prophete David, *"Irascimini et nolite peccare."* [540] Now understondeth that wikked Ire is in two maneres; that is to seyn, sodeyn Ire or hastif Ire, withoute avisement and consentynge of reson./ The menyng and the sens of this is, that the reson of a man ne consente nat to thilke sodeyn Ire; and thanne is it venial./ Another Ire is ful wikked, that comth of felonye of herte avysed and cast biforn, with wikked wil to do vengeance, and therto his resoun consenteth; and soothly this is deedly synne./ This Ire is so displesant to God that it troubleth his hous, and chaceth the Holy Goost out of mannes soule, and wasteth and destroyeth the liknesse of God, that is to seyn, the vertu that is in mannes soule,/ and put in hym the liknesse of the devel, and bynymeth the man fro God, that is his rightful lord. [545] This Ire is a ful gret plesaunce to the devel; for it is the develes fourneys, that is eschawfed with the fyr of helle./ For certes, right so as fyr is moore mighty to destroye erthely thynges than any oother element, right so Ire is myghty to destroye alle spirituel thynges./

Looke how that fyr of smale gleedes, that ben almost dede under asshen, wolen quike agayn when they ben touched with brymstoon; right so Ire wol everemo quyken agayn, when it is touched by the pride that is covered in mannes herte./ For certes, fyr ne may nat come out of no thyng, but if it were first in the same thyng naturelly, as fyr is drawen out of flyntes with steel./ And right so as pride is ofte tyme matere of Ire, right so is rancour norice and kepere of Ire. [550] Ther is a maner tree, as seith Seint Ysidre, that whan men maken fyr of thilke tree, and covere the coles of it with asshen, soothly the fyr of it wol lasten al a yeer or moore./ And right so fareth it of rancour; whan it is ones conceyved in the hertes of som men, certein, it wol lasten peraventure from oon Estre day unto another Estre day, and moore./ But certes, thilke man is ful fer fro the mercy of God al thilke while./

---

536. fervent: hot, violent.   yquyked: stirred up.   wole: desires.
537. eschawfynge: the heating.   moevynge: the stirring.   trouble: turbulent.   of resoun: rational.
539. jalousie of: zeal for.   wys man: see Ecclesiastes vii.4.   pley: jesting.
540. with: accompanied by.   debonairetee: kindness.   David: see Vulgate, Psalms iv.5.   *Irascimini et nolite peccare:* be ye angry, and sin not.
541. hastif: unexpected.   avisement: (the) consideration.
542. venial: pardonable.
543. felonye: evil intention.   avysed: considered.   cast: deliberated.   deedly: deadly, mortal.
544. displesant: offensive.   his hous: i.e., the soul.
545. put: (putteth) puts.   bynymeth: takes away.
546. fourneys: the hearth of a forge.   eschawfed: made hot.
548. looke how: just as.   gleedes: coals.   asshen: ashes.   quike: kindle.   everemo: always.   covered: hidden.
550. norice: nurse.
551. Seint Ysidre: see St. Isidore, *Etymologiae* XVII.vii.35.
552. Estre: Easter.

In this forseyde develes fourneys ther forgen three shrewes: Pride, that ay blow-
eth and encreesseth the fyr by chidynge and wikked wordes;/ thanne stant Envye,
and holdeth the hoote iren upon the herte of man with a peire of longe toonges of
long rancour; [555] and thanne stant the synne of Contumelie, or strif and cheeste,
and batereth and forgeth by vileyns reprevynges./ Certes, this cursed synne anoyeth
bothe to the man hymself and eek to his neighebor. For soothly, almoost al the
harm that any man dooth to his neighebor comth of wratthe./ For certes, out-
rageous wratthe dooth al that evere the devel hym comaundeth; for he ne spareth
neither Crist ne his sweete Moder./ And in his outrageous anger and ire, allas! allas!
ful many oon at that tyme feeleth in his herte ful wikkedly, bothe of Crist and eek
of alle his halwes./ Is nat this a cursed vice? Yis, certes. Allas! it bynymeth from
man his wit and his reson, and al his debonaire lif espirituel that sholde kepen his
soule. [560] Certes, it bynymeth eek Goddes due lordshipe, and that is mannes
soule, and the love of his neighebores. It stryveth eek alday agayn trouthe. It reveth
hym the quiete of his herte, and subverteth his soule./

Of Ire comen thise stynkynge engendrures: first, hate, that is oold wratthe; dis-
cord, thurgh which a man forsaketh his olde freend that he hath loved ful longe;/
and thanne cometh werre, and every manere of wrong that man dooth to his
neighebor, in body or in catel./ Of this cursed synne of Ire cometh eek man-
slaughtre. And understonde wel that homycide, that is manslaughtre, is in diverse
wise. Som manere of homycide is spirituel, and som is bodily./ Spirituel man-
slaughtre is in [thre] thynges. First by hate, as seith Seint John: "He that hateth
his brother is homycide." [565] Homycide is eek by bakbitynge, of whiche bak-
biteres seith Salomon that "they han two swerdes with whiche they sleen hire
neighebores." For soothly, as wikke is to bynyme hym his good name as his lyf./
Homycide is eek in yevynge of wikked conseil by fraude; as for to yeven conseil
to areysen wrongful custumes and taillages./ Of whiche seith Salomon: "Leon
rorynge and bere hongry ben like to the cruel lordshipes" in withholdynge or abreg-
gynge of the shepe (or the hyre), or of the wages of servauntz, or elles in usure, or
in withdrawynge of the almesse of povre folk./ For which the wise man seith,
"Fedeth hym that almoost dyeth for honger"; for soothly, but if thow feede hym,
thou sleest hym; and all thise ben deedly synnes./

Bodily manslaughtre is, whan thow sleest him with thy tonge in oother manere;

---

554. forgen: work at the forge. shrewes: scoundrels.
555. stant: stands. hoote: hot. peire: pair. toonges: tongs. long: prolonged.
556. cheeste: quarreling. batereth: beats, hammers. vileyns: evil. reprevynges: reproaches.
557. anoyeth to: injures.
559. of Crist: toward Christ. halwes: saints.
560. bynymeth: takes away. debonaire: gracious.
561. stryveth agayn: wages warfare against. alday: all the time. reveth hym: robs him of.
562. engendrures: offspring. oold: inveterate; deep-rooted.
563. werre: war. catel: property.
564. is in diverse wise: occurs in diverse ways.
565. spirituel manslaughtre: manslaughter in spirit (as opposed to manslaughter in act; see in
dede, line 571, below). [thre]: O' reads sixe. Seint John: see I John iii.15.
566. Salomon: cf. Proverbs xxv.18. sleen: slay. bynyme: take away.
567. areysen: levy. custumes: tributes. taillages: taxes.
568. Salomon: see Proverbs xxviii.15. bere: bear. lordshipes: rulers. abreggynge: reducing.
shepe: reward. usure: usury. withdrawynge: withholding. the almesse of: (his) alms for.
569. wise man: see Proverbs xxv.21. thou sleest: you slay.
570. with: by the use of. in oother: (but actually) in another.

as whan thou comandest to sleen a man, or elles yevest hym conseil to sleen a man. [570] Manslaughtre in dede is in foure maneres. That oon is by lawe, right as a justice dampneth hym that is coupable to the deeth. But lat the justice be war that he do it rightfully, and that he do it nat for delit to spille blood, but for kepynge of rightwisnesse./ Another homycide is doon for necessitee, as whan a man sleeth another in his defendaunt, and that he ne may noon ootherwise escape from his owene deeth./ But certeinly if he may escape withouten slaughtre of his adversarie, and sleeth hym, he dooth synne and he shal bere penance as for deedly synne./ Eek if a man, by caas or aventure, shete an arwe, or caste a stoon, with which he sleeth a man, he is homycide./ Eek if a womman by necligence overlyeth hire child in hir slepyng, it is homycide and deedly synne. [575] Eek whan man destour-beth concepcioun of a child, and maketh a womman outher bareyne by drynkynge of venemouse herbes thurgh which she may nat conceyve, or sleeth a child by drynkes, or elles putteth certeine material thynges in hire secree places to slee the child,/ or elles dooth unkyndely synne, by which man or womman shedeth hire nature in manere or in place ther as a child may nat be conceived, or elles if a woman have conceyved, and hurt hirself and sleeth the child, yet is it homycide./ What seye we eek of wommen that mordren hir children for drede of worldly shame? Certes, an horrible homicide./ Homycide is eek if a man approcheth to a womman by desir of lecherie, thurgh which the child is perissed, or elles smyteth a womman wityngly, thurgh which she leseth hir child. Alle thise been homycides and horrible dedly synnes./

Yet comen ther of Ire manye mo synnes, as wel in word as in thoght and in dede; as he that arretteth upon God, or blameth God of thyng of which he is hym-self gilty, or despiseth God and alle his halwes, as doon thise cursede hasardours in diverse contrees. [580] This cursed synne doon they, whan they feelen in hir herte ful wikkedly of God and his halwes./ Also whan they treten unreverently the sacre-ment of the auter, thilke synne is so greet that unnethe may it ben releessed, but that the mercy of God passeth alle his werkes; it is so greet, and he so benigne./

Thanne comth of Ire attry angre. Whan a man is sharply amonested in his shrifte to forleten synne,/ thanne wole he be angry, and answeren hokerly and angrily, and deffenden or excusen his synne by unstedefastnesse of his flessh; or elles he dide it

---

571. in dede: in act. right: just. justice: judge. coupable to the deeth: deserving to die. kepynge: preserving.

572. in his defendaunt: in his own defense, in self-defense. noon ootherwise: in no other way.

573. sleeth: slays. bere: suffer. as for: for.

574. shete: shoot. caste a stoon: see Numbers xxxv.17.

575. overlyeth: lies upon. slepyng: sleep.

576. destourbeth: prevents. outher: either. by drynkynge: by her drinking. drynkes: potions that produce abortion.

577. unkyndely: unnatural. shedeth: emits. nature: seminal fluid; orgastic fluid.

578. mordren: murder.

579. a womman: i.e., a pregnant woman. perissed: killed. wityngly: deliberately. leseth: loses.

580. arretteth: places the blame. halwes: saints. hasardours: gamblers.

581. of: toward.

582. treten: treat. auter: altar. unnethe: hardly. releessed: remitted. mercy: see Psalms cxlv.9 (Vulgate, cxliv.9). passeth: surpasses. greet: great.

583. attry: venomous. amonested: admonished. forleten: renounce.

584. hokerly: scornfully. deffenden . . . by: find excuses for his sin in. unstedefastnesse: in-stability; frailty.

for to holde compaignye with his felawes; or elles, he seith, the feend enticed hym;/ or elles he dide it for his youthe; or elles his compleccioun is so corageous that he may nat forbere; or elles it is his destinee, as he seith, unto a certein age; or elles, he seith, it cometh hym of gentillesse of his auncestres; and semblable thynges. [585] Alle thise manere of folk so wrappen hem in hir synnes that they ne wol nat delivere hemself. For soothly, no wight that excuseth hym wilfully of his synne may nat been delivered of his synne, til that he mekely biknoweth his synne./

After this, thanne cometh sweryng, that is expres agayn the comandement of God; and this bifalleth ofte of anger and of Ire./ God seith: "Thow shalt nat take the name of thy Lord God in veyn or in ydel." Also oure Lord Jhesu Crist seith, by the word of Seint Mathew,/ "Ne wol ye nat swere in alle manere; neither by hevene, for it is Goddes trone; ne by erthe, for it is the bench of his feet; ne by Jerusalem, for it is the citee of a greet kyng; ne by thyn heed, for thou mayst nat make an heer whit ne blak./ But seyeth by youre word 'ye, ye,' and 'nay, nay'; and what that is moore, it is of yvel,"—thus seith Crist. [590] For Cristes sake, ne swereth nat so synfully in dismembrynge of Crist by soule, herte, bones, and body. For certes, it semeth that ye thynke that the cursede Jewes ne dismembred nat ynough the preciouse persone of Crist, but ye dismembre hym moore./ And if so be that the lawe compelle yow to swere, thanne rule yow after the lawe of God in youre swerying, as seith Jeremye, *quarto capitulo:* "Thou shalt kepe three condicions: thou shalt swere in trouthe, in doom, and in rightwisnesse."/ This is to seyn, thou shalt swere sooth; for every lesynge is agayns Crist. For Crist is verray trouthe. And thynk wel this, that every greet swerere, nat compelled lawefully to swere, the wounde shal nat departe from his hous whil he useth swich unleveful swerying./ Thou shalt sweren eek in doom, whan thou art constreyned by thy domesman to witnessen the trouthe./ Eek thow shalt nat swere for envye, ne for favour, ne for meede, but for rightwisnesse, for declarynge of it, to the worshipe of God and helpyng of thyne evene-Cristene. [595] And therfore every man that taketh Goddes name in ydel, or falsly swereth with his mouth, or elles taketh on hym the name of Crist, to be called a Cristen man, and lyveth agayns Cristes lyvynge and his techynge, alle they taken Goddes name in ydel./ Looke eek what seith Seint Peter, *Actuum, quarto, Non est aliud nomen sub celo, etc.,* "Ther nys noon oother name," seith Seint Peter, "under hevene yeven to men, in which they mowe

585. for: because of. compleccioun: temperament. corageous: lascivious. unto: until.
586. wrappen hem: envelop themselves. ne wol . . . hemself: do not wish to free themselves. wilfully: perversely. biknoweth: acknowledges, confesses.
587. expres agayn: directly opposed to. bifalleth of: occurs because of.
588. God seith: see Exodus xx.7. ydel: vain. Crist: see Matthew v.34–37.
589. alle: any. of his feet: for his feet. heed: head. heer: hair.
590. word: utterance. is of: comes from.
591. persone: body.
592. Jeremye: see Jeremiah iv.2. doom: court.
593. sooth: truly. lesynge: lie. verray: the real. thynk: consider. greet: frequent. swerere: see Ecclesiasticus xxiii.12. lawefully: by law. wounde: plague. useth: practices. unleveful: illicit.
594. sweren in doom: take an oath in court. domesman: judge.
595. meede: reward; bribery. evene-Cristene: fellow Christian.
596. ydel: vain. agayns: contrary to. lyvynge: way of life.
597. looke: consider. Seint Peter: see Acts iv.12. mowe: may.

be saved"; that is to seyn, but the name of Jhesu Crist./ Take kepe eek how precious is the name of Crist, as seith Seint Paul, *ad Philipenses, secundo, In nomine Jhesu, etc.,* "that in the name of Jhesu every knee of hevenely creatures, or erthely, or of helle sholde bowe"; for it is so heigh and so worshipful that the cursede feend in helle sholde tremblen to heeren it ynempned./ Thanne semeth it that men that sweren so horribly by his blessed name, that they despise it moore boldely than dide the cursede Jewes, or elles the devel, that trembleth whan he heereth his name./

Now certes, sith that sweryng, but if it be lawefully doon, is so heighly deffended, muche worse is forsweryng falsly, and yet nedelees. [600]

What seye we eek of hem that deliten hem in sweryng, and holden it a gentrie or a manly dede to swere grete othes? And what of hem that of verray usage ne cesse nat to swere grete othes, al be the cause nat worth a straw? Certes, this is horrible synne./ Swerynge sodeynly withoute avysement is eek a synne./

But lat us go now to thilke horrible sweryng of adjuracioun and conjuracioun, as doon thise false enchauntours or nigromanciens in bacyns ful of water, or in a bright swerd, in a cercle, or in a fyr, or in a shulderboon of a sheep./ I kan nat seye but that they doon cursedly and dampnably agayns Crist and al the feith of holy chirche./

What seye we of hem that bileeven on divynailes, as by flight or by noyse of briddes, or of beestes, or by sort, by nigromancie, by dremes, by chirkynge of dores, or crakkynge of houses, by gnawynge of rattes, and swich manere wrecchednesse? [605] Certes, al this thyng is deffended by God and by holy chirche. For which they been acursed, til they come to amendement, that on swich filthe setten hire bileeve./ Charmes for woundes or maladie of men or of beestes, if they taken any effect, it may be peraventure that God suffreth it, for folk sholden yeve the moore feith and reverence to his name./

Now wol I speke of lesynges, which generally is fals signyficaunce of word, in entente to deceyven his evene-Cristene./ Som lesynge is of which ther comth noon avantage to no wight; and som lesynge turneth to the ese or profit of o man, and to damage of another man./ Another lesynge is for to saven his lyf or his catel. Another lesynge comth of delit for to lye, in which delit they wol forge a long tale, and peynten it with alle circumstaunces, where al the ground of the tale is fals. [610] Som lesynge comth, for he wole sustene his word; and som lesynge comth of reccheleesnesse withouten avisement; and semblable thynges./

---

598. **kepe:** notice. **Seint Paul:** see Philippians ii.10. **feend:** see James ii.19. **ynempned:** mentioned.

599. **despise:** revile. **boldely:** blasphemously.

600. **heighly deffended:** strictly forbidden. **forsweryng:** swearing falsely, perjury.

601. **gentrie:** noble act. **of verray usage:** out of sheer habit. **cesse to swere:** stop swearing.

602. **avysement:** thinking.

603. **adjuracioun:** exorcism. **conjuracioun:** magic spell. **nigromanciens:** necromancers.

605. **on divynailes:** in divination. **sort:** lots. **nigromancie:** necromancy. **chirkynge:** creaking. **crakkynge:** creaking. **wrecchednesse:** contemptible matters.

606. **deffended:** forbidden. **come to amendement:** i.e., are converted to Christian living. **bileeve:** belief.

607. **suffreth:** allows. **for:** so that.

608. **lesynges:** lying. **evene-Cristene:** fellow Christian.

609. **ese:** benefit.

610. **catel:** property. **with alle circumstaunces:** in full detail. **ground:** basis.

611. **for he:** because a man. **sustene:** support. **reccheleesnesse:** carelessness. **avisement:** forethought.

Lat us now touche the vice of flaterye, which ne comth nat gladly but for drede or for coveitise./ Flaterye is generally wrongful preisynge. Flatereres ben the develes norices, that norissen his children with milk of losengerie./ For sothe, Salomon seith that "flaterie is wors than detraccioun." For somtyme detraccion maketh an hauteyn man be the moore humble, for he dredeth detraccion; but certes flaterye maketh a man to enhauncen his herte and his contenaunce./ Flatereres ben the develes enchauntours; for they make a man to wene of hymself be lyk that he nys nat lyk. [615] They been lyk to Judas that bitraysed a man to sellen hym to his enemy, that is to the devel./ Flatereres been the develes chapelleyns, that syngen evere *Placebo.*/ I rekene flaterie in the vices of Ire; for ofte tyme, if o man be wrooth with another, thanne wole he flatere som wight to sustene hym in his querele./

Speke we now of swich cursynge as comth of irous herte. Malisoun generally may be seyd every maner power of harm. Swich cursynge bireveth man fro the regne of God, as seith Seint Paul./ And ofte tyme swich cursynge wrongfully retorneth agayn to hym that curseth, as a bryd that retorneth agayn to his owene nest. [620] And over alle thyng men oghten eschewe to cursen hire children and yeven to the devel hire engendrure, as ferforth as in hem is. Certes, it is greet peril and greet synne./

Lat us thanne speken of chidynge and reproche, whiche ben ful grete woundes in mannes herte, for they unsowen the semes of frendshipe in mannes herte./ For certes, unnethes may a man pleynly ben accorded with hym that hath hym openly revyled and repreved and disclaundred. This is a ful grisly synne, as Crist seith in the gospel./ And taak kepe now, that he that repreveth his neighebor, outher he repreveth hym by som harm of peyne that he hath on his body, as "mesel," "croked harlot," or by som synne that he dooth./ Now if he repreve hym by harm of peyne, thanne turneth the repreve to Jhesu Crist, for peyne is sent by the rightwys sonde of God, and by his suffrance, be it meselrie, or maheym, or maladie. [625] And if he repreve hym uncharitably of synne, as "thou holour," "thou dronkelewe harlot," and so forth, thanne aperteneth that to the rejoysynge of the devel, that evere hath joye that men doon synne./ And certes, chidynge may nat come but out of a vileyns herte. For after the habundance of the herte speketh the mouth ful ofte./ And ye

---

612. ne . . . for: usually occurs only because of.

613. norices: nurses. norissen: nurse. losengerie: flattery, deceit.

614. hauteyn: haughty. enhauncen: make arrogant.

615. wene of hymself be: think himself to be.

617. *Placebo:* see Summoner's Tale, l. 2075, and note.

618. wrooth: angry. to sustene: i.e., so that he will support.

619. irous: angry. malisoun: malediction. seyd: said to be. bireveth: takes away. Seint Paul: see I Corinthians vi.10.

621. over: above. eschewe: avoid. engendrure: offspring. as ferforth as in hem is: as far as in them lies.

622. unsowen: unsew. semes: seams.

623. unnethes: not easily; hardly. pleynly: fully. ben accorded: become reconciled. repreved: reproached. disclaundred: slandered. grisly: horrible. Crist: see Matthew v.22.

624. kepe: notice. outher: either. harm: disease; injury; physical affliction. mesel: leper. croked: crippled. harlot: scoundrel.

625. repreve: reproach. rightwys: righteous. sonde: sending. meselrie: leprosy. maheym: mutilation.

626. holour: lecher. dronkelewe: drunken. aperteneth: appertains.

627. vileyns: wicked. For . . . ofte: see Matthew xii.34. after: according to: habundance: fullness.

shul understonde that looke, by any wey, whan any man shal chastise another, that he be war from chidynge or reprevynge. For trewely, but he be war, he may ful lightly quyken the fyr of angre and of wratthe, which that he sholde quenche, and peraventure sleeth hym, that he myghte chastise with benignitee./ For as seith Salomon, "The amyable tonge is the tree of lyf," that is to seyn, of lyf espirituel; and soothly, a deslavee tonge sleeth the spirites of hym that repreveth and eek of hym that is repreved./ Loo, what seith Seint Augustyn: "Ther is nothyng so lyk the develes child as he that ofte chideth." Seint Paul seith eek, "[The] servant of God bihoveth nat to chide." [630] And how that chidynge be a vileyns thyng bitwixe alle manere folk, yet is it certes moost uncovenable bitwixe a man and his wyf; for there is nevere reste. And therfore seith Salomon, "An hous that is uncovered and droppynge, and a chidynge wyf, ben lyke."/ A man that is in a droppynge hous in manye places, though he eschewe the droppynge in o place, it droppeth on hym in another place. So fareth it by a chydynge wyf; but she chide hym in o place, she wol chide hym in another./ And therfore, "bettre is a morsel of breed with joye than an hous ful of delices with chidynge," seith Salomon./ Seint Paul seith: "O ye wommen, be ye subgetes to youre housbondes as bihoveth in God, and ye men loveth youre wyves." *Ad Colossenses, tertio.*/

Afterward speke we of scornynge, which is a wikked synne, and namely whan he scorneth a man for his goode werkes. [635] For certes, swiche scorneres faren lyk the foule tode, that may nat endure to smelle the soote savour of the vyne whanne it florissheth./ Thise scorneres ben partyng felawes with the devel; for they han joye whan the devel wynneth, and sorwe whan he leseth./ They ben adversaries of Jhesu Crist, for they haten that he loveth, that is to seyn, salvacioun of soule./

Speke we now of wikked conseil; for he that wikked conseil yeveth is a traytour. For he deceyveth hym that trusteth in hym, *ut Achitofel ad Absolonem.* But nathelees, yet is his wikked conseil first agayn hymself./ For, as seith the wise man, "Every fals lyvynge hath this propertee in hymself, that he that wole anoye another man, he anoyeth first hymself." [640] And men shul understonde that man shal nat taken his conseil of fals folk, ne of angry folk, or grevous folk, ne of folk that loven specially to muchel hir owene profit, ne to muche worldly folk, namely in conseilynge of soules./

---

628. **looke whan:** whenever. **be war from:** beware of. **reprevynge:** reproaching. **lightly:** quickly, easily. **benignitee:** graciousness.

629. **Salomon:** see Proverbs xv.4. **amyable:** pleasing. **deslavee:** unwashed, foul; unrestrained, immoderate. **sleeth:** slays.

630. **Seint Paul:** see II Timothy ii.24. **bihoveth:** ought.

631. **vileyns:** evil. **uncovenable:** inappropriate. **there:** i.e., in chiding. **reste:** freedom from molestation. **Salomon:** see Proverbs xxvii.15. **droppynge:** leaking. **lyke:** alike.

632. **droppynge hous:** a house leaking. **eschewe:** avoid. **fareth it by:** it goes with.

633. **delices:** fine foods. **Salomon:** see Proverbs xvii.1.

634. **Seint Paul:** see Colossians iii.18–19. **subgetes to:** subordinates of. **bihoveth:** is proper. **in:** with respect to.

635. **namely:** especially.

636. **faren:** behave. **tode:** toad. **soote:** sweet.

637. **partyng felawes:** (sharing fellows) partners. **leseth:** loses.

638. **that he loveth:** what he loves.

639. **Achitofel:** see II Samuel xvii.1 (Vulgate, Liber Secundus Regum xvii.1). **agayn:** against.

640. **fals lyvynge:** evil liver. **propertee:** trait. **anoye:** injure.

641. **grevous:** hostile. **to muchel:** too much. **to muche worldly:** too worldly.

Now comth the synne of hem that sowen and maken discord amonges folk, which is a synne that Crist hateth outrely. And no wonder is; for he deyde for to make concord./ And moore shame do they to Crist, than dide they that hym crucifiede; for God loveth bettre that frendshipe be amonges folk, than he dide his owene body, which that he yaf for unitee. Therfore ben they likned to the devel, that evere is aboute to maken discord./

Now comth the synne of double tonge; swiche as speken faire byforn folk, and wikkedly bihynde; or elles they maken semblant as though they speke of good entencioun, or elles in game and pley, and yet they speke of wikked entente./

Now comth biwreying of conseil, thurgh which a man is defamed; certes, unnethe may he restore the damage. [645]

Now comth manace, that is an open folye; for he that ofte manaceth, he threteth moore than he may perfourne ful ofte tyme./

Now cometh ydel wordes, that is withouten profit of hym that speketh tho wordes, and eek of hym that herkneth tho wordes. Or elles ydel wordes ben tho that ben nedelees, or withouten entente of naturel profit./ And al be it that ydel wordes ben somtyme venial synne, yet sholde men douten hem, for we shul yeve rekenynge of hem bifore God./

Now comth janglynge, that may nat been withoute synne. And, as seith Salomon, "It is a sygne of apert folye."/ And therfore a philosophre seyde, whan men axed hym how men sholde plese the peple, and he answerde, "Do manye goode werkes, and spek fewe jangles." [650]

After this comth the synne of japeres, that ben the develes apes; for they maken folk to laughe at hire japerie as folk doon at the gawdes of an ape. Swiche japeres deffendeth Seint Paul./ Looke how that vertuouse wordes and holy conforten hem that travaillen in the service of Crist, right so conforten the vileyns wordes and knakkes of japeris hem that travaillen in the service of the devel./

Thise ben the synnes that comen of the tonge, that comen of Ire and of othere synnes./

Sequitur remedium contra peccatum Ire.

The remedie agayns Ire is a vertu that men clepen Mansuetude, that is Debonairetee; and eek another vertu, that men clepen Pacience or Suffrance./

Debonairetee withdraweth and refreyneth the stirynges and the moevynges of mannes corage in his herte, in swich manere that they ne skippe nat out by angre

---

642. **outrely:** utterly.

643. **is aboute to maken:** is busy making.

644. **faire:** pleasantly; approvingly. **semblant:** pretence. **speke of:** spoke with.

645. **biwreying:** betrayal. **conseil:** secrets. **unnethe:** not easily; hardly.

646. **manace:** threatening. **threteth:** threatens.

647. **ydel:** foolish; sinful. **naturel:** ordinary.

648. **douten:** fear. **rekenynge:** see Matthew xii.36.

649. **janglynge:** chattering. **Salomon:** see Ecclesiastes v.2.

650. **jangles:** idle words.

651. **japeres:** jesters. **japerie:** jesting speech. **gawdes:** pranks. **deffendeth:** forbids. **Seint Paul:** see Ephesians v.4.

652. **looke how that:** just as. **travaillen:** work. **vileyns:** evil. **knakkes:** tricks.

654. **mansuetude:** meekness. **debonairetee:** humility. **suffrance:** long-suffering.

655. **withdraweth:** restrains. **refreyneth:** represses. **corage:** desire. **skippe:** leap. **by:** through the agency of.

ne by ire. [655] Suffrance suffreth swetely alle the anoyaunces and the wronges that men doon to man outward./ Seint Jerome seith thus of debonairetee, that "it dooth noon harm to no wight ne seith; ne for noon harm that men doon ne seyn, he ne eschawfeth nat agayns his resoun."/ This vertu somtyme comth of nature; for, as seith the philosophre, "A man is a quyk thyng, by nature debonaire and tretable to goodnesse; but whan debonairetee is enformed of grace, thanne is it the moore worth."/

Pacience, that is another remedie agayns Ire, is a vertu that suffreth swetely every mannes goodnesse, and is nat wrooth for noon harm that is doon to hym./ The philosophre seith that pacience is thilke vertu that suffreth debonairely alle the outrages of adversitee and every wikked word. [660] This vertu maketh a man lyk to God, and maketh hym Goddes owene deere child, as seith Crist. This vertu disconfiteth thyn enemy. And therfore seith the wise man, "If thow wolt venquysse thyn enemy, lerne to suffre."/ And thou shalt understonde that man suffreth foure manere of grevances in outward thynges, agayns the whiche foure he moot have foure manere of paciences./

The firste grevance is of wikkede wordes. Thilke suffrede Jhesu Crist withouten grucchyng, ful paciently, whan the Jewes despised hym and repreved hym ful ofte./ Suffre thou therfore paciently; for the wise man seith, "If thou stryve with a fool, though the fool be wrooth or though he laughe, algate thou shalt have no reste."/ That oother grevance outward is to have damage of thy catel. Theragayns suffred Crist ful paciently, whan he was despoyled of al that he hadde in this lyf, and that nas but his clothes. [665] The thridde grevance is a man to have harm in his body. That suffred Crist ful paciently in al his passioun./ The fourthe grevance is in outrageous labour in werkes. Wherfore I seye that folk that maken hir servantz to travaillen to grevously, or out of tyme, as on haly dayes, soothly they do greet synne./ Heer-agayns suffred Crist ful paciently and taughte us pacience, whan he baar upon his blissed shulder the croys upon which he sholde suffren despitous deth./

Heere may men lerne to be pacient; for certes noght oonly Cristen men ben pacient, for the love of Jhesu Crist, and for gerdoun of the blisful lyf that is perdurable, but certes, the olde payens that nevere were Cristene, commendeden and useden the vertu of pacience./

A philosophre upon a tyme, that wolde have beten his disciple for his grete trespas, for which he was greetly amoeved, and broghte a yerde to scoure the

---

656. outward: i.e., to the body or person (as opposed to the mind or spirit).

657. eschawfeth: becomes inflamed.

658. quyk: perceptive. thyng: being. tretable: amenable. enformed of: perfected by.

659. suffreth: permits.

660. suffreth: endures. debonairely: graciously; humbly.

661. Goddes child: i.e., a good Christian. Crist: see Matthew v.9. disconfiteth: vanquishes. wise man: see Dionysius Cato, Disticha de Moribus i.38. suffre: endure.

663. grucchyng: complaint. despised: reviled. repreved: reproached.

664. wise man: see Proverbs xxix.9. algate: nevertheless.

665. catel: property. Crist: see Matthew xxvii.35.

666. a man: for a man. harm: suffering.

667. outrageous: excessive. to grevously: too hard. tyme: proper time. greet: great.

668. croys: cross. despitous: cruel.

669. gerdoun: reward. payens: pagans.

670. beten: beaten. disciple: pupil. greetly amoeved: greatly provoked. yerde: stick. scoure: scourge, beat.

child; [670] and whan the child saugh the yerde, he seyde to his maister, "What thenke ye to do?" "I wol bete thee," quod the maister, "for thy correccioun."/ "For sothe," quod the child, "ye oghten first correcte yourself, that han lost al youre pacience for the gilt of a child."/ "For sothe," quod the maister al wepynge, "thow seyst sooth. Have thow the yerde, my deere sone, and correcte me for myn inpacience."/

Of pacience comth obedience, thurgh which a man is obedient to Crist and to alle hem to whiche he oghte to ben obedient in Crist./ And understond wel that obedience is perfit, whan that a man dooth gladly and hastily, with good herte entierly, all that he sholde do. [675] Obedience generally is to perfourne the doctrine of God and of his sovereyns, to whiche hym oghte to ben obeisaunt in alle rightwisnesse./

Sequitur de Accidia.

After the synnes of Envye and Ire, now wol I speken of the synne of Accidie. For Envye blyndeth the herte of a man, and Ire troubleth a man, and Accidie maketh hym hevy, thoghtful, and wraw./ Envye and Ire maken bitternesse in herte, which bitternesse is moder of Accidie, and bynymeth hym the love of alle goodnesse. Thanne is Accidie the angwissh of a trouble herte; and Seint Augustyn seith, "It is anoy of goodnesse and ioye of harm."/ Certes, this is a dampnable synne; for it dooth wrong to Jhesu Crist, in as muche as it bynymeth the service that men oghte doon to Crist with alle diligence, as seith Salomon./ But Accidie dooth no swich diligence. He dooth alle thyng with anoy, and with wrawnesse, slaknesse, and excusacioun, and with ydelnesse, and unlust; for which the book seith, "Acursed be he that dooth the service of God necligently." [680]

Thanne is Accidie enemy to everich estaat of man; for certes, the estaat of man is in three maneres./ Outher it is th'estaat of innocence, as was th'estaat of Adam biforn that he fil into synne; in which estaat he was holden to wirche as in heriynge and adowrynge of God./ Another estaat is the estaat of synful men, in which estaat men ben holden to laboure in preiynge to God for amendement of hire synnes, and that he wole graunte hem to risen out of hir synnes./ Another estaat is th'estaat of grace; in which estaat he is holden to werkes of penitence. And certes, to alle thise thynges is Accidie enemy and contrarie, for he loveth no bisynesse at al./ Now certes, this foule synne, Accidie, is eek a ful greet enemy to the liflode of the body; for it ne hath no purveaunce agayn temporel necessitee; for it forsleweth and for-

---

672. **correcte:** set right by punishment. **gilt:** offense.

675. **gladly:** willingly. **hastily:** eagerly.

676. **his:** i.e., one's. **obeisaunt:** obedient.

677. **accidie:** sloth. **hevy:** sluggish, indolent. **thoghtful:** moody. **wraw:** peevish; perverse.

678. **bynymeth hym:** takes away from one. **angwissh:** anxiety. **trouble:** troubled. **Seint Augustyn:** see line 484 and note, above. **anoy:** affliction.

679. **bynymeth:** takes away. **Salomon:** cf. Ecclesiastes ix.10.

680. **anoy:** displeasure. **wrawnesse:** perverseness. **excusacioun:** apology. **unlust:** disinclination to be active. **the book:** cf. Jeremiah xlviii.10.

681. **estaat of man:** period or state of man's existence. **maneres:** modes.

682. **outher:** either. **estaat:** period; state, condition. **fil:** fell. **holden:** constrained. **wirche:** work. **heriynge:** worship.

684. **holden:** bound. **bisynesse:** activity.

685. **liflode:** livelihood, sustenance. **purveaunce:** provision. **agayn:** in respect to. **forsleweth:** loses by sloth. **forsluggeth:** neglects through sluggishness

sluggeth and destroyeth alle goodes temporels by reccheleesnesse. [685]

The fourthe thyng is that Accidie is lyk hem that ben in the peyne of helle, by cause of hir slouthe and of hir hevynesse; for they that been dampned ben so bounde that they ne may neither wel do ne wel thynke./

Of Accidie comth first, that a man is anoyed and encombred for to doon any goodnesse, and maketh that God hath abhomynacion of swich Accidie, as seith Seint John./

Now comth Slouthe, that wol nat suffre noon hardnesse ne no penaunce. For soothly, Slouthe is so tendre and so delicat, as seith Salomon, that he wol nat suffre noon hardnesse ne penaunce, and therfore he shendeth al that he dooth./

Agayns this roten-herted synne of Accidie and Slouthe sholde men exercise hem-self to doon goode werkes, and manly and vertuously cacchen corage wel to doon, thynkynge that oure Lord Jhesu Crist quiteth every good dede, be it never so lite./ Usage of labour is a greet thyng, for it maketh, as seith Seint Bernard, the laborer to have stronge armes and harde synwes; and slouthe maketh hem feble and tendre. [690]

Thanne comth drede to bigynne to werke any goode werkes. For certes, he that is enclyned to synne, hym thynketh it is so greet an emprise for to undertake to doon werkes of goodnesse,/ and casteth in his herte that the circumstaunces of good-nesse ben so grevouse and so chargeaunt for to suffre, that he dar nat undertake to do werkes of goodnesse, as seith Seint Gregorie./

Now comth wanhope, that is despeir of the mercy of God, that comth somtyme of to muche outrageous sorwe, and somtyme of to muche drede, ymaginynge that he hath doon so muche synne that it wol nat availlen hym, though he wolde re-penten hym and forsake synne;/ thurgh which despeir or drede he abaundoneth al his herte to every maner synne, as seith Seint Augustin./ Which dampnable synne, if that it continue unto his ende, it is cleped synnyng in the Holy Goost. [695] This horrible synne is so perilous that he that is despeired, ther nys no felonye ne no synne that he douteth for to do; as shewed wel by Judas./ Certes, aboven alle synnes thanne is this synne moost displesant to Crist, and moost adversarie./ Soothly, he that despeireth hym is lyk the coward champioun recreant, that seith "creant" withoute nede, allas! allas! nedeles is he recreant and nedelees despeired./ Certes, the mercy of God is evere redy to the penitent, and is aboven alle his werkes./

---

685. reccheleesnesse: negligent carelessness.

686. slouthe: sloth. hevynesse: indolence.

687. is anoyed: feels weary; is reluctant. encombred: hindered. Seint John: cf. Revelation iii.16.

688. delicat: sensitive. Salomon: cf. Proverbs xviii.9; xx.4; xxi.25. hardnesse: hardship. shendeth: ruins.

689. manly: manfully. cacchen: take, get. thynkynge: calling to mind. quiteth: requites. lite: little.

690. usage: the habit. synwes: sinews.

691. werke: do. emprise: enterprise.

692. casteth: considers. chargeaunt: burdensome. for to suffre: to bear.

693. wanhope: hopelessness. to muche: too great. drede: fear.

694. Seint Augustin: cf. *De Natura et Gratia* cap. 35; *Sermo* xx.§3.

696. douteth: is afraid; hesitates. shewed: was shown.

697. displesant: offensive. adversarie: hostile.

698. despeireth hym: despairs. recreant: confessing oneself to be vanquished; cowardly. seith "creant": cries mercy; surrenders.

Allas! kan nat a man bithynke hym on the gospel of Seint Luc, 15, where as Crist seith that "as wel shal ther be joye in hevene upon a synful man that dooth penitence, as upon nynety and nyne rightful men that neden no penitence." [700] Looke forther, in the same gospel, the joye and the feeste of the goode man that hadde lost his sone, whan his sone with repentaunce was retourned to his fader./ Kan they nat remembren hem eek that, as seith Seint Luc, 23, how that the theef that was hanged bisyde Jhesu Crist, seyde: "Lord, remembre of me, whan thow comest into thy regne."/ "For sothe," seyde Crist, "I seye to thee, to-day shaltow be with me in paradys."/ Certes, ther is noon so horrible synne of man that it ne may in his lyf be destroyed by penitence, thurgh vertu of the passion and of the deeth of Crist./ Allas! what nedeth man thanne to ben despeired, sith that his mercy so redy is and large? Axe and have. [705]

Thanne cometh sompnolence, that is, sloggy slombrynge, which maketh a man be hevy and dul in body and in soule; and this synne comth of Slouthe./ And certes, the tyme that, by wey of resoun, men sholde nat slepe, that is by the morwe, but if ther were cause resonable./ For soothly, the morwe tyde is moost covenable a man to seye his preyeres, and for to thynken on God, and for to honoure God, and to yeven almesse to the povre that first cometh in the name of Crist./ Lo, what seith Salomon: "Whoso wol by the morwe awaken and seke me, he shal fynde."/

Thanne cometh necligence, or reccheleesnesse, that rekketh of no thyng. And how that ignoraunce be moder of alle harm, certes, necligence is the norice. [710] Necligence ne doth no fors, whan he shal doon a thyng, wheither he do it wel or baddely./

Of the remedie of thise two synnes, as seith the wise man, that "he that dredeth God, he spareth nat to doon that him oghte to doon."/ And he that loveth God, he wol doon diligence to plese God by his werkes, and abaundone hymself, with al his myght, wel for to doon./

Thanne comth ydelnesse, that is the yate of alle harmes. An ydel man is lyk to a place that hath no walles; the develes may entre on every syde, or sheten at hym at discovert, by temptacion on every syde./ This ydelnesse is the thurrok of alle wikked and vileyns thoughtes, and of alle jangles, trufles, and of alle ordure. [715] Certes, the hevene is yeven to hem that wol labouren, and nat to ydel folk. Eek David seith that "they ne be nat in the labour of men, ne they shul nat been

---

700. **bithynke hym on:** call to mind. **Seint Luc, 15:** verse 7.
701. **looke:** consider. **the same gospel:** verses 22–24. **feeste:** feast. **was retourned:** had returned.
702. **Seint Luc, 23:** verses 42–43. **regne:** kingdom.
705. **large:** generous. **axe:** ask; see Matthew vii.7; John xvi.24.
706. **sloggy:** sluggish. **hevy:** indolent.
707. **by the morwe:** in the morning.
708. **mowre tyde:** morning time. **covenable:** suitable. **almesse:** alms.
709. **Salomon:** see Proverbs viii.17.
710. **reccheleesnesse:** carelessness. **rekketh:** recks, cares. **how:** howsoever. **harm:** evil. **norice:** nurse.
711. **ne doth no fors:** has no regard for.
712. **wise man:** see Ecclesiastes vii.18 (Vulgate 19). **that him:** what he.
713. **doon diligence:** make an effort. **abaundone hymself:** devote himself fully.
714. **yate:** gate. **harmes:** sins. **sheten:** shoot. **at discovert:** (when he is) unprotected.
715. **thurrok:** bilge. **vileyns:** evil. **jangles:** chatter. **trufles:** trifles. **ordure:** filth.
716. **hevene:** cf. Matthew xi.12. **David:** see Psalms lxxiii.5 (Vulgate, lxxii.5). **be in:** partake of.

whipped with men," that is to seyn, in purgatorie./ Certes, thanne semeth it, they shul be tormented with the devel in helle, but if they doon penitence./

Thanne comth the synne that men clepen *tarditas,* as whan a man is to laterede or tariynge, er he wole turne to God; and certes, that is a greet folie. He is lyk hym that falleth in the dych, and wol nat arise./ And this vice comth of a fals hope, that he thynketh that he shal lyve longe; but that hope faileth ful ofte./

Thanne comth lachesse; that is he, that whan he biginneth any good werk, anon he wol forleten it and stynten; as doon they that han any wight to governe, and ne taken of hym namoore kepe, anon as they fynden any contrarie or any anoy. [720] Thise ben the newe sheepherdes that leten hir sheep wityngly go renne to the wolf that is in the breres, or do no fors of hir owene governaunce./ Of this comth poverte and destruccioun, bothe of spiritueel and temporel thynges.

Thanne comth a manere cooldnesse, that freseth al the herte of man./

Thanne comth undevocioun, thurgh which a man is so blent, as seith Seint Bernard, and hath swich langour in soule that he may neither rede ne singe in holy chirche, ne heere ne thynke of no devocioun, ne travaille with his handes in no good werk, that it nys to hym unsavory and al apalled./ Thanne wexeth he slough and slombry, and soone wol be wrooth, and soone is enclyned to hate and to envye./

Thanne comth the synne of worldly sorwe, swich as is cleped *tristicia,* that sleeth man, as seith Seint Paul. [725] For certes, swich sorwe werketh to the deeth of the soule and of the body also; for therof comth that a man is anoyed of his owene lif./ Wherfore swich sorwe shorteth ful ofte the lif of a man, er that his tyme be come by wey of kynde./

Remedium contra peccatum Accidie.

Agayns this horrible synne of Accidie, and the branches of the same, ther is a vertu that is called *fortitudo* or strengthe, that is an affeccioun thurgh which a man despiseth anoyouse thinges./ This vertu is so myghty and so vigorous that it dar withstonde myghtily and wisely kepen hymself fro perils that ben wikked, and wrastle agayn the assautes of the devel./ For it enhaunceth and enforceth the soule, right as Accidie abateth it and maketh it fieble. For this *fortitudo* may endure by long suffraunce the travailles that been covenable. [730]

This vertu hath manye speces; the firste is cleped magnanimitee, that is to seyn, greet corage. For certes, ther bihoveth greet corage agayns Accidie, lest that it ne

---

716. with: by.

718. to laterede: too tardy. tariynge: delaying.

720. lachesse: laziness. forleten: neglect. stynten: stop. anon as: as soon as. contrarie: hostile act. anoy: annoyance.

721. newe: modern. leten wityngly: deliberately allow. renne: run. breres: briers. do no fors: take no heed of. governaunce: guardianship; behavior.

722. freseth: freezes.

723. undevocioun: lack of devotion. blent: blinded. rede: read. heere: hear. travaille: labor. unsavory: unpleasant. apalled: distasteful.

724. slough: sluggish. slombry: slumbrous.

725. sleeth: slays. Seint Paul: see II Corinthians vii.10.

726. anoyed: weary.

727. by wey of kynde: naturally.

728. affeccioun: disposition. anoyouse: harmful.

729. withstonde: offer opposition. kepen: guard. assautes: assaults.

730. enhaunceth: uplifts. enforceth: strengthens. abateth: casts down. long suffraunce: long-suffering. travailles: hardships. covenable: fitting.

731. greet corage: great courage. bihoveth: is needed.

swolwe the soule by the synne of sorwe, or destroye it by wanhope./ This vertu
maketh folk undertake harde thynges and grevouse thynges, by hir owene wil,
wisely and resonably./ And for as muchel as the devel fighteth agayns a man
moore by queyntise and by sleighte than by strengthe, therfore a man shal with-
stonden hym by wit and by resoun and by discrecioun./ Thanne arn ther the ver-
tues of feith and hope in God and in his seintes, to acheve and acomplice the goode
werkes in the whiche he purposeth fermely to continue./ Thanne comth seuretee or
sikernesse; and that is whan a man ne douteth no travaille in tyme comynge of the
goode werkes that a man hath bigonne. [735] Thanne comth magnificence, that is
to seyn, whan a man dooth and perfourneth grete werkes of goodnesse; and that
is the ende why that men sholde do goode werkes, for in the acomplissynge of grete
goode werkes lith the grete gerdoun./ Thanne is ther constaunce, that is, stablenesse
of corage; and this sholde ben in herte by stedefast feith, and in mouth, and in
berynge, and in chiere, and in dede./ Eke ther ben mo speciale remedies against
Accidie in diverse werkes, and in consideracioun of the peynes of helle and of the
joyes of hevene, and in the trust of the grace of the Holy Goost, that wole yeve
hym mygt to perfourne his goode entente./

Sequitur de Avaricia.

After Accidie wol I speke of Avarice and of Coveitise, of which synne seith Seint
Paul that "the roote of alle harmes is Coveitise." *Ad Thimotheum, sexto.*/ For
soothly, whan the herte of a man is confounded in itself and troubled, and that the
soule hath lost the confort of God, thanne seketh he an ydel solas of worldly
thynges. [740]

Avarice, after the descripcioun of Seint Augustyn, is a likerousnesse in herte to
have erthely thynges./ Som oother folk seyn that Avarice is for to purchacen manye
erthely thynges, and no thyng yeve to hem that han nede./ And understond that
Avarice ne stant nat oonly in lond ne catel, but somtyme in science and in glorie,
and in every manere of outrageous thynges is Avarice and Coveitise./ And the
difference bitwixe Avarice and Coveitise is this: Coveitise is for to coveite swiche
thynges as thou hast nat; and Avarice is for to withholde and kepe swiche thynges
as thou hast, withoute rightful nede./ Soothly, this Avarice is a synne that is ful
dampnable; for al holy writ curseth it, and speketh agayns that vice; for it dooth
wrong to Jhesu Crist. [745] For it bireveth hym the love that men to hym owen,
and turneth it bakward agayns alle resoun,/ and maketh that the avaricious man
hath moore hope in his catel than in Jhesu Crist, and dooth moore observance in

---

731. **swolwe:** swallow. **wanhope:** despair.

732. **grevouse:** difficult.

733. **queyntise:** cunning, craft. **sleighte:** trickery. **withstonden:** offer opposition to. **wit:** intel-
ligence.

734. **arn:** are.

735. **seuretee:** confidence. **sikernesse:** sense of security. **douteth:** fears. **travaille:** hardship.
tyme comynge: the future. **of:** in connection with.

736. **magnificence:** great well-doing. **lith:** lies. **gerdoun:** reward.

737. **constaunce:** constancy. **corage:** spirit. **berynge:** bearing.

739. **Seint Paul:** see I Timothy vi.10. **harmes:** evils.

740. **confounded:** encumbered. **ydel:** empty. **solas:** solace.

741. **Seint Augustyn:** see *Enarratio in Psalmum xxxi* part ii.§5. **likerousnesse:** keen eagerness.

742. **purchacen:** acquire. **no thyng:** not at all.

743. **stant:** (standeth) stands. **catel:** goods. **science:** knowledge. **outrageous:** excessive.

746. **bireveth:** takes from.

kepynge of his tresor than he dooth to the service of Jhesu Crist./ And therfore seith Seint Paul *ad Ephesios, quinto,* that an avaricious man is in the thraldom of ydolatrie./

What difference is bitwixe an ydolastre and an avaricious man, but that an ydolastre, per aventure, ne hath but o mawmet or two, and the avaricious man hath manye? For certes, every floryn in his cofre is his mawmet./ And certes, the synne of mawmettrie is the firste thyng that God deffended in the ten comaundementz, as bereth witnesse in *Exodi capitulo vicesimo.* [750] "Thou shalt have no false goddes bifore me, ne thou shalt make to thee no grave thyng." Thus is an avaricious man, that loveth his tresor biforn God, an ydolastre,/ thurgh his cursed synne of avarice.

Of Coveitise comen thise harde lordshipes, thurgh whiche men ben distreyned by taylages, custumes, and cariages, moore than hire duetee or resoun is. And eek taken they of hire bonde-men amercimentz, whiche myghten moore resonably ben cleped extorcions than amercimentz./ Of whiche amercimentz and raunsonynge of bonde-men somme lordes stywardes seyn that it is rightful, for as muche as a cherl hath no temporel thyng that it ne is his lordes, as they seyn./ But certes, thise lordshipes doon wrong that bireven hire bondefolk thynges that they nevere yave hem. *Augustinus, de Civitate, libro nono./*

Sooth is that the condicioun of thraldom and the firste cause of thraldom is for synne. *Genesis, nono.* [755] Thus may ye seen that the gilt disserveth thraldom, but nat nature./ Wherfore thise lordes ne sholde nat muche glorifien hem in hir lordshipes, sith that by naturel condicion they ben nat lordes over thralles, but that thraldom comth first by the desert of synne./ And forther over, ther as the lawe seith that temporel goodes of bonde-folk ben the goodes of hir lordshipes, ye, that is for to understonde, the goodes of the emperour, to deffenden hem in hir right, but nat to robben hem ne reven hem./ And therfore seith Seneca, "Thy prudence sholde lyve benignely with thy thralles."/ Thilke that thou clepest thy thralles ben Goddes peple; for humble folk ben Cristes freendes; they ben contubernyal with the Lord. [760]

Thynk eek that of swich seed as cherles spryngen, of swich seed spryngen lordes. As wel may the cherl be saved as the lord./ The same deeth that taketh the cherl, swich deeth taketh the lord. Wherfore I rede, do right so with thy cherl, as thou

---

748. **Seint Paul:** see Ephesians v.5. **the thraldom of:** bondage to.

749. **ydolastre:** worshiper of idols. **o mawmet:** one idol. **cofre:** coffer.

750. **mawmettrie:** idolatry. **firste thyng:** see Exodus xx.3-4. **deffended:** prohibited.

751. **grave:** graven.

752. **harde:** severe. **distreyned:** oppressed. **taylages:** taxes. **custumes:** customs duties. **cariages:** tolls. **duetee:** obligation. **resoun:** i.e., reasonable. **bonde-men:** tenants; villeins; serfs. **amercimentz:** arbitrary fines.

753. **raunsonynge:** oppressing with exactions.

754. **bireven:** seize from. **yave:** gave. **Augustinus:** see *De Civitate Dei* xix.15.

755. **for synne:** because of sin. **Genesis:** see ix.18-27.

756. **gilt:** sin.

757. **by the desert of:** by reason of.

758. **reven:** despoil.

759-63. Cf. Seneca, *Epistola* xlvii. **benignely:** kindly.

760. **contubernyal:** intimate, familiar.

761. **of:** from. **cherles:** serfs.

762. **rede:** counsel.

woldest that thy lord dide with thee, if thou were in his plit./ Every synful man is a cherl to synne. I rede thee, certes, that thou, lord, werke in swich wise with thy cherles that they rather love thee than drede thee./ I woot wel ther is degree above degree, as reson is; and skile is that men do hir devoir ther as it is due; but certes, extorcions and despit of youre underlynges is dampnable./

And forther over, understoond wel that conquerours or tirauntz maken ful ofte thralles of hem that ben born of as roial blood as ben they that hem conqueren. [765] This name of thraldom was nevere erst kouth, til that Noe seyde that his sone Canaan sholde be thral to his bretheren for his synne./

What seye we thanne of hem that pilen and doon extorcions to holy chirche? Certes, the swerd that men yeven first to a knyght, whan he is newe dubbed, signifieth that he sholde deffenden holy chirche, and nat robben it ne pilen it; and whoso dooth is traitour to Crist./ And, as seith Seint Augustyn, "they ben the develes wolves that stranglen the sheep of Jhesu Crist"; and doon worse than wolves./ For soothly, whan the wolf hath ful his wombe, he stynteth to strangle sheep. But soothly, the pilours and destroyours of goodes of holy chirche ne do nat so, for they ne stynte nevere to pile./

Now as I have seyd, sith so is that synne was first cause of thraldom, thanne is it thus, that thilke tyme that al this world was in synne, thanne was al this world in thraldom and subjeccioun. [770] But certes, sith the time of grace cam, God ordeyned that som folk sholde be moore heigh in estaat and in degree, and som folk moore lough, and that everich sholde be served in his estaat./ And therfore in somme contrees, ther they byen thralles, whan they han turned hem to the feith, they maken hire thralles free out of thraldom. And therfore, certes, the lord oweth to his man that the man oweth to his lord./ The Pope calleth hymself servant of the servantz of God; but for as muche as the estaat of holy chirche ne myghte nat han be, ne the commune profit myghte nat han be kept, ne pees and rest in erthe, but if God hadde ordeyned that some men hadde hyer degree and som men lower,/ therfore was sovereyntee ordeyned, to kepe and mayntene and deffenden hire underlynges or hire subgetz in resoun, as ferforth as it lith in hire power, and nat to destroyen hem ne confounde./ Wherfore I seye that thilke lordes that ben lyk wolves, that devouren the possessiouns or the catel of povre folk wrongfully, withouten mercy or mesure, [775] they shul receyven, by the same mesure that they han mesured to povre folk, the mercy of Jhesu Crist, but if it be amended./

Now comth deceite bitwixe marchaunt and marchant. And thow shalt understonde that marchandise is in manye maneres; that oon is bodily, and that oother is goostly; that oon is honest and leveful, and that oother is deshonest and unleve-

---

762. plit: plight.

764. reson: i.e., reasonable. skile: i.e., right. devoir: duty. despit: contempt.

766. kouth: known. Noe: see Genesis ix.25–27.

767. pilen: rob, pillage.

769. wombe: belly. stynteth: ceases. pilours: pillagers.

771. lough: low. in his estaat: according to his rank.

772. byen: buy. thralles: slaves. turned: converted. that: that which, what.

773. servant: slave. han be: have been established. han be kept: have been preserved.

774. subgetz: subjects. in resoun: according to reason. as ferforth as: as far as. lith: (lieth) lies. confounde: harass.

775. catel: goods. mesure: moderation.

776. mesure: measure. mesured: meted out. it be amended: they make amends.

777. marchandise: buying and selling. bodily: material. goostly: spiritual. leveful: lawful.

ful./ Of thilke bodily marchandise that is leveful and honest is this: that, there as God hath ordeyned that a regne or a contree is suffisaunt to hymself, thanne is it honest and leveful that of habundaunce of this contree, that men helpe another contree that is moore nedy./ And therfore ther moote ben marchantz to bryngen fro that o contree to that oother hire marchandise./ That oother marchandise, that men haunten with fraude and trecherie and deceite, with lesynges and false othes, is cursed and dampnable. [780]

Espirituel marchandise is proprely symonye, that is, ententif desir to byen thyng espirituel, that is, thyng that aperteneth to the seintuarie of God and to cure of the soule./ This desir, if so be that a man do his diligence to parfournen it, al be it that his desir ne take noon effect, yet is it to hym a deedly synne; and if he be ordred, he is irreguler./ Certes symonye is cleped of Simon Magus, that wolde han boght for temporel catel the yifte that God hadde yeven, by the Holy Goost, to Seint Peter and to the apostles./ And therfore understond that bothe he that selleth and he that beyeth thynges espirituels been cleped symonyals, be it by catel, be it by procurynge, or by flesshly preyere of his freendes, flesshly freendes, or spirituel freendes./ Flesshly in two maneres; as by kynrede, or othere freendes. Soothly, if they praye for hym that is nat worthy and able, it is symonye, if he take the bene-fice; and if he be worthy and able, ther nys noon. [785] That oother manere is whan man or womman preyen for folk to avauncen hem, oonly for wikked flesshly affec-cioun that they han unto the persone; and that is foul symonye./ But certes, in service, for which men yeven thynges espirituels unto hir servantz, it moot ben understonde that the service moot ben honest, and elles nat; and eek that it be withouten bargaynynge, and that the persone be able./ For, as seith Seint Damasie, "Alle the synnes of the world, at regard of this synne, arn as thyng of noght." For it is the gretteste synne that may be, after the synne of Lucifer and of Antecrist./ For by this synne God forleseth the chirche and the soule that he boghte with his precious blood, by hem that yeven chirches to hem that ben nat digne./ For they putten in theves that stelen the soules of Jhesu Crist and destroyen his patri-moyne. [790] By swiche undigne preestes and curates han lewed men the lasse rev-erence of the sacramentz of holy chirche; and swiche yeveres of chirches putten out

---

778. **regne:** kingdom. **hymself:** itself.

779. **marchandise:** goods.

780. **marchandise:** buying and selling. **haunten:** practice. **lesynges:** lies.

781. **symonye:** simony, the buying or selling of ecclesiastical preferments, benefices, or emolu-ments. **ententif:** eager. **seintuarie:** sanctuary. **cure of the soule:** responsibility for spirituai welfare.

782. **do his diligence:** exert himself to the utmost. **parfournen:** fulfill. **ordred:** in holy orders; ordained. **irreguler:** disqualified.

783. **cleped of:** named after. **Simon Magus:** see Acts viii.17–24. **for:** with. **catel:** goods.

784. **beyeth:** buys. **symonyals:** simoniacs. **procurynge:** contriving. **flesshly:** earthly, worldly. **preyere:** entreaty. **spirituel:** ecclesiastical.

785. **kynrede:** kindred.

786. **folk:** i.e., a person. **to avauncen hem:** to be preferred to a benefice.

787. **moot:** must. **honest:** righteous. **bargaynynge:** fraudulent dealings. **able:** worthy.

788. **Seint Damasie:** Pope Damasus I (336–84); cf. St. Jerome, *Contra Hierosolymitanum* §8. **at regard of:** in comparison with. **arn:** are.

789. **forleseth:** loses completely. **boghte:** redeemed. **digne:** worthy.

790. **patrimoyne:** patrimony.

791. **by:** through. **undigne:** unworthy. **lewed:** ignorant. **yeveres:** givers.

the children of Crist, and putten into the chirche the develes owene sone./ They sellen the soules that lambes sholde kepen to the wolf that strangleth hem. And therfore shul they nevere han part of the pasture of lambes, that is the blisse of hevene./

Now comth hasardrie with his apurtenaunces, as tables and rafles, of which comth deceite, false othes, chidynges, and alle ravynes, blasphemynge and reneiynge of God, and hate of his neighebores, wast of goodes, mysspendynge of tyme, and somtyme manslaughtre./ Certes, hasardours ne mowe nat ben withouten greet synne whiles they haunte that craft./

Of Avarice comen eek lesynges, thefte, fals witnesse, and false othes. And ye shul understonde that thise ben grete synnes, and expres agayn the comaundementz of God, as I have seyd. [795]

Fals witnesse is in word and eek in dede. In word, as for to bireve thy neighebores goode name by thy fals witnessyng, or bireven hym his catel or his heritage by thy fals witnessyng, whan thou for ire, or for meede, or for envye, berest fals witnesse, or accusest hym or excusest hym by thy fals witnesse, or elles excusest thyself falsly./ Ware yow, questemongeres and notaries! Certes, for fals witnessyng was Susanna in ful gret sorwe and peyne, and many another mo./

The synne of thefte is eek expres agayns Goddes heeste, and that in two maneres, corporel or spirituel./ Corporel, as for to take thy neighebores catel agayn his wyl, be it by force or by sleighte, be it by met or by mesure;/ by stelyng eek of false enditementz upon hym, and in borwynge of thy neighebores catel, in entente nevere to payen and semblable thynges. [800] Espirituel thefte is sacrilege, that is to seyn, hurtynge of holy thynges, or of thynges sacred to Crist, in two maneres: by reson of the holy place, as chirches or chirche-hawes,/ for which every vileyns synne that men doon in swich places may be cleped sacrilege, or every violence in the semblable places; also, they that withdrawen falsly the rightes that longen to holy chirche./ And pleynly and generally, sacrilege is to reven holy thyng fro holy place, or unholy thyng out of holy place, or holy thing out of unholy place./

Relevacio contra peccatum Avaricie.

Now shul ye understonde that the releevynge of Avarice is misericorde, and pitee largely taken. And men myghten axe why that misericorde and pitee is releevynge of Avarice./ Certes, the avaricious man sheweth no pitee ne misericorde to the

---

792. **they that lambes sholde kepen:** those who ought to protect lambs. **han part of:** share.
793. **hasardrie:** gambling. **tables:** backgammon. **rafles:** a game played with three dice. **othes:** oaths. **chidynges:** quarrels. **ravynes:** robberies. **reneiynge:** renouncing.
794. **haunte:** practice.
795. **lesynges:** lies. **expres agayn:** directly opposed to.
796. **bireve:** take away. **bireven hym:** take away from him. **meede:** bribery.
797. **ware yow:** beware. **questemongeres:** conductors of inquests. **Susanna:** see Daniel xiii, or the apocryphal Book of Susannah.
798. **expres agayns:** directly opposed to. **heeste:** commandment. **corporel:** material.
799. **sleighte:** trickery. **met:** (false) measuring.
800. **stelyng of:** coming stealthily with. **semblable:** similar.
801. **chirche-hawes:** churchyards.
802. **vileyns:** wicked. **withdrawen:** withhold. **rightes:** titles, claims. **longen:** belong.
803. **reven:** rob.
804. **releevynge:** alleviation. **misericorde:** mercy. **largely:** generously. **taken:** used.

nedeful man, for he deliteth hym in the kepynge of his tresor, and nat in the rescowynge ne releevynge of his evene-Cristen. And therfore speke I first of misericorde. [805]

Thanne is misericorde, as seith the philosophre, a vertu by which the corage of a man is stired by the mysese of hym that is mysesed./ Upon which misericorde folweth pitee in parfournynge of charitable werkes of misericorde./ And certes, thise thynges moeven a man to misericorde of Jhesu Crist, that yaf hymself for oure gilt, and suffred deeth for misericorde, and forgaf us oure originale synnes,/ and therby relessed us fro the peynes of helle, and amenused the peynes of purgatorie by penitence, and yeveth grace wel to do, and atte laste the blisse of hevene./ The speces of misericorde ben, as for to lene and for to yeve, and to foryeven and relesse, and for to han pitee in herte and compassioun of the meschief of his evene-Cristene, and eek to chastise, there as nede is. [810]

Another manere of remedie agayns avarice is resonable largesse; but soothly, here bihoveth the consideracioun of the grace of Jhesu Crist, and of his temporel goodes, and eek of the goodes perdurables, that Crist yaf us;/ and eek to han remembrance of the deeth that he shal receyve, he noot whanne; and eek that he shal forgon al that he hath, save oonly that he hath despended in goode werkes./

But for as muche as som folk been unmesurable, men oghten eschue fool-largesse, that men clepen wast./ Certes, he that is fool-large ne yeveth nat his catel, but he leseth his catel. Soothly, what thyng that he yeveth for veyne glorie, as to mynstrals and to folk, for to beren his renoun in the world, he hath synne and noon almesse./ Certes, he leseth foule his good, that ne seketh with the yifte of his good nothyng but synne. [815] He is lyk to an hors that seketh rather to drynken drovy or trouble water than for to drynken water of the clere welle./ And for as muchel as they yeven ther as they sholde nat yeven, to hem aperteneth thilke malisoun that Crist shal yeven at the day of doom to hem that shullen been dampned./

Sequitur de Gulâ.

After Avarice comth Glotonye, which is expres eek agayn the comandement of God. Glotonye is unmesurable appetit to ete or to drynke, or elles to doon ynogh to the unmesurable appetit and desordeynee coveitise to ete or to drynke./ This synne corrumped al this world, as is wel shewed in the synne of Adam and of Eve.

---

805. **rescowynge**: rescuing. **evene-Cristen**: fellow Christian.

806. **stired**: stirred, moved. **mysese**: misery. **mysesed**: distressed.

808. **misericorde of**: compassion for. **gilt**: sins. **for misericorde**: for the sake of mercy.

809. **amenused**: reduced.

810. **lene**: lend. **relesse**: release (from obligation). **meschief**: distress. **evene-Cristene**: fellow Christian.

811. **largesse**: generosity. **bihoveth**: is needed. **perdurables**: everlasting.

812. **noot**: knows not. **despended in goode werkes**: i.e., distributed in charity to the poor.

813. **unmesurable**: immoderate. **eschue**: avoid. **fool-largesse**: foolish generosity.

814. **fool-large**: prodigal. **leseth**: loses. **almesse**: work of charity.

815. **foule**: foully, sinfully. **good**: goods.

816. **drovy**: stirred up, muddy. **trouble**: troubled.

817. **aperteneth**: belongs. **malisoun**: malediction, curse. **doom**: judgment.

818. **expres agayn**: directly opposed to. **unmesurable**: immoderate. **appetit**: desire. **doon ynogh to**: minister enough to satisfy. **desordeynee**: inordinate. **coveitise**: craving.

819. **corrumped**: corrupted.

Looke eek what seith Seint Paul of Glotonye:/ "Manye," seith Saint Paul, "goon, of whiche I have ofte seyd to yow, and now I seye it wepynge, that they ben the enemys of the croys of Crist; of whiche the ende is deeth, and of whiche hire wombe is hire god, and hire glorie in confusioun of hem that so savouren erthely thynges." [820] He that is usaunt to this synne of glotonye, he ne may no synne withstonde. He moot ben in servage of alle vices, for it is the develes hoord ther he hideth hym and resteth./

This synne hath manye speces. The firste is dronkenesse, that is the horrible sepulture of mannes resoun; and therfore, whan a man is dronken, he hath lost his resoun; and this is deedly synne./ But soothly, whan that a man is nat wont to strong drynke, and peraventure ne knoweth nat the strengthe of the drynke, or hath feblesse in his heed, or hath travailed, thurgh which he drynketh the moore, al be he sodeynly caught with drynke, it is no deedly synne, but venyal./ The seconde spece of glotonye is that the spirit of a man wexeth al trouble, for dronkenesse bireveth hym the discrecioun of his wit./ The thridde spece of glotonye is whan a man devoureth his mete, and hath no rightful manere of etynge. [825] The fourthe is whan, thurgh the grete habundaunce of his mete, the humours in his body ben distempred./ The fifthe is foryetelnesse by to muchel drynkynge; for which somtyme a man foryeteth er the morwe what he dide at even or on the nyght biforn./

In oother manere been distinct the speces of Glotonye, after Seint Gregorie. The firste is for to ete biforn tyme to ete. The seconde is whan a man get hym to delicat mete or drynke./ The thridde is whan men taken to muche over mesure. The fourthe is curiositee, with greet entente to maken and apparaillen his mete. The fifthe is for to eten to gredily./ Thise ben the fyve fyngres of the develes hand, by whiche he draweth folk to synne [830]

Remedium contra peccatum Gule.

Agayns Glotonye is the remedie abstinence, as seith Galien; but that holde I nat meritorie, if he do it oonly for the hele of his body. Seint Augustyn wole that abstinence be doon for vertu and with pacience./ "Abstinence," he seith, "is litel worth, but if a man have good wil therto, and but it be enforced by pacience and by charitee, and that men doon it for Godes sake, and in hope to have the blisse of hevene."/

---

819. **looke**: consider.
820. **Saint Paul**: see Philippians iii.18–19. **goon**: walk. **croys**: cross. **wombe**: belly. **confusioun**: shame. **savouren**: relish.
821. **usaunt**: addicted. **moot**: must. **servage of**: servitude to. **hoord**: hiding place.
822. **sepulture**: burial.
823. **wont**: accustomed. **heed**: head. **travailed**: labored. **caught with drynke**: drunk.
824. **wexeth**: becomes. **trouble**: confused. **bireveth**: robs.
825. **mete**: food.
827. **foryetelnesse**: forgetfulness. **morwe**: morning. **at even**: in the evening.
828. **after**: according to. **Seint Gregorie**: see *Moralium* Lib. xxx, c. xviii, §60. **to delicat**: too rich, too epicurean.
829. **to . . . mesure**: too much beyond moderation. **curiositee**: fastidiousness. **entente**: attention. **to . . . apparaillen**: to preparing and garnishing. **to gredily**: too greedily.
831. **Galien**: Galen. **meritorie**: meritorious. **hele**: health. **doon**: practiced.
832. **enforced**: strengthened. **doon**: practice.

The felawes of abstinence ben attemperaunce, that holdeth the meene in alle thynges; eek shame, that eschueth alle deshonestee; suffisance, that seketh no riche metes ne drynkes, ne dooth no fors of to outrageous apparailynge of mete;/ mesure also, that restreyneth by resoun the deslavee appetit of etynge; sobrenesse also, that restreyneth the outrage of drynke;/ sparynge also, that restreyneth the delicat ese to sitte longe at his mete and softely, wherfore some folk stonden of hir owene wyl to eten at the lasse leyser. [835]

Sequitur de Luxuria.

After Glotonye thanne comth Lecherie, for thise two synnes ben so ny cosyns that ofte tyme they wol nat departe./ God woot, this synne is ful displesaunt thyng to God; for he seyde hymself, "Do no lecherie." And therfore he putte grete peynes agayns this synne in the olde lawe./ If womman thral were taken in this synne, she sholde be beten with staves to the deeth; and if she were a gentil womman, she sholde be slayn with stones; and if she were a bisshoppes doghter, she sholde be brent, by Goddes comandement./ Further over, by the synne of lecherie God dreynte al the world at the diluve. And after that he brente fyve citees with thonder-leyt, and sank hem into helle./

Now lat us speke thanne of thilke stynkynge synne of Lecherie that men clepe avowtrie of wedded folk, that is to seyn, if that oon of hem be wedded, or elles bothe. [840] Seint John seith that avowtiers shullen ben in helle, in a stank bren-nynge of fyr and of brymston; in fyr, for lecherye; in brymston, for the stynk of hire ordure./ Certes, the brekynge of this sacrement is an horrible thyng. It was maked of God hymself in paradys, and confermed by Jhesu Crist, as witnesseth Seint Mathew in the gospel: "A man shal lete fader and moder, and taken hym to his wif, and they shullen be two in o flessh."/ This sacrement bitokneth the knyttynge togidre of Crist and of holy chirche./ And nat oonly that God forbad avowtrie in dede, but eek he comanded that thou sholdest nat coveite thy neighebores wyf./ "In this heste," seith Seint Augustyn, "is forboden alle manere coveitise to doon lecherie." Lo, what seith Seint Mathew in the gospel, that "whoso seeth a womman

---

833. **felawes:** companions. **attemperaunce:** moderation. **the meene:** the "golden mean." **eschueth:** avoids. **deshonestee:** dishonor; disgraceful conduct. **suffisance:** contentment. **dooth no fors:** has no regard for. **to outrageous:** too extravagant. **apparailynge:** preparation.

834. **deslavee:** unbridled. **outrage:** excess.

835. **sparynge:** frugality. **delicat:** voluptuous. **ese to sitte:** pleasure of sitting. **softely:** luxuriously. **lasse:** less. **leyser:** leisure.

836. **departe:** part company.

837. **Do:** see Exodus xx.14. **peynes:** punishments; see Leviticus xx.10–21. **the olde lawe:** i.e., the Mosaic dispensation.

838. **womman thral:** bondwoman; cf. Leviticus xix.20. **gentil womman:** cf. Deuteronomy xxii.21. **bisshoppes doghter:** cf. Leviticus xxi.9. **brent:** burned.

839. **by:** because of. **dreynte:** inundated. **diluve:** Noah's flood. **brente:** burned; see Genesis xix.24–25; Isaiah xix.18. **thonder-leyt:** lightning.

840. **avowtrie:** adultery.

841. **Seint John:** see Revelation xxi.8. **avowtiers:** adulterers. **stank:** pool. **ordure:** filth.

842. **maked of:** made by. **God:** see Genesis ii.22–24. **Crist:** see Matthew xix.5. **lete:** leave. **taken hym:** betake himself. **o:** one.

843. **knyttynge:** tying; joining. **Crist:** see Ephesians v.25.

844. **coveite:** lust after; see Exodus xx.17.

845. **heste:** commandment. **forboden:** forbidden. **coveitise:** craving. **Seint Mathew:** see Matthew v.28. **seeth:** looks at.

to coveitise of his lust, he hath doon lecherie with hire in his herte." [845] Here may ye seen that nat oonly the dede of this synne is forboden, but eek the desir to doon that synne./

This cursed synne anoyeth grevousliche hem that it haunten. And first to hire soule, for he obligeth it to synne and to peyne of deeth that is perdurable./ Unto the body anoyeth it grevously also, for it dreyeth hym, and wasteth him, and shent hym, and of his blood he maketh sacrifice to the feend of helle. It wasteth eek his catel and his substaunce./ And certes, if it be a foul thyng a man to waste his catel on wommen, yet is it a fouler thyng whan that, for swich ordure, wommen dispenden upon men hir catel and substaunce./ This synne, as seith the prophete, bireveth man and womman hir goode fame and al hire honour; and it is ful plesaunt to the devel, for therby wynneth he the mooste partie of this world. [850] And right as a marchant deliteth hym moost in chaffare that he hath moost avantage of, right so deliteth the fend in this ordure./

This is that oother hand of the devel with fyve fyngres to cacche the peple to his vileynye./ The firste fynger is the fool lookynge of the fool womman and of the fool man, that sleeth, right as the basilicok sleeth folk by the venym of his sighte; for the coveitise of eyen folweth the coveitise of the herte./ The seconde fynger is the vileyns touchynge in wikked manere. And therfore seith Salomon that "whoso toucheth and handleth a womman, he fareth lyk hym that handleth the scorpioun that styngeth and sodeynly sleeth thurgh his envenymynge"; as whoso toucheth warm pych, it shent his fyngres./ The thridde is foule wordes, that fareth lyk fyr, that right anon brenneth the herte. [855] The fourthe fynger is the kissynge; and trewely he were a greet fool that wolde kisse the mouth of a brennynge oven or of a fourneys./ And moore fooles ben they that kissen in vileynye, for that mouth is the mouth of helle; and namely thise olde dotardes holours, yet wol they kisse, though they may nat do, and smatre hem./ Certes, they ben lyk to houndes; for an hound, whan he comth by the roser or by othere beautees, though he may nat pisse, yet wole he heve up his leg, and make a contenaunce to pisse./ And for that many man weneth that he may nat synne, for no likerousnesse that he doth with his wyf, certes, that opinion is fals. God woot, a man may sleen hymself with his owene knyf, and make hymselve dronken of his owene tonne./ Certes, be it wyf,

---

845. **to coveitise:** in the ardent desire.
847. **anoyeth:** harms. **haunten:** practise. **obligeth:** constrains. **peyne:** punishment.
848. **dreyeth:** dries up. **shent:** ruins. **catel:** property.
849. **a man:** for a man. **ordure:** filth. **dispenden:** spend.
850. **bireveth:** takes away from. **mooste partie:** greatest part.
851. **chaffare:** trading. **avantage of:** profit from.
852. **to his vileynye:** i.e., so as to bring about their bondage to him.
853. **fool:** lascivious. **lookynge:** gaze. **sleeth:** slays. **basilicok:** basilisk, fabled to kill by its glance. **venym:** poison. **sighte:** glance. **coveitise:** craving.
854. **vileyns:** evil. **Salomon:** see Ecclesiasticus xxvi.10. **envenymynge:** poisoning (him) **pych:** pitch; see Ecclesiasticus xiii.1. **shent:** defiles.
855. **fareth:** act.
856. **fourneys:** furnace.
857. **vileynye:** wickedness. **dotardes:** senile. **holours:** lechers. **smatre hem:** defile themselves.
858. **roser:** rose-bush. **beautees:** beauties: Tyrwhitt, followed by other editors, printed **busshes,** which (though in no MS) may be correct. **heve:** heave. **contenaunce:** pretence.
859. **for that:** because. **sleen:** slay. **tonne:** tun, cask.

be it child, or any worldly thyng that he loveth biforn God, it is his mawmet, and
he is an ydolastre. [860] Man sholde loven his wyf by discrecioun, paciently and
atemprely; and thanne is she as though she were his suster./ The fifthe fynger of
the develes hand is the stynkynge dede of Leccherie./ Certes, the fyve fyngres
of Glotonye the feend put in the wombe of a man and with his fyve fingres of Lech-
erie he gripeth hym by the reynes, for to throwen hym into the fourneys of helle,/
ther as they shul han the fyr and the wormes that evere shul lasten, and wepynge
and wailynge, sharp hunger and thurst, grislynesse of develes, that shullen al totrede
hem withouten respit and withouten ende./

Of Leccherie, as I seyde, sourden diverse speces, as fornicacioun, that is bitwixe
man and womman that ben nat maried; and this is deedly synne, and agayns na-
ture [865] Al that is enemy and destruccioun to nature is agayns nature./ Parfay,
the resoun of a man telleth eek hym wel that it is deedly synne, for as muche as
God forbad leccherie. And Seint Paul yeveth hem the regne that nys dewe to no
wight but to hem that doon deedly synne./ Another synne of Leccherie is to bireve
a mayden of hir maydenhede; for he that so dooth, certes, he casteth a mayden out
of the hyeste degree that is in this present lif,/ and bireveth hire thilke precious
fruyt that the book clepeth the hundred fruyt. I ne kan seye it noon ootherweyes
in Englissh, but in Latyn it highte *Centesimus fructus.*/ Certes, he that so dooth is
cause of manye damages and vileynyes, mo than any man kan rekene; right as he
somtyme is cause of alle damages that beestes don in the feeld, that breketh the
hegge or the closure, thurgh which he destroyeth that may nat been restored. [870]
For certes, namoore may maydenhede be restored than an arm that is smyten fro
the body may retourne agayn to wexe./ She may have mercy, this woot I wel, if she
do penitence; but nevere shal it be that she nas corrupt./

And al be it so that I have spoken somwhat of avowtrie, it is good to shewen mo
perils that longen to avowtrie, for to eschue that foule synne./ Avowtrie in Latyn
is for to seyn, approchynge of oother mannes bed, thurgh which tho that whilom
weren o flessh abawndone hir bodyes to othere persones./ Of this synne, as seith the
wise man, folwen manye harmes. First, brekynge of feith; and certes, in feith is the
keye of Cristendom. [875] And whan that feith is broken and lorn, soothly Cristen-

---

860. **biforn:** more than. **mawmet:** idol. **ydolastre:** idolater.

861. **by discrecioun:** in moderation. **atemprely:** temperately. **suster:** see St. Jerome, *Contra Jovinianum* i.c.11.

863. **put:** (putteth) puts. **wombe:** belly. **gripeth:** grasps; ensnares. **reynes:** reins, "loins," the seat of generative power.

864. **fyr, wormes:** see Mark ix.44 (Vulgate 43). **grislynesse:** horribleness. **totrede:** trample upon.

865. **of:** from. **sourden:** arise.

866. **to:** of.

867. **Seint Paul:** see Galatians v.19–21. **dewe:** due.

868. **bireve:** rob. **maydenhede:** maidenhood.

869. **hundred fruyt:** cf. St. Jerome, *Contra Jovinianum* i.c.3. **noon ootherweyes:** in no other way.

870. **vileynyes:** shameful injuries. **hegge:** hedge. **closure:** fence, wall, or other barrier. **that:** that which.

871. **smyten:** smitten, cut. **wexe:** grow.

872. **corrupt:** defiled.

873. **avowtrie:** adultery. **shewen:** consider. **longen:** belong. **eschue:** avoid.

874. **tho:** those. **whilom:** formerly. **o:** one. **abawndone:** surrender.

875. **of:** from. **harmes:** evils. **Cristendom:** Christian doctrine; Christianity.

876. **lorn:** lost.

dom stant veyn and withouten fruyt./ This synne is eek a thefte; for thefte gen-
erally is for to reve a wight his thyng agayns his wille./ Certes, this is the fouleste
thefte that may be, whan a womman steleth hir body from hir housbonde, and
yeveth it to hire holour to defoulen hire; and steleth hir soule fro Crist, and yeveth
it to the devel./ This is a fouler thefte than for to breke a chirche and stele the
chalice; for thise avowtiers breken the temple of God spiritually, and stelen the
vessel of grace, that is the body and the soule, for which Crist shal destroyen hem,
as seith Seint Paul./ Soothly, of this thefte douted gretly Joseph, whan that his
lordes wyf preyed hym of vileynye, whan he seyde, "Lo, my lady, how my lord
hath take to me under my warde al that he hath in this world, ne no thyng of his
thynges is out of my power, but oonly ye, that ben his wyf. [880] And how sholde
I thanne do this wikkednesse and synne so horrible agayns God and agayns my
lord? God it forbeede!" Allas! al to litel is swich trouthe now yfounde./ The thridde
harm is the filthe thurgh which they breken the comandement of God, and de-
foulen the auctour of matrimoyne, that is Crist./ For certes, in so muche as the
sacrement of mariage is so noble and so digne, so muche is it gretter synne for to
breken it; for God made mariage in paradys, in the estaat of innocence, to mul-
tiplye mankynde to the service of God./ And therfore is the brekynge therof moore
grevous; of which brekynge comen false heires often tyme, that wrongfully ocupien
folkes heritages. And therfore wol Crist putte hem out of the regne of hevene, that
is heritage to goode folk./ Of this brekynge comth eek ofte tyme that folk unwar
wedden or synnen with hire owene kynrede, and namely thilke harlotes that
haunten bordels of thise fool wommen, that mowe be likned to a commune gonge,
where as men purgen hire ordure. [885] What seye we eek of putours that lyven by
the horrible synne of putrie, and constreyne wommen to yelden to hem a certeyn
rente of hire bodily puterie, ye, somtyme of his owene wyf or his child, as doon
thise bawdes? Certes, thise ben cursed synnes./ Understoond eek that Avowtrie is
set gladly in the ten comandementz bitwixe thefte and manslaughtre; for it is the
gretteste thefte that may be, for it is thefte of body and of soule./ And it is lyk to
homycide, for it kerveth atwo and breketh atwo hem that first were maked o flessh.
And therfore, by the olde lawe of God, they sholde be slayn./ But nathelees, by the
lawe of Jhesu Crist, that is lawe of pitee, whan he seyde to the womman that was
founden in avowtrie, and sholde han ben slayn with stones, after the wyl of the
Jewes, as was hir lawe, "Go," quod Jhesu Crist, "and have namoore wyl to synne,"

---

876. **stant:** stands; is. **veyn:** useless.

877. **reve a wight:** seize from a person. **thyng:** possession.

878. **steleth:** steals. **holour:** lecher. **defoulen:** defile.

879. **breke:** break into. **avowtiers:** adulterers. **Seint Paul:** see I Corinthians iii.17.

880. **douted of:** was fearful or anxious concerning. **Joseph:** see Genesis xxxix.8–9. **preyed hym of vileynye:** entreated him to do villainous evil. **take:** entrusted. **warde:** guardianship.

882. **auctour:** originator, founder.

883. **digne:** worthy. **multiplye:** cf. Genesis i.28.

885. **unwar:** without knowing it. **harlotes:** male lechers. **haunten:** frequent. **bordels:** brothels. **fool:** lascivious. **gonge:** privy.

886. **putours:** pimps. **putrie:** prostitution. **yelden:** pay. **rente of:** payment from. **bawdes:** procurers.

887. **avowtrie:** adultery. **gladly:** aptly.

888. **kerveth atwo:** cuts in two. **the olde lawe:** the Mosaic dispensation.

889. **the lawe of Jhesu Crist:** the new law; the Gospel dispensation. **the womman:** see John viii.3–11.

or, "wille namoore to do synne."/ Soothly the vengeaunce of Avowtrie is awarded to the peynes of helle, but if it be destourbed by penitence. [890]

Yet ben ther mo speces of this cursed synne; as whan that oon of hem is religious, or elles bothe; or of folk that ben entred into ordre, as subdekne, dekne, or preest, or hospitaliers. And evere the hyer that he is in ordre, the gretter is the synne./ The thynges that gretly agreggen hire synne is the brekynge of hire avow of chastitee, whan they receyved the ordre./ And forther over, sooth is that holy ordre is chief of al the tresor of God, and his especial signe and mark of chastitee, to shewe that they ben joyned to chastitee, which that is the moost precious lyf that is./ And thise ordred folk ben specially titled to God, and of the special meignee of God, for which, whan they doon deedly synne, they ben the special traytours of God and of his peple; for they lyven of the peple, to preye for the peple, and while they ben suche traitours, hir preyeres availlen nat to the peple./ Preestes ben aungels, as by the dignitee of hir mysterye; but for sothe, Seint Paul seith that Sathanas transformeth hym in an aungel of light. [895] Soothly, the preest that haunteth deedly synne, he may be likned to the aungel of derknesse transformed in the aungel of light. He semeth aungel of light, but for sothe he is aungel of derknesse./ Swiche preestes ben the sones of Helie, as sheweth in the Book of Kynges, that they weren the sones of Belial, that is, the devel./ Belial is to seyn, "withouten juge"; and so faren they; hem thynketh they ben free, and han no juge, namoore than hath a free bole that taketh which cow that hym liketh in the town./ So faren they by wommen. For right as a free bole is ynough for al a toun, right so is a wikked preest corrupcioun ynough for al a parisshe, or for al a contree./ Thise preestes, as seith the book, ne [coude] nat the mysterie of preesthod to the peple, ne God ne [knewe] they nat. They ne helde hem nat apayd, as seith the book, of soden flessh that was to hem offred, but they tooke by force the flessh that is rawe. [900] Certes, so thise shrewes ne holden hem nat apayed of roosted flessh and sode flessh, with which the peple feden hem in greet reverence, but they wole have raw flessh of folkes wyves and hir doghtres./ And certes, thise wommen that consenten to hire harlotrie doon greet wrong to Crist, and to holy chirche, and alle halwes, and to alle soules; for they bireven alle thise hym that sholde worshipe Crist and holy chirche, and preye for Cristene soules./ And therfore han swiche

---

890. **awarded to:** given into the jurisdiction of. **peynes:** punishments; tortures. **destourbed:** prevented.

891. **of hem:** of the parties. **is religious:** belongs to a religious order. **ordre:** holy orders; an order of monks or friars; a monastic society of knights. **hospitaliers:** knights hospitallers.

892. **agreggen:** aggravate, make worse. **avow:** vow.

894. **titled:** dedicated. **meignee:** household. **for which:** because of which. **lyven of:** live off.

895. **dignitee:** high spiritual worth. **mysterye:** ministry. **Seint Paul:** see II Corinthians xi.14. **transformeth hym in:** transforms himself into.

896. **haunteth:** practices.

897. **Helie:** Eli; see I Samuel ii.12 (Vulgate, Liber Primus Regum ii.12). **sheweth:** is shown.

898. **is to seyn:** means. **bole:** bull. **town:** field; farm.

899. **al a contree:** an entire district.

900. **the book:** the Bible, as in 897. **mysterie:** office. **helde hem nat apayd of:** were not satisfied with. **the book:** see I Samuel ii.15. **soden:** boiled.

901. **so:** just so. **shrewes:** scoundrels. **holden hem nat apayd of:** are not satisfied with. **flessh:** meat. **sode:** boiled. **greet:** great.

902. **harlotrie:** sexual immorality. **halwes:** saints. **bireven alle thise:** rob all these of.

preestes, and hire lemmanes eek that consenten to hir leccherie, the malisoun of al the court Cristien, til they come to amendement./

The thridde spece of avowtrie is somtyme bitwixe a man and his wyf, and that is whan they take no reward in hire assemblynge but oonly to hire flesshly delit, as seith Seint Jerome,/ and ne rekken of nothyng but that they ben assembled; by cause that they ben maried, al is good ynough, as thynketh to hem. [905] But in swich folk hath the devel power, as seyde the aungel Raphael to Thobie, for in hire assem-blynge they putten Jhesu Crist out of hire herte, and yeven hemself to alle ordure./

The fourthe spece is the assemblee of hem that ben of hire kynrede, or of hem that ben of oon affynytee, or elles with hem with whiche hir fadres or hir kynrede han deled in the synne of lecherie. This synne maketh hem lyk to houndes, that taken no kep to kynrede./ And certes, parentele is in two maneres, outher goostly or flesshly; goostly, as for to deelen with his godsibbes./ For right so as he that en-gendreth a child is his flesshly fader, right so is his godfader his fader espirituel. For which a womman may in no lasse synne assemblen with hire godsib than with hire owene flesshly brother./

The fifthe spece is thilke abhomynable synne, of which that no man unnethe oghte speke ne write; nathelees it is openly reherced in holy writ. [910] This cur-sednesse doon men and wommen in diverse entente and in diverse manere; but though that holy writ speke of horrible synne, certes holy writ may nat been de-fouled, namoore than the sonne that shyneth on the mixne./

Another synne aperteyneth to leccherie, that comth in slepynge, and this synne cometh ofte to hem that ben maydenes, and eek to hem that ben corrupt; and this synne men clepen polucioun, that comth in foure maneres./ Somtyme of langwis-synge of body, for the humours ben to ranke and to habundaunt in the body of man; somtyme of infermetee, for the fieblesse of the vertu retentif, as phisik maketh mencion; somtyme for surfeet of mete and drynke;/ and somtyme of vileyns thoghtes that ben enclosed in mannes mynde whan he gooth to slepe, which may nat ben withoute synne; for which men moste kepen hem wisely, or elles may men synnen ful grevously./

---

903. lemmanes: concubines. malisoun: malediction. court Cristien: ecclesiastical court. come to amendement: i.e., are converted to Christian living.

904. reward: regard. assemblynge: sexual union. but oonly: except. Seint Jerome: see *Contra Jovinianum* i.c.49.

905. rekken of: care for.

906. Raphael: see Tobias vi.17. ordure: filth.

907. of oon affynytee: related by marriage. deled in: had intercourse with. taken no kep to: take no heed of. kynrede: kinship.

908. parentele: kinship. goostly: spiritual. godsibbes: i.e., the children of one's godparents, or the godchildren of one's parents.

909. lasse: less

910. unnethe: scarcely. reherced: mentioned. holy writ: see Romans i.26–27.

911. defouled: defiled. mixne: dunghill.

912. maydenes: virgins. corrupt: defiled. polucioun: pollution; emission apart from coition.

913. langwissynge: faintness. for: because. to ranke: too copious. infermetee: infirmity. for: because of. vertu retentif: retentive virtue, the ability to retain the physical secretions. phisik: medical science. surfeet: surfeit, excess.

914. vileyns: sinful. for which: because of which. moste: must. kepen hem: look after them-selves.

Remedium contra peccatum luxurie.

Now comth the remedie agayns Leccherie, and that is generally chastitee and continence, that restreyneth alle the desordeynee moevynges that comen of flesshly talentes. [915] And evere the gretter merite shal he han, that moost restreyneth the wikkede eschawfynges of the ardour of this synne. And this is in two maneres, that is to seyn, chastitee in mariage, and chastitee of widwehod./

Now shaltow understonde that matrimoyne is leefful assemblynge of man and of womman that receyven by vertu of the sacrement the boond thurgh which they may nat be departed in al hir lyf, that is to seyn, whil that they lyven bothe./ This, as seith the book, is a ful greet sacrement. God maked it, as I have seyd, in paradys, and wolde hymself be born in mariage./ And for to halwen mariage he was at a weddynge, where as he turned water into wyn; which was the firste miracle that he wroghte in erthe biforn his disciples./ Trewe effect of mariage clenseth fornicacioun and replenysseth holy chirche of good lynage; for that is the ende of mariage; and it chaungeth deedly synne into venial synne bitwixe hem that ben ywedded, and maketh the hertes al oon of hem that ben ywedded, as wel as the bodies. [920]

This is verray mariage, that was establissed by God, er that synne bigan, whan naturel lawe was in his right poynt in paradys; and it was ordeyned that o man sholde have but o womman, and o womman but o man, as seith Seint Augustyn, by manye resouns./

First, for mariage is figured bitwixe Crist and holy chirche. And that oother is for a man is heved of a womman; algate, by ordinaunce it sholde be so./ For if a womman hadde mo men than oon, thanne sholde she have mo hevedes than oon, and that were an horrible thyng biforn God; and eek a womman ne myghte nat plese to many folk at ones. And also ther ne sholde nevere be pees ne reste amonges hem; for everich wolde axen his owene thyng./ And forther over, no man sholde knowe his owene engendrure, ne who sholde have his heritage; and the womman sholde ben the lasse biloved fro the tyme that she were conjoynt to many men./

Now comth how that a man sholde bere hym with his wif, and namely in two thynges, that is to seyn, in suffraunce and in reverence, as shewed Crist whan he made first womman. [925] For he ne made hire nat of the heved of Adam, for she

---

915. **desordeynee:** inordinate, excessive. **moevynges:** impulses. **talentes:** passions; appetites.

916. **moost:** most. **eschawfynges:** inflaming with passion.

917. **leefful:** lawful. **assemblynge:** union. **departed:** separated.

918. **book:** see Vulgate, *Ad Ephesios* v.32. **God:** see Genesis ii.22–24.

919. **halwen:** hallow. **weddynge:** see John ii. 1–11.

920. **effect:** consummation. **replenysseth:** replenishes. **of:** with. **lynage:** lineage. **maketh al oon:** unites.

921. **his right poynt:** its proper stage of development. **o:** one. **by:** for.

922. **for:** because. **figured:** figuratively expressed; see Ephesians v.23. **for:** because. **heved:** head; see I Corinthians xi.3. **algate:** at any rate. **ordinaunce:** (God's) ordinance or dispensation.

923. **to many:** too many. **ones:** once. **reste:** peace. **axen:** demand. **his owene thyng:** i.e., what concerned him.

924. **engendrure:** offspring. **lasse:** less. **conjoynt:** joined (in marriage) with.

925. **bere hym with:** behave towards. **suffraunce:** patient endurance.

926. **heved:** head.

sholde nat clayme to greet lordshipe./ For ther as the womman hath the maistrie, she maketh to muche desray. Ther neden none ensamples of this; the experience of day by day oghte suffise./ Also, certes, God ne made nat womman of the foot of Adam, for she ne sholde nat ben holden to lowe; for she kan nat paciently suffre. But God made womman of the ryb of Adam, for womman sholde be felawe unto man./ Man sholde bere hym to his wyf in feith, in trouthe, and in love, as seith Seint Paul, that a man sholde loven his wyf as Crist loved holy chirche, that loved it so wel that he deyde for it. So sholde a man for his wyf, if it were nede./

Now how that a womman sholde be subget to hire housbonde, that telleth Seint Peter. First, in obedience. [930] And eek, as seith the decree, a womman that is a wyf, as longe as she is a wyf, she hath noon auctoritee to swere ne to bere witnesse withoute leve of hir housbonde, that is hire lord; algate, he sholde be so by resoun./ She sholde eek serven hym in alle honestee, and ben attempree of hir array. I woot wel that they sholde setten hire entente to plesen hir housbondes, but nat by hire queyntise of array./ Seint Jerome seith that "wyves that ben apparailled in silk and in precious purpre ne mowe nat clothen hem in Jhesu Crist." Loke what seith Seint John eek in thys matere./ Seint Gregorie eek seith that "no wight seketh precious array but oonly for veyne glorie, to ben honoured the moore biforn the peple."/ It is a greet folye, a womman to have a fair array outward and in hirself be foul inward. [935] A wyf sholde eek be mesurable in lookynge and in berynge and in lawghynge, and discreet in all hire wordes and hire dedes./ And aboven alle worldly thynges she sholde loven hire housbonde with al hire herte, and to hym be trewe of hir body./ So sholde an housbonde eek be to his wyf. For sith that al the body is the housbondes, so sholde hire herte ben, or elles ther is bitwixe hem two, as in that, no parfit mariage./

Thanne shal men understonde that for thre thynges a man and his wyf flesshly mowen assemble. The firste is in entente of engendrure of children to the service of God; for certes that is the cause final of matrimoyne./ Another cause is to yelden everich of hem to oother the dette of hire bodies; for neither of hem hath power of his owene body. The thridde is for to eschewe leccherye and vileynye. The ferthe is for sothe deedly synne. [940] As to the firste, it is meritorie; the seconde also, for, as seith the decree, that she hath merite of chastitee that yeldeth to hire housbonde the dette of hir body, ye, though it be agayn hir likynge and the lust of hire herte./

---

926. **to greet:** too great.
927. **ther as:** where. **maketh to muche desray:** causes too much confusion.
928. **holden:** held. **to lowe:** too low. **felawe:** companion.
929. **bere hym to:** behave towards. **Seint Paul:** see Ephesians v.25.
930. **subget:** subject. **Seint Peter:** see I Peter iii.1.
931. **the decree:** the body of canon law. **leve:** permission. **algate:** at any rate.
932. **honestee:** propriety of behavior. **attempree:** modest. **array:** clothing. **setten hire entente to plesen:** give heed to pleasing. **queyntise:** elegance.
933. **apparailled:** dressed. **purpre:** purple. **Seint John:** cf. Revelation xvii.4; xviii.16.
934. **Seint Gregorie:** see line 414, above.
935. **a womman:** for a woman.
936. **mesurable:** modest. **lookynge:** appearance. **berynge:** behavior.
938. **as in that:** in that respect.
939. **mowen:** may. **assemble:** have intercourse. **engendrure:** begetting. **cause final:** the ultimate or basic purpose.
940. **cause:** motive. **yelden:** pay; see I Corinthians vii.3.
941. **meritorie:** meritorious. **yeldeth:** pays. **agayn:** against. **lust:** desire.

The thridde manere is venyal synne; and, trewely, scarsly may any of thise be withoute venial synne, for the corrupcion and for the delit./ The fourthe manere is for to understonde, if they assemble oonly for amorous love and for noon of the foreseyde causes, but for to accomplice thilke brennynge delit, they rekke nevere how ofte. Soothly it is deedly synne; and yet, with sorwe, somme folk wol peynen hem moore to doon than to hire appetit suffiseth./

The seconde manere of chastitee is for to ben a clene wydewe, and eschue the embracynges of man, and desiren the embracynge of Jhesu Crist./ Thise ben tho that han ben wyves and han forgoon hire housbondes, and eek wommen that han doon leccherie and ben releeved by penitence. [945] And certes, if that a wyf koude kepen hire al chaast by licence of hir housbonde, so that she yeve nevere noon occasion that he agilte, it were to hire a greet merite./ Thise manere wommen that observen chastitee moste be clene in herte as wel as in body and in thought, and mesurable in clothynge and in contenaunce, abstinent in etynge and drynknge, in spekynge, and in dede. And thanne is she the vessel or the boyste of the blissed Magdalene, that fulfilleth holy chirche of good odour./

The thridde manere of chastitee is virginitee, and it bihoveth that she be holy in herte and clene of body. Thanne is she spouse to Jhesu Crist, and she is the lyf of angeles./ She is the preisynge of this world, and she is as thise martirs in egalitee; she hath in hire that tonge may nat telle./ Virginitee baar oure Lord Jhesu Crist, and virgine was hymselve. [950]

Another remedie agayns Leccherie is specially to withdrawen swiche thynges as yeve occasion to thilke vileynye, as ese, etynge, and drynkynge. For certes, whan the pot boyleth strongly, the beste remedie is to withdrawe the fyr./ Slepynge longe in greet quiete is eek a greet norice to Leccherie./

Another remedie agayns Leccherie is that a man or a womman eschue the compaignye of hem by whiche he douteth to be tempted; for al be it so that the dede be withstonden, yet is ther greet temptacioun./ Soothly, a whit wal, although it ne brenne noght fully by stikynge of a candele, yet is the wal blak of the leyt./ Ful ofte tyme I rede that no man truste in his owene perfeccioun, but he be stronger than Sampson, holier than David, and wiser than Salomon. [955]

Now after that I have declared yow, as I kan, the sevene deedly synnes, and somme of hire braunches and hire remedies, soothly, if I koude, I wolde telle yow

942. for: because of.
943. accomplice: achieve. rekke: care. peynen hem: exert themselves. appetit: sexual craving.
945. forgoon: lost. doon: practised. releeved: relieved (of guilt).
946. licence: permission. agilte: sinned.
947. manere: kind of. moste: must. mesurable: modest. dede: deed. boyste: box. fulfilleth: fills.
948. bihoveth is necessary. lyf: beloved.
949. preisynge: i.e., worthy of the praise. egalitee: equanimity. that: that which.
950. baar: bore. virgine was hymselve: he himself was a virgin.
951. withdrawen: refrain from. ese: sensual gratification.
952. greet: great. norice: nurse.
953. eschue: avoid. douteth: fears. withstonden: resisted.
954. whit: white. brenne: be consumed by fire. stikynge: the sticking (against it). blak: i.e., blackened. of the leyt: from the flame.
955. ofte tyme: the comparison here introduced was a medieval commonplace. rede: read. but: unless.
956. declared yow: told you about.

the ten comandementz./ But so heigh a doctrine I lete to divines. Nathelees, I hope to God, they ben touched in this tretice, everich of hem alle./

Sequitur secunda pars Penitencie.

Now for as muche as the seconde partie of Penitence stant in Confessioun of mouth, as I bigan in the firste chapitre, I seye, Seint Augustyn seith:/ "Synne is every word and every dede, and al that men coveiten, agayn the lawe of Jhesu Crist; and this is for to synne in herte, in mouth, and in dede, by thy fyve wittes, that ben sighte, herynge, smellynge, tastynge or savourynge, and feelynge."/

Now is it good to understonde the circumstances that agreggen muchel every synne. [960] Thou shalt considere what thow art that doost the synne, wheither thou be male or female, yong or oold, gentil or thral, free or servant, hool or syk, wedded or sengle, ordred or unordred, wys or fool, clerk or seculer;/ if she be of thy kynrede, bodily or goostly, or noon; if any of thy kynrede have synned with hire, or noon; and manye mo thinges./

Another circumstaunce is this: wheither it be doon in fornicacioun or in avowtrie or noon; incest or noon; mayden or noon; in manere of homicide or noon; horrible grete synnes or smale; and how longe thou hast continued in synne./

The thridde circumstaunce is the place ther thou hast do synne; wheither in oother mennes hous or in thyn owene; in feeld or in chirche or in chirchehawe; in chirche dedicaat or noon./ For if the chirche be halwed, and man or womman spille his kynde inwith that place, by wey of synne or by wikked temptacioun, the chirche is entredited til it be reconsiled by the bysshop. [965] And the preest sholde be enterdited that dide swich a vileynye; to terme of al his lif he sholde namoore synge masse, and if he dide, he sholde doon deedly synne at every time that he so songe masse./

The fourthe circumstaunce is by whiche mediatours, or by whiche messagers, as for enticement, or for consentement to bere compaignye with felaweshipe; for many a wrecche, for to bere compaignye, wol go to the devel of helle./ For they that eggen or consenten to the synne ben parteners of the synne, and of the dampnacioun of the synnere./

The fifthe circumstaunce is how manye tymes that he hath synned, if it be in his mynde, and how ofte that he hath falle./ For he that ofte falleth in synne, he de-

---

957. lete: leave. divines: theologians.
958. stant in: consists in.
959. coveiten: desire sinfully. wittes: senses.
960. agreggen: aggravate, make worse.
961. gentil: nobly born. thral: in bondage. servant: in servitude. hool: sound. sengle: single. ordred: ordained; in orders. unordred: lay. clerk: cleric. seculer: secular.
962. goostly: spiritually. or noon: or not.
963. avowtrie: adultery. mayden: virgin.
964. do: committed. chirchehawe: churchyard. dedicaat: consecrated.
965. halwed: consecrated. kynde: seminal fluid; orgastic fluid. inwith: within. entredited: interdicted; cut off from religious privileges. reconsiled: purified.
966. to: for the. doon: commit. songe: sang.
967. mediatours: go-betweens. messagers: messengers. bere compaignye: have companionship. felaweshipe: good fellowship, revelry.
968. eggen: incite. consenten to: connive in.
969. falle: fallen.

spiseth the mercy of God, and encreesseth his synne, and is unkynde to Crist; and he wexeth the moore fieble to withstonde synne, and synneth the moore lightly, [970] and the latter ariseth, and is the moore eschew for to shryven hym, and namely to hym that is his confessour./ For which that folk, whan they falle agayn in hir olde folies, outher they forleten hir olde confessours al outrely, or elles they departen hir shrift in diverse places; but soothly, swich departed shrift deserveth no mercy of God of his synnes./

The sixte circumstaunce is why that a man synneth, as by which temptacioun; and if hymself procure thilke temptacioun, or by the excitynge of oother folk; or if he synne with a womman by force, or by hire owene assent;/ or if the womman, maugree hir hed, hath ben afforced, or noon. This shal she telle: for coveitise, or for poverte, and if it was hire procurynge, or noon; and swich manere harneys./

The seventhe circumstaunce is in what manere he hath doon his synne, or how that she hath suffred that folk han doon to hire. [975] And the same shal the man telle pleynly with alle circumstaunces; and wheither he hath synned with comune bordel wommen, or noon;/ or doon his synne in holy tymes, or noon; in fastyng tymes, or noon; or biforn his shrifte, or after his latter shrifte;/ and hath peraventure broken therfore his penance enjoyned; by whos help and whos conseil; by sorcerie or craft; al moste be toold./

Alle thise thynges, after that they ben grete or smale, engreggen the conscience of man. And eek the preest, that is thy juge, may the bettre ben avysed of his juggement in yevynge of thy penaunce, and that is after thy contricioun./ For understond wel that after tyme that a man hath defouled his baptesme by synne, if he wole come to salvacioun, ther is noon other wey but by penitence and shrifte and satisfaccioun; [980] and namely by the two, if ther be a confessour to which he may shriven hym, and the thridde, if he have lyf to parfournen it./

Thanne shal man looke and considere that if he wole maken a trewe and a profitable confessioun, ther moste be foure condiciouns./ First, it moot been in sorweful bitternesse of herte, as seyde the kyng Ezechias to God: "I wol remembre me alle the yeres of my lif in bitternesse of myn herte."/ This condicioun of bitternesse hath fyve signes. The firste is that confessioun moste be shamefast, nat for to covere ne hide his synne, for he hath agilt his God and defouled his soule./

---

970. **unkynde:** ungrateful. **lightly:** easily.

971. **the latter:** the later, the more slowly. **eschew:** shy, reluctant. **shryven hym:** confess.

972. **for which:** for which reason. **outher:** either. **forleten:** forsake. **outrely:** completely. **departen:** divide. **shrift:** confession. **departed** divided.

973. **procure:** bring about. **excitynge:** inciting.

974. **maugree hir hed:** in spite of all she could do. **afforced:** violated. **or noon:** or not. **for:** (whether) because of. **coveitise:** covetousness. **procurynge:** contriving. **harneys:** details of circumstance.

975. **suffred:** allowed. **that:** that which, what.

976. **pleynly:** fully. **bordel:** brothel.

977. **latter:** last.

978. **enjoyned:** (that had been) imposed. **craft:** trickery.

979. **after that:** in accordance as. **engreggen:** oppress. **ben avysed of:** take under advisement. **juggement:** decision. **after:** according to.

980. **after tyme that:** after. **defouled:** defiled.

981. **namely:** especially. **the two:** i.e., the former two. **have lyf:** lives.

983. **Ezechias:** Hezekiah; see Isaiah xxxviii.15.

984. **shamefast:** shamefaced. **agilt:** sinned against.

And herof seith Seint Augustyn: "The herte travailleth for shame of his synne"; and for he hath greet shamefastnesse, he is digne to have greet mercy of God. [985] Swich was the confessioun of the publican that wolde nat heven up his eyen to hevene, for he hadde offended God of hevene; for which shamefastnesse he hadde anon the mercy of God./ And therof seith Seint Augustyn that swich shamefast folk ben next foryevenesse and remissioun./ Another signe is humylitee in confessioun; of which seith Seint Peter, "Humbleth yow under the myght of God." The hond of God is myghty in confessioun, for therby God foryeveth thee thy synnes, for he allone hath the power./ And this humylitee shal ben in herte, and in signe outward; for right as he hath humylitee to God in his herte, right so sholde he humble his body outward to the preest, that sit in Goddes place./ For which in no manere, sith that Crist is sovereyn, and the preest meene and mediatour bitwixe Crist and the synnere, and the synnere is the laste by wey of resoun, [990] thanne sholde nat the synnere sitte as heighe as his confessour, but knele biforn hym or at his feet, but if maladie destourbe it. For he shal nat taken kepe who sit there, but in whos place that he sitteth./ A man that hath trespased to a lord, and comth for to axe mercy and maken his accord, and set him doun anon by the lord, men wolde holden hym outrageous, and nat worthy so soone for to have remissioun ne mercy./ The thridde signe is that thy shrift sholde be ful of teeris, if man may, and if man may nat wepe with his bodily eyen, lat hym wepe in herte./ Swich was the confession of Seint Peter, for after that he hadde forsake Jhesu Crist, he wente out and weep ful bitterly./ The fourthe signe is that he ne lette nat for shame to shewen his confessioun. [995] Swich was the confessioun of the Magdalene, that ne spared, for no shame of hem that weren atte feeste, for to go to oure Lord Jhesu Crist and biknowe to hym hire synne./ The fifthe signe is that a man or a womman be obeisant to receyven the penaunce that hym is enjoyned, for certes, Jhesu Crist, for the giltes of o man, was obedient to the deeth./

The seconde condicion of verray confession is that it be hastily doon. For certes, if a man hadde a deedly wounde, evere the lenger that he taried to warisshe hymself, the moore wolde it corrupte and haste hym to his deeth; and eek the wounde wolde be the wors for to heele./ And right so fareth synne that longe tyme is in a man unshewed./ Certes, a man oghte hastily shewen his synnes for manye causes;

---

985. **Seint Augustyn:** see [Pseudo-Augustine] *Liber de Vera et Falsa Poenitentia* I.10.§25. **travailleth:** labors. **greet:** great. **is digne:** deserves.

986. **publican:** see Luke xviii.13. **heven:** lift. **shamefastnesse:** feeling of shame. **anon:** at once.

987. **next:** nearest to.

988. **Seint Peter:** see I Peter v.6.

989. **sit:** (sitteth) sits.

990. **in no manere:** not in any way. **meene:** intermediary. **laste:** lowest.

991. **destourbe:** prevent. **taken kepe:** take heed. **sit:** sits.

992. **trespased to:** trespassed against. **set him:** (setteth him) sits.

994. **Seint Peter:** see Matthew xxvi.75. **weep:** wept.

995. **lette:** refrain.

996. **the Magdalene:** see Luke vii.37. **of hem:** in front of those. **biknowe:** confess.

997. **obeisant:** obedient. **giltes:** sins. **o man:** one man, i.e., Adam.

998. **hastily:** soon. **deedly:** deadly, mortal. **warisshe:** cure. **corrupte:** putrefy. **haste:** hasten. **heele:** heal.

999. **unshewed:** unconfessed.

1000. **shewen:** confess.

as for drede of deeth, that cometh ofte sodeynly, and no certeyn what tyme it shal be, ne in what place; and eek the drecchynge of o synne draweth in another; [1000] and eek the lenger that he tarieth, the ferther he is fro Crist. And if he abide to his laste day, scarsly may he shryven hym or remembre hym of his synnes or repenten hym, for the grevous maladie of his deeth./ And for as muche as he hath nat in his lyf herkned Jhesu Crist whanne he hath spoken, he shal crie to Jhesu Crist at his laste day, and scarsly wol he herkne hym./

And understond that this condicioun moste han foure thynges. Thy shrift moste be purveyed bifore and avysed; for wikked haste dooth no profit; and that a man konne shryve hym of his synnes, be it of pride, or of envye, and so forth with the speces and circumstances;/ and that he have comprehended in his mynde the nombre and the greetnesse of his synnes, and how longe that he hath leyn in synne;/ and eek that he be contrit of his synnes, and in stedefast purpos, by the grace of God, nevere eft to falle in synne; and eek that he drede and countrewaite hymself, that he fle the occasiouns of synne to whiche he is enclyned. [1005]

Also thou shalt shryve thee of alle thy synnes to o man, and nat a parcel to o man and a parcel to another; that is to understonde, in entente to departe thy confessioun, as for shame or drede; for it nys but stranglynge of thy soule./ For certes Jhesu Crist is entierly al good; in hym is noon imperfeccioun; and therfore outher he foryeveth al parfitly or elles never a deel./ I seye nat that if thow be assigned to the penitauncer for certein synne, that thow art bounde to shewen hym al the remenaunt of thy synnes, of whiche thow hast be shryven of thy curaat, but if it like thee of thyn humylitee; this is no departynge of shrifte./ Ne I seye nat, ther as I speke of divisioun of confessioun, that if thou have licence for to shryve thee to a discreet and an honest preest, where thee liketh, and by licence of thy curaat, that thow ne mayst wel shryve thee to him of alle thy synnes./ But lat no blotte be bihynde; lat no synne ben untoold, as fer as thow hast remembraunce. [1010] And whan thou shalt be shryven to thy curaat, telle hym eek alle the synnes that thow hast doon syn thou were last yshryven; this is no wikked entente of divisioun of shrifte./

Also the verray shrifte axeth certeine condiciouns. First, that thow shryve thee by thy free wil, noght constreyned, ne for shame of folk, ne for maladie, ne swiche thynges. For it is resoun that he that trespaseth by his free wyl, that by his free wyl he confesse his trespas;/ noon oother man shal telle his synne but he hymself; ne he shal nat nayte ne denye his synne, ne wratthe hym agayn the preest

---

1000. drecchynge: continuance. o: one.
1001. abide to: delays until. for: because of.
1002. herkned: listened to. he herkne: [Christ] listen to.
1003. moste: must. purveyed bifore: arranged beforehand. avysed: thought about.
1004. greetnesse: greatness. leyn: lain.
1005. contrit of: contrite for. nevere eft: never again. countrewaite: watch against.
1006. o: one. parcel: part. departe: divide.
1007. outher: either. never a deel: never a bit, not at all.
1008. penitauncer: confessor who assigns penance.
1010. be bihynde: be neglected.
1011. syn: since.
1012. resoun: according to reason; i.e., reasonable.
1013. nayte: disclaim. wratthe hym: be wrathful, be angry.

for his amonestynge to lete synne./ The seconde condicioun is that thy shrift be laweful, that is to seyn, that thow that shryvest thee, and eek the preest that hereth thy confessioun, ben verraily in the feith of holy chirche;/ and that a man ne be nat despeired of the mercy of Jhesu Crist, as Caym or Judas. [1015] And eek a man moot accusen hymself of his owene trespas, and nat another; but he shal blame and wyten hymself and his owene malice of his synne, and noon oother./ But nathelees, if that another man be occasioun or enticere of his synne, or the estaat of a persone be swich thurgh which his synne is agregged, or elles that he may nat pleynly shryven hym but he telle the persone with which he hath synned, thanne may he telle it,/ so that his entente be nat to bakbite the persone, but oonly to declaren his confessioun./

Thou ne shalt nat eek make no lesynges in thy confessioun, for humylitee, peraventure, to seyn that thou hast doon synnes of whiche thow were nevere gilty./ For Seint Augustyn seith, "If thou, by cause of humylitee, makest lesynges on thyself, though thow ne were nat in synne biforn, yet artow thanne in synne thurgh thy lesynges." [1020] Thou most eek shewe thy synne by thyn owene propre mouth, but thow be woxe dowmb, and nat by no lettre; for thow that hast doon the synne, thou shalt have the shame./ Thow shalt nat eek peynte thy confessioun by faire subtile wordes, to covere the moore thy synne; for thanne bigilestow thyself, and nat the preest. Thow most tellen it platly, be it nevere so foul ne so horrible./ Thow shalt eek shryve thee to a preest that is discreet to conseille thee; and eek thou shalt nat shryve thee for veyne glorie, ne for ypocrisye, ne for no cause but oonly for the doute of Jhesu Crist and the heele of thy soule./ Thow shalt nat eek renne to the preest sodeynly to tellen hym lightly thy synne, as whoso telleth a jape or a tale, but avysely and with greet devocioun./

And generally, shryve thee ofte. If thou ofte falle, ofte thou arise by confessioun. [1025] And though thou shryve thee ofter than ones of synne of which thou hast be shryven, it is the moore merite. And, as seith Seint Augustyn, thow shalt have the moore lightly relessyng and grace of God, bothe of synne and of peyne./ And certes, oones a yeere atte leeste wey it is laweful for to ben housled; for soothly ones a yeere alle thynges renovellen./

1013. amonestynge: admonition.   lete: leave.

1015. be despeired: lack hope.   Caym: Cain; see Genesis iv.14.   Judas: see Matthew xxvii.5.

1016. wyten: impute guilt to.   of: for.

1017. occasioun: cause.   enticere: instigator.   agregged: aggravated.   pleynly: fully.   but: unless.   which: whom.

1019. lesynges: lies.

1020. Seint Augustyn: see *Sermo* clxxxi.§4.

1021. be woxe: have become.   lettre: writing.   doon: committed.

1022. peynte: paint, color.   bigilestow: you deceive.   most: must.   platly: plainly, directly.

1023. doute: fear.   heele: healing.

1024. renne: run.   lightly: carelessly.   jape: joke.   avysely: with forethought.

1025. arise: may arise.

1026. ofter: more often.   ones: once.   be: been.   moore: greater.   Seint Augustyn: see [Pseudo-Augustine] *De Vera et Falsa Poenitentia* 1.9.§24.   the moore lightly: the more easily.   relessyng: remission.

1027. oones: once.   to ben housled: to receive the Communion.   renovellen: renew, are renewed.

Now have I toold of verray Confessioun, that is the seconde partie of Penitence./

Explicit secunda pars penitencie, et sequitur tercia pars eiusdem.

The thridde partie of Penitence is Satisfaccioun, and that stant generally in alm-
esse and in bodily peyne./ Now been ther thre manere of almesse: contricion of
herte, where a man offreth hymself to God; another is to han pitee of the defaute
of his neighebores. The thridde is in yevynge of good conseil and comfort, goostly and
bodily, where men han nede, and namely in sustenaunce of mannes foode. [1030]
And tak kep that a man hath nede of thise thinges generally: he hath nede of foode,
he hath nede of clothyng and herberwe, he hath nede of charitable conseil and
visitynge in prisone and in maladie, and sepulture of his dede body./ And if thow
mayst nat visite the nedeful with thy persone, visite hym by thy message and thy
yiftes./ Thise ben general almesses or werkes of charitee of hem that han temporel
richesse or discrecioun in conseilynge. Of thise werkes shaltow heren at the day of
doom./

Thise almesses shaltow doon of thyne owene propre thynges, and hastily and
prively, if thow mayst./ But nathelees, if thow mayst nat doon it prively, thow shalt
nat forbere to doon almesse though men seen it, so that it be nat doon for thank
of the world, but oonly for thank of Jhesu Crist. [1035] For, as witnesseth Seint
Mathew, *capitulo quinto,* "A citee may nat ben hyd that is set on a montayne, ne
men lighte nat a lanterne and put it under a busshel, but men sette it on a candle-
stikke to lighten the men in the hous./ Right so shal youre light lighten bifore men,
that they may seen youre goode werkes, and glorifie youre fader that is in hevene."/

Now as to speken of bodily peyne, it stant in preyeres, in wakynges, in fastynges,
in vertuouse techynges of orisouns./ Ye shul understonde that orisouns or preyeres
is for to seyn a pitous wyl of herte, that redresseth it in God and expresseth it by
word outward, to remoeven harmes and to han thynges espirituel and durable, and
somtyme temporel thynges; of whiche orisouns, certes, in the orison of the *Pater
noster* hath Jhesu Crist enclosed moost thynges./ Certes, it is privyleged of thre
thynges in his dignytee, for which it is moore digne than any oother preyere; for
that Jhesu Crist hymself maked it; [1040] and it is short, for it sholde be koud the
moore lightly, and for to withholden it the moore esily in herte, and helpen hymself

---

1029. **satisfaccioun:** the performance by a penitent of the penal and meritorious acts enjoined
by his confessor as payment of the temporal punishment due to his sin. **stant in:** consists of.
almesse: satisfaction.

1030. **defaute:** sinfulness. **goostly:** spiritual.

1031. **herberwe:** shelter. **maladie:** sickness. **sepulture:** burial.

1032. **nedeful:** needy. **with thy persone:** in person. **message:** messenger.

1033. **discrecioun:** sound judgment. **heren:** hear. **doom:** judgment.

1034. **almesses:** alms, works of charity. **doon of:** accomplish by means of. **hastily:** promptly.
prively: secretly.

1035. **forbere:** fail. **thank:** favor.

1036. **Seint Mathew:** see Matthew v.14–16. **lighten:** give light to.

1037. **lighten:** shine.

1038. **stant in:** consists of. **wakynges:** vigils.

1039. **is for to seyn:** signifies. **wyl of herte:** desire of the heart. **redresseth it in:** addresses
itself to. **harmes:** evils. **enclosed:** included.

1040. **privyleged of:** invested with. **dignytee:** worth.

1041. **for:** so that. **koud:** learned. **lightly:** easily. **withholden:** retain.

the ofter with the orisoun;/ and for a man sholde be the lasse wery to seyen it, and for a man may nat excusen hym to lerne it, it is so short and so esy; and for it comprehendeth in it self alle goode preyeres./ The exposicioun of this holy preyere, that is so excellent and digne, I bitake to thise maistres of theologie, save thus muchel wol I seyn; that whan thow prayest that God sholde foryeve thee thy giltes as thou foryevest hem that agilten to thee, be ful wel war that thow be nat out of charitee./ This holy orison amenuseth eek venyal synne, and therfore it aperteneth specially to penitence./

This preyere moste be trewely seyd, and in verray feith, and that men preye to God ordinatly and discreetly and devoutly; and alwey a man shal putten his wyl to be subget to the wille of God. [1045] This orisoun moste eek ben seyd with greet humblesse and ful pure; honestly, and nat to the anoyaunce of any man or womman. It moste eek ben continued with the werkes of charitee./ It avayleth eek agayn the vices of the soule; for, as seith Seint Jerome, "By fastynge ben saved the vices of the flessh, and by preyere the vices of the soule."/ After this, thou shalt understonde that bodily peyne stant in wakynge; for Jhesu Crist seith, "Waketh and preyeth, that ye ne entre in wikked temptacioun."/

Ye shul understanden also that fastynge stant in thre thynges: in forberynge of bodily mete and drynke, and in forberynge of worldly jolitee, and in forberynge of deedly synne; this is to seyn, that a man shal kepen hym fro deedly synne with al his myght./

And thou shalt understanden eek that God ordeyned fastynge, and to fastynge appertenen foure things: [1050] largenesse to povre folk; gladnesse of herte espirituel, nat to ben angry ne anoyed, ne grucche for he fasteth; and also resonable houre for to ete by mesure; that is for to seyn, a man shulde nat ete in untyme, ne sitte the lenger at his table for he fasteth./

Thanne shaltow understonde that bodily peyne stant in disciplyne or techynge, by word, or by writynge, or in ensample; also in werynge of heyres, or of stamyn, or of haubergeons on hire naked flessh, for Cristes sake, and swiche manere penances./ But war thee wel that swiche manere penaunces on thy flessh ne make nat thyn herte bitter or angry or anoyed of thyself; for bettre is to caste awey thyn heyre, than for to caste awey the swetenesse of Jhesu Crist./ And therfore seith

---

1041. **ofter:** more often.

1042. **for:** so that. **lasse:** less. **to lerne:** from learning.

1043. **exposicioun:** explanation. **bitake:** entrust. **giltes:** transgressions. **agilten to:** transgress against. **be out of:** lack.

1044. **amenuseth:** diminishes. **aperteneth:** belongs.

1045. **ordinatly:** properly.

1046. **moste:** must. **greet:** great. **pure:** purely. **honestly:** reverently. **continued with:** accompanied by.

1047. **saved:** avoided.

1048. **stant in:** consists of. **wakynge:** remaining awake for purposes of devotion; keeping vigil. **Crist:** see Matthew xxvi.41. **waketh:** watch; keep vigil.

1049. **forberynge of:** abstinence from. **jolitee:** pleasure; lust.

1050. **appertenen:** belong.

1051. **largenesse:** generosity. **grucche:** grumble, complain. **for:** because. **for to ete:** for eating. **by mesure:** in moderation. **in untyme:** at an unsuitable time. **for:** because.

1052. **werynge:** wearing. **heyres:** garments of haircloth. **stamyn:** a garment made of coarse worsted. **haubergeons:** garments of mail worn next to the skin for penance.

1053. **war thee wel:** take good care. **heyre:** hair-shirt.

Seint Paul, "Clothe yow, as they that been chosen of God, in herte of misericorde, debonairetee, suffraunce, and swich manere of clothynge"; of whiche Jhesu Crist is moore apayed than of heyres, or haubergeouns, or hauberkes./

Thanne is discipline eek in knokkynge of thy brest, in scourgynge with yerdes, in knelynges, in tribulacions, [1055] in suffrynge paciently wronges that ben doon to thee, and eek in pacient suffraunce of maladies, or lesynge of worldly catel, or of wyf, or of child, or othere freendes./

Thanne shaltow understonde whiche thynges destourben penaunce; and this is in foure maneres, that is, drede, shame, hope, and wanhope, that is, desperacion./ And for to speke first of drede; for which he weneth that he may suffre no penaunce;/ ther-agayns is remedie for to thynke that bodily penaunce is but short and litel at regard of the peyne of helle, that is cruel and so long that it lasteth withouten ende./

Now again the shame that a man hath to shryven hym, and namely thise ypocrites that wolden been holden so parfite that they han no nede to shryven hem; [1060] agayns that shame sholde a man thynke that, by wey of resoun, that he that hath nat ben ashamed to doon foule thinges, certes hym oghte nat ben ashamed to do faire thynges, and that is confessiouns./ A man sholde eek thynke that God seeth and woot alle his thoghtes and alle his werkes; to hym may no thyng ben hyd ne covered./ Men sholden eek remembren hem of the shame that is to come at the day of doom to hem that ben nat penitent and shryven in this present lyf./ For alle the creatures in hevene, in erthe, and in helle shullen seen apertly al that they hyden in this world./

Now for to speken of the hope of hem that ben necligent and slowe to shryven hem, it stant in two maneres. [1065] That oon is that he hopeth for to lyve longe and for to purchacen muche richesse for his delit, and thanne he wol shryven hym; and, as he seith, he may as hym semeth tymely ynough come to shrifte./ Another is of surquidrie that he hath in Cristes mercy./ Agayns the firste vice, he shal thynke that oure lif is in no sikernesse, and eek that alle the richesse in this world ben in aventure, and passen as a shadwe on the wal;/ and, as seith Seint Gregorie, that it aperteneth to the grete rightwisnesse of God that nevere shal the peyne stynte of

---

1054. Seint Paul: see Colossians iii.12. misericorde: mercy. debonairetee: kindness. suffraunce: long-suffering. of whiche: with which. apayed: pleased. hauberkes: chain mail worn over a hair-shirt as a form of penance.

1055. knokkynge: beating. yerdes: rods.

1056. suffraunce: endurance. lesynge: loss.

1057. destourben: hinder. wanhope: despair.

1058. weneth: believes. suffre: endure.

1059. ther-agayns: against that. at regard of: in comparison with.

1060. namely: especially. holden: held.

1062. seeth: sees. woot: knows. werkes: deeds.

1063. doom: judgment.

1064. apertly: openly.

1065. slowe: sluggish. stant in: consists of.

1066. purchacen: acquire. tymely: early.

1067. surquidrie: over-confidence.

1068. sikernesse: certainty. in aventure: in jeopardy, uncertain.

1069. Seint Gregorie: see *Moralium* lib.xxxiv, c.19.§36. it aperteneth: it is appropriate to. rightwisnesse: righteousness. stynte: cease.

hem that nevere wolde withdrawen hem fro synne, hir thankes, but ay continue in synne; for thilke perpetuel wil to do synne shul they han perpetuel peyne./

Wanhope is in two maneres: the firste wanhope is in the mercy of Crist; that oother is that they thynken that they ne myghte nat longe persevere in goodnesse. [1070] The firste wanhope comth of that he demeth that he hath synned so greetly and so ofte, and so longe leyn in synne, that he shal nat be saved./ Certes, agayns that cursed wanhope sholde he thynke that the passion of Jhesu Crist is moore strong for to unbynde than synne is strong for to bynde./ Agayns the seconde wanhope he shal thynke that as ofte as he falleth he may arise agayn by penitence. And though he never so longe have leyn in synne, the mercy of Crist is alwey redy to receiven hym to mercy./ Agayns the wanhope that he demeth that he sholde nat longe persevere in goodnesse, he shal thynke that the feblesse of the devel may nothyng doon, but if men wol suffren hym;/ and eek he shal han strengthe of the help of God, and of al holy chirche, and of the proteccioun of aungels, if hym list. [1075]

Thanne shal men understonde what is the fruyt of penaunce; and, after the word of Jhesu Crist, it is the endelees blisse of hevene,/ ther joye hath no contrarioustee of wo ne grevaunce; ther alle harmes ben passed of this present lyf; ther as is the sikernesse fro the peyne of helle; ther as is the blisful compaignye that rejoysen hem everemo, everich of otheres joye;/ ther as the body of man, that whilom was foul and derk, is moore cleer than the sonne; ther as the body, that whilom was syk, freele, and fieble, and mortal, is inmortal, and so strong and so hool that ther may no thyng apeyren it;/ ther as ne is neither hunger, thurst, ne coold, but every soule replenyssed with the sighte of the parfit knowynge of God./ This blisful regne may men purchace by poverte espirituel, and the glorie by lowenesse, the plentee of joye by hunger and thurst, and the reste by travaille, and the lyf by deeth and mortificacion of synne. [1080]

Heere taketh the makere
of this book his leve.

Now preye I to hem alle that herkne this litel tretys or rede, that if ther be any thyng in it that liketh hem, that therof they thanken oure Lord Jhesu Crist, of whom procedeth al wit and al goodnesse./ And if ther be any thyng that displese hem, I preye hem also that they arrette it to the defaute of myn unkonnynge, and nat to my wyl, that wolde fayn have seyd bettre if I hadde had konnynge./ For oure

---

1069. **hir thankes:** of their free will, willingly.

1070. **wanhope:** despair.

1071. **of that he demeth:** from his thinking. **greetly:** greatly. **leyn:** lain.

1074. **thynke:** call to mind. **doon:** accomplish. **suffren:** allow.

1076. **after:** according to.

1077. **contrarioustee of:** quality opposite to. **harmes:** evils. **ben passed:** are past. **sikernesse:** security. **everich of:** each in.

1078. **cleer:** bright. **freele:** frail. **hool:** sound. **apeyren:** impair, harm.

1079. **replenyssed:** filled.

1080. **purchace:** gain. **by:** through. **lowenesse:** humility. **plentee:** fullness. **travaille:** labor.

1082. **arrette:** impute, ascribe. **defaute:** fault, defect. **unkonnynge:** ignorance.

book seith, "Al that is writen is writen for oure doctrine," and that is myn entente./ Wherfore I biseke yow mekely, for the mercy of God, that ye preye for me that Crist have mercy on me and foryeve me my giltes;/ and namely of my translacions and enditynges of worldly vanitees, the whiche I revoke in my retracciouns: [1085] as is the book of Troilus; the book also of Fame; the book of the xxv. Ladies; the book of the Duchesse; the book of Seint Valentynes day of the Parlement of Briddes; the tales of Caunterbury, thilke that sownen into synne;/ the book of the Leoun; and many another book, if they were in my remembrance, and many a song and many a leccherous lay; that Crist for his grete mercy foryeve me the synne./ But of the translacion of Boece de Consolacione, and othere bookes of legendes of seintes, and omelies, and moralitee, and devocioun,/ that thanke I oure Lord Jhesu Crist and his blisful Moder, and alle the seintes of hevene,/ bisekynge hem that they from hennes forth unto my lyves ende sende me grace to biwayle my giltes, and to studie to the salvacioun of my soule, and graunte me grace of verray penitence, confessioun and satisfaccioun to doon in this present lyf, [1090] thurgh the benigne grace of hym that is kyng of kynges and preest of alle preestes, that boghte us with the precious blood of his herte;/ so that I may been oon of hem at the day of doom that shulle be saved. *Qui cum patre et Spiritu Sancto vivit et regnat Deus per omnia secula. Amen.*

HEERE IS ENDED THE BOOK OF THE TALES OF CAUNTERBURY, COMPILED BY GEFFREY CHAUCER, OF WHOS SOULE JHESU CRIST HAVE MERCY. AMEN.

·

1083. book: see I Timothy iii.16.

1084. giltes: sins.

1086. the book of Fame: *The House of Fame.* the book of the xxv. Ladies: *The Legend of Good Women.* sownen into: tend toward.

1087. the book of the Leoun: a lost work which may have been translated or adapted from Guillaume de Machaut's *Le Dit dou Lyon* or from *Le Dict du Lyon* of Eustache Deschamps.

1088. omelies: homilies, sermons.

1090. hennes forth: henceforth. studie to: meditate upon; be solicitous for.

1092. doom: judgment.

Comment on the Text

Basic Glossary

Comment on the Text

For the working basis of the text (including paragraphing, punctuation, and spelling) and for many other matters I am indebted to F. N. Robinson, who kindly and generously gave me permission to make use of his edition of *The Tales,* revising it in whatever ways seemed best to me. For the present edition I have been less conservative than he in admitting readings from Manly and Rickert; in fact the present text represents as accurately as possible Manly's "latest common original of all extant manuscripts" (O'), with the correction of all recognizable errors in the transmission to O' of Chaucer's own text (O). This has meant the acceptance of the headless nine-syllabled line, with stress on the first syllable, as characteristic of Chaucer's prosody; in commenting on Fragment I, line 217, Manly (Vol. III, p. 423) writes that Skeat, the Globe edition, and Robinson "adopt 'eek' from inadequate MS evidence to avoid a nine-syllabled line, but textual evidence is overwhelmingly in favor of Chaucer's frequent use of such lines in CT. In almost every case a reader sensitive to rhythmic effects will find justification for these lines in the increased speed of movement." The "Lydgatian line" (existing before Chaucer), of which Robinson admits a few examples (see p. 715, on IV, 1682), is recognized even more willingly by Manly (III, 425, on I, 741): "Chaucer seems not only to have allowed an extra syllable at the caesura, but sometimes, as here, to have omitted the unstressed syllable after the caesural pause." He likewise recognized that there are many examples of "final *e* pronounced before an initial vowel at the caesura for us to reject the evidence of the MSS here" (III, 436, on I, 2904). These and other types of lines have encouraged the insertion of a variety of such fillers as "eek," "that," and "ful" by scribes and editors. Unless emendations seem fairly certain I have not striven to use fillers to complete imperfect lines, of which a number occur in the unrevised portion of the Knight's Tale (after l. 2800) and elsewhere.

In attempting to recreate the text as Chaucer wrote it I have accepted a number of emendations suggested by Manly and others; for example, "chaunten" for "dauncen" in I, 2202 (Manly), "Scoler" for "Soler" in I, 3990 (Brewer), "Nath" for "Hath" in II, 49 (Manly), "nas" for "was" in II, 752 (Skeat), "worly" for "worthy" in VII, 917 (Burrow, *Chaucer Review,* 3 [1969], 170–73), "wright" for "wight" in III, 117 (Donaldson), "pace" for "pees" in III, 838 (Koch), and Manly's conjectures for I, 2963, III, 436, 462, and 1277. The more complicated emendations—"was gon" for "bigan" in VII, 3190, "as Ptholomee" for "Protholomee" in III, 2289 of O', and "of the monthe of Juyn" for "er the month of Juyn" in IV, 2133—are explained in footnotes.

The title, *The Tales of Canterbury,* is attested by the evidence of the manuscripts with headings and colophons in English (see Manly and Rickert, III, 528–30) and by the "retracciouns" in the final section of *The Tales,* entitled "Here taketh the makere of this book his leve." Headings and endings of the tales and links are from the Ellesmere manuscript.

I have adopted some of the spellings of the Hengwrt manuscript, which are generally used by Manly. But the following list of revisions of Robinson's text only rarely includes spellings, different forms of the same word, punctuation, and paragraphing, and—in the prose tales—insignificant transpositions of words; not noted are the French passages for the gaps in the *Melibee*, which are from the text prepared by J. B. Severs for *Sources and Analogues* (pp. 568–614).

Readings which differ from those of Robinson

Tale, Fragment, and Line	Robinson's Reading	Present Reading
Gen Prol, I, 11	nature	Nature
164	chapeleyne, and preestes thre.	chapeleyne.
171	belle.	belle
172	celle,	celle.
217	And eek	And
288	nas	was
342	nowher	nevere
346	thynke.	thynke,
375	were they	they were
421	where they	where
500	shal	sholde
558	bokeler	a bokeler
613	myster;	myster:
630	noon;	noon,
686	lay biforn	biforn
741	whoso that	whoso
752	to han been	to been
754	is	was
824	alle in a flok	in a flok
826	wateryng	Wateryng
KnT, I, 894	unto	to
927	And	Now
980	slough	wan
992	housbondes	freendes
1005	bodyes	the bodies
1031	This Palamon and his felawe Arcite	Dwellen this Palamon and eek Arcite
1039	fyner	fairer
1044	hym	it
1046	maked	maketh
1095	for to crye	to crye
1129	"It nere," quod he, "to thee no greet honour	"It were to thee," quod he, "no greet honour
1145	Nay,	Now
1154	And	But
1171	mayde, or wydwe	mayde, wydwe
1179	whil that they	whil they
1180	And	That

Tale, Fragment, and Line	Robinson's Reading	Present Reading
KtT, I, 1223	that day	the day
1260	witen	woot
	thing	thing that
1279	on his shynes	of his shynes
1320	man after his deeth	after his deeth man
1346	nevere mo he shal	nevere mo ne shal
1350	he moot	moot he
1406	unknowe.	unknowe,
1424	long	strong
1452	Thise seven yeer	This seven yeer
1573	after	afterward
1595	for	or
1637	Tho	To
1876	thonked	thonken
1880	To Thebes, with his olde walles wyde.	To Thebesward, with olde walles wyde.
2049	depeynted was	was depeynted
2104	or	and
2125	is	nys
2202	dauncen	[chaunten]
2222	of	to
2420	victorie	the victorie
2427	the ground anon	anon the ground
2488	But	And
2491	that	the
2519	fighte;	fighte:—
2528	was	is
2534	peple	the peple
2536	Tho	Thus
	wille.	wille:
2559	maces	mace
2602	in arrest;	in th'arest;
2642	ydrawe unto	ydrawen to
2657	no	nat
2758	hath now	hath
2788	alle circumstances	circumstances alle
2825	swich	swich a
2840	chaunge bothe up and doun,	up and doun,
2842	ensamples	ensample
2860	that	the
2865	comande anon	anon comande
2874	hadde he gloves	his gloves
2892	that weren grete	grete
2918	ful many	many
2920	that	how
2949	wyn, and milk	milk, and wyn
2956	Ne	And
2963	eek how that they	how they alle

Tale, Fragment, and Line	Robinson's Reading	Present Reading
KnT, I, 2982	hadde	hath
2999	wel abregge	abregge
3000	nedeth noght noon	nedeth noon
3003	by this ordre wel	wel by this ordre
3011	of	for
3018	From	Fro the
	to sprynge,	sprynge,
3019	we	ye
3026	may ye se	ye se
3032	men	ye
3052	up yolden is	is yolden up
3059	the flour	flour
3063	loved	loveth
3070	er that	er
3071	rede that	rede
3074	we	I
3078	wille	wille,
3099	this wyde world	this world
3104	al so	so
MiP, I, 3172	For Goddes love, demeth nat	Demeth nat, for Goddes love,
MiT, I, 3187	at	in
3217	the Kynges Noote	The Kynges Noote
3225	wylde and yong,	yong and wylde
3228	man	men
3236	barmclooth eek	barmclooth
3285	Why, lat be," quod she, "lat be, Nicholas,	Why, lat be! Quod ich, 'Lat be,' Nicholas,
3292	wol	wolde
3403	hym	hem
3418	thyng	nothyng
3470	of	up
3500	sette.	sette,
3501	He	And [no ¶]
3519	an hour	in an hour
3532	and	or
3541	hadde be levere	hadde levere
3566	spye	espye
3602	"allas" and "weylawey,"	"Allas and weylawey,"
3619	swogh;	swogh,
3620	He	And
3654	of solas	in solas
3761	cleped	clepen
3767	for	what,
3810	amydde	in
3813	And	That
3828	That yet	That
3850	this	the
RvP, I, 3876	whil	whil that

Tale, Fragment, and Line	Robinson's Reading	Present Reading
RvT, I, 3931	is in [misprint]	in
3953	bounden	wounde
3977	This	The
3990	Soler	Scoler
4001	craketh	craked
4003	this	the
4005	revelrye	reverye
4020	hem	hym
4026	"Symond," quod John, "by God,	"By God," quod John, "Symond,
4056	ne counte	counte
4066	thurgh thenne	thenne
4097	now	ye,
4127	John	this John
4128	this	that
4129	seyd, 'man	seye, 'Men
4160	John;	John. [¶ at 4161]
4166	two	a
4172	upon	on
4184	al this day	this day
IMLT, II, 14	of	at
49	Hath	[Nath]
MLT, II, 150	And	But
188	That	And
288	wal,	wal
408	telle,	telle;
409	And	He
	blis.	blis,
435	was	nas
489	peple	the peple
532	in	on
574	Converted	Converteth
577	many a	many
676	holde I	I holde
714	no bet	noon oother
728	taketh	tath
735	to al	of al
752	was	[nas]
862	looked	looketh
882	seel and eek	seel, and
938	nas	was
1058	swowned	swowneth
1059	excuseth	excused
1060	and alle his	and his
1124	his	this
1142	deeth	Deeth
MLE, II, 1170	hem [misprint?]	him
ShT, VII, 59	to pleye	and pleye

Tale, Fragment, and Line	Robinson's Reading	Present Reading
ShT, VII, 78	as wel	wel
120	how that it	how it
131	porthors here	*portehors*
135	porthors I yow swere	*portehors* I swere
157	gooth youre wey	goth awey
181	I am	am I
184	it myghte	myghte it
312	For that	That
337	gooth first	first goth
359	hire	yow
382	thus	that
394	axen	axe of
404	that	this
432	my	thy
433	endeth now	endeth
442	unto	in to
PrT, VII, 493	the	this
512	alday	alwey
553	than wolde	wolde
555	swetnesse hath	swetnesse
564	youre	oure
577	ther	ther as
625	the	his
636	masse	the masse
682	his	this
Thop, VII, 781	that	the
805		[omitted]
818	with thee	thee
835	For now I wol yow rowne	I wol yow rowne
917	worthy	worly
Mel, VII, 993	thou has lorn [misprint]	thou hast lorn
998	oure othere goodes	oure goodes
1000	right as	right so as
1011	to Melibeus	unto Melibeus
1022	for which	for the which
1023	this same cause	the same cause
1026	thy persone for to save	thy body for to save
1033	al be it so that	al be it that
1034	weaxen [misprint]	we axen
1042	bigynne	be bigonne
1051	seide to hym	seide hym
1058	God forbede	Goddes forbode
1070	And as to	And to
1073	many	ful many
1082	For if it so were	For if so were
1095	I shal shewe yow ful hoolsome	I shal shewe holsom
1098	by good conseil	by conseil

Tale, Fragment, and Line	Robinson's Reading	Present Reading
Mel, VII, 1099	wolde have al destroyed it.	wolde it al destroye.
1103	whan	whan that
1105	conseils	conseil
	nevere	neither
1109	manye of othre resons	manye othere resons
	conseils	conseil
1120	thyng	thynges
1130	roote	the roote
1134	ye ne may nat	ye may nat
	by a sodeyn thought	a sodeyn thought
1136	ye ne be nat	ye be nat
1148	the biwreiyng	thy biwreiyng
1172	ye oghte to eschewe	ye oghte eschewe
1178	to cacche with	to cacche
1180	of the wordes	of wordes
1181	the wordes	wordes
1185	where	where as
1206	or noon	or no
1213	For certes,	For
1218	Piers	Peter
1221	or noon	or no
1224	conseillours	conseil
1230	if so be	if it so be
1251	that [misprint]	than
1254	ye ne han nat	ye han nat
1269	for to anoye	to anoye
1273	sholde	shullen
	youre	thy
1284	thys	that
1288–89	in this wise:/ For	in this wise,/ for
1289	othere thynges.	othere thynges:
1311	wolt thider	wolt go thider
1337	and strongeste	and the strongeste
1387	thou shal [misprint]	thou shalt
1432	chastisynge of the	the chastisynge of
1455	a greet fool.	to greet a fool.
1471	and the vileynyes	and vileynyes
1496	whan we	whan that we
1505	the seintes	seintes
1520	I nam nat	I am nat
1553	and wel konne	and that wel konne
1571	And	And therfore
	bet it is	bettre is
1593	the greete heete.	the heete.
1594	nat yow over-muchel	yow nat over-muchel
1605	spende hem	spende
1621	ne sholde nat	sholde nat
1622	part to hem	hem part

Tale, Fragment, and Line	Robinson's Reading	Present Reading
Mel, VII, 1623	shullen	sholden
1656	of the peple	of peple
1659	this peple	the peple
1661	a fewe folk	fewe folk
1663	if he be	if it be
1696	seith, 'He	seith that 'he
1706	ne anger	ne of anger
1722	of youre assent	youre assent
1726	delibered	she delibered
1774	knowelecheth it	knowelecheth
1777	place that 'he	place, ''He is worthy to have remissioun and foryifnesse
	it, is worthy remissioun.'	it.'
1810	It standeth [misprint]	''It standeth
1815	punyssement	punysshynge
1825	strecchen hem	strecchen
1875	unto hem	to hem
MkP, VII, 1898	me forth	me
1960	ye	they
1989	unto	to
MkT, VII, 2000	wol I	I wol
2003	where	where as
2006	which that	which
2068	his	this
2071	were	was
2098	of	fro
2192	bad	made
2254	his [misprint]	hir
2265	a	the
2438	save	but
2473	like [misprint]	ilke
2481	how that	how
2521	he were	he was
2544	ful greet	greet
2564	dar	dorst
2592	Of	With
2641	quaked.	quaked,
2642	He was	He
2662	And yet	And
2720	Valerie	Valerius
2757	and eek	and
NPP, VII, 2792	or daun	daun
NPT, VII, 2854	an	any
2901	wolde han	han
2977	this	his
3037	that same	the same
3042	carte	carte heere
3057	this	this is

Tale, Fragment, and Line	Robinson's Reading	Present Reading
NPT, VII, 3076	But	But herkneth!
3084	for to	to
3085	byde	abyde
3093	And eek	And
3155	venymous	venymes
3190	bigan	[was gon]
3231	that yerd	the yerd
3248	that was[1]	that I was
3255	that dreem	the dreem
3301	yow	ye
3314	For that a	For a
3375	This	The
3411	am I	I am
3418	the cok	he
3428	ofter	any ofter
WBP, III, 7	have ywedded	han wedded
19	seyde he	he seyde,
37	were leveful unto	leveful were to
46	sothe,	sith
	al.	al,
56	ferforth as	fer as evere
84	nys	is
97	clene, body	clene in body
98	I nyl nat	ne wol I
100	nath	hath
117	wight	wright
122	Were	Was
127	This	That
149	I wol	wol I
154	I wol have	wol I have
182	The	Thise
184	it were	were
189	that	yet
192	is nat	nys
193	now wol I telle	thanne wol I telle yow
212	me yeven	yeven me
WBP, II, 231	wyf shal, if	wyf, if
232	Bere	Shal beren
	that the	the
244	thou chidest	ye chiden
280	hous	houses
288	Spoones and	Spoones,
316	to enquere or	enquere and
326	the hyeste	hyeste
327	nevere	nat
331	certeyn	certes

[1] "that was" is a misprint for "that it was": see Robinson's first edition (1933).

Tale, Fragment, and Line	Robinson's Reading	Present Reading
WBP, II, 333	wolde	wil
368	maner resemblances	resemblances
371	wommenes	wommanes
387	and yit	and I
388	hadde I	I hadde
391	blyve	ful blyve
394	unnethes myghte they	they myghte unnethe
402	whil that	whil
463	He	Ne
467	wommen	womman
580	But	'But
	he	ye
581	taught.	taught.'
584	this	that
585	I shal	shal I
600	a twenty	twenty
621	wys	wysely
622	I ne	I
624	or long, or	long,
685	on	in
836	and eek	and
838	pees	[pace]
WBT, III, 878	go now	go
882	bifel it	bifel
899	thanketh	thanked
907	tellen it	tellen it me
929	hertes been	herte is
1046	the olde	that olde
1052	thyng that	thyng
1063	and oold	old
1080	on the	on
1090	so	thus
1091	and eek	and
1096	tel me	tel
1129	goodnesse,	prowesse,
1169	that it	that
1189	have	to have
1248	Dooth	Do
1262	wol nat	noght wol
FrP, III, 1277	scole eek	scoles
1288	wol have	wol
1295	And eek	And
1300	my leeve	leeve
FrT, III, 1319	Thanne	And thanne
1322	nas	was
1324	wel wher that	wher
1332	the wommen	wommen
1333	oure	my

Tale, Fragment, and Line	Robinson's Reading	Present Reading
FrT, III, 1370	yknowe	knowe
1377	Rood for	For
1379	And happed	Happed
1421	how that	how
1527	to	to thee,
1542	The	This
1650	may it	may
1663	thise somonours hem	this somonour hym
1664	hir	his
	hem	hym
SuP, III, 1693	from	of
1694	ther	they
SuT, III, 1744	hym	hem
1754	ay hem	hem ay
1768	whos that	whos
1784	have I	I have
1828	over	on
1868	his	my
1950	spent	spended
1979	chirches may ye fynde,	chirches, may ye fynde
1991	aqueyntances nat	aqueyntance nat for
1993	hire	ire
1999	hooly and	holy,
2035	That	This
2108	For elles moste	Or elles mote
2111	wolde us fro this world	fro this world wolde us
2122	on-fire	a-fire
2125	yeve yow,	yeve,
2134	also muche	as muche
2137	by	upon
2140	put in	put
2176	this day	to-day
2178	is noon	ther nys
2204	thynke ye herby	thynketh yow therby
2212	disclaundre	diffame
	ther	wher
2226	the soun	a soun
2235	evere	ther
	litel and litel	lite and lite
2245	thynges	thyng of
2261	his	this
2262	doun	adoun
2289	dide or	or [as]
CIP, IV, 17	be that	be
36	deeth	Deeth
CIT, IV, 57	right at	at
128	thyn	youre
165	That what	What

Tale, Fragment, and Line	Robinson's Reading	Present Reading
CIT, IV, 257	By	Of
288	hir	the
308	hir lyves	my lyves
316	This	The
360	Am I	I am
413	in	on
445	this markys	the markys
547	to speken	speken
579	hadde	hath
583	ful softe	softe
588	whenne	whennes
653	at	of
687	wondred	wondreth
692	for crueel	of cruel
760	I tellen	telle I
888	take I	I take
916	and	and she
937	womman	wommen
1017	konnyngly	so konnyngly
1063	ne noon	noon
MeP, IV, 1223	large	a large
MeT, IV, 1301	if that	if
1305–06	And if thou take a wyf unto thy hoold, Ful lightly maystow been a cokewold.	And if thou take a wyf
1417	twenty	sixteen
1418	ful fayn	fayn
1511	that koude	koude
1545	I have	that I
1566	sayd	ysayd
1689	this word	that word
1776	ther	as
1780	as at	at
1806	Wolde . . . . wolde	Wol . . . wol
1809	hath	hadde
1923	se	to see
1960	And	He
1967	aventure	by adventure
1996	made	maked
1998	oonly but	but oonly
2108	myghte	myghtest
2125	ful sooth	sooth
2127	Love	love
2133	er the month of Juyn	[of] the monthe of [Juyn]
2140	alle his	his
2179	whan that	whan
2218	ful myrie	myrie
2232	stories	storie

Tale, Fragment, and Line	Robinson's Reading	Present Reading
MeT, IV, 2239	The tresons whiche that wommen doon to man	The treson whiche that womman dooth to man
2300	if that	if
SqP, IV, 2424	the	a
SqT, V, 16	longeth	longed
94	his contenaunce	contenaunce
105	Al be it	Al be
128	ful many	many
171	as stille	stille
178	this	the
201	of	a
202	they	han
211	men moun	men
226	into	unto
239	with	for
255	nys	is
266	this Cambyuskan	Cambyuskan
268	Toforn	Biforn
270	they sownen	ther sownen
291	the spices	spices
299	at a	a
317	telle yow	yow telle
326	been ydrawe ne	be ydrawe nor
330	by day	day
349	wolde	wol
359	nys	is
366	Ne	Nor
374	on	upon
406	the	this
430	swowneth	swowned
470	yfynde	fynde
477	of hir swough gan breyde	of swough gan abreyde
529	on	upon
533	al my	my
592	it happeth	happeth
597	seyde hym	seyde
657	which that	which
FkP, V, 726	to me	to
FkT, V, 999–1000		[Placed between 1006 and 1007.]
1067	seye	seye thus
1086	wheither	wher
1358	or elles	or
1408	whan that she had	whan she hadde
1430	swich a	swich
1541–44		[Placed between 1550 and 1551.]
PhT, VI, 91	tresons	tresoun
97	that	if
99	ne perisse	perisse

Tale, Fragment, and Line	Robinson's Reading	Present Reading
PhT, VI, 252	sholde	wolde
PdP, VI, 382	ymaad	ymaked
386	He	They
	in Goddes	a Goddes
387	him	hem
PdT, VI, 532	That they	They
581	Bledynge ay	Bledynge
646	knoweth	knowen
663	for to	to
709	al torente	they torente
727	lyf [misprint]	lyf.
736	in me	me
769	he cam	they came
773	that	the
777	what that	what
817	woot wel	woot
871	of hym	hym
911	names	name
941	Hoost heere	Hoost
SNP, VIII, 27	with rose	of rose
SNT, VIII, 137	it	I
180	whiche	whiche that
202	lettre	lettres
216	the	this
280	make [misprint?]	made
326	thyng	thynges
405	tobete	bete
500	it is	is a
524	ful	a ful
534	is	he
CYP, VIII, 558	under-nethe	under that
561	semed as	semed
563	it	he
572	hadde longe	longe hadde
621	at	of
625	turne it	turnen
627	this tale	thus
678	but	and
686	Which that	Which
698	his	this
719	as that	as
CYT, VIII, 803	purpos, if	craft, if that
836	oght hath	hath oght
856	ablucions	ablucioun
890	And thus by smel, and by	Lo thus by smellyng and
895	seyn that	seyn
918	lord is	is lord
928	ne was	was

Tale, Fragment, and Line	Robinson's Reading	Present Reading
CYT, VIII, 944	Although	And though
963	herd it	herd
994	Although that	Although
1003	nas	was
1005	I seye	seye I
1079	ne artow	artow
1087	as that	as
1094	whan that	whan
1118	to the	the
1122	name	the name
1123	to whiche	whiche that
1157	as that	as
1170	at wynne [misprint]	atwynne
1200	aboven it	above
1203	that	the
1207	brynge us	bryngeth
1215	ne wol	wol
1237	hope.	hope."
1239	pardee!"	pardee!
1242	that it	it
1260	he blew	blew
1276	this	his
1296	the	this
1335	if that	if
1336	it shal	shal it
1397	thise jayes	jayes
1403	unto	into
1432	knowlechyng."	knowlechyng";
1433	How be	How
1447	of secrees	of the secretes
McP, IX, 59	wolde telle	telle wolde
89	hym	it
99	O thou	O
McT, IX, 110	soone [misprint]	sonne
147	in ydel	for naught
157	for	by
185	wol	that wol
263	And	Hym
268	and gyterne	gyterne
280	smyteth	smytest
290	and	or
310	what that	what
PsP, X, 1	al ended	ended
5	was tho,	was, so
23	arte	artow
PsT, X, 91	every	at every
105	pilgrimages	pilgrimage
121	a man	man

Tale, Fragment, and Line	Robinson's Reading	Present Reading
PsT, X, 126	of the kyng	of
134	looke he	looke
157	the stynkynge	stynkynge
171	in	on
175	into	in
185	as dooth	as
191	And	As
	of the	of
197	as of alle	of alle
	the soule	soule
199	For he nys	For he is
211	by the word	in the word
213	as though they	as though men
220	ne water ne	ne water
225	and they may nat plese	ne they may nat plese
231	to have	have
256	Crist	Jhesu Crist
273	forfeted. And therfore resonably may be seyd of Jhesu in this manere:	forfeted:
277	and peyne	and of peyne
281	for oure felonies	by oure felonies
288	wel for to do [twice]	wel to do
291	for his werkes	that for his werkes
	that God	God
294	aperceyveth it wel	aperceyveth wel
308	a man	man
315	soothly	certes
320	thee of thy	hym of hise
329	to the sighte	to sight
337	as for to	as to
345	ne hadde no mete	hadde no mete
350	wexeth or	wexeth and
353	if it so be	if so be
361	fallen into deedly synne	falle in dedly synne
365	the love of thilke worldly thynges	thilke worldly thynges
371–72	synnes;/ soothly	synnes/ soothly
372	clerkes writen,	clerkes writen;
	that a man eteth	that man eteth
383	God, and for the love	God, or for the love
387	the sevene deedly synnes	deedly synnes
404	whan man	whan a man
405	his temporeel hynesse	temporel hynesse
	this worldly estaat	worldly estat
424	faren	that faren
427	were corrupt	ben corrupt
	or by oother	or oother

Tale, Fragment, and Line	Robinson's Reading	Present Reading
PsT, X, 433	in many a	many a
	and in to curious	in to curious
451	or in goodes	or goodes
454	richesse	richesses
470	yifte	yiftes
472	delices of a man ben	delices of a man is
473	the synne of Pride	Pride
478	humylitee is in his mouth	humylitee in his mouth
484	mannes prosperitee	mennes prosperitee
487	whan a man werreyeth	whan that a man werreyeth
	whan he woot	whan that he woot
491	mannes goodnesse and of his	mennes goodnesse and of hir
501	sholde man suffre	sholde men suffre
505	grucchyng sourdeth	it sourdeth
506	doon	to doon
515	remedie	the remedye
516	espiritueel, and that	spirituel that
565	sixe	[thre]
	an homycide	homycide
568	lordshipes	lordshipes''
572	is that is doon	is doon
576	drynkynge	drynkynge of
	by drynkes wilfully	by drynkes
581	of his halwes	his halwes
583	his synne	synne
595	declaracioun	declarynge
609	ese and profit	ese or profit
	to disese and damage	to damage
612	flaterynge	flaterye
614	flaterye, that maketh	flaterye maketh
616	bitraysen	bitraysed
628	which that he myghte	that he myghte
643	the which	which
650	how that	how
651	Swiche japes	Swiche japeres
653	othere synnes mo	othere synnes
654	callen Pacience	clepen Pacience
657	doon or seyn	doon ne seyn
663	despised	despised hym
669	for love	for the love
670	broghte a yerde to scoure with	and broghte a yerde to scoure
671	this child	the child
	ye do	ye to do
677	synne of Envye and of Ire	synnes of Envye and Ire
678	of troubled herte	of a trouble herte
709	wolde	wol
712	oghte doon	oghte to doon

Tale, Fragment, and Line	Robinson's Reading	Present Reading
PsT, X, 718	lyk to hym	lyk hym
720	shal	wol
722	of a man	of man
723	nys hym	nys to hym
727	of man	of a man
731	and the firste	the firste
732	to undertake	undertake
733	therfore men shal	therfore a man shal
743	thyng	thynges
752	this cursed synne	his cursed synne
758	nat for to robben	nat to robben
763	than drede	than drede thee
765	that thise conquerours	that conquerours
769	of the godes	of goodes
	no do nat so [misprint]	ne do nat so
771	estaat and in his degree.	estaat.
779	marchandises	marchandise
786	men or wommen	man or womman
788	and Antecrist	and of Antecrist
800	to payen it agayn	to payen
808	to the misericorde of Jhesu Crist; that he yaf	to misericorde of Jhesu Crist, that yaf
811–12	yaf to us;/ and to han	yaf us;/ and eek to han
812	whanne, where, ne how;	whanne;
814	he hath synne therof	he hath synne
820	that been the enemys	that they ben the enemys
841	for hire lecherye	for lecherye
858	[bushes]	beautees
861	though it were	though she were
864	and grymnesse	grislynesse
884	the moore grevous	moore grevous
886	yelden hem	yelden to hem
890	if so be that it	if it
891	subdekne, or dekne	subdekne, dekne
894	here preyer avayleth nat	hir preyeres availlen nat
900	ne konne nat	ne [coude] nat
	ne knowe they nat	ne [knewe] they nat
924	no man ne	no man
925	and reverence	and in reverence
931	that is wyf	that is a wyf
937	thyng	thynges
942	may ther any	may any
943	as if they assemble	if they assemble
947	contenaunce; and been	contenaunce,
	They been	And thanne is she
949	telle ne herte thynke.	telle.
955	and hoolier	holier
968	Wherfore	For

Tale, Fragment, and Line	Robinson's Reading	Present Reading
PsT, X, 997	enjoyned for his synnes,	enjoyned,
1002	ne hath nat	hath nat
1007	nys noon	is noon
	or never;	or elles never
1008	like to thee	like thee
1013	and that noon oother man	noon oother man shal
1018	ne be nat	be nat
1020	of thym humylitee	of humylitee
1021	the shame therfore	the shame
1027	certes	soothly
1028	toold yow	toold
1029	moost generally	generally
1030	of defaute	of the defaute
	neighebores; and the	neighebores. The
1032	and by thy yiftes	and they yiftes
1033	richesses	richesse
1039	And ye	Ye
1043	ne be nat	be nat
1051	for to ete; ete by mesure;	for to ete by mesure;
	at his table to ete	at his table
1059	that is so crueel	that is cruel
1061	shamed to doon foule thinges	ashamed to doon foule thinges
1065	that stant	it stant
1066	hym semeth thanne tymely ynough to come	he may as hym semeth tymely ynough come
1068	richesses	richesse

Basic Glossary

Since most of these words are glossed marginally only on their first few occurrences, the reader should become familiar with them, especially those marked with asterisks.

adoun: down
adrad: afraid
adoun: down
after: according to; after; afterwards, later
agast: terrified, aghast, afraid
agayn(s), ageyn, aye(y)n(s): against; towards; back; in reply; in return
ago, ago(o)n: gone; ago
al: all; quite
*****al, al be (that):** although, even if
al (the) day, alday: all the time, continually
algate(s): in all ways; entirely; always, at all times, under all circumstances; at any rate; nevertheless
alighte: alight; alighted
*****als, also:** as; also
amende: amend, improve, correct
an: an; on
and: and; if
*****anon:** at once, immediately
ap(p)ertene: appertain
artow: art thou, thou art
arwe: arrow
as: as; as if; like
as: (emphatic adverb introducing an imperative), e.g., **as lene it me:** (please) lend it to me.
assay: try; test; trial
atte: at the
atte leeste (way): at least
attemperaunce: temperance
atwo: in two
auctor: author
auctoritee: authority
avaunce: advance
aventure: chance; fate; adventure; misfortune, accident
aventures: adventures
avyse: advise
*****axe:** ask
ay: always, ever
aye(y)n(s): against; towards; back

ba(a)r: bore, carried; wore
bad: bade; urged; begged; requested; commanded, ordered
bareyne: barren
barge: vessel; boat
be(e)(n): be; are; been
be(e)st: beast
benedicite: bless us! bless you! bless my soul! (usually pronounced in three syllables: "ben-diss-tay" or "ben-dick-tay")
ber(e): bear
berie: bury
*****bet:** better
bete: beat
beth: are; (imperative) be
bise(e)ke: beseech, pray
bitide: happen (to), befall
bitwixe(n): between
blake: black
blisful: happy; blessed; beautiful, pleasing, praiseworthy
bo(o)n: bone
bord: board; table
boren: born
bountee: goodness, virtue
breke: break
brende: burned
brenne: burn
brent(e): burned
breste: burst; break
briddes: birds
brood: broad
bryd: bird
*****but, but if:** unless

*****can, kan, konne:** be able; know how; know; learn
care: sorrow, woe, distress; pain; harm; misfortune
careful: sorrowful
*****ca(a)s:** case; matter; situation; event, happening, experience; chance, fate; accident; **(as) in this cas:** in this situation, under these circumstances
catel: chattel, property, goods; money
caught: caught; caught up, grasped, seized
cause: cause; reason; purpose; occasion
*****certes:** certainly, surely
certeyn: certain(ly), sure(ly)
cesse: cease
cheere, chiere: face, countenance, facial expression; manner; mood; gladness, merriment; **make cheere:** be pleasant, friendly; show hospitality
good cheere: mirth
chees: chose
chees, cheseth: choose (imperative)
chese: choose
chiere: see **cheere**

*clepe(n): call

clerk: scholar; learned man; writer

cokewold: cuckold

come(n): come; came

*conseil: council; counsel; decision; plan; advice; secret(s), confidence(s)

conseillyng: counseling, etc.

contrarie: opposite; contradict

*corage: heart; spirit; courage; desire

cost: cost; outlay of money, expenditure, expense

coveite: covet; desire strongly

coveitise: covetousness; avarice; strong desire

curious: careful; concerned, eager; full of care; made with care

cursed: accursed; wicked

curteisly: in a courtly manner, courteously, politely

dam(p)ned: condemned; damned

darst: darest, dare

daun: (from Latin *dominus*, "lord") a title of respect

debonaire: gentle, gracious

dede: deed

*dede, deed: dead

*de(e)l: bit; every deel: completely, in every respect

defaute: fault, defect; lack

*degree: rank; social condition; state; in his degree: according to his rank

delit: delight, pleasure

*de(e)me: judge; decide; suppose

departe: depart; part; separate; divide

depe: deeply

dette: debt; yelde dette: pay (marital) debt

*devyse: devise; say; tell (of), relate; describe; conceive; imagine

d(e)ye: die

d(e)yd(e): died

dispence: spending; expenditure

displeasaunce: displeasure

disport: amusement; pleasure

disserved: deserved

*do, do(o)n: do; cause; make; doon make (etc.): cause to be made (etc.)

do: done, finished

dorste: durst, dared, would dare

dout: doubt; out of dout: beyond doubt

*drede: dread, fear; doubt; it is no drede: there is no doubt; without drede: without doubt

dresse: prepare; array

dreye: dry

dure: endure; last

dwelle: dwell, remain

ech: each

echo(o)n: each one

*eek, ek(e): also

eet: ate; ete: eat

effect: effect; result; outcome; upshot; purport

elles, ellis: else; otherwise

encre(e)s(s)e: increase

endite: indite, write, compose

endure: remain

enquere: inquire

ensample: example; parable

entente: purpose, intention; spirit; desire

*er: before; formerly

ernest: seriousness

erst: before; formerly

eschue: eschew, shun, avoid

ese: ease, comfort; pleasure, delight

espirtuel: spiritual

espye: search out; discover; notice

*estaat: state, condition; rank, standing

ete: eat; eet: ate

everemo: evermore

*everich: every, each; every one, each one

everichon: every one, each one; all

eyen: eyes

eyle: ail, trouble; what eyleth: what's the matter with

*falle: fall; befall, happen

falle, yfalle: fallen; happened

falshede: falseness, deceitfulness

*fare: fare; go; behave; act

faste: quickly; firmly; intensely; vigorously; etc.

fay, fey: faith

*fayn: glad(ly); willing(ly); eager(ly)

feend: fiend, devil, the Devil; evil spirit

feendly: fiendish

fel, fil: fell; befell, happened

felawe: fellow, companion

fer: far

ferde: fared; behaved; acted

ferthe: fourth

fe(e)ste: feast; festival; rejoicing; joy

fey: faith

feyne: feign

fil, fille: fell; befell, happened

flour: flower; flour

*folie: folly, foolishness; wrongdoing, sinfulness; lechery; madness

fond, foond: found

*for: because (of); for; in order that; despite

no fors: no matter

forseyde: aforesaid

forther over: furthermore; moreover

forthy: therefore

foryeve: forgive

foryifnesse: forgiveness

*foul: disagreeable; evil; miserable

foule, fowel: bird

*fre(e): free; noble; gracious; generous, liberal

*fro: from

ful: full; very

fulfil: fulfill; satisfy; accomplish; fill full, fill
atte fulle: fully

game: fun; jest; game; sport
***gan (to):** did (auxiliary); began (to)
gat: got
gentilesse: nobility of birth; nobility of character or manners; gentility; generosity; gentleness; graciousness, courtesy; kindness; compassion
gentle: noble; courteous; gentle; generous
gesse: suppose, think
gete(n): get; got
gilt: guilt; sin; **giltes:** sins
girdel: belt
glade: make glad
***go(on):** go; walk
good: good; goods, possessions; wealth
go(o)st: ghost, spirit
***gonne(n) (to):** did; began (to)
gret, greet: great
grisly: horrible, terrible, dreadful
gyde: guide; keep
***gyse:** guise, manner, way, fashion, custom

***han:** have
hap: chance
hap(pe): happen
hardy: bold; sturdy
hardynesse: boldness
***harm:** injury, damage, misfortune; evil; sin; grief; affliction, suffering, pain; disease; pity; **speke harm:** speak ill
harneys: equipment; armor
harrow!: a cry for help
hastif: hasty; requiring haste, urgent
***hasti(f)ly:** hastily, quickly; without delay; soon
hastow: (hast thou) have you, you have
heed: head
heede: heed
heele: heal; happiness, prosperity
heer(e): here
heigh: high
***hem:** them
hende: ready to hand; convenient, handy; pleasant; courteous, gentle; comely, fair
he(e)ng: hanged; hung
***hente:** seize, catch; seized, caught
***her, hir(e):** their
her(e): her
he(e)r: hair
he(e)re: hear
hert: hart
herte: heart
hevynesse: sorrow, sadness, grief
hewe: hue, color; complexion; appearance
***hight(e):** was (is) named; named
***hir(e), her:** their
hir(e): her
his: his; its
holde(n): hold; held; considered

holpen: helped
holwe: hollow
honde: hand
honest: honorable; fitting, proper; virtuous
honestee: virtue
hool: whole, complete, entire; sound, well; healed, cured; wholly
hoolly: wholly
hoost: host; army
humblesse: humility
hye: high
hym: him; to him; etc.

ich: I
***ilke:** same

jalous: jealous
jape: jest, joke; trick; **japes:** tricks, deceits
jolif, joly: gay; amorous; wanton; *joli*
juste: just; joust

***kan:** be able; know how; know; learn
ke(e)pe: keep; care, heed; look after, protect, guard; save; **take ke(e)pe:** take heed, take care
kemb(e)d: combed
kitte: cut
knave: servant (man or boy); commoner; foot-soldier; rogue, knave, villain
knave child: male child
***konne:** be able; know how; know; learn
konnyng: ability, skill
***koude:** knew; knew how to; could
kyn, kynrede: kindred, family

lad, ladde: led
lasse: less
***lat:** let
laurer: laurel
le(e)ste: least
atte leeste (way): at least
leet: let, leave
leeve, leve: dear
legen: lay
lemman: lover; sweetheart
lese: lose
***lest(e):** (with dative) please; it pleases; pleased; **us leste, etc:** it pleased us; we wished, we wanted; etc.
lete, lette, leet: let; leave
leve: leave; depart; permission
le(e)ve: dear
***levere:** liefer, rather; **me were lever,** etc.: I would rather, I had rather, etc.
leyser: leisure; opportunity
lief: dear, beloved
lightly: easily; readily; quickly
***like, liketh:** it please(s); **it liketh me:** it pleases me
likerous: lecherous

*list(e): it pleased, it pleases; me list, etc.: it pleases me; I wish; etc.
*lite, lyte: little
lith, lyth: lies
londe: land
longe: long; belong, pertain; longeth: belongs, pertains
looke: look; see; behold, lo; consider; make sure; looke that: see that, make sure that
lo(o)re: learning; knowledge; wisdom; advice
looth: loath, reluctant; loathsome, repulsive, distasteful; me (hym) be looth: it is repulsive to me (him); it displeases me (him); I don't (he doesn't) like
*lust: desire; pleasure; joy
lust(e): it pleases; it pleased
lusty: lusty; joyous; pleasant; vigorous; pleasure-loving
luxurie: lasciviousness, lust
lyth: lies
on lyve: alive

maad: made
maistow, maystow: (mayest thou) may you, you may
maistrie: mastery; domination; control; skill; knowledge
manace: menace; threat; threaten
maner(e): kind of; manner
many oon: many a one
maydenhede: maidenhood, virginity
mede: mead, meadow
men: men; but sometimes a weakened form of man, used in the indefinite sense: e.g., men seyth: one says
mery, murie: merry, pleasant
mescha(u)nce, myscha(u)nce: misfortune, disaster, ruin, bad luck; with meschaunce: bad luck (to him)!; curse (him)!
met(te): dream(ed)
met(te): met
*mete: food; dinner
*mo: more
moder: mother
mo(o)st(e): most; greatest
*moot(e), mote: may, must, ought to; so (also, ever) moot I: as I hope to
mordre: murder
morwe: morning; morrow
*most(e): must
mote: see moot(e)
*mowe: can; may
muche, muchel: much; many (a)
murye, myrie: merry

na: no
na mo, namo: no more; no one else
nam: (ne am) am not
*nameliche, namely: especially
namo, namoore: no more; no one else
*nas: (ne was) was not

*nat: not; nat right: not at all
nathelees: nevertheless
naught: not
it is no nay: it cannot be denied
*ne: not; nor
*nere: (ne were) were not
newe: newly, lately
no(u)ght: nothing; not; not at all
*nolde: (ne wolde) would not
nones, nonys: nonce; occasion; purpose
non, none, noon: none; no one; no
or noon: or not
noon oother: not otherwise
*noot: (ne woot) know(s) not
nothyng, no thyng: not at all
ny: nigh, near; nearly
*nys: (ne is) is not
*nyste: (ne wiste) knew not, did not know

o, oo, on, oon: one; (the) same
obeisaunce: obedience; submission; deference
of: (adv.) off; away
of: (prep.) of; off; from; by; with; for; about; some
oghte: ought
on lyve: alive
ones, onis: once
oon the: one of the
ordinaunce: decree; governance, control; plan
*outher: either
outrely: utterly; entirely; truly
over al, overal: everywhere

paas: pace; a paas: at a footpace, at a walk
pace, passe: go, proceed; pass (by, away); surpass
paraventure: peradventure, perhaps, by chance
pardee: (lit., "by God") pardieu; certainly
parfay: by my faith
parfit: perfect
parfourne: perform, carry out, complete
partie: part
passe: go; proceed; pass (by, away); surpass
pees: peace
perdurable: everlasting
perfourne: perform, carry out, complete
phisik: medicine
pitous: pitiful, deserving pity; pitying, tenderhearted, compassionate; sad
playn(e), pleyn(e): plain, clear; open; full
plesaunce: pleasure
pleyne: complain, lament
poverte: poverty
*povre: poor
predicacioun: preaching; sermon
pre(e)ve: prove
prime, pryme: 9 A.M.
priso(u)n: captivity; prison
privee, pryvee: secret(ly); intimate

prively, pryvely: secretly

privetee, pryvetee: secrecy; secret; secrets; private affairs; in privetee: secretly

*quit, quyt: requited; repaid

quite, quyte: requite; repay, pay back

*quod: said

*rather: sooner; rather

recche, rekke: heed, care

*re(e)d(e): advise, counsel

reed: red

regne: realm, kingdom, dominion; reign

rekene, rekne: reckon

rekke: heed, care

renne: run

renoun: renown

repreve: reprove, reproach

resoun: reason; as resoun is: as is agreeable to reason

reyse: raid; expedition

richesse: riches, wealth

right: very; just, quite

right as .... right so: just as .... just so

right no: not at all

right noght: not at all

rightwisnesse: righteousness

ronne: run

roos: rose

route: company, retinue

routhe: ruth, pity

sapience: wisdom

sauf: safe; saufly: safely

saugh: saw

savacioun: salvation

sclaundre: slander

seche, seke: seek, search

secree: secret; able to keep secrets

seistow: (sayest thou) you say, say you

seith: says

seke: seek, search

selde: seldom

sely: good; innocent; blessed; simple; poor, pitiable, foolish; hapless, unfortunate

semblable: similar

sene, seyn: seen

*sentence: sentence; opinion; maxim; sentiments; subject matter; sense, substance, meaning; insight

servage: servitude, bondage, slavery

set: seated

seyde: said

seye: say

seyn: seen

shaltow: you shall

shape: plan; prepare; arrange; (reflexive) set oneself, prepare

shape(n): destined, determined

sheene: shining, bright, fair

shet(te): shut

shrewe: curse; scoundrel, villain, rascal; wretch

shrift: confession

shrive: confess

sik(e): sick

*siker(ly): certain(ly), sure(ly), true, truly

*sit: (sitteth) sits

*sith(en): since

slayn: slain

*slee(n): slay; overcome with distress; destroy spiritually

sleight: trickery

sleepe, slepe(n): sleep

sleep, slepen: slept

slow: slew

smal: small; slender

smoot: smote

smyte: smite, strike, hit

so (that): provided that

sodeyn(lich): sudden(ly)

softe: softly; quietly; gently

solas: delight; pleasure; entertainment; refreshment

solempne: sumptuous; imposing; distinguished; important

*somde(e)l: somewhat

somme: sum

somtyme: once; sometimes; for a time

song: song; sang

*so(o)re: bitterly; sorely; pain; sorrow; misery

*sooth: true

*sooth, soothfastnesse, sothe: truth

so(o)the, soothly: truly

soun, sowne: sound

sovereyn: supreme; sovereign

spece: kind; sort; speces: species, kinds

spedde him: hastened

spicerye: spices (collectively)

sprad(de): spread

squier: squire

*stant: (standeth) stands

*stente, stinte, stynte: cease; stop; restrain; cease to tell

sterre: star

*sterte, stirte: started; started up; leaped; sprang; rushed

stonde(n): stand

storie: historical narrative or anecdote; history; story

strange, straunge: foreign; unknown; distant

strook: stroke

subget(z): subject(s)

subtle: subtle; clever; crafty, cunning

suffera(u)nce: long-suffering

suffre: permit; endure

suste(e)ne: sustain

suster: sister; sustren: sisters

swerd: sword

sweven(e): dream

*swich: such

swowne: swoon

syk(e): sick
*syn: since

taak: take
tempte: test
than(ne): then; than
*that: that; that which, what
the: the; thee
*thee: prosper; also (as, so) moot I thee(n): as I hope to prosper
theef: thief; villain, scoundrel
thennes: thence
*ther(e): there; where
ther as: where; whereas
*ther to, therto: besides; also; moreover
*thilke: the same, that same
this: this; this is; these
*tho: those; then
hym thoughte: it seemed to him (etc.); see thynke
thridde: third
thurgh: through
thynke: (impersonal verb, with dative pronoun and sometimes with subject it) seem; me thynketh, me thynketh it: it seems to me; yow thynketh: it seems to you; hym thoughte: it seemed to him (etc.)
til: until; to
*to: to; too
travaille: labor, work; suffering
tresor: treasure
trete: treat
trewe: true
trompe: trumpet
trone: throne
*trouthe: truth; good faith; pledge, troth, promise
*trowe: believe
tweye: two
twies: twice

*unnethe(s): not easily, with difficulty, hardly, scarcely
up: up; upon
up so doun: upside down
usage: custom
use: use; practice

vanitee: vanity, folly, foolishness, nonsense
*verray: true; faithful; veritable
viage: voyage; journey; travel
vileins: villainous; evil
vileynye: evil; rudeness; shameful speech or deed
vitaille: victuals, food, provisions
vouche sauf: vouchsafe, grant, permit

waite, wayte: watch, await
wan: won; wan
*war: aware; be (beth) war(e), a ware yow: beware, take warning

wax: became, grew into
weep: weep; wept
we(e)l: well, happy, lucky; fully; very
wele: welfare, well-being, prosperity; good fortune, joy
welle: well; spring; source
*wende: go, pass; walk
*wende: weened, thought, supposed; expected
wene: ween, think, suppose; expect
went: went; gone
wepe: weep
werche, werke, wirche: work; do; perform; act
wered: wore
werk: deed; act; work
werre: war
wex: wax
wexe(n): wax; grow; become
*what: what; why
wheither: whether; whichever; which (of two)
*wher: where; whether
wher as: where; whereas
which: which; who, whom; what; what kind of
which that: which; who
*whilom: once; once upon a time; formerly
wight: creature, being, person, man
wikke: wicked, evil
wil(le): will; desire; pleasure
wil(t), wol(t): will; desire; intend; wiltow: (wilt thou) will you
wise, wyse: wise, prudent; way, manner
*wist(e): known; knew
wit: wit; mind, understanding; judgment; wisdom
*wite: know
with: with; by
wo: woe; woeful
wol, wil; will; desire; intend
wolde: would
wolt: will
*wood: mad; enraged; furious
woost: knowest; woostou, wostow: (knowest thou) know you, you know
*wo(o)t: know; knows
worthy: distinguished; well to do; in good social standing
wrecche: wretched; wretch; wretched person
wro(u)ght: worked; wroght; created; made; performed; did
wrooth, wrothe: wroth, wrathful, stirred to wrath, very angry
wydwe: widow
wyf: woman; wife
wyl: will; desire; pleasure
wys: wise
wyse: wise, prudent; way, manner

*yaf: gave
*y-: sign of past participle (a few examples appear below)

ybore, yborn: born; borne, carried
ycleped: named, called
ydo ydo(o)n: done; ended; finished
ye: ye; yea
yen: eyes
*yeve(n): give(n)
*yif: if; give

yifte: gift
yive(n): give(n)
ynogh, ynow(e): enough
yronne: run
ysene, yseyn: seen
yvel(e): evil, evilly
*ywis: surely, certainly